FIRM BEHAVIOR AND
THE ORGANIZATION OF INDUSTRY

13 The Costs of Production

14 Firms in Competitive Markets

The theory of the firm sheds light on the decisions that lie behind supply in competitive markets.

15 Monopoly

16 Oligopoly

Firms with market power can cause market outcomes to be inefficient.

17 Monopolistic Competition

THE ECONOMICS OF LABOR MARKETS

18 The Markets for the Factors of Production

19 Earnings and Discrimination

These chapters examine the special features of labor markets, in which most people earn most of their income.

20 Income Inequality and Poverty

TOPICS FOR FURTHER STUDY

21 The Theory of Consumer Choice

22 Frontiers of Microeconomics

Additional topics in microeconomics include household decisionmaking, asymmetric information, political economy, and behavioral economics.

THOMSON

SOUTH-WESTERN

Principles of Microeconomics, 3e

N. Gregory Mankiw

Vice President, Editorial Director:
Jack W. Calhoun

Vice President, Editor-in-Chief:
Michael P. Roche

Publisher of Economics:
Michael B. Mercier

Senior Acquisitions Editor:
Peter Adams

Developmental Editor:
Jane Tufts

Contributing Editors:
Jeff Gilbreath
Sarah K. Dorger
Susanna C. Smart

Senior Marketing Manager:
Janet Hennies

Senior Marketing Coordinator:
Jenny Fruechtenicht

Production Editor:
Daniel C. Plofchan

Manufacturing Coordinator:
Sandee Milewski

Senior Media Technology Editor:
Vicky True

Media Developmental Editor:
Peggy Buskey

Media Production Editor:
Pam Wallace

Compositor:
Graphic Arts Center Indianapolis

Project Management:
Thistle Hill Publishing Services

Printer:
R.R. Donnelley
Willard, OH

Senior Design Project Manager:
Mike Stratton

Internal/Cover Designer:
Mike Stratton

Cover Illustration:
"Market Scene"
19th century French watercolor
Artist unknown
From a private collection

Cover Images:
PhotoDisc, Inc.

Internal Illustrator:
Roger Lundquist, AWS

Photography Manager:
John Hill

Photo Research:
Fred Middendorf
Marie LePage
Script Pict Ink, Ltd.

Library of Congress Control
Number: 2002111169

Package ISBN: 0-324-17188-9
Book ISBN: 0-324-26939-0

PRINCIPLES OF
MICROECONOMICS
THIRD EDITION

N. GREGORY MANKIW
HARVARD UNIVERSITY

THOMSON

SOUTH-WESTERN

Australia · Canada · Mexico · Singapore · Spain · United Kingdom · United States

ABOUT THE AUTHOR

JORDI CABRÉ

N. Gregory Mankiw is Professor of Economics at Harvard University. As a student, he studied economics at Princeton University and MIT. As a teacher, he has taught macroeconomics, microeconomics, statistics, and principles of economics. He even spent one summer long ago as a sailing instructor on Long Beach Island.

Professor Mankiw is a prolific writer and a regular participant in academic and policy debates. His work has been published in scholarly journals, such as the *American Economic Review, Journal of Political Economy,* and *Quarterly Journal of Economics,* and in more popular forums, such as *The New York Times, The Financial Times, The Wall Street Journal,* and *Fortune.* He is also author of the best-selling intermediate-level textbook *Macroeconomics* (Worth Publishers). In addition to his teaching, research, and writing, Professor Mankiw is a research associate of the National Bureau of Economic Research, an adviser to the Federal Reserve Bank of Boston and the Congressional Budget Office, and a member of the ETS test development committee for the advanced placement exam in economics.

Professor Mankiw lives in Wellesley, Massachusetts, with his wife and three children.

To Catherine, Nicholas, and Peter,
my other contributions to the next generation

During my 20-year career as a student, the course that excited me most was the two-semester sequence on the principles of economics that I took during my freshman year in college. It is no exaggeration to say that it changed my life.

I had grown up in a family that often discussed politics over the dinner table. The pros and cons of various solutions to society's problems generated fervent debate. But, in school, I had been drawn to the sciences. Whereas politics seemed vague, rambling, and subjective, science was analytic, systematic, and objective. While political debate continued without end, science made progress.

My freshman course on the principles of economics opened my eyes to a new way of thinking. Economics combines the virtues of politics and science. It is, truly, a social science. Its subject matter is society—how people choose to lead their lives and how they interact with one another. But it approaches the subject with the dispassion of a science. By bringing the methods of science to the questions of politics, economics tries to make progress on the challenges that all societies face.

I was drawn to write this book in the hope that I could convey some of the excitement about economics that I felt as a student in my first economics course. Economics is a subject in which a little knowledge goes a long way. (The same cannot be said, for instance, of the study of physics or the Japanese language.) Economists have a unique way of viewing the world, much of which can be taught in one or two semesters. My goal in this book is to transmit this way of thinking to the widest possible audience and to convince readers that it illuminates much about the world around them.

I believe that everyone should study the fundamental ideas that economics has to offer. One purpose of general education is to inform people about the world and thereby make them better citizens. The study of economics, as much as any discipline, serves this goal. Writing an economics textbook is, therefore, a great honor and a great responsibility. It is one way that economists can help promote better government and a more prosperous future. As the great economist Paul Samuelson put it, "I don't care who writes a nation's laws, or crafts its advanced treaties, if I can write its economics textbooks."

For Whom Is This Book Written?

It is tempting for a professional economist writing a textbook to take the economist's point of view and to emphasize those topics that fascinate him and other economists. I have done my best to avoid that temptation. I have tried to put myself in the position of someone seeing economics for the first time. My goal is to emphasize the material that *students* should and do find interesting about the study of the economy.

One result is that this book is briefer than many books used to introduce students to economics. As a student, I was (and unfortunately still am) a slow reader. I groaned whenever a professor gave the class a 1,000-page tome to read. Of course, my reaction was not unique. The Greek poet Callimachus put it succinctly: "Big book, big bore." Callimachus made that observation in 250 B.C., so he was probably not referring to an economics textbook, but today his sentiment is echoed around the world every semester when students first see their economics assignments. My goal in this book is to avoid that reaction by skipping the bells, whistles, and extraneous details that distract students from the key lessons.

Another result of this student orientation is that more of this book is devoted to applications and policy—and less to formal economic theory—than is the case with many other books written for the principles course. Throughout this book I have tried to return to applications and policy questions as often as possible. Most chapters include case studies illustrating how the principles of economics are applied. In addition, "In the News" boxes (most of which are new to this edition) offer excerpts from newspaper articles showing how economic ideas shed light on current issues facing society. After students finish their first course in economics, they should think about news stories from a new perspective and with greater insight.

What's New in the Third Edition?

Much has happened in the world since I wrote the last edition of this book. Over the past few years, another U.S. recession, a new president, a tax cut, corporate accounting scandals, a new European currency, and terrorist attacks have all altered the economic landscape. Because the teaching of economics has to stay current with an ever changing world, this new edition includes dozens of new case studies and boxes.

In addition to updating the book, I have also refined its coverage and pedagogy with input from many users of the previous edition. There are many changes, both large and small. For example, the basic presentation of supply and demand in Chapter 4 has been rearranged and improved. More important, this new edition contains two new chapters. A new chapter on the "Frontiers of Microeconomics" introduces students to the economics of asymmetric information, political economy, and behavioral economics. A new chapter on "The Basic Tools of Finance" develops the concepts of present value, risk management, and asset valuation. (Only the complete 36-chapter version of this book includes both of these chapters. See below for outlines of each of the five available versions.) These new chapters are optional, and instructors can skip them without loss of continuity. But adding these topics should give students a greater appreciation of the use and scope of economics.

All the changes that I made, and the many others that I considered, were evaluated in light of the benefits of brevity. Like most things that we study in economics, a student's time is a scarce resource. I always keep in mind a dictum from the great novelist Robertson Davies: "One of the most important things about writing is to boil it down and not bore the hell out of everybody."

How Is This Book Organized?

To write a brief and student-friendly book, I had to consider new ways to organize familiar material. What follows is a whirlwind tour of this text. The tour will, I hope, give instructors some sense of how the pieces fit together.

Introductory Material

Chapter 1, "Ten Principles of Economics," introduces students to the economist's view of the world. It previews some of the big ideas that recur throughout economics, such as opportunity cost, marginal decisionmaking, the role of incentives, the gains from trade, and the efficiency of market allocations. Throughout the book, I refer regularly to the *Ten Principles of Economics* introduced in Chapter 1 to remind students that these ideas are the foundation for all economics. An icon in the margin calls attention to these key, interconnected principles.

Chapter 2, "Thinking Like an Economist," examines how economists approach their field of study. It discusses the role of assumptions in developing a theory and introduces the concept of an economic model. It also discusses the role of economists in making policy. The appendix to this chapter offers a brief refresher course on how graphs are used and how they can be abused.

Chapter 3, "Interdependence and the Gains from Trade," presents the theory of comparative advantage. This theory explains why individuals trade with their neighbors, as well as why nations trade with other nations. Much of economics is about how market forces coordinate many individual production and consumption decisions. As a starting point for this analysis, students see in this chapter why specialization, interdependence, and trade can benefit everyone.

The Fundamental Tools of Supply and Demand

The next three chapters introduce the basic tools of supply and demand. Chapter 4, "The Market Forces of Supply and Demand," develops the supply curve, the demand curve, and the notion of market equilibrium. Chapter 5, "Elasticity and Its Application," introduces the concept of elasticity and uses it to analyze events in three different markets. Chapter 6, "Supply, Demand, and Government Policies," uses these tools to examine price controls, such as rent-control and minimum-wage laws, and tax incidence.

Chapter 7, "Consumers, Producers, and the Efficiency of Markets," extends the analysis of supply and demand using the concepts of consumer surplus and producer surplus. It begins by developing the link between consumers' willingness to pay and the demand curve, and the link between producers' costs of production and the supply curve. It then shows that the market equilibrium maximizes the sum of the producer and consumer surplus. Thus, students learn early about the efficiency of market allocations.

The next two chapters apply the concepts of producer and consumer surplus to questions of policy. Chapter 8, "Application: The Costs of Taxation," shows why taxation results in deadweight losses and what determines the size of those losses. Chapter 9, "Application: International Trade," considers who wins and who loses from international trade and presents the debate over protectionist trade policies.

More Microeconomics

Having examined why market allocations are often desirable, the book then considers how the government can sometimes improve on them. Chapter 10, "Externalities," explains how external effects such as pollution can render market outcomes inefficient and discusses the possible public and private solutions to those inefficiencies. Chapter 11, "Public Goods and Common Resources," considers the problems that arise when goods, such as national defense, have no market price. Chapter 12, "The Design of the Tax System," describes how the government raises the revenue necessary to pay for public goods. It presents some institutional background about the U.S. tax system and then discusses how the goals of efficiency and equity come into play when designing a tax system.

The next five chapters examine firm behavior and industrial organization. Chapter 13, "The Costs of Production," discusses what to include in a firm's costs, and it introduces cost curves. Chapter 14, "Firms in Competitive Markets," analyzes the behavior of price-taking firms and derives the market supply curve. Chapter 15, "Monopoly," discusses the behavior of a firm that is the sole seller in its market. It discusses the inefficiency of monopoly pricing, the possible policy responses, and the attempts by monopolies to price discriminate. Chapter 16, "Oligopoly," covers markets in which there are only a few sellers, using the prisoners' dilemma as the model for examining strategic interaction. Chapter 17, "Monopolistic Competition," looks at behavior in a market in which many sellers offer similar but differentiated products. It also discusses the debate over the effects of advertising.

The next three chapters present issues related to labor markets. Chapter 18, "The Markets for the Factors of Production," emphasizes the link between factor prices and marginal productivity. Chapter 19, "Earnings and Discrimination," discusses the determinants of equilibrium wages, including compensating differentials, human capital, and discrimination. Chapter 20, "Income Inequality and Poverty," examines the degree of inequality in U.S. society, alternative views about the government's role in changing the distribution of income, and various policies aimed at helping society's poorest members.

The next two chapters present optional material. Chapter 21, "The Theory of Consumer Choice," analyzes individual decisionmaking using budget constraints and indifference curves. Chapter 22, "Frontiers of Microeconomics," introduces the topics of asymmetric information, political economy, and behavioral economics. Many instructors may skip all or some of this material. Instructors who do cover these topics may choose to assign these chapters earlier than they are presented in the book, and I have written them to give instructors flexibility.

Learning Tools

The purpose of this book is to help students learn the fundamental lessons of economics and to show how such lessons can be applied to the world in which they live. Toward that end, I have used various learning tools that recur throughout the book.

Case Studies   Economic theory is useful and interesting only if it can be applied to understanding actual events and policies. This book, therefore, contains numerous case studies that apply the theory that has just been developed.

"In the News" Boxes   One benefit that students gain from studying economics is a new perspective and greater understanding about news from around the world. To highlight this benefit, I have included excerpts from many newspaper articles, some of which are opinion columns written by prominent economists. These articles, together with my brief introductions, show how basic economic theory can be applied. Most of these boxes are new to this edition.

"FYI" Boxes   These boxes provide additional material "for your information." Some of them offer a glimpse into the history of economic thought. Others clarify technical issues. Still others discuss supplementary topics that instructors might choose either to discuss or skip in their lectures.

Definitions of Key Concepts   When key concepts are introduced in the chapter, they are presented in **bold** typeface. In addition, their definitions are placed in the margins. This treatment should aid students in learning and reviewing the material.

Quick Quizzes   After each major section, students are offered a "quick quiz" to check their comprehension of what they have just learned. If students cannot readily answer these quizzes, they should stop and reread material before continuing.

Chapter Summaries   Each chapter ends with a brief summary that reminds students of the most important lessons that they have just learned. Later in their study it offers an efficient way to review for exams.

List of Key Concepts   A list of key concepts at the end of each chapter offers students a way to test their understanding of the new terms that have been introduced. Page references are included so that students can review the terms they do not understand.

Questions for Review   At the end of each chapter are questions for review that cover the chapter's primary lessons. Students can use these questions to check their comprehension and to prepare for exams.

Problems and Applications   Each chapter also contains a variety of problems and applications that ask students to apply the material they have learned. Some professors may use these questions for homework assignments. Others may use them as a starting point for classroom discussions.

Alternative Versions of the Books

The book you are holding in your hand is one of five versions of this book that are available for introducing students to economics. South-Western and I offer this menu of books because instructors differ in how much time they have and what topics they choose to cover. Here is a brief description of each:

- *Principles of Economics:* This complete version of the book contains all 36 chapters. It is designed for a two-semester introductory course that covers both microeconomics and macroeconomics.
- *Principles of Microeconomics:* This version contains 22 chapters and is designed for one-semester courses in introductory microeconomics.
- *Principles of Macroeconomics:* This version contains 23 chapters and is designed for one-semester courses in introductory macroeconomics. It contains a full development of the theory of supply and demand.
- *Brief Principles of Macroeconomics:* This shortened macro version of 18 chapters contains only one chapter on the basics of supply and demand. It is designed for those instructors who want to jump to the core topics of macroeconomics more quickly.
- *Essentials of Economics:* This version of the book contains 24 chapters. It is designed for one-semester survey courses that cover the basics of both microeconomics and macroeconomics.

The table on the next page shows precisely which chapters are included in each book. Instructors who wish more information about these alternative versions should contact their local South-Western representative.

Wall Street Journal Edition

One goal in teaching the principles of economics is to provide students with a better understanding of the world around them. Many instructors, therefore, encourage students to read about economic issues in the newspaper as they take the course. Those instructors may want to consider the special *Wall Street Journal Edition* of this text. This version is the same as the standard edition but includes a 15-week subscription to both the print and interactive versions of *The Wall Street Journal*. Students can activate their subscriptions simply by completing and mailing a business reply card inserted in the back of the book. Instructors with at least ten students who activate their subscriptions will automatically receive their own free subscription. Talk to your South-Western representative or call 1-800-423-0563 for details.

Supplements

South-Western offers various supplements for instructors and students who use this book. These resources make teaching the principles of economics easy for the professor and learning them easy for the student. David R. Hakes of the University of Northern Iowa, a dedicated teacher and economist, supervised the development of the supplements for this edition.

South-Western will provide copies of these supplements free of charge to those instructors qualified under its adoption policy. Please contact your sales

AVAILABLE VERSIONS

The Five Versions of This Book

Principles of Economics	Principles of Microeconomics	Principles of Macroeconomics	Brief Principles of Macroeconomics	Essentials of Economics
1 Ten Principles of Economics	X	X	X	X
2 Thinking Like an Economist	X	X	X	X
3 Interdependence and the Gains from Trade	X	X	X	X
4 The Market Forces of Supply and Demand	X	X	X	X
5 Elasticity and Its Application	X	X		X
6 Supply, Demand, and Government Policies	X	X		X
7 Consumers, Producers and the Efficiency of Markets	X	X		X
8 Applications: The Costs of Taxation	X	X		X
9 Application: International Trade	X	X		X
10 Externalities	X			X
11 Public Goods and Common Resources	X			X
12 The Design of the Tax System	X			
13 The Costs of Production	X			X
14 Firms in Competitive Markets	X			X
15 Monopoly	X			X
16 Oligopoly	X			
17 Monopolistic Competition	X			
18 The Markets for the Factors of Production	X			
19 Earnings and Discrimination	X			
20 Income Inequality and Poverty	X			
21 The Theory of Consumer Choice	X			
22 Frontiers of Microeconomics	X			
23 Measuring a Nation's Income		X	X	X
24 Measuring the Cost of Living		X	X	X
25 Production and Growth		X	X	X
26 Saving, Investment, and the Financial System		X	X	X
27 The Basic Tools of Finance		X	X	X
28 Unemployment and Its Natural Rate		X	X	X
29 The Monetary System		X	X	X
30 Money Growth and Inflation		X	X	X
31 Open-Economy Macroeconomics: Basic Concepts		X	X	
32 A Macroeconomic Theory of the Open Economy		X	X	
33 Aggregate Demand and Aggregate Supply		X	X	X
34 The Influence of Monetary and Fiscal Policy on Aggregate Demand		X	X	X
35 The Short-Run Tradeoff between Inflation and Unemployment		X	X	
36 Five Debates over Macroeconomic Policy		X	X	

Note: Chapter numbers refer to the complete book, *Principles of Economics.*

representative to learn how you may qualify, or call the Academic Resource Center at 1-800-423-0563.

For the Instructor   Teaching the principles of economics can be a demanding job. Often, classes are large and teaching assistants in short supply. The supplements designed for the instructor make that job less difficult and more fun.

Instructor's Manual with Solutions Manual and Classroom Activities   For lecture preparation, the Instructor's Manual, written by Linda Ghent (Eastern Illinois University), offers a detailed outline for each chapter of the text that provides learning objectives, identifies stumbling blocks that students may face, offers helpful teaching tips, and provides suggested in-classroom activities for a more cooperative learning experience. The Instructor's Manual also includes solutions to all end-of-chapter exercises, Quick Quizzes, Questions for Review, and Problems and Applications found in the text.

Instructor's Resource CD   Included on this CD-ROM are the key supplements designed to aid instructors: Instructor's Integrated Resource Guide, Instructor's Manual with Solutions Manual and Classroom Activities, PowerPoint® Lecture and Exhibit Slides, Transparency Masters, and the Test Bank in both ExamView® Computerized Testing Software and Microsoft Word for ease of use.

Instructor's Integrated Resource Guide   Intended for use in planning instruction, this laminated guide provides a quick reference to all of South-Western's resources for teaching a course in economic principles and makes suggestions for incorporating them into all phases of instruction.

Test Bank   Daniel K. Biederman (University of North Dakota), Ken McCormick (University of Northern Iowa), Bryce Kanago (University of Northern Iowa), Penny Kugler (Central Missouri State University), and Andrew Parkes (University of Northern Iowa) have updated and revised the Test Bank. It consists of more than 200 questions per chapter. Every question has been checked to ensure the accuracy and clarity of the answers and painstakingly revised to address the main text revisions. Included are multiple-choice, true/false, and short-answer questions that assess students' critical thinking skills. Easy, medium, and difficult questions outline the process that students must use to arrive at their answers: recall, application, and integration. Questions are organized by text section to help instructors pick and choose their selections with ease.

Supplemental Test Banks   In order to keep the pool of Test Bank questions fresh and relevant, an additional testing resource will be published annually.

ExamView®   ExamView Computerized Testing Software contains all of the questions in the printed test bank. This program is an easy-to-use test creation software compatible with Microsoft Windows. Instructors can add or edit questions, instructions, and answers, and can select questions by previewing them on the screen, selecting them randomly, or selecting them by number. Instructors can also create and administer quizzes on-line, whether over the Internet, a local area network (LAN), or a wide area network (WAN).

The "Ten Principles" Video Set Ken Witty, a talented documentary filmmaker, has produced a video series to illustrate the *Ten Principles of Economics* introduced in Chapter 1. Instructors can show these videos as an interesting and visually appealing introduction to topics discussed throughout the textbook.

PowerPoint Lecture and Exhibit Slides Available only on the Web site and the IRCD are two versions of the PowerPoint presentation. Professors can save valuable time as they prepare for class using this comprehensive lecture presentation. This supplement covers all the essential topics presented in each chapter of the book. Graphs, tables, lists, and concepts are developed sequentially, much as one might develop them on a blackboard. Additional examples and applications are used to reinforce major lessons. The slides are crisp, clear, and colorful. Instructors may adapt or add slides to customize their lectures. A separate exhibit presentation provides instructors with all of the tables and graphs from the main text. The slides are all available for download at the support Web site: http://mankiw.swlearning.com.

Transparency Acetates To help instructors build text images into their lectures, full-color transparency acetates for all important figures and tables in the third edition are available for use on an overhead projector. They are available to adopters upon request in both microeconomic and macroeconomic sets.

WebTutor WebTutor is an interactive, Web-based, student supplement on WebCT and/or BlackBoard that harnesses the power of the Internet to deliver innovative learning aids that actively engage students. The instructor can incorporate WebTutor as an integral part of the course, or the students can use it on their own as a study guide. Benefits to students include automatic and immediate feedback from quizzes and exams; interactive, multimedia-rich explanation of concepts; on-line exercises that reinforce what they've learned; flashcards that include audio support; and greater interaction and involvement through on-line discussion forums.

WebTutor Advantage More than just an interactive study guide, WebTutor Advantage delivers innovative learning aids that actively engage students. Benefits include automatic and immediate feedback from quizzes; interactive, multimedia-rich explanation of concepts, such as flash-animated graphing tutorials and graphing exercises that utilize an on-line graph-drawing tool; streaming video applications; on-line exercises; flashcards; and greater interaction and involvement through on-line discussion forums. Powerful instructor tools are also provided to assist communication and collaboration between students and faculty.

Instructor Resources on the Product Support Web Site This password-protected Web site (http://mankiw.swlearning.com) features the essential resources for instructors in downloadable format: the Instructor's Manual in Word, the Test Bank in Word, and PowerPoint Lecture and Exhibit Slides.

TextChoice   TextChoice is the home of Thomson Learning's online digital content. It provides the fastest, easiest way for you to create your own learning materials. You may select content from hundreds of our best-selling titles, choose material from one of our databases, and add your own material. Contact your South-Western/Thomson Learning sales representative for more information.

Favorite Ways to Learn Economics: Instructor's Edition   Authors David Anderson of Centre College and Jim Chasey of Homewood Flossmoor High School use experiments to bring economic education to life. This is a lab manual for the classroom and for individual study that contains experiments and problem sets that reinforce key economic concepts.

Economics: HITS on the Web, *Mankiw Edition with InfoTrac*   This resource booklet supports students' research efforts on the World Wide Web. This manual includes an introduction to the World Wide Web, browsing the Web, finding information on the World Wide Web, e-mail, e-mail discussion groups and newsgroups, and documenting Internet sources for research. It also provides Internet activities for each chapter of the Mankiw text as well as a list of the hottest economic sites on the Web. Each booklet provides the student with an access code for InfoTrac College Edition, a fully searchable on-line university library containing complete articles and their images. Its database allows access to hundreds of scholarly and popular publications—all reliable sources, including magazines, journals, encyclopedias, and newsletters.

Turner Learning/CNN Economics Video with Integration Guide   Professors can bring the real world into the classroom by using the Turner Learning/CNN Economics Video. This video provides current stories of economic interest. The accompanying integration guide provides a summary and discussion questions for each clip. The video is produced in cooperation with Turner Learning, Inc. Contact your South-Western/Thomson Learning sales representative for ordering information.

For the Student   South-Western also offers supplements for students who are studying the principles of economics. These supplements reinforce the basic lessons taught in this book and offer opportunities for additional practice and feedback.

Study Guide   David R. Hakes (University of Northern Iowa) has prepared a study guide that will enhance student success. Each chapter of the study guide includes learning objectives, a description of the chapter's context and purpose, a chapter review, key terms and definitions, advanced critical thinking questions, and helpful hints for understanding difficult concepts. Students can develop their understanding by doing the practice problems and short-answer questions, then assess their mastery of the key concepts with the self-test, which includes true/false and multiple-choice questions. Solutions to all problems are included in the study guide.

Mankiw Xtra! Web Site This site (http://mankiwxtra.swlearning.com) offers a robust set of on-line multimedia learning tools to help the student gain a deeper and richer understanding of economics, including:

- Diagnostic Pretests offer diagnostic self-assessment on student comprehension of each chapter and an individualized plan for directed study.
- The MAP (**M**ankiw **L**earning **A**ssistance **P**rogram) provides step-by-step instructions for each chapter's learning objectives to systematically guide the student to a deeper understanding of economic concepts.
- The Graphing Workshop is a one-stop learning resource for help in mastering the often difficult language of graphs. A unique learning system made up of graphing tutorials, interactive drawing tools, and exercises, it teaches the student how to interpret, reproduce, and explain graphs.
- CNN Video Clips and exercises let the student see economics in action in the real world, to help learn theoretical material by applying it to current events.
- Ask the Author Video Clips provide the student with an opportunity for review and clarification of difficult material.
- Xtra! Quizzing allows the student to create and to take randomly generated quizzes on the chapter of his or her choice.
- Economic Applications (e-con apps), including EconNews Online, EconDebate Online, and EconData Online, features help to deepen student understanding of theoretical concepts through hands-on exploration and analysis of the latest economic news stories, policy debates, and data.

PowerPoint Lecture Notes A booklet is available that contains the Lecture Presentation in PowerPoint (both the notes and the graphics) with space next to each slide for taking notes during class. This supplement allows students to focus on classroom activities by providing them with the confident knowledge that they have an excellent set of notes for future reference. Instructors who choose to customize their PowerPoint presentations and would like to do the same with their accompanying customized printed lecture notes can do so via South-Western/ Thomson Learning's custom publishing program.

Web Site Valuable resources for students can be found on the Internet at the Mankiw textbook support site: http://mankiw.swlearning.com. Students will find links to economics-related Internet sites, PowerPoint slides for their review, and a sample chapter from the study guide. Also, career listings for students, leading economic indicator information, and an economic URL database can be found at http://economics.swlearning.com.

Economics Alive! CD-ROMS These interactive multimedia study aids for economics are the high-tech, high-fun way to study economics. Through a combination of animated presentations, interactive graphing exercises, and simulations, the core principles of economics come to life and are driven home in an upbeat and entertaining way. This product is available in both micro and macro economics versions. Find out more at http://econalive.swlearning.com.

Favorite Ways to Learn Economics Authors David Anderson of Centre College and Jim Chasey of Homewood Flossmoor High School use experiments to bring economic education to life. This is a lab manual for the classroom and for individual study that contains experiments and problem sets that reinforce key economic concepts.

9/11: Economic Viewpoints The shape, pace, and spirit of the global economy has been greatly impacted by the events that occurred on September 11, 2001. South-Western now offers a new collection of essays that provides a variety of perspectives on the economic effects of these events. Each essay is written by one of South-Western's economics textbook authors, all of whom are highly regarded for both their academic and professional achievements. This unique collaboration results in one of the most cutting-edge resources available to help facilitate discussion of September 11th's impact within the context of economics courses.

Translations and Adaptations

I am delighted that versions of this book are (or will soon be) available in many of the world's languages. Currently scheduled translations include Chinese (in both standard and simple characters), Czech, French, Georgian, German, Greek, Indonesian, Italian, Japanese, Korean, Portuguese, Romanian, Russian, and Spanish. In addition, adaptations of the book for Canadian and Australian students are also available. Instructors who would like more information about these books should contact South-Western College Publishing.

Acknowledgments

In writing this book, I had the benefit of the input from many talented people. Let me begin by thanking those economics professors who read and commented on portions of the manuscript for this edition:

Uzo Agulefo,
  Northlake College
Josiah Baker,
  University of Central Florida
Charles A. Bennett,
  Gannon University
Joyce C. Bremer,
  Oakton Community College
Anne Bunton,
  Cottey College
Raymond L. Cohn,
  Illinois State University
Ron Cronovich,
  University of Nevada–Las Vegas
Susan Dadres,
  Southern Methodist University
Alan Deardorff,
  University of Michigan
Elizabeth Dickhaus,
  University of Missouri, St. Louis
Stratford M. Douglas,
  West Virginia University
Patricia J. Euzent,
  University of Central Florida

Ali Faegh,
  Houston Community College
Fred Foldvary,
  Santa Clara University
David Hakes,
  University of Northern Iowa
Andy Hanssen,
  Montana State University
Joseph Haslag,
  University of Missouri
F. Steb Hipple,
  East Tennessee State University
Brian T. Kench,
  University of New Hampshire
Jim Lee,
  Texas A&M University–Corpus Christi
Fiona C. Maclachlan,
  Manhattan College
Daniel R. Marburger,
  Arkansas State University
Pete Mavrokordatos,
  Tarrant County College–University of Phoenix
Carmen F. Menezes,
  University of Missouri

Thomas F. Pogue,
  University of Iowa
Gyan Pradhan,
  Westminster College
Ratha Ramoo,
  Diablo Valley College
Marlene M. Reed,
  Samford University
William Sander,
  DePaul University
Jonathan Sandy,
  University of San Diego

Sue Lynn Sasser,
  University of Central Oklahoma
William Seyfried,
  Winthrop University
Stanton Ullerich,
  Buena Vista University
John Volpe,
  Trinity College
William C. Wood,
  James Madison University
Bassam Yousif,
  California State University–Fullerton

Many professors contributed to the planning of this edition by reviewing the second edition. I am grateful for their suggestions and ideas:

James Q. Aylsworth,
  Lakeland Community College
Laurence Ball,
  Johns Hopkins University
James F. Booker,
  Alfred University
Gerry Boyle,
  National University of Ireland
Joyce C. Bremer,
  Oakton Community College
Anne Bunton,
  Cottey College
Catherine Carey,
  Western Kentucky University
Christopher M. Cornell,
  Fordham University
Dean Croushore,
  Federal Reserve Bank of Philadelphia
Anna Della Vale,
  Columbia University
Stratford Douglas,
  West Virginia University
Gerard D'Souza,
  West Virginia University
David A. Dyer,
  University of Central Florida
Sally G. Finch,
  The Westminster Schools
Eric Fisher,
  The Ohio State University
Yee-Tien Fu,
  National Chen-Chi University (Taiwan)
Sylvestre Gaudin,
  Oberlin College
Tommy Georgiades,
  DeVry Institute of Technology
Abhay Ghiara,
  DeVry Institute of Technology
Douglas Irwin,
  Dartmouth College

Brian T. Kench,
  University of New Hampshire
Richard Lotspeich,
  Indiana State University
Fiona Maclachlan,
  Manhattan College
Rodney A. Madsen,
  Long Beach City College
Daniel Marburger,
  Arkansas State University
Marlene M. Reed,
  Samford University
Stuart S. Rosenthal,
  Syracuse University
June Roux,
  Salem Community College
Juha Seppälä,
  University of Illinois
Genevieve Signoret,
  University of Arkansas
Henry Siu,
  Northwestern University
Dick Stanford,
  Furman University
John J. Stevens,
  University of Minnesota
Ginger H. Szabo,
  DeVry Institute of Technology
Soumaya Tohamy,
  Berry College
Randall E. Waldron,
  University of South Dakota
Michael Welker,
  Franciscan University (Ohio)
James D. Whitney,
  Occidental College
Bonnie Wilson,
  The University of Maryland, Baltimore County
Kathryn Wilson,
  Kent State University

I appreciate the diligence of the diary reviewers. Their insights while using the second edition have contributed significantly to the third:

Ugur Aker,
Hiram College
Charles A. Bennett,
Gannon University
Elizabeth Dickhaus,
University of Missouri, St. Louis
Sharon Eicher,
Kansas State University

Chris Johnson,
Texas A&M University
Mark Karscig,
Central Missouri State University
Gary Lynch,
Indiana University, Northwest
Sharon Ryan,
University of Missouri–Columbia

The accuracy of a textbook is critically important. Although I am, of course, responsible for any remaining errors, I am grateful to the following professors for reading through final manuscript and page proof with me:

Tibor Besedes,
Rutgers University
Ronald Elkins,
Central Washington University

Marlene M. Reed,
Samford University
Thomas Rhoads,
Towson University

The following instructors participated in on-line surveys conducted during the revision process, contributing to the development of the text and the supplements:

Seemi Ahmad,
Dutchess County Community College
Gwendolyn Alexander,
Fordham University
Shahina Amin,
University of Northern Iowa
Cynthia Bansak,
San Diego State University
Gerald Baumgardner,
Gettysburg College
Doris Bennett,
Jacksonville State University
Ralph Brown,
University of South Dakota
David Carr,
American University
Byron Chapman,
University of Georgia
Raymond L. Cohn,
Illinois State University
Richard H. Courtney,
St Mary's College of California
Peter R. Crabb,
Northwest Nazarene College
Patrick Crowley,
Texas A&M University–Corpus Christi
Maria DaCosta,
University of Wisconsin–Eau Claire
Susan Dadres,
Southern Methodist University
Alan Deardorff,
University of Michigan
Stacy Dickert-Conlin,
Syracuse University

David Eaton,
Murray State University
Ronald Elkins,
Central Washington University
Zaki Eusufzai,
Loyola Marymount University
Patricia Euzent,
University of Central Florida
Ali Faegh,
Houston Community College
Donald Fagan,
Daniel Webster College
Daniel Flores-Guri,
Skidmore College
Fred Foldvary,
Santa Clara University
Robert Francis,
Shoreline Community College
Mark Frank,
Sam Houston State University
Rachel Friedberg,
Brown University
Lisa Geib-Gunderson,
University of Maryland
Jeffrey Gerlach,
The College of William and Mary
Mark Gius,
Quinnipiac University
Raj Goel,
Illinois State University
Lisa Grobar,
California State University–Long Beach
Barnali Gupta,
Miami University (Ohio)

Andy Hanssen,
  Montana State University
F. Steb Hipple,
  East Tennessee State University
Tom Hyclak,
  Lehigh University
Hans Isakson,
  University of Northern Iowa
Kristin Kucsma,
  Seton Hall University
Reuben Kyle,
  Middle Tennessee State University
Rose LaMont,
  Modesto Junior College
Jim Lee,
  Texas A&M University–Corpus Christi
Mary Lesser,
  Iona College
Martin Ludlum,
  Oklahoma City Community College
Ken McCormick,
  University of Northern Iowa
Khalid Mehtabdin,
  The College of Saint Rose
Kusum Mundra,
  San Diego State University

David O'Gorman,
  Santa Fe Community College
Darrell Parker,
  Georgia Southern University
Min Qi,
  Kent State University
William Sander,
  DePaul University
Robert Schwab,
  University of Maryland
William Seyfried,
  Winthrop University
David Sisk,
  San Francisco State University
Peter Thiel,
  Paradise Valley Community College
Stanton Ullerich,
  Buena Vista University
Sharmila Vishwasrao,
  Florida Atlantic University
Larry Wilson,
  Sandhills Community College
Jeff Yankow,
  Furman University
Bassam Yousif,
  California State University–Fullerton

Market surveys were conducted in preparation for this third edition of the textbook and its supplements. I appreciate the time taken by my colleagues to contribute their comments and am grateful for the useful information that they provided.

The success of the first two editions of this textbook was due in part to the many reviewers who helped me shape the manuscript. I continue to be grateful for their comments:

Kathleen S. Adler
Ashraf Afifi
Douglas Agbetsiafa
Seemin Ahmad
Rasheed Al-Hmoud
Terence Alexander
Neil O. Alper
Christine Amsler
Lisa Anderson
Kim Andrews
Okechukwu Dennis
  Anyamele
Clyde Arnold
Mahmoud P. Arya
Aliakbar Ataiifar
Leonardo Auernheimer
Paul Azrak
Kevin Baird
Stephen A. Baker
William Barber
Dru Barker
Daniel Barszcz
Klaus Becker
Doris Bennett
David Black

Peter Boettke
Michael Boyd
Chuck Britton
Robert Brooker
Oscar Brookins
Doug Brown
Mary Bumgarner
Robert J. Burrus, Jr.
Rebecca Campbell
Catherine Carey
Michael Carter
Thomas Cate
Subir Chakrabarti
Kenneth S. Chapman
John Chilton
Joy Clark
Howard Cochran
Paul Comolli
Joyce Cooper
Ron Cronovich
Dean Croushore
Susan Dadres
Doug Dalenberg
Patrick Dalendina
Justino De La Cruz

Alan Deardorff
Mary E. Deily
Stacy Dickert-Conlin
Elizabeth Dickhaus
Amy Diduch
Vern Dobis
Veda Doss
Mike Dowd
Richard Easterlin
James Eden
John Edgren
Ronald Elkins
Steffany Ellis
S. Kirk Elwood
Amy Farmer
Rick Fenner
David Figlio
Lehman Fletcher
Richard Fowles
Thomas Fox
Joseph W. Franklin
Jim Gapinski
Gay Garesche
Linda Ghent
Philip Gibbs

Kirk Gifford
J. Robert Gillette
Robert Gitter
Mark Paul Gius
Darrell Glenn
Robert Godby
Stephan F. Gohmann
Patrick Gormely
Randy Grant
Philip Gregorowicz
James Grisham
Lisa Grobar
Kwabena Gyimah-
 Brempong
R. W. Hafer
David R. Hakes
Arne Hallam
Andrew Hanssen
Mehdi Haririan
Richard Harper
Robert Harris
James Hartley
Jac C. Heckelman
Ron Heisner
James Henderson
Jannett Highfill
Daniel Himarios
Jane Himarios
Norman Hollingsworth
Thomas Husted
Beth Ingram
Darius Irani
Dwight Israelsen
A. Andrew John
Brenda Johnson
Stephen D. Joyce
Leo Kahane
Brad Kamp
Demetri Kantarelis
Mark Karscig
Alexander Katkov
Diane Keenan
Manfred Keil
George Kelley
Mark Killingsworth
Philip King
Linda Kinney
Peter Klein
Charles Klingensmith
Morris Knapp
Todd Knoop

James Knudson
Faik Koray
Patricia Koss
Marie Kratochvil
Rajaram Krishnan
Robert Krol
Penny Kugler
Mike Kupilik
Bob Lawson
Dan LeClair
Danielle Lewis
Stephen Lile
Luis Locay
Thomas Maloy
Neela Manage
Mike Marlow
Don Matthews
Cynthia McCarty
Bruce McClung
Rob Roy McGregor
Eugene McKibben
Thomas Means
Michael Meeropol
Deborah Merrigan
Charles Michalopoulos
Jeffrey Miron
Marie T. Mora
George Nagy
Farzeen Nasri
Walter Nicholson
Stephen Nord
Farrokh Nourzad
Tony O'Brien
John O'Connell
Peter K. Olson
Z. Edward O'Relley
Jack W. Osman
Jan Palmer
Ransford Palmer
Chris Papageorgiou
Tim Perri
Timothy Petry
Harmanna Poen
Naga Pulikonda
James Ragan
Reza Ramazani
Arnold H. Raphaelson
William Rawson
Francis E. Raymond III
Christine Rider
Steve Robinson

Christina Romer
S. Scanlon Romer
Joshua L. Rosenbloom
Leola Ross
Rose Rubin
Daniel Rupp
Fred J. Ruppel
Lynda Rush
Simran Sahi
Jolyne Sanjak
Rolando Santos
Sue Lynn Sasser
Edward Scahill
Torsten Schmidt
Bruce Seaman
Stanley Sedo
Michael Seelye
Linda Shaffer
Alden Shiers
David Shorow
Charles Sicotte
Mike Smitka
John Sondey
Kwang Soo Cheong
G.A. Spiva
Dennis Starleaf
William K. Steen
E. Frank Stephenson
Edward Stuart
Charles Stull
James L. Swofford
Bryan Taylor
James Thornton
Deborah Thorsen
Arthur Tobin
Naor Bich Tran
Tony Uremovic
Sharmila Vishwasrao
Joseph Walka
Harold Warren
Jack R. Wegman
Stephen Weiler
James Wetzel
Steven L. Widener
Joan Wiggenhorn
William Wood
Linus Yamane
Abdi Zahedani
Joachim Zietz

A special thanks go to Karen Dynan, Douglas Elmendorf, and Dean Croushore, who drafted many of the problems and applications presented at the end of each chapter. Yvonne Zinfon, my assistant at Harvard, as usual went beyond the call of duty as this edition was being prepared. I am also grateful to Fuad Faridi, a Harvard undergraduate, for assisting me in the final stages of this project.

The team of editors who worked on this book improved it tremendously. Jane Tufts, developmental editor, provided truly spectacular editing—as she always does. Peter Adams, senior economics acquisitions editor, did a splendid job of overseeing the many people involved in such a large project. Sarah Dorger, developmental editor, assembled an excellent team to write the supplements while managing thousands of related details. Dan Plofchan, production editor, along with the staff at Thistle Hill Publishing Services and GAC Indianapolis, had the patience and dedication necessary to turn my manuscript into this book. OffCenter Concept House professionally executed the production of the print supplements. Mike Stratton, senior designer, gave this book its clean, friendly look. Michele Gitlin, copyeditor, refined my prose, and Alexandra Nickerson, indexer, prepared a careful and thorough index. Janet Hennies, senior marketing manager, worked long hours getting the word out to potential users of this book, even as she gave birth to a future reader of it. Tom Gay, formerly of Harcourt, was instrumental in early stages of planning. Jeff Gilbreath worked as development editor until his untimely death; we will miss him. The rest of the South-Western team was also consistently professional, enthusiastic, and dedicated: Jon Schneider, Jenny Fruechtenicht, Terron Sanders, Carrie Hochstrasser, Vicky True, Peggy Buskey, Pam Wallace, and Sandee Milewski.

I must also thank my "in house" editor—Deborah Mankiw. As the first reader of almost everything I write, she continued to offer just the right mix of criticism and encouragement.

Finally, I am grateful to my children, Catherine, Nicholas, and Peter. Their unpredictable visits to my study offered welcome relief from long spans of writing and rewriting. Although now they are only ten, eight, and four years old, someday they will grow up and study the principles of economics. I hope this book provides its readers some of the education and enlightenment that I wish for my own children.

N. Gregory Mankiw
October 2002

PREFACE: TO THE STUDENT

"Economics is a study of mankind in the ordinary business of life." So wrote Alfred Marshall, the great nineteenth-century economist, in his textbook, *Principles of Economics*. Although we have learned much about the economy since Marshall's time, this definition of economics is as true today as it was in 1890, when the first edition of his text was published.

Why should you, as a student at the beginning of the twenty-first century, embark on the study of economics? There are three reasons.

The first reason to study economics is that it will help you understand the world in which you live. There are many questions about the economy that might spark your curiosity. Why are apartments so hard to find in New York City? Why do airlines charge less for a round-trip ticket if the traveler stays over a Saturday night? Why is Robin Williams paid so much to star in movies? Why are living standards so meager in many African countries? Why do some countries have high rates of inflation while others have stable prices? Why are jobs easy to find in some years and hard to find in others? These are just a few of the questions that a course in economics will help you answer.

The second reason to study economics is that it will make you a more astute participant in the economy. As you go about your life, you make many economic decisions. While you are a student, you decide how many years to stay in school. Once you take a job, you decide how much of your income to spend, how much to save, and how to invest your savings. Someday you may find yourself running a small business or a large corporation, and you will decide what prices to charge for your products. The insights developed in the coming chapters will give you a new perspective on how best to make these decisions. Studying economics will not by itself make you rich, but it will give you some tools that may help in that endeavor.

The third reason to study economics is that it will give you a better understanding of the potential and limits of economic policy. As a voter, you help choose the policies that guide the allocation of society's resources. When deciding which policies to support, you may find yourself asking various questions about economics. What are the burdens associated with alternative forms of taxation? What are the effects of free trade with other countries? What is the best way to protect the environment? How does a government budget deficit affect the economy? These and similar questions are always on the minds of policymakers in mayors' offices, governors' mansions, and the White House.

Thus the principles of economics can be applied in many of life's situations. Whether the future finds you reading the newspaper, running a business, or sitting in the Oval Office, you will be glad that you studied economics.

N. Gregory Mankiw
October 2002

BRIEF CONTENTS

PART 1 **INTRODUCTION 1**

CHAPTER 1 Ten Principles of Economics 3
CHAPTER 2 Thinking Like an Economist 19
CHAPTER 3 Interdependence and the Gains from Trade 45

PART 2 **SUPPLY AND DEMAND I: HOW MARKETS WORK 61**

CHAPTER 4 The Market Forces of Supply and Demand 63
CHAPTER 5 Elasticity and Its Application 89
CHAPTER 6 Supply, Demand, and Government Policies 113

PART 3 **SUPPLY AND DEMAND II: MARKETS AND WELFARE 135**

CHAPTER 7 Consumers, Producers, and the Efficiency of Markets 137
CHAPTER 8 Application: The Costs of Taxation 159
CHAPTER 9 Application: International Trade 175

PART 4 **THE ECONOMICS OF THE PUBLIC SECTOR 201**

CHAPTER 10 Externalities 203

CHAPTER 11 Public Goods and Common Resources 223
CHAPTER 12 The Design of the Tax System 241

PART 5 **FIRM BEHAVIOR AND THE ORGANIZATION OF INDUSTRY 265**

CHAPTER 13 The Costs of Production 267
CHAPTER 14 Firms in Competitive Markets 289
CHAPTER 15 Monopoly 313
CHAPTER 16 Oligopoly 345
CHAPTER 17 Monopolistic Competition 373

PART 6 **THE ECONOMICS OF LABOR MARKETS 389**

CHAPTER 18 The Markets for the Factors of Production 391
CHAPTER 19 Earnings and Discrimination 411
CHAPTER 20 Income Inequality and Poverty 429

PART 7 **TOPICS FOR FURTHER STUDY 451**

CHAPTER 21 The Theory of Consumer Choice 453
CHAPTER 22 Frontiers of Microeconomics 479

Glossary 497

Index 501

TABLE OF CONTENTS

Preface: **To the Instructor** v
Preface: **To the Student** xxii

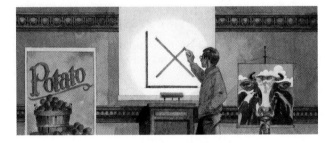

PART 1
INTRODUCTION 1

CHAPTER 1
TEN PRINCIPLES OF ECONOMICS 3

How People Make Decisions 4
  Principle #1: People Face Tradeoffs 4
  Principle #2: The Cost of Something
    Is What You Give Up to Get It 5
  Principle #3: Rational People Think at the Margin 6
  Principle #4: People Respond to Incentives 7

How People Interact 8
  Principle #5: Trade Can Make Everyone Better Off 8
  Principle #6: Markets Are Usually a Good Way
    to Organize Economic Activity 9
  FYI: Adam Smith and the Invisible Hand
  Principle #7: Governments Can Sometimes
    Improve Market Outcomes 10

How the Economy as a Whole Works 11
  Principle #8: A Country's Standard of Living
    Depends on Its Ability to Produce Goods
    and Services 11
  Principle #9: Prices Rise When the Government
    Prints Too Much Money 12
  Principle #10: Society Faces a Short-Run Tradeoff
    between Inflation and Unemployment 13
  FYI: How to Read This Book
Conclusion 15
Summary 15

Key Concepts 16
Questions for Review 16
Problems and Applications 16

CHAPTER 2
THINKING LIKE AN ECONOMIST 19

The Economist as Scientist 20
  The Scientific Method: Observation, Theory,
    and More Observation 21
  The Role of Assumptions 21
  Economic Models 22
  Our First Model: The Circular-Flow Diagram 23
  Our Second Model: The Production Possibilities
    Frontier 24
  Microeconomics and Macroeconomics 26

The Economist as Policy Adviser 28
  Positive versus Normative Analysis 28
  Economists in Washington 29

Why Economists Disagree 30
  Differences in Scientific Judgments 30
  Differences in Values 31
  Perception versus Reality 31

Let's Get Going 32
Summary 33
Key Concepts 33
Questions for Review 33
Problems and Applications 34

Appendix   Graphing: A Brief Review 36
  Graphs of a Single Variable 36
  Graphs of Two Variables: The Coordinate System 36
  Curves in the Coordinate System 37
  Slope 41
  Cause and Effect 42

CHAPTER 3
INTERDEPENDENCE AND THE GAINS FROM TRADE 45

A Parable for the Modern Economy 46
  Production Possibilities 46
  Specialization and Trade 48

Mankiw xtra!

CONGRATULATIONS!

Your purchase of this new textbook includes complimentary access to the Mankiw Xtra! Web Site (http://mankiwxtra.swlearning.com). This site offers a robust set of online multimedia learning tools to help you gain a deeper and richer understanding of economics, including:

DIAGNOSTIC PRETESTS

Innovative quizzes that offer diagnostic self-assessment on your comprehension of each chapter and an individualized plan for directed study.

THE MAP (Mankiw Learning Assistance Program)

Provides step-by-step instructions for each chapter's learning objectives to systematically guide you through deepening your understanding of concepts.

THE GRAPHING WORKSHOP

A one-stop learning resource for help in mastering the often difficult language of graphs. A unique learning system made up of graphing tutorials, interactive drawing tools, and exercises that teaches you how to interpret, reproduce, and explain graphs.

CNN VIDEO CLIPS

CNN video segments and exercises let you see economics in action, in the real world, to help you learn theoretical material by applying it to current events.

ASK THE AUTHOR VIDEO CLIPS

These video clips, featuring N. Gregory Mankiw, are extremely helpful for review and clarification on material if you have trouble understanding an in-class lecture.

XTRA! QUIZZING

You can create and take randomly-generated quizzes on whichever chapter(s) you wish to test yourself, and endlessly practice for exams.

ECONOMIC APPLICATIONS

EconNews Online, EconDebate Online, and EconData Online features help to deepen your understanding of theoretical concepts through hands-on exploration and analysis of the latest economic news stories, policy debates, and data.

Tear Out Card Missing?

If you did not buy a new textbook, the tear-out portion of this card may be missing, or the Access Code may not be valid. Access Codes can be used only once to register for access to Mankiw Xtra!, and are not transferable. You can choose to either buy a new book or purchase access to the Mankiw Xtra! site at http://mankiwxtra.swlearning.com.

HOW TO REGISTER YOUR SERIAL NUMBER

STEP 1 Launch a Web browser and go to http://mankiwxtra.swlearning.com

STEP 2 Click the "Register" button to enter your serial number.

STEP 3 Enter your serial number exactly as it appears here and create a unique User ID, or enter an existing User ID if you have previously registered for a different product via a serial number.

SERIAL NUMBER: SC-00116P60-NXTR

STEP 4 When prompted, create a password (or enter an existing password, if you have previously registered for a different product via a serial number). Submit the necessary information when prompted. Record your User ID and password in a secure location.

STEP 5 Once registered, follow the link to enter the product, or return to the URL above and select the "Enter" button. Note that the duration of your access to the product begins when registration is complete.

xtra!

THOMSON
SOUTH-WESTERN

For technical support, contact
1-800-423-0563
or email
support@thomsonlearning.cc

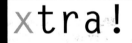

The Principle of Comparative Advantage 50
  Absolute Advantage 51
  Opportunity Cost and Comparative Advantage 51
  Comparative Advantage and Trade 52
  FYI: The Legacy of Adam Smith
    and David Ricardo

Applications of Comparative Advantage 54
  Should Tiger Woods Mow His Own Lawn? 54
  Should the United States Trade with
    Other Countries? 56
  IN THE NEWS: Who Has a Comparative Advantage in
    Producing Lamb?
Conclusion 56
Summary 57
Key Concepts 57
Questions for Review 57
Problems and Applications 57

PART 2
SUPPLY AND DEMAND I:
HOW MARKETS WORK 61

CHAPTER 4
THE MARKET FORCES OF SUPPLY AND DEMAND 63

Markets and Competition 64
  Competitive Markets 64
  Competition: Perfect and Otherwise 64

Demand 65
  The Demand Curve: The Relationship between Price and
    Quantity Demanded 65
  Market Demand versus Individual Demand 66
  Shifts in the Demand Curve 67
  CASE STUDY: Two Ways to Reduce the Quantity
    of Smoking Demanded

Supply 71
  The Supply Curve: The Relationship
    between Price and Quantity Supplied 71
  Market Supply versus Individual Supply 72
  Shifts in the Supply Curve 73

Supply and Demand Together 75
  Equilibrium 75
  Three Steps to Analyzing Changes in Equilibrium 77
  IN THE NEWS: Mother Nature Shifts the Supply
    Curve
Conclusion: How Prices Allocate Resources 83
Summary 84
Key Concepts 85
Questions for Review 85
Problems and Applications 86

CHAPTER 5
ELASTICITY AND ITS APPLICATION 89

The Elasticity of Demand 90
  The Price Elasticity of Demand and Its Determinants 90
  Computing the Price Elasticity of Demand 91
  The Midpoint Method: A Better Way to Calculate
    Percentage Changes and Elasticities 92
  The Variety of Demand Curves 94
  Total Revenue and the Price Elasticity of Demand 94
  Elasticity and Total Revenue along a Linear Demand
    Curve 96
  CASE STUDY: Pricing Admission to a Museum
  IN THE NEWS: On the Road with Elasticity
  Other Demand Elasticities 99

The Elasticity of Supply 100
  The Price Elasticity of Supply and Its Determinants 100
  Computing the Price Elasticity of Supply 101
  The Variety of Supply Curves 101

**Three Applications of Supply, Demand,
  and Elasticity** 104
  Can Good News for Farming Be Bad News for
    Farmers? 104
  Why Did OPEC Fail to Keep the Price of Oil High? 106
  Does Drug Interdiction Increase or Decrease
    Drug-Related Crime? 108
Conclusion 109
Summary 110
Key Concepts 110
Questions for Review 110
Problems and Applications 111

CHAPTER 6
SUPPLY, DEMAND, AND GOVERNMENT POLICIES 113

Controls on Prices 114
How Price Ceilings Affect Market Outcomes 114
CASE STUDY: Lines at the Gas Pump
IN THE NEWS: Does a Drought Need to Cause a Water
Shortage?
CASE STUDY: Rent Control in the Short Run and
Long Run
How Price Floors Affect Market Outcomes 120
CASE STUDY: The Minimum Wage
Evaluating Price Controls 123

Taxes 124
How Taxes on Buyers Affect Market Outcomes 124
How Taxes on Sellers Affect Market Outcomes 126
CASE STUDY: Can Congress Distribute the Burden of
a Payroll Tax?
Elasticity and Tax Incidence 128
CASE STUDY: Who Pays the Luxury Tax?

Conclusion 131
Summary 131
Key Concepts 131
Questions for Review 131
Problems and Applications 132

PART 3
SUPPLY AND DEMAND II:
MARKETS AND WELFARE 135

CHAPTER 7
CONSUMERS, PRODUCERS,
AND THE EFFICIENCY OF MARKETS 137

Consumer Surplus 138
Willingness to Pay 138
Using the Demand Curve to Measure Consumer
Surplus 139
How a Lower Price Raises Consumer Surplus 140
What Does Consumer Surplus Measure? 141

Producer Surplus 143
Cost and the Willingness to Sell 143
Using the Supply Curve to Measure Producer Surplus 144
How a Higher Price Raises Producer Surplus 146

Market Efficiency 147
The Benevolent Social Planner 147
Evaluating the Market Equilibrium 148
IN THE NEWS: Ticket Scalping
CASE STUDY: Should There Be a Market in Organs?
IN THE NEWS: How Pilgrims Embraced the Market
Conclusion: Market Efficiency and Market Failure 154
Summary 155
Key Concepts 155
Questions for Review 155
Problems and Applications 156

CHAPTER 8
APPLICATION: THE COSTS OF TAXATION 159

The Deadweight Loss of Taxation 160
How a Tax Affects Market Participants 161
Deadweight Losses and the Gains from Trade 163

The Determinants of the Deadweight Loss 164
CASE STUDY: The Deadweight Loss Debate
FYI: Henry George and the Land Tax

Deadweight Loss and Tax Revenue as Taxes Vary 167
CASE STUDY: The Laffer Curve and Supply-Side
Economics
Conclusion 171
Summary 172
Key Concepts 172
Questions for Review 172
Problems and Applications 172

CHAPTER 9
APPLICATION: INTERNATIONAL TRADE 175

The Determinants of Trade 176
The Equilibrium without Trade 176
The World Price and Comparative Advantage 177

The Winners and Losers from Trade 178
The Gains and Losses of an Exporting Country 178

The Gains and Losses of an Importing Country 180
The Effects of a Tariff 182
IN THE NEWS: Life in Isoland
The Effects of an Import Quota 185
The Lessons for Trade Policy 187
FYI: Other Benefits of International Trade

The Arguments for Restricting Trade 188
The Jobs Argument 188
The National-Security Argument 189
The Infant-Industry Argument 190
The Unfair-Competition Argument 190
IN THE NEWS: Trade Policy in India
The Protection-as-a-Bargaining-Chip Argument 191
CASE STUDY: Trade Agreements and the World Trade
   Organization
IN THE NEWS: Globalization

Conclusion 194

Summary 195

Key Concepts 196

Questions for Review 196

Problems and Applications 196

PART 4
THE ECONOMICS OF
THE PUBLIC SECTOR 201

CHAPTER 10
EXTERNALITIES 203

Externalities and Market Inefficiency 204
Welfare Economics: A Recap 205
Negative Externalities 206
Positive Externalities 207
CASE STUDY: Technology Spillovers and
   Industrial Policy

Private Solutions to Externalities 209
The Types of Private Solutions 209
The Coase Theorem 210
Why Private Solutions Do Not Always Work 211

Public Policies toward Externalities 212
Regulation 212
Pigovian Taxes and Subsidies 213
CASE STUDY: Why Is Gasoline Taxed So Heavily?
Tradable Pollution Permits 215
Objections to the Economic Analysis of Pollution 216
IN THE NEWS: Children as Externalities

Conclusion 217

Summary 218

Key Concepts 219

Questions for Review 220

Problems and Applications 220

CHAPTER 11
PUBLIC GOODS AND COMMON RESOURCES 223

The Different Kinds of Goods 224

Public Goods 225
The Free-Rider Problem 226
Some Important Public Goods 226
CASE STUDY: Are Lighthouses Public Goods?
The Difficult Job of Cost-Benefit Analysis 229
CASE STUDY: How Much Is a Life Worth?

Common Resources 231
The Tragedy of the Commons 231
Some Important Common Resources 232
IN THE NEWS: The Singapore Solution
CASE STUDY: Why the Cow Is Not Extinct
IN THE NEWS: Should Yellowstone Charge as Much as
   Disney World?

Conclusion: The Importance of Property Rights 236

Summary 237

Key Concepts 237

Questions for Review 237

Problems and Applications 237

CHAPTER 12
THE DESIGN OF THE TAX SYSTEM 241

A Financial Overview of the U.S. Government 242
The Federal Government 242
State and Local Government 246

Taxes and Efficiency 248
Deadweight Losses 248

CASE STUDY: Should Income or Consumption
   Be Taxed?
Administrative Burden   250
Marginal Tax Rates versus Average Tax Rates   250
CASE STUDY: Iceland's Natural Experiment
Lump-Sum Taxes   251
IN THE NEWS: How Taxes Affect Married Women

Taxes and Equity   253
   The Benefits Principle   254
   The Ability-to-Pay Principle   254
   CASE STUDY: How the Tax Burden Is Distributed
   CASE STUDY: Horizontal Equity and the Marriage Tax
   Tax Incidence and Tax Equity   258
   CASE STUDY: Who Pays the Corporate Income Tax?
   IN THE NEWS: The Case against Taxing
      Capital Income
Conclusion: The Tradeoff between Equity and
   Efficiency   260
Summary   261
Key Concepts   261
Questions for Review   262
Problems and Applications   262

PART 5

FIRM BEHAVIOR AND
THE ORGANIZATION OF INDUSTRY   265

CHAPTER 13
THE COSTS OF PRODUCTION   267

What Are Costs?   268
   Total Revenue, Total Cost, and Profit   268
   Costs as Opportunity Costs   268
   The Cost of Capital as an Opportunity Cost   269
   Economic Profit versus Accounting Profit   270
   IN THE NEWS: True Profit versus Fictitious Profit

Production and Costs   271

   The Production Function   272
   From the Production Function to the Total-Cost
      Curve   273

The Various Measures of Cost   275
   Fixed and Variable Costs   276
   Average and Marginal Cost   277
   Cost Curves and Their Shapes   278
   Typical Cost Curves   279

Costs in the Short Run and in the Long Run   280
   The Relationship between Short-Run and Long-Run
      Average Total Cost   280
   Economies and Diseconomies of Scale   283
   FYI: Lessons from a Pin Factory
Conclusion   284
Summary   285
Key Concepts   285
Questions for Review   285
Problems and Applications   286

CHAPTER 14
FIRMS IN COMPETITIVE MARKETS   289

What Is a Competitive Market?   290
   The Meaning of Competition   290
   The Revenue of a Competitive Firm   291

Profit Maximization and the Competitive Firm's Supply
   Curve   292
   A Simple Example of Profit Maximization   292
   The Marginal-Cost Curve and the Firm's Supply
      Decision   294
   The Firm's Short-Run Decision to Shut Down   295
   Spilt Milk and Other Sunk Costs   297
   CASE STUDY: Near-Empty Restaurants and Off-Season
      Miniature Golf
   The Firm's Long-Run Decision to Exit or Enter
      a Market   298
   Measuring Profit in Our Graph for the Competitive
      Firm   299

The Supply Curve in a Competitive Market   301
   The Short Run: Market Supply with a Fixed Number
      of Firms   301
   The Long Run: Market Supply with Entry and Exit   302
   Why Do Competitive Firms Stay in Business If They Make
      Zero Profit?   303
   A Shift in Demand in the Short Run and Long Run   304
   IN THE NEWS: Entry or Overinvestment?
   Why the Long-Run Supply Curve Might Slope
      Upward   304

Conclusion: Behind the Supply Curve 307

Summary 308

Key Concepts 308

Questions for Review 308

Problems and Applications 309

CHAPTER 15
MONOPOLY 313

Why Monopolies Arise 314
   Monopoly Resources 315
   CASE STUDY: The DeBeers Diamond Monopoly
   Government-Created Monopolies 316
   Natural Monopolies 316

How Monopolies Make Production
   and Pricing Decisions 318
   Monopoly versus Competition 318
   A Monopoly's Revenue 319
   Profit Maximization 321
   FYI: Why a Monopoly Does Not Have
     a Supply Curve
   A Monopoly's Profit 323
   CASE STUDY: Monopoly Drugs versus
     Generic Drugs

The Welfare Cost of Monopoly 325
   The Deadweight Loss 326
   The Monopoly's Profit: A Social Cost? 328

Public Policy toward Monopolies 329
   Increasing Competition with Antitrust Laws 329
   Regulation 330
   Public Ownership 331
   Doing Nothing 331
   IN THE NEWS: Public Transport and
     Private Enterprise

Price Discrimination 334
   A Parable about Pricing 334
   The Moral of the Story 335
   The Analytics of Price Discrimination 336
   Examples of Price Discrimination 337
   IN THE NEWS: Why People Pay More Than Dogs

Conclusion: The Prevalence of Monopoly 340

Summary 341

Key Concepts 341

Questions for Review 341

Problems and Applications 342

CHAPTER 16
OLIGOPOLY 345

Between Monopoly and Perfect Competition 346

Markets with Only a Few Sellers 347
   A Duopoly Example 348
   Competition, Monopolies, and Cartels 348
   IN THE NEWS: Modern Pirates
   The Equilibrium for an Oligopoly 349
   How the Size of an Oligopoly Affects
     the Market Outcome 352
   CASE STUDY: OPEC and the World Oil Market
   IN THE NEWS: The Growth of Oligopoly

Game Theory and the Economics of Cooperation 354
   The Prisoners' Dilemma 355
   Oligopolies as a Prisoners' Dilemma 356
   Other Examples of the Prisoners' Dilemma 357
   The Prisoners' Dilemma and the Welfare of Society 360
   Why People Sometimes Cooperate 361
   CASE STUDY: The Prisoners' Dilemma Tournament

Public Policy toward Oligopolies 362
   Restraint of Trade and the Antitrust Laws 363
   CASE STUDY: An Illegal Phone Call
   Controversies over Antitrust Policy 364
   CASE STUDY: The Microsoft Case
   IN THE NEWS: Antitrust in the New Economy

Conclusion 368

Summary 369

Key Concepts 369

Questions for Review 369

Problems and Applications 369

CHAPTER 17
MONOPOLISTIC COMPETITION 373

Competition with Differentiated Products 374
   The Monopolistically Competitive Firm
     in the Short Run 374
   The Long-Run Equilibrium 375
   Monopolistic versus Perfect Competition 377
   Monopolistic Competition and the Welfare of Society 379
   FYI: Is Excess Capacity a Social Problem?

Advertising 380
   The Debate over Advertising 381
   CASE STUDY: Advertising and the Price of Eyeglasses
   Advertising as a Signal of Quality 382

Brand Names 383
Conclusion 385
Summary 386
Key Concepts 386
Questions for Review 386
Problems and Applications 387

PART 6
THE ECONOMICS
OF LABOR MARKETS 389

CHAPTER 18
THE MARKETS FOR THE FACTORS OF PRODUCTION 391

The Demand for Labor 392
   The Competitive Profit-Maximizing Firm 393
   The Production Function
      and the Marginal Product of Labor 394
   The Value of the Marginal Product
      and the Demand for Labor 395
   FYI: Input Demand and Output Supply:
      Two Sides of the Same Coin
   What Causes the Labor Demand Curve to Shift? 397

The Supply of Labor 398
   The Tradeoff between Work and Leisure 398
   What Causes the Labor Supply Curve to Shift? 399

Equilibrium in the Labor Market 399
   Shifts in Labor Supply 400
   Shifts in Labor Demand 401
   CASE STUDY: Productivity and Wages
   FYI: Monopsony

The Other Factors of Production: Land and Capital 404
   Equilibrium in the Markets for Land and Capital 404
   FYI: What Is Capital Income?
   Linkages among the Factors of Production 406
   CASE STUDY: The Economics of the Black Death

Conclusion 408
Summary 408
Key Concepts 408
Questions for Review 409
Problems and Applications 409

CHAPTER 19
EARNINGS AND DISCRIMINATION 411

Some Determinants of Equilibrium Wages 412
   Compensating Differentials 412
   Human Capital 412
   CASE STUDY: The Increasing Value of Skills
   FYI: Looking for True Love? Go to School
   Ability, Effort, and Chance 414
   CASE STUDY: The Benefits of Beauty
   An Alternative View of Education: Signaling 416
   IN THE NEWS: Are Elite Colleges Worth
      the Cost?
   The Superstar Phenomenon 417
   Above-Equilibrium Wages: Minimum-Wage Laws,
      Unions, and Efficiency Wages 418

The Economics of Discrimination 420
   Measuring Labor-Market Discrimination 420
   Discrimination by Employers 422
   CASE STUDY: Segregated Streetcars and
      the Profit Motive
   Discrimination by Customers and Governments 423
   CASE STUDY: Discrimination in Sports

Conclusion 425
Summary 425
Key Concepts 426
Questions for Review 426
Problems and Applications 426

CHAPTER 20
INCOME INEQUALITY AND POVERTY 429

The Measurement of Inequality 430
   U.S. Income Inequality 430
   CASE STUDY: The Women's Movement and the Income
      Distribution
   CASE STUDY: Inequality Around the World
   The Poverty Rate 433
   Problems in Measuring Inequality 434
   Economic Mobility 436

The Political Philosophy of Redistributing Income 437
   Utilitarianism 437

Liberalism   438
Libertarianism   439

Policies to Reduce Poverty   440
Minimum-Wage Laws   441
Welfare   441
IN THE NEWS: Should the Government Try to Help
Poor Regions?
Negative Income Tax   443
In-Kind Transfers   444
Antipoverty Programs and Work Incentives   444
IN THE NEWS: School Vouchers

Conclusion   445
Summary   447
Key Concepts   448
Questions for Review   448
Problems and Applications   448

PART 7
TOPICS FOR FURTHER STUDY   451

CHAPTER 21
THE THEORY OF CONSUMER CHOICE   453

**The Budget Constraint: What the Consumer
Can Afford**   454

Preferences: What the Consumer Wants   456
Representing Preferences with Indifference Curves   456
Four Properties of Indifference Curves   457
Two Extreme Examples of Indifference Curves   458

Optimization: What the Consumer Chooses   460
The Consumer's Optimal Choices   461
FYI: Utility: An Alternative Way to Describe Preferences
and Optimization
How Changes in Income Affect the Consumer's
Choices   462
How Changes in Prices Affect the Consumer's Choices   463

Income and Substitution Effects   464
Deriving the Demand Curve   466

Three Applications   468
Do All Demand Curves Slope Downward?   468
How Do Wages Affect Labor Supply?   469
CASE STUDY: Income Effects on Labor Supply:
Historical Trends, Lottery Winners, and
the Carnegie Conjecture
How Do Interest Rates Affect Household Saving?   473
Conclusion: Do People Really Think This Way?   475
Summary   476
Key Concepts   476
Questions for Review   476
Problems and Applications   477

CHAPTER 22
FRONTIERS OF MICROECONOMICS   479

Asymmetric Information   480
Hidden Actions: Principals, Agents,
and Moral Hazard   480
Hidden Characteristics: Adverse Selection
and the Lemons Problem   481
Signaling to Convey Private Information   482
CASE STUDY: Gifts as Signals
Screening to Induce Information Revelation   483
Asymmetric Information and Public Policy   484

Political Economy   485
The Condorcet Voting Paradox   485
Arrow's Impossibility Theorem   486
The Median Voter Is King   487
Politicians Are People Too   488
IN THE NEWS: Farm Policy and Politics

Behavioral Economics   489
People Aren't Always Rational   489
People Care About Fairness   492
People Are Inconsistent over Time   493
Conclusion   493
Summary   494
Key Concepts   494
Questions for Review   494
Problems and Applications   495

Glossary   497
Index   501

1

INTRODUCTION

TEN PRINCIPLES OF ECONOMICS

The word *economy* comes from the Greek word for "one who manages a household." At first, this origin might seem peculiar. But, in fact, households and economies have much in common.

A household faces many decisions. It must decide which members of the household do which tasks and what each member gets in return: Who cooks dinner? Who does the laundry? Who gets the extra dessert at dinner? Who gets to choose what TV show to watch? In short, the household must allocate its scarce resources among its various members, taking into account each member's abilities, efforts, and desires.

Like a household, a society faces many decisions. A society must decide what jobs will be done and who will do them. It needs some people to grow food, other people to make clothing, and still others to design computer software. Once society has allocated people (as well as land, buildings, and machines) to various jobs, it must also allocate the output of goods and services that they produce. It must decide who will eat caviar and who will eat potatoes. It must decide who will drive a Ferrari and who will take the bus.

scarcity
the limited nature
of society's resources

economics
the study of how society
manages its scarce resources

The management of society's resources is important because resources are scarce. **Scarcity** means that society has limited resources and therefore cannot produce all the goods and services people wish to have. Just as a household cannot give every member everything he or she wants, a society cannot give every individual the highest standard of living to which he or she might aspire.

Economics is the study of how society manages its scarce resources. In most societies, resources are allocated not by a single central planner but through the combined actions of millions of households and firms. Economists therefore study how people make decisions: how much they work, what they buy, how much they save, and how they invest their savings. Economists also study how people interact with one another. For instance, they examine how the multitude of buyers and sellers of a good together determine the price at which the good is sold and the quantity that is sold. Finally, economists analyze forces and trends that affect the economy as a whole, including the growth in average income, the fraction of the population that cannot find work, and the rate at which prices are rising.

Although the study of economics has many facets, the field is unified by several central ideas. In the rest of this chapter, we look at *Ten Principles of Economics*. Don't worry if you don't understand them all at first, or if you don't find them completely convincing. In the coming chapters we will explore these ideas more fully. The ten principles are introduced here just to give you an overview of what economics is all about. You can think of this chapter as a "preview of coming attractions."

HOW PEOPLE MAKE DECISIONS

There is no mystery to what an "economy" is. Whether we are talking about the economy of Los Angeles, of the United States, or of the whole world, an economy is just a group of people interacting with one another as they go about their lives. Because the behavior of an economy reflects the behavior of the individuals who make up the economy, we start our study of economics with four principles of individual decisionmaking.

Principle #1: People Face Tradeoffs

The first lesson about making decisions is summarized in the adage: "There is no such thing as a free lunch." To get one thing that we like, we usually have to give up another thing that we like. Making decisions requires trading off one goal against another.

Consider a student who must decide how to allocate her most valuable resource—her time. She can spend all of her time studying economics; she can spend all of her time studying psychology; or she can divide her time between the two fields. For every hour she studies one subject, she gives up an hour she could have used studying the other. And for every hour she spends studying, she gives up an hour that she could have spent napping, bike riding, watching TV, or working at her part-time job for some extra spending money.

Or consider parents deciding how to spend their family income. They can buy food, clothing, or a family vacation. Or they can save some of the family income for retirement or the children's college education. When they choose to spend an extra dollar on one of these goods, they have one less dollar to spend on some other good.

When people are grouped into societies, they face different kinds of tradeoffs. The classic tradeoff is between "guns and butter." The more we spend on national defense (guns) to protect our shores from foreign aggressors, the less we can spend on consumer goods (butter) to raise our standard of living at home. Also important in modern society is the tradeoff between a clean environment and a high level of income. Laws that require firms to reduce pollution raise the cost of producing goods and services. Because of the higher costs, these firms end up earning smaller profits, paying lower wages, charging higher prices, or some combination of these three. Thus, while pollution regulations give us the benefit of a cleaner environment and the improved health that comes with it, they have the cost of reducing the incomes of the firms' owners, workers, and customers.

Another tradeoff society faces is between efficiency and equity. **Efficiency** means that society is getting the most it can from its scarce resources. **Equity** means that the benefits of those resources are distributed fairly among society's members. In other words, efficiency refers to the size of the economic pie, and equity refers to how the pie is divided. Often, when government policies are being designed, these two goals conflict.

Consider, for instance, policies aimed at achieving a more equal distribution of economic well-being. Some of these policies, such as the welfare system or unemployment insurance, try to help those members of society who are most in need. Others, such as the individual income tax, ask the financially successful to contribute more than others to support the government. Although these policies have the benefit of achieving greater equity, they have a cost in terms of reduced efficiency. When the government redistributes income from the rich to the poor, it reduces the reward for working hard; as a result, people work less and produce fewer goods and services. In other words, when the government tries to cut the economic pie into more equal slices, the pie gets smaller.

Recognizing that people face tradeoffs does not by itself tell us what decisions they will or should make. A student should not abandon the study of psychology just because doing so would increase the time available for the study of economics. Society should not stop protecting the environment just because environmental regulations reduce our material standard of living. The poor should not be ignored just because helping them distorts work incentives. Nonetheless, acknowledging life's tradeoffs is important because people are likely to make good decisions only if they understand the options that they have available.

efficiency
the property of society getting the most it can from its scarce resources

equity
the property of distributing economic prosperity fairly among the members of society

Principle #2: The Cost of Something Is What You Give Up to Get It

Because people face tradeoffs, making decisions requires comparing the costs and benefits of alternative courses of action. In many cases, however, the cost of some action is not as obvious as it might first appear.

Consider, for example, the decision whether to go to college. The benefit is intellectual enrichment and a lifetime of better job opportunities. But what is the cost? To answer this question, you might be tempted to add up the money you spend on tuition, books, room, and board. Yet this total does not truly represent what you give up to spend a year in college.

The first problem with this answer is that it includes some things that are not really costs of going to college. Even if you quit school, you would need a place to sleep and food to eat. Room and board are costs of going to college only to the extent that they are more expensive at college than elsewhere. Indeed, the cost of room and board at your school might be less than the rent and food expenses that you would pay living on your own. In this case, the savings on room and board are a benefit of going to college.

The second problem with this calculation of costs is that it ignores the largest cost of going to college—your time. When you spend a year listening to lectures, reading textbooks, and writing papers, you cannot spend that time working at a job. For most students, the wages given up to attend school are the largest single cost of their education.

opportunity cost
whatever must be given up to obtain some item

The **opportunity cost** of an item is what you give up to get that item. When making any decision, such as whether to attend college, decisionmakers should be aware of the opportunity costs that accompany each possible action. In fact, they usually are. College-age athletes who can earn millions if they drop out of school and play professional sports are well aware that their opportunity cost of college is very high. It is not surprising that they often decide that the benefit is not worth the cost.

Principle #3: Rational People Think at the Margin

Decisions in life are rarely black and white but usually involve shades of gray. At dinnertime, the decision you face is not between fasting or eating like a pig, but whether to take that extra spoonful of mashed potatoes. When exams roll around, your decision is not between blowing them off or studying 24 hours a day, but whether to spend an extra hour reviewing your notes instead of watching TV. Economists use the term **marginal changes** to describe small incremental adjustments to an existing plan of action. Keep in mind that "margin" means "edge," so marginal changes are adjustments around the edges of what you are doing.

marginal changes
small incremental adjustments to a plan of action

In many situations, people make the best decisions by thinking at the margin. Suppose, for instance, that you asked a friend for advice about how many years to stay in school. If he were to compare for you the lifestyle of a person with a Ph.D. to that of a grade school dropout, you might complain that this comparison is not helpful for your decision. You have some education already and most likely are deciding whether to spend an extra year or two in school. To make this decision, you need to know the additional benefits that an extra year in school would offer (higher wages throughout life and the sheer joy of learning) and the additional costs that you would incur (tuition and the forgone wages while you're in school). By comparing these *marginal benefits* and *marginal costs,* you can evaluate whether the extra year is worthwhile.

As another example, consider an airline deciding how much to charge passengers who fly standby. Suppose that flying a 200-seat plane across the country costs the airline $100,000. In this case, the average cost of each seat is $100,000/200, which is $500. One might be tempted to conclude that the airline should never sell a ticket for less than $500. In fact, however, the airline can raise its profits by thinking at the margin. Imagine that a plane is about to take off with ten empty seats, and a standby passenger is waiting at the gate willing to pay $300 for a seat. Should the airline sell it to him? Of course it should. If the plane has empty seats, the cost of adding one more passenger is minuscule. Although the *average* cost of flying a passenger is $500, the *marginal* cost is merely the cost of the bag of peanuts and can of soda that the extra passenger will consume. As long as the standby passenger pays more than the marginal cost, selling him a ticket is profitable.

As these examples show, individuals and firms can make better decisions by thinking at the margin. A rational decisionmaker takes an action if and only if the marginal benefit of the action exceeds the marginal cost.

Principle #4: People Respond to Incentives

Because people make decisions by comparing costs and benefits, their behavior may change when the costs or benefits change. That is, people respond to incentives. When the price of an apple rises, for instance, people decide to eat more pears and fewer apples because the cost of buying an apple is higher. At the same time, apple orchards decide to hire more workers and harvest more apples, because the benefit of selling an apple is also higher. As we will see, the effect of price on the behavior of buyers and sellers in a market—in this case, the market for apples—is crucial for understanding how the economy works.

Public policymakers should never forget about incentives, for many policies change the costs or benefits that people face and, therefore, alter behavior. A tax on gasoline, for instance, encourages people to drive smaller, more fuel-efficient cars. It also encourages people to take public transportation rather than drive and to live closer to where they work. If the tax were large enough, people would start driving electric cars.

When policymakers fail to consider how their policies affect incentives, they often end up with results they did not intend. For example, consider public policy regarding auto safety. Today all cars have seat belts, but that was not true 50 years ago. In the 1960s, Ralph Nader's book *Unsafe at Any Speed* generated much public concern over auto safety. Congress responded with laws requiring seat belts as standard equipment on new cars.

How does a seat belt law affect auto safety? The direct effect is obvious: When a person wears a seat belt, the probability of surviving a major auto accident rises. But that's not the end of the story, for the law also affects behavior by altering incentives. The relevant behavior here is the speed and care with which drivers operate their cars. Driving slowly and carefully is costly because it uses the driver's time and energy. When deciding how safely to drive, rational people compare the marginal benefit from safer driving to the marginal cost. They drive more slowly and carefully when the benefit of increased safety is high. It is no surprise, for instance, that people drive more slowly and carefully when roads are icy than when roads are clear.

Consider how a seat belt law alters a driver's cost–benefit calculation. Seat belts make accidents less costly because they reduce the likelihood of injury or death. In other words, seat belts reduce the benefits to slow and careful driving. People respond to seat belts as they would to an improvement in road conditions—by faster and less careful driving. The end result of a seat belt law, therefore, is a larger number of accidents. The decline in safe driving has a clear, adverse impact on pedestrians, who are more likely to find themselves in an accident but (unlike the drivers) don't have the benefit of added protection.

At first, this discussion of incentives and seat belts might seem like idle speculation. Yet, in a 1975 study, economist Sam Peltzman showed that the auto-safety laws have had many of these effects. According to Peltzman's evidence, these laws

Basketball star Kobe Bryant understood opportunity cost and incentives. Despite good high school grades and SAT scores, he decided to skip college and go straight to the pros, where he has earned millions of dollars as one of the NBA's top players.

produce both fewer deaths per accident and more accidents. The net result is little change in the number of driver deaths and an increase in the number of pedestrian deaths.

Peltzman's analysis of auto safety is an example of the general principle that people respond to incentives. Many incentives that economists study are more straightforward than those of the auto-safety laws. No one is surprised that people drive smaller cars in Europe, where gasoline taxes are high, than in the United States, where gasoline taxes are low. Yet, as the seat belt example shows, policies can have effects that are not obvious in advance. When analyzing any policy, we must consider not only the direct effects but also the indirect effects that work through incentives. If the policy changes incentives, it will cause people to alter their behavior.

QuickQuiz   List and briefly explain the four principles of individual decisionmaking.

HOW PEOPLE INTERACT

The first four principles discussed how individuals make decisions. As we go about our lives, many of our decisions affect not only ourselves but other people as well. The next three principles concern how people interact with one another.

Principle #5: Trade Can Make Everyone Better Off

You have probably heard on the news that the Japanese are our competitors in the world economy. In some ways this is true, for American and Japanese firms do produce many of the same goods. Ford and Toyota compete for the same customers in the market for automobiles. Compaq and Toshiba compete for the same customers in the market for personal computers.

Yet it is easy to be misled when thinking about competition among countries. Trade between the United States and Japan is not like a sports contest, where one side wins and the other side loses. In fact, the opposite is true: Trade between two countries can make each country better off.

To see why, consider how trade affects your family. When a member of your family looks for a job, he or she competes against members of other families who are looking for jobs. Families also compete against one another when they go shopping, because each family wants to buy the best goods at the lowest prices. So, in a sense, each family in the economy is competing with all other families.

Despite this competition, your family would not be better off isolating itself from all other families. If it did, your family would need to grow its own food, make its own clothes, and build its own home. Clearly, your family gains much from its ability to trade with others. Trade allows each person to specialize in the activities he or she does best, whether it is farming, sewing, or home building. By trading with others, people can buy a greater variety of goods and services at lower cost.

Countries as well as families benefit from the ability to trade with one another. Trade allows countries to specialize in what they do best and to enjoy a greater

"For $5 a week you can watch baseball without being nagged to cut the grass!"

variety of goods and services. The Japanese, as well as the French and the Egyptians and the Brazilians, are as much our partners in the world economy as they are our competitors.

Principle #6: Markets Are Usually a Good Way to Organize Economic Activity

The collapse of communism in the Soviet Union and Eastern Europe in the 1980s may be the most important change in the world during the past half century. Communist countries worked on the premise that central planners in the government were in the best position to guide economic activity. These planners decided what goods and services were produced, how much was produced, and who produced and consumed these goods and services. The theory behind central planning was that only the government could organize economic activity in a way that promoted economic well-being for the country as a whole.

Today, most countries that once had centrally planned economies have abandoned this system and are trying to develop market economies. In a **market economy,** the decisions of a central planner are replaced by the decisions of millions of firms and households. Firms decide whom to hire and what to make. Households decide which firms to work for and what to buy with their incomes. These firms and households interact in the marketplace, where prices and self-interest guide their decisions.

market economy
an economy that allocates resources through the decentralized decisions of many firms and households as they interact in markets for goods and services

At first glance, the success of market economies is puzzling. After all, in a market economy, no one is looking out for the economic well-being of society as a whole. Free markets contain many buyers and sellers of numerous goods and services, and all of them are interested primarily in their own well-being. Yet, despite decentralized decisionmaking and self-interested decisionmakers, market economies have proven remarkably successful in organizing economic activity in a way that promotes overall economic well-being.

In his 1776 book *An Inquiry into the Nature and Causes of the Wealth of Nations,* economist Adam Smith made the most famous observation in all of economics: Households and firms interacting in markets act as if they are guided by an "invisible hand" that leads them to desirable market outcomes. One of our goals in this book is to understand how this invisible hand works its magic. As you study economics, you will learn that prices are the instrument with which the invisible hand directs economic activity. Prices reflect both the value of a good to society and the cost to society of making the good. Because households and firms look at prices when deciding what to buy and sell, they unknowingly take into account the social benefits and costs of their actions. As a result, prices guide these individual decisionmakers to reach outcomes that, in many cases, maximize the welfare of society as a whole.

There is an important corollary to the skill of the invisible hand in guiding economic activity: When the government prevents prices from adjusting naturally to supply and demand, it impedes the invisible hand's ability to coordinate the millions of households and firms that make up the economy. This corollary explains why taxes adversely affect the allocation of resources: Taxes distort prices and thus the decisions of households and firms. It also explains the even greater harm caused by policies that directly control prices, such as rent control. And it explains the failure of communism. In communist countries, prices were not determined in the marketplace but were dictated by central planners. These planners lacked the information that gets reflected in prices when prices are free to respond to market forces. Central planners failed because they tried to run the economy with one hand tied behind their backs—the invisible hand of the marketplace.

Principle #7: Governments Can Sometimes Improve Market Outcomes

If the invisible hand of the market is so great, why do we need government? One answer is that the invisible hand needs government to protect it. Markets work only if property rights are enforced. A farmer won't grow food if he expects his crop to be stolen, and a restaurant won't serve meals unless it is assured that customers will pay before they leave. We all rely on government-provided police and courts to enforce our rights over the things we produce.

Yet there is another answer to why we need government: Although markets are usually a good way to organize economic activity, this rule has some important exceptions. There are two broad reasons for a government to intervene in the

FYI

ADAM SMITH AND THE INVISIBLE HAND

It may be only a coincidence that Adam Smith's great book *The Wealth of Nations* was published in 1776, the exact year American revolutionaries signed the Declaration of Independence. But the two documents do share a point of view that was prevalent at the time—that individuals are usually best left to their own devices, without the heavy hand of government guiding their actions. This political philosophy provides the intellectual basis for the market economy, and for free society more generally.

Why do decentralized market economies work so well? Is it because people can be counted on to treat one another with love and kindness? Not at all. Here is Adam Smith's description of how people interact in a market economy:

Adam Smith

Man has almost constant occasion for the help of his brethren, and it is vain for him to expect it from their benevolence only. He will be more likely to prevail if he can interest their self-love in his favor, and show them that it is for their own advantage to do for him what he requires of them. . . . It is not from the benevolence of the butcher, the brewer, or the baker that we expect our dinner, but from their regard to their own interest. . . .

Every individual . . . neither intends to promote the public interest, nor knows how much he is promoting it. . . . He intends only his own gain, and he is in this, as in many other cases, led by an invisible hand to promote an end which was no part of his intention. Nor is it always the worse for the society that it was no part of it. By pursuing his own interest he frequently promotes that of the society more effectually than when he really intends to promote it.

Smith is saying that participants in the economy are motivated by self-interest and that the "invisible hand" of the marketplace guides this self-interest into promoting general economic well-being.

Many of Smith's insights remain at the center of modern economics. Our analysis in the coming chapters will allow us to express Smith's conclusions more precisely and to analyze fully the strengths and weaknesses of the market's invisible hand.

economy—to promote efficiency and to promote equity. That is, most policies aim either to enlarge the economic pie or to change how the pie is divided.

Although the invisible hand usually leads markets to allocate resources efficiently, that is not always the case. Economists use the term **market failure** to refer to a situation in which the market on its own fails to produce an efficient allocation of resources. One possible cause of market failure is an **externality,** which is the impact of one person's actions on the well-being of a bystander. For instance, the classic example of an external cost is pollution. Another possible cause of market failure is **market power,** which refers to the ability of a single person (or small group) to unduly influence market prices. For example, if everyone in town needs water but there is only one well, the owner of the well is not subject to the rigorous competition with which the invisible hand normally keeps self-interest in check. In the presence of externalities or market power, well-designed public policy can enhance economic efficiency.

The invisible hand may also fail to ensure that economic prosperity is distributed equitably. A market economy rewards people according to their ability to produce things that other people are willing to pay for. The world's best basketball player earns more than the world's best chess player simply because people are willing to pay more to watch basketball than chess. The invisible hand does not ensure that everyone has sufficient food, decent clothing, and adequate health care. Many public policies, such as the income tax and the welfare system, aim to achieve a more equitable distribution of economic well-being.

To say that the government *can* improve on market outcomes at times does not mean that it always *will*. Public policy is made not by angels but by a political process that is far from perfect. Sometimes policies are designed simply to reward the politically powerful. Sometimes they are made by well-intentioned leaders who are not fully informed. One goal of the study of economics is to help you judge when a government policy is justifiable to promote efficiency or equity, and when it is not.

market failure
a situation in which a market left on its own fails to allocate resources efficiently

externality
the impact of one person's actions on the well-being of a bystander

market power
the ability of a single economic actor (or small group of actors) to have a substantial influence on market prices

QuickQuiz List and briefly explain the three principles concerning economic interactions.

HOW THE ECONOMY AS A WHOLE WORKS

We started by discussing how individuals make decisions and then looked at how people interact with one another. All these decisions and interactions together make up "the economy." The last three principles concern the workings of the economy as a whole.

Principle #8: A Country's Standard of Living Depends on Its Ability to Produce Goods and Services

The differences in living standards around the world are staggering. In 2000 the average American had an income of about $34,100. In the same year, the average Mexican earned $8,790, and the average Nigerian earned $800. Not surprisingly, this large variation in average income is reflected in various measures of the quality of life. Citizens of high-income countries have more TV sets, more cars, better nutrition, better health care, and longer life expectancy than citizens of low-income countries.

Changes in living standards over time are also large. In the United States, incomes have historically grown about 2 percent per year (after adjusting for changes in the cost of living). At this rate, average income doubles every 35 years. Over the past century, average income has risen about eightfold.

What explains these large differences in living standards among countries and over time? The answer is surprisingly simple. Almost all variation in living standards is attributable to differences in countries' **productivity**—that is, the amount of goods and services produced from each hour of a worker's time. In nations where workers can produce a large quantity of goods and services per unit of time, most people enjoy a high standard of living; in nations where workers are less productive, most people must endure a more meager existence. Similarly, the growth rate of a nation's productivity determines the growth rate of its average income.

The fundamental relationship between productivity and living standards is simple, but its implications are far-reaching. If productivity is the primary determinant of living standards, other explanations must be of secondary importance. For example, it might be tempting to credit labor unions or minimum-wage laws for the rise in living standards of American workers over the past century. Yet the real hero of American workers is their rising productivity. As another example, some commentators have claimed that increased competition from Japan and other countries explained the slow growth in U.S. incomes during the 1970s and 1980s. Yet the real villain was not competition from abroad but flagging productivity growth in the United States.

The relationship between productivity and living standards also has profound implications for public policy. When thinking about how any policy will affect living standards, the key question is how it will affect our ability to produce goods and services. To boost living standards, policymakers need to raise productivity by ensuring that workers are well educated, have the tools needed to produce goods and services, and have access to the best available technology.

Principle #9: Prices Rise When the Government Prints Too Much Money

In Germany in January 1921, a daily newspaper cost 0.30 marks. Less than two years later, in November 1922, the same newspaper cost 70,000,000 marks. All other prices in the economy rose by similar amounts. This episode is one of history's most spectacular examples of **inflation,** an increase in the overall level of prices in the economy.

Although the United States has never experienced inflation even close to that in Germany in the 1920s, inflation has at times been an economic problem. During the 1970s, for instance, the overall level of prices more than doubled, and President Gerald Ford called inflation "public enemy number one." By contrast, inflation in the 1990s was about 3 percent per year; at this rate it would take more than 20 years for prices to double. Because high inflation imposes various costs on society, keeping inflation at a low level is a goal of economic policymakers around the world.

What causes inflation? In almost all cases of large or persistent inflation, the culprit turns out to be the same—growth in the quantity of money. When a

---

productivity
the quantity of goods and services produced from each hour of a worker's time

inflation
an increase in the overall level of prices in the economy

"Well it may have been 68 cents when you got in line, but it's 74 cents now!"

government creates large quantities of the nation's money, the value of the money falls. In Germany in the early 1920s, when prices were on average tripling every month, the quantity of money was also tripling every month. Although less dramatic, the economic history of the United States points to a similar conclusion: The high inflation of the 1970s was associated with rapid growth in the quantity of money, and the low inflation of the 1990s was associated with slow growth in the quantity of money.

Principle #10: Society Faces a Short-Run Tradeoff between Inflation and Unemployment

When the government increases the amount of money in the economy, one result is inflation. Another result, at least in the short run, is a lower level of unemployment. The curve that illustrates this short-run tradeoff between inflation and unemployment is called the **Phillips curve,** after the economist who first examined this relationship.

The Phillips curve remains a controversial topic among economists, but most economists today accept the idea that society faces a short-run tradeoff between inflation and unemployment. This simply means that, over a period of a year or two, many economic policies push inflation and unemployment in opposite directions. Policymakers face this tradeoff regardless of whether inflation and unemployment both start out at high levels (as they were in the early 1980s), at low levels (as they were in the late 1990s), or someplace in between.

The tradeoff between inflation and unemployment is only temporary, but it can last for several years. The Phillips curve is, therefore, crucial for understanding

Phillips curve
a curve that shows the short-run tradeoff between inflation and unemployment

business cycle
fluctuations in economic activity, such as employment and production

many developments in the economy. In particular, it is important for understanding the **business cycle**—the irregular and largely unpredictable fluctuations in economic activity, as measured by the number of people employed or the production of goods and services.

Policymakers can exploit the short-run tradeoff between inflation and unemployment using various policy instruments. By changing the amount that the government spends, the amount it taxes, and the amount of money it prints, policymakers can influence the combination of inflation and unemployment that the economy experiences. Because these instruments of monetary and fiscal policy are potentially so powerful, how policymakers should use these instruments to control the economy, if at all, is a subject of continuing debate.

QuickQuiz   List and briefly explain the three principles that describe how the economy as a whole works.

HOW TO READ THIS BOOK

Economics is fun, but it can also be hard to learn. My aim in writing this text is to make it as fun and easy as possible. But you, the student, also have a role to play. Experience shows that if you are actively involved as you study this book, you will enjoy a better outcome, both on your exams and in the years that follow. Here are a few tips about how best to read this book.

1. *Summarize, don't highlight.* Running a yellow marker over the text is too passive an activity to keep your mind engaged. Instead, when you come to the end of a section, take a minute and summarize what you just learned in your own words, writing your summary in the wide margins we've provided. When you've finished the chapter, compare your summary with the one at the end of the chapter. Did you pick up the main points?

2. *Test yourself.* Throughout the book, Quick Quizzes offer instant feedback to find out if you've learned what you are supposed to. Take the opportunity. Write your answer in the book's margin. The quizzes are meant to test your basic comprehension. If you aren't sure your answer is right, you probably need to review the section.

3. *Practice, practice, practice.* At the end of each chapter, Questions for Review test your understanding, and Problems and Applications ask you to apply and extend the material. Perhaps your instructor will assign some of these exercises as homework. If so, do them. If not, do them anyway. The more you use your new knowledge, the more solid it becomes.

4. *Study in groups.* After you've read the book and worked the problems on your own, get together with classmates to discuss the material. You will learn from each other—an example of the gains from trade.

5. *Don't forget the real world.* In the midst of all the numbers, graphs, and strange new words, it is easy to lose sight of what economics is all about. The Case Studies and In the News boxes sprinkled throughout this book should help remind you. Don't skip them. They show how the theory is tied to events happening in all of our lives. If your study is successful, you won't be able to read a newspaper again without thinking about supply, demand, and the wonderful world of economics.

TABLE 1

Ten Principles of Economics

How People Make Decisions	#1: People Face Tradeoffs
	#2: The Cost of Something Is What You Give Up to Get It
	#3: Rational People Think at the Margin
	#4: People Respond to Incentives
How People Interact	#5: Trade Can Make Everyone Better Off
	#6: Markets Are Usually a Good Way to Organize Economic Activity
	#7: Governments Can Sometimes Improve Market Outcomes
How the Economy as a Whole Works	#8: A Country's Standard of Living Depends on Its Ability to Produce Goods and Services
	#9: Prices Rise When the Government Prints Too Much Money
	#10: Society Faces a Short-Run Tradeoff between Inflation and Unemployment

CONCLUSION

You now have a taste of what economics is all about. In the coming chapters we will develop many specific insights about people, markets, and economies. Mastering these insights will take some effort, but it is not an overwhelming task. The field of economics is based on a few basic ideas that can be applied in many different situations.

Throughout this book we will refer back to the *Ten Principles of Economics* highlighted in this chapter and summarized in Table 1. Whenever we do so, an icon will be displayed in the margin, as it is now. But even when that icon is absent, you should keep these building blocks in mind. Even the most sophisticated economic analysis is built using the ten principles introduced here.

SUMMARY

- The fundamental lessons about individual decisionmaking are that people face tradeoffs among alternative goals, that the cost of any action is measured in terms of forgone opportunities, that rational people make decisions by comparing marginal costs and marginal benefits, and that people change their behavior in response to the incentives they face.

- The fundamental lessons about interactions among people are that trade can be mutually beneficial, that markets are usually a good way

of coordinating trade among people, and that the government can potentially improve market outcomes if there is some market failure or if the market outcome is inequitable.

- The fundamental lessons about the economy as a whole are that productivity is the ultimate source of living standards, that money growth is the ultimate source of inflation, and that society faces a short-run tradeoff between inflation and unemployment.

KEY CONCEPTS

scarcity, p. 4
economics, p. 4
efficiency, p. 5
equity, p. 5
opportunity cost, p. 6

marginal changes, p. 6
market economy, p. 9
market failure, p. 11
externality, p. 11
market power, p. 11

productivity, p. 12
inflation, p. 12
Phillips curve, p. 13
business cycle, p. 14

QUESTIONS FOR REVIEW

1. Give three examples of important tradeoffs that you face in your life.

2. What is the opportunity cost of seeing a movie?

3. Water is necessary for life. Is the marginal benefit of a glass of water large or small?

4. Why should policymakers think about incentives?

5. Why isn't trade among countries like a game, with some winners and some losers?

6. What does the "invisible hand" of the marketplace do?

7. Explain the two main causes of market failure and give an example of each.

8. Why is productivity important?

9. What is inflation, and what causes it?

10. How are inflation and unemployment related in the short run?

PROBLEMS AND APPLICATIONS

1. Describe some of the tradeoffs faced by each of the following.
   a. a family deciding whether to buy a new car
   b. a member of Congress deciding how much to spend on national parks
   c. a company president deciding whether to open a new factory
   d. a professor deciding how much to prepare for class

2. You are trying to decide whether to take a vacation. Most of the costs of the vacation (airfare, hotel, forgone wages) are measured in dollars, but the benefits of the vacation are psychological. How can you compare the benefits to the costs?

3. You were planning to spend Saturday working at your part-time job, but a friend asks you to go skiing. What is the true cost of going skiing? Now suppose that you had been planning to spend the day studying at the library. What is the cost of going skiing in this case? Explain.

4. You win $100 in a basketball pool. You have a choice between spending the money now or putting it away for a year in a bank account that pays 5 percent interest. What is the opportunity cost of spending the $100 now?

5. The company that you manage has invested $5 million in developing a new product, but the development is not quite finished. At a recent meeting, your salespeople report that the introduction of competing products has reduced the expected sales of your new product to $3 million. If it would cost $1 million to finish development and make the product, should you go ahead and do so? What is the most that you should pay to complete development?

6. Three managers of the Magic Potion Company are discussing a possible increase in production. Each suggests a way to make this decision.

HARRY: We should examine whether our company's productivity—gallons of potion per worker—would rise or fall.

RON: We should examine whether our average cost—cost per worker—would rise or fall.

HERMIONE: We should examine whether the extra revenue from selling the additional potion would be greater or smaller than the extra costs.

Who do you think is right? Why?

7. The Social Security system provides income for people over age 65. If a recipient of Social Security decides to work and earn some income, the amount he or she receives in Social Security benefits is typically reduced.
   a. How does the provision of Social Security affect people's incentive to save while working?
   b. How does the reduction in benefits associated with higher earnings affect people's incentive to work past age 65?

8. A recent bill reforming the government's antipoverty programs limited many welfare recipients to only two years of benefits.
   a. How does this change affect the incentives for working?
   b. How might this change represent a tradeoff between equity and efficiency?

9. Your roommate is a better cook than you are, but you can clean more quickly than your roommate can. If your roommate did all of the cooking and you did all of the cleaning, would your chores take you more or less time than if you divided each task evenly? Give a similar example of how specialization and trade can make two countries both better off.

10. Suppose the United States adopted central planning for its economy, and you became the chief planner. Among the millions of decisions that you need to make for next year are how many compact discs to produce, what artists to record, and who should receive the discs.

    a. To make these decisions intelligently, what information would you need about the compact disc industry? What information would you need about each of the people in the United States?
    b. How would your decisions about CDs affect some of your other decisions, such as how many CD players to make or cassette tapes to produce? How might some of your other decisions about the economy change your views about CDs?

11. Explain whether each of the following government activities is motivated by a concern about equity or a concern about efficiency. In the case of efficiency, discuss the type of market failure involved.
    a. regulating cable TV prices
    b. providing some poor people with vouchers that can be used to buy food
    c. prohibiting smoking in public places
    d. breaking up Standard Oil (which once owned 90 percent of all oil refineries) into several smaller companies
    e. imposing higher personal income tax rates on people with higher incomes
    f. instituting laws against driving while intoxicated

12. Discuss each of the following statements from the standpoints of equity and efficiency.
    a. "Everyone in society should be guaranteed the best health care possible."
    b. "When workers are laid off, they should be able to collect unemployment benefits until they find a new job."

13. In what ways is your standard of living different from that of your parents or grandparents when they were your age? Why have these changes occurred?

14. Suppose Americans decide to save more of their incomes. If banks lend this extra saving to businesses, which use the funds to build new factories, how might this lead to faster growth in productivity? Who do you suppose benefits from the higher productivity? Is society getting a free lunch?

15. Imagine that you are a policymaker trying to decide whether to reduce the rate of inflation. To make an intelligent decision, what would you need to know about inflation, unemployment, and the tradeoff between them?

16. Look at a newspaper or at the Web site http://www.economist.com to find three stories about the economy that have been in the news lately. For each story, identify one (or more) of the *Ten Principles of Economics* discussed in this chapter that is relevant, and explain how it is relevant. Also, for each story, look through this book's table of contents and try to find a chapter that might shed light on the news event.

http://   For more study tools, please visit http://mankiwXtra.swlearning.com.

THINKING LIKE AN ECONOMIST

Every field of study has its own language and its own way of thinking. Mathematicians talk about axioms, integrals, and vector spaces. Psychologists talk about ego, id, and cognitive dissonance. Lawyers talk about venue, torts, and promissory estoppel.

Economics is no different. Supply, demand, elasticity, comparative advantage, consumer surplus, deadweight loss—these terms are part of the economist's language. In the coming chapters, you will encounter many new terms and some familiar words that economists use in specialized ways. At first, this new language may seem needlessly arcane. But, as you will see, its value lies in its ability to provide you a new and useful way of thinking about the world in which you live.

The single most important purpose of this book is to help you learn the economist's way of thinking. Of course, just as you cannot become a mathematician, psychologist, or lawyer overnight, learning to think like an economist will take some time. Yet with a combination of theory, case studies, and examples of economics in the news, this book will give you ample opportunity to develop and practice this skill.

Before delving into the substance and details of economics, it is helpful to have an overview of how economists approach the world. This chapter, therefore, discusses the field's methodology. What is distinctive about how economists confront a question? What does it mean to think like an economist?

THE ECONOMIST AS SCIENTIST

Economists try to address their subject with a scientist's objectivity. They approach the study of the economy in much the same way as a physicist approaches the study of matter and a biologist approaches the study of life: They devise theories, collect data, and then analyze these data in an attempt to verify or refute their theories.

To beginners, it can seem odd to claim that economics is a science. After all, economists do not work with test tubes or telescopes. The essence of science, however, is the *scientific method*—the dispassionate development and testing of theories about how the world works. This method of inquiry is as applicable to studying a nation's economy as it is to studying the earth's gravity or a species' evolution. As Albert Einstein once put it, "The whole of science is nothing more than the refinement of everyday thinking."

Although Einstein's comment is as true for social sciences such as economics as it is for natural sciences such as physics, most people are not accustomed to looking at society through the eyes of a scientist. Let's therefore discuss some of the ways in which economists apply the logic of science to examine how an economy works.

"I'm a social scientist, Michael. That means I can't explain electricity or anything like that, but if you ever want to know about people, I'm your man."

The Scientific Method: Observation, Theory, and More Observation

Isaac Newton, the famous seventeenth-century scientist and mathematician, allegedly became intrigued one day when he saw an apple fall from an apple tree. This observation motivated Newton to develop a theory of gravity that applies not only to an apple falling to the earth but to any two objects in the universe. Subsequent testing of Newton's theory has shown that it works well in many circumstances (although, as Einstein would later emphasize, not in all circumstances). Because Newton's theory has been so successful at explaining observation, it is still taught today in undergraduate physics courses around the world.

This interplay between theory and observation also occurs in the field of economics. An economist might live in a country experiencing rapid increases in prices and be moved by this observation to develop a theory of inflation. The theory might assert that high inflation arises when the government prints too much money. (As you may recall, this was one of the *Ten Principles of Economics* in Chapter 1.) To test this theory, the economist could collect and analyze data on prices and money from many different countries. If growth in the quantity of money were not at all related to the rate at which prices are rising, the economist would start to doubt the validity of his theory of inflation. If money growth and inflation were strongly correlated in international data, as in fact they are, the economist would become more confident in his theory.

Although economists use theory and observation like other scientists, they do face an obstacle that makes their task especially challenging: Experiments are often difficult in economics. Physicists studying gravity can drop many objects in their laboratories to generate data to test their theories. By contrast, economists studying inflation are not allowed to manipulate a nation's monetary policy simply to generate useful data. Economists, like astronomers and evolutionary biologists, usually have to make do with whatever data the world happens to give them.

To find a substitute for laboratory experiments, economists pay close attention to the natural experiments offered by history. When a war in the Middle East interrupts the flow of crude oil, for instance, oil prices skyrocket around the world. For consumers of oil and oil products, such an event depresses living standards. For economic policymakers, it poses a difficult choice about how best to respond. But for economic scientists, it provides an opportunity to study the effects of a key natural resource on the world's economies, and this opportunity persists long after the wartime increase in oil prices is over. Throughout this book, therefore, we consider many historical episodes. These episodes are valuable to study because they give us insight into the economy of the past and, more important, because they allow us to illustrate and evaluate economic theories of the present.

The Role of Assumptions

If you ask a physicist how long it would take for a marble to fall from the top of a ten-story building, she will answer the question by assuming that the marble falls in a vacuum. Of course, this assumption is false. In fact, the building is surrounded by air, which exerts friction on the falling marble and slows it down. Yet the physicist will correctly point out that friction on the marble is so small that its effect is negligible. Assuming the marble falls in a vacuum greatly simplifies the problem without substantially affecting the answer.

Economists make assumptions for the same reason: Assumptions can simplify the complex world and make it easier to understand. To study the effects of international trade, for example, we may assume that the world consists of only two countries and that each country produces only two goods. Of course, the real world consists of dozens of countries, each of which produces thousands of different types of goods. But by assuming two countries and two goods, we can focus our thinking. Once we understand international trade in an imaginary world with two countries and two goods, we are in a better position to understand international trade in the more complex world in which we live.

The art in scientific thinking—whether in physics, biology, or economics—is deciding which assumptions to make. Suppose, for instance, that we were dropping a beach ball rather than a marble from the top of the building. Our physicist would realize that the assumption of no friction is far less accurate in this case: Friction exerts a greater force on a beach ball than on a marble because a beach ball is much larger. The assumption that gravity works in a vacuum is reasonable for studying a falling marble but not for studying a falling beach ball.

Similarly, economists use different assumptions to answer different questions. Suppose that we want to study what happens to the economy when the government changes the number of dollars in circulation. An important piece of this analysis, it turns out, is how prices respond. Many prices in the economy change infrequently; the newsstand prices of magazines, for instance, are changed only every few years. Knowing this fact may lead us to make different assumptions when studying the effects of the policy change over different time horizons. For studying the short-run effects of the policy, we may assume that prices do not change much. We may even make the extreme and artificial assumption that all prices are completely fixed. For studying the long-run effects of the policy, however, we may assume that all prices are completely flexible. Just as a physicist uses different assumptions when studying falling marbles and falling beach balls, economists use different assumptions when studying the short-run and long-run effects of a change in the quantity of money.

Economic Models

High school biology teachers teach basic anatomy with plastic replicas of the human body. These models have all the major organs—the heart, the liver, the kidneys, and so on. The models allow teachers to show their students in a simple way how the important parts of the body fit together. Of course, these plastic models are not actual human bodies, and no one would mistake the model for a real person. These models are stylized, and they omit many details. Yet despite this lack of realism—indeed, because of this lack of realism—studying these models is useful for learning how the human body works.

Economists also use models to learn about the world, but instead of being made of plastic, they are most often composed of diagrams and equations. Like a biology teacher's plastic model, economic models omit many details to allow us to see what is truly important. Just as the biology teacher's model does not include all of the body's muscles and capillaries, an economist's model does not include every feature of the economy.

As we use models to examine various economic issues throughout this book, you will see that all the models are built with assumptions. Just as a physicist begins the analysis of a falling marble by assuming away the existence of friction, economists assume away many of the details of the economy that are irrelevant for studying the question at hand. All models—in physics, biology, or economics—simplify reality in order to improve our understanding of it.

Our First Model: The Circular-Flow Diagram

The economy consists of millions of people engaged in many activities—buying, selling, working, hiring, manufacturing, and so on. To understand how the economy works, we must find some way to simplify our thinking about all these activities. In other words, we need a model that explains, in general terms, how the economy is organized and how participants in the economy interact with one another.

Figure 1 presents a visual model of the economy, called a **circular-flow diagram.** In this model, the economy is simplified to include only two types of decision-makers—households and firms. Firms produce goods and services using inputs, such as labor, land, and capital (buildings and machines). These inputs are called the *factors of production.* Households own the factors of production and consume all the goods and services that the firms produce.

circular-flow diagram
a visual model of the economy that shows how dollars flow through markets among households and firms

FIGURE 1

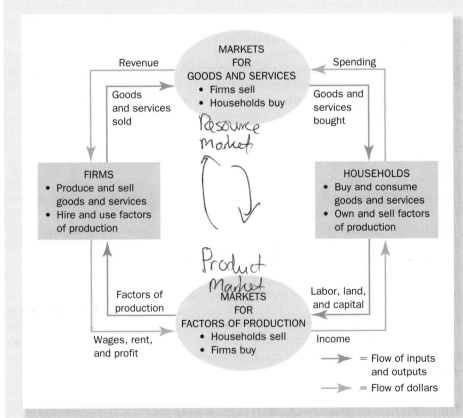

The Circular Flow

This diagram is a schematic representation of the organization of the economy. Decisions are made by households and firms. Households and firms interact in the markets for goods and services (where households are buyers and firms are sellers) and in the markets for the factors of production (where firms are buyers and households are sellers). The outer set of arrows shows the flow of dollars, and the inner set of arrows shows the corresponding flow of inputs and outputs.

Households and firms interact in two types of markets. In the *markets for goods and services,* households are buyers, and firms are sellers. In particular, households buy the output of goods and services that firms produce. In the *markets for the factors of production,* households are sellers, and firms are buyers. In these markets, households provide the inputs that the firms use to produce goods and services. The circular-flow diagram offers a simple way of organizing all the economic transactions that occur between households and firms in the economy.

The inner loop of the circular-flow diagram represents the flows of inputs and outputs. The households sell the use of their labor, land, and capital to the firms in the markets for the factors of production. The firms then use these factors to produce goods and services, which in turn are sold to households in the markets for goods and services. Hence, the factors of production flow from households to firms, and goods and services flow from firms to households.

The outer loop of the circular-flow diagram represents the corresponding flow of dollars. The households spend money to buy goods and services from the firms. The firms use some of the revenue from these sales to pay for the factors of production, such as the wages of their workers. What's left is the profit of the firm owners, who themselves are members of households. Hence, spending on goods and services flows from households to firms, and income in the form of wages, rent, and profit flows from firms to households.

Let's take a tour of the circular flow by following a dollar bill as it makes its way from person to person through the economy. Imagine that the dollar begins at a household, sitting in, say, your wallet. If you want to buy a cup of coffee, you take the dollar to one of the economy's markets for goods and services, such as your local Starbucks coffee shop. There you spend it on your favorite drink. When the dollar moves into the Starbucks cash register, it becomes revenue for the firm. The dollar doesn't stay at Starbucks for long, however, because the firm uses it to buy inputs in the markets for the factors of production. For instance, Starbucks might use the dollar to pay rent to its landlord for the space it occupies or to pay the wages of its workers. In either case, the dollar enters the income of some household and, once again, is back in someone's wallet. At that point, the story of the economy's circular flow starts once again.

The circular-flow diagram in Figure 1 is one simple model of the economy. It dispenses with details that, for some purposes, are significant. A more complex and realistic circular-flow model would include, for instance, the roles of government and international trade. Yet these details are not crucial for a basic understanding of how the economy is organized. Because of its simplicity, this circular-flow diagram is useful to keep in mind when thinking about how the pieces of the economy fit together.

Our Second Model: The Production Possibilities Frontier

Most economic models, unlike the circular-flow diagram, are built using the tools of mathematics. Here we consider one of the simplest such models, called the production possibilities frontier, and see how this model illustrates some basic economic ideas.

Although real economies produce thousands of goods and services, let's imagine an economy that produces only two goods—cars and computers. Together the car industry and the computer industry use all of the economy's factors of production. The **production possibilities frontier** is a graph that shows the various combinations of output—in this case, cars and computers—that the economy can possibly produce given the available factors of production and the available production technology that firms can use to turn these factors into output.

Figure 2 is an example of a production possibilities frontier. In this economy, if all resources were used in the car industry, the economy would produce 1,000 cars and no computers. If all resources were used in the computer industry, the economy would produce 3,000 computers and no cars. The two end points of the production possibilities frontier represent these extreme possibilities. If the economy were to divide its resources between the two industries, it could produce 700 cars and 2,000 computers, shown in the figure by point A. By contrast, the outcome at point D is not possible because resources are scarce: The economy does not have enough of the factors of production to support that level of output. In other words, the economy can produce at any point on or inside the production possibilities frontier, but it cannot produce at points outside the frontier.

An outcome is said to be *efficient* if the economy is getting all it can from the scarce resources it has available. Points on (rather than inside) the production possibilities frontier represent efficient levels of production. When the economy is producing at such a point, say point A, there is no way to produce more of one good without producing less of the other. Point B represents an *inefficient* outcome. For some reason, perhaps widespread unemployment, the economy is producing less than it could from the resources it has available: It is producing only 300 cars and 1,000 computers. If the source of the inefficiency were eliminated, the economy could move from point B to point A, increasing production of both cars (to 700) and computers (to 2,000).

production possibilities frontier
a graph that shows the combinations of output that the economy can possibly produce given the available factors of production and the available production technology

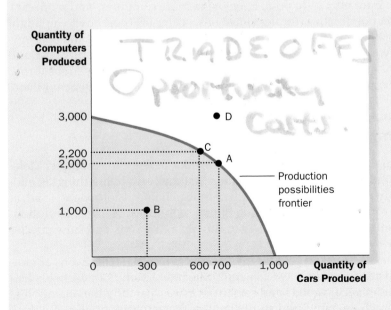

FIGURE 2

The Production Possibilities Frontier

The production possibilities frontier shows the combinations of output—in this case, cars and computers—that the economy can possibly produce. The economy can produce any combination on or inside the frontier. Points outside the frontier are not feasible given the economy's resources.

One of the *Ten Principles of Economics* discussed in Chapter 1 is that people face tradeoffs. The production possibilities frontier shows one tradeoff that society faces. Once we have reached the efficient points on the frontier, the only way of getting more of one good is to get less of the other. When the economy moves from point A to point C, for instance, society produces more computers but at the expense of producing fewer cars.

Another of the *Ten Principles of Economics* is that the cost of something is what you give up to get it. This is called the *opportunity cost*. The production possibilities frontier shows the opportunity cost of one good as measured in terms of the other good. When society reallocates some of the factors of production from the car industry to the computer industry, moving the economy from point A to point C, it gives up 100 cars to get 200 additional computers. In other words, when the economy is at point A, the opportunity cost of 200 computers is 100 cars.

Notice that the production possibilities frontier in Figure 2 is bowed outward. This means that the opportunity cost of cars in terms of computers depends on how much of each good the economy is producing. When the economy is using most of its resources to make cars, the production possibilities frontier is quite steep. Because even workers and machines best suited to making computers are being used to make cars, the economy gets a substantial increase in the number of computers for each car it gives up. By contrast, when the economy is using most of its resources to make computers, the production possibilities frontier is quite flat. In this case, the resources best suited to making computers are already in the computer industry, and each car the economy gives up yields only a small increase in the number of computers.

The production possibilities frontier shows the tradeoff between the production of different goods at a given time, but the tradeoff can change over time. For example, if a technological advance in the computer industry raises the number of computers that a worker can produce per week, the economy can make more computers for any given number of cars. As a result, the production possibilities frontier shifts outward, as in Figure 3. Because of this economic growth, society might move production from point A to point E, enjoying more computers and more cars.

The production possibilities frontier simplifies a complex economy to highlight and clarify some basic ideas. We have used it to illustrate some of the concepts mentioned briefly in Chapter 1: scarcity, efficiency, tradeoffs, opportunity cost, and economic growth. As you study economics, these ideas will recur in various forms. The production possibilities frontier offers one simple way of thinking about them.

Microeconomics and Macroeconomics

Many subjects are studied on various levels. Consider biology, for example. Molecular biologists study the chemical compounds that make up living things. Cellular biologists study cells, which are made up of many chemical compounds and, at the same time, are themselves the building blocks of living organisms. Evolutionary biologists study the many varieties of animals and plants and how species change gradually over the centuries.

Economics is also studied on various levels. We can study the decisions of individual households and firms. Or we can study the interaction of households and firms in markets for specific goods and services. Or we can study the operation of the economy as a whole, which is just the sum of the activities of all these decisionmakers in all these markets.

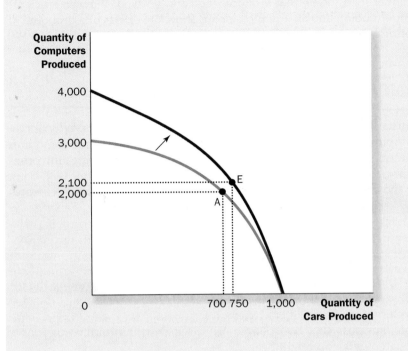

FIGURE 3

A Shift in the Production Possibilities Frontier

An economic advance in the computer industry shifts the production possibilities frontier outward, increasing the number of cars and computers the economy can produce.

The field of economics is traditionally divided into two broad subfields. **Microeconomics** is the study of how households and firms make decisions and how they interact in specific markets. **Macroeconomics** is the study of economy-wide phenomena. A microeconomist might study the effects of rent control on housing in New York City, the impact of foreign competition on the U.S. auto industry, or the effects of compulsory school attendance on workers' earnings. A macroeconomist might study the effects of borrowing by the federal government, the changes over time in the economy's rate of unemployment, or alternative policies to raise growth in national living standards.

Microeconomics and macroeconomics are closely intertwined. Because changes in the overall economy arise from the decisions of millions of individuals, it is impossible to understand macroeconomic developments without considering the associated microeconomic decisions. For example, a macroeconomist might study the effect of a cut in the federal income tax on the overall production of goods and services. To analyze this issue, he or she must consider how the tax cut affects the decisions of households about how much to spend on goods and services.

Despite the inherent link between microeconomics and macroeconomics, the two fields are distinct. In economics, as in biology, it may seem natural to begin with the smallest unit and build up. Yet doing so is neither necessary nor always the best way to proceed. Evolutionary biology is, in a sense, built upon molecular biology, since species are made up of molecules. Yet molecular biology and evolutionary biology are separate fields, each with its own questions and its own methods. Similarly, because microeconomics and macroeconomics address different questions, they sometimes take quite different approaches and are often taught in separate courses.

microeconomics
the study of how households and firms make decisions and how they interact in markets

macroeconomics
the study of economy-wide phenomena, including inflation, unemployment, and economic growth

QuickQuiz In what sense is economics like a science? • Draw a production possibilities frontier for a society that produces food and clothing. Show an efficient point, an inefficient point, and an infeasible point. Show the effects of a drought. • Define *microeconomics* and *macroeconomics*.

THE ECONOMIST AS POLICY ADVISER

Often economists are asked to explain the causes of economic events. Why, for example, is unemployment higher for teenagers than for older workers? Sometimes economists are asked to recommend policies to improve economic outcomes. What, for instance, should the government do to improve the economic well-being of teenagers? When economists are trying to explain the world, they are scientists. When they are trying to help improve it, they are policy advisers.

Positive versus Normative Analysis

To help clarify the two roles that economists play, we begin by examining the use of language. Because scientists and policy advisers have different goals, they use language in different ways.

For example, suppose that two people are discussing minimum-wage laws. Here are two statements you might hear:

POLLY: Minimum-wage laws cause unemployment.
NORMA: The government should raise the minimum wage.

Ignoring for now whether you agree with these statements, notice that Polly and Norma differ in what they are trying to do. Polly is speaking like a scientist: She is making a claim about how the world works. Norma is speaking like a policy adviser: She is making a claim about how she would like to change the world.

In general, statements about the world are of two types. One type, such as Polly's, is positive. **Positive statements** are descriptive. They make a claim about how the world *is*. A second type of statement, such as Norma's, is normative. **Normative statements** are prescriptive. They make a claim about how the world *ought to be*.

A key difference between positive and normative statements is how we judge their validity. We can, in principle, confirm or refute positive statements by examining evidence. An economist might evaluate Polly's statement by analyzing data on changes in minimum wages and changes in unemployment over time. By contrast, evaluating normative statements involves values as well as facts. Norma's statement cannot be judged using data alone. Deciding what is good or bad policy is not merely a matter of science. It also involves our views on ethics, religion, and political philosophy.

Of course, positive and normative statements may be related. Our positive views about how the world works affect our normative views about what policies are desirable. Polly's claim that the minimum wage causes unemployment, if true, might lead us to reject Norma's conclusion that the government should raise the minimum wage. Yet our normative conclusions cannot come from positive analysis alone; they involve value judgments as well.

positive statements
claims that attempt to describe the world as it is

normative statements
claims that attempt to prescribe how the world should be

As you study economics, keep in mind the distinction between positive and normative statements. Much of economics just tries to explain how the economy works. Yet often the goal of economics is to improve how the economy works. When you hear economists making normative statements, you know they have crossed the line from scientist to policy adviser.

Economists in Washington

President Harry Truman once said that he wanted to find a one-armed economist. When he asked his economists for advice, they always answered, "On the one hand, . . . On the other hand, ..."

Truman was right in realizing that economists' advice is not always straightforward. This tendency is rooted in one of the *Ten Principles of Economics* in Chapter 1: People face tradeoffs. Economists are aware that tradeoffs are involved in most policy decisions. A policy might increase efficiency at the cost of equity. It might help future generations but hurt current generations. An economist who says that all policy decisions are easy is an economist not to be trusted.

Truman was also not alone among presidents in relying on the advice of economists. Since 1946, the president of the United States has received guidance from the Council of Economic Advisers, which consists of three members and a staff of several dozen economists. The council, whose offices are just a few steps from the White House, has no duty other than to advise the president and to write the annual *Economic Report of the President*.

The president also receives input from economists in many administrative departments. Economists at the Department of Treasury help design tax policy. Economists at the Department of Labor analyze data on workers and those looking for work in order to help formulate labor-market policies. Economists at the Department of Justice help enforce the nation's antitrust laws.

Economists are also found outside the administrative branch of government. To obtain independent evaluations of policy proposals, Congress relies on the advice of the Congressional Budget Office, which is staffed by economists. The Federal Reserve, the institution that sets the nation's monetary policy, employs hundreds of economists to analyze economic developments in the United States and throughout the world. Table 1 lists the Web sites of some of these agencies.

The influence of economists on policy goes beyond their role as advisers: Their research and writings often affect policy indirectly. Economist John Maynard Keynes offered this observation:

"*Let's switch. I'll make the policy, you implement it, and he'll explain it.*"

TABLE 1

Web Sites

Here are the Web sites for a few of the government agencies that are responsible for collecting economic data and making economic policy.

Department of Commerce	http://www.commerce.gov
Bureau of Labor Statistics	http://www.bls.gov
Congressional Budget Office	http://www.cbo.gov
Federal Reserve Board	http://www.federalreserve.gov

The ideas of economists and political philosophers, both when they are right and when they are wrong, are more powerful than is commonly understood. Indeed, the world is ruled by little else. Practical men, who believe themselves to be quite exempt from intellectual influences, are usually the slaves of some defunct economist. Madmen in authority, who hear voices in the air, are distilling their frenzy from some academic scribbler of a few years back.

Although these words were written in 1935, they remain true today. Indeed, the "academic scribbler" now influencing public policy is often Keynes himself.

QuickQuiz Give an example of a positive statement and an example of a normative statement. • Name three parts of government that regularly rely on advice from economists.

WHY ECONOMISTS DISAGREE

"If all economists were laid end to end, they would not reach a conclusion." This quip from George Bernard Shaw is revealing. Economists as a group are often criticized for giving conflicting advice to policymakers. President Ronald Reagan once joked that if the game Trivial Pursuit were designed for economists, it would have 100 questions and 3,000 answers.

Why do economists so often appear to give conflicting advice to policymakers? There are two basic reasons:

- Economists may disagree about the validity of alternative positive theories about how the world works.
- Economists may have different values and, therefore, different normative views about what policy should try to accomplish.

Let's discuss each of these reasons.

Differences in Scientific Judgments

Several centuries ago, astronomers debated whether the earth or the sun was at the center of the solar system. More recently, meteorologists have debated whether the earth is experiencing global warming and, if so, why. Science is a search for understanding about the world around us. It is not surprising that as the search continues, scientists can disagree about the direction in which truth lies.

Economists often disagree for the same reason. Economics is a young science, and there is still much to be learned. Economists sometimes disagree because they have different hunches about the validity of alternative theories or about the size of important parameters.

For example, economists disagree about whether the government should levy taxes based on a household's income or its consumption (spending). Advocates of a switch from the current income tax to a consumption tax believe that the change would encourage households to save more, because income that is saved would not be taxed. Higher saving, in turn, would lead to more rapid growth in productivity and living standards. Advocates of the current income tax system believe that household saving would not respond much to a change in the tax laws. These two groups of economists hold different normative views about the tax system because they have different positive views about the responsiveness of saving to tax incentives.

Differences in Values

Suppose that Peter and Paul both take the same amount of water from the town well. To pay for maintaining the well, the town taxes its residents. Peter has income of $50,000 and is taxed $5,000, or 10 percent of his income. Paul has income of $10,000 and is taxed $2,000, or 20 percent of his income.

Is this policy fair? If not, who pays too much and who pays too little? Does it matter whether Paul's low income is due to a medical disability or to his decision to pursue a career in acting? Does it matter whether Peter's high income is due to a large inheritance or to his willingness to work long hours at a dreary job?

These are difficult questions on which people are likely to disagree. If the town hired two experts to study how the town should tax its residents to pay for the well, we would not be surprised if they offered conflicting advice.

This simple example shows why economists sometimes disagree about public policy. As we learned earlier in our discussion of normative and positive analysis, policies cannot be judged on scientific grounds alone. Economists give conflicting advice sometimes because they have different values. Perfecting the science of economics will not tell us whether it is Peter or Paul who pays too much.

Perception versus Reality

Because of differences in scientific judgments and differences in values, some disagreement among economists is inevitable. Yet one should not overstate the amount of disagreement. In many cases, economists do offer a united view.

Table 2 (p. 32) contains ten propositions about economic policy. In a survey of economists in business, government, and academia, these propositions were endorsed by an overwhelming majority of respondents. Most of these propositions would fail to command a similar consensus among the general public.

The first proposition in the table is about rent control. For reasons we will discuss later, almost all economists believe that rent control adversely affects the availability and quality of housing and is a very costly way of helping the most needy members of society. Nonetheless, many city governments choose to ignore the advice of economists and place ceilings on the rents that landlords may charge their tenants.

The second proposition in the table concerns tariffs and import quotas, two policies that restrict trade among nations. For reasons we will discuss more fully in later chapters, almost all economists oppose such barriers to free trade. Nonetheless, over the years, the president and Congress have chosen to restrict the import of certain goods. In 2002, for example, the Bush administration imposed large tariffs on steel to protect domestic steel producers from foreign competition. In this case, economists did offer united advice, but policymakers chose to ignore it.

TABLE 2

Ten Propositions about Which Most Economists Agree

Source: Richard M. Alston, J. R. Kearl, and Michael B. Vaughn, "Is There Consensus among Economists in the 1990s?" *American Economic Review* (May 1992): 203–209. Reprinted by permission.

Proposition (and percentage of economists who agree)
1. A ceiling on rents reduces the quantity and quality of housing available. (93%)
2. Tariffs and import quotas usually reduce general economic welfare. (93%)
3. Flexible and floating exchange rates offer an effective international monetary arrangement. (90%)
4. Fiscal policy (e.g., tax cut and/or government expenditure increase) has a significant stimulative impact on a less than fully employed economy. (90%)
5. If the federal budget is to be balanced, it should be done over the business cycle rather than yearly. (85%)
6. Cash payments increase the welfare of recipients to a greater degree than do transfers-in-kind of equal cash value. (84%)
7. A large federal budget deficit has an adverse effect on the economy. (83%)
8. A minimum wage increases unemployment among young and unskilled workers. (79%)
9. The government should restructure the welfare system along the lines of a "negative income tax." (79%)
10. Effluent taxes and marketable pollution permits represent a better approach to pollution control than imposition of pollution ceilings. (78%)

Why do policies such as rent control and trade barriers persist if the experts are united in their opposition? The reason may be that economists have not yet convinced the general public that these policies are undesirable. One purpose of this book is to make you understand the economist's view of these and other subjects and, perhaps, to persuade you that it is the right one.

QuickQuiz Why might economic advisers to the president disagree about a question of policy?

LET'S GET GOING

The first two chapters of this book have introduced you to the ideas and methods of economics. We are now ready to get to work. In the next chapter we start learning in more detail the principles of economic behavior and economic policy.

As you proceed through this book, you will be asked to draw on many of your intellectual skills. You might find it helpful to keep in mind some advice from the great economist John Maynard Keynes:

The study of economics does not seem to require any specialized gifts of an unusually high order. Is it not . . . a very easy subject compared with the higher branches of philosophy or pure science? An easy subject, at which very few excel! The paradox finds its explanation, perhaps, in that the master-economist must possess a rare *combination* of gifts. He must be mathematician, historian, statesman, philosopher—in some degree. He must understand symbols and speak in words. He must contemplate the particular in terms of the general, and touch abstract and concrete in the same flight of thought. He must study the present in the light of the past for the purposes of the future. No part of man's nature or his institutions must lie entirely outside his regard. He must be purposeful and disinterested in a simultaneous mood; as aloof and incorruptible as an artist, yet sometimes as near the earth as a politician.

It is a tall order. But with practice, you will become more and more accustomed to thinking like an economist.

SUMMARY

- Economists try to address their subject with a scientist's objectivity. Like all scientists, they make appropriate assumptions and build simplified models in order to understand the world around them. Two simple economic models are the circular-flow diagram and the production possibilities frontier.

- The field of economics is divided into two subfields: microeconomics and macroeconomics. Microeconomists study decisionmaking by households and firms and the interaction among households and firms in the marketplace. Macroeconomists study the forces and trends that affect the economy as a whole.

- A positive statement is an assertion about how the world *is*. A normative statement is an assertion about how the world *ought to be*. When economists make normative statements, they are acting more as policy advisers than scientists.

- Economists who advise policymakers offer conflicting advice either because of differences in scientific judgments or because of differences in values. At other times, economists are united in the advice they offer, but policymakers may choose to ignore it.

KEY CONCEPTS

circular-flow diagram, p. 23
production possibilities frontier, p. 25

microeconomics, p. 27
macroeconomics, p. 27
positive statements, p. 28

normative statements, p. 28

QUESTIONS FOR REVIEW

1. How is economics like a science?

2. Why do economists make assumptions?

3. Should an economic model describe reality exactly?

4. Draw and explain a production possibilities frontier for an economy that produces milk and cookies. What happens to this frontier if disease kills half of the economy's cow population?

5. Use a production possibilities frontier to describe the idea of "efficiency."

6. What are the two subfields into which economics is divided? Explain what each subfield studies.

7. What is the difference between a positive and a normative statement? Give an example of each.

8. What is the Council of Economic Advisers?

9. Why do economists sometimes offer conflicting advice to policymakers?

PROBLEMS AND APPLICATIONS

1. Describe some unusual language used in one of the other fields that you are studying. Why are these special terms useful?

2. One common assumption in economics is that the products of different firms in the same industry are indistinguishable. For each of the following industries, discuss whether this is a reasonable assumption.
   a. steel
   b. novels
   c. wheat
   d. fast food

3. Draw a circular-flow diagram. Identify the parts of the model that correspond to the flow of goods and services and the flow of dollars for each of the following activities.
   a. Sam pays a storekeeper $1 for a quart of milk.
   b. Sally earns $4.50 per hour working at a fast food restaurant.
   c. Serena spends $7 to see a movie.
   d. Stuart earns $10,000 from his 10 percent ownership of Acme Industrial.

4. Imagine a society that produces military goods and consumer goods, which we'll call "guns" and "butter."
   a. Draw a production possibilities frontier for guns and butter. Explain why it most likely has a bowed-out shape.
   b. Show a point that is impossible for the economy to achieve. Show a point that is feasible but inefficient.
   c. Imagine that the society has two political parties, called the Hawks (who want a strong military) and the Doves (who want a smaller military). Show a point on your production possibilities frontier that the Hawks might choose and a point the Doves might choose.
   d. Imagine that an aggressive neighboring country reduces the size of its military. As a result, both the Hawks and the Doves reduce their desired production of guns by the same amount. Which party would get the bigger "peace dividend," measured by the increase in butter production? Explain.

5. The first principle of economics discussed in Chapter 1 is that people face tradeoffs. Use a production possibilities frontier to illustrate society's tradeoff between a clean environment and the quantity of industrial output. What do you suppose determines the shape and position of the frontier? Show what happens to the frontier if engineers develop an automobile engine with almost no emissions.

6. Classify the following topics as relating to microeconomics or macroeconomics.
   a. a family's decision about how much income to save
   b. the effect of government regulations on auto emissions
   c. the impact of higher national saving on economic growth
   d. a firm's decision about how many workers to hire
   e. the relationship between the inflation rate and changes in the quantity of money

7. Classify each of the following statements as positive or normative. Explain.
   a. Society faces a short-run tradeoff between inflation and unemployment.
   b. A reduction in the rate of growth of money will reduce the rate of inflation.
   c. The Federal Reserve should reduce the rate of growth of money.
   d. Society ought to require welfare recipients to look for jobs.
   e. Lower tax rates encourage more work and more saving.

8. Classify each of the statements in Table 2 as positive, normative, or ambiguous. Explain.

9. If you were president, would you be more interested in your economic advisers' positive views or their normative views? Why?

10. The *Economic Report of the President* contains statistical information about the economy as well as the Council of Economic Advisers' analysis of current policy issues. Find a recent copy of this annual report at your library and read a chapter about an issue that interests you. Summarize the economic problem at hand and describe the council's recommended policy.

11. Who is the current chairman of the Federal Reserve? Who is the current chair of the Council

of Economic Advisers? Who is the current secretary of the treasury?

12. Would you expect economists to disagree less about public policy as time goes on? Why or why not? Can their differences be completely eliminated? Why or why not?

13. Look up one of the Web sites listed in Table 1. What recent economic trends or issues are addressed there?

http://   For more study tools, please visit http://mankiwXtra.swlearning.com.

APPENDIX
Graphing: A Brief Review

Many of the concepts that economists study can be expressed with numbers—the price of bananas, the quantity of bananas sold, the cost of growing bananas, and so on. Often these economic variables are related to one another. When the price of bananas rises, people buy fewer bananas. One way of expressing the relationships among variables is with graphs.

Graphs serve two purposes. First, when developing economic theories, graphs offer a way to visually express ideas that might be less clear if described with equations or words. Second, when analyzing economic data, graphs provide a way of finding how variables are in fact related in the world. Whether we are working with theory or with data, graphs provide a lens through which a recognizable forest emerges from a multitude of trees.

Numerical information can be expressed graphically in many ways, just as a thought can be expressed in words in many ways. A good writer chooses words that will make an argument clear, a description pleasing, or a scene dramatic. An effective economist chooses the type of graph that best suits the purpose at hand.

In this appendix we discuss how economists use graphs to study the mathematical relationships among variables. We also discuss some of the pitfalls that can arise in the use of graphical methods.

Graphs of a Single Variable

Three common graphs are shown in Figure A-1. The *pie chart* in panel (a) shows how total income in the United States is divided among the sources of income, including compensation of employees, corporate profits, and so on. A slice of the pie represents each source's share of the total. The *bar graph* in panel (b) compares income for four countries. The height of each bar represents the average income in each country. The *time-series graph* in panel (c) traces the rising productivity in the U.S. business sector over time. The height of the line shows output per hour in each year. You have probably seen similar graphs presented in newspapers and magazines.

Graphs of Two Variables: The Coordinate System

Although the three graphs in Figure A-1 are useful in showing how a variable changes over time or across individuals, such graphs are limited in how much they can tell us. These graphs display information only on a single variable. Economists are often concerned with the relationships between variables. Thus, they need to be able to display two variables on a single graph. The *coordinate system* makes this possible.

Suppose you want to examine the relationship between study time and grade point average. For each student in your class, you could record a pair of numbers: hours per week spent studying and grade point average. These numbers could then be placed in parentheses as an *ordered pair* and appear as a single point on the

Types of Graphs

The pie chart in panel (a) shows how U.S. national income is derived from various sources. The bar graph in panel (b) compares the average income in four countries. The time-series graph in panel (c) shows the productivity of labor in U.S. businesses from 1950 to 2000.

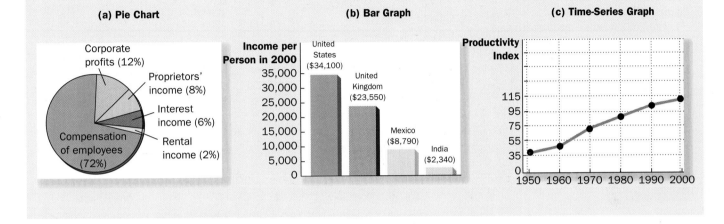

graph. Albert E., for instance, is represented by the ordered pair (25 hours/week, 3.5 GPA), while his "what-me-worry?" classmate Alfred E. is represented by the ordered pair (5 hours/week, 2.0 GPA).

We can graph these ordered pairs on a two-dimensional grid. The first number in each ordered pair, called the *x-coordinate*, tells us the horizontal location of the point. The second number, called the *y-coordinate*, tells us the vertical location of the point. The point with both an *x*-coordinate and a *y*-coordinate of zero is known as the *origin*. The two coordinates in the ordered pair tell us where the point is located in relation to the origin: *x* units to the right of the origin and *y* units above it.

Figure A-2 (p. 38) graphs grade point average against study time for Albert E., Alfred E., and their classmates. This type of graph is called a *scatterplot* because it plots scattered points. Looking at this graph, we immediately notice that points farther to the right (indicating more study time) also tend to be higher (indicating a better grade point average). Because study time and grade point average typically move in the same direction, we say that these two variables have a *positive correlation*. By contrast, if we were to graph party time and grades, we would likely find that higher party time is associated with lower grades; because these variables typically move in opposite directions, we would call this a *negative correlation*. In either case, the coordinate system makes the correlation between the two variables easy to see.

Curves in the Coordinate System

Students who study more do tend to get higher grades, but other factors also influence a student's grade. Previous preparation is an important factor, for instance,

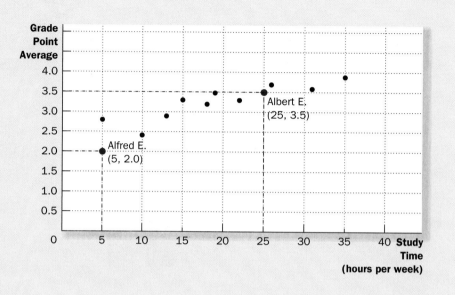

FIGURE A-2

Using the Coordinate System

Grade point average is measured on the vertical axis and study time on the horizontal axis. Albert E., Alfred E., and their classmates are represented by various points. We can see from the graph that students who study more tend to get higher grades.

as are talent, attention from teachers, even eating a good breakfast. A scatterplot like Figure A-2 does not attempt to isolate the effect that study has on grades from the effects of other variables. Often, however, economists prefer looking at how one variable affects another holding everything else constant.

To see how this is done, let's consider one of the most important graphs in economics—the *demand curve*. The demand curve traces out the effect of a good's price on the quantity of the good consumers want to buy. Before showing a demand curve, however, consider Table A-1, which shows how the number of novels that Emma buys depends on her income and on the price of novels. When novels are cheap, Emma buys them in large quantities. As they become more expensive, she borrows books from the library instead of buying them or chooses to go to the movies instead of reading. Similarly, at any given price, Emma buys more novels when she has a higher income. That is, when her income increases, she spends part of the additional income on novels and part on other goods.

We now have three variables—the price of novels, income, and the number of novels purchased—which is more than we can represent in two dimensions. To put the information from Table A-1 in graphical form, we need to hold one of the three variables constant and trace out the relationship between the other two. Because the demand curve represents the relationship between price and quantity demanded, we hold Emma's income constant and show how the number of novels she buys varies with the price of novels.

Suppose that Emma's income is $30,000 per year. If we place the number of novels Emma purchases on the *x*-axis and the price of novels on the *y*-axis, we can graphically represent the middle column of Table A-1. When the points that represent these entries from the table—(5 novels, $10), (9 novels, $9), and so on—are connected, they form a line. This line, pictured in Figure A-3, is known as Emma's demand curve for novels; it tells us how many novels Emma purchases at any

	Income		
Price	$20,000	$30,000	$40,000
$10	2 novels	5 novels	8 novels
9	6	9	12
8	10	13	16
7	14	17	20
6	18	21	24
5	22	25	28
	Demand curve, D_3	Demand curve, D_1	Demand curve, D_2

Novels Purchased by Emma

This table shows the number of novels Emma buys at various incomes and prices. For any given level of income, the data on price and quantity demanded can be graphed to produce Emma's demand curve for novels, as shown in Figures A-3 and A-4.

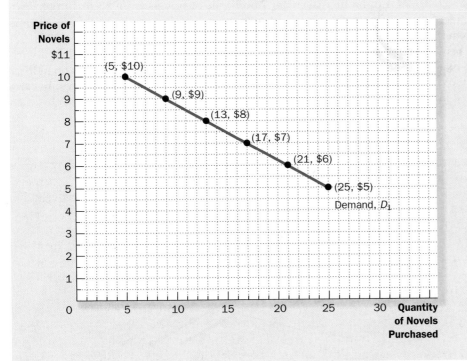

Demand Curve

The line D_1 shows how Emma's purchases of novels depend on the price of novels when her income is held constant. Because the price and the quantity demanded are negatively related, the demand curve slopes downward.

given price. The demand curve is downward sloping, indicating that a higher price reduces the quantity of novels demanded. Because the quantity of novels demanded and the price move in opposite directions, we say that the two variables are *negatively related*. (Conversely, when two variables move in the same direction, the curve relating them is upward sloping, and we say the variables are *positively related*.)

Now suppose that Emma's income rises to $40,000 per year. At any given price, Emma will purchase more novels than she did at her previous level of income. Just as earlier we drew Emma's demand curve for novels using the entries from the middle column of Table A-1, we now draw a new demand curve using the entries from the right-hand column of the table. This new demand curve (curve D_2) is pictured alongside the old one (curve D_1) in Figure A-4; the new curve is a similar line drawn farther to the right. We therefore say that Emma's demand curve for novels *shifts* to the right when her income increases. Likewise, if Emma's income were to fall to $20,000 per year, she would buy fewer novels at any given price and her demand curve would shift to the left (to curve D_3).

In economics, it is important to distinguish between *movements along a curve* and *shifts of a curve*. As we can see from Figure A-3, if Emma earns $30,000 per year and novels cost $8 apiece, she will purchase 13 novels per year. If the price of novels falls to $7, Emma will increase her purchases of novels to 17 per year. The demand curve, however, stays fixed in the same place. Emma still buys the same number of novels *at each price*, but as the price falls she moves along her demand curve from left to right. By contrast, if the price of novels remains fixed at $8 but her income rises to $40,000, Emma increases her purchases of novels from 13 to 16 per year. Because Emma buys more novels *at each price*, her demand curve shifts out, as shown in Figure A-4.

There is a simple way to tell when it is necessary to shift a curve. When a variable that is not named on either axis changes, the curve shifts. Income is on neither the x-axis nor the y-axis of the graph, so when Emma's income changes, her de-

---

FIGURE A-4

Shifting Demand Curves

The location of Emma's demand curve for novels depends on how much income she earns. The more she earns, the more novels she will purchase at any given price, and the farther to the right her demand curve will lie. Curve D_1 represents Emma's original demand curve when her income is $30,000 per year. If her income rises to $40,000 per year, her demand curve shifts to D_2. If her income falls to $20,000 per year, her demand curve shifts to D_3.

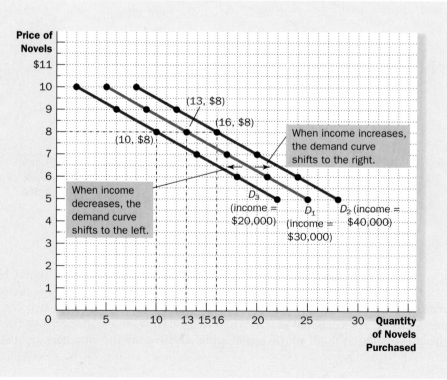

mand curve must shift. Any change that affects Emma's purchasing habits besides a change in the price of novels will result in a shift in her demand curve. If, for instance, the public library closes and Emma must buy all the books she wants to read, she will demand more novels at each price, and her demand curve will shift to the right. Or, if the price of movies falls and Emma spends more time at the movies and less time reading, she will demand fewer novels at each price, and her demand curve will shift to the left. By contrast, when a variable on an axis of the graph changes, the curve does not shift. We read the change as a movement along the curve.

Slope

One question we might want to ask about Emma is how much her purchasing habits respond to price. Look at the demand curve pictured in Figure A-5. If this curve is very steep, Emma purchases nearly the same number of novels regardless of whether they are cheap or expensive. If this curve is much flatter, Emma purchases many fewer novels when the price rises. To answer questions about how much one variable responds to changes in another variable, we can use the concept of *slope*.

The slope of a line is the ratio of the vertical distance covered to the horizontal distance covered as we move along the line. This definition is usually written out in mathematical symbols as follows:

$$\text{slope} = \frac{\Delta y}{\Delta x},$$

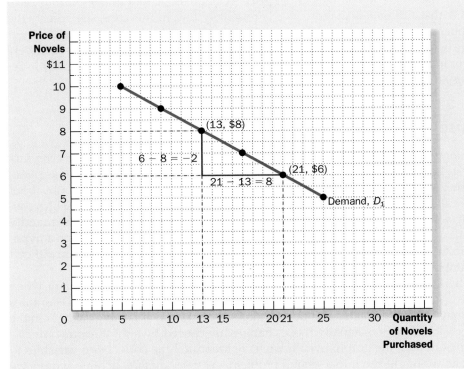

Calculating the Slope of a Line

To calculate the slope of the demand curve, we can look at the changes in the x- and y-coordinates as we move from the point (21 novels, $6) to the point (13 novels, $8). The slope of the line is the ratio of the change in the y-coordinate (−2) to the change in the x-coordinate (+8), which equals −1/4.

where the Greek letter Δ (delta) stands for the change in a variable. In other words, the slope of a line is equal to the "rise" (change in y) divided by the "run" (change in x). The slope will be a small positive number for a fairly flat upward-sloping line, a large positive number for a steep upward-sloping line, and a negative number for a downward-sloping line. A horizontal line has a slope of zero because in this case the y-variable never changes; a vertical line is said to have an infinite slope because the y-variable can take any value without the x-variable changing at all.

What is the slope of Emma's demand curve for novels? First of all, because the curve slopes down, we know the slope will be negative. To calculate a numerical value for the slope, we must choose two points on the line. With Emma's income at $30,000, she will purchase 21 novels at a price of $6 or 13 novels at a price of $8. When we apply the slope formula, we are concerned with the change between these two points; in other words, we are concerned with the difference between them, which lets us know that we will have to subtract one set of values from the other, as follows:

$$\text{slope} = \frac{\Delta y}{\Delta x} = \frac{\text{first } y\text{-coordinate} - \text{second } y\text{-coordinate}}{\text{first } x\text{-coordinate} - \text{second } x\text{-coordinate}} = \frac{6-8}{21-13} = \frac{-2}{8} = \frac{-1}{4}$$

Figure A-5 shows graphically how this calculation works. Try computing the slope of Emma's demand curve using two different points. You should get exactly the same result, $-1/4$. One of the properties of a straight line is that it has the same slope everywhere. This is not true of other types of curves, which are steeper in some places than in others.

The slope of Emma's demand curve tells us something about how responsive her purchases are to changes in the price. A small slope (a number close to zero) means that Emma's demand curve is relatively flat; in this case, she adjusts the number of novels she buys substantially in response to a price change. A larger slope (a number farther from zero) means that Emma's demand curve is relatively steep; in this case, she adjusts the number of novels she buys only slightly in response to a price change.

Cause and Effect

Economists often use graphs to advance an argument about how the economy works. In other words, they use graphs to argue about how one set of events *causes* another set of events. With a graph like the demand curve, there is no doubt about cause and effect. Because we are varying price and holding all other variables constant, we know that changes in the price of novels cause changes in the quantity Emma demands. Remember, however, that our demand curve came from a hypothetical example. When graphing data from the real world, it is often more difficult to establish how one variable affects another.

The first problem is that it is difficult to hold everything else constant when measuring how one variable affects another. If we are not able to hold variables constant, we might decide that one variable on our graph is causing changes in the other variable when actually those changes are caused by a third *omitted variable* not pictured on the graph. Even if we have identified the correct two variables to look at, we might run into a second problem—*reverse causality*. In other words, we might decide that A causes B when in fact B causes A. The omitted-variable and reverse-causality traps require us to proceed with caution when using graphs to draw conclusions about causes and effects.

Omitted Variables   To see how omitting a variable can lead to a deceptive graph, let's consider an example. Imagine that the government, spurred by public concern about the large number of deaths from cancer, commissions an exhaustive study from Big Brother Statistical Services, Inc. Big Brother examines many of the items found in people's homes to see which of them are associated with the risk of cancer. Big Brother reports a strong relationship between two variables: the number of cigarette lighters that a household owns and the probability that someone in the household will develop cancer. Figure A-6 shows this relationship.

What should we make of this result? Big Brother advises a quick policy response. It recommends that the government discourage the ownership of cigarette lighters by taxing their sale. It also recommends that the government require warning labels: "Big Brother has determined that this lighter is dangerous to your health."

In judging the validity of Big Brother's analysis, one question is paramount: Has Big Brother held constant every relevant variable except the one under consideration? If the answer is no, the results are suspect. An easy explanation for Figure A-6 is that people who own more cigarette lighters are more likely to smoke cigarettes and that cigarettes, not lighters, cause cancer. If Figure A-6 does not hold constant the amount of smoking, it does not tell us the true effect of owning a cigarette lighter.

This story illustrates an important principle: When you see a graph being used to support an argument about cause and effect, it is important to ask whether the movements of an omitted variable could explain the results you see.

Reverse Causality   Economists can also make mistakes about causality by misreading its direction. To see how this is possible, suppose the Association of American Anarchists commissions a study of crime in America and arrives at Figure A-7 (p. 44), which plots the number of violent crimes per thousand people in major cities against the number of police officers per thousand people. The anarchists

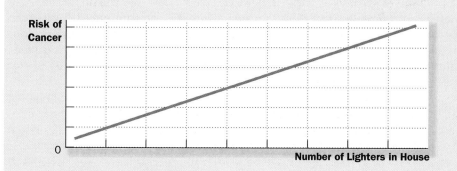

FIGURE A-6

Risk of Cancer

Number of Lighters in House

Graph with an Omitted Variable

The upward-sloping curve shows that members of households with more cigarette lighters are more likely to develop cancer. Yet we should not conclude that ownership of lighters causes cancer, because the graph does not take into account the number of cigarettes smoked.

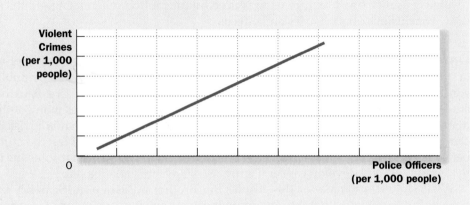

FIGURE A-7

Graph Suggesting Reverse Causality

The upward-sloping curve shows that cities with a higher concentration of police are more dangerous. Yet the graph does not tell us whether police cause crime or crime-plagued cities hire more police.

note the curve's upward slope and argue that because police increase rather than decrease the amount of urban violence, law enforcement should be abolished.

If we could run a controlled experiment, we would avoid the danger of reverse causality. To run an experiment, we would set the number of police officers in different cities randomly and then examine the correlation between police and crime. Figure A-7, however, is not based on such an experiment. We simply observe that more dangerous cities have more police officers. The explanation for this may be that more dangerous cities hire more police. In other words, rather than police causing crime, crime may cause police. Nothing in the graph itself allows us to establish the direction of causality.

It might seem that an easy way to determine the direction of causality is to examine which variable moves first. If we see crime increase and then the police force expand, we reach one conclusion. If we see the police force expand and then crime increase, we reach the other. Yet there is also a flaw with this approach: Often people change their behavior not in response to a change in their present conditions but in response to a change in their *expectations* of future conditions. A city that expects a major crime wave in the future, for instance, might well hire more police now. This problem is even easier to see in the case of babies and minivans. Couples often buy a minivan in anticipation of the birth of a child. The minivan comes before the baby, but we wouldn't want to conclude that the sale of minivans causes the population to grow!

There is no complete set of rules that says when it is appropriate to draw causal conclusions from graphs. Yet just keeping in mind that cigarette lighters don't cause cancer (omitted variable) and minivans don't cause larger families (reverse causality) will keep you from falling for many faulty economic arguments.

INTERDEPENDENCE AND
THE GAINS FROM TRADE

Consider your typical day. You wake up in the morning, and you pour yourself juice from oranges grown in Florida and coffee from beans grown in Brazil. Over breakfast, you watch a news program broadcast from New York on your television made in Japan. You get dressed in clothes made of cotton grown in Georgia and sewn in factories in Thailand. You drive to class in a car made of parts manufactured in more than a dozen countries around the world. Then you open up your economics textbook written by an author living in Massachusetts, published by a company located in Ohio, and printed on paper made from trees grown in Oregon.

Every day you rely on many people from around the world, most of whom you do not know, to provide you with the goods and services that you enjoy. Such interdependence is possible because people trade with one another. Those people who provide you with goods and services are not acting out of generosity or concern for your welfare. Nor is some government agency directing them to make what you want and to give it to you. Instead, people provide you and other consumers with the goods and services they produce because they get something in return.

In subsequent chapters we will examine how our economy coordinates the activities of millions of people with varying tastes and abilities. As a starting point for this analysis, here we consider the reasons for economic interdependence. One of the *Ten Principles of Economics* highlighted in Chapter 1 is that trade can make everyone better off. This principle explains why people trade with their neighbors and why nations trade with other nations. In this chapter we examine this principle more closely. What exactly do people gain when they trade with one another? Why do people choose to become interdependent?

A PARABLE FOR THE MODERN ECONOMY

To understand why people choose to depend on others for goods and services and how this choice improves their lives, let's look at a simple economy. Imagine that there are two goods in the world—meat and potatoes. And there are two people in the world—a cattle rancher and a potato farmer—each of whom would like to eat both meat and potatoes.

The gains from trade are most obvious if the rancher can produce only meat and the farmer can produce only potatoes. In one scenario, the rancher and the farmer could choose to have nothing to do with each other. But after several months of eating beef roasted, boiled, broiled, and grilled, the rancher might decide that self-sufficiency is not all it's cracked up to be. The farmer, who has been eating potatoes mashed, fried, baked, and scalloped, would likely agree. It is easy to see that trade would allow them to enjoy greater variety: Each could then have a steak with baked potato.

Although this scene illustrates most simply how everyone can benefit from trade, the gains would be similar if the rancher and the farmer were each capable of producing the other good, but only at great cost. Suppose, for example, that the potato farmer is able to raise cattle and produce meat, but that he is not very good at it. Similarly, suppose that the cattle rancher is able to grow potatoes, but that her land is not very well suited for it. In this case, it is easy to see that the farmer and the rancher can each benefit by specializing in what he or she does best and then trading with the other.

The gains from trade are less obvious, however, when one person is better at producing *every* good. For example, suppose that the rancher is better at raising cattle *and* better at growing potatoes than the farmer. In this case, should the rancher or farmer choose to remain self-sufficient? Or is there still reason for them to trade with each other? To answer this question, we need to look more closely at the factors that affect such a decision.

Production Possibilities

Suppose that the farmer and the rancher each work 8 hours a day and can devote this time to growing potatoes, raising cattle, or a combination of the two. Table 1 shows the amount of time each person requires to produce 1 ounce of each good. The farmer can produce an ounce of potatoes in 15 minutes and an ounce of meat in 60 minutes. The rancher, who is more productive in both activities, can produce an ounce of potatoes in 10 minutes and an ounce of meat in 20 minutes. The last columns in Table 1 show the amounts of meat or potatoes the farmer and rancher can produce if they work an 8-hour day, producing only that good.

Panel (a) of Figure 1 illustrates the amounts of meat and potatoes that the farmer can produce. If the farmer devotes all 8 hours of his time to potatoes, he produces

TABLE 1

	Minutes Needed to Make 1 Ounce of:		Amount of Meat or Potatoes Produced in 8 Hours	
	Meat	Potatoes	Meat	Potatoes
Farmer	60 min/oz	15 min/oz	8 oz	32 oz
Rancher	20 min/oz	10 min/oz	24 oz	48 oz

The Production Opportunities of the Farmer and the Rancher

FIGURE 1

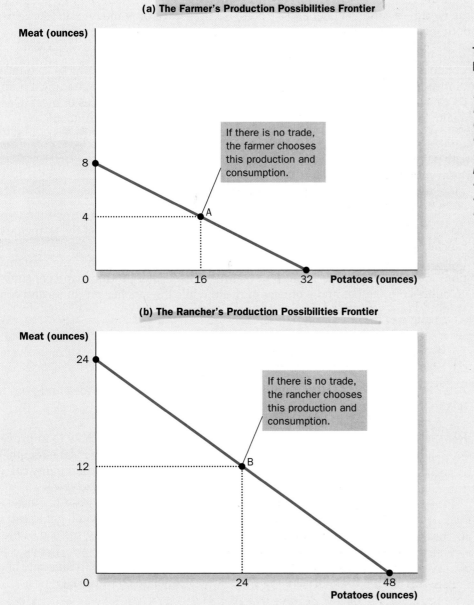

(a) The Farmer's Production Possibilities Frontier

Meat (ounces)

If there is no trade, the farmer chooses this production and consumption.

8

4 — A

0   16   32   Potatoes (ounces)

(b) The Rancher's Production Possibilities Frontier

Meat (ounces)

24

If there is no trade, the rancher chooses this production and consumption.

12 .... B

0   24   48
                          Potatoes (ounces)

The Production Possibilities Frontier

Panel (a) shows the combinations of meat and potatoes that the farmer can produce. Panel (b) shows the combinations of meat and potatoes that the rancher can produce. Both production possibilities frontiers are derived from Table 1 and the assumption that the farmer and rancher each work 8 hours a day.

32 ounces of potatoes (measured on the horizontal axis) and no meat. If he devotes all his time to meat, he produces 8 ounces of meat (measured on the vertical axis) and no potatoes. If the farmer divides his time equally between the two activities, spending 4 hours on each, he produces 16 ounces of potatoes and 4 ounces of meat. The figure shows these three possible outcomes and all others in between.

This graph is the farmer's production possibilities frontier. As we discussed in Chapter 2, a production possibilities frontier shows the various mixes of output that an economy can produce. It illustrates one of the *Ten Principles of Economics* in Chapter 1: People face tradeoffs. Here the farmer faces a tradeoff between producing meat and producing potatoes. You may recall that the production possibilities frontier in Chapter 2 was drawn bowed out; in that case, the tradeoff between the two goods depended on the amounts being produced. Here, however, the farmer's technology for producing meat and potatoes (as summarized in Table 1) allows him to switch between one good and the other at a constant rate. In this case, the production possibilities frontier is a straight line.

Panel (b) of Figure 1 shows the production possibilities frontier for the rancher. If the rancher devotes all 8 hours of her time to potatoes, she produces 48 ounces of potatoes and no meat. If she devotes all her time to meat, she produces 24 ounces of meat and no potatoes. If the rancher divides her time equally, spending 4 hours on each activity, she produces 24 ounces of potatoes and 12 ounces of meat. Once again, the production possibilities frontier shows all the possible outcomes.

If the farmer and rancher choose to be self-sufficient, rather than trade with each other, then each consumes exactly what he or she produces. In this case, the production possibilities frontier is also the consumption possibilities frontier. That is, without trade, Figure 1 shows the possible combinations of meat and potatoes that the farmer and rancher can each consume.

Although these production possibilities frontiers are useful in showing the tradeoffs that the farmer and rancher face, they do not tell us what the farmer and rancher will actually choose to do. To determine their choices, we need to know the tastes of the farmer and the rancher. Let's suppose they choose the combinations identified by points A and B in Figure 1: The farmer produces and consumes 16 ounces of potatoes and 4 ounces of meat, while the rancher produces and consumes 24 ounces of potatoes and 12 ounces of meat.

Specialization and Trade

After several years of eating combination B, the rancher gets an idea and goes to talk to the farmer:

RANCHER: Farmer, my friend, have I got a deal for you! I know how to improve life for both of us. I think you should stop producing meat altogether and devote all your time to growing potatoes. According to my calculations, if you work 8 hours a day growing potatoes, you'll produce 32 ounces of potatoes. If you give me 15 of those 32 ounces, I'll give you 5 ounces of meat in return. In the end, you'll get to eat 17 ounces of potatoes and 5 ounces of meat every day, instead of the 16 ounces of potatoes and 4 ounces of meat you now get. If you go along with my plan, you'll have more of *both* foods. [To illustrate her point, the rancher shows the farmer panel (a) of Figure 2.]

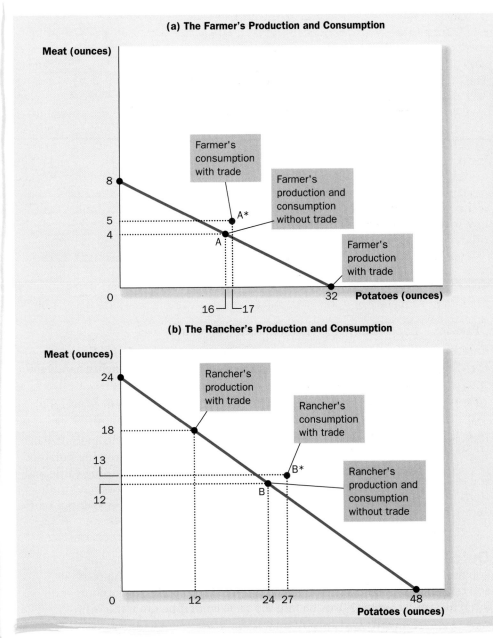

FIGURE 2

How Trade Expands the Set of Consumption Opportunities

The proposed trade between the farmer and the rancher offers each of them a combination of meat and potatoes that would be impossible in the absence of trade. In panel (a), the farmer gets to consume at point A* rather than point A. In panel (b), the rancher gets to consume at point B* rather than point B. Trade allows each to consume more meat and more potatoes.

FARMER: *(sounding skeptical)* That seems like a good deal for me. But I don't understand why you are offering it. If the deal is so good for me, it can't be good for you too.

RANCHER: Oh, but it is! Suppose I spend 6 hours a day raising cattle and 2 hours growing potatoes. Then I can produce 18 ounces of meat and 12 ounces of potatoes. After I give you 5 ounces of my meat in exchange for 15 ounces of your potatoes, I'll end up with 13 ounces of meat and 27 ounces of potatoes. So I will also consume more of both foods than I do now. [She points out panel (b) of Figure 2.]

TABLE 2

The Gains from Trade:
A Summary

	Farmer		Rancher	
	Meat	**Potatoes**	**Meat**	**Potatoes**
Without Trade:	*4 potatoes*	*4 oz meat*	*2 pot*	*16*	
Production and Consumption	4 oz	16 oz	12 oz	24 oz
With Trade:				
Production	0 oz	32 oz	18 oz	12 oz
Trade	Gets 5 oz	Gives 15 oz	Gives 5 oz	Gets 15 oz
Consumption	5 oz	17 oz	13 oz	27 oz
Gains from Trade:				
Increase in Consumption	+1 oz	+1 oz	+1 oz	+3 oz

FARMER: I don't know. . . . This sounds too good to be true.

RANCHER: It's really not as complicated as it seems at first. Here—I've summarized my proposal for you in a simple table. [The rancher hands the farmer a copy of Table 2.]

FARMER: *(after pausing to study the table)* These calculations seem correct, but I am puzzled. How can this deal make us both better off?

RANCHER: We can both benefit because trade allows each of us to specialize in doing what we do best. You will spend more time growing potatoes and less time raising cattle. I will spend more time raising cattle and less time growing potatoes. As a result of specialization and trade, each of us can consume more meat and more potatoes without working any more hours.

QuickQuiz   Draw an example of a production possibilities frontier for Robinson Crusoe, a shipwrecked sailor who spends his time gathering coconuts and catching fish. Does this frontier limit Crusoe's consumption of coconuts and fish if he lives by himself? Does he face the same limits if he can trade with natives on the island?

THE PRINCIPLE OF COMPARATIVE ADVANTAGE

The rancher's explanation of the gains from trade, though correct, poses a puzzle: If the rancher is better at both raising cattle and growing potatoes, how can the farmer ever specialize in doing what he does best? The farmer doesn't seem to do anything best. To solve this puzzle, we need to look at the principle of *comparative advantage*.

As a first step in developing this principle, consider the following question: In our example, who can produce potatoes at lower cost—the farmer or the rancher? There are two possible answers, and in these two answers lie the solution to our puzzle and the key to understanding the gains from trade.

Absolute Advantage

One way to answer the question about the cost of producing potatoes is to compare the inputs required by the two producers. Economists use the term **absolute advantage** when comparing the productivity of one person, firm, or nation to that of another. The producer that requires a smaller quantity of inputs to produce a good is said to have an absolute advantage in producing that good.

In our example, the rancher has an absolute advantage both in producing meat and in producing potatoes, because she requires less time than the farmer to produce a unit of either good. The rancher needs to input only 20 minutes to produce an ounce of meat, whereas the farmer needs 60 minutes. Similarly, the rancher needs only 10 minutes to produce an ounce of potatoes, whereas the farmer needs 15 minutes. Based on this information, we can conclude that the rancher has the lower cost of producing potatoes, if we measure cost in terms of the quantity of inputs.

absolute advantage
the comparison among producers of a good according to their productivity

Opportunity Cost and Comparative Advantage

There is another way to look at the cost of producing potatoes. Rather than comparing inputs required, we can compare the opportunity costs. Recall from Chapter 1 that the **opportunity cost** of some item is what we give up to get that item. In our example, we assumed that the farmer and the rancher each spend 8 hours a day working. Time spent producing potatoes, therefore, takes away from time available for producing meat. As the rancher and farmer reallocate time between producing the two goods, they move along their production possibility frontiers; they give up units of one good to produce units of the other. The opportunity cost measures the tradeoff between the two goods that each producer faces.

opportunity cost
whatever must be given up to obtain some item

Let's first consider the rancher's opportunity cost. According to Table 1, producing 1 ounce of potatoes takes her 10 minutes of work. When the rancher spends that 10 minutes producing potatoes, she spends 10 minutes less producing meat. Because the rancher needs 20 minutes to produce 1 ounce of meat, 10 minutes of work would yield ½ ounce of meat. Hence, the rancher's opportunity cost of producing 1 ounce of potatoes is ½ ounce of meat.

Now consider the farmer's opportunity cost. Producing 1 ounce of potatoes takes him 15 minutes. Because he needs 60 minutes to produce 1 ounce of meat, 15 minutes of work would yield ¼ ounce of meat. Hence, the farmer's opportunity cost of 1 ounce of potatoes is ¼ ounce of meat.

Table 3 (p. 52) shows the opportunity costs of meat and potatoes for the two producers. Notice that the opportunity cost of meat is the inverse of the opportunity cost of potatoes. Because 1 ounce of potatoes costs the rancher ½ ounce of meat, 1 ounce of meat costs the rancher 2 ounces of potatoes. Similarly, because 1 ounce of potatoes costs the farmer ¼ ounce of meat, 1 ounce of meat costs the farmer 4 ounces of potatoes.

TABLE 3		Opportunity Cost of:	
		1 Ounce of Meat	**1 Ounce of Potatoes**
The Opportunity Cost of Meat and Potatoes	Farmer	4 oz potatoes	¼ oz meat
	Rancher	2 oz potatoes	½ oz meat

comparative advantage
the comparison among producers of a good according to their opportunity cost

Economists use the term **comparative advantage** when describing the opportunity cost of two producers. The producer who gives up less of other goods to produce good X has the smaller opportunity cost of producing good X and is said to have a comparative advantage in producing it. In our example, the farmer has a lower opportunity cost of producing potatoes than does the rancher: An ounce of potatoes costs the farmer only ¼ ounce of meat, while it costs the rancher ½ ounce of meat. Conversely, the rancher has a lower opportunity cost of producing meat than does the farmer: An ounce of meat costs the rancher 2 ounces of potatoes, while it costs the farmer 4 ounces of potatoes. Thus, the farmer has a comparative advantage in growing potatoes, and the rancher has a comparative advantage in producing meat.

Although it is possible for one person to have an absolute advantage in both goods (as the rancher does in our example), it is impossible for one person to have a comparative advantage in both goods. Because the opportunity cost of one good is the inverse of the opportunity cost of the other, if a person's opportunity cost of one good is relatively high, his opportunity cost of the other good must be relatively low. Comparative advantage reflects the relative opportunity cost. Unless two people have exactly the same opportunity cost, one person will have a comparative advantage in one good, and the other person will have a comparative advantage in the other good.

Comparative Advantage and Trade

Differences in opportunity cost and comparative advantage create the gains from trade. When each person specializes in producing the good for which he or she has a comparative advantage, total production in the economy rises, and this increase in the size of the economic pie can be used to make everyone better off. In other words, as long as two people have different opportunity costs, each can benefit from trade by obtaining a good at a price that is lower than his or her opportunity cost of that good.

Consider the proposed deal from the viewpoint of the farmer. The farmer gets 5 ounces of meat in exchange for 15 ounces of potatoes. In other words, the farmer buys each ounce of meat for a price of 3 ounces of potatoes. This price of meat is lower than his opportunity cost for 1 ounce of meat, which is 4 ounces of potatoes. Thus, the farmer benefits from the deal because he gets to buy meat at a good price.

Now consider the deal from the rancher's viewpoint. The rancher buys 15 ounces of potatoes for a price of 5 ounces of meat. That is, the price of potatoes is

FYI

THE LEGACY OF ADAM SMITH AND DAVID RICARDO

Economists have long understood the principle of comparative advantage. Here is how the great economist Adam Smith put the argument:

It is a maxim of every prudent master of a family, never to attempt to make at home what it will cost him more to make than to buy. The tailor does not attempt to make his own shoes, but buys them of the shoemaker. The shoemaker does not attempt to make his own clothes but employs a tailor. The farmer attempts to make neither the one nor the other, but employs those different artificers. All of them find it for their interest to employ their whole industry in a way in which they have some advantage over their neighbors,

and to purchase with a part of its produce, or what is the same thing, with the price of part of it, whatever else they have occasion for.

This quotation is from Smith's 1776 book *An Inquiry into the Nature and Causes of the Wealth of Nations,* which was a landmark in the analysis of trade and economic interdependence.

Smith's book inspired David Ricardo, a millionaire stockbroker, to become an economist. In his 1817 book *Principles of Political Economy and Taxation,* Ricardo developed the principle of comparative advantage as we know it today. His defense of free trade was not a mere academic exercise. Ricardo put his economic beliefs to work as a member of the British Parliament, where he opposed the Corn Laws, which restricted the import of grain.

The conclusions of Adam Smith and David Ricardo on the gains from trade have held up well over time. Although economists often disagree on questions of policy, they are united in their support of free trade. Moreover, the central argument for free trade has not changed much in the past two centuries. Even though the field of economics has broadened its scope and refined its theories since the time of Smith and Ricardo, economists' opposition to trade restrictions is still based largely on the principle of comparative advantage.

David Ricardo

PHOTO: © BETTMANN/CORBIS

⅓ ounce of meat. This price of potatoes is lower than her opportunity cost of 1 ounce of potatoes, which is ½ ounce of meat. The rancher benefits because she gets to buy potatoes at a good price.

These benefits arise because each person concentrates on the activity for which he or she has the lower opportunity cost: The farmer spends more time growing potatoes, and the rancher spends more time producing meat. As a result, the total production of potatoes and the total production of meat both rise. In our example, potato production rises from 40 to 44 ounces, and meat production rises from 16 to 18 ounces. The farmer and rancher share the benefits of this increased production. The moral of the story of the farmer and the rancher should now be clear: *Trade can benefit everyone in society because it allows people to specialize in activities in which they have a comparative advantage.*

QuickQuiz Robinson Crusoe can gather 10 coconuts or catch 1 fish per hour. His friend Friday can gather 30 coconuts or catch 2 fish per hour. What is Crusoe's opportunity cost of catching one fish? What is Friday's? Who has an absolute advantage in catching fish? Who has a comparative advantage in catching fish?

APPLICATIONS OF COMPARATIVE ADVANTAGE

The principle of comparative advantage explains interdependence and the gains from trade. Because interdependence is so prevalent in the modern world, the principle of comparative advantage has many applications. Here are two examples, one fanciful and one of great practical importance.

Should Tiger Woods Mow His Own Lawn?

Tiger Woods spends a lot of time walking around on grass. One of the most talented golfers of all time, he can hit a drive and sink a putt in a way that most casual golfers only dream of doing. Most likely, he is talented at other activities too.

IN THE NEWS

WHO HAS A COMPARATIVE ADVANTAGE IN PRODUCING LAMB?

A common barrier to free trade among countries is tariffs, which are taxes on the import of goods from abroad. In the following opinion column, economist Douglas Irwin discusses a recent example of their use.

Lamb Tariffs Fleece U.S. Consumers

By Douglas A. Irwin

President Clinton dealt a serious blow to free trade last Wednesday, when he announced that the U.S. would impose stiff import tariffs on lamb from Australia and New Zealand. His decision undercuts American leadership and makes a mockery of the administration's claims that it favors free and fair trade.

U.S. sheep producers have long been dependent on government. For more than half a century, until Congress enacted farm-policy reforms in 1995, they received subsidies for wool. Having lost

that handout, saddled with high costs and inefficiencies, and facing domestic competition from chicken, beef, and pork, sheep producers sought to stop foreign competition by filing for import relief.

Almost all U.S. lamb imports come from Australia and New Zealand, major agricultural producers with a crushing comparative advantage. New Zealand has fewer than four million people but as many as 60 million sheep (compared with about seven million sheep in the U.S.). New Zealand's farmers have invested substantial resources in new technology and effective marketing, making them among the most efficient producers in the world. New Zealand also elim-

inated domestic agricultural subsidies in the free-market reforms of the 1950s, and is a free-trading country, on track to eliminate all import tariffs by 2006.

Rather than emulate this example, the American Sheep Industry Association, among others, filed an "escape clause" petition under the Trade Act of 1974, which allows temporary "breathing space" protection to import-competing industries. Under the escape-clause provision, a petitioning industry is required to present an adjustment plan to ensure that it undertakes steps to become competitive in the future. The tariff protection is usually limited and scheduled to be phased out.

For example, let's imagine that Woods can mow his lawn faster than anyone else. But just because he *can* mow his lawn fast, does this mean he *should?*

To answer this question, we can use the concepts of opportunity cost and comparative advantage. Let's say that Woods can mow his lawn in 2 hours. In that same 2 hours, he could film a television commercial for Nike and earn $10,000. By contrast, Forrest Gump, the boy next door, can mow Woods's lawn in 4 hours. In that same 4 hours, he could work at McDonald's and earn $20.

In this example, Woods's opportunity cost of mowing the lawn is $10,000 and Forrest's opportunity cost is $20. Woods has an absolute advantage in mowing lawns because he can do the work in less time. Yet Forrest has a comparative advantage in mowing lawns because he has the lower opportunity cost.

The gains from trade in this example are tremendous. Rather than mowing his own lawn, Woods should make the commercial and hire Forrest to mow the lawn.

The U.S. International Trade Commission determines whether imports are a cause of "serious injury" to the domestic industry and, if so, proposes a remedy, which the president has full discretion to adopt, change or reject. In February, the ITC did not find that the domestic industry had suffered "serious injury," but rather adopted the weaker ruling that imports were "a substantial cause of threat of serious injury." The ITC did not propose to roll back imports, only to impose a 20% tariff (declining over four years) on imports above last year's levels.

The administration at first appeared to be considering less restrictive measures. Australia and New Zealand even offered financial assistance to the U.S. producers, and the administration delayed any announcement and appeared to be working toward a compromise. But these hopes were completely dashed with the shocking final decision, in which the administration capitulated to the demands of the sheep industry and its advocates in Congress.

The congressional charge was led by Sen. Max Baucus (D., Mont.), a member of the Agriculture Committee whose sister, a sheep producer, had appeared before the ITC to press for higher tariffs. The administration opted for . . . [the following:] On top of existing tariffs, the president imposed a 9% tariff on *all* imports in the first year (declining to 6% and then 3% in years two and three), and a whopping 40% tariff on imports above last year's levels (dropping to 32% and 24%). . . .

The American Sheep Industry Association's president happily announced that the move will "bring some stability to the market." Whenever producers speak of bringing stability to the market, you know that consumers are getting fleeced.

The lamb decision, while little noticed at home, has been closely followed abroad. The decision undercuts the administration's free-trade rhetoric and harms its efforts to get other countries to open up their markets. Some import relief had been expected, but not so clearly protectionist as what finally materialized. The extreme decision has outraged farmers in Australia and New Zealand, and officials there have vowed to take the U.S. to a WTO dispute settlement panel.

The administration's timing could not have been worse. The decision came right after an Asia Pacific Economic Cooperation summit reaffirmed its commitment to reduce trade barriers, and a few months before the World Trade Organization's November meeting in Seattle, where the WTO is to launch a new round of multilateral trade negotiations. A principal U.S. objective at the summit is the reduction of agricultural protection in Europe and elsewhere.

In 1947, facing an election the next year, President Truman courageously resisted special interest pressure and vetoed a bill to impose import quotas on wool, which would have jeopardized the first postwar multilateral trade negotiations due to start later that year. In contrast, Mr. Clinton, though a lame duck, caved in to political pressure. If the U.S., whose booming economy is the envy of the world, cannot resist protectionism, how can it expect other countries to do so?

Source: *The Wall Street Journal,* July 12, 1999, p. A28. © 1999 by Dow Jones & Co. Inc. Reproduced with permission of DOW JONES & CO INC in the format Textbook via Copyright Clearance Center.

As long as Woods pays Forrest more than $20 and less than $10,000, both of them are better off.

Should the United States Trade with Other Countries?

Just as individuals can benefit from specialization and trade with one another, as the farmer and rancher did, so can populations of people in different countries. Many of the goods that Americans enjoy are produced abroad, and many of the goods produced in the United States are sold abroad. Goods produced abroad and sold domestically are called **imports**. Goods produced domestically and sold abroad are called **exports**.

To see how countries can benefit from trade, suppose there are two countries, the United States and Japan, and two goods, food and cars. Imagine that the two countries produce cars equally well: An American worker and a Japanese worker can each produce 1 car per month. By contrast, because the United States has more and better land, it is better at producing food: A U.S. worker can produce 2 tons of food per month, whereas a Japanese worker can produce only 1 ton of food per month.

The principle of comparative advantage states that each good should be produced by the country that has the smaller opportunity cost of producing that good. Because the opportunity cost of a car is 2 tons of food in the United States but only 1 ton of food in Japan, Japan has a comparative advantage in producing cars. Japan should produce more cars than it wants for its own use and export some of them to the United States. Similarly, because the opportunity cost of a ton of food is 1 car in Japan but only ½ car in the United States, the United States has a comparative advantage in producing food. The United States should produce more food than it wants to consume and export some of it to Japan. Through specialization and trade, both countries can have more food and more cars.

In reality, of course, the issues involved in trade among nations are more complex than this example suggests, as we will see in Chapter 9. Most important among these issues is that each country has many citizens with different interests. International trade can make some individuals worse off, even as it makes the country as a whole better off. When the United States exports food and imports cars, the impact on an American farmer is not the same as the impact on an American autoworker. Yet, contrary to the opinions sometimes voiced by politicians and political commentators, international trade is not like war, in which some countries win and others lose. Trade allows all countries to achieve greater prosperity.

QuickQuiz Suppose that the world's fastest typist happens to be trained in brain surgery. Should he do his own typing or hire a secretary? Explain.

CONCLUSION

The principle of comparative advantage shows that trade can make everyone better off. You should now understand more fully the benefits of living in an interdependent economy. But having seen why interdependence is desirable, you might

imports
goods produced abroad and sold domestically

exports
goods produced domestically and sold abroad

naturally ask how it is possible. How do free societies coordinate the diverse activities of all the people involved in their economies? What ensures that goods and services will get from those who should be producing them to those who should be consuming them?

In a world with only two people, such as the rancher and the farmer, the answer is simple: These two people can directly bargain and allocate resources between themselves. In the real world with billions of people, the answer is less obvious. We take up this issue in the next chapter, where we see that free societies allocate resources through the market forces of supply and demand.

SUMMARY

- Each person consumes goods and services produced by many other people both in our country and around the world. Interdependence and trade are desirable because they allow everyone to enjoy a greater quantity and variety of goods and services.

- There are two ways to compare the ability of two people in producing a good. The person who can produce the good with the smaller quantity of inputs is said to have an *absolute advantage* in producing the good. The person who has the smaller opportunity cost of producing the good is said to have a *comparative advantage*. The gains from trade are based on comparative advantage, not absolute advantage.

- Trade makes everyone better off because it allows people to specialize in those activities in which they have a comparative advantage.

- The principle of comparative advantage applies to countries as well as to people. Economists use the principle of comparative advantage to advocate free trade among countries.

KEY CONCEPTS

absolute advantage, p. 51
opportunity cost, p. 51

comparative advantage, p. 52
imports, p. 56

exports, p. 56

QUESTIONS FOR REVIEW

1. Explain how absolute advantage and comparative advantage differ.

2. Give an example in which one person has an absolute advantage in doing something but another person has a comparative advantage.

3. Is absolute advantage or comparative advantage more important for trade? Explain your

reasoning using the example in your answer to Question 2.

4. Will a nation tend to export or import goods for which it has a comparative advantage? Explain.

5. Why do economists oppose policies that restrict trade among nations?

PROBLEMS AND APPLICATIONS

1. Consider the farmer and the rancher from our example in this chapter. Explain why the farmer's opportunity cost of producing 1 ounce of meat is 4 ounces of potatoes. Explain why the rancher's opportunity cost

of producing 1 ounce of meat is 2 ounces of potatoes.

2. Maria can read 20 pages of economics in an hour. She can also read 50 pages of sociology in an hour. She spends 5 hours per day studying.

a. Draw Maria's production possibilities frontier for reading economics and sociology.

b. What is Maria's opportunity cost of reading 100 pages of sociology?

3. American and Japanese workers can each produce 4 cars a year. An American worker can produce 10 tons of grain a year, whereas a Japanese worker can produce 5 tons of grain a year. To keep things simple, assume that each country has 100 million workers.

a. For this situation, construct a table analogous to Table 1.

b. Graph the production possibilities frontier of the American and Japanese economies.

c. For the United States, what is the opportunity cost of a car? Of grain? For Japan, what is the opportunity cost of a car? Of grain? Put this information in a table analogous to Table 3.

d. Which country has an absolute advantage in producing cars? In producing grain?

e. Which country has a comparative advantage in producing cars? In producing grain?

f. Without trade, half of each country's workers produce cars and half produce grain. What quantities of cars and grain does each country produce?

g. Starting from a position without trade, give an example in which trade makes each country better off.

4. Pat and Kris are roommates. They spend most of their time studying (of course), but they leave some time for their favorite activities: making pizza and brewing root beer. Pat takes 4 hours to brew a gallon of root beer and 2 hours to make a pizza. Kris takes 6 hours to brew a gallon of root beer and 4 hours to make a pizza.

a. What is each roommate's opportunity cost of making a pizza? Who has the absolute advantage in making pizza? Who has the comparative advantage in making pizza?

b. If Pat and Kris trade foods with each other, who will trade away pizza in exchange for root beer?

c. The price of pizza can be expressed in terms of gallons of root beer. What is the highest price at which pizza can be traded that would make both roommates better off? What is the lowest price? Explain.

5. Suppose that there are 10 million workers in Canada, and that each of these workers can produce either 2 cars or 30 bushels of wheat in a year.

a. What is the opportunity cost of producing a car in Canada? What is the opportunity cost of producing a bushel of wheat in Canada? Explain the relationship between the opportunity costs of the two goods.

b. Draw Canada's production possibilities frontier. If Canada chooses to consume 10 million cars, how much wheat can it consume without trade? Label this point on the production possibilities frontier.

c. Now suppose that the United States offers to buy 10 million cars from Canada in exchange for 20 bushels of wheat per car. If Canada continues to consume 10 million cars, how much wheat does this deal allow Canada to consume? Label this point on your diagram. Should Canada accept the deal?

6. Consider a professor who is writing a book. The professor can both write the chapters and gather the needed data faster than anyone else at his university. Still, he pays a student to collect data at the library. Is this sensible? Explain.

7. England and Scotland both produce scones and sweaters. Suppose that an English worker can produce 50 scones per hour or 1 sweater per hour. Suppose that a Scottish worker can produce 40 scones per hour or 2 sweaters per hour.

a. Which country has the absolute advantage in the production of each good? Which country has the comparative advantage?

b. If England and Scotland decide to trade, which commodity will Scotland trade to England? Explain.

c. If a Scottish worker could produce only 1 sweater per hour, would Scotland still gain from trade? Would England still gain from trade? Explain.

8. The following table describes the production possibilities of two cities in the country of Baseballia:

	Pairs of Red Socks per Worker per Hour	Pairs of White Socks per Worker per Hour
Boston	3	3
Chicago	2	1

a. Without trade, what is the price of white socks (in terms of red socks) in Boston? What is the price in Chicago?

b. Which city has an absolute advantage in the production of each color sock? Which city has a comparative advantage in the production of each color sock?

c. If the cities trade with each other, which color sock will each export?

d. What is the range of prices at which trade can occur?

9. Suppose that all goods can be produced with fewer worker hours in Germany than in France.

a. In what sense is the cost of all goods lower in Germany than in France?

b. In what sense is the cost of some goods lower in France?

c. If Germany and France traded with each other, would both countries be better off as a result? Explain in the context of your answers to parts (a) and (b).

10. Are the following statements true or false? Explain in each case.

a. "Two countries can achieve gains from trade even if one of the countries has an absolute advantage in the production of all goods."

b. "Certain very talented people have a comparative advantage in everything they do."

c. "If a certain trade is good for one person, it can't be good for the other one."

http://   For more study tools, please visit http://mankiwXtra.swlearning.com.

2

SUPPLY AND DEMAND I:
HOW MARKETS WORK

THE MARKET FORCES
OF SUPPLY AND DEMAND

When a cold snap hits Florida, the price of orange juice rises in supermarkets throughout the country. When the weather turns warm in New England every summer, the price of hotel rooms in the Caribbean plummets. When a war breaks out in the Middle East, the price of gasoline in the United States rises, and the price of a used Cadillac falls. What do these events have in common? They all show the workings of supply and demand.

Supply and *demand* are the two words that economists use most often—and for good reason. Supply and demand are the forces that make market economies work. They determine the quantity of each good produced and the price at which it is sold. If you want to know how any event or policy will affect the economy, you must think first about how it will affect supply and demand.

This chapter introduces the theory of supply and demand. It considers how buyers and sellers behave and how they interact with one another. It shows how supply and demand determine prices in a market economy and how prices, in turn, allocate the economy's scarce resources.

MARKETS AND COMPETITION

market
a group of buyers and sellers of a particular good or service

The terms *supply* and *demand* refer to the behavior of people as they interact with one another in markets. A **market** is a group of buyers and sellers of a particular good or service. The buyers as a group determine the demand for the product, and the sellers as a group determine the supply of the product. Before discussing how buyers and sellers behave, let's first consider more fully what we mean by a "market" and the various types of markets we observe in the economy.

Competitive Markets

Markets take many forms. Sometimes markets are highly organized, such as the markets for many agricultural commodities. In these markets, buyers and sellers meet at a specific time and place, where an auctioneer helps set prices and arrange sales.

More often, markets are less organized. For example, consider the market for ice cream in a particular town. Buyers of ice cream do not meet together at any one time. The sellers of ice cream are in different locations and offer somewhat different products. There is no auctioneer calling out the price of ice cream. Each seller posts a price for an ice-cream cone, and each buyer decides how much ice cream to buy at each store.

Even though it is not organized, the group of ice-cream buyers and ice-cream sellers forms a market. Each buyer knows that there are several sellers from which to choose, and each seller is aware that his product is similar to that offered by other sellers. The price of ice cream and the quantity of ice cream sold are not determined by any single buyer or seller. Rather, price and quantity are determined by all buyers and sellers as they interact in the marketplace.

competitive market
a market in which there are many buyers and many sellers so that each has a negligible impact on the market price

The market for ice cream, like most markets in the economy, is highly competitive. A **competitive market** is a market in which there are many buyers and many sellers so that each has a negligible impact on the market price. Each seller of ice cream has limited control over the price because other sellers are offering similar products. A seller has little reason to charge less than the going price, and if he or she charges more, buyers will make their purchases elsewhere. Similarly, no single buyer of ice cream can influence the price of ice cream because each buyer purchases only a small amount.

In this chapter we examine how buyers and sellers interact in competitive markets. We see how the forces of supply and demand determine both the quantity of the good sold and its price.

Competition: Perfect and Otherwise

We assume in this chapter that markets are *perfectly competitive*. Perfectly competitive markets are defined by two primary characteristics: (1) the goods being offered for sale are all the same, and (2) the buyers and sellers are so numerous that no single buyer or seller can influence the market price. Because buyers and sellers in perfectly competitive markets must accept the price the market determines, they are said to be *price takers*.

There are some markets in which the assumption of perfect competition applies perfectly. In the wheat market, for example, there are thousands of farmers who sell wheat and millions of consumers who use wheat and wheat products. Because no single buyer or seller can influence the price of wheat, each takes the price as given.

Not all goods and services, however, are sold in perfectly competitive markets. Some markets have only one seller, and this seller sets the price. Such a seller is called a *monopoly*. Your local cable television company, for instance, may be a monopoly. Residents of your town probably have only one cable company from which to buy this service.

Some markets fall between the extremes of perfect competition and monopoly. One such market, called an *oligopoly*, has a few sellers that do not always compete aggressively. Airline routes are an example. If a route between two cities is serviced by only two or three carriers, the carriers may avoid rigorous competition so they can keep prices high. Another type of market is *monopolistically competitive*; it contains many sellers but each offers a slightly different product. Because the products are not exactly the same, each seller has some ability to set the price for its own product. An example is the market for magazines. Magazines compete with one another for readers and anyone can enter the market by starting a new one, but each magazine offers different articles and can set its own price.

Despite the diversity of market types we find in the world, we begin by studying perfect competition. Perfectly competitive markets are the easiest to analyze. Moreover, because some degree of competition is present in most markets, many of the lessons that we learn by studying supply and demand under perfect competition apply in more complicated markets as well.

QuickQuiz What is a market? • What are the characteristics of a competitive market?

DEMAND

We begin our study of markets by examining the behavior of buyers. To focus our thinking, let's keep in mind a particular good—ice cream.

The Demand Curve: The Relationship between Price and Quantity Demanded

The **quantity demanded** of any good is the amount of the good that buyers are willing and able to purchase. As we will see, many things determine the quantity demanded of any good, but when analyzing how markets work, one determinant plays a central role—the price of the good. If the price of ice cream rose to $20 per scoop, you would buy less ice cream. You might buy frozen yogurt instead. If the price of ice cream fell to $0.20 per scoop, you would buy more. Because the quantity demanded falls as the price rises and rises as the price falls, we say that the quantity demanded is *negatively related* to the price. This relationship between price and quantity demanded is true for most goods in the economy and, in fact, is

quantity demanded
the amount of a good that buyers are willing and able to purchase

FIGURE 1

Catherine's Demand Schedule and Demand Curve

The demand schedule shows the quantity demanded at each price. The demand curve, which graphs the demand schedule, shows how the quantity demanded of the good changes as its price varies. Because a lower price increases the quantity demanded, the demand curve slopes downward.

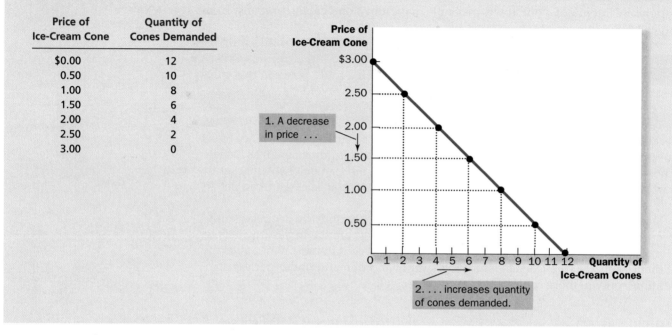

Price of Ice-Cream Cone	Quantity of Cones Demanded
$0.00	12
0.50	10
1.00	8
1.50	6
2.00	4
2.50	2
3.00	0

1. A decrease in price . . .

2. . . . increases quantity of cones demanded.

---

law of demand
the claim that, other things equal, the quantity demanded of a good falls when the price of the good rises

demand schedule
a table that shows the relationship between the price of a good and the quantity demanded

demand curve
a graph of the relationship between the price of a good and the quantity demanded

so pervasive that economists call it the **law of demand:** Other things equal, when the price of a good rises, the quantity demanded of the good falls, and when price falls, the quantity demanded rises.

The table in Figure 1 shows how many ice-cream cones Catherine buys each month at different prices of ice cream. If ice cream is free, Catherine eats 12 cones. At $0.50 per cone, Catherine buys 10 cones. As the price rises further, she buys fewer and fewer cones. When the price reaches $3.00, Catherine doesn't buy any ice cream at all. This table is a **demand schedule,** a table that shows the relationship between the price of a good and the quantity demanded, holding constant everything else that influences how much consumers of the good want to buy.

The graph in Figure 1 uses the numbers from the table to illustrate the law of demand. By convention, the price of ice cream is on the vertical axis, and the quantity of ice cream demanded is on the horizontal axis. The downward-sloping line relating price and quantity demanded is called the **demand curve.**

Market Demand versus Individual Demand

The demand curve in Figure 1 shows an individual's demand for a product. To analyze how markets work, we need to determine the *market demand,* which is the sum of all the individual demands for a particular good or service.

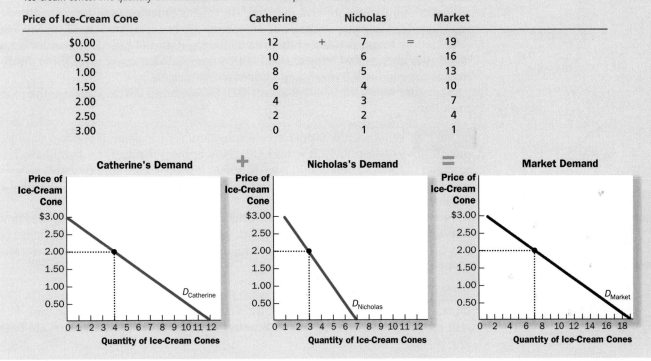

FIGURE 2

Market Demand as the Sum of Individual Demands

The quantity demanded in a market is the sum of the quantities demanded by all the buyers at each price. Thus, the market demand curve is found by adding horizontally the individual demand curves. At a price of $2, Catherine demands 4 ice-cream cones, and Nicholas demands 3 ice-cream cones. The quantity demanded in the market at this price is 7 cones.

Price of Ice-Cream Cone	Catherine		Nicholas		Market
$0.00	12	+	7	=	19
0.50	10		6		16
1.00	8		5		13
1.50	6		4		10
2.00	4		3		7
2.50	2		2		4
3.00	0		1		1

The table in Figure 2 shows the demand schedules for ice cream of two individuals—Catherine and Nicholas. At any price, Catherine's demand schedule tells us how much ice cream she buys, and Nicholas's demand schedule tells us how much ice cream he buys. The market demand at each price is the sum of the two individual demands.

The graph in Figure 2 shows the demand curves that correspond to these demand schedules. Notice that we sum the individual demand curves *horizontally* to obtain the market demand curve. That is, to find the total quantity demanded at any price, we add the individual quantities found on the horizontal axis of the individual demand curves. Because we are interested in analyzing how markets work, we will work most often with the market demand curve. The market demand curve shows how the total quantity demanded of a good varies as the price of the good varies, while all the other factors that affect how much consumers want to buy are held constant.

Shifts in the Demand Curve

The demand curve for ice cream shows how much ice cream people buy at any given price, holding constant the many other factors beyond price that influence consumers' buying decisions. As a result, this demand curve need not be stable over time. If something happens to alter the quantity demanded at any given price, the demand curve shifts. For example, suppose the American Medical Association discovered that people who regularly eat ice cream live longer, healthier lives. The discovery would raise the demand for ice cream. At any given price, buyers would now want to purchase a larger quantity of ice cream, and the demand curve for ice cream would shift.

Figure 3 illustrates shifts in demand. Any change that increases the quantity demanded at every price, such as our imaginary discovery by the American Medical Association, shifts the demand curve to the right and is called *an increase in demand*. Any change that reduces the quantity demanded at every price shifts the demand curve to the left and is called *a decrease in demand*.

There are many variables that can shift the demand curve. Here are the most important:

normal good
a good for which, other things equal, an increase in income leads to an increase in demand

Income   What would happen to your demand for ice cream if you lost your job one summer? Most likely, it would fall. A lower income means that you have less to spend in total, so you would have to spend less on some—and probably most—goods. If the demand for a good falls when income falls, the good is called a **normal good.**

inferior good
a good for which, other things equal, an increase in income leads to a decrease in demand

Not all goods are normal goods. If the demand for a good rises when income falls, the good is called an **inferior good.** An example of an inferior good might be bus rides. As your income falls, you are less likely to buy a car or take a cab, and more likely to ride the bus.

Prices of Related Goods   Suppose that the price of frozen yogurt falls. The law of demand says that you will buy more frozen yogurt. At the same time, you will probably buy less ice cream. Because ice cream and frozen yogurt are both

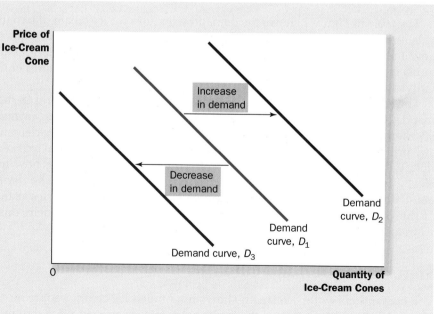

FIGURE 3

Shifts in the Demand Curve

Any change that raises the quantity that buyers wish to purchase at a given price shifts the demand curve to the right. Any change that lowers the quantity that buyers wish to purchase at a given price shifts the demand curve to the left.

cold, sweet, creamy desserts, they satisfy similar desires. When a fall in the price of one good reduces the demand for another good, the two goods are called **substitutes.** Substitutes are often pairs of goods that are used in place of each other, such as hot dogs and hamburgers, sweaters and sweatshirts, and movie tickets and video rentals.

Now suppose that the price of hot fudge falls. According to the law of demand, you will buy more hot fudge. Yet, in this case, you will buy more ice cream as well, because ice cream and hot fudge are often used together. When a fall in the price of one good raises the demand for another good, the two goods are called **complements.** Complements are often pairs of goods that are used together, such as gasoline and automobiles, computers and software, and peanut butter and jelly.

substitutes
two goods for which an increase in the price of one leads to an increase in the demand for the other

complements
two goods for which an increase in the price of one leads to a decrease in the demand for the other

Tastes   The most obvious determinant of your demand is your tastes. If you like ice cream, you buy more of it. Economists normally do not try to explain people's tastes because tastes are based on historical and psychological forces that are beyond the realm of economics. Economists do, however, examine what happens when tastes change.

Expectations   Your expectations about the future may affect your demand for a good or service today. For example, if you expect to earn a higher income next month, you may be more willing to spend some of your current savings buying ice cream. As another example, if you expect the price of ice cream to fall tomorrow, you may be less willing to buy an ice-cream cone at today's price.

Number of Buyers   Because market demand is derived from individual demands, it depends on all those factors that determine the demand of individual buyers, including buyers' incomes, tastes, expectations, and the prices of related goods. In addition, it depends on the number of buyers. If Peter, another consumer of ice cream, were to join Catherine and Nicholas, the quantity demanded in the market would be higher at every price and the demand curve would shift to the right.

Summary   The demand curve shows what happens to the quantity demanded of a good when its price varies, holding constant all the other variables that influence buyers. When one of these other variables changes, the demand curve shifts. Table 1 lists all the variables that influence how much consumers choose to buy of a good.

TABLE 1

Variables That Influence Buyers

This table lists the variables that affect how much consumers choose to buy of any good. Notice the special role that the price of the good plays: A change in the good's price represents a movement along the demand curve, whereas a change in one of the other variables shifts the demand curve.

Variable	A Change in This Variable . . .
Price	Represents a movement along the demand curve
Income	Shifts the demand curve
Prices of related goods	Shifts the demand curve
Tastes	Shifts the demand curve
Expectations	Shifts the demand curve
Number of buyers	Shifts the demand curve

Case Study

TWO WAYS TO REDUCE THE QUANTITY OF SMOKING DEMANDED

Public policymakers often want to reduce the amount that people smoke. There are two ways that policy can attempt to achieve this goal.

One way to reduce smoking is to shift the demand curve for cigarettes and other tobacco products. Public service announcements, mandatory health warnings on cigarette packages, and the prohibition of cigarette advertising on television are all policies aimed at reducing the quantity of cigarettes demanded at any given price. If successful, these policies shift the demand curve for cigarettes to the left, as in panel (a) of Figure 4.

Alternatively, policymakers can try to raise the price of cigarettes. If the government taxes the manufacture of cigarettes, for example, cigarette companies pass much of this tax on to consumers in the form of higher prices. A higher price encourages smokers to reduce the numbers of cigarettes they smoke. In this case,

---

FIGURE 4

Shifts in the Demand Curve versus Movements along the Demand Curve

If warnings on cigarette packages convince smokers to smoke less, the demand curve for cigarettes shifts to the left. In panel (a), the demand curve shifts from D_1 to D_2. At a price of $2 per pack, the quantity demanded falls from 20 to 10 cigarettes per day, as reflected by the shift from point A to point B. By contrast, if a tax raises the price of cigarettes, the demand curve does not shift. Instead, we observe a movement to a different point on the demand curve. In panel (b), when the price rises from $2 to $4, the quantity demanded falls from 20 to 12 cigarettes per day, as reflected by the movement from point A to point C.

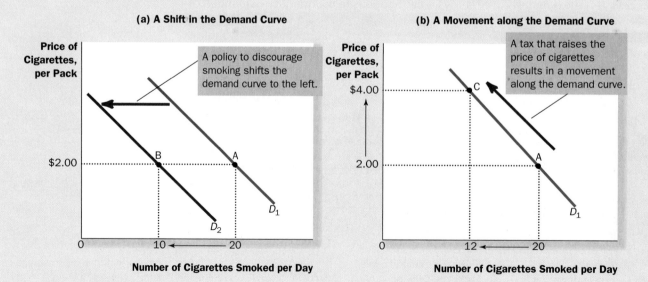

(a) A Shift in the Demand Curve

(b) A Movement along the Demand Curve

Number of Cigarettes Smoked per Day

the reduced amount of smoking does not represent a shift in the demand curve. Instead, it represents a movement along the same demand curve to a point with a higher price and lower quantity, as in panel (b) of Figure 4.

How much does the amount of smoking respond to changes in the price of cigarettes? Economists have attempted to answer this question by studying what happens when the tax on cigarettes changes. They have found that a 10 percent increase in the price causes a 4 percent reduction in the quantity demanded. Teenagers are found to be especially sensitive to the price of cigarettes: A 10 percent increase in the price causes a 12 percent drop in teenage smoking.

A related question is how the price of cigarettes affects the demand for illicit drugs, such as marijuana. Opponents of cigarette taxes often argue that tobacco and marijuana are substitutes, so that high cigarette prices encourage marijuana use. By contrast, many experts on substance abuse view tobacco as a "gateway drug" leading the young to experiment with other harmful substances. Most studies of the data are consistent with this view: They find that lower cigarette prices are associated with greater use of marijuana. In other words, tobacco and marijuana appear to be complements rather than substitutes. ●

QuickQuiz Make up an example of a demand schedule for pizza, and graph the implied demand curve. • Give an example of something that would shift this demand curve. • Would a change in the price of pizza shift this demand curve?

© ROYALTY-FREE/CORBIS

What is the best way to stop this?

SUPPLY

We now turn to the other side of the market and examine the behavior of sellers. Once again, to focus our thinking, let's consider the market for ice cream.

The Supply Curve: The Relationship between Price and Quantity Supplied

The **quantity supplied** of any good or service is the amount that sellers are willing and able to sell. There are many determinants of quantity supplied, but once again price plays a special role in our analysis. When the price of ice cream is high, selling ice cream is profitable, and so the quantity supplied is large. Sellers of ice cream work long hours, buy many ice-cream machines, and hire many workers. By contrast, when the price of ice cream is low, the business is less profitable, and so sellers produce less ice cream. At a low price, some sellers may even choose to shut down, and their quantity supplied falls to zero. Because the quantity supplied rises as the price rises and falls as the price falls, we say that the quantity supplied is *positively related* to the price of the good. This relationship between price and quantity supplied is called the **law of supply:** Other things equal, when the price of a good rises, the quantity supplied of the good also rises, and when the price falls, the quantity supplied falls as well.

quantity supplied
the amount of a good that sellers are willing and able to sell

law of supply
the claim that, other things equal, the quantity supplied of a good rises when the price of the good rises

FIGURE 5

Ben's Supply Schedule and Supply Curve

The supply schedule shows the quantity supplied at each price. This supply curve, which graphs the supply schedule, shows how the quantity supplied of the good changes as its price varies. Because a higher price increases the quantity supplied, the supply curve slopes upward.

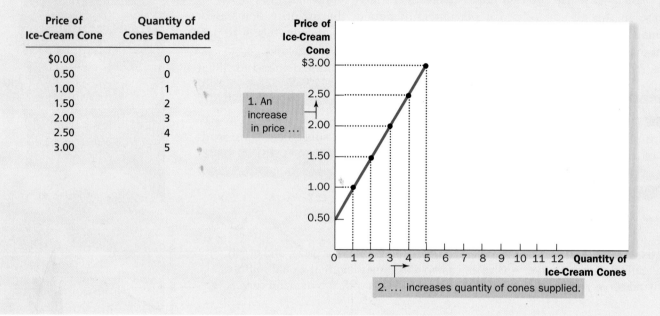

Price of Ice-Cream Cone	Quantity of Cones Demanded
$0.00	0
0.50	0
1.00	1
1.50	2
2.00	3
2.50	4
3.00	5

The table in Figure 5 shows the quantity supplied by Ben, an ice-cream seller, at various prices of ice cream. At a price below $1.00, Ben does not supply any ice cream at all. As the price rises, he supplies a greater and greater quantity. This is the **supply schedule,** a table that shows the relationship between the price of a good and the quantity supplied, holding constant everything else that influences how much producers of the good want to sell.

The graph in Figure 5 uses the numbers from the table to illustrate the law of supply. The curve relating price and quantity supplied is called the **supply curve.** The supply curve slopes upward because, other things equal, a higher price means a greater quantity supplied.

supply schedule
a table that shows the relationship between the price of a good and the quantity supplied

supply curve
a graph of the relationship between the price of a good and the quantity supplied

Market Supply versus Individual Supply

Just as market demand is the sum of the demands of all buyers, market supply is the sum of the supplies of all sellers. The table in Figure 6 shows the supply schedules for two ice-cream producers—Ben and Jerry. At any price, Ben's supply schedule tells us the quantity of ice cream Ben supplies, and Jerry's supply schedule tells us the quantity of ice cream Jerry supplies. The market supply is the sum of the two individual supplies.

FIGURE 6

Market Supply as the Sum of Individual Supplies

The quantity supplied in a market is the sum of the quantities supplied by all the sellers at each price. Thus, the market supply curve is found by adding horizontally the individual supply curves. At a price of $2, Ben supplies 3 ice-cream cones, and Jerry supplies 4 ice-cream cones. The quantity supplied in the market at this price is 7 cones.

Price of Ice-Cream Cone	Ben		Jerry		Market
$0.00	0	+	0	=	0
0.50	0		0		0
1.00	1		0		1
1.50	2		2		4
2.00	3		4		7
2.50	4		6		10
3.00	5		8		13

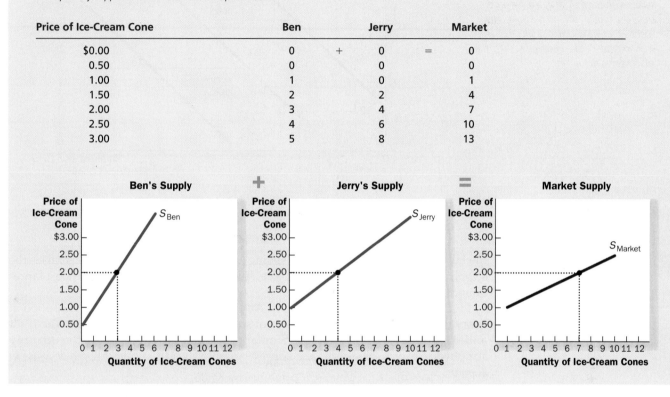

The graph in Figure 6 shows the supply curves that correspond to the supply schedules. As with demand curves, we sum the individual supply curves *horizontally* to obtain the market supply curve. That is, to find the total quantity supplied at any price, we add the individual quantities found on the horizontal axis of the individual supply curves. The market supply curve shows how the total quantity supplied varies as the price of the good varies.

Shifts in the Supply Curve

The supply curve for ice cream shows how much ice cream producers offer for sale at any given price, holding constant all the other factors beyond price that influence producers' decisions about how much to sell. This relationship can change over time, which is represented by a shift in the supply curve. For example, suppose the price of sugar falls. Because sugar is an input into producing ice cream,

FIGURE 7

Shifts in the Supply Curve

Any change that raises the quantity that sellers wish to produce at a given price shifts the supply curve to the right. Any change that lowers the quantity that sellers wish to produce at a given price shifts the supply curve to the left.

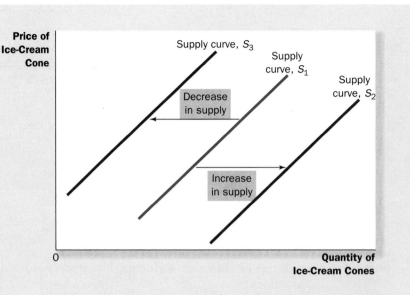

the fall in the price of sugar makes selling ice cream more profitable. This raises the supply of ice cream: At any given price, sellers are now willing to produce a larger quantity. Thus, the supply curve for ice cream shifts to the right.

Figure 7 illustrates shifts in supply. Any change that raises quantity supplied at every price, such as a fall in the price of sugar, shifts the supply curve to the right and is called *an increase in supply*. Similarly, any change that reduces the quantity supplied at every price shifts the supply curve to the left and is called *a decrease in supply*.

There are many variables that can shift the supply curve. Here are some of the most important:

Input Prices To produce its output of ice cream, sellers use various inputs: cream, sugar, flavoring, ice-cream machines, the buildings in which the ice cream is made, and the labor of workers to mix the ingredients and operate the machines. When the price of one or more of these inputs rises, producing ice cream is less profitable, and firms supply less ice cream. If input prices rise substantially, a firm might shut down and supply no ice cream at all. Thus, the supply of a good is negatively related to the price of the inputs used to make the good.

Technology The technology for turning the inputs into ice cream is yet another determinant of supply. The invention of the mechanized ice-cream machine, for example, reduced the amount of labor necessary to make ice cream. By reducing firms' costs, the advance in technology raised the supply of ice cream.

Expectations The amount of ice cream a firm supplies today may depend on its expectations of the future. For example, if it expects the price of ice cream to rise

TABLE 2

Variables That Influence Sellers

This table lists the variables that affect how much producers choose to sell of any good. Notice the special role that the price of the good plays: A change in the good's price represents a movement along the supply curve, whereas a change in one of the other variables shifts the supply curve.

Variable	A Change in This Variable . . .
Price	Represents a movement along the supply curve
Input prices	Shifts the supply curve
Technology	Shifts the supply curve
Expectations	Shifts the supply curve
Number of sellers	Shifts the supply curve

in the future, it will put some of its current production into storage and supply less to the market today.

Number of Sellers   Market supply depends on all those factors that influence the supply of individual sellers, such as the prices of inputs used to produce the good, the available technology, and expectations. In addition, the supply in a market depends on the number of sellers. If Ben or Jerry were to retire from the ice-cream business, the supply in the market would fall.

Summary   The supply curve shows what happens to the quantity supplied of a good when its price varies, holding constant all the other variables that influence sellers. When one of these other variables changes, the supply curve shifts. Table 2 lists all the variables that influence how much producers choose to sell of a good.

QuickQuiz Make up an example of a supply schedule for pizza, and graph the implied supply curve. • Give an example of something that would shift this supply curve. • Would a change in the price of pizza shift this supply curve?

SUPPLY AND DEMAND TOGETHER

Having analyzed supply and demand separately, we now combine them to see how they determine the quantity of a good sold in a market and its price.

Equilibrium

Figure 8 (p. 76) shows the market supply curve and market demand curve together. Notice that there is one point at which the supply and demand curves intersect. This point is called the market's **equilibrium.** The price at this intersection is called the **equilibrium price,** and the quantity is called the **equilibrium quantity.** Here

equilibrium
a situation in which the price has reached the level where quantity supplied equals quantity demanded

equilibrium price
the price that balances quantity supplied and quantity demanded

equilibrium quantity
the quantity supplied and the quantity demanded at the equilibrium price

FIGURE 8

The Equilibrium of Supply and Demand

The equilibrium is found where the supply and demand curves intersect. At the equilibrium price, the quantity supplied equals the quantity demanded. Here the equilibrium price is $2: At this price, 7 ice-cream cones are supplied, and 7 ice-cream cones are demanded.

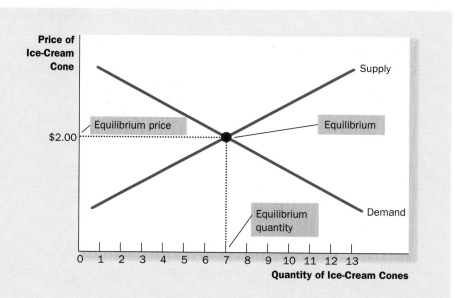

the equilibrium price is $2.00 per cone, and the equilibrium quantity is 7 ice-cream cones.

The dictionary defines the word *equilibrium* as a situation in which various forces are in balance—and this also describes a market's equilibrium. *At the equilibrium price, the quantity of the good that buyers are willing and able to buy exactly balances the quantity that sellers are willing and able to sell.* The equilibrium price is sometimes called the *market-clearing price* because, at this price, everyone in the market has been satisfied: Buyers have bought all they want to buy, and sellers have sold all they want to sell.

The actions of buyers and sellers naturally move markets toward the equilibrium of supply and demand. To see why, consider what happens when the market price is not equal to the equilibrium price.

Suppose first that the market price is above the equilibrium price, as in panel (a) of Figure 9. At a price of $2.50 per cone, the quantity of the good supplied (10 cones) exceeds the quantity demanded (4 cones). There is a **surplus** of the good: Suppliers are unable to sell all they want at the going price. A surplus is sometimes called a situation of *excess supply*. When there is a surplus in the ice-cream market, sellers of ice cream find their freezers increasingly full of ice cream they would like to sell but cannot. They respond to the surplus by cutting their prices. Falling prices, in turn, increase the quantity demanded and decrease the quantity supplied. Prices continue to fall until the market reaches the equilibrium.

Suppose now that the market price is below the equilibrium price, as in panel (b) of Figure 9. In this case, the price is $1.50 per cone, and the quantity of the good demanded exceeds the quantity supplied. There is a **shortage** of the good: Demanders are unable to buy all they want at the going price. A shortage is sometimes called a situation of *excess demand*. When a shortage occurs in the ice-cream market, buyers have to wait in long lines for a chance to buy one of the few cones

surplus
a situation in which quantity supplied is greater than quantity demanded

shortage
a situation in which quantity demanded is greater than quantity supplied

FIGURE 9

Markets Not in Equilibrium

In panel (a), there is a surplus. Because the market price of $2.50 is above the equilibrium price, the quantity supplied (10 cones) exceeds the quantity demanded (4 cones). Suppliers try to increase sales by cutting the price of a cone, and this moves the price toward its equilibrium level. In panel (b), there is a shortage. Because the market price of $1.50 is below the equilibrium price, the quantity demanded (10 cones) exceeds the quantity supplied (4 cones). With too many buyers chasing too few goods, suppliers can take advantage of the shortage by raising the price. Hence, in both cases, the price adjustment moves the market toward the equilibrium of supply and demand.

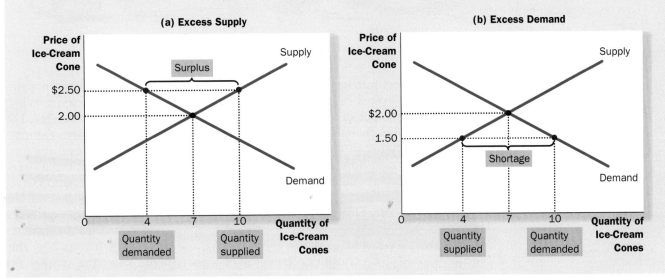

that are available. With too many buyers chasing too few goods, sellers can respond to the shortage by raising their prices without losing sales. As the price rises, quantity demanded falls, quantity supplied rises, and the market once again moves toward the equilibrium.

Thus, the activities of the many buyers and sellers automatically push the market price toward the equilibrium price. Once the market reaches its equilibrium, all buyers and sellers are satisfied, and there is no upward or downward pressure on the price. How quickly equilibrium is reached varies from market to market, depending on how quickly prices adjust. In most free markets, surpluses and shortages are only temporary because prices eventually move toward their equilibrium levels. Indeed, this phenomenon is so pervasive that it is called the **law of supply and demand:** The price of any good adjusts to bring the quantity supplied and quantity demanded for that good into balance.

law of supply and demand
the claim that the price of any good adjusts to bring the quantity supplied and the quantity demanded for that good into balance

Three Steps to Analyzing Changes in Equilibrium

So far we have seen how supply and demand together determine a market's equilibrium, which in turn determines the price of the good and the amount of the

good that buyers purchase and sellers produce. Of course, the equilibrium price and quantity depend on the position of the supply and demand curves. When some event shifts one of these curves, the equilibrium in the market changes. The analysis of such a change is called *comparative statics* because it involves comparing two unchanging situations—an initial and a new equilibrium.

When analyzing how some event affects a market, we proceed in three steps. First, we decide whether the event shifts the supply curve, the demand curve, or in some cases both curves. Second, we decide whether the curve shifts to the right or to the left. Third, we use the supply-and-demand diagram to compare the initial and the new equilibrium, which shows how the shift affects the equilibrium price and quantity. Table 3 summarizes these three steps. To see how this recipe is used, let's consider various events that might affect the market for ice cream.

Example: A Change in Demand   Suppose that one summer the weather is very hot. How does this event affect the market for ice cream? To answer this question, let's follow our three steps.

1. The hot weather affects the demand curve by changing people's taste for ice cream. That is, the weather changes the amount of ice cream that people want to buy at any given price. The supply curve is unchanged because the weather does not directly affect the firms that sell ice cream.

TABLE 3

A Three-Step Program for Analyzing Changes in Equilibrium

1. Decide whether the event shifts the supply or demand curve (or perhaps both).
2. Decide in which direction the curve shifts.
3. Use the supply-and-demand diagram to see how the shift changes the equilibrium price and quantity.

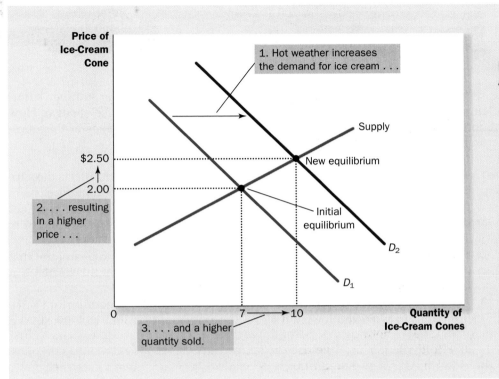

FIGURE 10

How an Increase in Demand Affects the Equilibrium

An event that raises quantity demanded at any given price shifts the demand curve to the right. The equilibrium price and the equilibrium quantity both rise. Here, an abnormally hot summer causes buyers to demand more ice cream. The demand curve shifts from D_1 to D_2, which causes the equilibrium price to rise from $2.00 to $2.50 and the equilibrium quantity to rise from 7 to 10 cones.

2. Because hot weather makes people want to eat more ice cream, the demand curve shifts to the right. Figure 10 shows this increase in demand as the shift in the demand curve from D_1 to D_2. This shift indicates that the quantity of ice cream demanded is higher at every price.

3. As Figure 10 shows, the increase in demand raises the equilibrium price from $2.00 to $2.50 and the equilibrium quantity from 7 to 10 cones. In other words, the hot weather increases the price of ice cream and the quantity of ice cream sold.

Shifts in Curves versus Movements along Curves   Notice that when hot weather drives up the price of ice cream, the quantity of ice cream that firms supply rises, even though the supply curve remains the same. In this case, economists say there has been an increase in "quantity supplied" but no change in "supply."

"Supply" refers to the position of the supply curve, whereas the "quantity supplied" refers to the amount suppliers wish to sell. In this example, supply does not change because the weather does not alter firms' desire to sell at any given price. Instead, the hot weather alters consumers' desire to buy at any given price and thereby shifts the demand curve. The increase in demand causes the equilibrium price to rise. When the price rises, the quantity supplied rises. This increase in quantity supplied is represented by the movement along the supply curve.

To summarize, a shift *in* the supply curve is called a "change in supply," and a shift *in* the demand curve is called a "change in demand." A movement *along* a fixed supply curve is called a "change in the quantity supplied," and a movement *along* a fixed demand curve is called a "change in the quantity demanded."

Example: A Change in Supply Suppose that, during another summer, a hurricane destroys part of the sugar cane crop and drives up the price of sugar. How does this event affect the market for ice cream? Once again, to answer this question, we follow our three steps.

1. The change in the price of sugar, an input into making ice cream, affects the supply curve. By raising the costs of production, it reduces the amount of ice cream that firms produce and sell at any given price. The demand curve does not change because the higher cost of inputs does not directly affect the amount of ice cream households wish to buy.
2. The supply curve shifts to the left because, at every price, the total amount that firms are willing and able to sell is reduced. Figure 11 illustrates this decrease in supply as a shift in the supply curve from S_1 to S_2.
3. As Figure 11 shows, the shift in the supply curve raises the equilibrium price from $2.00 to $2.50 and lowers the equilibrium quantity from 7 to 4 cones. As a

---

FIGURE 11

How a Decrease in Supply Affects the Equilibrium

An event that reduces quantity supplied at any given price shifts the supply curve to the left. The equilibrium price rises, and the equilibrium quantity falls. Here, an increase in the price of sugar (an input) causes sellers to supply less ice cream. The supply curve shifts from S_1 to S_2, which causes the equilibrium price of ice cream to rise from $2.00 to $2.50 and the equilibrium quantity to fall from 7 to 4 cones.

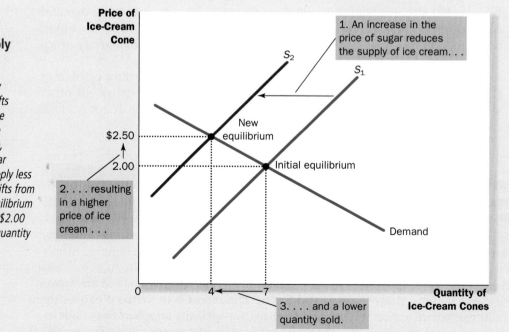

IN THE NEWS

MOTHER NATURE SHIFTS THE SUPPLY CURVE

According to our analysis, a natural disaster that reduces supply reduces the quantity sold and raises the price. Here's a recent example.

4-Day Cold Spell Slams California: Crops Devastated; Price of Citrus to Rise

By Todd S. Purdum

A brutal four-day freeze has destroyed more than a third of California's annual citrus crop, inflicting upwards of a half-billion dollars in damage and raising the prospect of tripled orange prices in supermarkets by next week.

Throughout the Golden State, cold, dry air from the Gulf of Alaska sent temperatures below freezing beginning Monday, with readings in the high teens and low 20's in agriculturally rich Central Valley early today—the worst cold spell since a 10-day freeze in 1990. Farmers frantically ran wind and irrigation machines overnight to keep trees warm, but officials pronounced a near total loss in the valley, and said perhaps half of the state's orange crop was lost as well....

California grows about 80 percent of the nation's oranges eaten as fruit, and 90 percent of lemons, and wholesalers said the retail prices of oranges could triple in the next few days. The price of lemons was certain to rise as well, but the price of orange juice should be less affected because most juice oranges are grown in Florida.

In some California markets, wholesalers reported that the price of navel or-

anges had increased to 90 cents a pound on Wednesday from 35 cents on Tuesday.

Source: *The New York Times,* December 25, 1998, p. A1. Copyright © 1998 by The New York Times Co. Reprinted by permission.

result of the sugar price increase, the price of ice cream rises, and the quantity of ice cream sold falls.

Example: A Change in Both Supply and Demand Now suppose that the heat wave and the hurricane occur during the same summer. To analyze this combination of events, we again follow our three steps.

1. We determine that both curves must shift. The hot weather affects the demand curve because it alters the amount of ice cream that households want to buy at any given price. At the same time, when the hurricane drives up sugar prices, it alters the supply curve for ice cream because it changes the amount of ice cream that firms want to sell at any given price.

FIGURE 12

A Shift in Both Supply and Demand

Here we observe a simultaneous increase in demand and decrease in supply. Two outcomes are possible. In panel (a), the equilibrium price rises from P_1 to P_2, and the equilibrium quantity rises from Q_1 to Q_2. In panel (b), the equilibrium price again rises from P_1 to P_2, but the equilibrium quantity falls from Q_1 to Q_2.

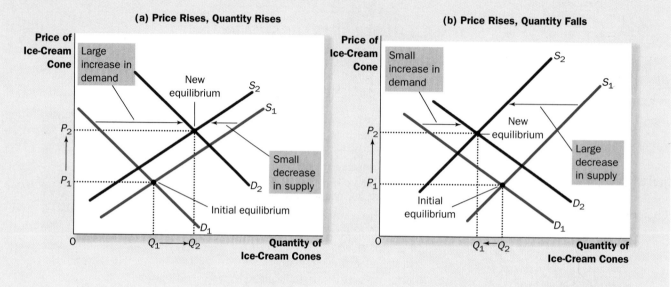

2. The curves shift in the same directions as they did in our previous analysis: The demand curve shifts to the right, and the supply curve shifts to the left. Figure 12 illustrates these shifts.

3. As Figure 12 shows, there are two possible outcomes that might result, depending on the relative size of the demand and supply shifts. In both cases, the equilibrium price rises. In panel (a), where demand increases substantially while supply falls just a little, the equilibrium quantity also rises. By contrast, in panel (b), where supply falls substantially while demand rises just a little, the equilibrium quantity falls. Thus, these events certainly raise the price of ice cream, but their impact on the amount of ice cream sold is ambiguous (that is, it could go either way).

Summary We have just seen three examples of how to use supply and demand curves to analyze a change in equilibrium. Whenever an event shifts the supply curve, the demand curve, or perhaps both curves, you can use these tools to predict how the event will alter the amount sold in equilibrium and the price at which the good is sold. Table 4 shows the predicted outcome for any combination of shifts in the two curves. To make sure you understand how to use the tools of supply and demand, pick a few entries in this table and make sure you can explain to yourself why the table contains the prediction it does.

TABLE 4

What Happens to Price and Quantity When Supply or Demand Shifts?

As a quick quiz, make sure you can explain each of the entries in this table using a supply-and-demand diagram.

	No Change in Supply	An Increase in Supply	A Decrease in Supply
No Change in Demand	*P* same *Q* same	*P* down *Q* up	*P* up *Q* down
An Increase in Demand	*P* up *Q* up	*P* ambiguous *Q* up	*P* up *Q* ambiguous
A Decrease in Demand	*P* down *Q* down	*P* down *Q* ambiguous	*P* ambiguous *Q* down

QuickQuiz Analyze what happens to the market for pizza if the price of tomatoes rises. • Analyze what happens to the market for pizza if the price of hamburgers falls.

CONCLUSION: HOW PRICES ALLOCATE RESOURCES

This chapter has analyzed supply and demand in a single market. Although our discussion has centered around the market for ice cream, the lessons learned here apply in most other markets as well. Whenever you go to a store to buy something, you are contributing to the demand for that item. Whenever you look for a job, you are contributing to the supply of labor services. Because supply and demand

"Two dollars."

"—and seventy-five cents."

are such pervasive economic phenomena, the model of supply and demand is a powerful tool for analysis. We will be using this model repeatedly in the following chapters.

One of the *Ten Principles of Economics* discussed in Chapter 1 is that markets are usually a good way to organize economic activity. Although it is still too early to judge whether market outcomes are good or bad, in this chapter we have begun to see how markets work. In any economic system, scarce resources have to be allocated among competing uses. Market economies harness the forces of supply and demand to serve that end. Supply and demand together determine the prices of the economy's many different goods and services; prices in turn are the signals that guide the allocation of resources.

For example, consider the allocation of beachfront land. Because the amount of this land is limited, not everyone can enjoy the luxury of living by the beach. Who gets this resource? The answer is: whoever is willing and able to pay the price. The price of beachfront land adjusts until the quantity of land demanded exactly balances the quantity supplied. Thus, in market economies, prices are the mechanism for rationing scarce resources.

Similarly, prices determine who produces each good and how much is produced. For instance, consider farming. Because we need food to survive, it is crucial that some people work on farms. What determines who is a farmer and who is not? In a free society, there is no government planning agency making this decision and ensuring an adequate supply of food. Instead, the allocation of workers to farms is based on the job decisions of millions of workers. This decentralized system works well because these decisions depend on prices. The prices of food and the wages of farmworkers (the price of their labor) adjust to ensure that enough people choose to be farmers.

If a person had never seen a market economy in action, the whole idea might seem preposterous. Economies are large groups of people engaged in many interdependent activities. What prevents decentralized decisionmaking from degenerating into chaos? What coordinates the actions of the millions of people with their varying abilities and desires? What ensures that what needs to get done does in fact get done? The answer, in a word, is *prices*. If market economies are guided by an invisible hand, as Adam Smith famously suggested, then the price system is the baton that the invisible hand uses to conduct the economic orchestra.

SUMMARY

- Economists use the model of supply and demand to analyze competitive markets. In a competitive market, there are many buyers and sellers, each of whom has little or no influence on the market price.

- The demand curve shows how the quantity of a good demanded depends on the price. According to the law of demand, as the price of a good falls, the quantity demanded rises. Therefore, the demand curve slopes downward.

- In addition to price, other determinants of how much consumers want to buy include income, the prices of substitutes and complements, tastes, expectations, and the number of buyers. If one of these factors changes, the demand curve shifts.

- The supply curve shows how the quantity of a good supplied depends on the price. According to the law of supply, as the price of a good rises, the quantity supplied rises. Therefore, the supply curve slopes upward.

- In addition to price, other determinants of how much producers want to sell include input prices, technology, expectations, and the number of sellers. If one of these factors changes, the supply curve shifts.

- The intersection of the supply and demand curves determines the market equilibrium. At the equilibrium price, the quantity demanded equals the quantity supplied.

- The behavior of buyers and sellers naturally drives markets toward their equilibrium. When the market price is above the equilibrium price, there is a surplus of the good, which causes the market price to fall. When the market price is below the equilibrium price, there is a shortage, which causes the market price to rise.

- To analyze how any event influences a market, we use the supply-and-demand diagram to examine how the event affects the equilibrium price and quantity. To do this we follow three steps. First, we decide whether the event shifts the supply curve or the demand curve (or both). Second, we decide which direction the curve shifts. Third, we compare the new equilibrium with the initial equilibrium.

- In market economies, prices are the signals that guide economic decisions and thereby allocate scarce resources. For every good in the economy, the price ensures that supply and demand are in balance. The equilibrium price then determines how much of the good buyers choose to purchase and how much sellers choose to produce.

KEY CONCEPTS

market, p. 64
competitive market, p. 64
quantity demanded, p. 65
law of demand, p. 66
demand schedule, p. 66
demand curve, p. 66
normal good, p. 68

inferior good, p. 68
substitutes, p. 69
complements, p. 69
quantity supplied, p. 71
law of supply, p. 71
supply schedule, p. 72
supply curve, p. 72

equilibrium, p. 75
equilibrium price, p. 75
equilibrium quantity, p. 75
surplus, p. 76
shortage, p. 76
law of supply and demand, p. 77

QUESTIONS FOR REVIEW

1. What is a competitive market? Briefly describe the types of markets other than perfectly competitive markets.

2. What determines the quantity of a good that buyers demand?

3. What are the demand schedule and the demand curve, and how are they related? Why does the demand curve slope downward?

4. Does a change in consumers' tastes lead to a movement along the demand curve or a shift in the demand curve? Does a change in price lead to a movement along the demand curve or a shift in the demand curve?

5. Popeye's income declines and, as a result, he buys more spinach. Is spinach an inferior or a normal good? What happens to Popeye's demand curve for spinach?

6. What determines the quantity of a good that sellers supply?

7. What are the supply schedule and the supply curve, and how are they related? Why does the supply curve slope upward?

8. Does a change in producers' technology lead to a movement along the supply curve or a shift in the supply curve? Does a change in price lead to a movement along the supply curve or a shift in the supply curve?

9. Define the equilibrium of a market. Describe the forces that move a market toward its equilibrium.

10. Beer and pizza are complements because they are often enjoyed together. When the price of beer rises, what happens to the supply, demand, quantity supplied, quantity demanded, and the price in the market for pizza?

11. Describe the role of prices in market economies.

PROBLEMS AND APPLICATIONS

1. Explain each of the following statements using supply-and-demand diagrams.
   a. When a cold snap hits Florida, the price of orange juice rises in supermarkets throughout the country.
   b. When the weather turns warm in New England every summer, the prices of hotel rooms in Caribbean resorts plummet.
   c. When a war breaks out in the Middle East, the price of gasoline rises, while the price of a used Cadillac falls.

2. "An increase in the demand for notebooks raises the quantity of notebooks demanded, but not the quantity supplied." Is this statement true or false? Explain.

3. Consider the market for minivans. For each of the events listed here, identify which of the determinants of demand or supply are affected. Also indicate whether demand or supply is increased or decreased. Then show the effect on the price and quantity of minivans.
   a. People decide to have more children.
   b. A strike by steelworkers raises steel prices.
   c. Engineers develop new automated machinery for the production of minivans.
   d. The price of sports utility vehicles rises.
   e. A stock-market crash lowers people's wealth.

4. During the 1990s, technological advances reduced the cost of computer chips. How do you think this affected the market for computers? For computer software? For typewriters?

5. Using supply-and-demand diagrams, show the effect of the following events on the market for sweatshirts.
   a. A hurricane in South Carolina damages the cotton crop.
   b. The price of leather jackets falls.
   c. All colleges require morning calisthenics in appropriate attire.
   d. New knitting machines are invented.

6. Suppose that in the year 2005 the number of births is temporarily high. How does this baby boom affect the price of baby-sitting services in 2010 and 2020? (Hint: 5-year-olds need baby-sitters, whereas 15-year-olds can be baby-sitters.)

7. Ketchup is a complement (as well as a condiment) for hot dogs. If the price of hot dogs rises, what happens to the market for ketchup? For tomatoes? For tomato juice? For orange juice?

8. The case study presented in the chapter discussed cigarette taxes as a way to reduce smoking. Now think about the markets for other tobacco products such as cigars and chewing tobacco.
   a. Are these goods substitutes or complements for cigarettes?
   b. Using a supply-and-demand diagram, show what happens in the markets for cigars and chewing tobacco if the tax on cigarettes is increased.
   c. If policymakers wanted to reduce total tobacco consumption, what policies could they combine with the cigarette tax?

9. The market for pizza has the following demand and supply schedules:

Price	Quantity Demanded	Quantity Supplied
$4	135	26
5	104	53
6	81	81
7	68	98
8	53	110
9	39	121

Graph the demand and supply curves. What is the equilibrium price and quantity in this market? If the actual price in this market were *above* the equilibrium price, what would drive the market toward the equilibrium? If the actual

price in this market were *below* the equilibrium price, what would drive the market toward the equilibrium?

10. Because bagels and cream cheese are often eaten together, they are complements.
   a. We observe that both the equilibrium price of cream cheese and the equilibrium quantity of bagels have risen. What could be responsible for this pattern—a fall in the price of flour or a fall in the price of milk? Illustrate and explain your answer.
   b. Suppose instead that the equilibrium price of cream cheese has risen but the equilibrium quantity of bagels has fallen. What could be responsible for this pattern—a rise in the price of flour or a rise in the price of milk? Illustrate and explain your answer.

11. Suppose that the price of basketball tickets at your college is determined by market forces. Currently, the demand and supply schedules are as follows:

Price	Quantity Demanded	Quantity Supplied
$4	10,000	8,000
8	8,000	8,000
12	6,000	8,000
16	4,000	8,000
20	2,000	8,000

   a. Draw the demand and supply curves. What is unusual about this supply curve? Why might this be true?
   b. What are the equilibrium price and quantity of tickets?

c. Your college plans to increase total enrollment next year by 5,000 students. The additional students will have the following demand schedule:

Price	Quantity Demanded
$4	4,000
8	3,000
12	2,000
16	1,000
20	0

Now add the old demand schedule and the demand schedule for the new students to calculate the new demand schedule for the entire college. What will be the new equilibrium price and quantity?

12. An article in *The New York Times* described a successful marketing campaign by the French champagne industry. The article noted that "many executives felt giddy about the stratospheric champagne prices. But they also feared that such sharp price increases would cause demand to decline, which would then cause prices to plunge." What mistake are the executives making in their analysis of the situation? Illustrate your answer with a graph.

13. Market research has revealed the following information about the market for chocolate bars: The demand schedule can be represented by the equation $Q^D = 1,600 - 300P$, where Q^D is the quantity demanded and P is the price. The supply schedule can be represented by the equation $Q^S = 1,400 + 700P$, where Q^S is the quantity supplied. Calculate the equilibrium price and quantity in the market for chocolate bars.

14. What do we mean by a perfectly competitive market? Do you think that the example of ice cream used in this chapter fits this description? Is there another type of market that better characterizes the market for ice cream?

http://

For more study tools, please visit http://mankiwXtra.swlearning.com.

ELASTICITY AND ITS APPLICATION

Imagine yourself as a Kansas wheat farmer. Because you earn all your income from selling wheat, you devote much effort to making your land as productive as it can be. You monitor weather and soil conditions, check your fields for pests and disease, and study the latest advances in farm technology. You know that the more wheat you grow, the more you will have to sell after the harvest, and the higher will be your income and your standard of living.

One day Kansas State University announces a major discovery. Researchers in its agronomy department have devised a new hybrid of wheat that raises the amount farmers can produce from each acre of land by 20 percent. How should you react to this news? Should you use the new hybrid? Does this discovery make you better off or worse off than you were before? In this chapter we will see that these questions can have surprising answers. The surprise will come from applying the most basic tools of economics—supply and demand—to the market for wheat.

The previous chapter introduced supply and demand. In any competitive market, such as the market for wheat, the upward-sloping supply curve represents the behavior of sellers, and the downward-sloping demand curve represents the behavior of buyers. The price of the good adjusts to bring the quantity supplied and quantity demanded of the good into balance. To apply this basic analysis to understand the impact of the agronomists' discovery, we must first develop one more tool: the concept of *elasticity*. Elasticity, a measure of how much buyers and sellers respond to changes in market conditions, allows us to analyze supply and demand with greater precision. When studying how some event or policy affects a market, we can discuss not only the direction of the effects but their magnitude as well.

THE ELASTICITY OF DEMAND

When we introduced demand in Chapter 4, we noted that consumers usually buy more of a good when its price is lower, when their incomes are higher, when the prices of substitutes for the good are higher, or when the prices of complements of the good are lower. Our discussion of demand was qualitative, not quantitative. That is, we discussed the direction in which quantity demanded moves, but not the size of the change. To measure how much consumers respond to changes in these variables, economists use the concept of **elasticity.**

elasticity
a measure of the responsiveness of quantity demanded or quantity supplied to one of its determinants

The Price Elasticity of Demand and Its Determinants

The law of demand states that a fall in the price of a good raises the quantity demanded. The **price elasticity of demand** measures how much the quantity demanded responds to a change in price. Demand for a good is said to be *elastic* if the quantity demanded responds substantially to changes in the price. Demand is said to be *inelastic* if the quantity demanded responds only slightly to changes in the price.

The price elasticity of demand for any good measures how willing consumers are to move away from the good as its price rises. Thus, the elasticity reflects the many economic, social, and psychological forces that shape consumer tastes. Based on experience, however, we can state some general rules about what determines the price elasticity of demand.

price elasticity of demand
a measure of how much the quantity demanded of a good responds to a change in the price of that good, computed as the percentage change in quantity demanded divided by the percentage change in price

Availability of Close Substitutes   Goods with close substitutes tend to have more elastic demand because it is easier for consumers to switch from that good to others. For example, butter and margarine are easily substitutable. A small increase in the price of butter, assuming the price of margarine is held fixed, causes the quantity of butter sold to fall by a large amount. By contrast, because eggs are a food without a close substitute, the demand for eggs is less elastic than the demand for butter.

Necessities versus Luxuries   Necessities tend to have inelastic demands, whereas luxuries have elastic demands. When the price of a visit to the doctor rises, people will not dramatically alter the number of times they go to the doctor, although they might go somewhat less often. By contrast, when the price of sailboats rises, the quantity of sailboats demanded falls substantially. The reason is that most people view doctor visits as a necessity and sailboats as a luxury. Of course, whether a good is a necessity or a luxury depends not on the intrinsic properties of the good but on the preferences of the buyer. For an avid sailor with little concern over his health, sailboats might be a necessity with inelastic demand and doctor visits a luxury with elastic demand.

Definition of the Market   The elasticity of demand in any market depends on how we draw the boundaries of the market. Narrowly defined markets tend to have more elastic demand than broadly defined markets, because it is easier to find close substitutes for narrowly defined goods. For example, food, a broad category, has a fairly inelastic demand because there are no good substitutes for food. Ice cream, a more narrow category, has a more elastic demand because it is easy to substitute other desserts for ice cream. Vanilla ice cream, a very narrow category, has a very elastic demand because other flavors of ice cream are almost perfect substitutes for vanilla.

Time Horizon   Goods tend to have more elastic demand over longer time horizons. When the price of gasoline rises, the quantity of gasoline demanded falls only slightly in the first few months. Over time, however, people buy more fuel-efficient cars, switch to public transportation, and move closer to where they work. Within several years, the quantity of gasoline demanded falls substantially.

Computing the Price Elasticity of Demand

Now that we have discussed the price elasticity of demand in general terms, let's be more precise about how it is measured. Economists compute the price elasticity of demand as the percentage change in the quantity demanded divided by the percentage change in the price. That is,

$$\text{Price elasticity of demand} = \frac{\text{Percentage change in quantity demanded}}{\text{Percentage change in price}}.$$

For example, suppose that a 10 percent increase in the price of an ice-cream cone causes the amount of ice cream you buy to fall by 20 percent. We calculate your elasticity of demand as

$$\text{Price elasticity of demand} = \frac{20 \text{ percent}}{10 \text{ percent}} = 2.$$

In this example, the elasticity is 2, reflecting that the change in the quantity demanded is proportionately twice as large as the change in the price.

Because the quantity demanded of a good is negatively related to its price, the percentage change in quantity will always have the opposite sign as the percentage change in price. In this example, the percentage change in price is a *positive* 10 percent (reflecting an increase), and the percentage change in quantity demanded is a *negative* 20 percent (reflecting a decrease). For this reason, price elasticities of demand are sometimes reported as negative numbers. In this book we follow the common practice of dropping the minus sign and reporting all price elasticities as positive numbers. (Mathematicians call this the *absolute value*.) With this convention, a larger price elasticity implies a greater responsiveness of quantity demanded to price.

The Midpoint Method: A Better Way to Calculate Percentage Changes and Elasticities

If you try calculating the price elasticity of demand between two points on a demand curve, you will quickly notice an annoying problem: The elasticity from point A to point B seems different from the elasticity from point B to point A. For example, consider these numbers:

Point A:	Price = $4	Quantity = 120
Point B:	Price = $6	Quantity = 80

Going from point A to point B, the price rises by 50 percent, and the quantity falls by 33 percent, indicating that the price elasticity of demand is 33/50, or 0.66. By contrast, going from point B to point A, the price falls by 33 percent, and the quantity rises by 50 percent, indicating that the price elasticity of demand is 50/33, or 1.5.

One way to avoid this problem is to use the *midpoint method* for calculating elasticities. The standard way to compute a percentage change is to divide the change by the initial level. By contrast, the midpoint method computes a percentage change by dividing the change by the midpoint (or average) of the initial and final levels. For instance, $5 is the midpoint of $4 and $6. Therefore, according to the midpoint method, a change from $4 to $6 is considered a 40 percent rise, because $(6 - 4)/5 \times 100 = 40$. Similarly, a change from $6 to $4 is considered a 40 percent fall.

Because the midpoint method gives the same answer regardless of the direction of change, it is often used when calculating the price elasticity of demand between two points. In our example, the midpoint between point A and point B is:

Midpoint:	Price = $5	Quantity = 100

According to the midpoint method, when going from point A to point B, the price rises by 40 percent, and the quantity falls by 40 percent. Similarly, when going from point B to point A, the price falls by 40 percent, and the quantity rises by 40 percent. In both directions, the price elasticity of demand equals 1.

We can express the midpoint method with the following formula for the price elasticity of demand between two points, denoted (Q_1, P_1) and (Q_2, P_2):

$$\text{Price elasticity of demand} = \frac{(Q_2 - Q_1)/[(Q_2 + Q_1)/2]}{(P_2 - P_1)/[(P_2 + P_1)/2]}.$$

The numerator is the percentage change in quantity computed using the midpoint method, and the denominator is the percentage change in price computed using

FIGURE 1

The Price Elasticity of Demand

The price elasticity of demand determines whether the demand curve is steep or flat. Note that all percentage changes are calculated using the midpoint method.

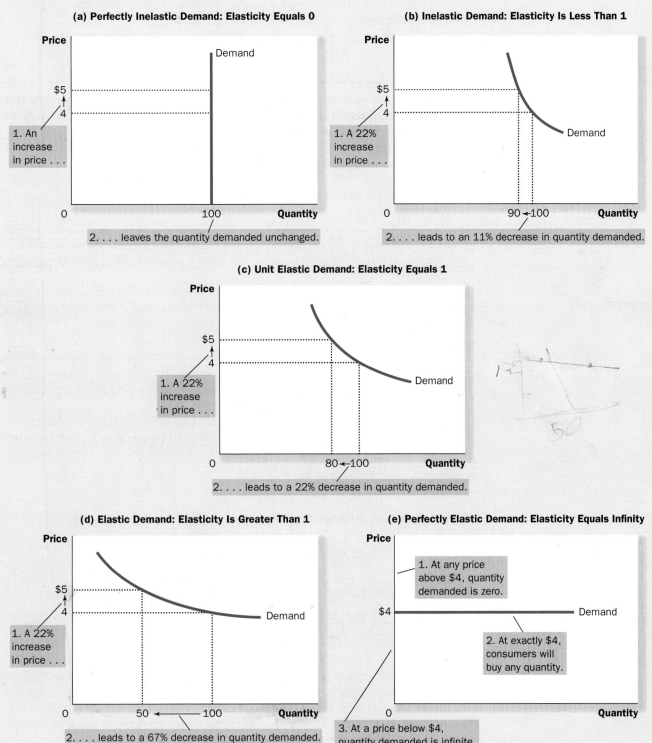

(a) Perfectly Inelastic Demand: Elasticity Equals 0

Price

Demand

$5

4

1. An increase in price . . .

0   100   Quantity

2. . . . leaves the quantity demanded unchanged.

(b) Inelastic Demand: Elasticity Is Less Than 1

Price

$5

4

1. A 22% increase in price . . .

Demand

0   90 100   Quantity

2. . . . leads to an 11% decrease in quantity demanded.

(c) Unit Elastic Demand: Elasticity Equals 1

Price

$5

4

1. A 22% increase in price . . .

Demand

0   80 100   Quantity

2. . . . leads to a 22% decrease in quantity demanded.

(d) Elastic Demand: Elasticity Is Greater Than 1

Price

$5

4

1. A 22% increase in price . . .

Demand

0   50   100   Quantity

2. . . . leads to a 67% decrease in quantity demanded.

(e) Perfectly Elastic Demand: Elasticity Equals Infinity

Price

1. At any price above $4, quantity demanded is zero.

$4   Demand

2. At exactly $4, consumers will buy any quantity.

0   Quantity

3. At a price below $4, quantity demanded is infinite.

the midpoint method. If you ever need to calculate elasticities, you should use this formula.

In this book, however, we rarely perform such calculations. For most of our purposes, what elasticity represents—the responsiveness of quantity demanded to price—is more important than how it is calculated.

The Variety of Demand Curves

Economists classify demand curves according to their elasticity. Demand is *elastic* when the elasticity is greater than 1, so that quantity moves proportionately more than the price. Demand is *inelastic* when the elasticity is less than 1, so that quantity moves proportionately less than the price. If the elasticity is exactly 1, so that quantity moves the same amount proportionately as price, demand is said to have *unit elasticity.*

Because the price elasticity of demand measures how much quantity demanded responds to changes in the price, it is closely related to the slope of the demand curve. The following rule of thumb is a useful guide: The flatter the demand curve that passes through a given point, the greater the price elasticity of demand. The steeper the demand curve that passes through a given point, the smaller the price elasticity of demand.

Figure 1 (p. 93) shows five cases. In the extreme case of a zero elasticity shown in panel (a), demand is *perfectly inelastic,* and the demand curve is vertical. In this case, regardless of the price, the quantity demanded stays the same. As the elasticity rises, the demand curve gets flatter and flatter, as shown in panels (b), (c), and (d). At the opposite extreme shown in panel (e), demand is *perfectly elastic.* This occurs as the price elasticity of demand approaches infinity and the demand curve becomes horizontal, reflecting the fact that very small changes in the price lead to huge changes in the quantity demanded.

Finally, if you have trouble keeping straight the terms *elastic* and *inelastic,* here's a memory trick for you: Inelastic curves, such as in panel (a) of Figure 1, look like the letter *I*. Elastic curves, as in panel (e), look like the letter *E*. This is not a deep insight, but it might help on your next exam.

Total Revenue and the Price Elasticity of Demand

total revenue
the amount paid by buyers and received by sellers of a good, computed as the price of the good times the quantity sold

When studying changes in supply or demand in a market, one variable we often want to study is **total revenue,** the amount paid by buyers and received by sellers of the good. In any market, total revenue is $P \times Q$, the price of the good times the quantity of the good sold. We can show total revenue graphically, as in Figure 2. The height of the box under the demand curve is P, and the width is Q. The area of this box, $P \times Q$, equals the total revenue in this market. In Figure 2, where $P = \$4$ and $Q = 100$, total revenue is $\$4 \times 100$, or $\$400$.

How does total revenue change as one moves along the demand curve? The answer depends on the price elasticity of demand. If demand is inelastic, as in Figure 3, then an increase in the price causes an increase in total revenue. Here an increase in price from $\$1$ to $\$3$ causes the quantity demanded to fall only from 100 to 80, and so total revenue rises from $\$100$ to $\$240$. An increase in price raises $P \times Q$ because the fall in Q is proportionately smaller than the rise in P.

FIGURE 2

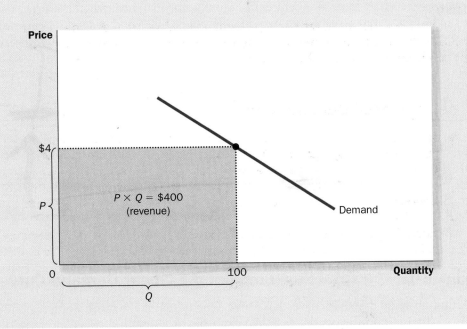

Total Revenue

The total amount paid by buyers, and received as revenue by sellers, equals the area of the box under the demand curve, P × Q. Here, at a price of $4, the quantity demanded is 100, and total revenue is $400.

FIGURE 3

How Total Revenue Changes When Price Changes: Inelastic Demand

With an inelastic demand curve, an increase in the price leads to a decrease in quantity demanded that is proportionately smaller. Therefore, total revenue (the product of price and quantity) increases. Here, an increase in the price from $1 to $3 causes the quantity demanded to fall from 100 to 80, and total revenue rises from $100 to $240.

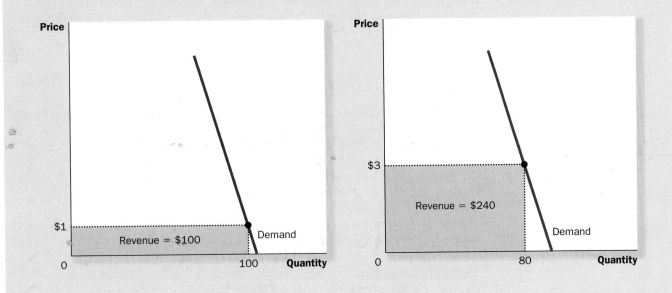

We obtain the opposite result if demand is elastic: An increase in the price causes a decrease in total revenue. In Figure 4, for instance, when the price rises from $4 to $5, the quantity demanded falls from 50 to 20, and so total revenue falls from $200 to $100. Because demand is elastic, the reduction in the quantity demanded is so great that it more than offsets the increase in the price. That is, an increase in price reduces $P \times Q$ because the fall in Q is proportionately greater than the rise in P.

Although the examples in these two figures are extreme, they illustrate a general rule:

- When demand is inelastic (a price elasticity less than 1), price and total revenue move in the same direction.
- When demand is elastic (a price elasticity greater than 1), price and total revenue move in opposite directions.
- If demand is unit elastic (a price elasticity exactly equal to 1), total revenue remains constant when the price changes.

Elasticity and Total Revenue along a Linear Demand Curve

Although some demand curves have an elasticity that is the same along the entire curve, that is not always the case. An example of a demand curve along which elasticity changes is a straight line, as shown in Figure 5. A linear demand curve

---

How Total Revenue Changes When Price Changes: Elastic Demand

With an elastic demand curve, an increase in the price leads to a decrease in quantity demanded that is proportionately larger. Therefore, total revenue (the product of price and quantity) decreases. Here, an increase in the price from $4 to $5 causes the quantity demanded to fall from 50 to 20, so total revenue falls from $200 to $100.

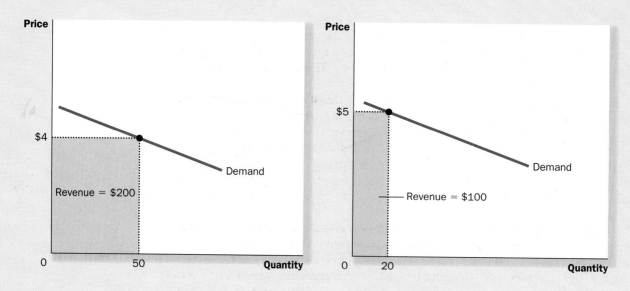

FIGURE 5

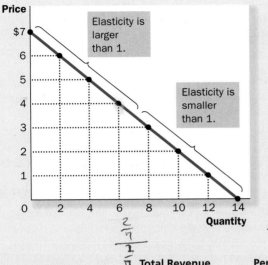

Elasticity of a Linear Demand Curve

The slope of a linear demand curve is constant, but its elasticity is not. The demand schedule in the table was used to calculate the price elasticity of demand by the midpoint method. At points with a low price and high quantity, the demand curve is inelastic. At points with a high price and low quantity, the demand curve is elastic.

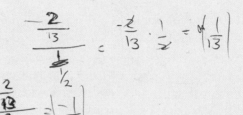

Price	Quantity	Total Revenue (Price × Quantity)	Percent Change in Price	Percent Change in Quantity	Elasticity	Description
$7	0	$ 0				
			15	200	13.0	Elastic
6	2	12				
			18	67	3.7	Elastic
5	4	20				
			22	40	1.8	Elastic
4	6	24				
			29	29	1.0	Unit elastic
3	8	24				
			40	22	0.6	Inelastic
2	10	20				
			67	18	0.3	Inelastic
1	12	12				
			200	15	0.1	Inelastic
0	14	0				

has a constant slope. Recall that slope is defined as "rise over run," which here is the ratio of the change in price ("rise") to the change in quantity ("run"). This particular demand curve's slope is constant because each $1 increase in price causes the same 2-unit decrease in the quantity demanded.

Even though the slope of a linear demand curve is constant, the elasticity is not. The reason is that the slope is the ratio of *changes* in the two variables, whereas the elasticity is the ratio of *percentage changes* in the two variables. You can see this by looking at the table in Figure 5, which shows the demand schedule for the linear demand curve in the graph. The table uses the midpoint method to calculate the price elasticity of demand. At points with a low price and high quantity, the demand curve is inelastic. At points with a high price and low quantity, the demand curve is elastic.

The table also presents total revenue at each point on the demand curve. These numbers illustrate the relationship between total revenue and elasticity. When the price is $1, for instance, demand is inelastic, and a price increase to $2 raises total revenue. When the price is $5, demand is elastic, and a price increase to $6 reduces total revenue. Between $3 and $4, demand is exactly unit elastic, and total revenue is the same at these two prices.

IN THE NEWS

ON THE ROAD WITH ELASTICITY

How should a firm that operates a private toll road set a price for its service? As the following article makes clear, answering this question requires an understanding of the demand curve and its elasticity.

For Whom the Booth Tolls, Price Really Does Matter

By Steven Pearlstein

All businesses face a similar question: What price for their product will generate the maximum profit?

The answer is not always obvious: Raising the price of something often has the effect of reducing sales as price-sensitive consumers seek alternatives or simply do without. For every product, the extent of that sensitivity is different. The trick is to find the point for each where the ideal tradeoff between profit margin and sales volume is achieved.

Right now, the developers of a new private toll road between Leesburg and Washington-Dulles International Airport are trying to discern the magic point. The group originally projected that it could charge nearly $2 for the 14-mile one-way trip, while attracting 34,000 trips on an average day from overcrowded public roads such as nearby Route 7. But after spending $350 million to build their much heralded "Greenway," they

If the price of admission were higher, how much smaller would this crowd be?

Case Study

PRICING ADMISSION TO A MUSEUM

You are curator of a major art museum. Your director of finance tells you that the museum is running short of funds and suggests that you consider changing the price of admission to increase total revenue. What do you do? Do you raise the price of admission, or do you lower it?

The answer depends on the elasticity of demand. If the demand for visits to the museum is inelastic, then an increase in the price of admission would increase total revenue. But if the demand is elastic, then an increase in price would cause the number of visitors to fall by so much that total revenue would decrease. In this case, you should cut the price. The number of visitors would rise by so much that total revenue would increase.

To estimate the price elasticity of demand, you would need to turn to your statisticians. They might use historical data to study how museum attendance varied from year to year as the admission price changed. Or they might use data on attendance at the various museums around the country to see how the admission price affects attendance. In studying either of these sets of data, the statisticians would need to take account of other factors that affect attendance—weather,

discovered to their dismay that only about a third that number of commuters were willing to pay that much to shave 20 minutes off their daily commute. . . .

It was only when the company, in desperation, lowered the toll to $1 that it came even close to attracting the expected traffic flows.

Although the Greenway still is losing money, it is clearly better off at this new point on the demand curve than it was when it first opened. Average daily revenue today is $22,000, compared with $14,875 when the "special introductory" price was $1.75. And with traffic still light even at rush hour, it is possible that the owners may lower tolls even further in search of higher revenue.

After all, when the price was lowered by 45 percent last spring, it generated a 200 percent increase in volume three months later. If the same ratio applies

again, lowering the toll another 25 percent would drive the daily volume up to 38,000 trips, and daily revenue up to nearly $29,000.

The problem, of course, is that the same ratio usually does not apply at every price point, which is why this pricing business is so tricky. . . .

Clifford Winston of the Brookings Institution and John Calfee of the American Enterprise Institute have considered the toll road's dilemma. . . .

Last year, the economists conducted an elaborate market test with 1,170 people across the country who were each presented with a series of options in which they were, in effect, asked to make a personal tradeoff between less commuting time and higher tolls.

In the end, they concluded that the people who placed the highest value on reducing their commuting time already

had done so by finding public transportation, living closer to their work, or selecting jobs that allowed them to commute at off-peak hours.

Conversely, those who commuted significant distances had a higher tolerance for traffic congestion and were willing to pay only 20 percent of their hourly pay to save an hour of their time.

Overall, the Winston/Calfee findings help explain why the Greenway's original toll and volume projections were too high: By their reckoning, only commuters who earned at least $30 an hour (about $60,000 a year) would be willing to pay $2 to save 20 minutes.

Source: *The Washington Post,* October 24, 1996, p. E1. Copyright © 1996, *The Washington Post.* Reprinted by permission.

population, size of collection, and so forth—to isolate the effect of price. In the end, such data analysis would provide an estimate of the price elasticity of demand, which you could use in deciding how to respond to your financial problem. ●

Other Demand Elasticities

In addition to the price elasticity of demand, economists also use other elasticities to describe the behavior of buyers in a market.

The Income Elasticity of Demand   The **income elasticity of demand** measures how the quantity demanded changes as consumer income changes. It is calculated as the percentage change in quantity demanded divided by the percentage change in income. That is,

$$\text{Income elasticity of demand} = \frac{\text{Percentage change in quantity demanded}}{\text{Percentage change in income}}.$$

income elasticity of demand
a measure of how much the quantity demanded of a good responds to a change in consumers' income, computed as the percentage change in quantity demanded divided by the percentage change in income

As we discussed in Chapter 4, most goods are *normal goods:* Higher income raises quantity demanded. Because quantity demanded and income move in the same direction, normal goods have positive income elasticities. A few goods, such as bus rides, are *inferior goods:* Higher income lowers the quantity demanded. Because quantity demanded and income move in opposite directions, inferior goods have negative income elasticities.

Even among normal goods, income elasticities vary substantially in size. Necessities, such as food and clothing, tend to have small income elasticities because consumers, regardless of how low their incomes, choose to buy some of these goods. Luxuries, such as caviar and diamonds, tend to have large income elasticities because consumers feel that they can do without these goods altogether if their income is too low.

cross-price elasticity of demand
a measure of how much the quantity demanded of one good responds to a change in the price of another good, computed as the percentage change in quantity demanded of the first good divided by the percentage change in the price of the second good

The Cross-Price Elasticity of Demand

The **cross-price elasticity of demand** measures how the quantity demanded of one good changes as the price of another good changes. It is calculated as the percentage change in quantity demanded of good 1 divided by the percentage change in the price of good 2. That is,

$$\text{Cross-price elasticity of demand} = \frac{\text{Percentage change in quantity demanded of good 1}}{\text{Percentage change in the price of good 2}}.$$

Whether the cross-price elasticity is a positive or negative number depends on whether the two goods are substitutes or complements. As we discussed in Chapter 4, substitutes are goods that are typically used in place of one another, such as hamburgers and hot dogs. An increase in hot dog prices induces people to grill hamburgers instead. Because the price of hot dogs and the quantity of hamburgers demanded move in the same direction, the cross-price elasticity is positive. Conversely, complements are goods that are typically used together, such as computers and software. In this case, the cross-price elasticity is negative, indicating that an increase in the price of computers reduces the quantity of software demanded.

QuickQuiz Define the price elasticity of demand. • Explain the relationship between total revenue and the price elasticity of demand.

THE ELASTICITY OF SUPPLY

When we introduced supply in Chapter 4, we noted that producers of a good offer to sell more of it when the price of the good rises, when their input prices fall, or when their technology improves. To turn from qualitative to quantitative statements about quantity supplied, we once again use the concept of elasticity.

price elasticity of supply
a measure of how much the quantity supplied of a good responds to a change in the price of that good, computed as the percentage change in quantity supplied divided by the percentage change in price

The Price Elasticity of Supply and Its Determinants

The law of supply states that higher prices raise the quantity supplied. The **price elasticity of supply** measures how much the quantity supplied responds to changes in the price. Supply of a good is said to be *elastic* if the quantity supplied responds substantially to changes in the price. Supply is said to be *inelastic* if the quantity supplied responds only slightly to changes in the price.

The price elasticity of supply depends on the flexibility of sellers to change the amount of the good they produce. For example, beachfront land has an inelastic supply because it is almost impossible to produce more of it. By contrast, manufactured goods, such as books, cars, and televisions, have elastic supplies because the firms that produce them can run their factories longer in response to a higher price.

In most markets, a key determinant of the price elasticity of supply is the time period being considered. Supply is usually more elastic in the long run than in the short run. Over short periods of time, firms cannot easily change the size of their factories to make more or less of a good. Thus, in the short run, the quantity supplied is not very responsive to the price. By contrast, over longer periods, firms can build new factories or close old ones. In addition, new firms can enter a market, and old firms can shut down. Thus, in the long run, the quantity supplied can respond substantially to price changes.

Computing the Price Elasticity of Supply

Now that we have some idea about what the price elasticity of supply is, let's be more precise. Economists compute the price elasticity of supply as the percentage change in the quantity supplied divided by the percentage change in the price. That is,

$$\text{Price elasticity of supply} = \frac{\text{Percentage change in quantity supplied}}{\text{Percentage change in price}}.$$

For example, suppose that an increase in the price of milk from $2.85 to $3.15 a gallon raises the amount that dairy farmers produce from 9,000 to 11,000 gallons per month. Using the midpoint method, we calculate the percentage change in price as

$$\text{Percentage change in price} = (3.15 - 2.85)/3.00 \times 100 = 10 \text{ percent.}$$

Similarly, we calculate the percentage change in quantity supplied as

$$\text{Percentage change in quantity supplied} = (11,000 - 9,000)/10,000 \times 100 = 20 \text{ percent.}$$

In this case, the price elasticity of supply is

$$\text{Price elasticity of supply} = \frac{20 \text{ percent}}{10 \text{ percent}} = 2.0.$$

In this example, the elasticity of 2 reflects the fact that the quantity supplied moves proportionately twice as much as the price.

The Variety of Supply Curves

Because the price elasticity of supply measures the responsiveness of quantity supplied to the price, it is reflected in the appearance of the supply curve. Figure 6 (p. 102) shows five cases. In the extreme case of a zero elasticity, as shown in

FIGURE 6

The Price Elasticity of Supply

The price elasticity of supply determines whether the supply curve is steep or flat. Note that all percentage changes are calculated using the midpoint method.

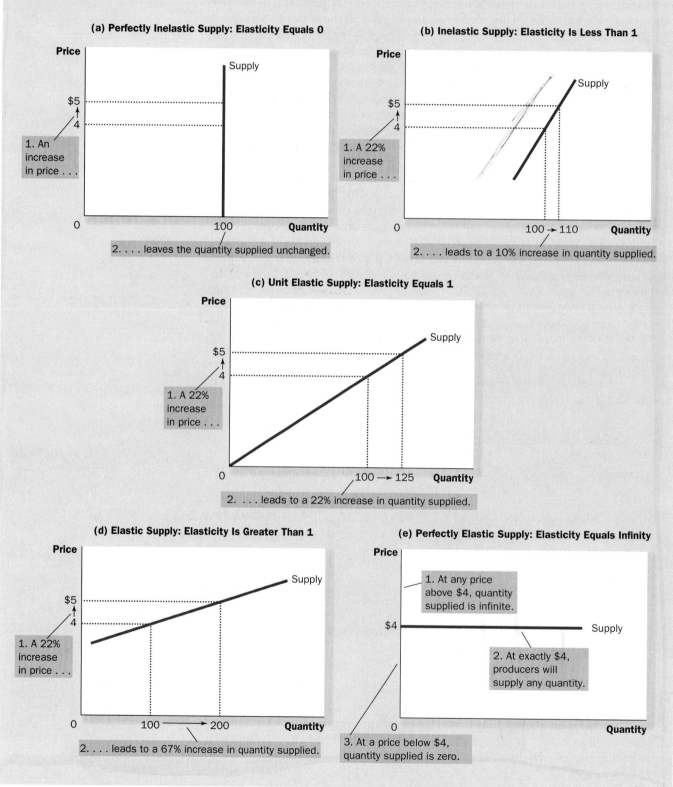

(a) Perfectly Inelastic Supply: Elasticity Equals 0

Price

Supply

$5

4

1. An increase in price . . .

0   100   Quantity

2. . . . leaves the quantity supplied unchanged.

(b) Inelastic Supply: Elasticity Is Less Than 1

Price

Supply

$5

4

1. A 22% increase in price . . .

0   100 → 110   Quantity

2. . . . leads to a 10% increase in quantity supplied.

(c) Unit Elastic Supply: Elasticity Equals 1

Price

Supply

$5

4

1. A 22% increase in price . . .

0   100 → 125   Quantity

2. . . . leads to a 22% increase in quantity supplied.

(d) Elastic Supply: Elasticity Is Greater Than 1

Price

Supply

$5

4

1. A 22% increase in price . . .

0   100 → 200   Quantity

2. . . . leads to a 67% increase in quantity supplied.

(e) Perfectly Elastic Supply: Elasticity Equals Infinity

Price

1. At any price above $4, quantity supplied is infinite.

$4

Supply

2. At exactly $4, producers will supply any quantity.

0   Quantity

3. At a price below $4, quantity supplied is zero.

panel (a), supply is *perfectly inelastic* and the supply curve is vertical. In this case, the quantity supplied is the same regardless of the price. As the elasticity rises, the supply curve gets flatter, which shows that the quantity supplied responds more to changes in the price. At the opposite extreme shown in panel (e), supply is *perfectly elastic*. This occurs as the price elasticity of supply approaches infinity and the supply curve becomes horizontal, meaning that very small changes in the price lead to very large changes in the quantity supplied.

In some markets, the elasticity of supply is not constant but varies over the supply curve. Figure 7 shows a typical case for an industry in which firms have factories with a limited capacity for production. For low levels of quantity supplied, the elasticity of supply is high, indicating that firms respond substantially to changes in the price. In this region, firms have capacity for production that is not being used, such as plants and equipment sitting idle for all or part of the day. Small increases in price make it profitable for firms to begin using this idle capacity. As the quantity supplied rises, firms begin to reach capacity. Once capacity is fully used, increasing production further requires the construction of new plants. To induce firms to incur this extra expense, the price must rise substantially, so supply becomes less elastic.

Figure 7 presents a numerical example of this phenomenon. When the price rises from $3 to $4 (a 29 percent increase, according to the midpoint method), the quantity supplied rises from 100 to 200 (a 67 percent increase). Because quantity supplied moves proportionately more than the price, the supply curve has elasticity greater than 1. By contrast, when the price rises from $12 to $15 (a 22 percent increase), the quantity supplied rises from 500 to 525 (a 5 percent increase). In this case, quantity supplied moves proportionately less than the price, so the elasticity is less than 1.

FIGURE 7

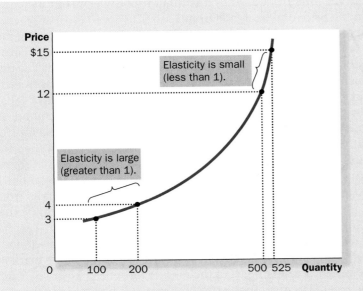

How the Price Elasticity of Supply Can Vary

Because firms often have a maximum capacity for production, the elasticity of supply may be very high at low levels of quantity supplied and very low at high levels of quantity supplied. Here, an increase in price from $3 to $4 increases the quantity supplied from 100 to 200. Because the increase in quantity supplied of 67 percent (computed using the midpoint method) is larger than the increase in price of 29 percent, the supply curve is elastic in this range. By contrast, when the price rises from $12 to $15, the quantity supplied rises only from 500 to 525. Because the increase in quantity supplied of 5 percent is smaller than the increase in price of 22 percent, the supply curve is inelastic in this range.

QuickQuiz Define the price elasticity of supply. • Explain why the price elasticity of supply might be different in the long run than in the short run.

THREE APPLICATIONS OF SUPPLY, DEMAND, AND ELASTICITY

Can good news for farming be bad news for farmers? Why did OPEC fail to keep the price of oil high? Does drug interdiction increase or decrease drug-related crime? At first, these questions might seem to have little in common. Yet all three questions are about markets, and all markets are subject to the forces of supply and demand. Here we apply the versatile tools of supply, demand, and elasticity to answer these seemingly complex questions.

Can Good News for Farming Be Bad News for Farmers?

Let's now return to the question posed at the beginning of this chapter: What happens to wheat farmers and the market for wheat when university agronomists discover a new wheat hybrid that is more productive than existing varieties? Recall from Chapter 4 that we answer such questions in three steps. First, we examine whether the supply or demand curve shifts. Second, we consider which direction the curve shifts. Third, we use the supply-and-demand diagram to see how the market equilibrium changes.

In this case, the discovery of the new hybrid affects the supply curve. Because the hybrid increases the amount of wheat that can be produced on each acre of land, farmers are now willing to supply more wheat at any given price. In other words, the supply curve shifts to the right. The demand curve remains the same because consumers' desire to buy wheat products at any given price is not affected by the introduction of a new hybrid. Figure 8 shows an example of such a change. When the supply curve shifts from S_1 to S_2, the quantity of wheat sold increases from 100 to 110, and the price of wheat falls from $3 to $2.

But does this discovery make farmers better off? As a first cut to answering this question, consider what happens to the total revenue received by farmers. Farmers' total revenue is $P \times Q$, the price of the wheat times the quantity sold. The discovery affects farmers in two conflicting ways. The hybrid allows farmers to produce more wheat (Q rises), but now each bushel of wheat sells for less (P falls).

Whether total revenue rises or falls depends on the elasticity of demand. In practice, the demand for basic foodstuffs such as wheat is usually inelastic, for these items are relatively inexpensive and have few good substitutes. When the demand curve is inelastic, as it is in Figure 8, a decrease in price causes total revenue to fall. You can see this in the figure: The price of wheat falls substantially, whereas the quantity of wheat sold rises only slightly. Total revenue falls from $300 to $220. Thus, the discovery of the new hybrid lowers the total revenue that farmers receive for the sale of their crops.

If farmers are made worse off by the discovery of this new hybrid, why do they adopt it? The answer to this question goes to the heart of how competitive markets work. Because each farmer is a small part of the market for wheat, he or she takes the price of wheat as given. For any given price of wheat, it is better to use the new

FIGURE 8

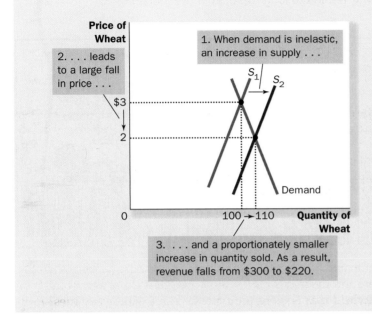

Price of Wheat

2. . . . leads to a large fall in price . . .

1. When demand is inelastic, an increase in supply . . .

An Increase in Supply in the Market for Wheat

When an advance in farm technology increases the supply of wheat from S_1 to S_2, the price of wheat falls. Because the demand for wheat is inelastic, the increase in the quantity sold from 100 to 110 is proportionately smaller than the decrease in the price from $3 to $2. As a result, farmers' total revenue falls from $300 ($3 × 100) to $220 ($2 × 110).

3. . . . and a proportionately smaller increase in quantity sold. As a result, revenue falls from $300 to $220.

hybrid in order to produce and sell more wheat. Yet when all farmers do this, the supply of wheat rises, the price falls, and farmers are worse off.

Although this example may at first seem only hypothetical, in fact it helps to explain a major change in the U.S. economy over the past century. Two hundred years ago, most Americans lived on farms. Knowledge about farm methods was sufficiently primitive that most of us had to be farmers to produce enough food. Yet, over time, advances in farm technology increased the amount of food that each farmer could produce. This increase in food supply, together with inelastic food demand, caused farm revenues to fall, which in turn encouraged people to leave farming.

A few numbers show the magnitude of this historic change. As recently as 1950, there were 10 million people working on farms in the United States, representing 17 percent of the labor force. In 2000, fewer than 3 million people worked on farms, or 2 percent of the labor force. This change coincided with tremendous advances in farm productivity: Despite the 70 percent drop in the number of farmers, U.S. farms produced more than twice the output of crops and livestock in 2000 as they did in 1950.

This analysis of the market for farm products also helps to explain a seeming paradox of public policy: Certain farm programs try to help farmers by inducing them not to plant crops on all of their land. Why do these programs do this? Their purpose is to reduce the supply of farm products and thereby raise prices. With inelastic demand for their products, farmers as a group receive greater total revenue if they supply a smaller crop to the market. No single farmer would choose to leave his land fallow on his own because each takes the market price as given. But if all farmers do so together, each of them can be better off.

When analyzing the effects of farm technology or farm policy, it is important to keep in mind that what is good for farmers is not necessarily good for society as a whole. Improvement in farm technology can be bad for farmers who become increasingly unnecessary, but it is surely good for consumers who pay less for food. Similarly, a policy aimed at reducing the supply of farm products may raise the incomes of farmers, but it does so at the expense of consumers.

Why Did OPEC Fail to Keep the Price of Oil High?

Many of the most disruptive events for the world's economies over the past several decades have originated in the world market for oil. In the 1970s members of the Organization of Petroleum Exporting Countries (OPEC) decided to raise the world price of oil in order to increase their incomes. These countries accomplished this goal by jointly reducing the amount of oil they supplied. From 1973 to 1974, the price of oil (adjusted for overall inflation) rose more than 50 percent. Then, a few years later, OPEC did the same thing again. The price of oil rose 14 percent in 1979, followed by 34 percent in 1980, and another 34 percent in 1981.

Yet OPEC found it difficult to maintain a high price. From 1982 to 1985, the price of oil steadily declined at about 10 percent per year. Dissatisfaction and disarray soon prevailed among the OPEC countries. In 1986 cooperation among OPEC members completely broke down, and the price of oil plunged 45 percent. In 1990 the price of oil (adjusted for overall inflation) was back to where it began in 1970, and it stayed at that low level throughout most of the 1990s.

This episode shows how supply and demand can behave differently in the short run and in the long run. In the short run, both the supply and demand for oil are relatively inelastic. Supply is inelastic because the quantity of known oil reserves and the capacity for oil extraction cannot be changed quickly. Demand is inelastic because buying habits do not respond immediately to changes in price. Many drivers with old gas-guzzling cars, for instance, will just pay the higher price. Thus,

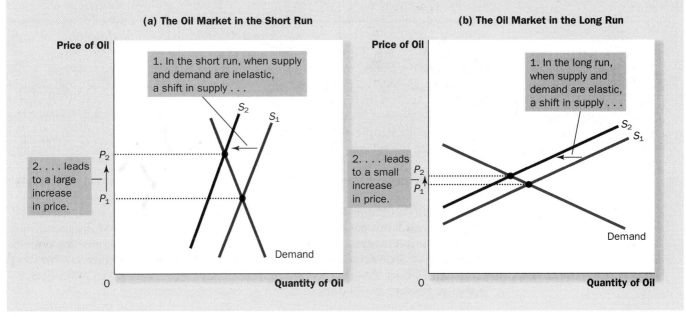

FIGURE 9

A Reduction in Supply in the World Market for Oil

When the supply of oil falls, the response depends on the time horizon. In the short run, supply and demand are relatively inelastic, as in panel (a). Thus, when the supply curve shifts from S_1 to S_2, the price rises substantially. By contrast, in the long run, supply and demand are relatively elastic, as in panel (b). In this case, the same size shift in the supply curve (S_1 to S_2) causes a smaller increase in the price.

(a) The Oil Market in the Short Run

Price of Oil

1. In the short run, when supply and demand are inelastic, a shift in supply . . .

S_2 S_1

P_2

2. . . . leads to a large increase in price.

P_1

Demand

0   Quantity of Oil

(b) The Oil Market in the Long Run

Price of Oil

1. In the long run, when supply and demand are elastic, a shift in supply . . .

S_2 S_1

2. . . . leads to a small increase in price.

P_2

P_1

Demand

0   Quantity of Oil

as panel (a) of Figure 9 shows, the short-run supply and demand curves are steep. When the supply of oil shifts from S_1 to S_2, the price increase from P_1 to P_2 is large.

The situation is very different in the long run. Over long periods of time, producers of oil outside of OPEC respond to high prices by increasing oil exploration and by building new extraction capacity. Consumers respond with greater conservation, for instance by replacing old inefficient cars with newer efficient ones. Thus, as panel (b) of Figure 9 shows, the long-run supply and demand curves are more elastic. In the long run, the shift in the supply curve from S_1 to S_2 causes a much smaller increase in the price.

This analysis shows why OPEC succeeded in maintaining a high price of oil only in the short run. When OPEC countries agreed to reduce their production of oil, they shifted the supply curve to the left. Even though each OPEC member sold less oil, the price rose by so much in the short run that OPEC incomes rose. By contrast, in the long run when supply and demand are more elastic, the same reduction in supply, measured by the horizontal shift in the supply curve, caused a smaller increase in the price. Thus, OPEC's coordinated reduction in supply proved less profitable in the long run.

OPEC still exists today, and it has from time to time succeeded at reducing supply and raising prices. But the price of oil (adjusted for overall inflation) has never returned to the peak reached in 1981. The cartel now seems to understand that raising prices is easier in the short run than in the long run.

Does Drug Interdiction Increase or Decrease Drug-Related Crime?

A persistent problem facing our society is the use of illegal drugs, such as heroin, cocaine, ecstasy, and crack. Drug use has several adverse effects. One is that drug dependency can ruin the lives of drug users and their families. Another is that drug addicts often turn to robbery and other violent crimes to obtain the money needed to support their habit. To discourage the use of illegal drugs, the U.S. government devotes billions of dollars each year to reduce the flow of drugs into the country. Let's use the tools of supply and demand to examine this policy of drug interdiction.

Suppose the government increases the number of federal agents devoted to the war on drugs. What happens in the market for illegal drugs? As is usual, we answer this question in three steps. First, we consider whether the supply or demand curve shifts. Second, we consider the direction of the shift. Third, we see how the shift affects the equilibrium price and quantity.

Although the purpose of drug interdiction is to reduce drug use, its direct impact is on the sellers of drugs rather than the buyers. When the government stops some drugs from entering the country and arrests more smugglers, it raises the cost of selling drugs and, therefore, reduces the quantity of drugs supplied at any given price. The demand for drugs—the amount buyers want at any given price—is not changed. As panel (a) of Figure 10 shows, interdiction shifts the supply curve to the left from S_1 to S_2 and leaves the demand curve the same. The equilibrium price of drugs rises from P_1 to P_2, and the equilibrium quantity falls from Q_1 to Q_2. The fall in the equilibrium quantity shows that drug interdiction does reduce drug use.

But what about the amount of drug-related crime? To answer this question, consider the total amount that drug users pay for the drugs they buy. Because few drug addicts are likely to break their destructive habits in response to a higher price, it is likely that the demand for drugs is inelastic, as it is drawn in the figure. If demand is inelastic, then an increase in price raises total revenue in the drug market. That is, because drug interdiction raises the price of drugs proportionately more than it reduces drug use, it raises the total amount of money that drug users pay for drugs. Addicts who already had to steal to support their habits would have an even greater need for quick cash. Thus, drug interdiction could increase drug-related crime.

Because of this adverse effect of drug interdiction, some analysts argue for alternative approaches to the drug problem. Rather than trying to reduce the supply of drugs, policymakers might try to reduce the demand by pursuing a policy of drug education. Successful drug education has the effects shown in panel (b) of Figure 10. The demand curve shifts to the left from D_1 to D_2. As a result, the equilibrium quantity falls from Q_1 to Q_2, and the equilibrium price falls from P_1 to P_2. Total revenue, which is price times quantity, also falls. Thus, in contrast to drug interdiction, drug education can reduce both drug use and drug-related crime.

Advocates of drug interdiction might argue that the effects of this policy are different in the long run than in the short run, because the elasticity of demand may depend on the time horizon. The demand for drugs is probably inelastic over short periods of time because higher prices do not substantially affect drug use by established addicts. But demand may be more elastic over longer periods of time

FIGURE 10

Policies to Reduce the Use of Illegal Drugs

Drug interdiction reduces the supply of drugs from S_1 to S_2, as in panel (a). If the demand for drugs is inelastic, then the total amount paid by drug users rises, even as the amount of drug use falls. By contrast, drug education reduces the demand for drugs from D_1 to D_2, as in panel (b). Because both price and quantity fall, the amount paid by drug users falls.

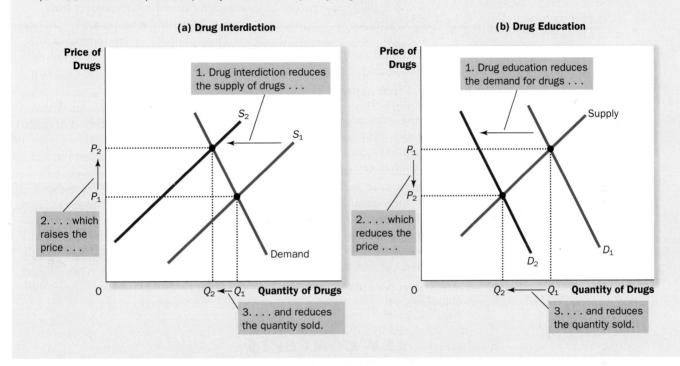

(a) Drug Interdiction

1. Drug interdiction reduces the supply of drugs . . .

2. . . . which raises the price . . .

3. . . . and reduces the quantity sold.

(b) Drug Education

1. Drug education reduces the demand for drugs . . .

2. . . . which reduces the price . . .

3. . . . and reduces the quantity sold.

because higher prices would discourage experimentation with drugs among the young and, over time, lead to fewer drug addicts. In this case, drug interdiction would increase drug-related crime in the short run while decreasing it in the long run.

QuickQuiz   How might a drought that destroys half of all farm crops be good for farmers? If such a drought is good for farmers, why don't farmers destroy their own crops in the absence of a drought?

Conclusion

According to an old quip, even a parrot can become an economist simply by learning to say "supply and demand." These last two chapters should have convinced you that there is much truth in this statement. The tools of supply and demand allow you to analyze many of the most important events and policies that shape the economy. You are now well on your way to becoming an economist (or, at least, a well-educated parrot).

SUMMARY

- The price elasticity of demand measures how much the quantity demanded responds to changes in the price. Demand tends to be more elastic if close substitutes are available, if the good is a luxury rather than a necessity, if the market is narrowly defined, or if buyers have substantial time to react to a price change.

- The price elasticity of demand is calculated as the percentage change in quantity demanded divided by the percentage change in price. If the elasticity is less than 1, so that quantity demanded moves proportionately less than the price, demand is said to be inelastic. If the elasticity is greater than 1, so that quantity demanded moves proportionately more than the price, demand is said to be elastic.

- Total revenue, the total amount paid for a good, equals the price of the good times the quantity sold. For inelastic demand curves, total revenue rises as price rises. For elastic demand curves, total revenue falls as price rises.

- The income elasticity of demand measures how much the quantity demanded responds to changes in consumers' income. The cross-price elasticity of demand measures how much the quantity demanded of one good responds to changes in the price of another good.

- The price elasticity of supply measures how much the quantity supplied responds to changes in the price. This elasticity often depends on the time horizon under consideration. In most markets, supply is more elastic in the long run than in the short run.

- The price elasticity of supply is calculated as the percentage change in quantity supplied divided by the percentage change in price. If the elasticity is less than 1, so that quantity supplied moves proportionately less than the price, supply is said to be inelastic. If the elasticity is greater than 1, so that quantity supplied moves proportionately more than the price, supply is said to be elastic.

- The tools of supply and demand can be applied in many different kinds of markets. This chapter uses them to analyze the market for wheat, the market for oil, and the market for illegal drugs.

KEY CONCEPTS

elasticity, p. 90
price elasticity of demand, p. 90
total revenue, p. 94

income elasticity of demand, p. 99
cross-price elasticity of demand, p. 100

price elasticity of supply, p. 100

QUESTIONS FOR REVIEW

1. Define the price elasticity of demand and the income elasticity of demand.

2. List and explain some of the determinants of the price elasticity of demand.

3. If the elasticity is greater than 1, is demand elastic or inelastic? If the elasticity equals 0, is demand perfectly elastic or perfectly inelastic?

4. On a supply-and-demand diagram, show equilibrium price, equilibrium quantity, and the total revenue received by producers.

5. If demand is elastic, how will an increase in price change total revenue? Explain.

6. What do we call a good whose income elasticity is less than 0?

7. How is the price elasticity of supply calculated? Explain what this measures.

8. What is the price elasticity of supply of Picasso paintings?

9. Is the price elasticity of supply usually larger in the short run or in the long run? Why?

10. In the 1970s, OPEC caused a dramatic increase in the price of oil. What prevented it from maintaining this high price through the 1980s?

PROBLEMS AND APPLICATIONS

1. For each of the following pairs of goods, which good would you expect to have more elastic demand and why?
   a. required textbooks or mystery novels
   b. Beethoven recordings or classical music recordings in general
   c. heating oil during the next six months or heating oil during the next five years
   d. root beer or water

2. Suppose that business travelers and vacationers have the following demand for airline tickets from New York to Boston:

Price	Quantity Demanded (business travelers)	Quantity Demanded (vacationers)
$150	2,100	1,000
200	2,000	800
250	1,900	600
300	1,800	400

   a. As the price of tickets rises from $200 to $250, what is the price elasticity of demand for (i) business travelers and (ii) vacationers? (Use the midpoint method in your calculations.)
   b. Why might vacationers have a different elasticity than business travelers?

3. Suppose that your demand schedule for compact discs is as follows:

Price	Quantity Demanded (income = $10,000)	Quantity Demanded (income = $12,000)
$ 8	40	50
10	32	45
12	24	30
14	16	20
16	8	12

   a. Use the midpoint method to calculate your price elasticity of demand as the price of compact discs increases from $8 to $10 if (i) your income is $10,000, and (ii) your income is $12,000.
   b. Calculate your income elasticity of demand as your income increases from $10,000 to $12,000 if (i) the price is $12, and (ii) the price is $16.

4. Emily has decided always to spend one-third of her income on clothing.

   a. What is her income elasticity of clothing demand?
   b. What is her price elasticity of clothing demand?
   c. If Emily's tastes change and she decides to spend only one-fourth of her income on clothing, how does her demand curve change? What are her income elasticity and price elasticity now?

5. *The New York Times* reported (Feb. 17, 1996, p. 25) that subway ridership declined after a fare increase: "There were nearly four million fewer riders in December 1995, the first full month after the price of a token increased 25 cents to $1.50, than in the previous December, a 4.3 percent decline."
   a. Use these data to estimate the price elasticity of demand for subway rides.
   b. According to your estimate, what happens to the Transit Authority's revenue when the fare rises?
   c. Why might your estimate of the elasticity be unreliable?

6. Two drivers—Tom and Jerry—each drive up to a gas station. Before looking at the price, each places an order. Tom says, "I'd like 10 gallons of gas." Jerry says, "I'd like $10 of gas." What is each driver's price elasticity of demand?

7. Economists have observed that spending on restaurant meals declines more during economic downturns than does spending on food to be eaten at home. How might the concept of elasticity help to explain this phenomenon?

8. Consider public policy aimed at smoking.
   a. Studies indicate that the price elasticity of demand for cigarettes is about 0.4. If a pack of cigarettes currently costs $2 and the government wants to reduce smoking by 20 percent, by how much should it increase the price?
   b. If the government permanently increases the price of cigarettes, will the policy have a larger effect on smoking one year from now or five years from now?
   c. Studies also find that teenagers have a higher price elasticity than do adults. Why might this be true?

9. Would you expect the price elasticity of *demand* to be larger in the market for all ice cream or the market for vanilla ice cream? Would you expect the price elasticity of *supply* to be larger in the market for all ice cream or the market for vanilla ice cream? Be sure to explain your answers.

10. Pharmaceutical drugs have an inelastic demand, and computers have an elastic demand. Suppose that technological advance doubles the supply of both products (that is, the quantity supplied at each price is twice what it was).
    a. What happens to the equilibrium price and quantity in each market?
    b. Which product experiences a larger change in price?
    c. Which product experiences a larger change in quantity?
    d. What happens to total consumer spending on each product?

11. Beachfront resorts have an inelastic supply, and automobiles have an elastic supply. Suppose that a rise in population doubles the demand for both products (that is, the quantity demanded at each price is twice what it was).
    a. What happens to the equilibrium price and quantity in each market?
    b. Which product experiences a larger change in price?
    c. Which product experiences a larger change in quantity?
    d. What happens to total consumer spending on each product?

12. Several years ago, flooding along the Missouri and Mississippi rivers destroyed thousands of acres of wheat.
    a. Farmers whose crops were destroyed by the floods were much worse off, but farmers whose crops were not destroyed benefited from the floods. Why?
    b. What information would you need about the market for wheat to assess whether farmers as a group were hurt or helped by the floods?

13. Explain why the following might be true: A drought around the world raises the total revenue that farmers receive from the sale of grain, but a drought only in Kansas reduces the total revenue that Kansas farmers receive.

14. Because better weather makes farmland more productive, farmland in regions with good weather conditions is more expensive than farmland in regions with bad weather conditions. Over time, however, as advances in technology have made all farmland more productive, the price of farmland (adjusted for overall inflation) has fallen. Use the concept of elasticity to explain why productivity and farmland prices are positively related across space but negatively related over time.

http:// For more study tools, please visit http://mankiwXtra.swlearning.com.

SUPPLY, DEMAND,
AND GOVERNMENT POLICIES

Economists have two roles. As scientists, they develop and test theories to explain the world around them. As policy advisers, they use their theories to help change the world for the better. The focus of the preceding two chapters has been scientific. We have seen how supply and demand determine the price of a good and the quantity of the good sold. We have also seen how various events shift supply and demand and thereby change the equilibrium price and quantity.

This chapter offers our first look at policy. Here we analyze various types of government policy using only the tools of supply and demand. As you will see, the analysis yields some surprising insights. Policies often have effects that their architects did not intend or anticipate.

We begin by considering policies that directly control prices. For example, rent-control laws dictate a maximum rent that landlords may charge tenants. Minimum-wage laws dictate the lowest wage that firms may pay workers. Price controls are usually enacted when policymakers believe that the market price of a good or service is unfair to buyers or sellers. Yet, as we will see, these policies can generate inequities of their own.

After our discussion of price controls, we next consider the impact of taxes. Policymakers use taxes both to influence market outcomes and to raise revenue for public purposes. Although the prevalence of taxes in our economy is obvious, their effects are not. For example, when the government levies a tax on the amount that firms pay their workers, do the firms or the workers bear the burden of the tax? The answer is not at all clear—until we apply the powerful tools of supply and demand.

CONTROLS ON PRICES

To see how price controls affect market outcomes, let's look once again at the market for ice cream. As we saw in Chapter 4, if ice cream is sold in a competitive market free of government regulation, the price of ice cream adjusts to balance supply and demand: At the equilibrium price, the quantity of ice cream that buyers want to buy exactly equals the quantity that sellers want to sell. To be concrete, suppose the equilibrium price is $3 per cone.

Not everyone may be happy with the outcome of this free-market process. Let's say the American Association of Ice-Cream Eaters complains that the $3 price is too high for everyone to enjoy a cone a day (their recommended diet). Meanwhile, the National Organization of Ice-Cream Makers complains that the $3 price—the result of "cutthroat competition"—is too low and is depressing the incomes of its members. Each of these groups lobbies the government to pass laws that alter the market outcome by directly controlling the price of an ice-cream cone.

Of course, because buyers of any good always want a lower price while sellers want a higher price, the interests of the two groups conflict. If the Ice-Cream Eaters are successful in their lobbying, the government imposes a legal maximum on the price at which ice cream can be sold. Because the price is not allowed to rise above this level, the legislated maximum is called a **price ceiling.** By contrast, if the Ice-Cream Makers are successful, the government imposes a legal minimum on the price. Because the price cannot fall below this level, the legislated minimum is called a **price floor.** Let us consider the effects of these policies in turn.

price ceiling
a legal maximum on the price at which a good can be sold

price floor
a legal minimum on the price at which a good can be sold

How Price Ceilings Affect Market Outcomes

When the government, moved by the complaints and campaign contributions of the Ice-Cream Eaters, imposes a price ceiling on the market for ice cream, two outcomes are possible. In panel (a) of Figure 1, the government imposes a price ceiling of $4 per cone. In this case, because the price that balances supply and demand ($3) is below the ceiling, the price ceiling is *not binding.* Market forces naturally move the economy to the equilibrium, and the price ceiling has no effect on the price or the quantity sold.

Panel (b) of Figure 1 shows the other, more interesting, possibility. In this case, the government imposes a price ceiling of $2 per cone. Because the equilibrium price of $3 is above the price ceiling, the ceiling is a *binding constraint* on the market. The forces of supply and demand tend to move the price toward the equilibrium price, but when the market price hits the ceiling, it can rise no further. Thus, the market price equals the price ceiling. At this price, the quantity of ice cream demanded (125 cones in the figure) exceeds the quantity supplied (75 cones). There

FIGURE 1

A Market with a Price Ceiling

In panel (a), the government imposes a price ceiling of $4. Because the price ceiling is above the equilibrium price of $3, the price ceiling has no effect, and the market can reach the equilibrium of supply and demand. In this equilibrium, quantity supplied and quantity demanded both equal 100 cones. In panel (b), the government imposes a price ceiling of $2. Because the price ceiling is below the equilibrium price of $3, the market price equals $2. At this price, 125 cones are demanded and only 75 are supplied, so there is a shortage of 50 cones.

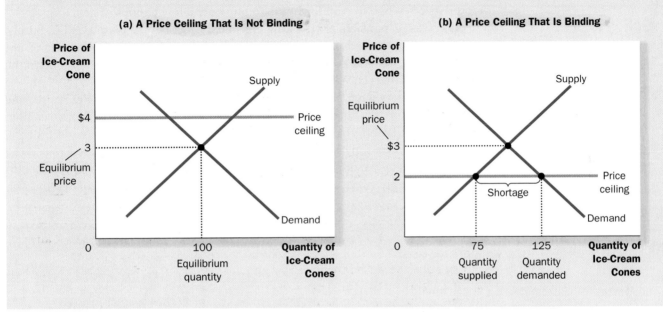

(a) A Price Ceiling That Is Not Binding

(b) A Price Ceiling That Is Binding

is a shortage of ice cream, so some people who want to buy ice cream at the going price are unable to.

When a shortage of ice cream develops because of this price ceiling, some mechanism for rationing ice cream will naturally develop. The mechanism could be long lines: Buyers who are willing to arrive early and wait in line get a cone, while those unwilling to wait do not. Alternatively, sellers could ration ice cream according to their own personal biases, selling it only to friends, relatives, or members of their own racial or ethnic group. Notice that even though the price ceiling was motivated by a desire to help buyers of ice cream, not all buyers benefit from the policy. Some buyers do get to pay a lower price, although they may have to wait in line to do so, but other buyers cannot get any ice cream at all.

This example in the market for ice cream shows a general result: *When the government imposes a binding price ceiling on a competitive market, a shortage of the good arises, and sellers must ration the scarce goods among the large number of potential buyers.* The rationing mechanisms that develop under price ceilings are rarely desirable. Long lines are inefficient, because they waste buyers' time. Discrimination according to seller bias is both inefficient (because the good does not necessarily go to the buyer who values it most highly) and potentially unfair. By contrast, the rationing mechanism in a free, competitive market is both efficient and impersonal. When the market for ice cream reaches its equilibrium, anyone who wants to pay the market price can get a cone. Free markets ration goods with prices.

Case Study

LINES AT THE GAS PUMP

As we discussed in the preceding chapter, in 1973 the Organization of Petroleum Exporting Countries (OPEC) raised the price of crude oil in world oil markets. Because crude oil is the major input used to make gasoline, the higher oil prices reduced the supply of gasoline. Long lines at gas stations became commonplace, and motorists often had to wait for hours to buy only a few gallons of gas.

What was responsible for the long gas lines? Most people blame OPEC. Surely, if OPEC had not raised the price of crude oil, the shortage of gasoline would not have occurred. Yet economists blame U.S. government regulations that limited the price oil companies could charge for gasoline.

Figure 2 shows what happened. As shown in panel (a), before OPEC raised the price of crude oil, the equilibrium price of gasoline P_1 was below the price ceiling. The price regulation, therefore, had no effect. When the price of crude oil rose, however, the situation changed. The increase in the price of crude oil raised the cost of producing gasoline, and this reduced the supply of gasoline. As panel (b) shows, the supply curve shifted to the left from S_1 to S_2. In an unregulated market,

---

FIGURE 2

The Market for Gasoline with a Price Ceiling

Panel (a) shows the gasoline market when the price ceiling is not binding because the equilibrium price, P_1, is below the ceiling. Panel (b) shows the gasoline market after an increase in the price of crude oil (an input into making gasoline) shifts the supply curve to the left from S_1 to S_2. In an unregulated market, the price would have risen from P_1 to P_2. The price ceiling, however, prevents this from happening. At the binding price ceiling, consumers are willing to buy Q_D, but producers of gasoline are willing to sell only Q_S. The difference between quantity demanded and quantity supplied, $Q_D - Q_S$, measures the gasoline shortage.

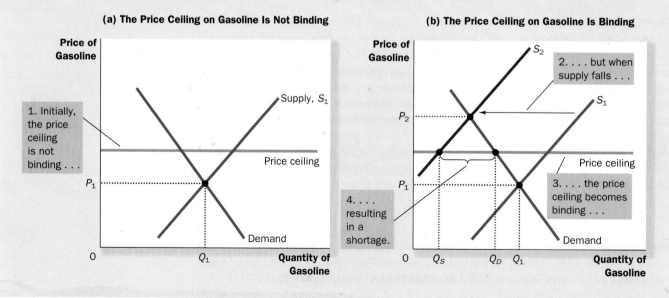

this shift in supply would have raised the equilibrium price of gasoline from P_1 to P_2, and no shortage would have resulted. Instead, the price ceiling prevented the price from rising to the equilibrium level. At the price ceiling, producers were willing to sell Q_S, and consumers were willing to buy Q_D. Thus, the shift in supply caused a severe shortage at the regulated price.

Eventually, the laws regulating the price of gasoline were repealed. Lawmakers came to understand that they were partly responsible for the many hours Americans lost waiting in line to buy gasoline. Today, when the price of crude oil changes, the price of gasoline can adjust to bring supply and demand into equilibrium. ●

Case Study
RENT CONTROL IN THE SHORT RUN AND LONG RUN

One common example of a price ceiling is rent control. In many cities, the local government places a ceiling on rents that landlords may charge their tenants. The goal of this policy is to help the poor by making housing more affordable. Economists often criticize rent control, arguing that it is a highly inefficient way to help the poor raise their standard of living. One economist called rent control "the best way to destroy a city, other than bombing."

The adverse effects of rent control are less apparent to the general population because these effects occur over many years. In the short run, landlords have a fixed number of apartments to rent, and they cannot adjust this number quickly as market conditions change. Moreover, the number of people searching for housing in a city may not be highly responsive to rents in the short run because people take time to adjust their housing arrangements. Therefore, the short-run supply and demand for housing are relatively inelastic.

Panel (a) of Figure 3 (p. 118) shows the short-run effects of rent control on the housing market. As with any binding price ceiling, rent control causes a shortage. Yet because supply and demand are inelastic in the short run, the initial shortage caused by rent control is small. The primary effect in the short run is to reduce rents.

The long-run story is very different because the buyers and sellers of rental housing respond more to market conditions as time passes. On the supply side, landlords respond to low rents by not building new apartments and by failing to maintain existing ones. On the demand side, low rents encourage people to find their own apartments (rather than living with their parents or sharing apartments with roommates) and induce more people to move into a city. Therefore, both supply and demand are more elastic in the long run.

Panel (b) of Figure 3 illustrates the housing market in the long run. When rent control depresses rents below the equilibrium level, the quantity of apartments supplied falls substantially, and the quantity of apartments demanded rises substantially. The result is a large shortage of housing.

In cities with rent control, landlords use various mechanisms to ration housing. Some landlords keep long waiting lists. Others give a preference to tenants without children. Still others discriminate on the basis of race. Sometimes, apartments

FIGURE 3

Rent Control in the Short Run and in the Long Run

Panel (a) shows the short-run effects of rent control: Because the supply and demand for apartments are relatively inelastic, the price ceiling imposed by a rent-control law causes only a small shortage of housing. Panel (b) shows the long-run effects of rent control: Because the supply and demand for apartments are more elastic, rent control causes a large shortage.

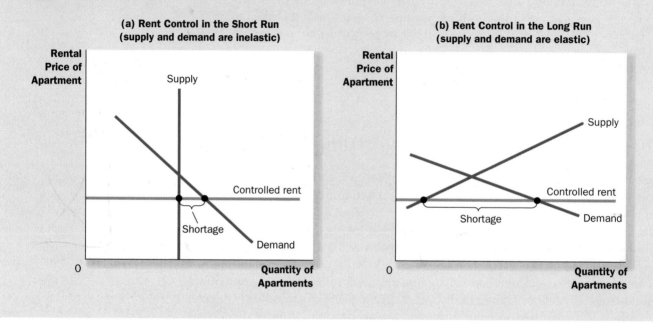

are allocated to those willing to offer under-the-table payments to building super-intendents. In essence, these bribes bring the total price of an apartment (including the bribe) closer to the equilibrium price.

To understand fully the effects of rent control, we have to remember one of the *Ten Principles of Economics* from Chapter 1: People respond to incentives. In free markets, landlords try to keep their buildings clean and safe because desirable apartments command higher prices. By contrast, when rent control creates short-ages and waiting lists, landlords lose their incentive to respond to tenants' con-cerns. Why should a landlord spend his money to maintain and improve his property when people are waiting to get in as it is? In the end, tenants get lower rents, but they also get lower-quality housing.

Policymakers often react to the effects of rent control by imposing additional regulations. For example, there are laws that make racial discrimination in hous-ing illegal and require landlords to provide minimally adequate living conditions. These laws, however, are difficult and costly to enforce. By contrast, when rent control is eliminated and a market for housing is regulated by the forces of com-petition, such laws are less necessary. In a free market, the price of housing adjusts to eliminate the shortages that give rise to undesirable landlord behavior. ●

IN THE NEWS

DOES A DROUGHT NEED TO CAUSE A WATER SHORTAGE?

During the summer of 1999, the east coast of the United States experienced unusually little rain and a shortage of water. The following article suggests a way that the shortage could have been averted.

Trickle-Down Economics
By Terry L. Anderson and Clay J. Landry

Water shortages are being blamed on the drought in the East, but that's giving Mother Nature a bum rap. Certainly the drought is the immediate cause, but the real culprit is regulations that don't allow markets and prices to equalize demand and supply.

The similarity between water and gasoline is instructive. The energy crisis of the 1970s, too, was blamed on nature's stingy supply of oil, but in fact it was the actions of the Organization of Petroleum Exporting Countries, combined with price controls, that was the main cause of the shortages. . . .

Once again, regulators are responding to shortages—in this case of water—with controls and regulations rather than allowing the market to work. Cities are restricting water usage; some have even gone so far as to prohibit restaurants from serving water except if the customer asks for a glass. But although cities initially saw declines in water use, some are starting to report increases in consumption. This has prompted some police departments to collect lists of residents suspected of wasting water.

There's a better answer than sending out the cops. Market forces could ensure

plentiful water availability even in drought years. Contrary to popular belief, the supply of water is no more fixed than the supply of oil. Like all resources, water supplies change in response to economic growth and to the price. In developing countries, despite population growth, the percentage of people with access to safe drinking water has increased to 74 percent in 1994 from 44 percent in 1980. Rising incomes have given those countries the wherewithal to supply potable water.

Supplies also increase when current users have an incentive to conserve their surplus in the marketplace. California's drought-emergency water bank illustrates this. The bank allows farmers to lease water from other users during dry spells. In 1991, the first year the bank was tried, when the price was $125 per acre-foot (326,000 gallons), supply exceeded demand by two to one. That is, many more people wanted to sell their water than wanted to buy.

Data from every corner of the world show that when cities raise the price of water by 10 percent, water use goes down by as much as 12 percent. When the price of agricultural water goes up 10 percent, usage goes down by 20 percent. . . .

Unfortunately, Eastern water users do not pay realistic prices for water. Accord-

ing to the American Water Works Association, only 2 percent of municipal water suppliers adjust prices seasonally. . . .

Even more egregious, Eastern water laws bar people from buying and selling water. Just as tradable pollution permits established under the Clean Air Act have encouraged polluters to find efficient ways to reduce emissions, tradable water rights can encourage conservation and increase supplies. It is mainly a matter of following the lead of Western water courts that have quantified water rights and Western legislatures that have allowed trades.

By making water a commodity and unleashing market forces, policymakers can ensure plentiful water supplies for all. New policies won't make droughts disappear, but they will ease the pain they impose by priming the invisible pump of water markets.

How Price Floors Affect Market Outcomes

To examine the effects of another kind of government price control, let's return to the market for ice cream. Imagine now that the government is persuaded by the pleas of the National Organization of Ice-Cream Makers. In this case, the government might institute a price floor. Price floors, like price ceilings, are an attempt by the government to maintain prices at other than equilibrium levels. Whereas a price ceiling places a legal maximum on prices, a price floor places a legal minimum.

When the government imposes a price floor on the ice-cream market, two outcomes are possible. If the government imposes a price floor of $2 per cone when the equilibrium price is $3, we obtain the outcome in panel (a) of Figure 4. In this case, because the equilibrium price is above the floor, the price floor is not binding. Market forces naturally move the economy to the equilibrium, and the price floor has no effect.

Panel (b) of Figure 4 shows what happens when the government imposes a price floor of $4 per cone. In this case, because the equilibrium price of $3 is below the floor, the price floor is a binding constraint on the market. The forces of supply and demand tend to move the price toward the equilibrium price, but when the market price hits the floor, it can fall no further. The market price equals the price floor. At this floor, the quantity of ice cream supplied (120 cones) exceeds the quantity demanded (80 cones). Some people who want to sell ice cream at the going price are unable to. *Thus, a binding price floor causes a surplus.*

FIGURE 4

A Market with a Price Floor

In panel (a), the government imposes a price floor of $2. Because this is below the equilibrium price of $3, the price floor has no effect. The market price adjusts to balance supply and demand. At the equilibrium, quantity supplied and quantity demanded both equal 100 cones. In panel (b), the government imposes a price floor of $4, which is above the equilibrium price of $3. Therefore, the market price equals $4. Because 120 cones are supplied at this price and only 80 are demanded, there is a surplus of 40 cones.

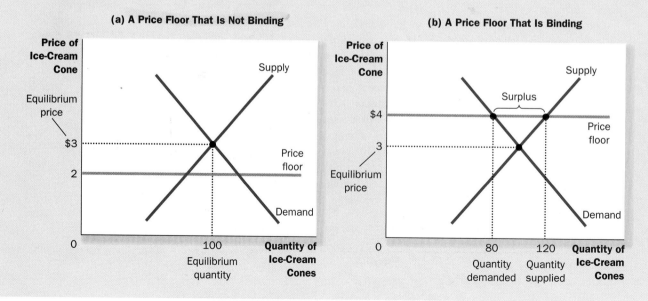

(a) A Price Floor That Is Not Binding

(b) A Price Floor That Is Binding

Just as price ceilings and shortages can lead to undesirable rationing mechanisms, so can price floors and surpluses. In the case of a price floor, some sellers are unable to sell all they want at the market price. The sellers who appeal to the personal biases of the buyers, perhaps due to racial or familial ties, are better able to sell their goods than those who do not. By contrast, in a free market, the price serves as the rationing mechanism, and sellers can sell all they want at the equilibrium price.

Case Study
THE MINIMUM WAGE

An important example of a price floor is the minimum wage. Minimum-wage laws dictate the lowest price for labor that any employer may pay. The U.S. Congress first instituted a minimum wage with the Fair Labor Standards Act of 1938 to ensure workers a minimally adequate standard of living. In 2002 the minimum wage according to federal law was $5.15 per hour, and some state laws imposed higher minimum wages.

To examine the effects of a minimum wage, we must consider the market for labor. Panel (a) of Figure 5 shows the labor market which, like all markets, is subject to the forces of supply and demand. Workers determine the supply of labor, and firms determine the demand. If the government doesn't intervene, the wage normally adjusts to balance labor supply and labor demand.

FIGURE 5

How the Minimum Wage Affects the Labor Market

Panel (a) shows a labor market in which the wage adjusts to balance labor supply and labor demand. Panel (b) shows the impact of a binding minimum wage. Because the minimum wage is a price floor, it causes a surplus: The quantity of labor supplied exceeds the quantity demanded. The result is unemployment.

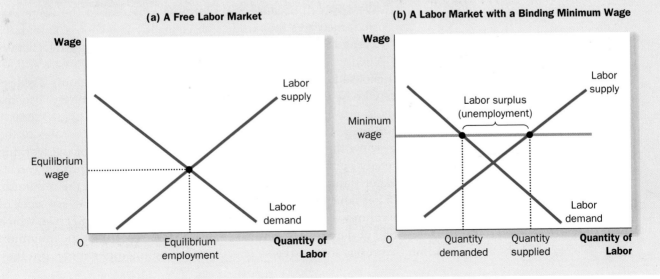

Panel (b) of Figure 5 shows the labor market with a minimum wage. If the minimum wage is above the equilibrium level, as it is here, the quantity of labor supplied exceeds the quantity demanded. The result is unemployment. Thus, the minimum wage raises the incomes of those workers who have jobs, but it lowers the incomes of those workers who cannot find jobs.

To fully understand the minimum wage, keep in mind that the economy contains not a single labor market, but many labor markets for different types of workers. The impact of the minimum wage depends on the skill and experience of the worker. Workers with high skills and much experience are not affected, because their equilibrium wages are well above the minimum. For these workers, the minimum wage is not binding.

The minimum wage has its greatest impact on the market for teenage labor. The equilibrium wages of teenagers are low because teenagers are among the least skilled and least experienced members of the labor force. In addition, teenagers are often willing to accept a lower wage in exchange for on-the-job training. (Some teenagers are willing to work as "interns" for no pay at all. Because internships pay nothing, however, the minimum wage does not apply to them. If it did, these jobs might not exist.) As a result, the minimum wage is more often binding for teenagers than for other members of the labor force.

Many economists have studied how minimum-wage laws affect the teenage labor market. These researchers compare the changes in the minimum wage over time with the changes in teenage employment. Although there is some debate about how much the minimum wage affects employment, the typical study finds that a 10 percent increase in the minimum wage depresses teenage employment between 1 and 3 percent. In interpreting this estimate, note that a 10 percent increase in the minimum wage does not raise the average wage of teenagers by 10 percent. A change in the law does not directly affect those teenagers who are already paid well above the minimum, and enforcement of minimum-wage laws is not perfect. Thus, the estimated drop in employment of 1 to 3 percent is significant.

In addition to altering the quantity of labor demanded, the minimum wage also alters the quantity supplied. Because the minimum wage raises the wage that teenagers can earn, it increases the number of teenagers who choose to look for jobs. Studies have found that a higher minimum wage influences which teenagers are employed. When the minimum wage rises, some teenagers who are still attending school choose to drop out and take jobs. These new dropouts displace other teenagers who had already dropped out of school and who now become unemployed.

The minimum wage is a frequent topic of political debate. Advocates of the minimum wage view the policy as one way to raise the income of the working poor. They correctly point out that workers who earn the minimum wage can afford only a meager standard of living. In 2002, for instance, when the minimum wage was $5.15 per hour, two adults working 40 hours a week for every week of the year at minimum-wage jobs had a total annual income of only $21,424, which was less than half of the median family income. Many advocates of the minimum wage admit that it has some adverse effects, including unemployment, but they believe that these effects are small and that, all things considered, a higher minimum wage makes the poor better off.

Opponents of the minimum wage contend that it is not the best way to combat poverty. They note that a high minimum wage causes unemployment, encourages teenagers to drop out of school, and prevents some unskilled workers from getting the on-the-job training they need. Moreover, opponents of the minimum wage point out that the minimum wage is a poorly targeted policy. Not all minimum-wage workers are heads of households trying to help their families escape poverty. In fact, fewer than a third of minimum-wage earners are in families with incomes below the poverty line. Many are teenagers from middle-class homes working at part-time jobs for extra spending money. ●

Evaluating Price Controls

One of the *Ten Principles of Economics* discussed in Chapter 1 is that markets are usually a good way to organize economic activity. This principle explains why economists usually oppose price ceilings and price floors. To economists, prices are not the outcome of some haphazard process. Prices, they contend, are the result of the millions of business and consumer decisions that lie behind the supply and demand curves. Prices have the crucial job of balancing supply and demand and, thereby, coordinating economic activity. When policymakers set prices by legal decree, they obscure the signals that normally guide the allocation of society's resources.

Another one of the *Ten Principles of Economics* is that governments can sometimes improve market outcomes. Indeed, policymakers are led to control prices because they view the market's outcome as unfair. Price controls are often aimed at helping the poor. For instance, rent-control laws try to make housing affordable for everyone, and minimum-wage laws try to help people escape poverty.

Yet price controls often hurt those they are trying to help. Rent control may keep rents low, but it also discourages landlords from maintaining their buildings and makes housing hard to find. Minimum-wage laws may raise the incomes of some workers, but they also cause other workers to be unemployed.

Helping those in need can be accomplished in ways other than controlling prices. For instance, the government can make housing more affordable by paying a fraction of the rent for poor families. Unlike rent control, such rent subsidies do not reduce the quantity of housing supplied and, therefore, do not lead to housing shortages. Similarly, wage subsidies raise the living standards of the working poor without discouraging firms from hiring them. An example of a wage subsidy is the *earned income tax credit*, a government program that supplements the incomes of low-wage workers.

Although these alternative policies are often better than price controls, they are not perfect. Rent and wage subsidies cost the government money and, therefore, require higher taxes. As we see in the next section, taxation has costs of its own.

QuickQuiz Define *price ceiling* and *price floor*, and give an example of each. Which leads to a shortage? Which leads to a surplus? Why?

TAXES

All governments—from the federal government in Washington, D.C., to the local governments in small towns—use taxes to raise revenue for public projects, such as roads, schools, and national defense. Because taxes are such an important policy instrument, and because they affect our lives in many ways, the study of taxes is a topic to which we return several times throughout this book. In this section we begin our study of how taxes affect the economy.

To set the stage for our analysis, imagine that a local government decides to hold an annual ice-cream celebration—with a parade, fireworks, and speeches by town officials. To raise revenue to pay for the event, it decides to place a $0.50 tax on the sale of ice-cream cones. When the plan is announced, our two lobbying groups swing into action. The National Organization of Ice-Cream Makers claims that its members are struggling to survive in a competitive market, and it argues that *buyers* of ice cream should have to pay the tax. The American Association of Ice-Cream Eaters claims that consumers of ice cream are having trouble making ends meet, and it argues that *sellers* of ice cream should pay the tax. The town mayor, hoping to reach a compromise, suggests that half the tax be paid by the buyers and half be paid by the sellers.

To analyze these proposals, we need to address a simple but subtle question: When the government levies a tax on a good, who bears the burden of the tax? The people buying the good? The people selling the good? Or, if buyers and sellers share the tax burden, what determines how the burden is divided? Can the government simply legislate the division of the burden, as the mayor is suggesting, or is the division determined by more fundamental forces in the economy? Economists use the term **tax incidence** to refer to the distribution of a tax burden. As we will see, some surprising lessons about tax incidence arise just by applying the tools of supply and demand.

tax incidence
the manner in which the burden of a tax is shared among participants in a market

How Taxes on Buyers Affect Market Outcomes

We first consider a tax levied on buyers of a good. Suppose, for instance, that our local government passes a law requiring buyers of ice-cream cones to send $0.50 to the government for each ice-cream cone they buy. How does this law affect the buyers and sellers of ice cream? To answer this question, we can follow the three steps in Chapter 4 for analyzing supply and demand: (1) We decide whether the law affects the supply curve or demand curve. (2) We decide which way the curve shifts. (3) We examine how the shift affects the equilibrium.

Step One The initial impact of the tax is on the demand for ice cream. The supply curve is not affected because, for any given price of ice cream, sellers have the same incentive to provide ice cream to the market. By contrast, buyers now have to pay a tax to the government (as well as the price to the sellers) whenever they buy ice cream. Thus, the tax shifts the demand curve for ice cream.

Step Two The direction of the shift is easy to determine. Because the tax on buyers makes buying ice cream less attractive, buyers demand a smaller quantity of ice cream at every price. As a result, the demand curve shifts to the left (or, equivalently, downward), as shown in Figure 6.

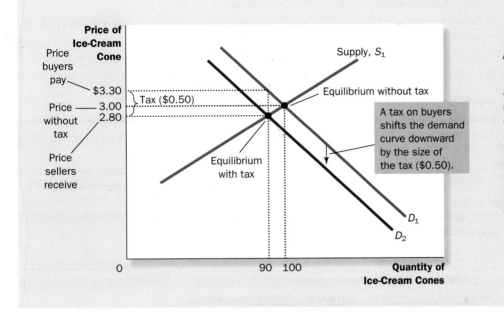

FIGURE 6

A Tax on Buyers

When a tax of $0.50 is levied on buyers, the demand curve shifts down by $0.50 from D_1 to D_2. The equilibrium quantity falls from 100 to 90 cones. The price that sellers receive falls from $3.00 to $2.80. The price that buyers pay (including the tax) rises from $3.00 to $3.30. Even though the tax is levied on buyers, buyers and sellers share the burden of the tax.

We can, in this case, be precise about how much the curve shifts. Because of the $0.50 tax levied on buyers, the effective price to buyers is now $0.50 higher than the market price (whatever the market price happens to be). For example, if the market price of a cone happened to be $2.00, the effective price to buyers would be $2.50. Because buyers look at their total cost including the tax, they demand a quantity of ice cream as if the market price were $0.50 higher than it actually is. In other words, to induce buyers to demand any given quantity, the market price must now be $0.50 lower to make up for the effect of the tax. Thus, the tax shifts the demand curve *downward* from D_1 to D_2 by exactly the size of the tax ($0.50).

Step Three Having determined how the demand curve shifts, we can now see the effect of the tax by comparing the initial equilibrium and the new equilibrium. You can see in the figure that the equilibrium price of ice cream falls from $3.00 to $2.80 and the equilibrium quantity falls from 100 to 90 cones. Because sellers sell less and buyers buy less in the new equilibrium, the tax on ice cream reduces the size of the ice-cream market.

Implications We can now return to the question of tax incidence: Who pays the tax? Although buyers send the entire tax to the government, buyers and sellers share the burden. Because the market price falls from $3.00 to $2.80 when the tax is introduced, sellers receive $0.20 less for each ice-cream cone than they did without the tax. Thus, the tax makes sellers worse off. Buyers pay sellers a lower price ($2.80), but the effective price including the tax rises from $3.00 before the tax to $3.30 with the tax ($2.80 + $0.50 = $3.30). Thus, the tax also makes buyers worse off.

To sum up, the analysis yields two lessons:

- Taxes discourage market activity. When a good is taxed, the quantity of the good sold is smaller in the new equilibrium.
- Buyers and sellers share the burden of taxes. In the new equilibrium, buyers pay more for the good, and sellers receive less.

How Taxes on Sellers Affect Market Outcomes

Now consider a tax levied on sellers of a good. Suppose the local government passes a law requiring sellers of ice-cream cones to send $0.50 to the government for each cone they sell. What are the effects of this law? Again, we apply our three steps.

Step One In this case, the immediate impact of the tax is on the sellers of ice cream. Because the tax is not levied on buyers, the quantity of ice cream demanded at any given price is the same; thus, the demand curve does not change. By contrast, the tax on sellers makes the ice-cream business less profitable at any given price, so it shifts the supply curve.

Step Two Because the tax on sellers raises the cost of producing and selling ice cream, it reduces the quantity supplied at every price. The supply curve shifts to the left (or, equivalently, upward).

Once again, we can be precise about the magnitude of the shift. For any market price of ice cream, the effective price to sellers—the amount they get to keep after paying the tax—is $0.50 lower. For example, if the market price of a cone happened to be $2.00, the effective price received by sellers would be $1.50. Whatever the market price, sellers will supply a quantity of ice cream as if the price were $0.50 lower than it is. Put differently, to induce sellers to supply any given quantity, the market price must now be $0.50 higher to compensate for the effect of the tax. Thus, as shown in Figure 7, the supply curve shifts *upward* from S_1 to S_2 by exactly the size of the tax ($0.50).

FIGURE 7

A Tax on Sellers

When a tax of $0.50 is levied on sellers, the supply curve shifts up by $0.50 from S_1 to S_2. The equilibrium quantity falls from 100 to 90 cones. The price that buyers pay rises from $3.00 to $3.30. The price that sellers receive (after paying the tax) falls from $3.00 to $2.80. Even though the tax is levied on sellers, buyers and sellers share the burden of the tax.

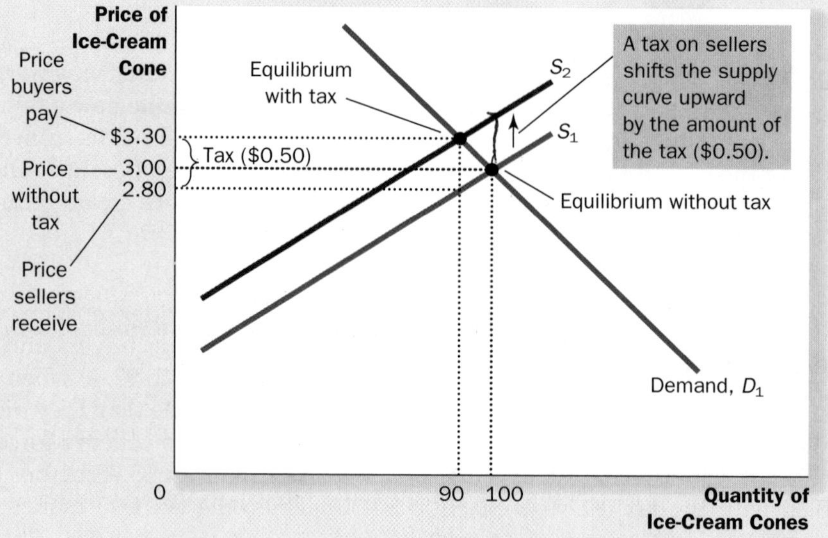

Step Three   Having determined how the supply curve shifts, we can now compare the initial and the new equilibrium. The figure shows that the equilibrium price of ice cream rises from $3.00 to $3.30, and the equilibrium quantity falls from 100 to 90 cones. Once again, the tax reduces the size of the ice-cream market. And once again, buyers and sellers share the burden of the tax. Because the market price rises, buyers pay $0.30 more for each cone than they did before the tax was enacted. Sellers receive a higher price than they did without the tax, but the effective price (after paying the tax) falls from $3.00 to $2.80.

Implications   If you compare Figures 6 and 7, you will notice a surprising conclusion: *Taxes on buyers and taxes on sellers are equivalent*. In both cases, the tax places a wedge between the price that buyers pay and the price that sellers receive. The wedge between the buyers' price and the sellers' price is the same, regardless of whether the tax is levied on buyers or sellers. In either case, the wedge shifts the relative position of the supply and demand curves. In the new equilibrium, buyers and sellers share the burden of the tax. The only difference between taxes on buyers and taxes on sellers is who sends the money to the government.

The equivalence of these two taxes is easy to understand if we imagine that the government collects the $0.50 ice-cream tax in a bowl on the counter of each ice-cream store. When the government levies the tax on buyers, the buyer is required to place $0.50 in the bowl every time a cone is bought. When the government levies the tax on sellers, the seller is required to place $0.50 in the bowl after the sale of each cone. Whether the $0.50 goes directly from the buyer's pocket into the bowl, or indirectly from the buyer's pocket into the seller's hand and then into the bowl, does not matter. Once the market reaches its new equilibrium, buyers and sellers share the burden, regardless of how the tax is levied.

Case Study

CAN CONGRESS DISTRIBUTE THE BURDEN OF A PAYROLL TAX?

If you have ever received a paycheck, you probably noticed that taxes were deducted from the amount you earned. One of these taxes is called FICA, an acronym for the Federal Insurance Contribution Act. The federal government uses the revenue from the FICA tax to pay for Social Security and Medicare, the income support and health care programs for the elderly. FICA is an example of a *payroll tax*, which is a tax on the wages that firms pay their workers. In 2002, the total FICA tax for the typical worker was 15.3 percent of earnings.

Who do you think bears the burden of this payroll tax—firms or workers? When Congress passed this legislation, it tried to mandate a division of the tax burden. According to the law, half of the tax is paid by firms, and half is paid by workers. That is, half of the tax is paid out of firm revenue, and half is deducted from workers' paychecks. The amount that shows up as a deduction on your pay stub is the worker contribution.

Our analysis of tax incidence, however, shows that lawmakers cannot so easily dictate the distribution of a tax burden. To illustrate, we can analyze a payroll tax as merely a tax on a good, where the good is labor and the price is the wage. The

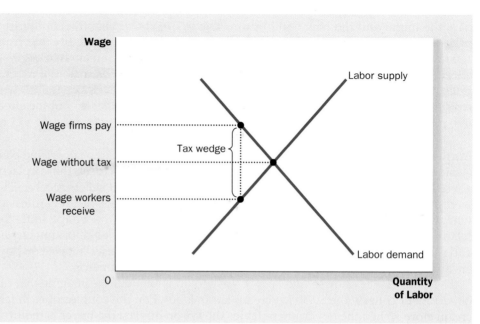

FIGURE 8

A Payroll Tax

A payroll tax places a wedge between the wage that workers receive and the wage that firms pay. Comparing wages with and without the tax, you can see that workers and firms share the tax burden. This division of the tax burden between workers and firms does not depend on whether the government levies the tax on workers, levies the tax on firms, or divides the tax equally between the two groups.

key feature of the payroll tax is that it places a wedge between the wage that firms pay and the wage that workers receive. Figure 8 shows the outcome. When a payroll tax is enacted, the wage received by workers falls, and the wage paid by firms rises. In the end, workers and firms share the burden of the tax, much as the legislation requires. Yet this division of the tax burden between workers and firms has nothing to do with the legislated division: The division of the burden in Figure 8 is not necessarily fifty-fifty, and the same outcome would prevail if the law levied the entire tax on workers or if it levied the entire tax on firms.

This example shows that the most basic lesson of tax incidence is often overlooked in public debate. Lawmakers can decide whether a tax comes from the buyer's pocket or from the seller's, but they cannot legislate the true burden of a tax. Rather, tax incidence depends on the forces of supply and demand. ●

Elasticity and Tax Incidence

When a good is taxed, buyers and sellers of the good share the burden of the tax. But how exactly is the tax burden divided? Only rarely will it be shared equally. To see how the burden is divided, consider the impact of taxation in the two markets in Figure 9. In both cases, the figure shows the initial demand curve, the initial supply curve, and a tax that drives a wedge between the amount paid by buyers and the amount received by sellers. (Not drawn in either panel of the figure is the new supply or demand curve. Which curve shifts depends on whether the tax is levied on buyers or sellers. As we have seen, this is irrelevant for the incidence of the tax.) The difference in the two panels is the relative elasticity of supply and demand.

Panel (a) of Figure 9 shows a tax in a market with very elastic supply and relatively inelastic demand. That is, sellers are very responsive to changes in the price

FIGURE 9

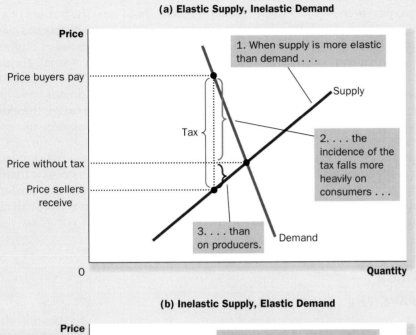

How the Burden of a Tax Is Divided

In panel (a), the supply curve is elastic, and the demand curve is inelastic. In this case, the price received by sellers falls only slightly, while the price paid by buyers rises substantially. Thus, buyers bear most of the burden of the tax. In panel (b), the supply curve is inelastic, and the demand curve is elastic. In this case, the price received by sellers falls substantially, while the price paid by buyers rises only slightly. Thus, sellers bear most of the burden of the tax.

(a) Elastic Supply, Inelastic Demand

1. When supply is more elastic than demand . . .

2. . . . the incidence of the tax falls more heavily on consumers . . .

3. . . . than on producers.

Supply

Demand

Tax

Price buyers pay

Price without tax

Price sellers receive

Price

Quantity

(b) Inelastic Supply, Elastic Demand

1. When demand is more elastic than supply . . .

3. . . . than on consumers.

2. . . . the incidence of the tax falls more heavily on producers . . .

Supply

Demand

Tax

Price buyers pay

Price without tax

Price sellers receive

Price

Quantity

of the good (so the supply curve is relatively flat), whereas buyers are not very responsive (so the demand curve is relatively steep). When a tax is imposed on a market with these elasticities, the price received by sellers does not fall much, so sellers bear only a small burden. By contrast, the price paid by buyers rises substantially, indicating that buyers bear most of the burden of the tax.

Panel (b) of Figure 9 shows a tax in a market with relatively inelastic supply and very elastic demand. In this case, sellers are not very responsive to changes in the price (so the supply curve is steeper), while buyers are very responsive (so the demand curve is flatter). The figure shows that when a tax is imposed, the price paid

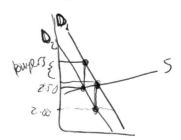

by buyers does not rise much, while the price received by sellers falls substantially. Thus, sellers bear most of the burden of the tax.

The two panels of Figure 9 show a general lesson about how the burden of a tax is divided: *A tax burden falls more heavily on the side of the market that is less elastic.* Why is this true? In essence, the elasticity measures the willingness of buyers or sellers to leave the market when conditions become unfavorable. A small elasticity of demand means that buyers do not have good alternatives to consuming this particular good. A small elasticity of supply means that sellers do not have good alternatives to producing this particular good. When the good is taxed, the side of the market with fewer good alternatives cannot easily leave the market and must, therefore, bear more of the burden of the tax.

We can apply this logic to the payroll tax discussed in the previous case study. Most labor economists believe that the supply of labor is much less elastic than the demand. This means that workers, rather than firms, bear most of the burden of the payroll tax. In other words, the distribution of the tax burden is not at all close to the fifty-fifty split that lawmakers intended.

Case Study

WHO PAYS THE LUXURY TAX?

In 1990, Congress adopted a new luxury tax on items such as yachts, private airplanes, furs, jewelry, and expensive cars. The goal of the tax was to raise revenue from those who could most easily afford to pay. Because only the rich could afford to buy such extravagances, taxing luxuries seemed a logical way of taxing the rich.

Yet, when the forces of supply and demand took over, the outcome was quite different from what Congress intended. Consider, for example, the market for yachts. The demand for yachts is quite elastic. A millionaire can easily not buy a yacht; she can use the money to buy a bigger house, take a European vacation, or leave a larger bequest to her heirs. By contrast, the supply of yachts is relatively inelastic, at least in the short run. Yacht factories are not easily converted to alternative uses, and workers who build yachts are not eager to change careers in response to changing market conditions.

Our analysis makes a clear prediction in this case. With elastic demand and inelastic supply, the burden of a tax falls largely on the suppliers. That is, a tax on yachts places a burden largely on the firms and workers who build yachts because they end up getting a lower price for their product. The workers, however, are not wealthy. Thus, the burden of a luxury tax falls more on the middle class than on the rich.

The mistaken assumptions about the incidence of the luxury tax quickly became apparent after the tax went into effect. Suppliers of luxuries made their congressional representatives well aware of the economic hardship they experienced, and Congress repealed most of the luxury tax in 1993. ●

© HANS GEORG ROTH/CORBIS

"If this boat were any more expensive, we'd be playing golf."

QuickQuiz   In a supply-and-demand diagram, show how a tax on car buyers of $1,000 per car affects the quantity of cars sold and the price of cars. In another diagram, show how a tax on car sellers of $1,000 per car affects the quantity of cars sold and the price of cars. In both of your diagrams, show the change in the price paid by car buyers and the change in price received by car sellers.

CONCLUSION

The economy is governed by two kinds of laws: the laws of supply and demand and the laws enacted by governments. In this chapter we have begun to see how these laws interact. Price controls and taxes are common in various markets in the economy, and their effects are frequently debated in the press and among policy-makers. Even a little bit of economic knowledge can go a long way toward under-standing and evaluating these policies.

In subsequent chapters we will analyze many government policies in greater detail. We will examine the effects of taxation more fully, and we will consider a broader range of policies than we considered here. Yet the basic lessons of this chapter will not change: When analyzing government policies, supply and de-mand are the first and most useful tools of analysis.

SUMMARY

- A price ceiling is a legal maximum on the price of a good or service. An example is rent control. If the price ceiling is below the equilibrium price, the quantity demanded exceeds the quantity supplied. Because of the resulting shortage, sellers must in some way ration the good or service among buyers.

- A price floor is a legal minimum on the price of a good or service. An example is the minimum wage. If the price floor is above the equilibrium price, the quantity supplied exceeds the quantity demanded. Because of the resulting surplus, buyers' demands for the good or service must in some way be rationed among sellers.

- When the government levies a tax on a good, the equilibrium quantity of the good falls. That is, a tax on a market shrinks the size of the market.

- A tax on a good places a wedge between the price paid by buyers and the price received by sellers. When the market moves to the new equilibrium, buyers pay more for the good and sellers receive less for it. In this sense, buyers and sellers share the tax burden. The incidence of a tax (that is, the division of the tax burden) does not depend on whether the tax is levied on buyers or sellers.

- The incidence of a tax depends on the price elasticities of supply and demand. The burden tends to fall on the side of the market that is less elastic because that side of the market can respond less easily to the tax by changing the quantity bought or sold.

KEY CONCEPTS

price ceiling, p. 114   price floor, p. 114   tax incidence, p. 124

QUESTIONS FOR REVIEW

1. Give an example of a price ceiling and an example of a price floor.

2. Which causes a shortage of a good—a price ceiling or a price floor? Which causes a surplus?

3. What mechanisms allocate resources when the price of a good is not allowed to bring supply and demand into equilibrium?

4. Explain why economists usually oppose controls on prices.

5. What is the difference between a tax paid by buyers and a tax paid by sellers?

6. How does a tax on a good affect the price paid by buyers, the price received by sellers, and the quantity sold?

7. What determines how the burden of a tax is divided between buyers and sellers? Why?

PROBLEMS AND APPLICATIONS

1. Lovers of classical music persuade Congress to impose a price ceiling of $40 per ticket. Does this policy get more or fewer people to attend classical music concerts?

2. The government has decided that the free-market price of cheese is too low.
   a. Suppose the government imposes a binding price floor in the cheese market. Use a supply-and-demand diagram to show the effect of this policy on the price of cheese and the quantity of cheese sold. Is there a shortage or surplus of cheese?
   b. Farmers complain that the price floor has reduced their total revenue. Is this possible? Explain.
   c. In response to farmers' complaints, the government agrees to purchase all of the surplus cheese at the price floor. Compared to the basic price floor, who benefits from this new policy? Who loses?

3. A recent study found that the demand and supply schedules for Frisbees are as follows:

Price per Frisbee	Quantity Demanded	Quantity Supplied
$11	1 million	15 million
10	2	12
9	4	9
8	6	6
7	8	3
6	10	1

   a. What are the equilibrium price and quantity of Frisbees?
   b. Frisbee manufacturers persuade the government that Frisbee production improves scientists' understanding of aerodynamics and thus is important for national security. A concerned Congress votes to impose a price floor $2 above the equilibrium price. What is the new market price? How many Frisbees are sold?
   c. Irate college students march on Washington and demand a reduction in the price of Frisbees. An even more concerned Congress votes to repeal the price floor and impose a price ceiling $1 below the former price floor. What is the new market price? How many Frisbees are sold?

4. Suppose the federal government requires beer drinkers to pay a $2 tax on each case of beer purchased. (In fact, both the federal and state governments impose beer taxes of some sort.)
   a. Draw a supply-and-demand diagram of the market for beer without the tax. Show the price paid by consumers, the price received by producers, and the quantity of beer sold. What is the difference between the price paid by consumers and the price received by producers?
   b. Now draw a supply-and-demand diagram for the beer market with the tax. Show the price paid by consumers, the price received by producers, and the quantity of beer sold. What is the difference between the price paid by consumers and the price received by producers? Has the quantity of beer sold increased or decreased?

5. A senator wants to raise tax revenue and make workers better off. A staff member proposes raising the payroll tax paid by firms and using part of the extra revenue to reduce the payroll tax paid by workers. Would this accomplish the senator's goal?

6. If the government places a $500 tax on luxury cars, will the price paid by consumers rise by

more than $500, less than $500, or exactly $500? Explain.

7. Congress and the president decide that the United States should reduce air pollution by reducing its use of gasoline. They impose a $0.50 tax for each gallon of gasoline sold.
   a. Should they impose this tax on producers or consumers? Explain carefully, using a supply-and-demand diagram.
   b. If the demand for gasoline were more elastic, would this tax be more effective or less effective in reducing the quantity of gasoline consumed? Explain with both words and a diagram.
   c. Are consumers of gasoline helped or hurt by this tax? Why?
   d. Are workers in the oil industry helped or hurt by this tax? Why?

8. A case study in this chapter discusses the federal minimum-wage law.
   a. Suppose the minimum wage is above the equilibrium wage in the market for unskilled labor. Using a supply-and-demand diagram of the market for unskilled labor, show the market wage, the number of workers who are employed, and the number of workers who are unemployed. Also show the total wage payments to unskilled workers.
   b. Now suppose the secretary of labor proposes an increase in the minimum wage. What effect would this increase have on employment? Does the change in employment depend on the elasticity of demand, the elasticity of supply, both elasticities, or neither?
   c. What effect would this increase in the minimum wage have on unemployment? Does the change in unemployment depend on the elasticity of demand, the elasticity of supply, both elasticities, or neither?
   d. If the demand for unskilled labor were inelastic, would the proposed increase in the minimum wage raise or lower total wage

payments to unskilled workers? Would your answer change if the demand for unskilled labor were elastic?

9. Consider the following policies, each of which is aimed at reducing violent crime by reducing the use of guns. Illustrate each of these proposed policies in a supply-and-demand diagram of the gun market.
   a. a tax on gun buyers
   b. a tax on gun sellers
   c. a price floor on guns
   d. a tax on ammunition

10. The U.S. government administers two programs that affect the market for cigarettes. Media campaigns and labeling requirements are aimed at making the public aware of the dangers of cigarette smoking. At the same time, the Department of Agriculture maintains a price-support program for tobacco farmers, which raises the price of tobacco above the equilibrium price.
    a. How do these two programs affect cigarette consumption? Use a graph of the cigarette market in your answer.
    b. What is the combined effect of these two programs on the price of cigarettes?
    c. Cigarettes are also heavily taxed. What effect does this tax have on cigarette consumption?

11. A subsidy is the opposite of a tax. With a $0.50 tax on the buyers of ice-cream cones, the government collects $0.50 for each cone purchased; with a $0.50 subsidy for the buyers of ice-cream cones, the government pays buyers $0.50 for each cone purchased.
    a. Show the effect of a $0.50 per cone subsidy on the demand curve for ice-cream cones, the effective price paid by consumers, the effective price received by sellers, and the quantity of cones sold.
    b. Do consumers gain or lose from this policy? Do producers gain or lose? Does the government gain or lose?

http:// For more study tools, please visit http://mankiwXtra.swlearning.com.

3

SUPPLY AND DEMAND II: MARKETS AND WELFARE

CONSUMERS, PRODUCERS, AND THE EFFICIENCY OF MARKETS

When consumers go to grocery stores to buy their turkeys for Thanksgiving dinner, they may be disappointed that the price of turkey is as high as it is. At the same time, when farmers bring to market the turkeys they have raised, they wish the price of turkey were even higher. These views are not surprising: Buyers always want to pay less, and sellers always want to get paid more. But is there a "right price" for turkey from the standpoint of society as a whole?

In previous chapters we saw how, in market economies, the forces of supply and demand determine the prices of goods and services and the quantities sold. So far, however, we have described the way markets allocate scarce resources without directly addressing the question of whether these market allocations are desirable. In other words, our analysis has been *positive* (what is) rather than *normative* (what should be). We know that the price of turkey adjusts to ensure that the quantity of turkey supplied equals the quantity of turkey demanded. But, at this equilibrium, is the quantity of turkey produced and consumed too small, too large, or just right?

welfare economics
the study of how the allocation of
resources affects economic well-being

In this chapter we take up the topic of **welfare economics,** the study of how the allocation of resources affects economic well-being. We begin by examining the benefits that buyers and sellers receive from taking part in a market. We then examine how society can make these benefits as large as possible. This analysis leads to a profound conclusion: The equilibrium of supply and demand in a market maximizes the total benefits received by buyers and sellers.

As you may recall from Chapter 1, one of the *Ten Principles of Economics* is that markets are usually a good way to organize economic activity. The study of welfare economics explains this principle more fully. It also answers our question about the right price of turkey: The price that balances the supply and demand for turkey is, in a particular sense, the best one because it maximizes the total welfare of turkey consumers and turkey producers.

CONSUMER SURPLUS

We begin our study of welfare economics by looking at the benefits buyers receive from participating in a market.

Willingness to Pay

Imagine that you own a mint-condition recording of Elvis Presley's first album. Because you are not an Elvis Presley fan, you decide to sell it. One way to do so is to hold an auction.

Four Elvis fans show up for your auction: John, Paul, George, and Ringo. Each of them would like to own the album, but there is a limit to the amount that each is willing to pay for it. Table 1 shows the maximum price that each of the four possible buyers would pay. Each buyer's maximum is called his **willingness to pay,** and it measures how much that buyer values the good. Each buyer would be eager to buy the album at a price less than his willingness to pay, would refuse to buy the album at a price more than his willingness to pay, and would be indifferent about buying the album at a price exactly equal to his willingness to pay.

To sell your album, you begin the bidding at a low price, say $10. Because all four buyers are willing to pay much more, the price rises quickly. The bidding stops when John bids $80 (or slightly more). At this point, Paul, George, and Ringo

willingness to pay
the maximum amount that a buyer
will pay for a good

TABLE 1

Four Possible Buyers' Willingness to Pay

Buyer	Willingness to Pay
John	$100
Paul	80
George	70
Ringo	50

have dropped out of the bidding, because they are unwilling to bid any more than $80. John pays you $80 and gets the album. Note that the album has gone to the buyer who values the album most highly.

What benefit does John receive from buying the Elvis Presley album? In a sense, John has found a real bargain: He is willing to pay $100 for the album but pays only $80 for it. We say that John receives *consumer surplus* of $20. **Consumer surplus** is the amount a buyer is willing to pay for a good minus the amount the buyer actually pays for it.

consumer surplus
a buyer's willingness to pay minus the amount the buyer actually pays

Consumer surplus measures the benefit to buyers of participating in a market. In this example, John receives a $20 benefit from participating in the auction because he pays only $80 for a good he values at $100. Paul, George, and Ringo get no consumer surplus from participating in the auction, because they left without the album and without paying anything.

Now consider a somewhat different example. Suppose that you had two identical Elvis Presley albums to sell. Again, you auction them off to the four possible buyers. To keep things simple, we assume that both albums are to be sold for the same price and that no buyer is interested in buying more than one album. Therefore, the price rises until two buyers are left.

In this case, the bidding stops when John and Paul bid $70 (or slightly higher). At this price, John and Paul are each happy to buy an album, and George and Ringo are not willing to bid any higher. John and Paul each receive consumer surplus equal to his willingness to pay minus the price. John's consumer surplus is $30, and Paul's is $10. John's consumer surplus is higher now than it was previously, because he gets the same album but pays less for it. The total consumer surplus in the market is $40.

Using the Demand Curve to Measure Consumer Surplus

Consumer surplus is closely related to the demand curve for a product. To see how they are related, let's continue our example and consider the demand curve for this rare Elvis Presley album.

We begin by using the willingness to pay of the four possible buyers to find the demand schedule for the album. The table in Figure 1 (p. 140) shows the demand schedule that corresponds to Table 1. If the price is above $100, the quantity demanded in the market is 0, because no buyer is willing to pay that much. If the price is between $80 and $100, the quantity demanded is 1, because only John is willing to pay such a high price. If the price is between $70 and $80, the quantity demanded is 2, because both John and Paul are willing to pay the price. We can continue this analysis for other prices as well. In this way, the demand schedule is derived from the willingness to pay of the four possible buyers.

The graph in Figure 1 shows the demand curve that corresponds to this demand schedule. Note the relationship between the height of the demand curve and the buyers' willingness to pay. At any quantity, the price given by the demand curve shows the willingness to pay of the *marginal buyer*, the buyer who would leave the market first if the price were any higher. At a quantity of 4 albums, for instance, the demand curve has a height of $50, the price that Ringo (the marginal buyer) is willing to pay for an album. At a quantity of 3 albums, the demand curve has a height of $70, the price that George (who is now the marginal buyer) is willing to pay.

FIGURE 1

The Demand Schedule and the Demand Curve

The table shows the demand schedule for the buyers in Table 1. The graph shows the corresponding demand curve. Note that the height of the demand curve reflects buyers' willingness to pay.

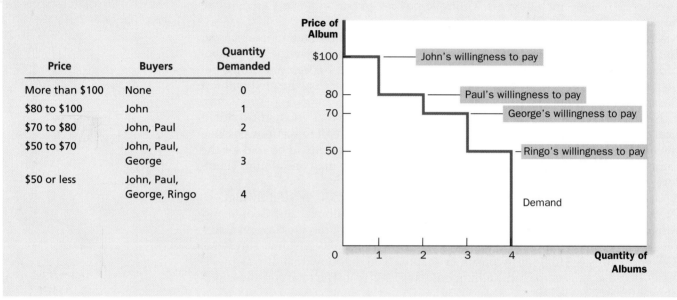

Price	Buyers	Quantity Demanded
More than $100	None	0
$80 to $100	John	1
$70 to $80	John, Paul	2
$50 to $70	John, Paul, George	3
$50 or less	John, Paul, George, Ringo	4

Because the demand curve reflects buyers' willingness to pay, we can also use it to measure consumer surplus. Figure 2 uses the demand curve to compute consumer surplus in our example. In panel (a), the price is $80 (or slightly above), and the quantity demanded is 1. Note that the area above the price and below the demand curve equals $20. This amount is exactly the consumer surplus we computed earlier when only 1 album is sold.

Panel (b) of Figure 2 shows consumer surplus when the price is $70 (or slightly above). In this case, the area above the price and below the demand curve equals the total area of the two rectangles: John's consumer surplus at this price is $30 and Paul's is $10. This area equals a total of $40. Once again, this amount is the consumer surplus we computed earlier.

The lesson from this example holds for all demand curves: *The area below the demand curve and above the price measures the consumer surplus in a market*. The reason is that the height of the demand curve measures the value buyers place on the good, as measured by their willingness to pay for it. The difference between this willingness to pay and the market price is each buyer's consumer surplus. Thus, the total area below the demand curve and above the price is the sum of the consumer surplus of all buyers in the market for a good or service.

How a Lower Price Raises Consumer Surplus

Because buyers always want to pay less for the goods they buy, a lower price makes buyers of a good better off. But how much does buyers' well-being rise in

FIGURE 2

Measuring Consumer Surplus with the Demand Curve

In panel (a), the price of the good is $80, and the consumer surplus is $20. In panel (b), the price of the good is $70, and the consumer surplus is $40.

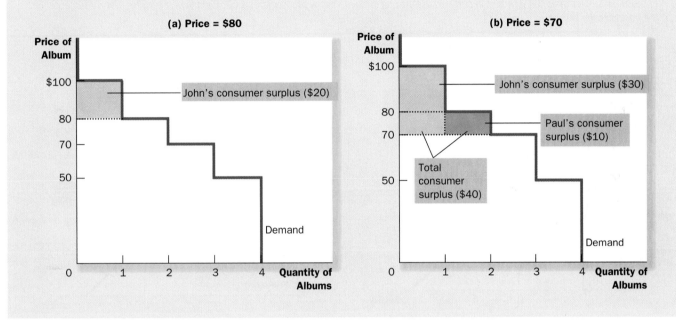

response to a lower price? We can use the concept of consumer surplus to answer this question precisely.

Figure 3 (p. 142) shows a typical downward-sloping demand curve. Although this demand curve appears somewhat different in shape from the steplike demand curves in our previous two figures, the ideas we have just developed apply nonetheless: Consumer surplus is the area above the price and below the demand curve. In panel (a), consumer surplus at a price of P_1 is the area of triangle ABC.

Now suppose that the price falls from P_1 to P_2, as shown in panel (b). The consumer surplus now equals area ADF. The increase in consumer surplus attributable to the lower price is the area BCFD.

This increase in consumer surplus is composed of two parts. First, those buyers who were already buying Q_1 of the good at the higher price P_1 are better off because they now pay less. The increase in consumer surplus of existing buyers is the reduction in the amount they pay; it equals the area of the rectangle BCED. Second, some new buyers enter the market because they are now willing to buy the good at the lower price. As a result, the quantity demanded in the market increases from Q_1 to Q_2. The consumer surplus these newcomers receive is the area of the triangle CEF.

What Does Consumer Surplus Measure?

Our goal in developing the concept of consumer surplus is to make normative judgments about the desirability of market outcomes. Now that you have seen

FIGURE 3

How the Price Affects Consumer Surplus

In panel (a), the price is P_1, the quantity demanded is Q_1, and consumer surplus equals the area of the triangle ABC. When the price falls from P_1 to P_2, as in panel (b), the quantity demanded rises from Q_1 to Q_2, and the consumer surplus rises to the area of the triangle ADF. The increase in consumer surplus (area BCFD) occurs in part because existing consumers now pay less (area BCED) and in part because new consumers enter the market at the lower price (area CEF).

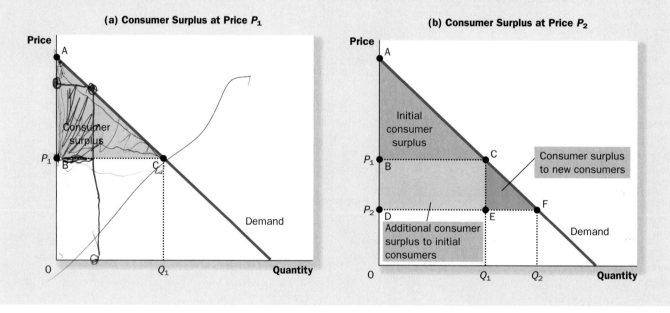

what consumer surplus is, let's consider whether it is a good measure of economic well-being.

Imagine that you are a policymaker trying to design a good economic system. Would you care about the amount of consumer surplus? Consumer surplus, the amount that buyers are willing to pay for a good minus the amount they actually pay for it, measures the benefit that buyers receive from a good *as the buyers themselves perceive it.* Thus, consumer surplus is a good measure of economic well-being if policymakers want to respect the preferences of buyers.

In some circumstances, policymakers might choose not to care about consumer surplus because they do not respect the preferences that drive buyer behavior. For example, drug addicts are willing to pay a high price for heroin. Yet we would not say that addicts get a large benefit from being able to buy heroin at a low price (even though addicts might say they do). From the standpoint of society, willingness to pay in this instance is not a good measure of the buyers' benefit, and consumer surplus is not a good measure of economic well-being, because addicts are not looking after their own best interests.

In most markets, however, consumer surplus does reflect economic well-being. Economists normally presume that buyers are rational when they make decisions and that their preferences should be respected. In this case, consumers are the best judges of how much benefit they receive from the goods they buy.

QuickQuiz Draw a demand curve for turkey. In your diagram, show a price of turkey and the consumer surplus that results from that price. Explain in words what this consumer surplus measures.

PRODUCER SURPLUS

We now turn to the other side of the market and consider the benefits sellers receive from participating in a market. As you will see, our analysis of sellers' welfare is similar to our analysis of buyers' welfare.

Cost and the Willingness to Sell

Imagine now that you are a homeowner, and you need to get your house painted. You turn to four sellers of painting services: Mary, Frida, Georgia, and Grandma. Each painter is willing to do the work for you if the price is right. You decide to take bids from the four painters and auction off the job to the painter who will do the work for the lowest price.

Each painter is willing to take the job if the price she would receive exceeds her cost of doing the work. Here the term **cost** should be interpreted as the painters' opportunity cost: It includes the painters' out-of-pocket expenses (for paint, brushes, and so on) as well as the value that the painters place on their own time. Table 2 shows each painter's cost. Because a painter's cost is the lowest price she would accept for her work, cost is a measure of her willingness to sell her services. Each painter would be eager to sell her services at a price greater than her cost, would refuse to sell her services at a price less than her cost, and would be indifferent about selling her services at a price exactly equal to her cost.

When you take bids from the painters, the price might start off high, but it quickly falls as the painters compete for the job. Once Grandma has bid $600 (or slightly less), she is the sole remaining bidder. Grandma is happy to do the job for this price, because her cost is only $500. Mary, Frida, and Georgia are unwilling to do the job for less than $600. Note that the job goes to the painter who can do the work at the lowest cost.

What benefit does Grandma receive from getting the job? Because she is willing to do the work for $500 but gets $600 for doing it, we say that she receives *producer*

cost
the value of everything a seller must give up to produce a good

---

TABLE 2

The Costs of Four Possible Sellers

Seller	Cost
Mary	$900
Frida	800
Georgia	600
Grandma	500

producer surplus
the amount a seller is paid for a good minus the seller's cost

surplus of $100. **Producer surplus** is the amount a seller is paid minus the cost of production. Producer surplus measures the benefit to sellers of participating in a market.

Now consider a somewhat different example. Suppose that you have two houses that need painting. Again, you auction off the jobs to the four painters. To keep things simple, let's assume that no painter is able to paint both houses and that you will pay the same amount to paint each house. Therefore, the price falls until two painters are left.

In this case, the bidding stops when Georgia and Grandma each offer to do the job for a price of $800 (or slightly less). At this price, Georgia and Grandma are willing to do the work, and Mary and Frida are not willing to bid a lower price. At a price of $800, Grandma receives producer surplus of $300, and Georgia receives producer surplus of $200. The total producer surplus in the market is $500.

Using the Supply Curve to Measure Producer Surplus

Just as consumer surplus is closely related to the demand curve, producer surplus is closely related to the supply curve. To see how, let's continue our example.

We begin by using the costs of the four painters to find the supply schedule for painting services. The table in Figure 4 shows the supply schedule that corresponds to the costs in Table 2. If the price is below $500, none of the four painters is willing to do the job, so the quantity supplied is zero. If the price is between $500 and $600, only Grandma is willing to do the job, so the quantity supplied is 1.

FIGURE 4

The Supply Schedule and the Supply Curve

The table shows the supply schedule for the sellers in Table 2. The graph shows the corresponding supply curve. Note that the height of the supply curve reflects sellers' costs.

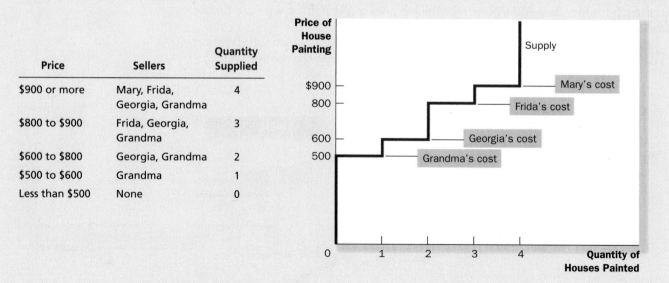

Price	Sellers	Quantity Supplied
$900 or more	Mary, Frida, Georgia, Grandma	4
$800 to $900	Frida, Georgia, Grandma	3
$600 to $800	Georgia, Grandma	2
$500 to $600	Grandma	1
Less than $500	None	0

If the price is between $600 and $800, Grandma and Georgia are willing to do the job, so the quantity supplied is 2, and so on. Thus, the supply schedule is derived from the costs of the four painters.

The graph in Figure 4 shows the supply curve that corresponds to this supply schedule. Note that the height of the supply curve is related to the sellers' costs. At any quantity, the price given by the supply curve shows the cost of the *marginal seller*, the seller who would leave the market first if the price were any lower. At a quantity of 4 houses, for instance, the supply curve has a height of $900, the cost that Mary (the marginal seller) incurs to provide her painting services. At a quantity of 3 houses, the supply curve has a height of $800, the cost that Frida (who is now the marginal seller) incurs.

Because the supply curve reflects sellers' costs, we can use it to measure producer surplus. Figure 5 uses the supply curve to compute producer surplus in our example. In panel (a), we assume that the price is $600. In this case, the quantity supplied is 1. Note that the area below the price and above the supply curve equals $100. This amount is exactly the producer surplus we computed earlier for Grandma.

Panel (b) of Figure 5 shows producer surplus at a price of $800. In this case, the area below the price and above the supply curve equals the total area of the two rectangles. This area equals $500, the producer surplus we computed earlier for Georgia and Grandma when two houses needed painting.

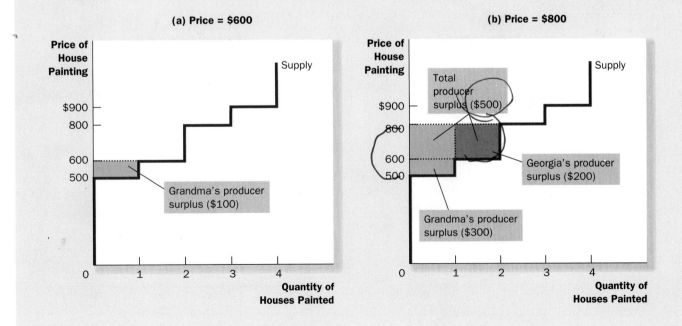

FIGURE 5

Measuring Producer Surplus with the Supply Curve

In panel (a), the price of the good is $600, and the producer surplus is $100. In panel (b), the price of the good is $800, and the producer surplus is $500.

The lesson from this example applies to all supply curves: *The area below the price and above the supply curve measures the producer surplus in a market.* The logic is straightforward: The height of the supply curve measures sellers' costs, and the difference between the price and the cost of production is each seller's producer surplus. Thus, the total area is the sum of the producer surplus of all sellers.

How a Higher Price Raises Producer Surplus

You will not be surprised to hear that sellers always want to receive a higher price for the goods they sell. But how much does sellers' well-being rise in response to a higher price? The concept of producer surplus offers a precise answer to this question.

Figure 6 shows a typical upward-sloping supply curve. Even though this supply curve differs in shape from the steplike supply curves in the previous figure, we measure producer surplus in the same way: Producer surplus is the area below the price and above the supply curve. In panel (a), the price is P_1, and producer surplus is the area of triangle ABC.

FIGURE 6

How the Price Affects Producer Surplus

In panel (a), the price is P_1, the quantity demanded is Q_1, and producer surplus equals the area of the triangle ABC. When the price rises from P_1 to P_2, as in panel (b), the quantity supplied rises from Q_1 to Q_2, and the producer surplus rises to the area of the triangle ADF. The increase in producer surplus (area BCFD) occurs in part because existing producers now receive more (area BCED) and in part because new producers enter the market at the higher price (area CEF).

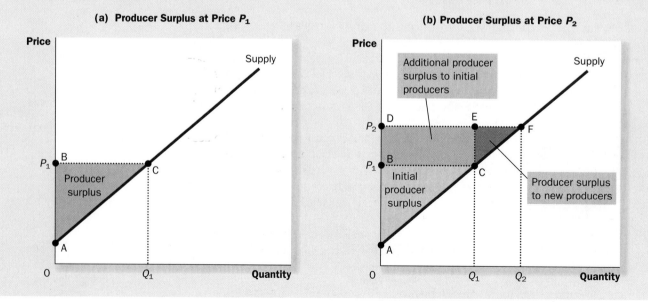

Panel (b) shows what happens when the price rises from P_1 to P_2. Producer surplus now equals area ADF. This increase in producer surplus has two parts. First, those sellers who were already selling Q_1 of the good at the lower price P_1 are better off because they now get more for what they sell. The increase in producer surplus for existing sellers equals the area of the rectangle BCED. Second, some new sellers enter the market because they are now willing to produce the good at the higher price, resulting in an increase in the quantity supplied from Q_1 to Q_2. The producer surplus of these newcomers is the area of the triangle CEF.

As this analysis shows, we use producer surplus to measure the well-being of sellers in much the same way as we use consumer surplus to measure the well-being of buyers. Because these two measures of economic welfare are so similar, it is natural to use them together. And, indeed, that is exactly what we do in the next section.

QuickQuiz Draw a supply curve for turkey. In your diagram, show a price of turkey and the producer surplus that results from that price. Explain in words what this producer surplus measures.

MARKET EFFICIENCY

Consumer surplus and producer surplus are the basic tools that economists use to study the welfare of buyers and sellers in a market. These tools can help us address a fundamental economic question: Is the allocation of resources determined by free markets in any way desirable?

The Benevolent Social Planner

To evaluate market outcomes, we introduce into our analysis a new, hypothetical character, called the benevolent social planner. The benevolent social planner is an all-knowing, all-powerful, well-intentioned dictator. The planner wants to maximize the economic well-being of everyone in society. What do you suppose this planner should do? Should he just leave buyers and sellers at the equilibrium that they reach naturally on their own? Or can he increase economic well-being by altering the market outcome in some way?

To answer this question, the planner must first decide how to measure the economic well-being of a society. One possible measure is the sum of consumer and producer surplus, which we call *total surplus*. Consumer surplus is the benefit that buyers receive from participating in a market, and producer surplus is the benefit that sellers receive. It is therefore natural to use total surplus as a measure of society's economic well-being.

To better understand this measure of economic well-being, recall how we measure consumer and producer surplus. We define consumer surplus as

Consumer surplus = Value to buyers − Amount paid by buyers.

Similarly, we define producer surplus as

$$\text{Producer surplus} = \text{Amount received by sellers} - \text{Cost to sellers.}$$

When we add consumer and producer surplus together, we obtain

$$\text{Total surplus} = \text{Value to buyers} - \text{Amount paid by buyers} \\ + \text{Amount received by sellers} - \text{Cost to sellers.}$$

The amount paid by buyers equals the amount received by sellers, so the middle two terms in this expression cancel each other. As a result, we can write total surplus as

$$\text{Total surplus} = \text{Value to buyers} - \text{Cost to sellers.}$$

Total surplus in a market is the total value to buyers of the goods, as measured by their willingness to pay, minus the total cost to sellers of providing those goods.

If an allocation of resources maximizes total surplus, we say that the allocation exhibits **efficiency.** If an allocation is not efficient, then some of the gains from trade among buyers and sellers are not being realized. For example, an allocation is inefficient if a good is not being produced by the sellers with lowest cost. In this case, moving production from a high-cost producer to a low-cost producer will lower the total cost to sellers and raise total surplus. Similarly, an allocation is inefficient if a good is not being consumed by the buyers who value it most highly. In this case, moving consumption of the good from a buyer with a low valuation to a buyer with a high valuation will raise total surplus.

In addition to efficiency, the social planner might also care about **equity**—the fairness of the distribution of well-being among the various buyers and sellers. In essence, the gains from trade in a market are like a pie to be distributed among the market participants. The question of efficiency is whether the pie is as big as possible. The question of equity is whether the pie is divided fairly. Evaluating the equity of a market outcome is more difficult than evaluating the efficiency. Whereas efficiency is an objective goal that can be judged on strictly positive grounds, equity involves normative judgments that go beyond economics and enter into the realm of political philosophy.

In this chapter we concentrate on efficiency as the social planner's goal. Keep in mind, however, that real policymakers often care about equity as well. That is, they care about both the size of the economic pie and how the pie gets sliced and distributed among members of society.

efficiency
the property of a resource allocation of maximizing the total surplus received by all members of society

equity
the fairness of the distribution of well-being among the members of society

Evaluating the Market Equilibrium

Figure 7 shows consumer and producer surplus when a market reaches the equilibrium of supply and demand. Recall that consumer surplus equals the area above the price and under the demand curve and producer surplus equals the area below the price and above the supply curve. Thus, the total area between the

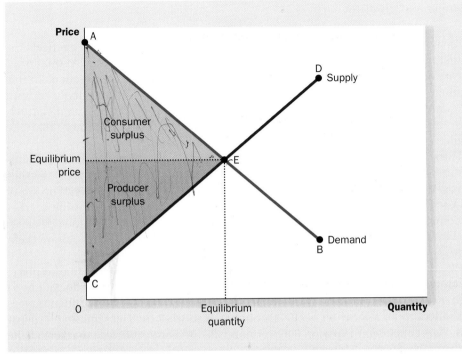

FIGURE 7

Consumer and Producer Surplus in the Market Equilibrium

Total surplus—the sum of consumer and producer surplus—is the area between the supply and demand curves up to the equilibrium quantity.

supply and demand curves up to the point of equilibrium represents the total surplus in this market.

Is this equilibrium allocation of resources efficient? Does it maximize total surplus? To answer these questions, keep in mind that when a market is in equilibrium, the price determines which buyers and sellers participate in the market. Those buyers who value the good more than the price (represented by the segment AE on the demand curve) choose to buy the good; those buyers who value it less than the price (represented by the segment EB) do not. Similarly, those sellers whose costs are less than the price (represented by the segment CE on the supply curve) choose to produce and sell the good; those sellers whose costs are greater than the price (represented by the segment ED) do not.

These observations lead to two insights about market outcomes:

1. Free markets allocate the supply of goods to the buyers who value them most highly, as measured by their willingness to pay.
2. Free markets allocate the demand for goods to the sellers who can produce them at least cost.

Thus, given the quantity produced and sold in a market equilibrium, the social planner cannot increase economic well-being by changing the allocation of consumption among buyers or the allocation of production among sellers.

But can the social planner raise total economic well-being by increasing or decreasing the quantity of the good? The answer is no, as stated in this third insight about market outcomes:

3. Free markets produce the quantity of goods that maximizes the sum of consumer and producer surplus.

To see why this is true, consider Figure 8. Recall that the demand curve reflects the value to buyers and that the supply curve reflects the cost to sellers. At quantities below the equilibrium level, the value to buyers exceeds the cost to sellers. In this region, increasing the quantity raises total surplus, and it continues to do so until the quantity reaches the equilibrium level. Beyond the equilibrium quantity, however, the value to buyers is less than the cost to sellers. Producing more than the equilibrium quantity would, therefore, lower total surplus.

These three insights about market outcomes tell us that the equilibrium of supply and demand maximizes the sum of consumer and producer surplus. In other words, the equilibrium outcome is an efficient allocation of resources. The job of the benevolent social planner is, therefore, very easy: He can leave the market outcome just as he finds it. This policy of leaving well enough alone goes by the French expression *laissez-faire*, which literally translated means "allow them to do."

We can now better appreciate Adam Smith's invisible hand of the marketplace, which we first discussed in Chapter 1. The benevolent social planner doesn't need to alter the market outcome because the invisible hand has already guided buyers and sellers to an allocation of the economy's resources that maximizes total surplus. This conclusion explains why economists often advocate free markets as the best way to organize economic activity.

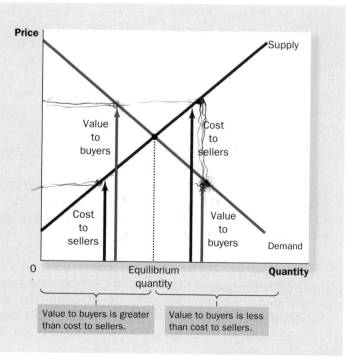

FIGURE 8

The Efficiency of the Equilibrium Quantity

At quantities less than the equilibrium quantity, the value to buyers exceeds the cost to sellers. At quantities greater than the equilibrium quantity, the cost to sellers exceeds the value to buyers. Therefore, the market equilibrium maximizes the sum of producer and consumer surplus.

IN THE NEWS

TICKET SCALPING

To allocate resources efficiently, an economy must get goods to the consumers who value them most highly. Sometimes this job falls to ticket scalpers.

Tickets? Supply Meets Demand on Sidewalk

By John Tierney

Ticket scalping has been very good to Kevin Thomas, and he makes no apologies. He sees himself as a classic American entrepreneur: a high school dropout from the Bronx who taught himself a trade, works seven nights a week, earns $40,000 a year, and at age twenty-six has $75,000 in savings, all by providing a public service outside New York's theaters and sports arenas.

He has just one complaint. "I've been busted about 30 times in the last year," he said one recent evening, just after making $280 at a Knicks game. "You learn to deal with it—I give the cops a fake name, and I pay the fines when I have to, but I don't think it's fair. I look at scalping like working as a stockbroker, buying low and selling high. If people are willing to pay me the money, what kind of problem is that?"

It is a significant problem to public officials in New York and New Jersey, who are cracking down on street scalpers like Mr. Thomas and on licensed ticket brokers. Undercover officers are enforcing new restrictions on reselling tickets at marked-up prices, and the attorneys general of the two states are pressing well-publicized cases against more than a dozen ticket brokers.

But economists tend to see scalping from Mr. Thomas's perspective. To them, the governments' crusade makes about as much sense as the old campaigns by Communist authorities against "profiteering." Economists argue that the restrictions inconvenience the public, reduce the audience for cultural and sports events, waste the police's time, deprive New York City of tens of millions of dollars of tax revenue, and actually drive up the cost of many tickets.

"It is always good politics to pose as defender of the poor by declaring high prices illegal," says William J. Baumol, the director of the C. V. Starr Center for Applied Economics at New York University. "I expect politicians to try to solve the AIDS crisis by declaring AIDS illegal as well. That would be harmless, because nothing would happen, but when you outlaw high prices you create real problems."

Dr. Baumol was one of the economists who came up with the idea of selling same-day Broadway tickets for half price at the TKTS booth in Times Square, which theater owners thought dangerously radical when the booth opened in 1973. But the owners have profited by finding a new clientele for tickets that would have gone unsold, an illustration of the free-market tenet that both buyers and sellers ultimately benefit when price is adjusted to meet demand.

Economists see another illustration of that lesson at the Museum of Modern Art, where people wait in line for up to two hours to buy tickets for the Matisse exhibit. But there is an alternative on the sidewalk: Scalpers who evade the police have been selling the $12.50 tickets to the show at prices ranging from $20 to $50.

The invisible hand at work

"You don't have to put a very high value on your time to pay $10 or $15 to avoid standing in line for two hours for a Matisse ticket," said Richard H. Thaler, an economist at Cornell University. "Some people think it's fairer to make everyone stand in line, but that forces everyone to engage in a totally unproductive activity, and it discriminates in favor of people who have the most free time. Scalping gives other people a chance, too. I can see no justification for outlawing it." . . .

Legalizing scalping, however, would not necessarily be good news for everyone. Mr. Thomas, for instance, fears that the extra competition might put him out of business. But after 16 years—he started at age ten outside of Yankee Stadium—he is thinking it might be time for a change anyway.

Source: *The New York Times,* December 26, 1992, p. A1. Copyright © 1992 by The New York Times Co. Reprinted by permission.

Case Study

SHOULD THERE BE A MARKET IN ORGANS?

On April 12, 2001, the front page of *The Boston Globe* ran the headline "How a Mother's Love Helped Save Two Lives." The newspaper told the story of Susan Stephens, a woman whose son needed a kidney transplant. When the doctor learned that the mother's kidney was not compatible, he proposed a novel solution: If Stephens donated one of her kidneys to a stranger, her son would move to the top of the kidney waiting list. The mother accepted the deal, and soon two patients had the transplant they were waiting for.

The ingenuity of the doctor's proposal and the nobility of the mother's act cannot be doubted. But the story raises many intriguing questions. If the mother could trade a kidney for a kidney, would the hospital allow her to trade a kidney for an expensive, experimental cancer treatment that she could not afford otherwise? Should she be allowed to exchange her kidney for free tuition for her son at the hospital's medical school? Should she be able to sell her kidney so she can use the cash to trade in her old Chevy for a new Lexus?

As a matter of public policy, people are not allowed to sell their organs. In essence, in the market for organs, the government has imposed a price ceiling of zero. The result, as with any binding price ceiling, is a shortage of the good. The deal in the Stephens case did not fall under this prohibition because no cash changed hands.

Many economists believe that there would be large benefits to allowing a free market in organs. People are born with two kidneys, but they usually need only one. Meanwhile, a few people suffer from illnesses that leave them without any working kidney. Despite the obvious gains from trade, the current situation is dire: The average wait for a kidney transplant is 3½ years, and about 6,000 Americans die every year because a kidney cannot be found. If those needing a kidney were allowed to buy one from those who have two, the price would rise to balance supply and demand. Sellers would be better off with the extra cash in their pockets. Buyers would be better off with the organ they need to save their lives. The shortage of kidneys would disappear.

Such a market would lead to an efficient allocation of resources, but critics of this plan worry about fairness. A market for organs, they argue, would benefit the rich at the expense of the poor, because organs would then be allocated to those most willing and able to pay. But you can also question the fairness of the current system. Now, most of us walk around with an extra organ that we don't really need, while some of our fellow citizens are dying to get one. Is that fair? ●

QuickQuiz Draw the supply and demand for turkey. In the equilibrium, show producer and consumer surplus. Explain why producing more turkey would lower total surplus.

IN THE NEWS

HOW PILGRIMS EMBRACED THE MARKET

The next time you sit down for Thanksgiving dinner, perhaps you should give thanks not only for the turkey on your plate but also for the economic system in which you live.

Thanksgiving Pays Homage to the Invisible Hand

By Caroline Baum

Most Americans think of Thanksgiving as a time to gather with friends and family and celebrate with a huge feast. If children know anything about the origins of the national holiday, declared each year by presidential proclamation, it's that the Pilgrims were grateful for a good harvest in their new land and set aside this day to give thanks.

What they don't know is that things weren't always so good for the Pilgrims, who came to the new world from England (via Holland) to escape religious persecution. Their first winters after they landed at Plymouth Rock in 1620 and established the Plymouth Bay colony were harsh. The weather was lousy and crop yields were poor. Half the Pilgrims died or returned to England.

Those who remained went hungry. Despite their deep religious convictions, the colonists took to stealing from one another. In the spring of 1623, following three grueling winters and widespread famine, Governor Bradford and the others "began to think how they might raise as much as they could, and obtain a better crop than they had done, that they might not still thus languish in misery," Bradford relates in his history.

One of the traditions the Pilgrims brought with them from England was something called "farming in common." The colonists pooled the fruits of their labor, and the harvest was rationed among them.

The idea that "the taking away of property, and bringing them into common community was found to breed too much confusion and discontent, and retard much employment that would have been to their benefit and comfort."

Young and able men resented working hard for other men and their wives, without any compensation.

So after three winters of starvation, Bradford instituted a new policy when it came time to plant in the spring of 1623. He set aside a plot of land for each family, allowing each to "plant for his own particular, and in that regard trust to them selves."

For the colonists, the results were nothing short of miraculous. The women went willingly into the field, carrying their young children with them. Those who previously claimed to be too ill or weak to work were eager to till their own soil. . . .

Yet it was no miracle. Without knowing it, Bradford and the Pilgrims discovered what Eastern Europe learned—the hard way—more than 350 years later: socialism doesn't work. Deprived of property rights and lacking economic incentives to work, produce and save, human beings behave in a predictable manner. . . .

Pretty soon, the colonists had more than enough food for their own needs and started to trade their excess corn for other commodities, such as furs.

After three winters of famine, the Pilgrims viewed their times of plenty as a stroke of good fortune when they were merely responding to market signals. Even before there was an official market, the invisible hand was at work.

Thanksgiving is a time to give thanks for our system of government, which allows the invisible hand to guide and protect us.

Source: Bloomberg News, (on-line at http://www.bloomberg.com), November 21, 2001. Reprinted with permission.

CONCLUSION: MARKET EFFICIENCY AND MARKET FAILURE

This chapter introduced the basic tools of welfare economics—consumer and producer surplus—and used them to evaluate the efficiency of free markets. We showed that the forces of supply and demand allocate resources efficiently. That is, even though each buyer and seller in a market is concerned only about his or her own welfare, they are together led by an invisible hand to an equilibrium that maximizes the total benefits to buyers and sellers.

A word of warning is in order. To conclude that markets are efficient, we made several assumptions about how markets work. When these assumptions do not hold, our conclusion that the market equilibrium is efficient may no longer be true. As we close this chapter, let's consider briefly two of the most important of these assumptions.

First, our analysis assumed that markets are perfectly competitive. In the world, however, competition is sometimes far from perfect. In some markets, a single buyer or seller (or a small group of them) may be able to control market prices. This ability to influence prices is called *market power.* Market power can cause markets to be inefficient because it keeps the price and quantity away from the equilibrium of supply and demand.

Second, our analysis assumed that the outcome in a market matters only to the buyers and sellers in that market. Yet, in the world, the decisions of buyers and sellers sometimes affect people who are not participants in the market at all. Pollution is the classic example of a market outcome that affects people not in the market. Such side effects, called *externalities,* cause welfare in a market to depend on more than just the value to the buyers and the cost to the sellers. Because buyers and sellers do not take these side effects into account when deciding how much to consume and produce, the equilibrium in a market can be inefficient from the standpoint of society as a whole.

Market power and externalities are examples of a general phenomenon called *market failure*—the inability of some unregulated markets to allocate resources efficiently. When markets fail, public policy can potentially remedy the problem and increase economic efficiency. Microeconomists devote much effort to studying when market failure is likely and what sorts of policies are best at correcting market failures. As you continue your study of economics, you will see that the tools of welfare economics developed here are readily adapted to that endeavor.

Despite the possibility of market failure, the invisible hand of the marketplace is extraordinarily important. In many markets, the assumptions we made in this chapter work well, and the conclusion of market efficiency applies directly. Moreover, our analysis of welfare economics and market efficiency can be used to shed light on the effects of various government policies. In the next two chapters we apply the tools we have just developed to study two important policy issues—the welfare effects of taxation and of international trade.

SUMMARY

- Consumer surplus equals buyers' willingness to pay for a good minus the amount they actually pay for it, and it measures the benefit buyers get from participating in a market. Consumer surplus can be computed by finding the area below the demand curve and above the price.

- Producer surplus equals the amount sellers receive for their goods minus their costs of production, and it measures the benefit sellers get from participating in a market. Producer surplus can be computed by finding the area below the price and above the supply curve.

- An allocation of resources that maximizes the sum of consumer and producer surplus is said to be efficient. Policymakers are often concerned with the efficiency, as well as the equity, of economic outcomes.

- The equilibrium of supply and demand maximizes the sum of consumer and producer surplus. That is, the invisible hand of the marketplace leads buyers and sellers to allocate resources efficiently.

- Markets do not allocate resources efficiently in the presence of market failures such as market power or externalities.

KEY CONCEPTS

welfare economics, p. 138
willingness to pay, p. 138
consumer surplus, p. 139

cost, p. 143
producer surplus, p. 144
efficiency, p. 148

equity, p. 148

QUESTIONS FOR REVIEW

1. Explain how buyers' willingness to pay, consumer surplus, and the demand curve are related.

2. Explain how sellers' costs, producer surplus, and the supply curve are related.

3. In a supply-and-demand diagram, show producer and consumer surplus in the market equilibrium.

4. What is efficiency? Is it the only goal of economic policymakers?

5. What does the invisible hand do?

6. Name two types of market failure. Explain why each may cause market outcomes to be inefficient.

PROBLEMS AND APPLICATIONS

1. An early freeze in California sours the lemon crop. What happens to consumer surplus in the market for lemons? What happens to consumer surplus in the market for lemonade? Illustrate your answers with diagrams.

2. Suppose the demand for French bread rises. What happens to producer surplus in the market for French bread? What happens to producer surplus in the market for flour? Illustrate your answer with diagrams.

3. It is a hot day, and Bert is thirsty. Here is the value he places on a bottle of water:

Value of first bottle	$7
Value of second bottle	5
Value of third bottle	3
Value of fourth bottle	1

    a. From this information, derive Bert's demand schedule. Graph his demand curve for bottled water.

    b. If the price of a bottle of water is $4, how many bottles does Bert buy? How much consumer surplus does Bert get from his purchases? Show Bert's consumer surplus in your graph.

    c. If the price falls to $2, how does quantity demanded change? How does Bert's consumer surplus change? Show these changes in your graph.

4. Ernie owns a water pump. Because pumping large amounts of water is harder than pumping small amounts, the cost of producing a bottle of water rises as he pumps more. Here is the cost he incurs to produce each bottle of water:

Cost of first bottle	$1
Cost of second bottle	3
Cost of third bottle	5
Cost of fourth bottle	7

    a. From this information, derive Ernie's supply schedule. Graph his supply curve for bottled water.

    b. If the price of a bottle of water is $4, how many bottles does Ernie produce and sell? How much producer surplus does Ernie get from these sales? Show Ernie's producer surplus in your graph.

    c. If the price rises to $6, how does quantity supplied change? How does Ernie's producer surplus change? Show these changes in your graph.

5. Consider a market in which Bert from Problem 3 is the buyer and Ernie from Problem 4 is the seller.

    a. Use Ernie's supply schedule and Bert's demand schedule to find the quantity supplied and quantity demanded at prices of $2, $4, and $6. Which of these prices brings supply and demand into equilibrium?

    b. What are consumer surplus, producer surplus, and total surplus in this equilibrium?

    c. If Ernie produced and Bert consumed one fewer bottle of water, what would happen to total surplus?

    d. If Ernie produced and Bert consumed one additional bottle of water, what would happen to total surplus?

6. The cost of producing stereo systems has fallen over the past several decades. Let's consider some implications of this fact.

    a. Use a supply-and-demand diagram to show the effect of falling production costs on the price and quantity of stereos sold.

    b. In your diagram, show what happens to consumer surplus and producer surplus.

    c. Suppose the supply of stereos is very elastic. Who benefits most from falling production costs—consumers or producers of stereos?

7. There are four consumers willing to pay the following amounts for haircuts:

    Jerry: $7   Oprah: $2   Ricki: $8   Montel: $5

There are four haircutting businesses with the following costs:

Firm A: $3   Firm B: $6   Firm C: $4   Firm D: $2

Each firm has the capacity to produce only one haircut. For efficiency, how many haircuts should be given? Which businesses should cut hair, and which consumers should have their hair cut? How large is the maximum possible total surplus?

8. Suppose a technological advance reduces the cost of making computers.
   a. Use a supply-and-demand diagram to show what happens to price, quantity, consumer surplus, and producer surplus in the market for computers.
   b. Computers and adding machines are substitutes. Use a supply-and-demand diagram to show what happens to price, quantity, consumer surplus, and producer surplus in the market for adding machines. Should adding machine producers be happy or sad by the technological advance in computers?
   c. Computers and software are complements. Use a supply-and-demand diagram to show what happens to price, quantity, consumer surplus, and producer surplus in the market for software. Should software producers be happy or sad about the technological advance in computers?
   d. Does this analysis help explain why software producer Bill Gates is one of the world's richest men?

9. Consider how health insurance affects the quantity of health care services performed. Suppose that the typical medical procedure has a cost of $100, yet a person with health insurance pays only $20 out-of-pocket when she chooses to have an additional procedure performed. Her insurance company pays the remaining $80. (The insurance company will recoup the $80 through higher premiums for everybody, but the share paid by this individual is small.)
   a. Draw the demand curve in the market for medical care. (In your diagram, the horizontal axis should represent the number of medical procedures.) Show the quantity of procedures demanded if each procedure has a price of $100.
   b. On your diagram, show the quantity of procedures demanded if consumers pay only $20 per procedure. If the cost of each procedure to society is truly $100, and if individuals have health insurance as just described, will the number of procedures performed maximize total surplus? Explain.
   c. Economists often blame the health insurance system for excessive use of medical care. Given your analysis, why might the use of care be viewed as "excessive"?
   d. What sort of policies might prevent this excessive use?

10. Many parts of California experienced a severe drought in the late 1980s and early 1990s.
    a. Use a diagram of the water market to show the effects of the drought on the equilibrium price and quantity of water.
    b. Many communities did not allow the price of water to change, however. What is the effect of this policy on the water market? Show on your diagram any surplus or shortage that arises.
    c. A 1991 op-ed piece in *The Wall Street Journal* stated that "all Los Angeles residents are required to cut their water usage by 10 percent as of March 1 and another 5 percent starting May 1, based on their 1986 consumption levels." The author criticized this policy on both efficiency and equity grounds, saying "not only does such a policy reward families who 'wasted' more water back in 1986, it does little to encourage consumers who could make more drastic reductions, [and] . . . punishes consumers who cannot so readily reduce their water use." In what way is the

Los Angeles system for allocating water inefficient? In what way does the system seem unfair?

d. Suppose instead that Los Angeles allowed the price of water to increase until the quantity demanded equaled the quantity supplied. Would the resulting allocation of water be more efficient? In your view, would it be more or less fair than the proportionate reductions in water use mentioned in the newspaper article? What could be done to make the market solution more fair?

http://   For more study tools, please visit http://mankiwXtra.swlearning.com.

APPLICATION: THE COSTS OF TAXATION

Taxes are often a source of heated political debate. In 1776 the anger of the American colonies over British taxes sparked the American Revolution. More than two centuries later Ronald Reagan was elected president on a platform of large cuts in personal income taxes, and during his eight years in the White House the top tax rate on income fell from 70 percent to 28 percent. In 1992 Bill Clinton was elected in part because incumbent George Bush had broken his 1988 campaign promise, "Read my lips: no new taxes." At least in this regard, the younger George Bush did not follow in his father's footsteps: As a candidate he promised a tax cut, and as president he made sure to deliver.

We began our study of taxes in Chapter 6. There we saw how a tax on a good affects its price and the quantity sold and how the forces of supply and demand divide the burden of a tax between buyers and sellers. In this chapter we extend this analysis and look at how taxes affect welfare, the economic well-being of participants in a market.

The effects of taxes on welfare might at first seem obvious. The government enacts taxes to raise revenue, and that revenue must come out of someone's pocket. As we saw in Chapter 6, both buyers and sellers are worse off when a good is

*"You know, the idea of taxation **with** representation doesn't appeal to me very much, either."*

taxed: A tax raises the price buyers pay and lowers the price sellers receive. Yet to understand fully how taxes affect economic well-being, we must compare the reduced welfare of buyers and sellers to the amount of revenue the government raises. The tools of consumer and producer surplus allow us to make this comparison. The analysis will show that the costs of taxes to buyers and sellers exceeds the revenue raised by the government.

THE DEADWEIGHT LOSS OF TAXATION

We begin by recalling one of the surprising lessons from Chapter 6: It does not matter whether a tax on a good is levied on buyers or sellers of the good. When a tax is levied on buyers, the demand curve shifts downward by the size of the tax; when it is levied on sellers, the supply curve shifts upward by that amount. In either case, when the tax is enacted, the price paid by buyers rises, and the price received by sellers falls. In the end, buyers and sellers share the burden of the tax, regardless of how it is levied.

Figure 1 shows these effects. To simplify our discussion, this figure does not show a shift in either the supply or demand curve, although one curve must shift. Which curve shifts depends on whether the tax is levied on sellers (the supply curve shifts) or buyers (the demand curve shifts). In this chapter, we can simplify the graphs by not bothering to show the shift. The key result for our purposes here is that the tax places a wedge between the price buyers pay and the price sellers receive. Because of this tax wedge, the quantity sold falls below the level that would be sold without a tax. In other words, a tax on a good causes the size of the market for the good to shrink. These results should be familiar from Chapter 6.

FIGURE 1

The Effects of a Tax

A tax on a good places a wedge between the price that buyers pay and the price that sellers receive. The quantity of the good sold falls.

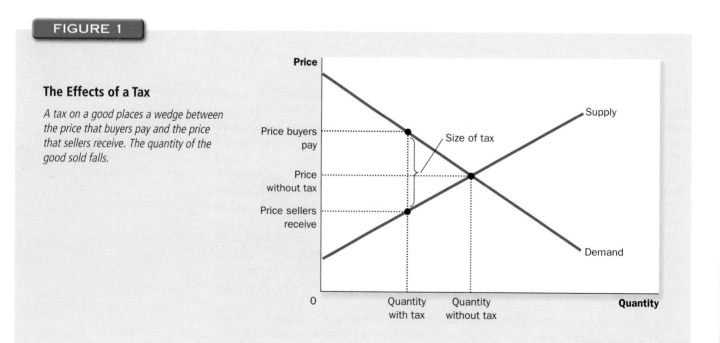

How a Tax Affects Market Participants

Now let's use the tools of welfare economics to measure the gains and losses from a tax on a good. To do this, we must take into account how the tax affects buyers, sellers, and the government. The benefit received by buyers in a market is measured by consumer surplus—the amount buyers are willing to pay for the good minus the amount they actually pay for it. The benefit received by sellers in a market is measured by producer surplus—the amount sellers receive for the good minus their costs. These are precisely the measures of economic welfare we used in Chapter 7.

What about the third interested party, the government? If T is the size of the tax and Q is the quantity of the good sold, then the government gets total tax revenue of $T \times Q$. It can use this tax revenue to provide services, such as roads, police, and public education, or to help the needy. Therefore, to analyze how taxes affect economic well-being, we use tax revenue to measure the government's benefit from the tax. Keep in mind, however, that this benefit actually accrues not to government but to those on whom the revenue is spent.

Figure 2 shows that the government's tax revenue is represented by the rectangle between the supply and demand curves. The height of this rectangle is the size of the tax, T, and the width of the rectangle is the quantity of the good sold, Q. Because a rectangle's area is its height times its width, this rectangle's area is $T \times Q$, which equals the tax revenue.

Welfare without a Tax To see how a tax affects welfare, we begin by considering welfare before the government has imposed a tax. Figure 3 (p. 162) shows the supply-and-demand diagram and marks the key areas with the letters A through F.

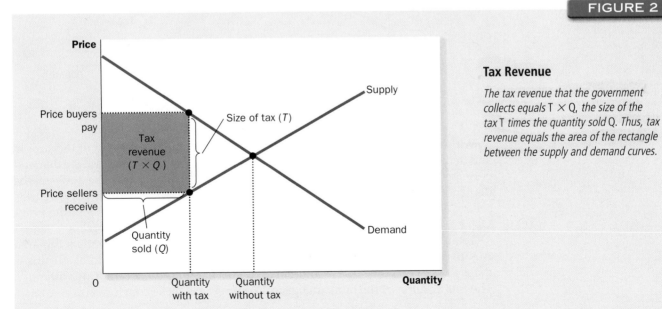

FIGURE 2

Tax Revenue

The tax revenue that the government collects equals T × Q, the size of the tax T times the quantity sold Q. Thus, tax revenue equals the area of the rectangle between the supply and demand curves.

FIGURE 3

How a Tax Affects Welfare

A tax on a good reduces consumer surplus (by the area B + C) and producer surplus (by the area D + E). Because the fall in producer and consumer surplus exceeds tax revenue (area B + D), the tax is said to impose a deadweight loss (area C + E).

	Without Tax	With Tax	Change
Consumer Surplus	A + B + C	A	−(B + C)
Producer Surplus	D + E + F	F	−(D + E)
Tax Revenue	None	B + D	+(B + D)
Total Surplus	A + B + C + D + E + F	A + B + D + F	−(C + E)

The area C + E shows the fall in total surplus and is the deadweight loss of the tax.

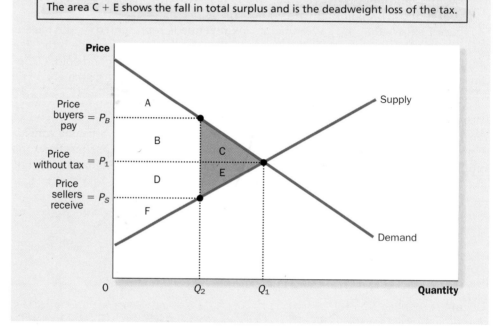

Without a tax, the price and quantity are found at the intersection of the supply and demand curves. The price is P_1, and the quantity sold is Q_1. Because the demand curve reflects buyers' willingness to pay, consumer surplus is the area between the demand curve and the price, A + B + C. Similarly, because the supply curve reflects sellers' costs, producer surplus is the area between the supply curve and the price, D + E + F. In this case, because there is no tax, tax revenue equals zero.

Total surplus—the sum of consumer and producer surplus—equals the area A + B + C + D + E + F. In other words, as we saw in Chapter 7, total surplus is the area between the supply and demand curves up to the equilibrium quantity. The first column of the table in Figure 3 summarizes these conclusions.

Welfare with a Tax   Now consider welfare after the tax is enacted. The price paid by buyers rises from P_1 to P_B, so consumer surplus now equals only area A (the area below the demand curve and above the buyer's price). The price received by sellers falls from P_1 to P_S, so producer surplus now equals only area F (the area above the supply curve and below the seller's price). The quantity sold falls from Q_1 to Q_2, and the government collects tax revenue equal to the area B + D.

To compute total surplus with the tax, we add consumer surplus, producer surplus, and tax revenue. Thus, we find that total surplus is area A + B + D + F. The second column of the table provides a summary.

Changes in Welfare   We can now see the effects of the tax by comparing welfare before and after the tax is enacted. The third column in the table in Figure 3 shows the changes. The tax causes consumer surplus to fall by the area B + C and producer surplus to fall by the area D + E. Tax revenue rises by the area B + D. Not surprisingly, the tax makes buyers and sellers worse off and the government better off.

The change in total welfare includes the change in consumer surplus (which is negative), the change in producer surplus (which is also negative), and the change in tax revenue (which is positive). When we add these three pieces together, we find that total surplus in the market falls by the area C + E. Thus, *the losses to buyers and sellers from a tax exceed the revenue raised by the government*. The fall in total surplus that results when a tax (or some other policy) distorts a market outcome is called the **deadweight loss**. The area C + E measures the size of the deadweight loss.

To understand why taxes impose deadweight losses, recall one of the *Ten Principles of Economics* in Chapter 1: People respond to incentives. In Chapter 7 we saw that markets normally allocate scarce resources efficiently. That is, the equilibrium of supply and demand maximizes the total surplus of buyers and sellers in a market. When a tax raises the price to buyers and lowers the price to sellers, however, it gives buyers an incentive to consume less and sellers an incentive to produce less than they otherwise would. As buyers and sellers respond to these incentives, the size of the market shrinks below its optimum. Thus, because taxes distort incentives, they cause markets to allocate resources inefficiently.

deadweight loss
the fall in total surplus that results from a market distortion, such as a tax

Deadweight Losses and the Gains from Trade

To gain some intuition for why taxes result in deadweight losses, consider an example. Imagine that Joe cleans Jane's house each week for $100. The opportunity cost of Joe's time is $80, and the value of a clean house to Jane is $120. Thus, Joe and Jane each receive a $20 benefit from their deal. The total surplus of $40 measures the gains from trade in this particular transaction.

Now suppose that the government levies a $50 tax on the providers of cleaning services. There is now no price that Jane can pay Joe that will leave both of them better off after paying the tax. The most Jane would be willing to pay is $120, but then Joe would be left with only $70 after paying the tax, which is less than his $80 opportunity cost. Conversely, for Joe to receive his opportunity cost of $80, Jane would need to pay $130, which is above the $120 value she places on a clean house. As a result, Jane and Joe cancel their arrangement. Joe goes without the income, and Jane lives in a dirtier house.

The tax has made Joe and Jane worse off by a total of $40, because they have lost this amount of surplus. At the same time, the government collects no revenue from Joe and Jane because they decide to cancel their arrangement. The $40 is pure deadweight loss: It is a loss to buyers and sellers in a market not offset by an increase in government revenue. From this example, we can see the ultimate source of deadweight losses: *Taxes cause deadweight losses because they prevent buyers and sellers from realizing some of the gains from trade.*

The area of the triangle between the supply and demand curves (area C + E in Figure 3) measures these losses. This loss can be seen most easily in Figure 4 by recalling that the demand curve reflects the value of the good to consumers and that the supply curve reflects the costs of producers. When the tax raises the price to buyers to P_B and lowers the price to sellers to P_S, the marginal buyers and sellers leave the market, so the quantity sold falls from Q_1 to Q_2. Yet, as the figure shows, the value of the good to these buyers still exceeds the cost to these sellers. As in our example with Joe and Jane, the gains from trade—the difference between buyers' value and sellers' cost—is less than the tax. Thus, these trades do not get made once the tax is imposed. The deadweight loss is the surplus lost because the tax discourages these mutually advantageous trades.

QuickQuiz Draw the supply and demand curve for cookies. If the government imposes a tax on cookies, show what happens to the quantity sold, the price paid by buyers, and the price paid by sellers. In your diagram, show the deadweight loss from the tax. Explain the meaning of the deadweight loss.

THE DETERMINANTS OF THE DEADWEIGHT LOSS

What determines whether the deadweight loss from a tax is large or small? The answer is the price elasticities of supply and demand, which measure how much the quantity supplied and quantity demanded respond to changes in the price.

FIGURE 4

The Deadweight Loss

When the government imposes a tax on a good, the quantity sold falls from Q_1 to Q_2. As a result, some of the potential gains from trade among buyers and sellers do not get realized. These lost gains from trade create the deadweight loss.

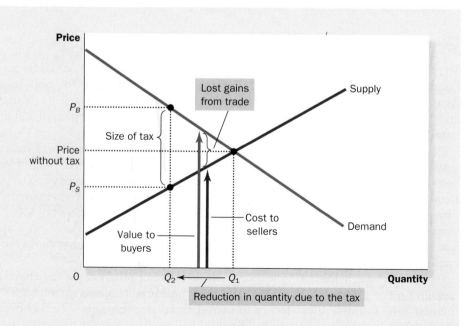

Let's consider first how the elasticity of supply affects the size of the dead-weight loss. In the top two panels of Figure 5, the demand curve and the size of the tax are the same. The only difference in these figures is the elasticity of the supply curve. In panel (a), the supply curve is relatively inelastic: Quantity supplied

FIGURE 5

Tax Distortions and Elasticities

In panels (a) and (b), the demand curve and the size of the tax are the same, but the price elasticity of supply is different. Notice that the more elastic the supply curve, the larger the deadweight loss of the tax. In panels (c) and (d), the supply curve and the size of the tax are the same, but the price elasticity of demand is different. Notice that the more elastic the demand curve, the larger the deadweight loss of the tax.

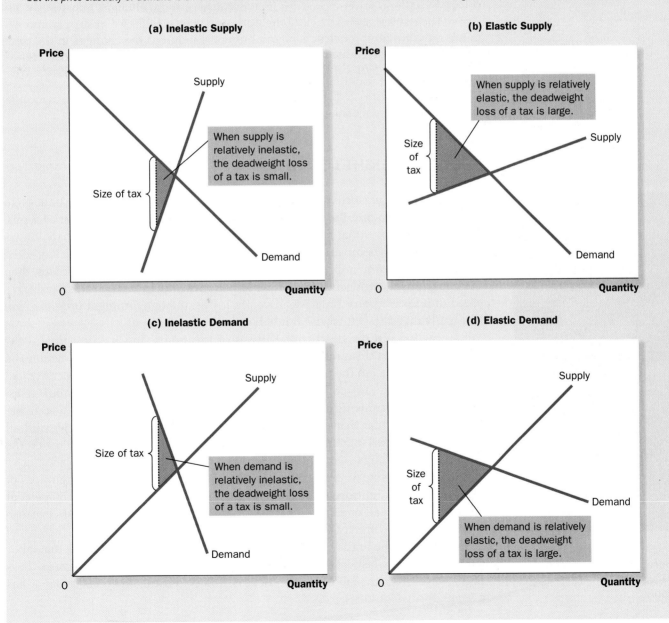

responds only slightly to changes in the price. In panel (b), the supply curve is relatively elastic: Quantity supplied responds substantially to changes in the price. Notice that the deadweight loss, the area of the triangle between the supply and demand curves, is larger when the supply curve is more elastic.

Similarly, the bottom two panels of Figure 5 show how the elasticity of demand affects the size of the deadweight loss. Here the supply curve and the size of the tax are held constant. In panel (c) the demand curve is relatively inelastic, and the deadweight loss is small. In panel (d) the demand curve is more elastic, and the deadweight loss from the tax is larger.

The lesson from this figure is easy to explain. A tax has a deadweight loss because it induces buyers and sellers to change their behavior. The tax raises the price paid by buyers, so they consume less. At the same time, the tax lowers the price received by sellers, so they produce less. Because of these changes in behavior, the size of the market shrinks below the optimum. The elasticities of supply and demand measure how much sellers and buyers respond to the changes in the price and, therefore, determine how much the tax distorts the market outcome. Hence, *the greater the elasticities of supply and demand, the greater the deadweight loss of a tax.*

Case Study

THE DEADWEIGHT LOSS DEBATE

Supply, demand, elasticity, deadweight loss—all this economic theory is enough to make your head spin. But believe it or not, these ideas go to the heart of a profound political question: How big should the government be? The debate hinges on these concepts because the larger the deadweight loss of taxation, the larger the cost of any government program. If taxation entails large deadweight losses, then these losses are a strong argument for a leaner government that does less and taxes less. But if taxes impose small deadweight losses, then government programs are less costly than they otherwise might be.

So how big are the deadweight losses of taxation? This is a question about which economists disagree. To see the nature of this disagreement, consider the most important tax in the U.S. economy—the tax on labor. The Social Security tax, the Medicare tax, and, to a large extent, the federal income tax are labor taxes. Many state governments also tax labor earnings. A labor tax places a wedge between the wage that firms pay and the wage that workers receive. If we add all forms of labor taxes together, the *marginal tax rate* on labor income—the tax on the last dollar of earnings—is almost 50 percent for many workers.

Although the size of the labor tax is easy to determine, the deadweight loss of this tax is less straightforward. Economists disagree about whether this 50 percent labor tax has a small or a large deadweight loss. This disagreement arises because economists hold different views about the elasticity of labor supply.

Economists who argue that labor taxes are not very distorting believe that labor supply is fairly inelastic. Most people, they claim, would work full-time regardless of the wage. If so, the labor supply curve is almost vertical, and a tax on labor has a small deadweight loss.

"Here's what I think about the elasticity of labor supply."

Economists who argue that labor taxes are highly distorting believe that labor supply is more elastic. They admit that some groups of workers may supply their labor inelastically but claim that many other groups respond more to incentives. Here are some examples:

- Many workers can adjust the number of hours they work—for instance, by working overtime. The higher the wage, the more hours they choose to work.
- Some families have second earners—often married women with children—with some discretion over whether to do unpaid work at home or paid work in the marketplace. When deciding whether to take a job, these second earners compare the benefits of being at home (including savings on the cost of child care) with the wages they could earn.
- Many of the elderly can choose when to retire, and their decisions are partly based on the wage. Once they are retired, the wage determines their incentive to work part-time.
- Some people consider engaging in illegal economic activity, such as the drug trade, or working at jobs that pay "under the table" to evade taxes. Economists call this the *underground economy*. In deciding whether to work in the underground economy or at a legitimate job, these potential criminals compare what they can earn by breaking the law with the wage they can earn legally.

In each of these cases, the quantity of labor supplied responds to the wage (the price of labor). Thus, the decisions of these workers are distorted when their labor earnings are taxed. Labor taxes encourage workers to work fewer hours, second earners to stay at home, the elderly to retire early, and the unscrupulous to enter the underground economy.

These two views of labor taxation persist to this day. Indeed, whenever you see two political candidates debating whether the government should provide more services or reduce the tax burden, keep in mind that part of the disagreement may rest on different views about the elasticity of labor supply and the deadweight loss of taxation. ●

QuickQuiz The demand for beer is more elastic than the demand for milk. Would a tax on beer or a tax on milk have larger deadweight loss? Why?

DEADWEIGHT LOSS AND TAX REVENUE AS TAXES VARY

Taxes rarely stay the same for long periods of time. Policymakers in local, state, and federal governments are always considering raising one tax or lowering another. Here we consider what happens to the deadweight loss and tax revenue when the size of a tax changes.

HENRY GEORGE AND THE LAND TAX

Is there an ideal tax? Henry George, the nineteenth-century American economist and social philosopher, thought so. In his 1879 book *Progress and Poverty*, George argued that the government should raise all its revenue from a tax on land. This "single tax" was, he claimed, both equitable and efficient. George's ideas won him a large political following, and in 1886 he lost a close race for mayor of New York City (although he finished well ahead of Republican candidate Theodore Roosevelt).

George's proposal to tax land was motivated largely by a concern over the distribution of economic well-being. He deplored the "shocking contrast between monstrous wealth and debasing want" and thought landowners benefited more than they should from the rapid growth in the overall economy.

George's arguments for the land tax can be understood using the tools of modern economics. Consider first supply and demand in the market for renting land. As immigration causes the population to rise and technological progress causes incomes to grow, the demand for land rises over time. Yet because the amount of land is fixed, the supply is perfectly inelastic. Rapid increases in demand together with inelastic supply lead to large increases in the equilibrium rents on land, so that economic growth makes rich landowners even richer.

Henry George

Now consider the incidence of a tax on land. As we first saw in Chapter 6, the burden of a tax falls more heavily on the side of the market that is less elastic. A tax on land takes this principle to an extreme. Because the elasticity of supply is zero, the landowners bear the entire burden of the tax.

Consider next the question of efficiency. As we just discussed, the deadweight loss of a tax depends on the elasticities of supply and demand. Again, a tax on land is an extreme case. Because supply is perfectly inelastic, a tax on land does not alter the market allocation. There is no deadweight loss, and the government's tax revenue exactly equals the loss of the landowners.

Although taxing land may look attractive in theory, it is not as straightforward in practice as it may appear. For a tax on land not to distort economic incentives, it must be a tax on raw land. Yet the value of land often comes from improvements, such as clearing trees, providing sewers, and building roads. Unlike the supply of raw land, the supply of improvements has an elasticity greater than zero. If a land tax were imposed on improvements, it would distort incentives. Landowners would respond by devoting fewer resources to improving their land.

Today, few economists support George's proposal for a single tax on land. Not only is taxing improvements a potential problem, but the tax would not raise enough revenue to pay for the much larger government we have today. Yet many of George's arguments remain valid. Here is the assessment of the eminent economist Milton Friedman a century after George's book:

"In my opinion, the least bad tax is the property tax on the unimproved value of land, the Henry George argument of many, many years ago."

Figure 6 shows the effects of a small, medium, and large tax, holding constant the market's supply and demand curves. The deadweight loss—the reduction in total surplus that results when the tax reduces the size of a market below the optimum—equals the area of the triangle between the supply and demand curves. For the small tax in panel (a), the area of the deadweight loss triangle is quite small. But as the size of a tax rises in panels (b) and (c), the deadweight loss grows larger and larger.

Indeed, the deadweight loss of a tax rises even more rapidly than the size of the tax. The reason is that the deadweight loss is an area of a triangle, and an area of a triangle depends on the *square* of its size. If we double the size of a tax, for instance, the base and height of the triangle double, so the deadweight loss rises by a factor of 4. If we triple the size of a tax, the base and height triple, so the deadweight loss rises by a factor of 9.

FIGURE 6

Deadweight Loss and Tax Revenue from Three Taxes of Different Size

The deadweight loss is the reduction in total surplus due to the tax. Tax revenue is the amount of the tax times the amount of the good sold. In panel (a), a small tax has a small deadweight loss and raises a small amount of revenue. In panel (b), a somewhat larger tax has a larger deadweight loss and raises a larger amount of revenue. In panel (c), a very large tax has a very large deadweight loss, but because it has reduced the size of the market so much, the tax raises only a small amount of revenue.

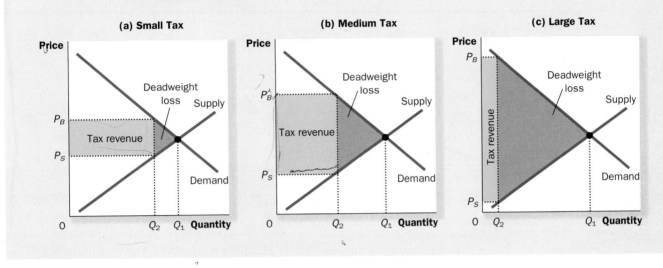

The government's tax revenue is the size of the tax times the amount of the good sold. As Figure 6 shows, tax revenue equals the area of the rectangle between the supply and demand curves. For the small tax in panel (a), tax revenue is small. As the size of a tax rises from panel (a) to panel (b), tax revenue grows. But as the size of the tax rises further from panel (b) to panel (c), tax revenue falls because the higher tax drastically reduces the size of the market. For a very large tax, no revenue would be raised, because people would stop buying and selling the good altogether.

Figure 7 (p. 170) summarizes these results. In panel (a) we see that as the size of a tax increases, its deadweight loss quickly gets larger. By contrast, panel (b) shows that tax revenue first rises with the size of the tax; but then, as the tax gets larger, the market shrinks so much that tax revenue starts to fall.

Case Study

THE LAFFER CURVE AND SUPPLY-SIDE ECONOMICS

One day in 1974, economist Arthur Laffer sat in a Washington restaurant with some prominent journalists and politicians. He took out a napkin and drew a figure on it to show how tax rates affect tax revenue. It looked much like panel (b) of our Figure 7. Laffer then suggested that the United States was on the downward-sloping side of this curve. Tax rates were so high, he argued, that reducing them would actually raise tax revenue.

FIGURE 7

How Deadweight Loss and Tax Revenue Vary with the Size of a Tax

Panel (a) shows that as the size of a tax grows larger, the deadweight loss grows larger. Panel (b) shows that tax revenue first rises, then falls. This relationship is sometimes called the Laffer curve.

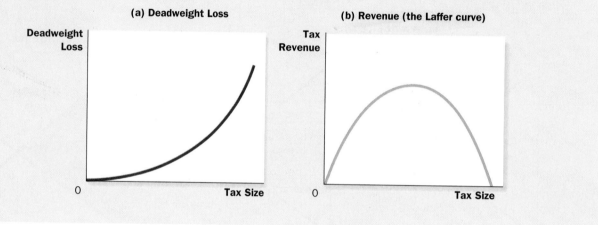

Most economists were skeptical of Laffer's suggestion. The idea that a cut in tax rates could raise tax revenue was correct as a matter of economic theory, but there was more doubt about whether it would do so in practice. There was little evidence for Laffer's view that U.S. tax rates had in fact reached such extreme levels.

Nonetheless, the *Laffer curve* (as it became known) captured the imagination of Ronald Reagan. David Stockman, budget director in the first Reagan administration, offers the following story:

> [Reagan] had once been on the Laffer curve himself. "I came into the Big Money making pictures during World War II," he would always say. At that time the wartime income surtax hit 90 percent. "You could only make four pictures and then you were in the top bracket," he would continue. "So we all quit working after four pictures and went off to the country." High tax rates caused less work. Low tax rates caused more. His experience proved it.

When Reagan ran for president in 1980, he made cutting taxes part of his platform. Reagan argued that taxes were so high that they were discouraging hard work. He argued that lower taxes would give people the proper incentive to work, which would raise economic well-being and perhaps even tax revenue. Because the cut in tax rates was intended to encourage people to increase the quantity of labor they supplied, the views of Laffer and Reagan became known as *supply-side economics*.

Subsequent history failed to confirm Laffer's conjecture that lower tax rates would raise tax revenue. When Reagan cut taxes after he was elected, the result was less tax revenue, not more. Revenue from personal income taxes (per person, adjusted for inflation) fell by 9 percent from 1980 to 1984, even though average

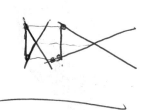

income (per person, adjusted for inflation) grew by 4 percent over this period. The tax cut, together with policymakers' unwillingness to restrain spending, began a long period during which the government spent more than it collected in taxes. Throughout Reagan's two terms in office, and for many years thereafter, the government ran large budget deficits.

Yet Laffer's argument is not completely without merit. Although an overall cut in tax rates normally reduces revenue, some taxpayers at some times may be on the wrong side of the Laffer curve. In the 1980s, tax revenue collected from the richest Americans, who face the highest tax rates, did rise when their taxes were cut. The idea that cutting taxes can raise revenue may be correct if applied to those taxpayers facing the highest tax rates. In addition, Laffer's argument may be more plausible when applied to other countries, where tax rates are much higher than in the United States. In Sweden in the early 1980s, for instance, the typical worker faced a marginal tax rate of about 80 percent. Such a high tax rate provides a substantial disincentive to work. Studies have suggested that Sweden would indeed have raised more tax revenue if it had lowered its tax rates.

These ideas arise frequently in political debate. When Bill Clinton moved into the White House in 1993, he increased the federal income tax rates on high-income taxpayers to about 40 percent. Some economists criticized the policy, arguing that the plan would not yield as much revenue as the Clinton administration estimated. They claimed that the administration did not fully take into account how taxes alter behavior. Conversely, when Bob Dole challenged Bill Clinton in the election of 1996, Dole proposed cutting personal income taxes. Although Dole rejected the idea that tax cuts would completely pay for themselves, he did claim that 28 percent of the tax cut would be recouped because lower tax rates would lead to more rapid economic growth. Economists debated whether Dole's 28 percent projection was reasonable, excessively optimistic, or (as Laffer might suggest) excessively pessimistic.

Policymakers disagree about these issues in part because they disagree about the size of the relevant elasticities. The more elastic that supply and demand are in any market, the more taxes in that market distort behavior, and the more likely it is that a tax cut will raise tax revenue. There is no debate, however, about the general lesson: How much revenue the government gains or loses from a tax change cannot be computed just by looking at tax rates. It also depends on how the tax change affects people's behavior. ●

QuickQuiz If the government doubles the tax on gasoline, can you be sure that revenue from the gasoline tax will rise? Can you be sure that the deadweight loss from the gasoline tax will rise? Explain.

CONCLUSION

Taxes, Oliver Wendell Holmes once said, are the price we pay for a civilized society. Indeed, our society cannot exist without some form of taxes. We all expect the government to provide us certain services, such as roads, parks, police, and national defense. These public services require tax revenue.

This chapter has shed some light on how high the price of civilized society can be. One of the *Ten Principles of Economics* discussed in Chapter 1 is that markets are usually a good way to organize economic activity. When the government imposes taxes on buyers or sellers of a good, however, society loses some of the benefits of market efficiency. Taxes are costly to market participants not only because taxes transfer resources from those participants to the government, but also because they alter incentives and distort market outcomes.

SUMMARY

- A tax on a good reduces the welfare of buyers and sellers of the good, and the reduction in consumer and producer surplus usually exceeds the revenue raised by the government. The fall in total surplus—the sum of consumer surplus, producer surplus, and tax revenue—is called the deadweight loss of the tax.

- Taxes have deadweight losses because they cause buyers to consume less and sellers to produce less, and this change in behavior shrinks the size of the market below the level that maximizes total surplus. Because the elasticities of supply and demand measure how much market participants respond to market conditions, larger elasticities imply larger deadweight losses.

- As a tax grows larger, it distorts incentives more, and its deadweight loss grows larger. Tax revenue first rises with the size of a tax. Eventually, however, a larger tax reduces tax revenue because it reduces the size of the market.

KEY CONCEPTS

deadweight loss, p. 163

QUESTIONS FOR REVIEW

1. What happens to consumer and producer surplus when the sale of a good is taxed? How does the change in consumer and producer surplus compare to the tax revenue? Explain.

2. Draw a supply-and-demand diagram with a tax on the sale of the good. Show the deadweight loss. Show the tax revenue.

3. How do the elasticities of supply and demand affect the deadweight loss of a tax? Why do they have this effect?

4. Why do experts disagree about whether labor taxes have small or large deadweight losses?

5. What happens to the deadweight loss and tax revenue when a tax is increased?

PROBLEMS AND APPLICATIONS

1. The market for pizza is characterized by a downward-sloping demand curve and an upward-sloping supply curve.
   a. Draw the competitive market equilibrium. Label the price, quantity, consumer surplus, and producer surplus. Is there any deadweight loss? Explain.
   b. Suppose that the government forces each pizzeria to pay a $1 tax on each pizza sold. Illustrate the effect of this tax on the pizza market, being sure to label the consumer surplus, producer surplus, government revenue, and deadweight loss. How does each area compare to the pre-tax case?
   c. If the tax were removed, pizza eaters and sellers would be better off, but the government would lose tax revenue. Suppose that consumers and producers voluntarily transferred some of their gains to the government. Could all parties (including the government) be better off than they were

with a tax? Explain using the labeled areas in your graph.

2. Evaluate the following two statements. Do you agree? Why or why not?
   a. "If the government taxes land, wealthy landowners will pass the tax on to their poorer renters."
   b. "If the government taxes apartment buildings, wealthy landlords will pass the tax on to their poorer renters."

3. Evaluate the following two statements. Do you agree? Why or why not?
   a. "A tax that has no deadweight loss cannot raise any revenue for the government."
   b. "A tax that raises no revenue for the government cannot have any deadweight loss."

4. Consider the market for rubber bands.
   a. If this market has very elastic supply and very inelastic demand, how would the burden of a tax on rubber bands be shared between consumers and producers? Use the tools of consumer surplus and producer surplus in your answer.
   b. If this market has very inelastic supply and very elastic demand, how would the burden of a tax on rubber bands be shared between consumers and producers? Contrast your answer with your answer to part (a).

5. Suppose that the government imposes a tax on heating oil.
   a. Would the deadweight loss from this tax likely be greater in the first year after it is imposed or in the fifth year? Explain.
   b. Would the revenue collected from this tax likely be greater in the first year after it is imposed or in the fifth year? Explain.

6. After economics class one day, your friend suggests that taxing food would be a good way to raise revenue because the demand for food is quite inelastic. In what sense is taxing food a "good" way to raise revenue? In what sense is it not a "good" way to raise revenue?

7. Senator Daniel Patrick Moynihan once introduced a bill that would levy a 10,000 percent tax on certain hollow-tipped bullets.
   a. Do you expect that this tax would raise much revenue? Why or why not?

   b. Even if the tax would raise no revenue, what might be Senator Moynihan's reason for proposing it?

8. The government places a tax on the purchase of socks.
   a. Illustrate the effect of this tax on equilibrium price and quantity in the sock market. Identify the following areas both before and after the imposition of the tax: total spending by consumers, total revenue for producers, and government tax revenue.
   b. Does the price received by producers rise or fall? Can you tell whether total receipts for producers rise or fall? Explain.
   c. Does the price paid by consumers rise or fall? Can you tell whether total spending by consumers rises or falls? Explain carefully. (Hint: Think about elasticity.) If total consumer spending falls, does consumer surplus rise? Explain.

9. Suppose the government currently raises $100 million through a $0.01 tax on widgets, and another $100 million through a $0.10 tax on gadgets. If the government doubled the tax rate on widgets and eliminated the tax on gadgets, would it raise more money than today, less money, or the same amount of money? Explain.

10. Most states tax the purchase of new cars. Suppose that New Jersey currently requires car dealers to pay the state $100 for each car sold, and plans to increase the tax to $150 per car next year.
    a. Illustrate the effect of this tax increase on the quantity of cars sold in New Jersey, the price paid by consumers, and the price received by producers.
    b. Create a table that shows the levels of consumer surplus, producer surplus, government revenue, and total surplus both before and after the tax increase.
    c. What is the change in government revenue? Is it positive or negative?
    d. What is the change in deadweight loss? Is it positive or negative?
    e. Give one reason why the demand for cars in New Jersey might be fairly elastic. Does this make the additional tax more or less likely to increase government revenue? How might states try to reduce the elasticity of demand?

11. Several years ago the British government imposed a "poll tax" that required each person to pay a flat amount to the government independent of his or her income or wealth. What is the effect of such a tax on economic efficiency? What is the effect on economic equity? Do you think this was a popular tax?

12. This chapter analyzed the welfare effects of a tax on a good. Consider now the opposite policy. Suppose that the government *subsidizes* a good: For each unit of the good sold, the government pays $2 to the buyer. How does the subsidy affect consumer surplus, producer surplus, tax revenue, and total surplus? Does a subsidy lead to a deadweight loss? Explain.

13. (This problem uses some high school algebra and is challenging.) Suppose that a market is described by the following supply and demand equations:

$$Q^S = 2P$$
$$Q^D = 300 - P$$

a. Solve for the equilibrium price and the equilibrium quantity.

b. Suppose that a tax of T is placed on buyers, so the new demand equation is

$$Q^D = 300 - (P + T).$$

Solve for the new equilibrium. What happens to the price received by sellers, the price paid by buyers, and the quantity sold?

c. Tax revenue is $T \times Q$. Use your answer to part (b) to solve for tax revenue as a function of T. Graph this relationship for T between 0 and 300.

d. The deadweight loss of a tax is the area of the triangle between the supply and demand curves. Recalling that the area of a triangle is $1/2 \times$ base $\times$ height, solve for deadweight loss as a function of T. Graph this relationship for T between 0 and 300. (Hint: Looking sideways, the base of the deadweight loss triangle is T, and the height is the difference between the quantity sold with the tax and the quantity sold without the tax.)

e. The government now levies a tax on this good of $200 per unit. Is this a good policy? Why or why not? Can you propose a better policy?

http://

For more study tools, please visit http://mankiwXtra.swlearning.com.

APPLICATION: INTERNATIONAL TRADE

If you check the labels on the clothes you are now wearing, you will probably find that some of your clothes were made in another country. A century ago the textiles and clothing industry was a major part of the U.S. economy, but that is no longer the case. Faced with foreign competitors that could produce quality goods at low cost, many U.S. firms found it increasingly difficult to produce and sell textiles and clothing at a profit. As a result, they laid off their workers and shut down their factories. Today, much of the textiles and clothing that Americans consume is imported from abroad.

The story of the textiles industry raises important questions for economic policy: How does international trade affect economic well-being? Who gains and who loses from free trade among countries, and how do the gains compare to the losses?

Chapter 3 introduced the study of international trade by applying the principle of comparative advantage. According to this principle, all countries can benefit from trading with one another because trade allows each country to specialize in doing what it does best. But the analysis in Chapter 3 was incomplete. It did not explain how the international marketplace achieves these gains from trade or how the gains are distributed among various economic actors.

We now return to the study of international trade and take up these questions. Over the past several chapters, we have developed many tools for analyzing how markets work: supply, demand, equilibrium, consumer surplus, producer surplus, and so on. With these tools we can learn more about the effects of international trade on economic well-being.

THE DETERMINANTS OF TRADE

Consider the market for steel. The steel market is well suited to examining the gains and losses from international trade: Steel is made in many countries around the world, and there is much world trade in steel. Moreover, the steel market is one in which policymakers often consider (and sometimes implement) trade restrictions to protect domestic steel producers from foreign competitors. We examine here the steel market in the imaginary country of Isoland.

The Equilibrium without Trade

As our story begins, the Isolandian steel market is isolated from the rest of the world. By government decree, no one in Isoland is allowed to import or export steel, and the penalty for violating the decree is so large that no one dares try.

Because there is no international trade, the market for steel in Isoland consists solely of Isolandian buyers and sellers. As Figure 1 shows, the domestic price adjusts to balance the quantity supplied by domestic sellers and the quantity

FIGURE 1

The Equilibrium without International Trade

When an economy cannot trade in world markets, the price adjusts to balance domestic supply and demand. This figure shows consumer and producer surplus in an equilibrium without international trade for the steel market in the imaginary country of Isoland.

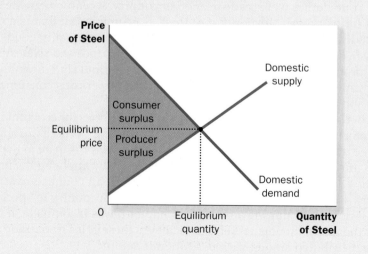

demanded by domestic buyers. The figure shows the consumer and producer surplus in the equilibrium without trade. The sum of consumer and producer surplus measures the total benefits that buyers and sellers receive from the steel market.

Now suppose that, in an election upset, Isoland elects a new president. The president campaigned on a platform of "change" and promised the voters bold new ideas. Her first act is to assemble a team of economists to evaluate Isolandian trade policy. She asks them to report back on three questions:

- If the government allowed Isolandians to import and export steel, what would happen to the price of steel and the quantity of steel sold in the domestic steel market?
- Who would gain from free trade in steel and who would lose, and would the gains exceed the losses?
- Should a tariff (a tax on steel imports) or an import quota (a limit on steel imports) be part of the new trade policy?

After reviewing supply and demand in their favorite textbook (this one, of course), the Isolandian economics team begins its analysis.

The World Price and Comparative Advantage

The first issue our economists take up is whether Isoland is likely to become a steel importer or a steel exporter. In other words, if free trade were allowed, would Isolandians end up buying or selling steel in world markets?

To answer this question, the economists compare the current Isolandian price of steel to the price of steel in other countries. We call the price prevailing in world markets the **world price**. If the world price of steel is higher than the domestic price, then Isoland would become an exporter of steel once trade is permitted. Isolandian steel producers would be eager to receive the higher prices available abroad and would start selling their steel to buyers in other countries. Conversely, if the world price of steel is lower than the domestic price, then Isoland would become an importer of steel. Because foreign sellers offer a better price, Isolandian steel consumers would quickly start buying steel from other countries.

In essence, comparing the world price and the domestic price before trade indicates whether Isoland has a comparative advantage in producing steel. The domestic price reflects the opportunity cost of steel: It tells us how much an Isolandian must give up to get one unit of steel. If the domestic price is low, the cost of producing steel in Isoland is low, suggesting that Isoland has a comparative advantage in producing steel relative to the rest of the world. If the domestic price is high, then the cost of producing steel in Isoland is high, suggesting that foreign countries have a comparative advantage in producing steel.

As we saw in Chapter 3, trade among nations is ultimately based on comparative advantage. That is, trade is beneficial because it allows each nation to specialize in doing what it does best. By comparing the world price and the domestic price before trade, we can determine whether Isoland is better or worse at producing steel than the rest of the world.

world price
the price of a good that prevails in the world market for that good

QuickQuiz The country Autarka does not allow international trade. In Autarka, you can buy a wool suit for 3 ounces of gold. Meanwhile, in neighboring countries, you can buy the same suit for 2 ounces of gold. If Autarka were to allow free trade, would it import or export suits?

THE WINNERS AND LOSERS FROM TRADE

To analyze the welfare effects of free trade, the Isolandian economists begin with the assumption that Isoland is a small economy compared to the rest of the world so that its actions have a negligible effect on world markets. The small-economy assumption has a specific implication for analyzing the steel market: If Isoland is a small economy, then the change in Isoland's trade policy will not affect the world price of steel. The Isolandians are said to be *price takers* in the world economy. That is, they take the world price of steel as given. They can sell steel at this price and be exporters or buy steel at this price and be importers.

The small-economy assumption is not necessary to analyze the gains and losses from international trade. But the Isolandian economists know from experience that this assumption greatly simplifies the analysis. They also know that the basic lessons do not change in the more complicated case of a large economy.

The Gains and Losses of an Exporting Country

Figure 2 shows the Isolandian steel market when the domestic equilibrium price before trade is below the world price. Once free trade is allowed, the domestic price rises to equal the world price. No seller of steel would accept less than the world price, and no buyer would pay more than the world price.

With the domestic price now equal to the world price, the domestic quantity supplied differs from the domestic quantity demanded. The supply curve shows the quantity of steel supplied by Isolandian sellers. The demand curve shows the

---

FIGURE 2

International Trade in an Exporting Country

Once trade is allowed, the domestic price rises to equal the world price. The supply curve shows the quantity of steel produced domestically, and the demand curve shows the quantity consumed domestically. Exports from Isoland equal the difference between the domestic quantity supplied and the domestic quantity demanded at the world price.

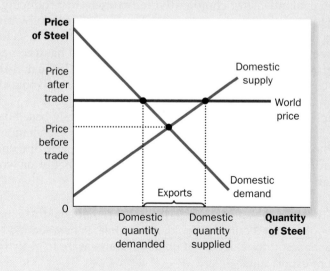

quantity of steel demanded by Isolandian buyers. Because the domestic quantity supplied is greater than the domestic quantity demanded, Isoland sells steel to other countries. Thus, Isoland becomes a steel exporter.

Although domestic quantity supplied and domestic quantity demanded differ, the steel market is still in equilibrium because there is now another participant in the market: the rest of the world. One can view the horizontal line at the world price as representing the demand for steel from the rest of the world. This demand curve is perfectly elastic because Isoland, as a small economy, can sell as much steel as it wants at the world price.

Now consider the gains and losses from opening up trade. Clearly, not everyone benefits. Trade forces the domestic price to rise to the world price. Domestic producers of steel are better off because they can now sell steel at a higher price, but domestic consumers of steel are worse off because they have to buy steel at a higher price.

To measure these gains and losses, we look at the changes in consumer and producer surplus, which are shown in the graph and table in Figure 3. Before trade is allowed, the price of steel adjusts to balance domestic supply and domestic demand. Consumer surplus, the area between the demand curve and the before-trade

FIGURE 3

How Free Trade Affects Welfare in an Exporting Country

When the domestic price rises to equal the world price, sellers are better off (producer surplus rises from C to B + C + D), and buyers are worse off (consumer surplus falls from A + B to A). Total surplus rises by an amount equal to area D, indicating that trade raises the economic well-being of the country as a whole.

	Before Trade	After Trade	Change
Consumer Surplus	A + B	A	−B
Producer Surplus	C	B + C + D	+(B + D)
Total Surplus	A + B + C	A + B + C + D	+D

The area D shows the increase in total surplus and represents the gains from trade.

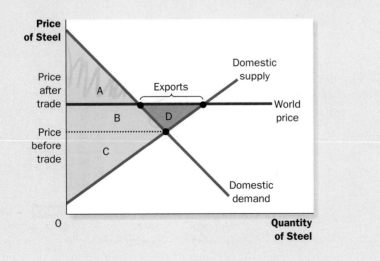

price, is area A + B. Producer surplus, the area between the supply curve and the before-trade price, is area C. Total surplus before trade, the sum of consumer and producer surplus, is area A + B + C.

After trade is allowed, the domestic price rises to the world price. Consumer surplus is area A (the area between the demand curve and the world price). Producer surplus is area B + C + D (the area between the supply curve and the world price). Thus, total surplus with trade is area A + B + C + D.

These welfare calculations show who wins and who loses from trade in an exporting country. Sellers benefit because producer surplus increases by the area B + D. Buyers are worse off because consumer surplus decreases by the area B. Because the gains of sellers exceed the losses of buyers by the area D, total surplus in Isoland increases.

This analysis of an exporting country yields two conclusions:

- When a country allows trade and becomes an exporter of a good, domestic producers of the good are better off, and domestic consumers of the good are worse off.
- Trade raises the economic well-being of a nation in the sense that the gains of the winners exceed the losses of the losers.

The Gains and Losses of an Importing Country

Now suppose that the domestic price before trade is above the world price. Once again, after free trade is allowed, the domestic price must equal the world price. As Figure 4 shows, the domestic quantity supplied is less than the domestic quantity

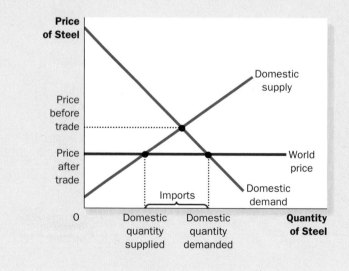

FIGURE 4

International Trade in an Importing Country

Once trade is allowed, the domestic price falls to equal the world price. The supply curve shows the amount produced domestically, and the demand curve shows the amount consumed domestically. Imports equal the difference between the domestic quantity demanded and the domestic quantity supplied at the world price.

demanded. The difference between the domestic quantity demanded and the domestic quantity supplied is bought from other countries, and Isoland becomes a steel importer.

In this case, the horizontal line at the world price represents the supply of the rest of the world. This supply curve is perfectly elastic because Isoland is a small economy and, therefore, can buy as much steel as it wants at the world price.

Now consider the gains and losses from trade. Once again, not everyone benefits. When trade forces the domestic price to fall, domestic consumers are better off (they can now buy steel at a lower price), and domestic producers are worse off (they now have to sell steel at a lower price). Changes in consumer and producer surplus measure the size of the gains and losses, as shown in the graph and table in Figure 5. Before trade, consumer surplus is area A, producer surplus is area B + C, and total surplus is area A + B + C. After trade is allowed, consumer surplus is area A + B + D, producer surplus is area C, and total surplus is area A + B + C + D.

These welfare calculations show who wins and who loses from trade in an importing country. Buyers benefit because consumer surplus increases by the

FIGURE 5

How Free Trade Affects Welfare in an Importing Country

When the domestic price falls to equal the world price, buyers are better off (consumer surplus rises from A to A + B + D), and sellers are worse off (producer surplus falls from B + C to C). Total surplus rises by an amount equal to area D, indicating that trade raises the economic well-being of the country as a whole.

	Before Trade	After Trade	Change
Consumer Surplus	A	A + B + D	+(B + D)
Producer Surplus	B + C	C	−B
Total Surplus	A + B + C	A + B + C + D	+D

The area D shows the increase in total surplus and represents the gains from trade.

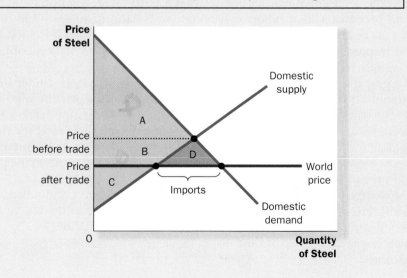

area B + D. Sellers are worse off because producer surplus falls by the area B. The gains of buyers exceed the losses of sellers, and total surplus increases by the area D.

This analysis of an importing country yields two conclusions parallel to those for an exporting country:

- When a country allows trade and becomes an importer of a good, domestic consumers of the good are better off, and domestic producers of the good are worse off.
- Trade raises the economic well-being of a nation in the sense that the gains of the winners exceed the losses of the losers.

Having completed our analysis of trade, we can better understand one of the *Ten Principles of Economics* in Chapter 1: Trade can make everyone better off. If Isoland opens up its steel market to international trade, that change will create winners and losers, regardless of whether Isoland ends up exporting or importing steel. In either case, however, the gains of the winners exceed the losses of the losers, so the winners could compensate the losers and still be better off. In this sense, trade *can* make everyone better off. But *will* trade make everyone better off? Probably not. In practice, compensation for the losers from international trade is rare. Without such compensation, opening up to international trade is a policy that expands the size of the economic pie, while perhaps leaving some participants in the economy with a smaller slice.

We can now see why the debate over trade policy is so often contentious. Whenever a policy creates winners and losers, the stage is set for a political battle. Nations sometimes fail to enjoy the gains from trade simply because the losers from free trade have more political clout than the winners. The losers lobby for trade restrictions, such as tariffs and import quotas.

The Effects of a Tariff

tariff
a tax on goods produced abroad and sold domestically

The Isolandian economists next consider the effects of a **tariff**—a tax on imported goods. The economists quickly realize that a tariff on steel will have no effect if Isoland becomes a steel exporter. If no one in Isoland is interested in importing steel, a tax on steel imports is irrelevant. The tariff matters only if Isoland becomes a steel importer. Concentrating their attention on this case, the economists compare welfare with and without the tariff.

The graph in Figure 6 shows the Isolandian market for steel. Under free trade, the domestic price equals the world price. A tariff raises the price of imported steel above the world price by the amount of the tariff. Domestic suppliers of steel, who compete with suppliers of imported steel, can now sell their steel for the world price plus the amount of the tariff. Thus, the price of steel—both imported and domestic—rises by the amount of the tariff and is, therefore, closer to the price that would prevail without trade.

The change in price affects the behavior of domestic buyers and sellers. Because the tariff raises the price of steel, it reduces the domestic quantity demanded from Q_1^D to Q_2^D and raises the domestic quantity supplied from Q_1^S to Q_2^S. *Thus, the tariff reduces the quantity of imports and moves the domestic market closer to its equilibrium without trade.*

FIGURE 6

The Effects of a Tariff

A tariff reduces the quantity of imports and moves a market closer to the equilibrium that would exist without trade. Total surplus falls by an amount equal to area D + F. These two triangles represent the deadweight loss from the tariff.

	Before Tariff	After Tariff	Change
Consumer Surplus	A + B + C + D + E + F	A + B	−(C + D + E + F)
Producer Surplus	G	C + G	+C
Government Revenue	None	E	+E
Total Surplus	A + B + C + D + E + F + G	A + B + C + E + G	−(D + F)

The area D + F shows the fall in total surplus and represents the deadweight loss of the tariff.

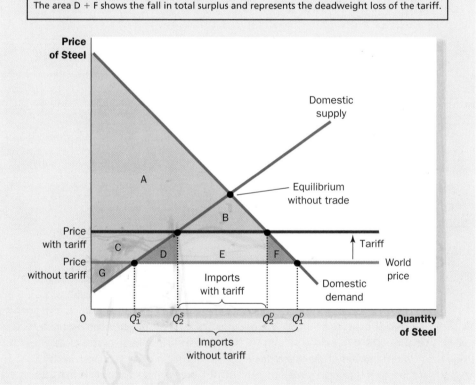

Now consider the gains and losses from the tariff. Because the tariff raises the domestic price, domestic sellers are better off, and domestic buyers are worse off. In addition, the government raises revenue. To measure these gains and losses, we look at the changes in consumer surplus, producer surplus, and government revenue. These changes are summarized in the table in Figure 6.

Before the tariff, the domestic price equals the world price. Consumer surplus, the area between the demand curve and the world price, is area A + B + C + D + E + F. Producer surplus, the area between the supply curve and the world price, is area G.

Government revenue equals zero. Total surplus—the sum of consumer surplus, producer surplus, and government revenue—is area A + B + C + D + E + F + G.

Once the government imposes a tariff, the domestic price exceeds the world price by the amount of the tariff. Consumer surplus is now area A + B. Producer surplus is area C + G. Government revenue, which is the quantity of after-tariff imports times the size of the tariff, is the area E. Thus, total surplus with the tariff is area A + B + C + E + G.

To determine the total welfare effects of the tariff, we add the change in consumer surplus (which is negative), the change in producer surplus (positive), and the change in government revenue (positive). We find that total surplus in the market decreases by the area D + F. This fall in total surplus is called the *deadweight loss* of the tariff.

A tariff causes a deadweight loss simply because a tariff is a type of tax. Like most taxes, it distorts incentives and pushes the allocation of scarce resources away from the optimum. In this case, we can identify two effects. First, the tariff on

IN THE NEWS

LIFE IN ISOLAND

Our story about the steel industry and the debate over trade policy in Isoland is just a parable. Or is it?

Bush Puts Tariffs of as Much as 30% on Steel Imports

By David E. Sanger

President Bush took some of the broadest federal action in two decades to protect a major American industry today, imposing tariffs of up to 30 percent on most types of steel imported into the United States from Europe, Asia, and South America. The tariffs will last three years, he said, to give American steel producers time to consolidate operations and stem layoffs.

Mr. Bush's action is likely to send the price of steel up sharply, perhaps as much as 10 percent, a cost American consumers will ultimately bear in higher prices for autos, appliances, and housing. The United States imports about a quarter of the steel it consumes. . . .

Within minutes of the White House announcement, America's European allies and Japan said they would almost certainly challenge the action before the World Trade Organization, setting the stage for a major trade fight with many of the same countries Mr. Bush is trying to hold together in the fractious fight against terrorism. . . .

Mr. Bush is an avowed free trader, and many members of his economic team—including Lawrence Lindsey, who runs the National Economic Council, and Glenn Hubbard, the chairman of the council of economic advisors—warned of the risks to both his free-trade credentials and the broader economy. In the past his trade representative, Robert B. Zoellick, compared raising tariffs to raising taxes, and while the White House officials sidestepped such comparisons today they admitted that the result would be greater costs to consumers.

steel raises the price of steel that domestic producers can charge above the world price and, as a result, encourages them to increase production of steel (from Q_1^S to Q_2^S). Second, the tariff raises the price that domestic steel buyers have to pay and, therefore, encourages them to reduce consumption of steel (from Q_1^D to Q_2^D). Area D represents the deadweight loss from the overproduction of steel, and area F represents the deadweight loss from the underconsumption. The total deadweight loss of the tariff is the sum of these two triangles.

The Effects of an Import Quota

The Isolandian economists next consider the effects of an **import quota**—a limit on the quantity of imports. In particular, imagine that the Isolandian government distributes a limited number of import licenses. Each license gives the license holder the right to import 1 ton of steel into Isoland from abroad. The Isolandian economists want to compare welfare under a policy of free trade and welfare with the addition of this import quota.

The graph and table in Figure 7 (p. 186) show how an import quota affects the Isolandian market for steel. Because the import quota prevents Isolandians from buying as much steel as they want from abroad, the supply of steel is no longer perfectly elastic at the world price. Instead, as long as the price of steel in Isoland is above the world price, the license holders import as much as they are permitted, and the total supply of steel in Isoland equals the domestic supply plus the quota amount. That is, the supply curve above the world price is shifted to the right by exactly the amount of the quota. (The supply curve below the world price does not shift because, in this case, importing is not profitable for the license holders.)

The price of steel in Isoland adjusts to balance supply (domestic plus imported) and demand. As the figure shows, the quota causes the price of steel to rise above the world price. The domestic quantity demanded falls from Q_1^D to Q_2^D, and the domestic quantity supplied rises from Q_1^S to Q_2^S. Not surprisingly, the import quota reduces steel imports.

Now consider the gains and losses from the quota. Because the quota raises the domestic price above the world price, domestic sellers are better off, and domestic buyers are worse off. In addition, the license holders are better off because they make a profit from buying at the world price and selling at the higher domestic price. To measure these gains and losses, we look at the changes in consumer surplus, producer surplus, and license-holder surplus.

Before the government imposes the quota, the domestic price equals the world price. Consumer surplus, the area between the demand curve and the world price, is area A + B + C + D + E' + E'' + F. Producer surplus, the area between the supply curve and the world price, is area G. The surplus of license holders equals zero because there are no licenses. Total surplus, the sum of consumer, producer, and license-holder surplus, is area A + B + C + D + E' + E'' + F + G.

After the government imposes the import quota and issues the licenses, the domestic price exceeds the world price. Domestic consumers get surplus equal to area A + B, and domestic producers get surplus equal to area C + G. The license holders make a profit on each unit imported equal to the difference between the Isolandian price of steel and the world price. Their surplus equals this price differential times the quantity of imports. Thus, it equals the area of the rectangle E' + E''. Total surplus with the quota is the area A + B + C + E' + E'' + G.

import quota
a limit on the quantity of a good that can be produced abroad and sold domestically

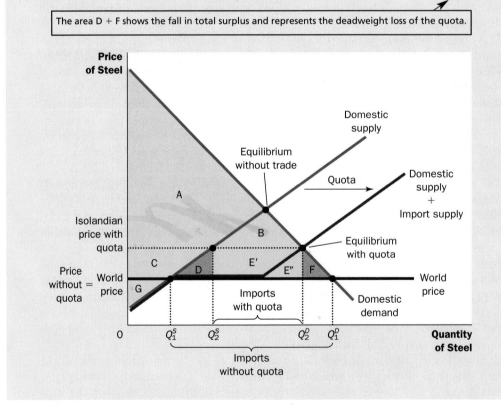

FIGURE 7

The Effects of an Import Quota

An import quota, like a tariff, reduces the quantity of imports and moves a market closer to the equilibrium that would exist without trade. Total surplus falls by an amount equal to area D + F. These two triangles represent the deadweight loss from the quota. In addition, the import quota transfers E' + E" to whoever holds the import licenses.

	Before Quota	After Quota	Change
Consumer Surplus	A + B + C + D + E' + E" + F	A + B	−(C + D + E' + E" + F)
Producer Surplus	G	C + G	+C
License-Holder Surplus	None	E' + E"	+(E' + E")
Total Surplus	A + B + C + D + E' + E" + F + G	A + B + C + E' + E" + G	−(D + F)

The area D + F shows the fall in total surplus and represents the deadweight loss of the quota.

To see how total welfare changes with the imposition of the quota, we add the change in consumer surplus (which is negative), the change in producer surplus (positive), and the change in license-holder surplus (positive). We find that total surplus in the market decreases by the area D + F. This area represents the deadweight loss of the import quota.

This analysis should seem somewhat familiar. Indeed, if you compare the analysis of import quotas in Figure 7 with the analysis of tariffs in Figure 6, you will see that they are essentially identical. *Both tariffs and import quotas raise the domestic price of the good, reduce the welfare of domestic consumers, increase the welfare of domestic producers, and cause deadweight losses.* There is only one difference between these two types of trade restriction: A tariff raises revenue for the government (area E in Figure 6), whereas an import quota creates surplus for license holders (area E' + E" in Figure 7).

Tariffs and import quotas can be made to look even more similar. Suppose that the government tries to capture the license-holder surplus for itself by charging a fee for the licenses. A license to sell 1 ton of steel is worth exactly the difference between the Isolandian price of steel and the world price, and the government can set the license fee as high as this price differential. If the government does this, the license fee for imports works exactly like a tariff: Consumer surplus, producer surplus, and government revenue are exactly the same under the two policies.

In practice, however, countries that restrict trade with import quotas rarely do so by selling the import licenses. For example, the U.S. government has at times pressured Japan to "voluntarily" limit the sale of Japanese cars in the United States. In this case, the Japanese government allocates the import licenses to Japanese firms, and the surplus from these licenses (area E' + E") accrues to those firms. This kind of import quota is, from the standpoint of U.S. welfare, strictly worse than a U.S. tariff on imported cars. Both a tariff and an import quota raise prices, restrict trade, and cause deadweight losses, but at least the tariff produces revenue for the U.S. government rather than for Japanese auto companies.

Although in our analysis so far import quotas and tariffs appear to cause similar deadweight losses, a quota can potentially cause an even larger deadweight loss, depending on the mechanism used to allocate the import licenses. Suppose that when Isoland imposes a quota, everyone understands that the licenses will go to those who spend the most resources lobbying the Isolandian government. In this case, there is an implicit license fee—the cost of lobbying. The revenues from this fee, however, rather than being collected by the government, are spent on lobbying expenses. The deadweight losses from this type of quota include not only the losses from overproduction (area D) and underconsumption (area F) but also whatever part of the license-holder surplus (area E' + E") is wasted on the cost of lobbying.

The Lessons for Trade Policy

The team of Isolandian economists can now write to the new president:

Dear Madam President,

You asked us three questions about opening up trade. After much hard work, we have the answers.

Question: If the government allowed Isolandians to import and export steel, what would happen to the price of steel and the quantity of steel sold in the domestic steel market?

Answer: Once trade is allowed, the Isolandian price of steel would be driven to equal the price prevailing around the world.

If the world price is now higher than the Isolandian price, our price would rise. The higher price would reduce the amount of steel Isolandians consume and raise the amount of steel that Isolandians produce. Isoland would, therefore, become a steel exporter. This occurs because, in this case, Isoland would have a comparative advantage in producing steel.

Conversely, if the world price is now lower than the Isolandian price, our price would fall. The lower price would raise the amount of steel that

Isolandians consume and lower the amount of steel that Isolandians produce. Isoland would, therefore, become a steel importer. This occurs because, in this case, other countries would have a comparative advantage in producing steel.

Question: Who would gain from free trade in steel and who would lose, and would the gains exceed the losses?

Answer: The answer depends on whether the price rises or falls when trade is allowed. If the price rises, producers of steel gain, and consumers of steel lose. If the price falls, consumers gain, and producers lose. In both cases, the gains are larger than the losses. Thus, free trade raises the total welfare of Isolandians.

Question: Should a tariff or an import quota be part of the new trade policy?

Answer: A tariff, like most taxes, has deadweight losses: The revenue raised would be smaller than the losses to the buyers and sellers. In this case, the deadweight losses occur because the tariff would move the economy closer to our current no-trade equilibrium. An import quota works much like a tariff and would cause similar deadweight losses. The best policy, from the standpoint of economic efficiency, would be to allow trade without a tariff or an import quota.

We hope you find these answers helpful as you decide on your new policy.

Your faithful servants,
Isolandian economics team

QuickQuiz   Draw the supply and demand curve for wool suits in the country of Autarka. When trade is allowed, the price of a suit falls from 3 to 2 ounces of gold. In your diagram, what is the change in consumer surplus, the change in producer surplus, and the change in total surplus? How would a tariff on suit imports alter these effects?

THE ARGUMENTS FOR RESTRICTING TRADE

The letter from the economics team persuades the new president of Isoland to consider opening up trade in steel. She notes that the domestic price is now high compared to the world price. Free trade would, therefore, cause the price of steel to fall and hurt domestic steel producers. Before implementing the new policy, she asks Isolandian steel companies to comment on the economists' advice.

Not surprisingly, the steel companies are opposed to free trade in steel. They believe that the government should protect the domestic steel industry from foreign competition. Let's consider some of the arguments they might give to support their position and how the economics team would respond.

The Jobs Argument

Opponents of free trade often argue that trade with other countries destroys domestic jobs. In our example, free trade in steel would cause the price of steel to fall, reducing the quantity of steel produced in Isoland and thus reducing employment in the Isolandian steel industry. Some Isolandian steelworkers would lose their jobs.

Yet free trade creates jobs at the same time that it destroys them. When Isolandians buy steel from other countries, those countries obtain the resources to buy

OTHER BENEFITS OF INTERNATIONAL TRADE

Our conclusions so far have been based on the standard analysis of international trade. As we have seen, there are winners and losers when a nation opens itself up to trade, but the gains to the winners exceed the losses of the losers. Yet the case for free trade can be made even stronger. There are several other economic benefits of trade beyond those emphasized in the standard analysis.

Here, in a nutshell, are some of these other benefits:

- *Increased variety of goods:* Goods produced in different countries are not exactly the same. German beer, for instance, is not the same as American beer. Free trade gives consumers in all countries greater variety from which to choose.
- *Lower costs through economies of scale:* Some goods can be produced at low cost only if they are produced in large quantities—

a phenomenon called *economies of scale.* A firm in a small country cannot take full advantage of economies of scale if it can sell only in a small domestic market. Free trade gives firms access to larger world markets and allows them to realize economies of scale more fully.

- *Increased competition:* A company shielded from foreign competitors is more likely to have market power, which in turn gives it the ability to raise prices above competitive levels. This is a type of market failure. Opening up trade fosters competition and gives the invisible hand a better chance to work its magic.
- *Enhanced flow of ideas:* The transfer of technological advances around the world is often thought to be linked to international trade in the goods that embody those advances. The best way for a poor, agricultural nation to learn about the computer revolution, for instance, is to buy some computers from abroad, rather than trying to make them domestically.

Thus, free international trade increases variety for consumers, allows firms to take advantage of economies of scale, makes markets more competitive, and facilitates the spread of technology. If the Isolandian economists thought these effects were important, their advice to their president would be even more forceful.

---

other goods from Isoland. Isolandian workers would move from the steel industry to those industries in which Isoland has a comparative advantage. Although the transition may impose hardship on some workers in the short run, it allows Isolandians as a whole to enjoy a higher standard of living.

Opponents of trade are often skeptical that trade creates jobs. They might respond that *everything* can be produced more cheaply abroad. Under free trade, they might argue, Isolandians could not be profitably employed in any industry. As Chapter 3 explains, however, the gains from trade are based on comparative advantage, not absolute advantage. Even if one country is better than another country at producing everything, each country can still gain from trading with the other. Workers in each country will eventually find jobs in the industry in which that country has a comparative advantage.

The National-Security Argument

When an industry is threatened with competition from other countries, opponents of free trade often argue that the industry is vital for national security. In our example, Isolandian steel companies might point out that steel is used to make guns and tanks. Free trade would allow Isoland to become dependent on foreign countries to supply steel. If a war later broke out, Isoland might be unable to produce enough steel and weapons to defend itself.

Berry's World

"You like protectionism as a 'working man.' How about as a consumer?"

Economists acknowledge that protecting key industries may be appropriate when there are legitimate concerns over national security. Yet they fear that this argument may be used too quickly by producers eager to gain at consumers' expense. The U.S. watchmaking industry, for instance, long argued that it was vital for national security, claiming that its skilled workers would be necessary in wartime. Certainly, it is tempting for those in an industry to exaggerate their role in national defense to obtain protection from foreign competition.

The Infant-Industry Argument

New industries sometimes argue for temporary trade restrictions to help them get started. After a period of protection, the argument goes, these industries will mature and be able to compete with foreign competitors. Similarly, older industries sometimes argue that they need temporary protection to help them adjust to new conditions. For example, General Motors Chairman Roger Smith once argued for temporary protection "to give U.S. automakers turnaround time to get the domestic industry back on its feet."

Economists are often skeptical about such claims. The primary reason is that the infant-industry argument is difficult to implement in practice. To apply protection successfully, the government would need to decide which industries will eventually be profitable and decide whether the benefits of establishing these industries exceed the costs to consumers of protection. Yet "picking winners" is extraordinarily difficult. It is made even more difficult by the political process, which often awards protection to those industries that are politically powerful. And once a powerful industry is protected from foreign competition, the "temporary" policy is hard to remove.

In addition, many economists are skeptical about the infant-industry argument even in principle. Suppose, for instance, that the Isolandian steel industry is young and unable to compete profitably against foreign rivals. Yet there is reason to believe that the industry can be profitable in the long run. In this case, the owners of the firms should be willing to incur temporary losses to obtain the eventual profits. Protection is not necessary for an industry to grow. Firms in various industries—such as many Internet firms today—incur temporary losses in the hope of growing and becoming profitable in the future. And many of them succeed, even without protection from foreign competition.

The Unfair-Competition Argument

A common argument is that free trade is desirable only if all countries play by the same rules. If firms in different countries are subject to different laws and regulations, then it is unfair (the argument goes) to expect the firms to compete in the international marketplace. For instance, suppose that the government of Neighborland subsidizes its steel industry by giving steel companies large tax breaks. The Isolandian steel industry might argue that it should be protected from this foreign competition because Neighborland is not competing fairly.

Would it, in fact, hurt Isoland to buy steel from another country at a subsidized price? Certainly, Isolandian steel producers would suffer, but Isolandian steel consumers would benefit from the low price. Moreover, the case for free trade is no different: The gains of the consumers from buying at the low price would exceed the losses of the producers. Neighborland's subsidy to its steel industry may be a bad policy, but it is the taxpayers of Neighborland who bear the burden. Isoland can benefit from the opportunity to buy steel at a subsidized price.

IN THE NEWS

TRADE POLICY IN INDIA

India is among the world's poorest countries. The government's trade policy is one of the reasons.

Chicken Shows Difficulty of Exporting Food to India

By Celia W. Dugger

NEW DELHI—Americans love succulent chicken breasts dressed up in every conceivable way, while Indians relish a savory tandoori drumstick brandished easily in one hand or a spicy chicken curry enriched by the marrow of the leg bone.

For Perdue Farms, America's No. 3 chicken producer, this divergence in culinary tastes seems a heaven-sent opportunity. While selling white meat at a premium to Americans, it could ship inexpensive, unwanted dark meat to India.

So as India prepared to lift its longstanding ban on chicken imports next year in a deal worked out with American trade negotiators, Perdue began developing a strategy to sell leg portions in this potentially huge new market, home to as many as 150 million middle-class consumers.

But India does not have a reputation as one of the world's most protected economies for nothing. There is still a deep ambivalence here about foreign investment and trade, and India has taken a decidedly cautious approach to globalization. Over the last decade, it has let in ever more foreign goods and lowered barriers to trade, cutting average tariffs from 128 percent to 40 percent. Still, India has some of the world's highest tariffs.

Sure enough, as the domestic chicken industry considered the fearsome prospect of cheap imported dark meat, its lobbyists began to protest. The government hastily agreed last month to raise the tariff on chicken legs from 35 percent to 100 percent. . . .

Many Indians, from hard-line Hindu nationalists to Nehruvian socialists, believe India must shield its small producers,

Are American chickens a threat to Indian prosperity?

even at the expense of higher prices for consumers and lower-quality goods.

Source: *The New York Times,* June 14, 2000, pp. C1, C6. Copyright © 2000 by The New York Times Co. Reprinted with permission.

PHOTO: © TONY ARRUZA/CORBIS

The Protection-as-a-Bargaining-Chip Argument

Another argument for trade restrictions concerns the strategy of bargaining. Many policymakers claim to support free trade but, at the same time, argue that trade restrictions can be useful when we bargain with our trading partners. They claim that the threat of a trade restriction can help remove a trade restriction already imposed by a foreign government. For example, Isoland might threaten to impose a tariff on steel unless Neighborland removes its tariff on wheat. If Neighborland responds to this threat by removing its tariff, the result can be freer trade.

IN THE NEWS

GLOBALIZATION

The movement toward free world trade—sometimes called globalization—has some vocal opponents, but as this article discusses, they are not always well informed.

Hearts and Heads

By Paul Krugman

There is an old European saying: anyone who is not a socialist before he is 30 has no heart, anyone who is still a socialist after he is 30 has no head. Suitably updated, this applies perfectly to the movement against globalization—the movement that made its big splash in Seattle back in 1999 and is doing its best to disrupt the Summit of the Americas in Quebec City this weekend.

The facts of globalization are not always pretty. If you buy a product made in a third-world country, it was produced by workers who are paid incredibly little by Western standards and probably work under awful conditions. Anyone who is not bothered by those facts, at least some of the time, has no heart.

But that doesn't mean the demonstrators are right. On the contrary: anyone who thinks that the answer to world poverty is simple outrage against global trade has no head—or chooses not to

use it. The anti-globalization movement already has a remarkable track record of hurting the very people and causes it claims to champion. . . .

Could anything be worse than having children work in sweatshops? Alas, yes. In 1993, child workers in Bangladesh were found to be producing clothing for Wal-Mart, and Senator Tom Harkin proposed legislation banning imports from countries employing underage workers. The direct result was that Bangladeshi textile factories stopped employing

The problem with this bargaining strategy is that the threat may not work. If it doesn't work, the country has a difficult choice. It can carry out its threat and implement the trade restriction, which would reduce its own economic welfare. Or it can back down from its threat, which would cause it to lose prestige in international affairs. Faced with this choice, the country would probably wish that it had never made the threat in the first place.

Case Study

TRADE AGREEMENTS AND THE WORLD TRADE ORGANIZATION

A country can take one of two approaches to achieving free trade. It can take a *unilateral* approach and remove its trade restrictions on its own. This is the approach that Great Britain took in the nineteenth century and that Chile and South Korea have taken in recent years. Alternatively, a country can take a *multilateral* approach and reduce its trade restrictions while other countries do the same. In other words, it can bargain with its trading partners in an attempt to reduce trade restrictions around the world.

children. But did the children go back to school? Did they return to happy homes? Not according to Oxfam, which found that the displaced child workers ended up in even worse jobs, or on the streets—and that a significant number were forced into prostitution.

The point is that third-world countries aren't poor because their export workers earn low wages; it's the other way around. Because the countries are poor, even what look to us like bad jobs at bad wages are almost always much better than the alternatives: millions of Mexicans are migrating to the north of the country to take the low-wage export jobs that outrage opponents of NAFTA. And those jobs wouldn't exist if the wages were much higher: the same factors that make poor countries poor—low productivity, bad infrastructure, general social disorganization—mean that such countries can compete on world markets only if they pay wages much lower than those paid in the West.

Of course, opponents of globalization have heard this argument, and they have answers. At a conference last week, I heard paeans to the superiority of traditional rural lifestyles over modern, urban life—a claim that not only flies in the face of the clear fact that many peasants flee to urban jobs as soon as they can, but that (it seems to me) has a disagreeable element of cultural condescension, especially given the overwhelming preponderance of white faces in the crowds of demonstrators. (Would you want to live in a pre-industrial village?) I also heard claims that rural poverty in the third world is mainly the fault of multinational corporations—which is just plain wrong, but is a convenient belief if you want to think of globalization as an unmitigated evil.

The most sophisticated answer was that the movement doesn't want to stop exports—it just wants better working conditions and higher wages.

But it's not a serious position. Third-world countries desperately need their

export industries—they cannot retreat to an imaginary rural Arcadia. They can't have those export industries unless they are allowed to sell goods produced under conditions that Westerners find appalling, by workers who receive very low wages. And that's a fact the anti-globalization activists refuse to accept.

So who are the bad guys? The activists are getting the images they wanted from Quebec City: leaders sitting inside their fortified enclosure, with thousands of police protecting them from the outraged masses outside. But images can deceive. Many of the people inside that chain-link fence are sincerely trying to help the world's poor. And the people outside the fence, whatever their intentions, are doing their best to make the poor even poorer.

Source: *The New York Times,* April 22, 2001, OP-ED WK/p. 17. Copyright © 2001 by The New York Times Co. Reprinted by permission.

One important example of the multilateral approach is the North American Free Trade Agreement (NAFTA), which in 1993 lowered trade barriers among the United States, Mexico, and Canada. Another is the General Agreement on Tariffs and Trade (GATT), which is a continuing series of negotiations among many of the world's countries with the goal of promoting free trade. The United States helped to found GATT after World War II in response to the high tariffs imposed during the Great Depression of the 1930s. Many economists believe that the high tariffs contributed to the economic hardship during that period. GATT has successfully reduced the average tariff among member countries from about 40 percent after World War II to about 5 percent today.

The rules established under GATT are now enforced by an international institution called the World Trade Organization (WTO). The WTO was established in 1995 and has its headquarters in Geneva, Switzerland. As of January 2002, 144 countries have joined the organization, accounting for 97 percent of world trade. The functions of the WTO are to administer trade agreements, provide a forum for negotiations, and handle disputes that arise among member countries.

What are the pros and cons of the multilateral approach to free trade? One advantage is that the multilateral approach has the potential to result in freer trade than a unilateral approach because it can reduce trade restrictions abroad as well as at home. If international negotiations fail, however, the result could be more restricted trade than under a unilateral approach.

In addition, the multilateral approach may have a political advantage. In most markets, producers are fewer and better organized than consumers—and thus wield greater political influence. Reducing the Isolandian tariff on steel, for example, may be politically difficult if considered by itself. The steel companies would oppose free trade, and the users of steel who would benefit are so numerous that organizing their support would be difficult. Yet suppose that Neighborland promises to reduce its tariff on wheat at the same time that Isoland reduces its tariff on steel. In this case, the Isolandian wheat farmers, who are also politically powerful, would back the agreement. Thus, the multilateral approach to free trade can sometimes win political support when a unilateral reduction cannot. ●

QuickQuiz   The textile industry of Autarka advocates a ban on the import of wool suits. Describe five arguments its lobbyists might make. Give a response to each of these arguments.

CONCLUSION

Economists and the general public often disagree about free trade. In May 2000, for example, the U.S. Congress debated whether to grant China "Permanent Normal Trade Relations," which would keep trade barriers low between the two countries. The public was split on the issue. In a *Wall Street Journal* poll, 48 percent agreed with the statement that, "Foreign trade is bad for the U.S. economy, as cheap imports hurt wages and cost jobs." Only 34 percent agreed that "Foreign trade is good for the U.S. economy, resulting in economic growth and jobs for Americans." By contrast, economists overwhelmingly supported the proposal. They viewed free trade as a way of allocating production efficiently and raising living standards in both countries. In the end, Congress agreed with the economists, and the bill passed the House of Representatives by a vote of 237 to 197.

Economists view the United States as an ongoing experiment that confirms the virtues of free trade. Throughout its history, the United States has allowed unrestricted trade among the states, and the country as a whole has benefited from the specialization that trade allows. Florida grows oranges, Texas pumps oil, California makes wine, and so on. Americans would not enjoy the high standard of living they do today if people could consume only those goods and services produced in their own states. The world could similarly benefit from free trade among countries.

To better understand economists' view of trade, let's continue our parable. Suppose that the country of Isoland ignores the advice of its economics team and decides not to allow free trade in steel. The country remains in the equilibrium without international trade.

Then, one day, some Isolandian inventor discovers a new way to make steel at very low cost. The process is quite mysterious, however, and the inventor insists on keeping it a secret. What is odd is that the inventor doesn't need any workers or iron ore to make steel. The only input he requires is wheat.

The inventor is hailed as a genius. Because steel is used in so many products, the invention lowers the cost of many goods and allows all Isolandians to enjoy a higher standard of living. Workers who had previously produced steel do suffer when their factories close, but eventually they find work in other industries. Some become farmers and grow the wheat that the inventor turns into steel. Others enter new industries that emerge as a result of higher Isolandian living standards. Everyone understands that the displacement of these workers is an inevitable part of progress.

After several years, a newspaper reporter decides to investigate this mysterious new steel process. She sneaks into the inventor's factory and learns that the inventor is a fraud. The inventor has not been making steel at all. Instead, he has been smuggling wheat abroad in exchange for steel from other countries. The only thing that the inventor had discovered was the gains from international trade.

When the truth is revealed, the government shuts down the inventor's operation. The price of steel rises, and workers return to jobs in steel factories. Living standards in Isoland fall back to their former levels. The inventor is jailed and held up to public ridicule. After all, he was no inventor. He was just an economist.

SUMMARY

- The effects of free trade can be determined by comparing the domestic price without trade to the world price. A low domestic price indicates that the country has a comparative advantage in producing the good and that the country will become an exporter. A high domestic price indicates that the rest of the world has a comparative advantage in producing the good and that the country will become an importer.

- When a country allows trade and becomes an exporter of a good, producers of the good are better off, and consumers of the good are worse off. When a country allows trade and becomes an importer of a good, consumers are better off, and producers are worse off. In both cases, the gains from trade exceed the losses.

- A tariff—a tax on imports—moves a market closer to the equilibrium that would exist without trade and, therefore, reduces the gains from trade. Although domestic producers are better off and the government raises revenue, the losses to consumers exceed these gains.

- An import quota—a limit on imports—has effects that are similar to those of a tariff. Under a quota, however, the holders of the import licenses receive the revenue that the government would collect with a tariff.

- There are various arguments for restricting trade: protecting jobs, defending national security, helping infant industries, preventing unfair competition, and responding to foreign trade restrictions. Although some of these arguments have some merit in some cases, economists believe that free trade is usually the better policy.

KEY CONCEPTS

world price, p. 177   tariff, p. 182   import quota, p. 185

QUESTIONS FOR REVIEW

1. What does the domestic price that prevails without international trade tell us about a nation's comparative advantage?

2. When does a country become an exporter of a good? An importer?

3. Draw the supply-and-demand diagram for an importing country. What is consumer surplus and producer surplus before trade is allowed? What is consumer surplus and producer surplus with free trade? What is the change in total surplus?

4. Describe what a tariff is, and describe its economic effects.

5. What is an import quota? Compare its economic effects with those of a tariff.

6. List five arguments often given to support trade restrictions. How do economists respond to these arguments?

7. What is the difference between the unilateral and multilateral approaches to achieving free trade? Give an example of each.

PROBLEMS AND APPLICATIONS

1. The United States represents a small part of the world orange market.
   a. Draw a diagram depicting the equilibrium in the U.S. orange market without international trade. Identify the equilibrium price, equilibrium quantity, consumer surplus, and producer surplus.
   b. Suppose that the world orange price is below the U.S. price before trade, and that the U.S. orange market is now opened to trade. Identify the new equilibrium price, quantity consumed, quantity produced domestically, and quantity imported. Also show the change in the surplus of domestic consumers and producers. Has domestic total surplus increased or decreased?

2. The world price of wine is below the price that would prevail in the United States in the absence of trade.
   a. Assuming that American imports of wine are a small part of total world wine production, draw a graph for the U.S. market for wine under free trade. Identify consumer surplus, producer surplus, and total surplus in an appropriate table.
   b. Now suppose that an unusual shift of the Gulf Stream leads to an unseasonably cold summer in Europe, destroying much of the grape harvest there. What effect does this shock have on the world price of wine? Using your graph and table from part (a), show the effect on consumer surplus, producer

surplus, and total surplus in the United States. Who are the winners and losers? Is the United States as a whole better or worse off?

3. The world price of cotton is below the no-trade price in country A and above the no-trade price in country B. Using supply-and-demand diagrams and welfare tables such as those in the chapter, show the gains from trade in each country. Compare your results for the two countries.

4. Suppose that Congress imposes a tariff on imported autos to protect the U.S. auto industry from foreign competition. Assuming that the U.S. is a price taker in the world auto market, show on a diagram: the change in the quantity of imports, the loss to U.S. consumers, the gain to U.S. manufacturers, government revenue, and the deadweight loss associated with the tariff. The loss to consumers can be decomposed into three pieces: a transfer to domestic producers, a transfer to the government, and a deadweight loss. Use your diagram to identify these three pieces.

5. According to an article in *The New York Times* (Nov. 5, 1993), "many Midwest wheat farmers oppose the [North American] free trade agreement [NAFTA] as much as many corn farmers support it." For simplicity, assume that the United States is a small country in the markets for both corn and wheat, and that without the free trade agreement, the United States would not trade these commodities internationally. (Both of these assumptions are false, but they do not affect the qualitative responses to the following questions.)
   a. Based on this report, do you think the world wheat price is above or below the U.S. no-trade wheat price? Do you think the world corn price is above or below the U.S. no-trade corn price? Now analyze the welfare consequences of NAFTA in both markets.
   b. Considering both markets together, does NAFTA make U.S. farmers as a group better or worse off? Does it make U.S. consumers as a group better or worse off? Does it make the United States as a whole better or worse off?

6. Imagine that winemakers in the state of Washington petitioned the state government to tax wines imported from California. They argue that this tax would both raise tax revenue for the state government and raise employment in the Washington State wine industry. Do you agree with these claims? Is it a good policy?

7. Senator Ernest Hollings once wrote that "consumers *do not* benefit from lower-priced imports. Glance through some mail-order catalogs and you'll see that consumers pay exactly the same price for clothing whether it is U.S.-made or imported." Comment.

8. Write a brief essay advocating or criticizing each of the following policy positions.
   a. The government should not allow imports if foreign firms are selling below their costs of production (a phenomenon called "dumping").
   b. The government should temporarily stop the import of goods for which the domestic industry is new and struggling to survive.
   c. The government should not allow imports from countries with weaker environmental regulations than ours.

9. Suppose that a technological advance in Japan lowers the world price of televisions.

a. Assume the U.S. is an importer of televisions and there are no trade restrictions. How does the technological advance affect the welfare of U.S. consumers and U.S. producers? What happens to total surplus in the United States?

b. Now suppose the United States has a quota on television imports. How does the Japanese technological advance affect the welfare of U.S. consumers, U.S. producers, and the holders of import licenses?

10. When the government of Tradeland decides to impose an import quota on foreign cars, three proposals are suggested: (1) Sell the import licenses in an auction. (2) Distribute the licenses randomly in a lottery. (3) Let people wait in line and distribute the licenses on a first-come, first-served basis. Compare the effects of these policies. Which policy do you think has the largest deadweight losses? Which policy has the smallest deadweight losses? Why? (Hint: The government's other ways of raising tax revenue all cause deadweight losses themselves.)

11. An article about sugar beet growers in *The Wall Street Journal* (June 26, 1990) explained that "the government props up domestic sugar prices by curtailing imports of lower-cost sugar. Producers are guaranteed a 'market stabilization price' of $0.22 a pound, about $0.09 higher than the current world market price." The government maintains the higher price by imposing an import quota.

a. Illustrate the effect of this quota on the U.S. sugar market. Label the relevant prices and quantities under free trade and under the quota.

b. Analyze the effects of the sugar quota using the tools of welfare analysis.

c. The article also comments that "critics of the sugar program say that [the quota] has deprived numerous sugar-producing nations in the Caribbean, Latin America, and Far East of export earnings, harmed their economies, and caused political instability, while increasing Third World demand for U.S. foreign aid." Our usual welfare analysis includes only gains and losses to U.S. consumers and producers. What role do you think the gains or losses to people in other countries should play in our economic policymaking?

d. The article continues that "at home, the sugar program has helped make possible the spectacular rise of the high-fructose corn syrup industry." Why has the sugar program had this effect? (Hint: Are sugar and corn syrup substitutes or complements?)

12. (This question is challenging.) Consider a small country that exports steel. Suppose that a "pro-trade" government decides to subsidize the export of steel by paying a certain amount for each ton sold abroad. How does this export subsidy affect the domestic price of steel, the quantity of steel produced, the quantity of steel consumed, and the quantity of steel exported?

How does it affect consumer surplus, producer surplus, government revenue, and total surplus? (Hint: The analysis of an export subsidy is similar to the analysis of a tariff.)

13. What trade disputes or trade agreements have been in the news lately? In this case, who do you think are the winners and losers from free trade? Which group has more political clout?

Note: Places to look for this information include the Web sites of the World Trade Organization (http://www.wto.org), the U.S. International Trade Commission (http://www.usitc.gov), and the International Trade Administration in the Department of Commerce (http://www.ita.doc.gov).

http:// For more study tools, please visit http://mankiwXtra.swlearning.com.

4

THE ECONOMICS OF THE PUBLIC SECTOR

10

EXTERNALITIES

Firms that make and sell paper also create, as a by-product of the manufacturing process, a chemical called dioxin. Scientists believe that once dioxin enters the environment, it raises the population's risk of cancer, birth defects, and other health problems.

Is the production and release of dioxin a problem for society? In Chapters 4 through 9 we examined how markets allocate scarce resources with the forces of supply and demand, and we saw that the equilibrium of supply and demand is typically an efficient allocation of resources. To use Adam Smith's famous metaphor, the "invisible hand" of the marketplace leads self-interested buyers and sellers in a market to maximize the total benefit that society derives from that market. This insight is the basis for one of the *Ten Principles of Economics* in Chapter 1: Markets are usually a good way to organize economic activity. Should we conclude, therefore, that the invisible hand prevents firms in the paper market from emitting too much dioxin?

Markets do many things well, but they do not do everything well. In this chapter we begin our study of another one of the *Ten Principles of Economics:* Governments can sometimes improve market outcomes. We examine why markets sometimes fail

externality
the uncompensated impact of one person's actions on the well-being of a bystander

to allocate resources efficiently, how government policies can potentially improve the market's allocation, and what kinds of policies are likely to work best.

The market failures examined in this chapter fall under a general category called *externalities*. An **externality** arises when a person engages in an activity that influences the well-being of a bystander and yet neither pays nor receives any compensation for that effect. If the impact on the bystander is adverse, it is called a *negative externality*; if it is beneficial, it is called a *positive externality*. In the presence of externalities, society's interest in a market outcome extends beyond the well-being of buyers and sellers who participate in the market; it also includes the well-being of bystanders who are affected indirectly. Because buyers and sellers neglect the external effects of their actions when deciding how much to demand or supply, the market equilibrium is not efficient when there are externalities. That is, the equilibrium fails to maximize the total benefit to society as a whole. The release of dioxin into the environment, for instance, is a negative externality. Self-interested paper firms will not consider the full cost of the pollution they create and, therefore, will emit too much pollution unless the government prevents or discourages them from doing so.

Externalities come in many varieties, as do the policy responses that try to deal with the market failure. Here are some examples:

- The exhaust from automobiles is a negative externality because it creates smog that other people have to breathe. As a result of this externality, drivers tend to pollute too much. The federal government attempts to solve this problem by setting emission standards for cars. It also taxes gasoline to reduce the amount that people drive.
- Restored historic buildings convey a positive externality because people who walk or ride by them can enjoy their beauty and the sense of history that these buildings provide. Building owners do not get the full benefit of restoration and, therefore, tend to discard older buildings too quickly. Many local governments respond to this problem by regulating the destruction of historic buildings and by providing tax breaks to owners who restore them.
- Barking dogs create a negative externality because neighbors are disturbed by the noise. Dog owners do not bear the full cost of the noise and, therefore, tend to take too few precautions to prevent their dogs from barking. Local governments address this problem by making it illegal to "disturb the peace."
- Research into new technologies provides a positive externality because it creates knowledge that other people can use. Because inventors cannot capture the full benefits of their inventions, they tend to devote too few resources to research. The federal government addresses this problem partially through the patent system, which gives inventors an exclusive use over their inventions for a period of time.

In each of these cases, some decisionmaker fails to take account of the external effects of his or her behavior. The government responds by trying to influence this behavior to protect the interests of bystanders.

EXTERNALITIES AND MARKET INEFFICIENCY

In this section we use the tools from Chapter 7 to examine how externalities affect economic well-being. The analysis shows precisely why externalities cause markets to allocate resources inefficiently. Later in the chapter we examine various ways in which private actors and public policymakers may remedy this type of market failure.

Welfare Economics: A Recap

We begin by recalling the key lessons of welfare economics from Chapter 7. To make our analysis concrete, we will consider a specific market—the market for aluminum. Figure 1 shows the supply and demand curves in the market for aluminum.

As you should recall from Chapter 7, the supply and demand curves contain important information about costs and benefits. The demand curve for aluminum reflects the value of aluminum to consumers, as measured by the prices they are willing to pay. At any given quantity, the height of the demand curve shows the willingness to pay of the marginal buyer. In other words, it shows the value to the consumer of the last unit of aluminum bought. Similarly, the supply curve reflects the costs of producing aluminum. At any given quantity, the height of the supply curve shows the cost of the marginal seller. In other words, it shows the cost to the producer of the last unit of aluminum sold.

In the absence of government intervention, the price adjusts to balance the supply and demand for aluminum. The quantity produced and consumed in the market equilibrium, shown as Q_{MARKET} in Figure 1, is efficient in the sense that it maximizes the sum of producer and consumer surplus. That is, the market allocates resources in a way that maximizes the total value to the consumers who buy and use aluminum minus the total costs to the producers who make and sell aluminum.

FIGURE 1

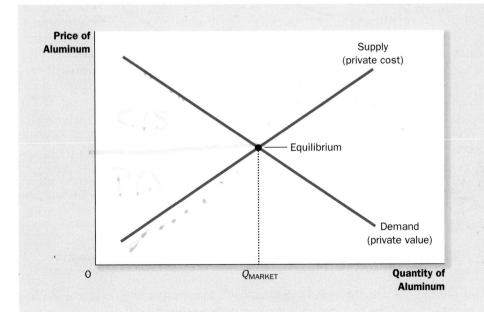

The Market for Aluminum

The demand curve reflects the value to buyers, and the supply curve reflects the costs of sellers. The equilibrium quantity, Q_{MARKET}, maximizes the total value to buyers minus the total costs of sellers. In the absence of externalities, therefore, the market equilibrium is efficient.

Negative Externalities

Now let's suppose that aluminum factories emit pollution: For each unit of aluminum produced, a certain amount of smoke enters the atmosphere. Because this smoke creates a health risk for those who breathe the air, it is a negative externality. How does this externality affect the efficiency of the market outcome?

Because of the externality, the cost to *society* of producing aluminum is larger than the cost to the aluminum producers. For each unit of aluminum produced, the *social cost* includes the private costs of the aluminum producers plus the costs to those bystanders affected adversely by the pollution. Figure 2 shows the social cost of producing aluminum. The social-cost curve is above the supply curve because it takes into account the external costs imposed on society by aluminum producers. The difference between these two curves reflects the cost of the pollution emitted.

What quantity of aluminum should be produced? To answer this question, we once again consider what a benevolent social planner would do. The planner wants to maximize the total surplus derived from the market—the value to consumers of aluminum minus the cost of producing aluminum. The planner understands, however, that the cost of producing aluminum includes the external costs of the pollution.

The planner would choose the level of aluminum production at which the demand curve crosses the social-cost curve. This intersection determines the optimal amount of aluminum from the standpoint of society as a whole. Below this level of production, the value of the aluminum to consumers (as measured by the height of the demand curve) exceeds the social cost of producing it (as measured by the height of the social-cost curve). The planner does not produce more than this level because the social cost of producing additional aluminum exceeds the value to consumers.

"All I can say is that if being a leading manufacturer means being a leading polluter, so be it."

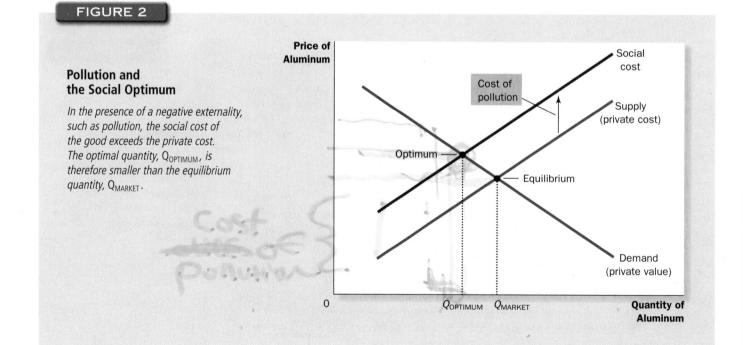

FIGURE 2

Pollution and the Social Optimum

In the presence of a negative externality, such as pollution, the social cost of the good exceeds the private cost. The optimal quantity, $Q_{OPTIMUM}$, is therefore smaller than the equilibrium quantity, Q_{MARKET}.

Note that the equilibrium quantity of aluminum, Q_{MARKET}, is larger than the socially optimal quantity, $Q_{OPTIMUM}$. The reason for this inefficiency is that the market equilibrium reflects only the private costs of production. In the market equilibrium, the marginal consumer values aluminum at less than the social cost of producing it. That is, at Q_{MARKET} the demand curve lies below the social-cost curve. Thus, reducing aluminum production and consumption below the market equilibrium level raises total economic well-being.

How can the social planner achieve the optimal outcome? One way would be to tax aluminum producers for each of aluminum sold. The tax would shift the supply curve for aluminum upward by the size of the tax. If the tax accurately reflected the social cost of smoke released into the atmosphere, the new supply curve would coincide with the social-cost curve. In the new market equilibrium, aluminum producers would produce the socially optimal quantity of aluminum.

The use of such a tax is called **internalizing the externality** because it gives buyers and sellers in the market an incentive to take account of the external effects of their actions. Aluminum producers would, in essence, take the costs of pollution into account when deciding how much aluminum to supply because the tax would make them pay for these external costs. The policy is based on one of the *Ten Principles of Economics:* People respond to incentives. Later in this chapter we consider other ways in which policymakers can deal with externalities.

> **internalizing an externality**
> altering incentives so that people take account of the external effects of their actions

Positive Externalities

Although some activities impose costs on third parties, others yield benefits. For example, consider education. Education yields positive externalities because a more educated population leads to better government, which benefits everyone. Notice that the productivity benefit of education is not necessarily an externality: The consumer of education reaps most of the benefit in the form of higher wages. But if some of the productivity benefits of education spill over and benefit other people, then this effect would count as a positive externality as well.

The analysis of positive externalities is similar to the analysis of negative externalities. As Figure 3 (p. 208) shows, the demand curve does not reflect the value to society of the good. Because the social value is greater than the private value, the social-value curve lies above the demand curve. The optimal quantity is found where the social-value curve and the supply curve (which represents costs) intersect. Hence, the socially optimal quantity is greater than the quantity determined by the private market.

Once again, the government can correct the market failure by inducing market participants to internalize the externality. The appropriate response in the case of positive externalities is exactly the opposite to the case of negative externalities. To move the market equilibrium closer to the social optimum, a positive externality requires a subsidy. In fact, that is exactly the policy the government follows: Education is heavily subsidized through public schools and government scholarships.

To summarize: *Negative externalities lead markets to produce a larger quantity than is socially desirable. Positive externalities lead markets to produce a smaller quantity than is socially desirable. To remedy the problem, the government can internalize the externality by taxing goods that have negative externalities and subsidizing goods that have positive externalities.*

FIGURE 3

Education and the Social Optimum

In the presence of a positive externality, the social value of the good exceeds the private value. The optimal quantity, $Q_{OPTIMUM}$, is therefore larger than the equilibrium quantity, Q_{MARKET}.

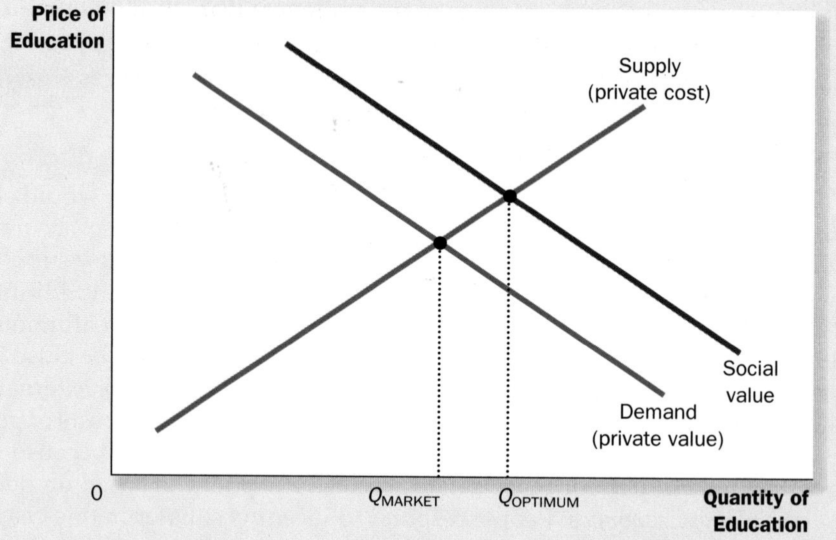

Case Study

TECHNOLOGY SPILLOVERS AND INDUSTRIAL POLICY

Consider the market for industrial robots. Robots are at the frontier of a rapidly changing technology. Whenever a firm builds a robot, there is some chance that it will discover a new and better design. This new design will benefit not only this firm but society as a whole because the design will enter society's pool of technological knowledge. This type of positive externality is called a *technology spillover.*

In this case, the government can internalize the externality by subsidizing the production of robots. If the government paid firms a subsidy for each robot produced, the supply curve would shift down by the amount of the subsidy, and this shift would increase the equilibrium quantity of robots. To ensure that the market equilibrium equals the social optimum, the subsidy should equal the value of the technology spillover.

How large are technology spillovers, and what do they imply for public policy? This is an important question because technological progress is the key to why living standards rise over time. Yet it is also a difficult question on which economists often disagree.

Some economists believe that technology spillovers are pervasive and that the government should encourage those industries that yield the largest spillovers. For instance, these economists argue that if making computer chips yields greater spillovers than making potato chips, then the government should use the tax laws to encourage the production of computer chips relative to the production of potato chips. Government intervention in the economy that aims to promote technology-enhancing industries is sometimes called *industrial policy.*

Other economists are skeptical about industrial policy. Even if technology spillovers are common, the success of an industrial policy requires that the government be able to measure the size of the spillovers from different markets. This measurement problem is difficult at best. Moreover, without precise measurements, the political system may end up subsidizing those industries with the most political clout, rather than those that yield the largest positive externalities.

Another way to deal with technology spillovers is patent protection. The patent laws protect the rights of inventors by giving them exclusive use of their inventions for a period of time. When a firm makes a technological breakthrough, it can patent the idea and capture much of the economic benefit for itself. The patent is said to internalize the externality by giving the firm a *property right* over its invention. If other firms want to use the new technology, they would have to obtain permission from the inventing firm and pay it some royalty. Thus, the patent system gives firms a greater incentive to engage in research and other activities that advance technology. ●

QuickQuiz Give an example of a negative externality and a positive externality. • Explain why market outcomes are inefficient in the presence of externalities.

PRIVATE SOLUTIONS TO EXTERNALITIES

We have discussed why externalities lead markets to allocate resources inefficiently, but have mentioned only briefly how this inefficiency can be remedied. In practice, both private actors and public policymakers respond to externalities in various ways. All of the remedies share the goal of moving the allocation of resources closer to the social optimum. In this section we examine private solutions.

The Types of Private Solutions

Although externalities tend to cause markets to be inefficient, government action is not always needed to solve the problem. In some circumstances, people can develop private solutions.

Sometimes, the problem of externalities is solved with moral codes and social sanctions. Consider, for instance, why most people do not litter. Although there are laws against littering, these laws are not vigorously enforced. Most people do not litter just because it is the wrong thing to do. The Golden Rule taught to most children says, "Do unto others as you would have them do unto you." This moral injunction tells us to take account of how our actions affect other people. In economic terms, it tells us to internalize externalities.

Another private solution to externalities is charities, many of which are established to deal with externalities. For example, the Sierra Club, whose goal is to protect the environment, is a nonprofit organization funded with private donations. As another example, colleges and universities receive gifts from alumni, corporations, and foundations in part because education has positive externalities for society.

The private market can often solve the problem of externalities by relying on the self-interest of the relevant parties. Sometimes the solution takes the form of integrating different types of business. For example, consider an apple grower and a beekeeper who are located next to each other. Each business confers a positive externality on the other: By pollinating the flowers on the trees, the bees help the orchard produce apples. At the same time, the bees use the nectar they get from the apple trees to produce honey. Nonetheless, when the apple grower is deciding how many trees to plant and the beekeeper is deciding how many bees to keep, they neglect the positive externality. As a result, the apple grower plants too few trees and the beekeeper keeps too few bees. These externalities could be internalized if the beekeeper bought the apple orchard or if the apple grower bought the beehives: Both activities would then take place within the same firm, and this single firm could choose the optimal number of trees and bees. Internalizing externalities is one reason that some firms are involved in different types of business.

Another way for the private market to deal with external effects is for the interested parties to enter into a contract. In the foregoing example, a contract between the apple grower and the beekeeper can solve the problem of too few trees and too few bees. The contract can specify the number of trees, the number of bees, and perhaps a payment from one party to the other. By setting the right number of trees and bees, the contract can solve the inefficiency that normally arises from these externalities and make both parties better off.

The Coase Theorem

Coase theorem
the proposition that if private parties can bargain without cost over the allocation of resources, they can solve the problem of externalities on their own

How effective is the private market in dealing with externalities? A famous result, called the **Coase theorem** after economist Ronald Coase, suggests that it can be very effective in some circumstances. According to the Coase theorem, if private parties can bargain without cost over the allocation of resources, then the private market will always solve the problem of externalities and allocate resources efficiently.

To see how the Coase theorem works, consider an example. Suppose that Dick owns a dog named Spot. Spot barks and disturbs Jane, Dick's neighbor. Dick gets a benefit from owning the dog, but the dog confers a negative externality on Jane. Should Dick be forced to send Spot to the pound, or should Jane have to suffer sleepless nights because of Spot's barking?

Consider first what outcome is socially efficient. A social planner, considering the two alternatives, would compare the benefit that Dick gets from the dog to the cost that Jane bears from the barking. If the benefit exceeds the cost, it is efficient for Dick to keep the dog and for Jane to live with the barking. Yet if the cost exceeds the benefit, then Dick should get rid of the dog.

According to the Coase theorem, the private market will reach the efficient outcome on its own. How? Jane can simply offer to pay Dick to get rid of the dog. Dick will accept the deal if the amount of money Jane offers is greater than the benefit of keeping the dog.

By bargaining over the price, Dick and Jane can always reach the efficient outcome. For instance, suppose that Dick gets a $500 benefit from the dog and Jane bears an $800 cost from the barking. In this case, Jane can offer Dick $600 to get rid of the dog, and Dick will gladly accept. Both parties are better off than they were before, and the efficient outcome is reached.

It is possible, of course, that Jane would not be willing to offer any price that Dick would accept. For instance, suppose that Dick gets a $1,000 benefit from the dog and Jane bears an $800 cost from the barking. In this case, Dick would turn down any offer below $1,000, while Jane would not offer any amount above $800. Therefore, Dick ends up keeping the dog. Given these costs and benefits, however, this outcome is efficient.

So far, we have assumed that Dick has the legal right to keep a barking dog. In other words, we have assumed that Dick can keep Spot unless Jane pays him enough to induce him to give up the dog voluntarily. How different would the outcome be, on the other hand, if Jane had the legal right to peace and quiet?

According to the Coase theorem, the initial distribution of rights does not matter for the market's ability to reach the efficient outcome. For instance, suppose that Jane can legally compel Dick to get rid of the dog. Although having this right works to Jane's advantage, it probably will not change the outcome. In this case, Dick can offer to pay Jane to allow him to keep the dog. If the benefit of the dog to Dick exceeds the cost of the barking to Jane, then Dick and Jane will strike a bargain in which Dick keeps the dog.

Although Dick and Jane can reach the efficient outcome regardless of how rights are initially distributed, the distribution of rights is not irrelevant: It determines the distribution of economic well-being. Whether Dick has the right to a barking dog or Jane the right to peace and quiet determines who pays whom in the final bargain. But, in either case, the two parties can bargain with each other and solve the externality problem. Dick will end up keeping the dog only if the benefit exceeds the cost.

To sum up: *The Coase theorem says that private economic actors can solve the problem of externalities among themselves. Whatever the initial distribution of rights, the interested parties can always reach a bargain in which everyone is better off and the outcome is efficient.*

Why Private Solutions Do Not Always Work

Despite the appealing logic of the Coase theorem, private actors on their own often fail to resolve the problems caused by externalities. The Coase theorem applies only when the interested parties have no trouble reaching and enforcing an agreement. In the world, however, bargaining does not always work, even when a mutually beneficial agreement is possible.

Sometimes the interested parties fail to solve an externality problem because of **transaction costs**, the costs that parties incur in the process of agreeing to and following through on a bargain. In our example, imagine that Dick and Jane speak different languages so that, to reach an agreement, they will need to hire a translator. If the benefit of solving the barking problem is less than the cost of the translator, Dick and Jane might choose to leave the problem unsolved. In more realistic examples, the transaction costs are the expenses not of translators but of the lawyers required to draft and enforce contracts.

transaction costs
the costs that parties incur in the process of agreeing and following through on a bargain

At other times bargaining simply breaks down. The recurrence of wars and labor strikes shows that reaching agreement can be difficult and that failing to reach agreement can be costly. The problem is often that each party tries to hold out for a better deal. For example, suppose that Dick gets a $500 benefit from the dog, and Jane bears an $800 cost from the barking. Although it is efficient for Jane to pay

Dick to get rid of the dog, there are many prices that could lead to this outcome. Dick might demand $750, and Jane might offer only $550. As they haggle over the price, the inefficient outcome with the barking dog persists.

Reaching an efficient bargain is especially difficult when the number of interested parties is large because coordinating everyone is costly. For example, consider a factory that pollutes the water of a nearby lake. The pollution confers a negative externality on the local fishermen. According to the Coase theorem, if the pollution is inefficient, then the factory and the fishermen could reach a bargain in which the fishermen pay the factory not to pollute. If there are many fishermen, however, trying to coordinate them all to bargain with the factory may be almost impossible.

When private bargaining does not work, the government can sometimes play a role. The government is an institution designed for collective action. In this example, the government can act on behalf of the fishermen, even when it is impractical for the fishermen to act for themselves. In the next section, we examine how the government can try to remedy the problem of externalities.

QuickQuiz Give an example of a private solution to an externality. • What is the Coase theorem? • Why are private economic actors sometimes unable to solve the problems caused by an externality?

PUBLIC POLICIES TOWARD EXTERNALITIES

When an externality causes a market to reach an inefficient allocation of resources, the government can respond in one of two ways. *Command-and-control policies* regulate behavior directly. *Market-based policies* provide incentives so that private decisionmakers will choose to solve the problem on their own.

Regulation

The government can remedy an externality by making certain behaviors either required or forbidden. For example, it is a crime to dump poisonous chemicals into the water supply. In this case, the external costs to society far exceed the benefits to the polluter. The government therefore institutes a command-and-control policy that prohibits this act altogether.

In most cases of pollution, however, the situation is not this simple. Despite the stated goals of some environmentalists, it would be impossible to prohibit all polluting activity. For example, virtually all forms of transportation—even the horse—produce some undesirable polluting by-products. But it would not be sensible for the government to ban all transportation. Thus, instead of trying to eradicate pollution altogether, society has to weigh the costs and benefits to decide the kinds and quantities of pollution it will allow. In the United States, the Environmental Protection Agency (EPA) is the government agency with the task of developing and enforcing regulations aimed at protecting the environment.

Environmental regulations can take many forms. Sometimes the EPA dictates a maximum level of pollution that a factory may emit. Other times the EPA requires that firms adopt a particular technology to reduce emissions. In all cases, to design good rules, the government regulators need to know the details about specific industries and about the alternative technologies that those industries could adopt. This information is often difficult for government regulators to obtain.

Pigovian Taxes and Subsidies

Instead of regulating behavior in response to an externality, the government can use market-based policies to align private incentives with social efficiency. For instance, as we saw earlier, the government can internalize the externality by taxing activities that have negative externalities and subsidizing activities that have positive externalities. Taxes enacted to correct the effects of negative externalities are called **Pigovian taxes,** after economist Arthur Pigou (1877–1959), an early advocate of their use.

Economists usually prefer Pigovian taxes over regulations as a way to deal with pollution because such taxes can reduce pollution at a lower cost to society. To see why, let us consider an example.

Suppose that two factories—a paper mill and a steel mill—are each dumping 500 tons of glop into a river each year. The EPA decides that it wants to reduce the amount of pollution. It considers two solutions:

- Regulation: The EPA could tell each factory to reduce its pollution to 300 tons of glop per year.
- Pigovian tax: The EPA could levy a tax on each factory of $50,000 for each ton of glop it emits.

The regulation would dictate a level of pollution, whereas the tax would give factory owners an economic incentive to reduce pollution. Which solution do you think is better?

Most economists would prefer the tax. They would first point out that a tax is just as effective as a regulation in reducing the overall level of pollution. The EPA can achieve whatever level of pollution it wants by setting the tax at the appropriate level. The higher the tax, the larger the reduction in pollution. Indeed, if the tax is high enough, the factories will close down altogether, reducing pollution to zero.

The reason why economists would prefer the tax is that it reduces pollution more efficiently. The regulation requires each factory to reduce pollution by the same amount, but an equal reduction is not necessarily the least expensive way to clean up the water. It is possible that the paper mill can reduce pollution at lower cost than the steel mill. If so, the paper mill would respond to the tax by reducing pollution substantially to avoid the tax, whereas the steel mill would respond by reducing pollution less and paying the tax.

In essence, the Pigovian tax places a price on the right to pollute. Just as markets allocate goods to those buyers who value them most highly, a Pigovian tax allocates pollution to those factories that face the highest cost of reducing it. Whatever the level of pollution the EPA chooses, it can achieve this goal at the lowest total cost using a tax.

Economists also argue that Pigovian taxes are better for the environment. Under the command-and-control policy of regulation, the factories have no reason to

Pigovian tax
a tax enacted to correct the effects of a negative externality

reduce emission further once they have reached the target of 300 tons of glop. By contrast, the tax gives the factories an incentive to develop cleaner technologies, because a cleaner technology would reduce the amount of tax the factory has to pay.

Pigovian taxes are unlike most other taxes. As we discussed in Chapter 8, most taxes distort incentives and move the allocation of resources away from the social optimum. The reduction in economic well-being—that is, in consumer and producer surplus—exceeds the amount of revenue the government raises, resulting in a deadweight loss. By contrast, when externalities are present, society also cares about the well-being of the bystanders who are affected. Pigovian taxes correct incentives for the presence of externalities and thereby move the allocation of resources closer to the social optimum. Thus, while Pigovian taxes raise revenue for the government, they also enhance economic efficiency.

Case Study

WHY IS GASOLINE TAXED SO HEAVILY?

In many countries, gasoline is among the most heavily taxed goods in the economy. In the United States, for instance, almost half of what drivers pay for gasoline goes to the gas tax. In many European countries, the tax is even larger, and the price of gasoline is three or four times the U.S. price.

Why is this tax so common? One possible answer is that the gas tax is a Pigovian tax aimed at correcting three negative externalities associated with driving:

- *Congestion:* If you have ever been stuck in bumper-to-bumper traffic, you have probably wished that there were fewer cars on the road. A gasoline tax keeps congestion down by encouraging people to take public transportation, carpool more often, and live closer to work.
- *Accidents:* Whenever a person buys a large car or a sport utility vehicle, he makes himself safer, but he puts his neighbors at risk. According the National Highway Traffic Safety Administration, a person driving a typical car is five times as likely to die if hit by a sport utility vehicle than if hit by another car. The gas tax is an indirect way of making people pay when their large, gas-guzzling vehicles impose risk on others, which in turn makes them take account of this risk when choosing what vehicle to purchase.
- *Pollution:* The burning of fossil fuels such as gasoline is widely believed to be the cause of global warming. Experts disagree about how dangerous this threat is, but there is no doubt that the gas tax reduces the risk by reducing the use of gasoline.

So the gas tax, rather than causing deadweight losses like most taxes, actually makes the economy work better. It means less traffic congestion, safer roads, and a cleaner environment. ●

"If the gas tax were any larger, I'd take the bus."

Tradable Pollution Permits

Returning to our example of the paper mill and the steel mill, let us suppose that, despite the advice of its economists, the EPA adopts the regulation and requires each factory to reduce its pollution to 300 tons of glop per year. Then one day, after the regulation is in place and both mills have complied, the two firms go to the EPA with a proposal. The steel mill wants to increase its emission of glop by 100 tons. The paper mill has agreed to reduce its emission by the same amount if the steel mill pays it $5 million. Should the EPA allow the two factories to make this deal?

From the standpoint of economic efficiency, allowing the deal is good policy. The deal must make the owners of the two factories better off, because they are voluntarily agreeing to it. Moreover, the deal does not have any external effects because the total amount of pollution remains the same. Thus, social welfare is enhanced by allowing the paper mill to sell its right to pollute to the steel mill.

The same logic applies to any voluntary transfer of the right to pollute from one firm to another. If the EPA allows firms to make these deals, it will, in essence, have created a new scarce resource: pollution permits. A market to trade these permits will eventually develop, and that market will be governed by the forces of supply and demand. The invisible hand will ensure that this new market efficiently allocates the right to pollute. The firms that can reduce pollution only at high cost will be willing to pay the most for the pollution permits. The firms that can reduce pollution at low cost will prefer to sell whatever permits they have.

One advantage of allowing a market for pollution permits is that the initial allocation of pollution permits among firms does not matter from the standpoint of economic efficiency. The logic behind this conclusion is similar to that behind the Coase theorem. Those firms that can reduce pollution most easily would be willing to sell whatever permits they get, and those firms that can reduce pollution only at high cost would be willing to buy whatever permits they need. As long as there is a free market for the pollution rights, the final allocation will be efficient whatever the initial allocation.

Although reducing pollution using pollution permits may seem quite different from using Pigovian taxes, in fact the two policies have much in common. In both cases, firms pay for their pollution. With Pigovian taxes, polluting firms must pay a tax to the government. With pollution permits, polluting firms must pay to buy the permit. (Even firms that already own permits must pay to pollute: The opportunity cost of polluting is what they could have received by selling their permits on the open market.) Both Pigovian taxes and pollution permits internalize the externality of pollution by making it costly for firms to pollute.

The similarity of the two policies can be seen by considering the market for pollution. Both panels in Figure 4 (p. 216) show the demand curve for the right to pollute. This curve shows that the lower the price of polluting, the more firms will choose to pollute. In panel (a), the EPA uses a Pigovian tax to set a price for pollution. In this case, the supply curve for pollution rights is perfectly elastic (because firms can pollute as much as they want by paying the tax), and the position of the demand curve determines the quantity of pollution. In panel (b), the EPA sets a quantity of pollution by issuing pollution permits. In this case, the supply curve for pollution rights is perfectly inelastic (because the quantity of pollution is fixed by the number of permits), and the position of the demand curve determines the price of pollution. Hence, for any given demand curve for pollution, the EPA can

FIGURE 4

The Equivalence of Pigovian Taxes and Pollution Permits

In panel (a), the EPA sets a price on pollution by levying a Pigovian tax, and the demand curve determines the quantity of pollution. In panel (b), the EPA limits the quantity of pollution by limiting the number of pollution permits, and the demand curve determines the price of pollution. The price and quantity of pollution are the same in the two cases.

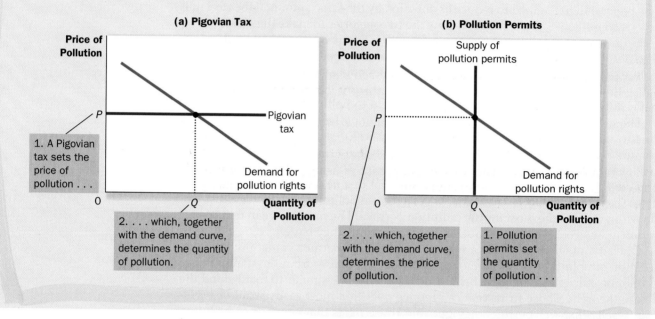

achieve any point on the demand curve either by setting a price with a Pigovian tax or by setting a quantity with pollution permits.

In some circumstances, however, selling pollution permits may be better than levying a Pigovian tax. Suppose the EPA wants no more than 600 tons of glop to be dumped into the river. But, because the EPA does not know the demand curve for pollution, it is not sure what size tax would achieve that goal. In this case, it can simply auction off 600 pollution permits. The auction price would yield the appropriate size of the Pigovian tax.

The idea of the government auctioning off the right to pollute may at first sound like a creature of some economist's imagination. And, in fact, that is how the idea began. But increasingly the EPA has used the system as a way to control pollution. Pollution permits, like Pigovian taxes, are now widely viewed as a cost-effective way to keep the environment clean.

Objections to the Economic Analysis of Pollution

"We cannot give anyone the option of polluting for a fee." This comment by former Senator Edmund Muskie reflects the view of some environmentalists. Clean air and clean water, they argue, are fundamental human rights that should not be debased by considering them in economic terms. How can you put a price on clean air and clean water? The environment is so important, they claim, that we should protect it as much as possible, regardless of the cost.

Economists have little sympathy with this type of argument. To economists, good environmental policy begins by acknowledging the first of the *Ten Principles of Economics* in Chapter 1: People face tradeoffs. Certainly, clean air and clean water have value. But their value must be compared to their opportunity cost—that is, to what one must give up to obtain them. Eliminating all pollution is impossible. Trying to eliminate all pollution would reverse many of the technological advances that allow us to enjoy a high standard of living. Few people would be willing to accept poor nutrition, inadequate medical care, or shoddy housing to make the environment as clean as possible.

Economists argue that some environmental activists hurt their own cause by not thinking in economic terms. A clean environment is a good like other goods. Like all normal goods, it has a positive income elasticity: Rich countries can afford a cleaner environment than poor ones and, therefore, usually have more rigorous environmental protection. In addition, like most other goods, clean air and water obey the law of demand: The lower the price of environmental protection, the more the public will want. The economic approach of using pollution permits and Pigovian taxes reduces the cost of environmental protection and should, therefore, increase the public's demand for a clean environment.

QuickQuiz A glue factory and a steel mill emit smoke containing a chemical that is harmful if inhaled in large amounts. Describe three ways the town government might respond to this externality. What are the pros and cons of each of your solutions?

CONCLUSION

The invisible hand is powerful but not omnipotent. A market's equilibrium maximizes the sum of producer and consumer surplus. When the buyers and sellers in the market are the only interested parties, this outcome is efficient from the standpoint of society as a whole. But when there are external effects, such as pollution, evaluating a market outcome requires taking into account the well-being of third parties as well. In this case, the invisible hand of the marketplace may fail to allocate resources efficiently.

In some cases, people can solve the problem of externalities on their own. The Coase theorem suggests that the interested parties can bargain among themselves and agree on an efficient solution. Sometimes, however, an efficient outcome cannot be reached, perhaps because the large number of interested parties makes bargaining difficult.

When people cannot solve the problem of externalities privately, the government often steps in. Yet, even now, society should not abandon market forces entirely. Rather, the government can address the problem by requiring decision-makers to bear the full costs of their actions. Pigovian taxes on emissions and pollution permits, for instance, are designed to internalize the externality of pollution. More and more, they are the policy of choice for those interested in protecting the environment. Market forces, properly redirected, are often the best remedy for market failure.

IN THE NEWS

CHILDREN AS EXTERNALITIES

This tongue-in-cheek editorial from The Economist, *an international newsmagazine, calls attention to a common externality that is not fully appreciated.*

Mum's the Word: When Children Should Be Screened and Not Heard

We live in increasingly intolerant times. Signs proliferate demanding no smoking, no spitting, no parking, even no walking. . . . Posh clubs and restaurants have long had "no jeans" rules, but these days you can be too smart. Some London hostelries have "no suits" policies, for fear that boisterous city traders in suits might spoil the atmosphere. Environmentalists have long demanded all sorts of bans on cars. Mobile telephones are the latest target: some trains, airline lounges, restaurants, and even golf courses are being designated "no phone" areas.

If intolerance really has to be the spirit of this age, *The Economist* would like to suggest restrictions on another source of noise pollution: children. Lest you dismiss this as mere prejudice, we can even produce a good economic argument for it. Smoking, driving, and mobile phones all cause what economists call "negative externalities." That is, the costs of these activities to other people tend to exceed the costs to the individuals of their proclivities. The invisible hand of the market fumbles, leading resources astray. Thus, because a driver's private motoring costs do not reflect the costs he imposes on others in the form of pollution and congestion, he uses the car more than is socially desirable. Likewise, it is argued, smokers take too little care to ensure that their acrid fumes do not damage other people around them.

Governments typically respond to such market failures in two ways. One is higher taxes, to make polluters pay the full cost of their anti-social behavior. The other is regulation, such as emission standards or bans on smoking in public places. Both approaches might work for children.

For children, just like cigarettes or mobile phones, clearly impose a negative externality on people who are near them.

SUMMARY

- When a transaction between a buyer and seller directly affects a third party, the effect is called an externality. Negative externalities, such as pollution, cause the socially optimal quantity in a market to be less than the equilibrium quantity. Positive externalities, such as technology spillovers, cause the socially optimal quantity to be greater than the equilibrium quantity.

- Those affected by externalities can sometimes solve the problem privately. For instance, when one business confers an externality on another business, the two businesses can internalize the externality by merging. Alternatively, the interested parties can solve the problem by negotiating a contract. According to the Coase theorem, if people can bargain without cost, then they can always reach an agreement in which resources are allocated efficiently. In many cases, however, reaching a bargain among the many interested parties is difficult, so the Coase theorem does not apply.

Anybody who has suffered a 12-hour flight with a bawling baby in the row immediately ahead, or a bored youngster viciously kicking their seat from behind, will grasp this as quickly as they would love to grasp the youngster's neck. Here is a clear case of market failure: parents do not bear the full costs (indeed young babies travel free), so they are too ready to take their noisy brats with them. Where is the invisible hand when it is needed to administer a good smack?

The solution is obvious. All airlines, trains, and restaurants should create child-free zones. Put all those children at the back of the plane and parents might make more effort to minimize their noise pollution. And instead of letting children pay less and babies go free, they should be charged (or taxed) more than adults, with the revenues used to subsidize seats immediately in front of the war-zone.

Passengers could then request a no-children seat, just as they now ask for a no-smoking one. As more women choose not to have children and the number of older people without young children increases, the demand for child-free travel will expand. Well, yes, it is a bit intolerant—but why shouldn't parents be treated as badly as smokers? And at least there is an obvious airline to pioneer the scheme: Virgin.

- When private parties cannot adequately deal with external effects, such as pollution, the government often steps in. Sometimes the government prevents socially inefficient activity by regulating behavior. Other times it internalizes an externality using Pigovian taxes.

Another public policy is to issue permits. For instance, the government could protect the environment by issuing a limited number of pollution permits. The end result of this policy is largely the same as imposing Pigovian taxes on polluters.

KEY CONCEPTS

externality, p. 204
internalizing an externality, p. 207

Coase theorem, p. 210
transaction costs, p. 211

Pigovian tax, p. 213

QUESTIONS FOR REVIEW

1. Give an example of a negative externality and an example of a positive externality.

2. Use a supply-and-demand diagram to explain the effect of a negative externality in production.

3. In what way does the patent system help society solve an externality problem?

4. List some of the ways that the problems caused by externalities can be solved without government intervention.

5. Imagine that you are a nonsmoker sharing a room with a smoker. According to the Coase theorem, what determines whether your roommate smokes in the room? Is this outcome efficient? How do you and your roommate reach this solution?

6. What are Pigovian taxes? Why do economists prefer them over regulations as a way to protect the environment from pollution?

PROBLEMS AND APPLICATIONS

1. There are two ways to protect your car from theft. The Club makes it difficult for a car thief to take your car. Lojack makes it easier for the police to catch a car thief after he has stolen it. Which of these types of protection conveys a negative externality on other car owners? Which conveys a positive externality? Do you think there are any policy implications of your analysis?

2. Do you agree with the following statements? Why or why not?
   a. "The benefits of Pigovian taxes as a way to reduce pollution have to be weighed against the deadweight losses that these taxes cause."
   b. "When deciding whether to levy a Pigovian tax on consumers or producers, the government should be careful to levy the tax on the side of the market generating the externality."

3. Consider the market for fire extinguishers.
   a. Why might fire extinguishers exhibit positive externalities?
   b. Draw a graph of the market for fire extinguishers, labeling the demand curve, the social-value curve, the supply curve, and the social-cost curve.
   c. Indicate the market equilibrium level of output and the efficient level of output. Give an intuitive explanation for why these quantities differ.
   d. If the external benefit is $10 per extinguisher, describe a government

policy that would result in the efficient outcome.

4. Contributions to charitable organizations are deductible under the federal income tax. In what way does this government policy encourage private solutions to externalities?

5. Ringo loves playing rock and roll music at high volume. Luciano loves opera and hates rock and roll. Unfortunately, they are next-door neighbors in an apartment building with paper-thin walls.
   a. What is the externality here?
   b. What command-and-control policy might the landlord impose? Could such a policy lead to an inefficient outcome?
   c. Suppose the landlord lets the tenants do whatever they want. According to the Coase theorem, how might Ringo and Luciano reach an efficient outcome on their own? What might prevent them from reaching an efficient outcome?

6. It is rumored that the Swiss government subsidizes cattle farming, and that the subsidy is larger in areas with more tourist attractions. Can you think of a reason why this policy might be efficient?

7. Greater consumption of alcohol leads to more motor vehicle accidents and, thus, imposes costs on people who do not drink and drive.
   a. Illustrate the market for alcohol, labeling the demand curve, the social-value curve,

the supply curve, the social-cost curve, the market equilibrium level of output, and the efficient level of output.

b. On your graph, shade the area corresponding to the deadweight loss of the market equilibrium. (Hint: The deadweight loss occurs because some units of alcohol are consumed for which the social cost exceeds the social value.) Explain.

8. Many observers believe that the levels of pollution in our economy are too high.

a. If society wishes to reduce overall pollution by a certain amount, why is it efficient to have different amounts of reduction at different firms?

b. Command-and-control approaches often rely on uniform reductions among firms. Why are these approaches generally unable to target the firms that should undertake bigger reductions?

c. Economists argue that appropriate Pigovian taxes or tradable pollution rights will result in efficient pollution reduction. How do these approaches target the firms that should undertake bigger reductions?

9. The Pristine River has two polluting firms on its banks. Acme Industrial and Creative Chemicals each dump 100 tons of glop into the river each year. The cost of reducing glop emissions per ton equals $10 for Acme and $100 for Creative. The local government wants to reduce overall pollution from 200 tons to 50 tons.

a. If the government knew the cost of reduction for each firm, what reductions would it impose to reach its overall goal? What would be the cost to each firm and the total cost to the firms together?

b. In a more typical situation, the government would not know the cost of pollution reduction at each firm. If the government decided to reach its overall goal by imposing uniform reductions on the firms, calculate the reduction made by each firm, the cost to each firm, and the total cost to the firms together.

c. Compare the total cost of pollution reduction in parts (a) and (b). If the government does not know the cost of reduction for

each firm, is there still some way for it to reduce pollution to 50 tons at the total cost you calculated in part (a)? Explain.

10. "A fine is a tax for doing something wrong. A tax is a fine for doing something right." Discuss.

11. Figure 4 shows that for any given demand curve for the right to pollute, the government can achieve the same outcome either by setting a price with a Pigovian tax or by setting a quantity with pollution permits. Suppose there is a sharp improvement in the technology for controlling pollution.

a. Using graphs similar to those in Figure 4, illustrate the effect of this development on the demand for pollution rights.

b. What is the effect on the price and quantity of pollution under each regulatory system? Explain.

12. Suppose that the government decides to issue tradable permits for a certain form of pollution.

a. Does it matter for economic efficiency whether the government distributes or auctions the permits? Does it matter in any other ways?

b. If the government chooses to distribute the permits, does the allocation of permits among firms matter for efficiency? Does it matter in any other ways?

13. The primary cause of global warming is carbon dioxide, which enters the atmosphere in varying amounts from different countries but is distributed equally around the globe within a year. In an article in *The Boston Globe* (July 3, 1990), Martin and Kathleen Feldstein argue that the correct approach to global warming is "not to ask individual countries to stabilize their emissions of carbon dioxide at current levels," as some have suggested. Instead, they argue that "carbon dioxide emissions should be reduced in countries where the costs are least, and the countries that bear that burden should be compensated by the rest of the world."

a. Why is international cooperation necessary to reach an efficient outcome?

b. Is it possible to devise a compensation scheme such that all countries would be better off than under a system of uniform emission reductions? Explain.

14. Some people object to market-based policies to reduce pollution, claiming that they place a dollar value on cleaning our air and water. Economists reply that society *implicitly* places a dollar value on environmental cleanup even under command-and-control policies. Discuss why this is true.

15. (This problem is challenging.) There are three industrial firms in Happy Valley.

Firm	Initial Pollution Level	Cost of Reducing Pollution by 1 Unit
A	70 units	$20
B	80	25
C	50	10

The government wants to reduce pollution to 120 units, so it gives each firm 40 tradable pollution permits.

a. Who sells permits and how many do they sell? Who buys permits and how many do they buy? Briefly explain why the sellers and buyers are each willing to do so. What is the total cost of pollution reduction in this situation?

b. How much higher would the costs of pollution reduction be if the permits could not be traded?

http:// For more study tools, please visit http://mankiwXtra.swlearning.com.

PUBLIC GOODS
AND COMMON RESOURCES

An old song lyric maintains that "the best things in life are free." A moment's thought reveals a long list of goods that the songwriter could have had in mind. Nature provides some of them, such as rivers, mountains, beaches, lakes, and oceans. The government provides others, such as playgrounds, parks, and parades. In each case, people do not pay a fee when they choose to enjoy the benefit of the good.

Free goods provide a special challenge for economic analysis. Most goods in our economy are allocated in markets, where buyers pay for what they receive and sellers are paid for what they provide. For these goods, prices are the signals that guide the decisions of buyers and sellers. When goods are available free of charge, however, the market forces that normally allocate resources in our economy are absent.

In this chapter we examine the problems that arise for goods without market prices. Our analysis will shed light on one of the *Ten Principles of Economics* in Chapter 1: Governments can sometimes improve market outcomes. When a good does not have a price attached to it, private markets cannot ensure that the good is produced and consumed in the proper amounts. In such cases, government policy can potentially remedy the market failure and raise economic well-being.

THE DIFFERENT KINDS OF GOODS

How well do markets work in providing the goods that people want? The answer to this question depends on the good being considered. As we discussed in Chapter 7, we can rely on the market to provide the efficient number of ice-cream cones: The price of ice-cream cones adjusts to balance supply and demand, and this equilibrium maximizes the sum of producer and consumer surplus. Yet, as we discussed in Chapter 10, we cannot rely on the market to prevent aluminum manufacturers from polluting the air we breathe: Buyers and sellers in a market typically do not take account of the external effects of their decisions. Thus, markets work well when the good is ice cream, but they work badly when the good is clean air.

In thinking about the various goods in the economy, it is useful to group them according to two characteristics:

- Is the good **excludable?** Can people be prevented from using the good?
- Is the good **rival?** Does one person's use of the good diminish another person's ability to use it?

Using these two characteristics, Figure 1 divides goods into four categories:

1. **Private goods** are both excludable and rival. Consider an ice-cream cone, for example. An ice-cream cone is excludable because it is possible to prevent someone from eating an ice-cream cone—you just don't give it to him. An

excludability
the property of a good whereby a person can be prevented from using it

rivalry
the property of a good whereby one person's use diminishes other people's use

private goods
goods that are both excludable and rival

FIGURE 1

Four Types of Goods

Goods can be grouped into four categories according to two questions: (1) Is the good excludable? That is, can people be prevented from using it? (2) Is the good rival? That is, does one person's use of the good diminish other people's use of it? This diagram gives examples of goods in each of the four categories.

		Rival?	
		Yes	**No**
Excludable?	**Yes**	**Private Goods** • Ice-cream cones • Clothing • Congested toll roads	**Natural Monopolies** • Fire protection • Cable TV • Uncongested toll roads
	No	**Common Resources** • Fish in the ocean • The environment • Congested nontoll roads	**Public Goods** • Tornado siren • National defense • Uncongested nontoll roads

ice-cream cone is rival because if one person eats an ice-cream cone, another person cannot eat the same cone. Most goods in the economy are private goods like ice-cream cones. When we analyzed supply and demand in Chapters 4, 5, and 6 and the efficiency of markets in Chapters 7, 8, and 9, we implicitly assumed that goods were both excludable and rival.

2. **Public goods** are neither excludable nor rival. That is, people cannot be prevented from using a public good, and one person's use of a public good does not reduce another person's ability to use it. For example, a tornado siren in a small town is a public good. Once the siren sounds, it is impossible to prevent any single person from hearing it. Moreover, when one person gets the benefit of the warning, he does not reduce the benefit to anyone else.

   public goods
   goods that are neither excludable nor rival

3. **Common resources** are rival but not excludable. For example, fish in the ocean are a rival good: When one person catches fish, there are fewer fish for the next person to catch. Yet these fish are not an excludable good because, given the vast size of an ocean, it is difficult to stop fishermen from taking fish out of it.

   common resources
   goods that are rival but not excludable

4. When a good is excludable but not rival, it is an example of a *natural monopoly*. For instance, consider fire protection in a small town. It is easy to exclude people from using this good: The fire department can just let their house burn down. Yet fire protection is not rival. Firefighters spend much of their time waiting for a fire, so protecting an extra house is unlikely to reduce the protection available to others. In other words, once a town has paid for the fire department, the additional cost of protecting one more house is small. In Chapter 15 we give a more complete definition of natural monopolies and study them in some detail.

In this chapter we examine goods that are not excludable and, therefore, are available to everyone free of charge: public goods and common resources. As we will see, this topic is closely related to the study of externalities. For both public goods and common resources, externalities arise because something of value has no price attached to it. If one person were to provide a public good, such as a tornado siren, other people would be better off, and yet they could not be charged for this benefit. Similarly, when one person uses a common resource, such as the fish in the ocean, other people are worse off, and yet they are not compensated for this loss. Because of these external effects, private decisions about consumption and production can lead to an inefficient allocation of resources, and government intervention can potentially raise economic well-being.

QuickQuiz Define *public goods* and *common resources*, and give an example of each.

PUBLIC GOODS

To understand how public goods differ from other goods and what problems they present for society, let's consider an example: a fireworks display. This good is not excludable because it is impossible to prevent someone from seeing fireworks, and it is not rival because one person's enjoyment of fireworks does not reduce anyone else's enjoyment of them.

The Free-Rider Problem

The citizens of Smalltown, U.S.A., like seeing fireworks on the Fourth of July. Each of the town's 500 residents places a $10 value on the experience. The cost of putting on a fireworks display is $1,000. Because the $5,000 of benefits exceed the $1,000 of costs, it is efficient for Smalltown residents to have a fireworks display on the Fourth of July.

Would the private market produce the efficient outcome? Probably not. Imagine that Ellen, a Smalltown entrepreneur, decided to put on a fireworks display. Ellen would surely have trouble selling tickets to the event because her potential customers would quickly figure out that they could see the fireworks even without a ticket. Because fireworks are not excludable, people have an incentive to be free riders. A **free rider** is a person who receives the benefit of a good but avoids paying for it.

One way to view this market failure is that it arises because of an externality. If Ellen did put on the fireworks display, she would confer an external benefit on those who saw the display without paying for it. When deciding whether to put on the display, Ellen ignores these external benefits. Even though a fireworks display is socially desirable, it is not privately profitable. As a result, Ellen makes the socially inefficient decision not to put on the display.

Although the private market fails to supply the fireworks display demanded by Smalltown residents, the solution to Smalltown's problem is obvious: The local government can sponsor a Fourth of July celebration. The town council can raise everyone's taxes by $2 and use the revenue to hire Ellen to produce the fireworks. Everyone in Smalltown is better off by $8—the $10 in value from the fireworks minus the $2 tax bill. Ellen can help Smalltown reach the efficient outcome as a public employee even though she could not do so as a private entrepreneur.

The story of Smalltown is simplified, but it is also realistic. In fact, many local governments in the United States do pay for fireworks on the Fourth of July. Moreover, the story shows a general lesson about public goods: Because public goods are not excludable, the free-rider problem prevents the private market from supplying them. The government, however, can potentially remedy the problem. If the government decides that the total benefits exceed the costs, it can provide the public good and pay for it with tax revenue, making everyone better off.

Some Important Public Goods

There are many examples of public goods. Here we consider three of the most important.

National Defense The defense of the country from foreign aggressors is a classic example of a public good. Once the country is defended, it is impossible to prevent any single person from enjoying the benefit of this defense. Moreover, when

free rider
a person who receives the benefit of a good but avoids paying for it

"I like the concept if we can do it with no new taxes."

one person enjoys the benefit of national defense, he does not reduce the benefit to anyone else. Thus, national defense is neither excludable nor rival.

National defense is also one of the most expensive public goods. In 2002 the U.S. federal government spent a total of $348 billion on national defense, or about $1,200 per person. People disagree about whether this amount is too small or too large, but almost no one doubts that some government spending for national defense is necessary. Even economists who advocate small government agree that the national defense is a public good the government should provide.

Basic Research The creation of knowledge is a public good. If a mathematician proves a new theorem, the theorem enters the general pool of knowledge that anyone can use without charge. Because knowledge is a public good, profit-seeking firms tend to free ride on the knowledge created by others and, as a result, devote too few resources to creating new knowledge.

In evaluating the appropriate policy toward knowledge creation, it is important to distinguish general knowledge from specific, technological knowledge. Specific, technological knowledge, such as the invention of a better battery, can be patented. The inventor thus obtains much of the benefit of his invention, although certainly not all of it. By contrast, a mathematician cannot patent a theorem; such general knowledge is freely available to everyone. In other words, the patent system makes specific, technological knowledge excludable, whereas general knowledge is not excludable.

The government tries to provide the public good of general knowledge in various ways. Government agencies, such as the National Institutes of Health and the National Science Foundation, subsidize basic research in medicine, mathematics, physics, chemistry, biology, and even economics. Some people justify government funding of the space program on the grounds that it adds to society's pool of knowledge. Certainly, many private goods, including bullet-proof vests and the instant drink Tang, use materials that were first developed by scientists and engineers trying to land a man on the moon. Determining the appropriate level of governmental support for these endeavors is difficult because the benefits are hard to measure. Moreover, the members of Congress who appropriate funds for research usually have little expertise in science and, therefore, are not in the best position to judge what lines of research will produce the largest benefits.

Fighting Poverty Many government programs are aimed at helping the poor. The welfare system (officially called Temporary Assistance for Needy Families) provides a small income for some poor families. Similarly, the Food Stamp program subsidizes the purchase of food for those with low incomes, and various government housing programs make shelter more affordable. These antipoverty programs are financed by taxes on families that are financially more successful.

Economists disagree among themselves about what role the government should play in fighting poverty. Here we note one important argument: Advocates of antipoverty programs claim that fighting poverty is a public good.

Suppose that everyone prefers to live in a society without poverty. Even if this preference is strong and widespread, fighting poverty is not a "good" that the private market can provide. No single individual can eliminate poverty because the problem is so large. Moreover, private charity is hard pressed to solve the problem: People who do not donate to charity can free ride on the generosity of others. In this case, taxing the wealthy to raise the living standards of the poor can make everyone better off. The poor are better off because they now enjoy a higher standard of living, and those paying the taxes are better off because they enjoy living in a society with less poverty.

What kind of good?

Case Study

ARE LIGHTHOUSES PUBLIC GOODS?

Some goods can switch between being public goods and being private goods depending on the circumstances. For example, a fireworks display is a public good if performed in a town with many residents. Yet if performed at a private amusement park, such as Walt Disney World, a fireworks display is more like a private good because visitors to the park pay for admission.

Another example is a lighthouse. Economists have long used lighthouses as an example of a public good. Lighthouses are used to mark specific locations so that passing ships can avoid treacherous waters. The benefit that the lighthouse provides to the ship captain is neither excludable nor rival, so each captain has an incentive to free ride by using the lighthouse to navigate without paying for the service. Because of this free-rider problem, private markets usually fail to provide the lighthouses that ship captains need. As a result, most lighthouses today are operated by the government.

In some cases, however, lighthouses may be closer to private goods. On the coast of England in the nineteenth century, some lighthouses were privately owned and operated. Instead of trying to charge ship captains for the service, however, the owner of the lighthouse charged the owner of the nearby port. If the port owner did not pay, the lighthouse owner turned off the light, and ships avoided that port.

In deciding whether something is a public good, one must determine the number of beneficiaries and whether these beneficiaries can be excluded from using the good. A free-rider problem arises when the number of beneficiaries is large and exclusion of any one of them is impossible. If a lighthouse benefits many ship captains, it is a public good. Yet if it primarily benefits a single port owner, it is more like a private good. ●

The Difficult Job of Cost-Benefit Analysis

So far we have seen that the government provides public goods because the private market on its own will not produce an efficient quantity. Yet deciding that the government must play a role is only the first step. The government must then determine what kinds of public goods to provide and in what quantities.

Suppose that the government is considering a public project, such as building a new highway. To judge whether to build the highway, it must compare the total benefits of all those who would use it to the costs of building and maintaining it. To make this decision, the government might hire a team of economists and engineers to conduct a study, called a **cost-benefit analysis,** the goal of which is to estimate the total costs and benefits of the project to society as a whole.

Cost-benefit analysts have a tough job. Because the highway will be available to everyone free of charge, there is no price with which to judge the value of the highway. Simply asking people how much they would value the highway is not reliable: Quantifying benefits is difficult using the results from a questionnaire, and respondents have little incentive to tell the truth. Those who would use the highway have an incentive to exaggerate the benefit they receive to get the highway built. Those who would be harmed by the highway have an incentive to exaggerate the costs to them to prevent the highway from being built.

The efficient provision of public goods is, therefore, intrinsically more difficult than the efficient provision of private goods. Private goods are provided in the market. Buyers of a private good reveal the value they place on it by the prices they are willing to pay. Sellers reveal their costs by the prices they are willing to accept. By contrast, cost-benefit analysts do not observe any price signals when evaluating whether the government should provide a public good. Their findings on the costs and benefits of public projects are, therefore, rough approximations at best.

cost-benefit analysis
a study that compares the costs and benefits to society of providing a public good

Case Study
HOW MUCH IS A LIFE WORTH?

Imagine that you have been elected to serve as a member of your local town council. The town engineer comes to you with a proposal: The town can spend $10,000 to build and operate a traffic light at a town intersection that now has only a stop sign. The benefit of the traffic light is increased safety. The engineer estimates, based on data from similar intersections, that the traffic light would reduce the risk of a fatal traffic accident over the lifetime of the traffic light from 1.6 to 1.1 percent. Should you spend the money for the new light?

To answer this question, you turn to cost-benefit analysis. But you quickly run into an obstacle: The costs and benefits must be measured in the same units if you are to compare them meaningfully. The cost is measured in dollars, but the benefit—the possibility of saving a person's life—is not directly monetary. To make your decision, you have to put a dollar value on a human life.

At first, you may be tempted to conclude that a human life is priceless. After all, there is probably no amount of money that you could be paid to voluntarily give up your life or that of a loved one. This suggests that a human life has an infinite dollar value.

For the purposes of cost-benefit analysis, however, this answer leads to non-sensical results. If we truly placed an infinite value on human life, we should be placing traffic lights on every street corner. Similarly, we should all be driving large cars with all the latest safety features, instead of smaller ones with fewer safety features. Yet traffic lights are not at every corner, and people sometimes choose to buy small cars without side-impact air bags or antilock brakes. In both our public and private decisions, we are at times willing to risk our lives to save some money.

Once we have accepted the idea that a person's life does have an implicit dollar value, how can we determine what that value is? One approach, sometimes used by courts to award damages in wrongful-death suits, is to look at the total amount of money a person would have earned if he or she had lived. Economists are often critical of this approach. It has the bizarre implication that the life of a retired or disabled person has no value.

A better way to value human life is to look at the risks that people are voluntarily willing to take and how much they must be paid for taking them. Mortality risk varies across jobs, for example. Construction workers in high-rise buildings face greater risk of death on the job than office workers do. By comparing wages in risky and less risky occupations, controlling for education, experience, and other determinants of wages, economists can get some sense about what value people put on their own lives. Studies using this approach conclude that the value of a human life is about $10 million.

We can now return to our original example and respond to the town engineer. The traffic light reduces the risk of fatality by 0.5 percentage points. Thus, the expected benefit from having the traffic light is 0.005 × $10 million, or $50,000. This estimate of the benefit well exceeds the cost of $10,000, so you should approve the project. ●

QuickQuiz   What is the *free-rider problem?* • Why does the free-rider problem induce the government to provide public goods? • How should the government decide whether to provide a public good?

COMMON RESOURCES

Common resources, like public goods, are not excludable: They are available free of charge to anyone who wants to use them. Common resources are, however, rival: One person's use of the common resource reduces other people's ability to use it. Thus, common resources give rise to a new problem. Once the good is provided, policymakers need to be concerned about how much it is used. This problem is best understood from the classic parable called the **Tragedy of the Commons.**

Tragedy of the Commons
a parable that illustrates why common resources get used more than is desirable from the standpoint of society as a whole

The Tragedy of the Commons

Consider life in a small medieval town. Of the many economic activities that take place in the town, one of the most important is raising sheep. Many of the town's families own flocks of sheep and support themselves by selling the sheep's wool, which is used to make clothing.

As our story begins, the sheep spend much of their time grazing on the land surrounding the town, called the Town Common. No family owns the land. Instead, the town residents own the land collectively, and all the residents are allowed to graze their sheep on it. Collective ownership works well because land is plentiful. As long as everyone can get all the good grazing land they want, the Town Common is not a rival good, and allowing residents' sheep to graze for free causes no problems. Everyone in town is happy.

As the years pass, the population of the town grows, and so does the number of sheep grazing on the Town Common. With a growing number of sheep and a fixed amount of land, the land starts to lose its ability to replenish itself. Eventually, the land is grazed so heavily that it becomes barren. With no grass left on the Town Common, raising sheep is impossible, and the town's once prosperous wool industry disappears. Many families lose their source of livelihood.

What causes the tragedy? Why do the shepherds allow the sheep population to grow so large that it destroys the Town Common? The reason is that social and private incentives differ. Avoiding the destruction of the grazing land depends on the collective action of the shepherds. If the shepherds acted together, they could reduce the sheep population to a size that the Town Common can support. Yet no single family has an incentive to reduce the size of its own flock because each flock represents only a small part of the problem.

In essence, the Tragedy of the Commons arises because of an externality. When one family's flock grazes on the common land, it reduces the quality of the land available for other families. Because people neglect this negative externality when deciding how many sheep to own, the result is an excessive number of sheep.

If the tragedy had been foreseen, the town could have solved the problem in various ways. It could have regulated the number of sheep in each family's flock, internalized the externality by taxing sheep, or auctioned off a limited number of sheep-grazing permits. That is, the medieval town could have dealt with the problem of overgrazing in the way that modern society deals with the problem of pollution.

In the case of land, however, there is a simpler solution. The town can divide up the land among town families. Each family can enclose its parcel of land with a fence and then protect it from excessive grazing. In this way, the land becomes a private good rather than a common resource. This outcome in fact occurred during the enclosure movement in England in the seventeenth century.

The Tragedy of the Commons is a story with a general lesson: When one person uses a common resource, he diminishes other people's enjoyment of it. Because of this negative externality, common resources tend to be used excessively. The government can solve the problem by reducing use of the common resource through regulation or taxes. Alternatively, the government can sometimes turn the common resource into a private good.

This lesson has been known for thousands of years. The ancient Greek philosopher Aristotle pointed out the problem with common resources: "What is common to many is taken least care of, for all men have greater regard for what is their own than for what they possess in common with others."

Some Important Common Resources

There are many examples of common resources. In almost all cases, the same problem arises as in the Tragedy of the Commons: Private decisionmakers use the com-

IN THE NEWS

THE SINGAPORE SOLUTION

Tolls are a simple way to solve the problem of road congestion and, according to some economists, are not used as much as they should be. In this opinion column, economist Lester Thurow describes Singapore's success in dealing with congestion.

Economics of Road Pricing

By Lester C. Thurow

Start with a simple observational truth. No city has ever been able to solve its congestion and pollution problems by building more roads.

Some of the world's cities have built a lot of roads (Los Angeles) and some have very few (Shanghai only recently has had a lot of autos) but the degrees of congestion and pollution don't differ very much. More roads simply encourage more people to use their cars, to live farther away from work, and thus use more road space. . . . A recent analysis of congestion problems in London came to the conclusion that London could tear the entire central city down to make room for roads and would still have something approaching gridlock.

Economists have always had a theoretical answer for auto congestion and pollution problems—road pricing. Charge people for using roads based on what roads they use, what time of day and year they use those roads, and the degree to which pollution problems exist at the time they are using those roads. Set prices at the levels that yield the optimal amounts of usage.

Until Singapore decided to try, no city had ever had the nerve to use road pricing. Many ideas seem good theoretically but have some hidden unexpected flaws. Singapore now has more than a decade of experience. The system works! There are no unexpected flaws. Singapore is the only city on the face of the earth

mon resource too much. Governments often regulate behavior or impose fees to mitigate the problem of overuse.

Clean Air and Water As we discussed in Chapter 10, markets do not adequately protect the environment. Pollution is a negative externality that can be remedied with regulations or with Pigovian taxes on polluting activities. One can view this market failure as an example of a common-resource problem. Clean air and clean water are common resources like open grazing land, and excessive pollution is like excessive grazing. Environmental degradation is a modern Tragedy of the Commons.

Congested Roads Roads can be either public goods or common resources. If a road is not congested, then one person's use does not affect anyone else. In this case, use is not rival, and the road is a public good. Yet if a road is congested, then use of that road yields a negative externality. When one person drives on the road, it becomes more crowded, and other people must drive more slowly. In this case, the road is a common resource.

without congestion and auto-induced pollution problems.

In Singapore a series of toll booths surrounds the central core of the city. To drive into the city, each car must pay a toll based on the roads being used, the time of day when the driving will occur, and that day's pollution problem. Prices are raised and lowered to get optimal usage.

In addition, Singapore calculates the maximum number of cars that can be supported without pollution outside of the central city and auctions off the rights to license new cars each month. Different types of plates allow different degrees of usage. A plate that allows one to use their car at any time is much more expensive than a plate that only allows one to use their car on weekends—a time when congestion problems are much less intense. Prices depend on supply and demand.

With this system Singapore ends up not wasting resources on infrastructure projects that won't cure congestion and pollution problems. The revenue collected from the system is used to lower other taxes.

If that is so, why then did London reject road pricing in its recent report on its auto congestion and pollution problems? They feared that such a system would be seen as too much interference from the heavy hand of government and that the public would not put up with a system that allows the rich to drive more than the poor.

Both arguments ignore the fact that we already have toll roads, but new technologies now also make it possible to avoid both problems.

Using bar codes and debit cards, a city can install bar code readers at different points around the city. As any car goes by each point a certain amount is deducted from the driver's debit card account depending upon weather, time of day, and location.

Inside the car, the driver has a meter that tells him how much he has been charged and how much remains in his debit card account. . . .

If one is an egalitarian and thinks that driving privileges should be distributed equally (i.e., not based upon income) then each auto can be given a specified debit card balance every year and those who are willing to drive less can sell their unused balances to those that want to drive more.

Instead of giving the city extra tax revenue, this system gives those who are willing to live near work or to use public transit an income supplement. Since poor people drive less than rich people, the system ends up being an egalitarian redistribution of income from the rich to the poor.

Source: *The Boston Globe*, February 28, 1995, p. 40. Copyright 1995 by GLOBE NEWSPAPER CO (MA). Reproduced with permission of GLOBE NEWSPAPER CO (MA) in the format Textbook via Copyright Clearance Center.

One way for the government to address the problem of road congestion is to charge drivers a toll. A toll is, in essence, a Pigovian tax on the externality of congestion. Often, as in the case of local roads, tolls are not a practical solution because the cost of collecting them is too high.

Sometimes congestion is a problem only at certain times of day. If a bridge is heavily traveled only during rush hour, for instance, the congestion externality is larger during this time than during other times of day. The efficient way to deal with these externalities is to charge higher tolls during rush hour. This toll would provide an incentive for drivers to alter their schedules and would reduce traffic when congestion is greatest.

Another policy that responds to the problem of road congestion, discussed in a case study in the previous chapter, is the tax on gasoline. Gasoline is a complementary good to driving: An increase in the price of gasoline tends to reduce the quantity of driving demanded. Therefore, a gasoline tax reduces road congestion. A gasoline tax, however, is an imperfect solution to road congestion. The problem is that the gasoline tax affects other decisions besides the amount of driving on congested roads. For example, the gasoline tax discourages driving on noncongested roads, even though there is no congestion externality for these roads.

Fish, Whales, and Other Wildlife   Many species of animals are common resources. Fish and whales, for instance, have commercial value, and anyone can go to the ocean and catch whatever is available. Each person has little incentive to maintain the species for the next year. Just as excessive grazing can destroy the Town Common, excessive fishing and whaling can destroy commercially valuable marine populations.

The ocean remains one of the least regulated common resources. Two problems prevent an easy solution. First, many countries have access to the oceans, so any solution would require international cooperation among countries that hold different values. Second, because the oceans are so vast, enforcing any agreement is difficult. As a result, fishing rights have been a frequent source of international tension among normally friendly countries.

Within the United States, various laws aim to protect fish and other wildlife. For example, the government charges for fishing and hunting licenses, and it restricts the lengths of the fishing and hunting seasons. Fishermen are often required to throw back small fish, and hunters can kill only a limited number of animals. All these laws reduce the use of a common resource and help maintain animal populations.

Case Study
WHY THE COW IS NOT EXTINCT

Throughout history, many species of animals have been threatened with extinction. When Europeans first arrived in North America, more than 60 million buffalo roamed the continent. Yet hunting the buffalo was so popular during the nineteenth century that by 1900 the animal's population fell to about 400 before the government stepped in to protect the species. In some African countries today, the elephant faces a similar challenge, as poachers kill the animals for the ivory in their tusks.

Yet not all animals with commercial value face this threat. The cow, for example, is a valuable source of food, but no one worries that the cow will soon be extinct. Indeed, the great demand for beef seems to ensure that the species will continue to thrive.

IN THE NEWS

SHOULD YELLOWSTONE CHARGE AS MUCH AS DISNEY WORLD?

National parks, like roads, can be either public goods or common resources. If congestion is not a problem, a visit to a park is not rival. Yet once a park becomes popular, it suffers from the same problem as the Town Common. In this opinion column, an economist argues for the use of higher entrance fees to solve the problem.

Save the Parks, and Make a Profit

By Allen R. Sanderson

It is common knowledge that our national parks are overcrowded, deteriorating, and broke. Some suggest that we address these problems by requiring reservations, closing some areas, or asking Congress to increase financing to the National Park Service. But to an economist, there is a more obvious solution: Raise the entrance fees.

When the National Park Service was established in 1916, the admission price to Yellowstone for a family of five arriving by car was $7.50; today, the price is only $10. Had the 1916 price been adjusted for inflation, the comparable 1995 fee would be $120 a day—about what that family would pay for a day of rides at Disney World, . . . or to see a professional football game.

No wonder our national parks are overrun and overtrampled. We are treating our natural and historical treasures as free goods when they are not. We are ignoring the costs of maintaining these places and rationing by congestion— when it gets too crowded, no more visitors are allowed—perhaps the most inefficient way to allocate scarce resources. The price of a family's day in a national park has not kept pace with most other forms of recreation. Systemwide, it barely averages a dollar a person. . . .

An increase in daily user fees to, say, $20 per person would either reduce the overcrowding and deterioration in our parks by cutting down on the number of visitors or it would substantially raise fee revenues for the Park Service (assuming that legislation was passed that would let the park system keep this money). Greater revenue is the more likely out-

come. After spending several hundred dollars to reach Yellowstone Park, few people would be deterred by another $20.

The added revenues would bring more possibilities for outdoor recreation, both through expansion of the National Park Service and by encouraging private entrepreneurs to carve out and operate their own parks, something they cannot do alongside a public competitor giving away his product well below cost.

It is time to put our money where our Patagonia outfits are: Either we value the Grand Canyon and Yosemite and won't complain about paying a realistic entrance fee, or we don't really value them and shouldn't wring our hands over their present sorry state and likely sorrier fate.

Source: *The New York Times*, September 30, 1995, p. 19. Copyright © 1995 by The New York Times Co. Reprinted by permission.

"Will the market protect me?"

Why is the commercial value of ivory a threat to the elephant, while the commercial value of beef is a guardian of the cow? The reason is that elephants are a common resource, whereas cows are a private good. Elephants roam freely without any owners. Each poacher has a strong incentive to kill as many elephants as he can find. Because poachers are numerous, each poacher has only a slight incentive to preserve the elephant population. By contrast, cows live on ranches that are privately owned. Each rancher takes great effort to maintain the cow population on his ranch because he reaps the benefit of these efforts.

Governments have tried to solve the elephant's problem in two ways. Some countries, such as Kenya, Tanzania, and Uganda, have made it illegal to kill elephants and sell their ivory. Yet these laws have been hard to enforce, and elephant populations have continued to dwindle. By contrast, other countries, such as Botswana, Malawi, Namibia, and Zimbabwe, have made elephants a private good by allowing people to kill elephants, but only those on their own property. Landowners now have an incentive to preserve the species on their own land, and as a result, elephant populations have started to rise. With private ownership and the profit motive now on its side, the African elephant might someday be as safe from extinction as the cow. ●

QuickQuiz   Why do governments try to limit the use of common resources?

CONCLUSION: THE IMPORTANCE OF PROPERTY RIGHTS

In this chapter and the previous one, we have seen there are some "goods" that the market does not provide adequately. Markets do not ensure that the air we breathe is clean or that our country is defended from foreign aggressors. Instead, societies rely on the government to protect the environment and to provide for the national defense.

Although the problems we considered in these chapters arise in many different markets, they share a common theme. In all cases, the market fails to allocate resources efficiently because *property rights* are not well established. That is, some item of value does not have an owner with the legal authority to control it. For example, although no one doubts that the "good" of clean air or national defense is valuable, no one has the right to attach a price to it and profit from its use. A factory pollutes too much because no one charges the factory for the pollution it emits. The market does not provide for national defense because no one can charge those who are defended for the benefit they receive.

When the absence of property rights causes a market failure, the government can potentially solve the problem. Sometimes, as in the sale of pollution permits, the solution is for the government to help define property rights and thereby unleash market forces. Other times, as in the restriction on hunting seasons, the solution is for the government to regulate private behavior. Still other times, as in the provision of national defense, the solution is for the government to supply a good that the market fails to supply. In all cases, if the policy is well planned and well run, it can make the allocation of resources more efficient and thus raise economic well-being.

SUMMARY

- Goods differ in whether they are excludable and whether they are rival. A good is excludable if it is possible to prevent someone from using it. A good is rival if one person's use of the good reduces other people's ability to use the same unit of the good. Markets work best for private goods, which are both excludable and rival. Markets do not work as well for other types of goods.

- Public goods are neither rival nor excludable. Examples of public goods include fireworks displays, national defense, and the creation of fundamental knowledge. Because people are not

charged for their use of the public good, they have an incentive to free ride when the good is provided privately. Therefore, governments provide public goods, making their decision about the quantity based on cost-benefit analysis.

- Common resources are rival but not excludable. Examples include common grazing land, clean air, and congested roads. Because people are not charged for their use of common resources, they tend to use them excessively. Therefore, governments try to limit the use of common resources.

KEY CONCEPTS

excludability, p. 224
rivalry, p. 224
private goods, p. 224

public goods, p. 225
common resources, p. 225
free rider, p. 226

cost-benefit analysis, p. 229
Tragedy of the Commons, p. 231

QUESTIONS FOR REVIEW

1. Explain what is meant by a good being "excludable." Explain what is meant by a good being "rival." Is a pizza excludable? Is it rival?

2. Define and give an example of a public good. Can the private market provide this good on its own? Explain.

3. What is cost-benefit analysis of public goods? Why is it important? Why is it hard?

4. Define and give an example of a common resource. Without government intervention, will people use this good too much or too little? Why?

PROBLEMS AND APPLICATIONS

1. The text says that both public goods and common resources involve externalities.
   a. Are the externalities associated with public goods generally positive or negative? Use examples in your answer. Is the free-market

quantity of public goods generally greater or less than the efficient quantity?
   b. Are the externalities associated with common resources generally positive or negative? Use examples in your

answer. Is the free-market use of common resources generally greater or less than the efficient use?

2. Think about the goods and services provided by your local government.
   a. Using the classification in Figure 1, explain what category each of the following goods falls into:
      • police protection
      • snow plowing
      • education
      • rural roads
      • city streets
   b. Why do you think the government provides items that are not public goods?

3. Charlie loves watching *Teletubbies* on his local public TV station, but he never sends any money to support the station during their fund-raising drives.
   a. What name do economists have for Charlie?
   b. How can the government solve the problem caused by people like Charlie?
   c. Can you think of ways the private market can solve this problem? How does the existence of cable TV alter the situation?

4. The text states that private firms will not undertake the efficient amount of basic scientific research.
   a. Explain why this is so. In your answer, classify basic research in one of the categories shown in Figure 1.
   b. What sort of policy has the United States adopted in response to this problem?
   c. It is often argued that this policy increases the technological capability of American producers relative to that of foreign firms. Is this argument consistent with your classification of basic research in part (a)? (Hint: Can excludability apply to some potential beneficiaries of a public good and not others?)

5. Why is there litter along most highways but rarely in people's yards?

6. The Washington, D.C., metro system (subway) charges higher fares during rush hours than during the rest of the day. Why might it do this?

7. Timber companies in the United States cut down many trees on publicly owned land and many trees on privately owned land. Discuss the likely efficiency of logging on each type of land in the absence of government regulation. How do you think the government should regulate logging on publicly owned lands? Should similar regulations apply to privately owned land?

8. An *Economist* article (Mar. 19, 1994) states: "In the past decade, most of the rich world's fisheries have been exploited to the point of near-exhaustion." The article continues with an analysis of the problem and a discussion of possible private and government solutions.
   a. "Do not blame fishermen for overfishing. They are behaving rationally, as they have always done." In what sense is "overfishing" rational for fishermen?
   b. "A community, held together by ties of obligation and mutual self-interest, can manage a common resource on its own." Explain how such management can work in principle, and what obstacles it faces in the real world.
   c. "Until 1976 most world fish stocks were open to all comers, making conservation almost impossible. Then an international agreement extended some aspects of [national] jurisdiction from 12 to 200 miles offshore." Using the concept of property rights, discuss how this agreement reduces the scope of the problem.
   d. The article notes that many governments come to the aid of suffering fishermen in ways that encourage increased fishing. How

do such policies encourage a vicious cycle of overfishing?

e. "Only when fishermen believe they are assured a long-term and exclusive right to a fishery are they likely to manage it in the same far-sighted way as good farmers manage their land." Defend this statement.

f. What other policies to reduce overfishing might be considered?

9. In a market economy, information about the quality or function of goods and services is a valuable good in its own right. How does the private market provide this information? Can you think of any way in which the government plays a role in providing this information?

10. Do you think the Internet is a public good? Why or why not?

11. High-income people are willing to pay more than lower-income people to avoid the risk of death. For example, they are more likely to pay for safety features on cars. Do you think cost-benefit analysts should take this fact into account when evaluating public projects? Consider, for instance, a rich town and a poor town, both of which are considering the installation of a traffic light. Should the rich town use a higher dollar value for a human life in making this decision? Why or why not?

http://

For more study tools, please visit http://mankiwXtra.swlearning.com.

THE DESIGN OF THE TAX SYSTEM

Al "Scarface" Capone, the notorious 1920s gangster and crime boss, was never convicted for his many violent crimes. Yet eventually he did go to jail—for tax evasion. He had neglected to heed Ben Franklin's observation that "in this world nothing is certain but death and taxes."

When Franklin made this claim in 1789, the average American paid less than 5 percent of his income in taxes, and that remained true for the next hundred years. Over the course of the twentieth century, however, taxes became ever more important in the life of the typical person. Today, all taxes taken together—including personal income taxes, corporate income taxes, payroll taxes, sales taxes, and property taxes—use up about a third of the average American's income. In many European countries, the tax bite is even larger.

Taxes are inevitable because we as citizens expect the government to provide us with various goods and services. The previous two chapters have started to shed light on one of the *Ten Principles of Economics* from Chapter 1: The government can sometimes improve market outcomes. When the government remedies an externality (such as air pollution), provides a public good (such as national defense), or regulates the use of a common resource (such as fish in a public lake), it can raise economic well-being. Yet the benefits of government come with costs. For the government to perform these and its many other functions, it needs to raise revenue through taxation.

We began our study of taxation in earlier chapters, where we saw how a tax on a good affects supply and demand for that good. In Chapter 6 we saw that a tax reduces the quantity sold in a market, and we examined how the burden of a tax is shared by buyers and sellers, depending on the elasticities of supply and demand. In Chapter 8 we examined how taxes affect economic well-being. We learned that taxes cause *deadweight losses:* The reduction in consumer and producer surplus resulting from a tax exceeds the revenue raised by the government.

In this chapter we build on these lessons to discuss the design of a tax system. We begin with a financial overview of the U.S. government. When thinking about the tax system, it is useful to know some basic facts about how the U.S. government raises and spends money. We then consider the fundamental principles of taxation. Most people agree that taxes should impose as small a cost on society as possible and that the burden of taxes should be distributed fairly. That is, the tax system should be both *efficient* and *equitable.* As we will see, however, stating these goals is easier than achieving them.

A FINANCIAL OVERVIEW OF THE U.S. GOVERNMENT

How much of the nation's income does the government take as taxes? Figure 1 shows government revenue, including federal, state, and local governments, as a percentage of total income for the U.S. economy. It shows that, over time, the government has taken a larger and larger share of total income. In 1902, the government collected 7 percent of total income; in 2000, it collected 31 percent. In other words, as the economy's income has grown, the government has grown even more.

Table 1 compares the tax burden for several major countries, as measured by the central government's tax revenue as a percentage of the nation's total income. The United States is in the middle of the pack. The U.S. tax burden is low compared to many European countries, but it is high compared to many other nations around the world. Poor countries, such as India and Pakistan, usually have relatively low tax burdens. This fact is consistent with the evidence in Figure 1 of a growing tax burden over time: As a nation gets richer, the government typically takes a larger share of income in taxes.

The overall size of government tells only part of the story. Behind the total dollar figures lie thousands of individual decisions about taxes and spending. To understand the government's finances more fully, let's look at how the total breaks down into some broad categories.

The Federal Government

The U.S. federal government collects about two-thirds of the taxes in our economy. It raises this money in a number of ways, and it finds even more ways to spend it.

FIGURE 1

Government Revenue as a Percentage of GDP

This figure shows revenue of the federal government and of state and local governments as a percentage of gross domestic product (GDP), which measures total income in the economy. It shows that the government plays a large role in the U.S. economy and that its role has grown over time.

Source: *Historical Statistics of the United States; Economic Report of the President, 2002; and author's calculations.*

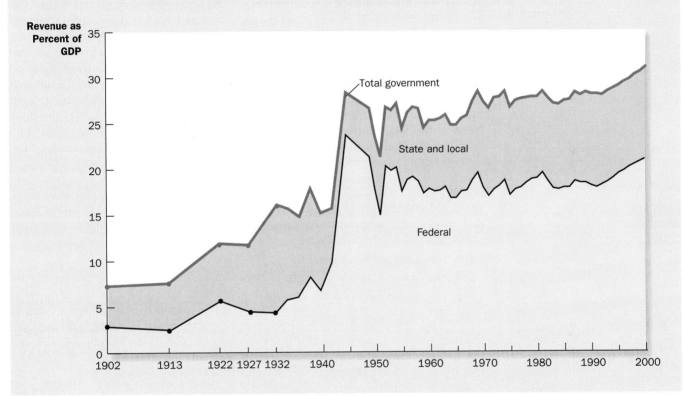

TABLE 1

Central Government Tax Revenue as a Percent of GDP

Source: *World Development Report 1998/99.*

France	38.8%	Russia	17.4
United Kingdom	33.7	Pakistan	15.3
Germany	29.4	Indonesia	14.7
Brazil	19.7	Mexico	12.8
United States	19.3	India	10.3
Canada	18.5		

Receipts   Table 2 shows the receipts of the federal government in 2001. Total receipts that year were $1,991 billion, a number so large that it is hard to comprehend. To bring this astronomical number down to earth, we can divide it by the size of the U.S. population, which was about 285 million in 2001. We then find that the average American paid $6,986 to the federal government.

The largest source of revenue for the federal government is the individual income tax. As April 15 approaches every year, almost every American family fills out a tax form to determine how much income tax it owes the government. Each family is required to report its income from all sources: wages from working, interest on savings, dividends from corporations in which it owns shares, profits from any small businesses it operates, and so on. The family's *tax liability* (how much it owes) is then based on its total income.

A family's income tax liability is not simply proportional to its income. Instead, the law requires a more complicated calculation. Taxable income is computed as total income minus an amount based on the number of dependents (primarily children) and minus certain expenses that policymakers have deemed "deductible" (such as mortgage interest payments and charitable giving). Then the tax liability is calculated from taxable income using the schedule shown in Table 3.

This table presents the *marginal tax rate*—the tax rate applied to each additional dollar of income. Because the marginal tax rate rises as income rises, higher-income families pay a larger percentage of their income in taxes. Note that each tax rate in the table applies only to income within the associated range, not to a person's entire income. For example, a person with an income of a million dollars still pays only 15 percent of the first $27,050. (We discuss the concept of marginal tax rate more fully later in this chapter.)

Almost as important to the federal government as the individual income tax are payroll taxes. A *payroll tax* is a tax on the wages that a firm pays its workers. Table 2 calls this revenue *social insurance taxes* because the revenue from these taxes is earmarked to pay for Social Security and Medicare. Social Security is an income-support program, designed primarily to maintain the living standards of the elderly. Medicare is the government health program for the elderly. Table 2 shows that the average American paid $2,435 in social insurance taxes in 2001.

Next in magnitude, but much smaller than either individual income taxes or social insurance taxes, is the corporate income tax. A *corporation* is a business that is

---

TABLE 2

Receipts of the Federal Government: 2001

Source: *Economic Report of the President,* 2002, table B-81, p. 416.

Tax	Amount (billions)	Amount per Person	Percent of Receipts
Individual income taxes	$ 994	$3,488	50%
Social insurance taxes	694	2,435	35
Corporate income taxes	151	530	8
Other	152	533	8
Total	$1,991	$6,986	100%

TABLE 3

The Federal Income Tax Rates: 2001

This table shows the marginal tax rates for an unmarried taxpayer. The taxes owed by a taxpayer depend on all the marginal tax rates up to his or her income level. For example, a taxpayer with income of $50,000 pays 15 percent of the first $27,050 of income, and then 27.5 percent of the rest.

On Taxable Income . . .	The Tax Rate Is . . .
Up to $27,050	15.0%
From $27,050 to $65,550	27.5
From $65,550 to $136,750	30.5
From $136,750 to $297,350	35.5
Over $297,350	39.1

set up as a separate legal entity. The government taxes each corporation based on its profit—the amount the corporation receives for the goods or services it sells minus the costs of producing those goods or services. Notice that corporate profits are, in essence, taxed twice. They are taxed once by the corporate income tax when the corporation earns the profits; they are taxed a second time by the individual income tax when the corporation uses its profits to pay dividends to its shareholders.

The last category, labeled "other" in Table 2, makes up 8 percent of receipts. This category includes *excise taxes*, which are taxes on specific goods like gasoline, cigarettes, and alcoholic beverages. It also includes various small items, such as estate taxes and customs duties.

Spending Table 4 shows the spending of the federal government in 2001. Total spending was $1,864 billion, or $6,540 per person. This table also shows how the federal government's spending was divided among major categories.

The largest category in Table 4 is Social Security, which represents mostly transfer payments to the elderly. (A *transfer payment* is a government payment not made

TABLE 4

Spending of the Federal Government: 2001

Source: *Economic Report of the President,* 2002, table B-81, p. 416.

Category	Amount (billions)	Amount per Person	Percent of Spending
Social Security	$ 433	$1,519	23%
National defense	309	1,084	17
Income security	270	947	14
Net interest	206	723	11
Medicare	217	761	12
Health	173	607	9
Other	256	898	14
Total	$1,864	$6,540	100%

in exchange for a good or service.) This category made up 23 percent of spending by the federal government in 2001 and is growing in importance. The reason for its growth is that increases in life expectancy and decreases in birthrates have caused the elderly population to grow more rapidly than the total population. Most analysts expect this trend to continue for many years into the future.

The second largest category of spending is national defense. This includes both the salaries of military personnel and the purchases of military equipment such as guns, fighter jets, and warships. Spending on national defense fluctuates over time as international tensions and the political climate change. Not surprisingly, spending on national defense rises substantially during wars.

The third category is spending on income security, which includes transfer payments to poor families. One program is Temporary Assistance for Needy Families (TANF), often simply called "welfare." Another is the Food Stamp program, which gives poor families vouchers that they can use to buy food. The federal government pays some of this money to state and local governments, which administer the programs under federal guidelines.

A bit smaller than spending on income security is net interest. When a person borrows from a bank, the bank requires the borrower to pay interest for the loan. The same is true when the government borrows from the public. The more indebted the government, the larger the amount it must spend in interest payments.

Medicare, the next category in Table 4, is the government's health plan for the elderly. Spending in this category has risen substantially over time for two reasons. First, the elderly population has grown more quickly than the overall population. Second, the cost of health care has risen more rapidly than the cost of other goods and services.

The next category is health spending other than Medicare. This includes Medicaid, the federal health program for the poor. It also includes spending on medical research, such as through the National Institutes of Health.

The "other" category in Table 4 consists of many less expensive functions of government. It includes, for example, the federal court system, the space program, and farm-support programs, as well as the salaries of Congress and the president.

You might have noticed that total receipts of the federal government shown in Table 2 exceed total spending shown in Table 4 by $127 billion. Such an excess of receipts over spending is called a **budget surplus.** When receipts fall short of spending, the government is said to run a **budget deficit.** The government finances the budget deficit by borrowing from the public. When the government runs a budget surplus, it uses the excess receipts to reduce its outstanding debts.

budget surplus
an excess of government receipts over government spending

budget deficit
an excess of government spending over government receipts

State and Local Government

State and local governments collect about 40 percent of all taxes paid. Let's look at how they obtain tax revenue and how they spend it.

Receipts   Table 5 shows the receipts of U.S. state and local governments. Total receipts for 1999 were $1,434 billion. Based on the 1999 population of about 272 million, this equals $5,271 per person. The table also shows how this total is broken down into different kinds of taxes.

The two most important taxes for state and local governments are sales taxes and property taxes. Sales taxes are levied as a percentage of the total amount spent at retail stores. Every time a customer buys something, he or she pays the storekeeper an extra amount that the storekeeper remits to the government. (Some

TABLE 5

Receipts of State and Local Governments: 1999

Source: *Economic Report of the President,* 2002, table B-86, p. 421.

Tax	Amount (billions)	Amount per Person	Percent of Receipts
Sales taxes	$ 291	$1,070	20%
Property taxes	240	882	17
Individual income taxes	189	695	13
Corporate income taxes	34	125	2
From federal government	271	996	19
Other	409	1,504	29
Total	$1,434	$5,271	100%

states exclude certain items that are considered necessities, such as food and clothing.) Property taxes are levied as a percentage of the estimated value of land and structures, and are paid by property owners. Together these two taxes make up more than a third of all receipts of state and local governments.

State and local governments also levy individual and corporate income taxes. In many cases, state and local income taxes are similar to federal income taxes. In other cases, they are quite different. For example, some states tax income from wages less heavily than income earned in the form of interest and dividends. Some states do not tax income at all.

State and local governments also receive substantial funds from the federal government. To some extent, the federal government's policy of sharing its revenue with state governments redistributes funds from high-income states (who pay more taxes) to low-income states (who receive more benefits). Often these funds are tied to specific programs that the federal government wants to subsidize.

Finally, state and local governments receive much of their receipts from various sources included in the "other" category in Table 5. These include fees for fishing and hunting licenses, tolls from roads and bridges, and fares for public buses and subways.

Spending   Table 6 (p. 248) shows the total spending of state and local governments in 1999 and its breakdown among the major categories.

By far the biggest single expenditure for state and local governments is education. Local governments pay for the public schools, which educate most students from kindergarten to high school. State governments contribute to the support of public universities. In 1999 education accounted for a third of the spending of state and local governments.

The second largest category of spending is for public welfare, which includes transfer payments to the poor. This category includes some federal programs that are administered by state and local governments. The next category is highways, which includes the building of new roads and the maintenance of existing ones. The "other" category in Table 6 includes the many additional services provided by state and local governments, such as libraries, police, garbage removal, fire protection, park maintenance, and snow removal.

TABLE 6

Spending of State and Local Governments: 1999

Source: *Economic Report of the President,* 2002, table B-86, p. 421.

Category	Amount (billions)	Amount per Person	Percent of Spending
Education	$ 483	$1,776	34%
Public welfare	219	805	16
Highways	93	341	7
Other	607	2,232	43
Total	$1,402	$5,154	100%

QuickQuiz What are the two most important sources of tax revenue for the federal government? • What are the two most important sources of tax revenue for state and local governments?

TAXES AND EFFICIENCY

Now that we have seen how the U.S. government at various levels raises and spends money, let's consider how one might evaluate its tax policy. Obviously, the aim of a tax system is to raise revenue for the government. But there are many ways to raise any given amount of money. In designing a tax system, policymakers have two objectives: efficiency and equity.

One tax system is more efficient than another if it raises the same amount of revenue at a smaller cost to taxpayers. What are the costs of taxes to taxpayers? The most obvious cost is the tax payment itself. This transfer of money from the taxpayer to the government is an inevitable feature of any tax system. Yet taxes also impose two other costs, which well-designed tax policy tries to avoid or, at least, minimize:

- The deadweight losses that result when taxes distort the decisions that people make
- The administrative burdens that taxpayers bear as they comply with the tax laws

An efficient tax system is one that imposes small deadweight losses and small administrative burdens.

Deadweight Losses

One of the *Ten Principles of Economics* is that people respond to incentives, and this includes incentives provided by the tax system. If the government taxes ice cream, people eat less ice cream and more frozen yogurt. If the government taxes housing, people live in smaller houses and spend more of their income on other things. If the government taxes labor earnings, people work less and enjoy more leisure.

Because taxes distort incentives, they entail deadweight losses. As we first discussed in Chapter 8, the deadweight loss of a tax is the reduction in economic well-being of taxpayers in excess of the amount of revenue raised by the government. The deadweight loss is the inefficiency that a tax creates as people allocate resources according to the tax incentive rather than the true costs and benefits of the goods and services that they buy and sell.

To recall how taxes cause deadweight losses, consider an example. Suppose that Joe places an $8 value on a pizza, and Jane places a $6 value on it. If there is no tax on pizza, the price of pizza will reflect the cost of making it. Let's suppose that the price of pizza is $5, so both Joe and Jane choose to buy one. Both consumers get some surplus of value over the amount paid. Joe gets consumer surplus of $3, and Jane gets consumer surplus of $1. Total surplus is $4.

Now suppose that the government levies a $2 tax on pizza and the price of pizza rises to $7. Joe still buys a pizza, but now he has consumer surplus of only $1. Jane now decides not to buy a pizza because its price is higher than its value to her. The government collects tax revenue of $2 on Joe's pizza. Total consumer surplus has fallen by $3 (from $4 to $1). Because total surplus has fallen by more than the tax revenue, the tax has a deadweight loss. In this case, the deadweight loss is $1.

Notice that the deadweight loss comes not from Joe, the person who pays the tax, but from Jane, the person who doesn't. The reduction of $2 in Joe's surplus exactly offsets the amount of revenue the government collects. The deadweight loss arises because the tax causes Jane to alter her behavior. When the tax raises the price of pizza, Jane is worse off, and yet there is no offsetting revenue to the government. This reduction in Jane's welfare is the deadweight loss of the tax.

BERRY'S WORLD REPRINTED BY PERMISSION OF UNITED FEATURE SYNDICATE, INC.

© 1977 by NEA, Inc.

"I was gonna fix the place up, but if I did the city would just raise my taxes!"

Case Study

SHOULD INCOME OR CONSUMPTION BE TAXED?

When taxes induce people to change their behavior—such as inducing Jane to buy less pizza—the taxes cause deadweight losses and make the allocation of resources less efficient. As we have already seen, much government revenue comes from the individual income tax. In a case study in Chapter 8, we discussed how this tax discourages people from working as hard as they otherwise might. Another inefficiency caused by this tax is that it discourages people from saving.

Consider a person 25 years old who is considering saving $100. If he puts this money in a savings account that earns 8 percent and leaves it there, he would have $2,172 when he retires at age 65. Yet if the government taxes one-fourth of his interest income each year, the effective interest rate is only 6 percent. After 40 years of earning 6 percent, the $100 grows to only $1,029, less than half of what it would have been without taxation. Thus, because interest income is taxed, saving is much less attractive.

Some economists advocate eliminating the current tax system's disincentive toward saving by changing the basis of taxation. Rather than taxing the amount of income that people *earn*, the government could tax the amount that people *spend*. Under this proposal, all income that is saved would not be taxed until the saving is later spent. This alternative system, called a *consumption tax*, would not distort people's saving decisions.

This idea has some support from policymakers. Several members of Congress have advocated replacing the current income tax system with a consumption tax.

Moreover, various provisions of the current tax code already make the tax system a bit like a consumption tax. Taxpayers can put a limited amount of their saving into special accounts—such as Individual Retirement Accounts, Keogh plans, and 401(k) plans—that escape taxation until the money is withdrawn at retirement. For people who do most of their saving through these retirement accounts, their tax bill is, in effect, based on their consumption rather than their income. ●

Administrative Burden

If you ask the typical person on April 15 for an opinion about the tax system, you might hear about the headache of filling out tax forms. The administrative burden of any tax system is part of the inefficiency it creates. This burden includes not only the time spent in early April filling out forms but also the time spent throughout the year keeping records for tax purposes and the resources the government has to use to enforce the tax laws.

Many taxpayers—especially those in higher tax brackets—hire tax lawyers and accountants to help them with their taxes. These experts in the complex tax laws fill out the tax forms for their clients and help clients arrange their affairs in a way that reduces the amount of taxes owed. This behavior is legal tax avoidance, which is different from illegal tax evasion.

Critics of our tax system say that these advisers help their clients avoid taxes by abusing some of the detailed provisions of the tax code, often dubbed "loopholes." In some cases, loopholes are congressional mistakes: They arise from ambiguities or omissions in the tax laws. More often, they arise because Congress has chosen to give special treatment to specific types of behavior. For example, the U.S. federal tax code gives preferential treatment to investors in municipal bonds because Congress wanted to make it easier for state and local governments to borrow money. To some extent, this provision benefits states and localities; to some extent, it benefits high-income taxpayers. Most loopholes are well known by those in Congress who make tax policy, but what looks like a loophole to one taxpayer may look like a justifiable tax deduction to another.

The resources devoted to complying with the tax laws are a type of deadweight loss. The government gets only the amount of taxes paid. By contrast, the taxpayer loses not only this amount but also the time and money spent documenting, computing, and avoiding taxes.

The administrative burden of the tax system could be reduced by simplifying the tax laws. Yet simplification is often politically difficult. Most people are ready to simplify the tax code by eliminating the loopholes that benefit others, yet few are eager to give up the loopholes that they use. In the end, the complexity of the tax law results from the political process as various taxpayers with their own special interests lobby for their causes.

average tax rate
total taxes paid divided by total income

marginal tax rate
the extra taxes paid on an additional dollar of income

Marginal Tax Rates versus Average Tax Rates

When discussing the efficiency and equity of income taxes, economists distinguish between two notions of the tax rate: the average and the marginal. The **average tax rate** is total taxes paid divided by total income. The **marginal tax rate** is the extra taxes paid on an additional dollar of income.

For example, suppose that the government taxes 20 percent of the first $50,000 of income and 50 percent of all income above $50,000. Under this tax, a person who makes $60,000 pays a tax of $15,000: 20 percent of the first $50,000 (0.20 × $50,000 = $10,000) plus 50 percent of the next $10,000 (0.50 × $10,000 = $5,000). For this person, the average tax rate is $15,000/$60,000, or 25 percent. But the marginal tax rate is 50 percent. If the taxpayer earned an additional dollar of income, that dollar would be subject to the 50 percent tax rate, so the amount the taxpayer would owe to the government would rise by $0.50.

The marginal and average tax rates each contain a useful piece of information. If we are trying to gauge the sacrifice made by a taxpayer, the average tax rate is more appropriate because it measures the fraction of income paid in taxes. By contrast, if we are trying to gauge how much the tax system distorts incentives, the marginal tax rate is more meaningful. One of the *Ten Principles of Economics* in Chapter 1 is that rational people think at the margin. A corollary to this principle is that the marginal tax rate measures how much the tax system discourages people from working. If you are thinking of working an extra few hours, the marginal tax rate determines how much the government takes of your additional earnings. It is the marginal tax rate, therefore, that determines the deadweight loss of an income tax.

Case Study
ICELAND'S NATURAL EXPERIMENT

In the 1980s, Iceland changed its tax system in a way that, as a side effect, provided a natural experiment to show how taxes affect an economy. Before the reform, people paid taxes based on their *previous* year's income. After the reform, people paid taxes based on their *current* income. Thus, taxes in 1987 were based on 1986 income, but taxes in 1988 were based on 1988 income. Income earned in 1987 was never taxed. For this one year of transition, the marginal income tax rate fell to zero.

As reported in a December 2001 article in the *American Economic Review*, the citizens of Iceland took advantage of this tax holiday. Total hours worked rose by about 3 percent in 1987 and then fell back to its normal level in 1988. The production of goods and services in 1987 (as measured by real GDP) was 4 percent higher than the average of the year before and the year after. This episode confirms one of the *Ten Principles of Economics:* People respond to incentives.

The fall in the Icelandic marginal tax rate was for one year only, and this fact surely influenced the response. On the one hand, some people may have put off vacations and worked overtime to take advantage of the temporary incentive. On the other hand, no one would alter career plans, and no business would restructure its work environment, in response to an incentive that would soon disappear. A permanent change in a marginal tax rate could have either a smaller or a larger incentive effect than a temporary change. ●

Lump-Sum Taxes

Suppose the government imposes a tax of $4,000 on everyone. That is, everyone owes the same amount, regardless of earnings or any actions that a person might take. Such a tax is called a **lump-sum tax.**

lump-sum tax
a tax that is the same amount for every person

A lump-sum tax shows clearly the difference between average and marginal tax rates. For a taxpayer with income of $20,000, the average tax rate of a $4,000 lump-sum tax is 20 percent; for a taxpayer with income of $40,000, the average tax rate is 10 percent. For both taxpayers, the marginal tax rate is zero because no tax is owed on an additional dollar of income.

A lump-sum tax is the most efficient tax possible. Because a person's decisions do not alter the amount owed, the tax does not distort incentives and, therefore, does not cause deadweight losses. Because everyone can easily compute the amount owed and because there is no benefit to hiring tax lawyers and accountants, the lump-sum tax imposes a minimal administrative burden on taxpayers.

If lump-sum taxes are so efficient, why do we rarely observe them in the real world? The reason is that efficiency is only one goal of the tax system. A lump-sum tax would take the same amount from the poor and the rich, an outcome most people would view as unfair. To understand the tax systems that we observe, in the next section, we consider the other major goal of tax policy: equity.

IN THE NEWS

HOW TAXES AFFECT MARRIED WOMEN

Taxes cause deadweight losses when they distort behavior. The labor supply of married women is one example.

The U.S. Tax System Is Discouraging Married Women from Working

By Virginia Postrel

The single women of "Sex and the City" read the New York Times wedding announcements and mock a bride who was "until recently" employed as an account executive. Now that she's found an investment banker to marry, they scoff, she doesn't have to pretend to be interested in her career. These independent women are contemptuous of such behavior. They're looking for love, not a meal ticket.

But maybe the new Mrs. Investment Banker doesn't deserve their scorn. Maybe she's just a rational "economic woman," responding to incentives.

Marriage has kicked her into the highest bracket. With federal, state, and Social Security taxes, she's now losing about half of every dollar she earns—starting with the very first one. You've got to really love your work to do it for half price.

The Census Bureau recently said that both spouses now work in 51 percent of married couples with wives of childbearing age—the first time that number has surpassed 50 percent since the bureau started tracking it. More wives would work if our progressive income tax structure didn't sock second earners with high marginal rates.

"There is a relationship between taxes and labor-force participation," said Nada Eissa, an economist at the University of California at Berkeley and the National Bureau of Economic Research. "We think it's fairly strong. In fact, we think it's strongest for married women," who are usually the family's secondary earners and are more likely to consider not working outside the home.

QuickQuiz What is meant by the *efficiency* of a tax system? • What can make a tax system inefficient?

TAXES AND EQUITY

Ever since American colonists dumped imported tea into Boston harbor to protest high British taxes, tax policy has generated some of the most heated debates in American politics. The heat is rarely fueled by questions of efficiency. Instead, it arises from disagreements over how the tax burden should be distributed. Senator Russell Long once mimicked the public debate with this ditty:

Don't tax you.
Don't tax me.
Tax that fella behind the tree.

Far more than men or single women, married women act like supply siders. Cut their marginal tax rates, and they get jobs. Raise their taxes, and they stay home.

By disproportionately punishing married women's work, the tax system distorts women's personal choices. And by discouraging valuable work, it lowers our overall standard of living.

This is a tax story you won't hear from politicians. The "marriage penalty" debate tends to frame the issue as one of family formation: How does the tax code affect a couple's decision to marry? But marriage isn't primarily an economic decision.

The more pertinent question is how does the tax code affect a married woman's decision to work? There are obvious political reasons not to ask that. Democrats don't want to admit that soak-the-rich taxation wallops working wives, lest they split feminists and redistributionists. And Republicans don't want to admit that cutting taxes will lead more married women to get jobs, lest they split

economic libertarians and social conservatives. So everyone stays mum.

But the empirical evidence is pretty clear. Tax rates are a feminist issue.

Professor Eissa has studied how the tax bite affects behavior. . . . In a 1995 paper for the National Bureau of Economic Research, she looked at how married women responded to the Tax Reform Act of 1986. That law created a natural experiment. It chopped the top marginal tax rate to 28 percent, from 50 percent, but had only a minor impact on middle-income taxpayers. That gave her an opportunity to compare the responses of different groups of wives before and after the change.

Before it, the women in the 99th percentile of family income (the top 1 percent) on average paid about 52 cents in taxes on the first dollar they earned. In some states, a wife who earned less than $30,000 a year could have paid in taxes as much as 70 cents of the first dollar she earned.

The 1986 law flattened federal rates and, as a result, slashed the average

marginal rate faced by such wives to 38 percent. The percentage of these married women who worked jumped from 46 percent to 55 percent—a 19 percent increase—and those who had jobs increased their hours 13 percent.

To make sure this increase was caused by the tax change rather than other trends, Professor Eissa compared it with the behavior of women in the 75th percentile, who got a much smaller tax cut. Their labor-force participation and hours worked also rose, but by significantly less—a 7 percent jump in those working and a 9 percent increase in hours worked.

Since 1986, rates have become steeper, as Washington pursued increased revenue and lost interest in supply-side incentives. . . . Once a woman is married, it seems, the tax laws don't really want her to work.

Source: *The New York Times*, November 2, 2000, p. C2. Copyright © 2000 by The New York Times Co. Reprinted by permission.

Of course, if we are to rely on the government to provide some of the goods and services we want, taxes must fall on someone. In this section we consider the equity of a tax system. How should the burden of taxes be divided among the population? How do we evaluate whether a tax system is fair? Everyone agrees that the tax system should be equitable, but there is much disagreement about what equity means and how the equity of a tax system can be judged.

The Benefits Principle

benefits principle
the idea that people should pay taxes based on the benefits they receive from government services

One principle of taxation, called the **benefits principle,** states that people should pay taxes based on the benefits they receive from government services. This principle tries to make public goods similar to private goods. It seems fair that a person who often goes to the movies pays more in total for movie tickets than a person who rarely goes. Similarly, a person who gets great benefit from a public good should pay more for it than a person who gets little benefit.

The gasoline tax, for instance, is sometimes justified using the benefits principle. In some states, revenues from the gasoline tax are used to build and maintain roads. Because those who buy gasoline are the same people who use the roads, the gasoline tax might be viewed as a fair way to pay for this government service.

The benefits principle can also be used to argue that wealthy citizens should pay higher taxes than poorer ones. Why? Simply because the wealthy benefit more from public services. Consider, for example, the benefits of police protection from theft. Citizens with much to protect get greater benefit from police than do those with less to protect. Therefore, according to the benefits principle, the wealthy should contribute more than the poor to the cost of maintaining the police force. The same argument can be used for many other public services, such as fire protection, national defense, and the court system.

It is even possible to use the benefits principle to argue for antipoverty programs funded by taxes on the wealthy. As we discussed in Chapter 11, people prefer living in a society without poverty, suggesting that antipoverty programs are a public good. If the wealthy place a greater dollar value on this public good than members of the middle class do, perhaps just because the wealthy have more to spend, then, according to the benefits principle, they should be taxed more heavily to pay for these programs.

The Ability-to-Pay Principle

ability-to-pay principle
the idea that taxes should be levied on a person according to how well that person can shoulder the burden

vertical equity
the idea that taxpayers with a greater ability to pay taxes should pay larger amounts

horizontal equity
the idea that taxpayers with similar abilities to pay taxes should pay the same amount

Another way to evaluate the equity of a tax system is called the **ability-to-pay principle,** which states that taxes should be levied on a person according to how well that person can shoulder the burden. This principle is sometimes justified by the claim that all citizens should make an "equal sacrifice" to support the government. The magnitude of a person's sacrifice, however, depends not only on the size of his tax payment but also on his income and other circumstances. A $1,000 tax paid by a poor person may require a larger sacrifice than a $10,000 tax paid by a rich one.

The ability-to-pay principle leads to two corollary notions of equity: vertical equity and horizontal equity. **Vertical equity** states that taxpayers with a greater ability to pay taxes should contribute a larger amount. **Horizontal equity** states that taxpayers with similar abilities to pay should contribute the same amount. Although these notions of equity are widely accepted, applying them to evaluate a tax system is rarely straightforward.

TABLE 7

Three Tax Systems

| Income | Proportional Tax | | Regressive Tax | | Progressive Tax | |
	Amount of Tax	Percent of Income	Amount of Tax	Percent of Income	Amount of Tax	Percent of Income
$ 50,000	$12,500	25%	$15,000	30%	$10,000	20%
100,000	25,000	25	25,000	25	25,000	25
200,000	50,000	25	40,000	20	60,000	30

Vertical Equity   If taxes are based on ability to pay, then richer taxpayers should pay more than poorer taxpayers. But how much more should the rich pay? Much of the debate over tax policy concerns this question.

Consider the three tax systems in Table 7. In each case, taxpayers with higher incomes pay more. Yet the systems differ in how quickly taxes rise with income. The first system is called **proportional** because all taxpayers pay the same fraction of income. The second system is called **regressive** because high-income taxpayers pay a smaller fraction of their income, even though they pay a larger amount. The third system is called **progressive** because high-income taxpayers pay a larger fraction of their income.

Which of these three tax systems is most fair? There is no obvious answer, and economic theory does not offer any help in trying to find one. Equity, like beauty, is in the eye of the beholder.

proportional tax
a tax for which high-income and low-income taxpayers pay the same fraction of income

regressive tax
a tax for which high-income taxpayers pay a smaller fraction of their income than do low-income taxpayers

progressive tax
a tax for which high-income taxpayers pay a larger fraction of their income than do low-income taxpayers

Case Study

HOW THE TAX BURDEN IS DISTRIBUTED

Much debate over tax policy concerns whether the wealthy pay their fair share. There is no objective way to make this judgment. In evaluating the issue for yourself, however, it is useful to know how much families of different incomes pay under the current tax system.

Table 8 (p. 256) presents some data on how all federal taxes are distributed among income classes. To construct this table, families are ranked according to their income and placed into five groups of equal size, called *quintiles*. The table also presents data on the richest 1 percent of Americans, who have an annual income of at least $245,700.

The second column of the table shows the average income of each group. The poorest one-fifth of families had average income of $11,400, and the richest one-fifth had average income of $167,500. The richest 1 percent had average income of just over $1 million.

The next column of the table shows total taxes as a percent of income. As you can see, the U.S. federal tax system is progressive. The poorest fifth of families paid 5.3 percent of their incomes in taxes, and the richest paid 27.4 percent. The top 1 percent paid 32.7 percent of their incomes.

TABLE 8

The Burden of Federal Taxes.

Source: Congressional Budget Office. Estimates are based on the tax law as of 2000. Dollar figures are in 1997 dollars.

Quintile	Average Income	Taxes as a Percent of Income	Percent of All Income	Percent of All Taxes
Lowest	$11,400	5.3%	4.0%	0.9%
Second	28,600	12.8	9.0	5.2
Middle	45,100	16.7	13.9	10.4
Fourth	65,600	20.0	20.2	18.1
Highest	167,500	27.4	53.2	65.4
Top 1%	1,016,900	32.7	15.8	23.1

The fourth and fifth columns compare the distribution of income and the distribution of taxes. The poorest quintile earns 4.0 percent of all income and pays 0.9 percent of all taxes. The richest quintile earns 53.2 percent of all income and pays 65.4 percent of all taxes. The richest 1 percent (which, remember, is 1/20th the size of each quintile) earns 15.8 percent of all income and pays 23.1 percent of all taxes.

This table on taxes is a good starting point for understanding the burden of government, but the picture it offers is incomplete. Although it includes all the taxes that flow from households to the federal government, it fails to include the transfer payments, such as Social Security and welfare, that flow from the federal government back to households.

Studies that include both taxes and transfers show more progressivity. The richest group of families still pays about one-quarter of its income to the government, even after transfers are subtracted. By contrast, poor families typically receive more in transfers than they pay in taxes. The average tax rate of the poorest quintile, rather than being 5.3 percent as in the table, is approximately *negative* 30 percent. In other words, their income is about 30 percent higher than it would be without government taxes and transfers. The lesson is clear: To understand fully the progressivity of government policies, one must take account of both what people pay and what they receive. ●

Horizontal Equity　If taxes are based on ability to pay, then similar taxpayers should pay similar amounts of taxes. But what determines if two taxpayers are similar? Families differ in many ways. To evaluate whether a tax code is horizontally equitable, one must determine which differences are relevant for a family's ability to pay and which differences are not.

Suppose the Smith and Jones families each have income of $50,000. The Smiths have no children, but Mr. Smith has an illness that causes medical expenses of $20,000. The Joneses are in good health, but they have four children. Two of the Jones children are in college, generating tuition bills of $30,000. Would it be fair for these two families to pay the same tax because they have the same income? Would it be more fair to give the Smiths a tax break to help them offset their high medical expenses? Would it be more fair to give the Joneses a tax break to help them with their tuition expenses?

There are no easy answers to these questions. In practice, the U.S. income tax is filled with special provisions that alter a family's tax based on its specific circumstances.

Case Study
HORIZONTAL EQUITY AND THE MARRIAGE TAX

The treatment of marriage provides an important example of how difficult it is to achieve horizontal equity in practice. Consider two couples who are exactly the same except that one couple is married and the other couple is not. A peculiar feature of the U.S. income tax code is that these two couples pay different taxes. The reason that marriage affects the tax liability of a couple is that the tax law treats a married couple as a single taxpayer. When a man and woman get married, they stop paying taxes as individuals and start paying taxes as a family. If the man and woman have similar incomes, their total tax liability rises when they get married.

To see how this "marriage tax" works, consider the following example of a progressive income tax. Suppose that the government taxes 25 percent of all income above $10,000. Income below $10,000 is excluded from taxation. Let's see how this system treats two different couples.

Consider first Sam and Sally. Sam is a struggling poet and earns no income, whereas Sally is a lawyer and earns $100,000 a year. Before getting married, Sam pays no tax. Sally pays 25 percent of $90,000 ($100,000 minus the $10,000 exclusion), which is $22,500. After getting married, their tax bill is the same. In this case, the income tax neither encourages nor discourages marriage.

Now consider John and Joan, two college professors each earning $50,000 a year. Before getting married, they each pay a tax of $10,000 (25 percent of $40,000), or a total of $20,000. After getting married, they have a total income of $100,000, and so they owe a tax of 25 percent of $90,000, or $22,500. Thus, when John and Joan get married, their tax bill rises by $2,500. This increase is called the marriage tax.

We can fix the problem for John and Joan by raising the income exclusion from $10,000 to $20,000 for married couples. But this change would create another problem. In this case, Sam and Sally would pay a tax after getting married of only $20,000, which is $2,500 less than they paid when they were single. Eliminating the marriage tax for John and Joan would create a marriage subsidy for Sam and Sally.

In practice, the U.S. tax code is an uneasy compromise that includes a combination of marriage taxes and marriage subsidies. According to a study by the Congressional Budget Office, 42 percent of married couples pay a marriage tax, averaging 2.0 percent of their income, while 51 percent of married couples pay lower taxes by virtue of being wed, averaging 2.3 percent of their income. Whether a couple is better off married or shacked up (from a tax standpoint) depends on how earnings are split between the two partners. If a man and woman have similar

"And do you promise to love, honor, and cherish each other, and to pay the United States government more in taxes as a married couple than you would have paid if you had just continued living together?"

incomes (like John and Joan), their wedding will most likely raise their tax bill. But a marriage subsidy is likely if one partner earns much more than the other, and especially if only one of them has earnings (like Sam and Sally).

This problem has no simple solution. To see why, try designing an income tax with the following four properties:

- Two married couples with the same total income should pay the same tax.
- When two people get married, their total tax bill should not change.
- A person or family with no income should pay no taxes.
- High-income taxpayers should pay a higher fraction of their incomes than low-income taxpayers.

All four of these properties are appealing, yet it is impossible to satisfy all of them simultaneously. Any income tax that satisfies the first three must violate the fourth. The only income tax that satisfies the first three properties is a proportional tax.

Some economists have advocated abolishing the marriage penalty by making individuals rather than the family the taxpaying unit, a policy that many European countries follow. This alternative might seem more equitable because it would treat married and unmarried couples the same. Yet this change would give up on the first of these properties: Families with the same total income could end up paying different taxes. For example, if each married couple paid taxes as if they were not married, then Sam and Sally would pay $22,500, and John and Joan would pay $20,000, even though both couples have the same total income. Whether this alternative tax system is more or less fair than the current marriage tax is hard to say. ●

Tax Incidence and Tax Equity

Tax incidence—the study of who bears the burden of taxes—is central to evaluating tax equity. As we first saw in Chapter 6, the person who bears the burden of a tax is not always the person who gets the tax bill from the government. Because taxes alter supply and demand, they alter equilibrium prices. As a result, they affect people beyond those who, according to statute, actually pay the tax. When evaluating the vertical and horizontal equity of any tax, it is important to take account of these indirect effects.

Many discussions of tax equity ignore the indirect effects of taxes and are based on what economists mockingly call the *flypaper theory* of tax incidence. According to this theory, the burden of a tax, like a fly on flypaper, sticks wherever it first lands. This assumption, however, is rarely valid.

For example, a person not trained in economics might argue that a tax on expensive fur coats is vertically equitable because most buyers of furs are wealthy. Yet if these buyers can easily substitute other luxuries for furs, then a tax on furs might only reduce the sale of furs. In the end, the burden of the tax will fall more on those who make and sell furs than on those who buy them. Because most workers who make furs are not wealthy, the equity of a fur tax could be quite different from what the flypaper theory indicates.

IN THE NEWS

THE CASE AGAINST TAXING CAPITAL INCOME

In this opinion column, an economist takes aim at the current tax system's treatment of capital income—that is, income earned on savings. Do you think his argument is based on efficiency or equity?

You Too Could Face 95 Percent Taxation

By Steven E. Landsburg

Once upon a time, a man went to work and earned a dollar. He used the dollar to buy a share of stock. The stock paid a dividend of 10 cents a year, 10 percent being the going rate of return in the land.

Thanks to wise corporate management, the dividend eventually doubled to 20 cents a year, causing the stock price to double as well. The man sold his share for $2, which he put in the bank. Eventually, his children inherited the money and reinvested it in the same company. They used their 20-cent annual dividend to purchase goods and services, happily ever after.

That was a fairy tale. Here is the reality:

Once upon a time, a man went to work and earned a dollar. After paying state and federal income taxes, he was left with 50 cents. He used the 50 cents to buy half a share of stock. When the stock price doubled, he sold his half-share for a dollar, paid a 10-cent tax on the capital gain, and put the remaining 90 cents in the bank. Eventually, his children inherited the money, paid 50 cents in inheritance tax, and reinvested the remaining 40 cents in the original company.

The company continued to earn a 10-percent rate of return, of which half went to pay corporate income and excise taxes. The children therefore received an annual dividend of 5 percent, which came to two cents a year. After paying personal income tax on the dividend, they were left with a penny a year in income. They used part of that penny to purchase goods and services, and the rest to pay sales taxes. . . .

After a series of perfectly reasonable economic choices, this family has lost 95 percent of its income to taxes. Ninety-five percent! From 20 cents down to a penny! How could such a thing happen? Simple: by taxing the same income five times.

Some aspects of multiple taxation are widely recognized, but others aren't. Everyone knows about the "double taxation" of corporate income: first when it's earned and then when it's paid out as dividends. But not everyone realizes that capital gains are always caused by expectations of future income. That means that the capital-gains tax amounts to a third tax on income that's already slated to be taxed twice. Taxing both dividends and capital gains is like fining drivers for speeding and then fining them again for having a high speedometer reading.

More important, each of these taxes—along with the inheritance tax and, for that matter, any tax at all on capital income—is ultimately a disguised tax on labor. That's because Marx was right: Capital is the embodiment of past labor. Today's capital income is a deferred reward for yesterday's hard work.

Tax that reward and you're taxing the work that made it possible.

A tax on capital—whether it comes in the form of a tax on dividends, corporate income, capital gains, or inheritance—is equivalent not just to a tax on labor but to a highly discriminatory tax on labor. It penalizes the labor of the young (who have many years of saving ahead of them) far more heavily than the labor of the old (who tend to spend their income as it arrives). So not only are people penalized for working, they're penalized doubly for working early in life.

A tax on labor discourages work. A tax on capital discourages work disproportionately among the young, distorting saving decisions and retarding economic growth. So a tax on capital has all the disadvantages of an extra tax on labor, and more besides. . . .

All of which suggests that we'd be better off with a single tax on labor income and no taxes at all on corporate income, dividends, capital gains, or inheritance. A growing body of research supports that suggestion. . . . The best thinking confirms common sense: Five taxes are at least four too many.

Source: *The Wall Street Journal*, March 5, 2001, p. A22. © 2001 by Dow Jones & Co. Inc. Reproduced with permission of DOW JONES CO INC in the format Textbook via Copyright Clearance Center.

This worker pays part of the corporate income tax.

Case Study

WHO PAYS THE CORPORATE INCOME TAX?

The corporate income tax provides a good example of the importance of tax incidence for tax policy. The corporate tax is popular among voters. After all, corporations are not people. Voters are always eager to have their taxes reduced and have some impersonal corporation pick up the tab.

But before deciding that the corporate income tax is a good way for the government to raise revenue, we should consider who bears the burden of the corporate tax. This is a difficult question on which economists disagree, but one thing is certain: *People pay all taxes.* When the government levies a tax on a corporation, the corporation is more like a tax collector than a taxpayer. The burden of the tax ultimately falls on people—the owners, customers, or workers of the corporation.

Many economists believe that workers and customers bear much of the burden of the corporate income tax. To see why, consider an example. Suppose that the U.S. government decides to raise the tax on the income earned by car companies. At first, this tax hurts the owners of the car companies, who receive less profit. But, over time, these owners will respond to the tax. Because producing cars is less profitable, they invest less in building new car factories. Instead, they invest their wealth in other ways—for example, by buying larger houses or by building factories in other industries or other countries. With fewer car factories, the supply of cars declines, as does the demand for autoworkers. Thus, a tax on corporations making cars causes the price of cars to rise and the wages of autoworkers to fall.

The corporate income tax shows how dangerous the flypaper theory of tax incidence can be. The corporate income tax is popular in part because it appears to be paid by rich corporations. Yet those who bear the ultimate burden of the tax—the customers and workers of corporations—are often not rich. If the true incidence of the corporate tax were more widely known, this tax might be less popular among voters. ●

QuickQuiz Explain the *benefits principle* and the *ability-to-pay principle.* ● What are *vertical equity* and *horizontal equity?* ● Why is studying tax incidence important for determining the equity of a tax system?

CONCLUSION: THE TRADEOFF BETWEEN EQUITY AND EFFICIENCY

Almost everyone agrees that equity and efficiency are the two most important goals of the tax system. But often these two goals conflict. Many proposed changes in the tax laws increase efficiency while reducing equity, or increase equity while reducing efficiency. People disagree about tax policy often because they attach different weights to these two goals.

The recent history of tax policy shows how political leaders differ in their views on equity and efficiency. When Ronald Reagan was elected president in

1980, the marginal tax rate on the earnings of the richest Americans was 50 percent. On interest income, the marginal tax rate was 70 percent. Reagan argued that such high tax rates greatly distorted economic incentives to work and save. In other words, he claimed that these high tax rates cost too much in terms of economic efficiency. Tax reform was, therefore, a high priority of his administration. Reagan signed into law large cuts in tax rates in 1981 and then again in 1986. When Reagan left office in 1989, the richest Americans faced a marginal tax rate of only 28 percent.

The pendulum of political debate swings both ways. When Bill Clinton ran for president in 1992, he argued that the rich were not paying their fair share of taxes. In other words, the low tax rates on the rich violated his view of vertical equity. In 1993 President Clinton signed into law a bill that raised the tax rates on the richest Americans to about 40 percent. When George W. Bush ran for president, he reprised many of Reagan's themes. Soon after moving into the White House in 2001, he fulfilled his campaign pledge of reversing part of the Clinton tax increase. When the Bush tax cut is fully phased in, the highest tax will be 35 percent.

Economics alone cannot determine the best way to balance the goals of efficiency and equity. This issue involves political philosophy as well as economics. But economists do have an important role in the political debate over tax policy: They can shed light on the tradeoffs that society faces and can help us avoid policies that sacrifice efficiency without any benefit in terms of equity.

SUMMARY

- The U.S. government raises revenue using various taxes. The most important taxes for the federal government are individual income taxes and payroll taxes for social insurance. The most important taxes for state and local governments are sales taxes and property taxes.

- The efficiency of a tax system refers to the costs it imposes on taxpayers. There are two costs of taxes beyond the transfer of resources from the taxpayer to the government. The first is the distortion in the allocation of resources that arises as taxes alter incentives and behavior. The second is the administrative burden of complying with the tax laws.

- The equity of a tax system concerns whether the tax burden is distributed fairly among the population. According to the benefits principle, it is fair for people to pay taxes based on the benefits they receive from the government. According to the ability-to-pay principle, it is fair for people to pay taxes based on their capability to handle the financial burden. When evaluating the equity of a tax system, it is important to remember a lesson from the study of tax incidence: The distribution of tax burdens is not the same as the distribution of tax bills.

- When considering changes in the tax laws, policymakers often face a tradeoff between efficiency and equity. Much of the debate over tax policy arises because people give different weights to these two goals.

KEY CONCEPTS

budget surplus, p. 246
budget deficit, p. 246
average tax rate, p. 250
marginal tax rate, p. 250

lump-sum tax, p. 251
benefits principle, p. 254
ability-to-pay principle, p. 254
vertical equity, p. 254

horizontal equity, p. 254
proportional tax, p. 255
regressive tax, p. 255
progressive tax, p. 255

QUESTIONS FOR REVIEW

1. Over the past century, has government grown more or less slowly than the rest of the economy?

2. What are the two most important sources of revenue for the U.S. federal government?

3. Explain how corporate profits are taxed twice.

4. Why is the burden of a tax to taxpayers greater than the revenue received by the government?

5. Why do some economists advocate taxing consumption rather than income?

6. Give two arguments why wealthy taxpayers should pay more taxes than poor taxpayers.

7. What is the concept of horizontal equity, and why is it hard to apply?

PROBLEMS AND APPLICATIONS

1. Government spending in the United States has grown as a share of national income over time. What changes in our economy and our society might explain this trend? Do you expect the trend to continue?

2. In a published source or on the Internet, find out whether the U.S. federal government had a budget deficit or surplus last year. What do policymakers expect to happen over the next few years? (Hint: The Web site of the Congressional Budget Office is http://www.cbo.gov.)

3. The information in many of the tables in this chapter is taken from the *Economic Report of the President*, which appears annually. Using a recent issue of the report at your library or on the Internet, answer the following questions and provide some numbers to support your answers. (Hint: The Web site of the government printing office is http://www.gpo.gov.)

   a. Figure 1 shows that government revenue as a percentage of total income has increased over time. Is this increase primarily attributable to changes in federal government revenue or in state and local government revenue?

   b. Looking at the combined revenue of the federal government and state and local governments, how has the composition of total revenue changed over time? Are personal income taxes more or less important? Social insurance taxes? Corporate profits taxes?

   c. Looking at the combined expenditures of the federal government and state and local governments, how have the relative shares of transfer payments and purchases of goods and services changed over time?

4. The chapter states that the elderly population in the United States is growing more rapidly than the total population. In particular, the number of workers is rising slowly, while the number of retirees is rising quickly. Concerned about the future of Social Security, some members of Congress propose a "freeze" on the program.

   a. If total expenditures were frozen, what would happen to benefits per retiree? To tax payments per worker? (Assume that Social Security taxes and receipts are balanced in each year.)

   b. If benefits per retiree were frozen, what would happen to total expenditures? To tax payments per worker?

   c. If tax payments per worker were frozen, what would happen to total expenditures? To benefits per retiree?

   d. What do your answers to parts (a), (b), and (c) imply about the difficult decisions faced by policymakers?

5. Suppose you are a typical person in the U.S. economy. You pay 4 percent of your income in a state income tax and 15.3 percent of your labor earnings in federal payroll taxes (employer and employee shares combined). You also pay federal income taxes as in Table 3. How much tax of each type do you pay if you earn $20,000 a year? Taking all taxes into account, what are your average and marginal tax rates? What happens to your tax bill and to your average and marginal tax rates if your income rises to $40,000?

6. Some states exclude necessities, such as food and clothing, from their sales tax. Other states do not. Discuss the merits of this exclusion. Consider both efficiency and equity.

7. Explain how individuals' behavior is affected by the following features of the federal tax code.
   a. Contributions to charity are tax deductible.
   b. Sales of beer are taxed.
   c. Interest that a homeowner pays on a mortgage is tax deductible.
   d. Realized capital gains are taxed, but accrued gains are not. (When someone owns a share of stock that rises in value, she has an "accrued" capital gain. If she sells the share, she has a "realized" gain.)

8. Suppose that your state raises its sales tax from 5 percent to 6 percent. The state revenue commissioner forecasts a 20 percent increase in sales tax revenue. Is this plausible? Explain.

9. Consider two of the income security programs in the United States: Temporary Assistance for Needy Families (TANF) and the Earned Income Tax Credit (EITC).
   a. When a woman with children and very low income earns an extra dollar, she receives less in TANF benefits. What do you think is the effect of this feature of TANF on the labor supply of low-income women? Explain.
   b. The EITC provides greater benefits as low-income workers earn more income (up to a point). What do you think is the effect of this program on the labor supply of low-income individuals? Explain.
   c. What are the disadvantages of eliminating TANF and allocating the savings to the EITC?

10. The Tax Reform Act of 1986 eliminated the deductibility of interest payments on consumer debt (mostly credit cards and auto loans) but maintained the deductibility of interest payments on mortgages and home equity loans. What do you think happened to the relative amounts of borrowing through consumer debt and home equity debt?

11. Categorize each of the following funding schemes as examples of the benefits principle or the ability-to-pay principle.
    a. Visitors to many national parks pay an entrance fee.
    b. Local property taxes support elementary and secondary schools.
    c. An airport trust fund collects a tax on each plane ticket sold and uses the money to improve airports and the air traffic control system.

12. Any income tax schedule embodies two types of tax rates—average tax rates and marginal tax rates.
    a. The average tax rate is defined as total taxes paid divided by income. For the proportional tax system presented in Table 7, what are the average tax rates for people earning $50,000, $100,000, and $200,000? What are the corresponding average tax rates in the regressive and progressive tax systems?
    b. The marginal tax rate is defined as the extra taxes paid on additional income divided by the increase in income. Calculate the marginal tax rate for the proportional tax system as income rises from $50,000 to $100,000. Calculate the marginal tax rate as income rises from $100,000 to $200,000. Calculate the corresponding marginal tax rates for the regressive and progressive tax systems.
    c. Describe the relationship between average tax rates and marginal tax rates for each of these three systems. In general, which rate is relevant for someone deciding whether to accept a job that pays slightly more than her current job? Which rate is relevant for judging the vertical equity of a tax system?

13. What is the efficiency justification for taxing consumption rather than income? If the United States were to adopt a consumption tax, do you think that would make the U.S. tax system more or less progressive? Explain.

14. If a salesman takes a client to lunch, part of the cost of the lunch is a deductible business expense for his company. Some members of Congress have argued that this feature of the tax code benefits relatively wealthy businesspeople and should be eliminated. Yet their arguments have been met with greater opposition from eating and drinking establishments than from companies themselves. Explain.

5

FIRM BEHAVIOR AND
THE ORGANIZATION OF INDUSTRY

THE COSTS OF PRODUCTION

The economy is made up of thousands of firms that produce the goods and services you enjoy every day: General Motors produces automobiles, General Electric produces lightbulbs, and General Mills produces breakfast cereals. Some firms, such as these three, are large; they employ thousands of workers and have thousands of stockholders who share in the firms' profits. Other firms, such as the local barbershop or candy store, are small; they employ only a few workers and are owned by a single person or family.

In previous chapters we used the supply curve to summarize firms' production decisions. According to the law of supply, firms are willing to produce and sell a greater quantity of a good when the price of the good is higher, and this response leads to a supply curve that slopes upward. For analyzing many questions, the law of supply is all you need to know about firm behavior.

In this chapter and the ones that follow, we examine firm behavior in more detail. This topic will give you a better understanding of what decisions lie behind the supply curve in a market. In addition, it will introduce you to a part of economics called *industrial organization*—the study of how firms' decisions regarding prices and quantities depend on the market conditions they face. The town in which you live, for instance, may have several pizzerias but only one cable television company. How does this difference in the number of firms affect the prices in these markets and the efficiency of the market outcomes? The field of industrial organization addresses exactly this question.

Before we turn to these issues, however, we need to discuss the costs of production. All firms, from Delta Air Lines to your local deli, incur costs as they make the goods and services that they sell. As we will see in the coming chapters, a firm's costs are a key determinant of its production and pricing decisions. In this chapter, we define some of the variables that economists use to measure a firm's costs, and we consider the relationships among them. A word of warning: This topic can seem dry and technical. But it provides a crucial foundation for the fascinating topics that follow.

WHAT ARE COSTS?

We begin our discussion of costs at Hungry Helen's Cookie Factory. Helen, the owner of the firm, buys flour, sugar, chocolate chips, and other cookie ingredients. She also buys the mixers and ovens and hires workers to run this equipment. She then sells the resulting cookies to consumers. By examining some of the issues that Helen faces in her business, we can learn some lessons about costs that apply to all firms in the economy.

Total Revenue, Total Cost, and Profit

We begin with the firm's objective. To understand what decisions a firm makes, we must understand what it is trying to do. It is conceivable that Helen started her firm because of an altruistic desire to provide the world with cookies or, perhaps, out of love for the cookie business. More likely, Helen started her business to make money. Economists normally assume that the goal of a firm is to maximize profit, and they find that this assumption works well in most cases.

What is a firm's profit? The amount that the firm receives for the sale of its output (cookies) is called its **total revenue**. The amount that the firm pays to buy inputs (flour, sugar, workers, ovens, etc.) is called its **total cost**. Helen gets to keep any revenue that is not needed to cover costs. **Profit** is a firm's total revenue minus its total cost. That is,

total revenue
the amount a firm receives for the sale of its output

total cost
the market value of the inputs a firm uses in production

profit
total revenue minus total cost

$$\text{Profit} = \text{Total revenue} - \text{Total cost}.$$

Helen's objective is to make her firm's profit as large as possible.

To see how a firm goes about maximizing profit, we must consider fully how to measure its total revenue and its total cost. Total revenue is the easy part: It equals the quantity of output the firm produces times the price at which it sells its output. If Helen produces 10,000 cookies and sells them at $2 a cookie, her total revenue is $20,000. By contrast, the measurement of a firm's total cost is more subtle.

Costs as Opportunity Costs

When measuring costs at Hungry Helen's Cookie Factory or any other firm, it is important to keep in mind one of the *Ten Principles of Economics* from Chapter 1:

The cost of something is what you give up to get it. Recall that the *opportunity cost* of an item refers to all those things that must be forgone to acquire that item. When economists speak of a firm's cost of production, they include all the opportunity costs of making its output of goods and services.

A firm's opportunity costs of production are sometimes obvious and sometimes less so. When Helen pays $1,000 for flour, that $1,000 is an opportunity cost because Helen can no longer use that $1,000 to buy something else. Similarly, when Helen hires workers to make the cookies, the wages she pays are part of the firm's costs. Because these costs require the firm to pay out some money, they are called **explicit costs.** By contrast, some of a firm's opportunity costs, called **implicit costs,** do not require a cash outlay. Imagine that Helen is skilled with computers and could earn $100 per hour working as a programmer. For every hour that Helen works at her cookie factory, she gives up $100 in income, and this forgone income is also part of her costs.

This distinction between explicit and implicit costs highlights an important difference between how economists and accountants analyze a business. Economists are interested in studying how firms make production and pricing decisions. Because these decisions are based on both explicit and implicit costs, economists include both when measuring a firm's costs. By contrast, accountants have the job of keeping track of the money that flows into and out of firms. As a result, they measure the explicit costs but often ignore the implicit costs.

The difference between economists and accountants is easy to see in the case of Hungry Helen's Cookie Factory. When Helen gives up the opportunity to earn money as a computer programmer, her accountant will not count this as a cost of her cookie business. Because no money flows out of the business to pay for this cost, it never shows up on the accountant's financial statements. An economist, however, will count the forgone income as a cost because it will affect the decisions that Helen makes in her cookie business. For example, if Helen's wage as a computer programmer rises from $100 to $500 per hour, she might decide that running her cookie business is too costly and choose to shut down the factory to become a full-time computer programmer.

explicit costs
input costs that require an outlay of money by the firm

implicit costs
input costs that do not require an outlay of money by the firm

The Cost of Capital as an Opportunity Cost

An important implicit cost of almost every business is the opportunity cost of the financial capital that has been invested in the business. Suppose, for instance, that Helen used $300,000 of her savings to buy her cookie factory from the previous owner. If Helen had instead left this money deposited in a savings account that pays an interest rate of 5 percent, she would have earned $15,000 per year. To own her cookie factory, therefore, Helen has given up $15,000 a year in interest income. This forgone $15,000 is one of the implicit opportunity costs of Helen's business.

As we have already noted, economists and accountants treat costs differently, and this is especially true in their treatment of the cost of capital. An economist views the $15,000 in interest income that Helen gives up every year as a cost of her business, even though it is an implicit cost. Helen's accountant, however, will not show this $15,000 as a cost because no money flows out of the business to pay for it.

To further explore the difference between economists and accountants, let's change the example slightly. Suppose now that Helen did not have the entire $300,000 to buy the factory but, instead, used $100,000 of her own savings and borrowed $200,000 from a bank at an interest rate of 5 percent. Helen's accountant, who

[Handwritten notes in left margin:]

Economic Profit

$$P = R - C(Ex + Im)$$

Accounting Profit

$$P = R - C(Ex)$$

only measures explicit costs, will now count the $10,000 interest paid on the bank loan every year as a cost because this amount of money now flows out of the firm. By contrast, according to an economist, the opportunity cost of owning the business is still $15,000. The opportunity cost equals the interest on the bank loan (an explicit cost of $10,000) plus the forgone interest on savings (an implicit cost of $5,000).

Economic Profit versus Accounting Profit

economic profit
total revenue minus total cost, including both explicit and implicit costs

accounting profit
total revenue minus total explicit cost

Now let's return to the firm's objective—profit. Because economists and accountants measure costs differently, they also measure profit differently. An economist measures a firm's **economic profit** as the firm's total revenue minus all the opportunity costs (explicit and implicit) of producing the goods and services sold. An accountant measures the firm's **accounting profit** as the firm's total revenue minus only the firm's explicit costs.

Figure 1 summarizes this difference. Notice that because the accountant ignores the implicit costs, accounting profit is usually larger than economic profit. For a business to be profitable from an economist's standpoint, total revenue must cover all the opportunity costs, both explicit and implicit.

QuickQuiz Farmer McDonald gives banjo lessons for $20 an hour. One day, he spends 10 hours planting $100 worth of seeds on his farm. What opportunity cost has he incurred? What cost would his accountant measure? If these seeds will yield

[Handwritten notes:] Imp $200 ← Opp · → ex $100 ← E = NO ⊘ (100) R = 200 ↑ 100 ↑

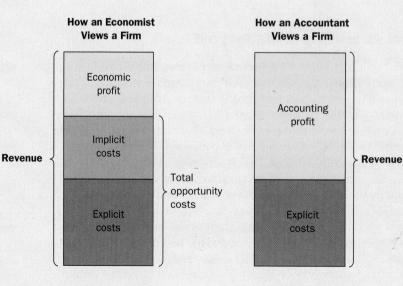

FIGURE 1

Economists versus Accountants

Economists include all opportunity costs when analyzing a firm, whereas accountants measure only explicit costs. Therefore, economic profit is smaller than accounting profit.

How an Economist Views a Firm

Revenue {
- Economic profit
- Implicit costs } Total opportunity costs
- Explicit costs

How an Accountant Views a Firm

- Accounting profit
- Explicit costs
} Revenue

$200 worth of crops, does McDonald earn an accounting profit? Does he earn an economic profit?

PRODUCTION AND COSTS

Firms incur costs when they buy inputs to produce the goods and services that they plan to sell. In this section we examine the link between a firm's production process and its total cost. Once again, we consider Hungry Helen's Cookie Factory.

IN THE NEWS

TRUE PROFIT VERSUS FICTITIOUS PROFIT

The analysis of firm behavior begins with the measurement of revenue, costs, and profits. In 2001 and 2002, this topic made the news when several major companies were revealed to have lied about these key measures of performance.

Flavors of Fraud

By Paul Krugman

So you're the manager of an ice cream parlor. It's not very profitable, so how can you get rich? Each of the big business scandals uncovered so far suggests a different strategy for executive self-dealing.

First there's the Enron strategy. You sign contracts to provide customers with an ice cream cone a day for the next 30 years. You deliberately underestimate the cost of providing each cone; then you book all the projected profits on those future ice cream sales as part of this year's bottom line. Suddenly you appear to have a highly profitable business, and you can sell shares in your store at inflated prices.

Then there's the Dynegy strategy. Ice cream sales aren't profitable, but you convince investors that they will be profitable in the future. Then you enter into a quiet agreement with another ice cream parlor down the street: each of you will buy hundreds of cones from the other every day. Or rather, pretend to buy—no need to go to the trouble of actually moving all those cones back and forth. The result is that you appear to be a big player in a coming business, and can sell shares at inflated prices. . . .

Finally, there's the WorldCom strategy. Here you don't create imaginary sales; you make real costs disappear, by pretending that operating expenses—cream, sugar, chocolate syrup—are part of the purchase price of a new refrigerator. So your unprofitable business seems, on paper, to be a highly profitable business that borrows money only to finance its purchases of new equipment. And you can sell shares at inflated prices.

Oh, I almost forgot: How do you enrich yourself personally? The easiest way is to give yourself lots of stock options, so that you benefit from those inflated prices. . . .

I'm not saying that all U.S. corporations are corrupt. But it's clear that executives who want to be corrupt have faced few obstacles. Auditors weren't interested in giving a hard time to companies that gave them lots of consulting income; bank executives weren't interested in giving a hard time to companies that, as we've learned in the Enron case, let them in on some of those lucrative side deals. And elected officials, kept compliant by campaign contributions and other inducements, kept the regulators from doing their job.

Source: *The New York Times*, June 28, 2002, p. A27. Copyright © 2002 by The New York Times Co. Reprinted by permission.

In the analysis that follows, we make an important simplifying assumption: We assume that the size of Helen's factory is fixed and that Helen can vary the quantity of cookies produced only by changing the number of workers. This assumption is realistic in the short run, but not in the long run. That is, Helen cannot build a larger factory overnight, but she can do so within a year or so. This analysis, therefore, should be viewed as describing the production decisions that Helen faces in the short run. We examine the relationship between costs and time horizon more fully later in the chapter.

The Production Function

Table 1 shows how the quantity of cookies Helen's factory produces per hour depends on the number of workers. As you see in the first two columns, if there are no workers in the factory, Helen produces no cookies. When there is 1 worker, she produces 50 cookies. When there are 2 workers, she produces 90 cookies, and so on. Figure 2 presents a graph of these two columns of numbers. The number of workers is on the horizontal axis, and the number of cookies produced is on the vertical axis. This relationship between the quantity of inputs (workers) and quantity of output (cookies) is called the **production function.**

production function
the relationship between quantity of inputs used to make a good and the quantity of output of that good

One of the *Ten Principles of Economics* introduced in Chapter 1 is that rational people think at the margin. As we will see in future chapters, this idea is the key to understanding the decision a firm makes about how many workers to hire and how much output to produce. To take a step toward understanding these decisions, the third column in the table gives the marginal product of a worker. The **marginal product** of any input in the production process is the increase in the quantity of output obtained from one additional unit of that input. When the number of workers goes from 1 to 2, cookie production increases from 50 to 90, so the marginal product of the second worker is 40 cookies. And when the number of workers goes from 2 to 3, cookie production increases from 90 to 120, so the marginal product of the third worker is 30 cookies.

marginal product
the increase in output that arises from an additional unit of input

TABLE 1

A Production Function and Total Cost: Hungry Helen's Cookie Factory

Number of Workers	Output (quantity of cookies produced per hour)	Marginal Product of Labor	Cost of Factory	Cost of Workers	Total Cost of Inputs (cost of factory + cost of workers)
0	0		$30	$ 0	$30
		50			
1	50		30	10	40
		40			
2	90		30	20	50
		30			
3	120		30	30	60
		20			
4	140		30	40	70
		10			
5	150		30	50	80

FIGURE 2

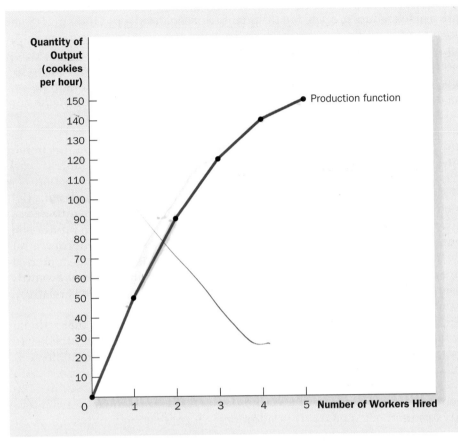

Hungry Helen's Production Function

A production function shows the relationship between the number of workers hired and the quantity of output produced. Here the number of workers hired (on the horizontal axis) is from the first column in Table 1, and the quantity of output produced (on the vertical axis) is from the second column. The production function gets flatter as the number of workers increases, which reflects diminishing marginal product.

Notice that as the number of workers increases, the marginal product declines. The second worker has a marginal product of 40 cookies, the third worker has a marginal product of 30 cookies, and the fourth worker has a marginal product of 20 cookies. This property is called **diminishing marginal product.** At first, when only a few workers are hired, they have easy access to Helen's kitchen equipment. As the number of workers increases, additional workers have to share equipment and work in more crowded conditions. Hence, as more and more workers are hired, each additional worker contributes less to the production of cookies.

Diminishing marginal product is also apparent in Figure 2. The production function's slope ("rise over run") tells us the change in Helen's output of cookies ("rise") for each additional input of labor ("run"). That is, the slope of the production function measures the marginal product of a worker. As the number of workers increases, the marginal product declines, and the production function becomes flatter.

diminishing marginal product the property whereby the marginal product of an input declines as the quantity of the input increases

From the Production Function to the Total-Cost Curve

The last three columns of Table 1 show Helen's cost of producing cookies. In this example, the cost of Helen's factory is $30 per hour, and the cost of a worker is $10 per hour. If she hires 1 worker, her total cost is $40. If she hires 2 workers, her total cost is $50, and so on. With this information, the table now shows how the number of workers Helen hires is related to the quantity of cookies she produces and to her total cost of production.

Our goal in the next several chapters is to study firms' production and pricing decisions. For this purpose, the most important relationship in Table 1 is between quantity produced (in the second column) and total costs (in the sixth column). Figure 3 graphs these two columns of data with the quantity produced on the horizontal axis and total cost on the vertical axis. This graph is called the *total-cost curve*.

Now compare the total-cost curve in Figure 3 with the production function in Figure 2. These two curves are opposite sides of the same coin. The total-cost curve gets steeper as the amount produced rises, whereas the production function gets flatter as production rises. These changes in slope occur for the same reason. High production of cookies means that Helen's kitchen is crowded with many workers. Because the kitchen is crowded, each additional worker adds less to production, reflecting diminishing marginal product. Therefore, the production function is relatively flat. But now turn this logic around: When the kitchen is crowded, producing an additional cookie requires a lot of additional labor and is thus very costly. Therefore, when the quantity produced is large, the total-cost curve is relatively steep.

FIGURE 3

Hungry Helen's Total-Cost Curve

A total-cost curve shows the relationship between the quantity of output produced and total cost of production. Here the quantity of output produced (on the horizontal axis) is from the second column in Table 1, and the total cost (on the vertical axis) is from the sixth column. The total-cost curve gets steeper as the quantity of output increases because of diminishing marginal product.

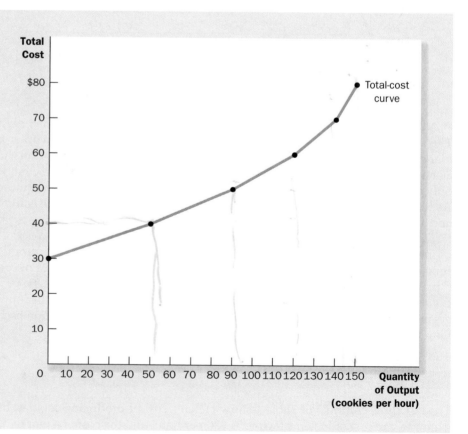

QuickQuiz If Farmer Jones plants no seeds on his farm, he gets no harvest. If he plants 1 bag of seeds, he gets 3 bushels of wheat. If he plants 2 bags, he gets 5 bushels. If he plants 3 bags, he gets 6 bushels. A bag of seeds costs $100, and seeds are his only cost. Use these data to graph the farmer's production function and total-cost curve. Explain their shapes.

THE VARIOUS MEASURES OF COST

Our analysis of Hungry Helen's Cookie Factory demonstrated how a firm's total cost reflects its production function. From data on a firm's total cost, we can derive several related measures of cost, which will turn out to be useful when we analyze production and pricing decisions in future chapters. To see how these related measures are derived, we consider the example in Table 2. This table presents cost data on Helen's neighbor: Thirsty Thelma's Lemonade Stand.

The first column of the table shows the number of glasses of lemonade that Thelma might produce, ranging from 0 to 10 glasses per hour. The second column shows Thelma's total cost of producing lemonade. Figure 4 (p. 276) plots Thelma's total-cost curve. The quantity of lemonade (from the first column) is on the

TABLE 2

The Various Measures of Cost: Thirsty Thelma's Lemonade Stand

Quantity of Lemonade (glasses per hour)	Total Cost	Fixed Cost	Variable Cost	Average Fixed Cost	Average Variable Cost	Average Total Cost	Marginal Cost
0	$3.00	$3.00	$0.00	—	—	—	
							$0.30
1	3.30	3.00	0.30	$3.00	$0.30	$3.30	
							0.50
2	3.80	3.00	0.80	1.50	0.40	1.90	
							0.70
3	4.50	3.00	1.50	1.00	0.50	1.50	
							0.90
4	5.40	3.00	2.40	0.75	0.60	1.35	
							1.10
5	6.50	3.00	3.50	0.60	0.70	1.30	
							1.30
6	7.80	3.00	4.80	0.50	0.80	1.30	
							1.50
7	9.30	3.00	6.30	0.43	0.90	1.33	
							1.70
8	11.00	3.00	8.00	0.38	1.00	1.38	
							1.90
9	12.90	3.00	9.90	0.33	1.10	1.43	
							2.10
10	15.00	3.00	12.00	0.30	1.20	1.50	

FIGURE 4

Thirsty Thelma's Total-Cost Curve

Here the quantity of output produced (on the horizontal axis) is from the first column in Table 2, and the total cost (on the vertical axis) is from the second column. As in Figure 3, the total-cost curve gets steeper as the quantity of output increases because of diminishing marginal product.

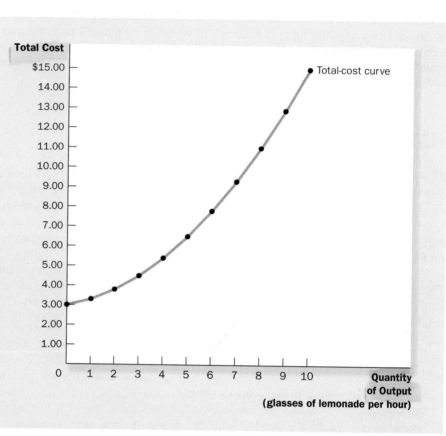

horizontal axis, and total cost (from the second column) is on the vertical axis. Thirsty Thelma's total-cost curve has a shape similar to Hungry Helen's. In particular, it becomes steeper as the quantity produced rises, which (as we have discussed) reflects diminishing marginal product.

Fixed and Variable Costs

fixed costs
costs that do not vary with the quantity of output produced

Thelma's total cost can be divided into two types. Some costs, called **fixed costs**, do not vary with the quantity of output produced. They are incurred even if the firm produces nothing at all. Thelma's fixed costs include any rent she pays because this cost is the same regardless of how much lemonade Thelma produces. Similarly, if Thelma needs to hire a full-time bookkeeper to pay bills, regardless of the quantity of lemonade produced, the bookkeeper's salary is a fixed cost. The third column in Table 2 shows Thelma's fixed cost, which in this example is $3.00.

variable costs
costs that do vary with the quantity of output produced

Some of the firm's costs, called **variable costs**, change as the firm alters the quantity of output produced. Thelma's variable costs include the cost of lemons, sugar, paper cups, and straws: The more lemonade Thelma makes, the more of these items she needs to buy. Similarly, if Thelma has to hire more workers to make more lemonade, the salaries of these workers are variable costs. The fourth column of the table shows Thelma's variable cost. The variable cost is 0 if she produces nothing, $0.30 if she produces 1 glass of lemonade, $0.80 if she produces 2 glasses, and so on.

A firm's total cost is the sum of fixed and variable costs. In Table 2, total cost in the second column equals fixed cost in the third column plus variable cost in the fourth column.

Average and Marginal Cost

As the owner of her firm, Thelma has to decide how much to produce. A key part of this decision is how her costs will vary as she changes the level of production. In making this decision, Thelma might ask her production supervisor the following two questions about the cost of producing lemonade:

- How much does it cost to make the typical glass of lemonade?
- How much does it cost to increase production of lemonade by 1 glass?

Although at first these two questions might seem to have the same answer, they do not. Both answers will turn out to be important for understanding how firms make production decisions.

To find the cost of the typical unit produced, we would divide the firm's costs by the quantity of output it produces. For example, if the firm produces 2 glasses per hour, its total cost is $3.80, and the cost of the typical glass is $3.80/2, or $1.90. Total cost divided by the quantity of output is called **average total cost**. Because total cost is just the sum of fixed and variable costs, average total cost can be expressed as the sum of average fixed cost and average variable cost. **Average fixed cost** is the fixed cost divided by the quantity of output, and **average variable cost** is the variable cost divided by the quantity of output.

Although average total cost tells us the cost of the typical unit, it does not tell us how much total cost will change as the firm alters its level of production. The last column in Table 2 shows the amount that total cost rises when the firm increases production by 1 unit of output. This number is called **marginal cost.** For example, if Thelma increases production from 2 to 3 glasses, total cost rises from $3.80 to $4.50, so the marginal cost of the third glass of lemonade is $4.50 minus $3.80, or $0.70.

It may be helpful to express these definitions mathematically:

$$\text{Average total cost} = \text{Total cost} / \text{Quantity}$$
$$ATC = TC/Q$$

and

$$\text{Marginal cost} = \text{Change in total cost} / \text{Change in quantity}$$
$$MC = \Delta TC / \Delta Q.$$

Here Δ, the Greek letter *delta*, represents the change in a variable. These equations show how average total cost and marginal cost are derived from total cost. *Average total cost tells us the cost of a typical unit of output if total cost is divided evenly over all the units produced. Marginal cost tells us the increase in total cost that arises from producing an additional unit of output.* As we will see more fully in the next chapter, Thelma, our lemonade entrepreneur, will find the concepts of average total cost and marginal cost useful when deciding how much lemonade to produce.

average total cost
total cost divided by the quantity of output

average fixed cost
fixed costs divided by the quantity of output

average variable cost
variable costs divided by the quantity of output

marginal cost
the increase in total cost that arises from an extra unit of production

Cost Curves and Their Shapes

Just as in previous chapters we found graphs of supply and demand useful when analyzing the behavior of markets, we will find graphs of average and marginal cost useful when analyzing the behavior of firms. Figure 5 graphs Thelma's costs using the data from Table 2. The horizontal axis measures the quantity the firm produces, and the vertical axis measures marginal and average costs. The graph shows four curves: average total cost (ATC), average fixed cost (AFC), average variable cost (AVC), and marginal cost (MC).

The cost curves shown here for Thirsty Thelma's Lemonade Stand have some features that are common to the cost curves of many firms in the economy. Let's examine three features in particular: the shape of marginal cost, the shape of average total cost, and the relationship between marginal and average total cost.

Rising Marginal Cost   Thirsty Thelma's marginal cost rises with the quantity of output produced. This reflects the property of diminishing marginal product. When Thelma is producing a small quantity of lemonade, she has few workers, and much of her equipment is not being used. Because she can easily put these idle resources to use, the marginal product of an extra worker is large, and the marginal cost of an extra glass of lemonade is small. By contrast, when Thelma is producing a large quantity of lemonade, her stand is crowded with workers, and most of her equipment is fully utilized. Thelma can produce more lemonade by adding

FIGURE 5

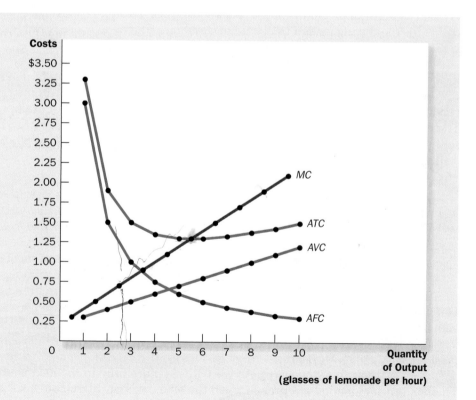

Thirsty Thelma's Average-Cost and Marginal-Cost Curves

This figure shows the average total cost (ATC), average fixed cost (AFC), average variable cost (AVC), and marginal cost (MC) for Thirsty Thelma's Lemonade Stand. All of these curves are obtained by graphing the data in Table 2. These cost curves show three features that are typical of many firms: (1) Marginal cost rises with the quantity of output. (2) The average-total-cost curve is U-shaped. (3) The marginal-cost curve crosses the average-total-cost curve at the minimum of average total cost.

workers, but these new workers have to work in crowded conditions and may have to wait to use the equipment. Therefore, when the quantity of lemonade being produced is already high, the marginal product of an extra worker is low, and the marginal cost of an extra glass of lemonade is large.

U-Shaped Average Total Cost   Thirsty Thelma's average-total-cost curve is U-shaped. To understand why this is so, remember that average total cost is the sum of average fixed cost and average variable cost. Average fixed cost always declines as output rises because the fixed cost is getting spread over a larger number of units. Average variable cost typically rises as output increases because of diminishing marginal product. Average total cost reflects the shapes of both average fixed cost and average variable cost. As shown in Figure 5, at very low levels of output, such as 1 or 2 glasses per hour, average total cost is high because the fixed cost is spread over only a few units. Average total cost then declines as output increases until the firm's output reaches 5 glasses of lemonade per hour, when average total cost falls to $1.30 per glass. When the firm produces more than 6 glasses, average total cost starts rising again because average variable cost rises substantially.

The bottom of the U-shape occurs at the quantity that minimizes average total cost. This quantity is sometimes called the **efficient scale** of the firm. For Thirsty Thelma, the efficient scale is 5 or 6 glasses of lemonade. If she produces more or less than this amount, her average total cost rises above the minimum of $1.30.

efficient scale
the quantity of output that minimizes average total cost

The Relationship between Marginal Cost and Average Total Cost   If you look at Figure 5 (or back at Table 2), you will see something that may be surprising at first. *Whenever marginal cost is less than average total cost, average total cost is falling. Whenever marginal cost is greater than average total cost, average total cost is rising.* This feature of Thirsty Thelma's cost curves is not a coincidence from the particular numbers used in the example: It is true for all firms.

To see why, consider an analogy. Average total cost is like your cumulative grade point average. Marginal cost is like the grade in the next course you will take. If your grade in your next course is less than your grade point average, your grade point average will fall. If your grade in your next course is higher than your grade point average, your grade point average will rise. The mathematics of average and marginal costs is exactly the same as the mathematics of average and marginal grades.

This relationship between average total cost and marginal cost has an important corollary: *The marginal-cost curve crosses the average-total-cost curve at its minimum.* Why? At low levels of output, marginal cost is below average total cost, so average total cost is falling. But after the two curves cross, marginal cost rises above average total cost. For the reason we have just discussed, average total cost must start to rise at this level of output. Hence, this point of intersection is the minimum of average total cost. As you will see in the next chapter, this point of minimum average total cost plays a key role in the analysis of competitive firms.

Typical Cost Curves

In the examples we have studied so far, the firms exhibit diminishing marginal product and, therefore, rising marginal cost at all levels of output. Yet actual firms are often a bit more complicated than this. In many firms, diminishing marginal product does not start to occur immediately after the first worker is hired. Depending on the production process, the second or third worker might have higher marginal product than the first because a team of workers can divide tasks and work more productively than a single worker. Such firms would first experience increasing marginal product for a while before diminishing marginal product sets in.

The table in Figure 6 shows the cost data for such a firm, called Big Bob's Bagel Bin. These data are used in the graphs. Panel (a) shows how total cost (TC) depends on the quantity produced, and panel (b) shows average total cost (ATC), average fixed cost (AFC), average variable cost (AVC), and marginal cost (MC). In the range of output from 0 to 4 bagels per hour, the firm experiences increasing marginal product, and the marginal-cost curve falls. After 5 bagels per hour, the firm starts to experience diminishing marginal product, and the marginal-cost curve starts to rise. This combination of increasing then diminishing marginal product also makes the average-variable-cost curve U-shaped.

Despite these differences from our previous example, Big Bob's cost curves share the three properties that are most important to remember:

- Marginal cost eventually rises with the quantity of output.
- The average-total-cost curve is U-shaped.
- The marginal-cost curve crosses the average-total-cost curve at the minimum of average total cost.

QuickQuiz Suppose Honda's total cost of producing 4 cars is $225,000 and its total cost of producing 5 cars is $250,000. What is the average total cost of producing 5 cars? What is the marginal cost of the fifth car? • Draw the marginal-cost curve and the average-total-cost curve for a typical firm, and explain why these curves cross where they do.

COSTS IN THE SHORT RUN AND IN THE LONG RUN

We noted at the beginning of this chapter that a firm's costs might depend on the time horizon being examined. Let's examine more precisely why this might be the case.

The Relationship between Short-Run and Long-Run Average Total Cost

For many firms, the division of total costs between fixed and variable costs depends on the time horizon. Consider, for instance, a car manufacturer, such as Ford Motor Company. Over a period of only a few months, Ford cannot adjust the number or sizes of its car factories. The only way it can produce additional cars is to hire more workers at the factories it already has. The cost of these factories is, therefore, a fixed cost in the short run. By contrast, over a period of several years, Ford can expand the size of its factories, build new factories, or close old ones. Thus, the cost of its factories is a variable cost in the long run.

FIGURE 6

Big Bob's Cost Curves

Many firms, like Big Bob's Bagel Bin, experience increasing marginal product before diminishing marginal product and, therefore, have cost curves shaped like those in this figure. Panel (a) shows how total cost (TC) depends on the quantity produced. Panel (b) shows how average total cost (ATC), average fixed cost (AFC), average variable cost (AVC), and marginal cost (MC) depend on the quantity produced. These curves are derived by graphing the data from the table. Notice that marginal cost and average variable cost fall for a while before starting to rise.

Quantity of Bagels (per hour)	Total Cost	Fixed Cost	Variable Cost	Average Fixed Cost	Average Variable Cost	Average Total Cost	Marginal Cost
Q	TC = FC + VC	FC	VC	AFC = FC/Q	AVC = VC/Q	ATC = TC/Q	MC = ΔTC/ΔQ
0	$ 2.00	$2.00	$ 0.00	—	—	—	
							$1.00
1	3.00	2.00	1.00	$2.00	$1.00	$3.00	
							0.80
2	3.80	2.00	1.80	1.00	0.90	1.90	
							0.60
3	4.40	2.00	2.40	0.67	0.80	1.47	
							0.40
4	4.80	2.00	2.80	0.50	0.70	1.20	
							0.40
5	5.20	2.00	3.20	0.40	0.64	1.04	
							0.60
6	5.80	2.00	3.80	0.33	0.63	0.96	
							0.80
7	6.60	2.00	4.60	0.29	0.66	0.95	
							1.00
8	7.60	2.00	5.60	0.25	0.70	0.95	
							1.20
9	8.80	2.00	6.80	0.22	0.76	0.98	
							1.40
10	10.20	2.00	8.20	0.20	0.82	1.02	
							1.60
11	11.80	2.00	9.80	0.18	0.89	1.07	
							1.80
12	13.60	2.00	11.60	0.17	0.97	1.14	
							2.00
13	15.60	2.00	13.60	0.15	1.05	1.20	
							2.20
14	17.80	2.00	15.80	0.14	1.13	1.27	

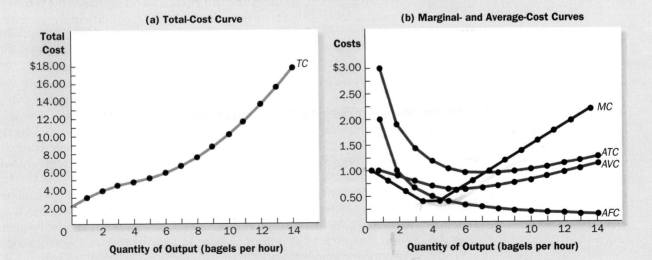

(a) Total-Cost Curve

(b) Marginal- and Average-Cost Curves

FIGURE 7

Average Total Cost in the Short and Long Runs

Because fixed costs are variable in the long run, the average-total-cost curve in the short run differs from the average-total-cost curve in the long run.

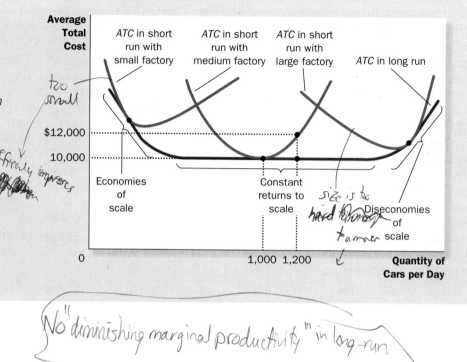

[handwritten annotations: "too small", "effecily improves", "size is too hard change turnover", "No 'diminishing marginal productivity' in long-run."]

Because many decisions are fixed in the short run but variable in the long run, a firm's long-run cost curves differ from its short-run cost curves. Figure 7 shows an example. The figure presents three short-run average-total-cost curves—for a small, medium, and large factory. It also presents the long-run average-total-cost curve. As the firm moves along the long-run curve, it is adjusting the size of the factory to the quantity of production.

This graph shows how short-run and long-run costs are related. The long-run average-total-cost curve is a much flatter U-shape than the short-run average-total-cost curve. In addition, all the short-run curves lie on or above the long-run curve. These properties arise because firms have greater flexibility in the long run. In essence, in the long run, the firm gets to choose which short-run curve it wants to use. But in the short run, it has to use whatever short-run curve it chose in the past.

The figure shows an example of how a change in production alters costs over different time horizons. When Ford wants to increase production from 1,000 to 1,200 cars per day, it has no choice in the short run but to hire more workers at its existing medium-sized factory. Because of diminishing marginal product, average total cost rises from $10,000 to $12,000 per car. In the long run, however, Ford can expand both the size of the factory and its workforce, and average total cost returns to $10,000.

How long does it take for a firm to get to the long run? The answer depends on the firm. It can take a year or longer for a major manufacturing firm, such as a car company, to build a larger factory. By contrast, a person running a lemonade stand can go and buy a larger pitcher within an hour or less. There is, therefore, no single answer about how long it takes a firm to adjust its production facilities.

Economies and Diseconomies of Scale

The shape of the long-run average-total-cost curve conveys important information about the technology for producing a good. When long-run average total cost declines as output increases, there are said to be **economies of scale**. When long-run average total cost rises as output increases, there are said to be **diseconomies of scale**. When long-run average total cost does not vary with the level of output, there are said to be **constant returns to scale**. In this example, Ford has economies of scale at low levels of output, constant returns to scale at intermediate levels of output, and diseconomies of scale at high levels of output.

What might cause economies or diseconomies of scale? Economies of scale often arise because higher production levels allow *specialization* among workers, which permits each worker to become better at his or her assigned tasks. For instance, modern assembly-line production requires a large number of workers. If Ford were producing only a small quantity of cars, it could not take advantage of this approach and would have higher average total cost. Diseconomies of scale can arise because of *coordination problems* that are inherent in any large organization. The more cars Ford produces, the more stretched the management team becomes, and the less effective the managers become at keeping costs down.

economies of scale
the property whereby long-run average total cost falls as the quantity of output increases

diseconomies of scale
the property whereby long-run average total cost rises as the quantity of output increases

constant returns to scale
the property whereby long-run average total cost stays the same as the quantity of output changes

FYI

LESSONS FROM A PIN FACTORY

"Jack of all trades, master of none." This well-known adage helps explain why firms sometimes experience economies of scale. A person who tries to do everything usually ends up doing nothing very well. If a firm wants its workers to be as productive as they can be, it is often best to give each a limited task that he or she can master. But this is possible only if a firm employs many workers and produces a large quantity of output.

In his celebrated book *An Inquiry into the Nature and Causes of the Wealth of Nations*, Adam Smith described a visit he made to a pin factory. Smith was impressed by the specialization among the workers and the resulting economies of scale. He wrote:

One man draws out the wire, another straightens it, a third cuts it, a fourth points it, a fifth grinds it at the top for receiving the head;

to make the head requires two or three distinct operations; to put it on is a peculiar business; to whiten it is another; it is even a trade by itself to put them into paper.

Smith reported that because of this specialization, the pin factory produced thousands of pins per worker every day. He conjectured that if the workers had chosen to work separately, rather than as a team of specialists, "they certainly could not each of them make twenty, perhaps not one pin a day." In other words, because of specialization, a large pin factory could achieve higher output per worker and lower average cost per pin than a small pin factory.

The specialization that Smith observed in the pin factory is prevalent in the modern economy. If you want to build a house, for instance, you could try to do all the work yourself. But most people turn to a builder, who in turn hires carpenters, plumbers, electricians, painters, and many other types of workers. These workers specialize in particular jobs, and this allows them to become better at their jobs than if they were generalists. Indeed, the use of specialization to achieve economies of scale is one reason modern societies are as prosperous as they are.

This analysis shows why long-run average-total-cost curves are often U-shaped. At low levels of production, the firm benefits from increased size because it can take advantage of greater specialization. Coordination problems, meanwhile, are not yet acute. By contrast, at high levels of production, the benefits of specialization have already been realized, and coordination problems become more severe as the firm grows larger. Thus, long-run average total cost is falling at low levels of production because of increasing specialization and rising at high levels of production because of increasing coordination problems.

QuickQuiz If Boeing produces 9 jets per month, its long-run total cost is $9.0 million per month. If it produces 10 jets per month, its long-run total cost is $9.5 million per month. Does Boeing exhibit economies or diseconomies of scale?

CONCLUSION

The purpose of this chapter has been to develop some tools that we can use to study how firms make production and pricing decisions. You should now understand what economists mean by the term *costs* and how costs vary with the quantity of output a firm produces. To refresh your memory, Table 3 summarizes some of the definitions we have encountered.

TABLE 3

The Many Types of Cost: A Summary

Term	Definition	Mathematical Description
Explicit costs	Costs that require an outlay of money by the firm	—
Implicit costs	Costs that do not require an outlay of money by the firm	—
Fixed costs	Costs that do not vary with the quantity of output produced	FC
Variable costs	Costs that do vary with the quantity of output produced	VC
Total cost	The market value of all the inputs that a firm uses in production	$TC = FC + VC$
Average fixed cost	Fixed costs divided by the quantity of output	$AFC = FC/Q$
Average variable cost	Variable costs divided by the quantity of output	$AVC = VC/Q$
Average total cost	Total cost divided by the quantity of output	$ATC = TC/Q$
Marginal cost	The increase in total cost that arises from an extra unit of production	$MC = \Delta TC/\Delta Q$

By themselves, of course, a firm's cost curves do not tell us what decisions the firm will make. But they are an important component of that decision, as we will begin to see in the next chapter.

SUMMARY

- The goal of firms is to maximize profit, which equals total revenue minus total cost.

- When analyzing a firm's behavior, it is important to include all the opportunity costs of production. Some of the opportunity costs, such as the wages a firm pays its workers, are explicit. Other opportunity costs, such as the wages the firm owner gives up by working in the firm rather than taking another job, are implicit.

- A firm's costs reflect its production process. A typical firm's production function gets flatter as the quantity of an input increases, displaying the property of diminishing marginal product. As a result, a firm's total-cost curve gets steeper as the quantity produced rises.

- A firm's total costs can be divided between fixed costs and variable costs. Fixed costs are costs that do not change when the firm alters the quantity of output produced. Variable costs are costs that do change when the firm alters the quantity of output produced.

- From a firm's total cost, two related measures of cost are derived. Average total cost is total cost divided by the quantity of output. Marginal cost is the amount by which total cost rises if output increases by 1 unit.

- When analyzing firm behavior, it is often useful to graph average total cost and marginal cost. For a typical firm, marginal cost rises with the quantity of output. Average total cost first falls as output increases and then rises as output increases further. The marginal-cost curve always crosses the average-total-cost curve at the minimum of average total cost.

- A firm's costs often depend on the time horizon being considered. In particular, many costs are fixed in the short run but variable in the long run. As a result, when the firm changes its level of production, average total cost may rise more in the short run than in the long run.

KEY CONCEPTS

total revenue, p. 268
total cost, p. 268
profit, p. 268
explicit costs, p. 269
implicit costs, p. 269
economic profit, p. 270
accounting profit, p. 270

production function, p. 272
marginal product, p. 272
diminishing marginal
    product, p. 273
fixed costs, p. 276
variable costs, p. 276
average total cost, p. 277

average fixed cost, p. 277
average variable cost, p. 277
marginal cost, p. 277
efficient scale, p. 279
economies of scale, p. 283
diseconomies of scale, p. 283
constant returns to scale, p. 283

QUESTIONS FOR REVIEW

1. What is the relationship between a firm's total revenue, profit, and total cost?

2. Give an example of an opportunity cost that an accountant might not count as a cost. Why would the accountant ignore this cost?

3. What is marginal product, and what does it mean if it is diminishing?

4. Draw a production function that exhibits diminishing marginal product of labor. Draw the associated total-cost curve. (In both cases, be sure

to label the axes.) Explain the shapes of the two curves you have drawn.

5. Define total cost, average total cost, and marginal cost. How are they related?

6. Draw the marginal-cost and average-total-cost curves for a typical firm. Explain why the curves have the shapes that they do and why they cross where they do.

7. How and why does a firm's average-total-cost curve differ in the short run and in the long run?

8. Define *economies of scale* and explain why they might arise. Define *diseconomies of scale* and explain why they might arise.

PROBLEMS AND APPLICATIONS

1. This chapter discusses many types of costs: opportunity cost, total cost, fixed cost, variable cost, average total cost, and marginal cost. Fill in the type of cost that best completes each phrase below:
   a. The true cost of taking some action is its
      _____.
   b. _____ is falling when marginal cost is below it, and rising when marginal cost is above it.
   c. A cost that does not depend on the quantity produced is a(n) _____.
   d. In the ice-cream industry in the short run, _____ includes the cost of cream and sugar, but not the cost of the factory.
   e. Profits equal total revenue less _____.
   f. The cost of producing an extra unit of output is the _____.

2. Your aunt is thinking about opening a hardware store. She estimates that it would cost $500,000 per year to rent the location and buy the stock. In addition, she would have to quit her $50,000 per year job as an accountant.
   a. Define opportunity cost.
   b. What is your aunt's opportunity cost of running a hardware store for a year? If your aunt thought she could sell $510,000 worth of merchandise in a year, should she open the store? Explain.

3. Suppose that your college charges you separately for tuition and for room and board.

   a. What is a cost of attending college that is not an opportunity cost?
   b. What is an explicit opportunity cost of attending college? tuition
   c. What is an implicit opportunity cost of attending college? room+board you could get living somewhere else

4. A commercial fisherman notices the following relationship between hours spent fishing and the quantity of fish caught:

Hours	Quantity of Fish (in pounds)
0	0
1	10
2	18
3	24
4	28
5	30

   a. What is the marginal product of each hour spent fishing?
   b. Use these data to graph the fisherman's production function. Explain its shape.
   c. The fisherman has a fixed cost of $10 (his pole). The opportunity cost of his time is $5 per hour. Graph the fisherman's total-cost curve. Explain its shape.

5. Nimbus, Inc., makes brooms and then sells them door-to-door. Here is the relationship between the number of workers and Nimbus's output in a given day:

Workers	Output	Marginal Product	Total Cost	Average Total Cost	Marginal Cost
0	0		200		100
		20			
1	20		300	300	100
		30			
2	50		400	200	
		40			
3	90		500		
		30			
4	120		600		
		20			
5	140		700		
		10			
6	150		800		
		5			
7	155		900		

a. Fill in the column of marginal products. What pattern do you see? How might you explain it?

b. A worker costs $100 a day, and the firm has fixed costs of $200. Use this information to fill in the column for total cost.

c. Fill in the column for average total cost. (Recall that $ATC = TC/Q$.) What pattern do you see?

d. Now fill in the column for marginal cost. (Recall that $MC = \Delta TC/\Delta Q$.) What pattern do you see?

e. Compare the column for marginal product and the column for marginal cost. Explain the relationship.

f. Compare the column for average total cost and the column for marginal cost. Explain the relationship.

6. Suppose that you and your roommate have started a bagel delivery service on campus. List some of your fixed costs and describe why they are fixed. List some of your variable costs and describe why they are variable.

7. Consider the following cost information for a pizzeria:

Q (dozens)	Total Cost	Variable Cost
0	$300	$ 0
1	350	50
2	390	90
3	420	120
4	450	150
5	490	190
6	540	240

a. What is the pizzeria's fixed cost?

b. Construct a table in which you calculate the marginal cost per dozen pizzas using the information on total cost. Also calculate the marginal cost per dozen pizzas using the information on variable cost. What is the relationship between these sets of numbers? Comment.

8. You are thinking about setting up a lemonade stand. The stand itself costs $200. The ingredients for each cup of lemonade cost $0.50.

a. What is your fixed cost of doing business? What is your variable cost per cup?

b. Construct a table showing your total cost, average total cost, and marginal cost for output levels varying from 0 to 10 gallons. (Hint: There are 16 cups in a gallon.) Draw the three cost curves.

9. Your cousin Vinnie owns a painting company with fixed costs of $200 and the following schedule for variable costs:

Quantity of Houses Painted per Month	1	2	3	4	5	6	7
Variable Costs	$10	$20	$40	$80	$160	$320	$640

Calculate average fixed cost, average variable cost, and average total cost for each quantity. What is the efficient scale of the painting company?

10. Healthy Harry's Juice Bar has the following cost schedules:

Q (vats)	Variable Cost	Total Cost
0	$ 0	$ 30
1	10	40
2	25	55
3	45	75
4	70	100
5	100	130
6	135	165

a. Calculate average variable cost, average total cost, and marginal cost for each quantity.

b. Graph all three curves. What is the relationship between the marginal-cost curve and the average-total-cost curve? Between the marginal-cost curve and the average-variable-cost curve? Explain.

11. Consider the following table of long-run total cost for three different firms:

Quantity	1	2	3	4	5	6	7
Firm A	$60	$70	$80	$90	$100	$110	$120
Firm B	11	24	39	56	75	96	119
Firm C	21	34	49	66	85	106	129

Does each of these firms experience economies of scale or diseconomies of scale?

http:// For more study tools, please visit http://mankiwXtra.swlearning.com.

FIRMS IN COMPETITIVE MARKETS

If your local gas station raised the price it charges for gasoline by 20 percent, it would see a large drop in the amount of gasoline it sold. Its customers would quickly switch to buying their gasoline at other gas stations. By contrast, if your local water company raised the price of water by 20 percent, it would see only a small decrease in the amount of water it sold. People might water their lawns less often and buy more water-efficient shower heads, but they would be hard pressed to reduce water consumption greatly and would be unlikely to find another supplier. The difference between the gasoline market and the water market is obvious: There are many firms pumping gasoline, but there is only one firm pumping water. As you might expect, this difference in market structure shapes the pricing and production decisions of the firms that operate in these markets.

In this chapter we examine the behavior of competitive firms, such as your local gas station. You may recall that a market is competitive if each buyer and seller is small compared to the size of the market and, therefore, has little ability to influence market prices. By contrast, if a firm can influence the market price of the good it sells, it is said to have *market power*. Later in the book, we examine the behavior of firms with market power, such as your local water company.

Our analysis of competitive firms in this chapter will shed light on the decisions that lie behind the supply curve in a competitive market. Not surprisingly, we will find that a market supply curve is tightly linked to firms' costs of production. (Indeed, this general insight should be familiar to you from our analysis in Chapter 7.) But among a firm's various costs—fixed, variable, average, and marginal—which ones are most relevant for its decision about the quantity to supply at any given price? We will see that all these measures of cost play important and interrelated roles.

WHAT IS A COMPETITIVE MARKET?

Our goal in this chapter is to examine how firms make production decisions in competitive markets. As a background for this analysis, we begin by considering what a competitive market is.

The Meaning of Competition

competitive market
a market with many buyers and sellers trading identical products so that each buyer and seller is a price taker

Although we already discussed the meaning of competition in Chapter 4, let's review the lesson briefly. A **competitive market,** sometimes called a *perfectly competitive market*, has two characteristics:

- There are many buyers and many sellers in the market.
- The goods offered by the various sellers are largely the same.

As a result of these conditions, the actions of any single buyer or seller in the market have a negligible impact on the market price. Each buyer and seller takes the market price as given.

An example is the market for milk. No single buyer of milk can influence the price of milk because each buyer purchases a small amount relative to the size of the market. Similarly, each seller of milk has limited control over the price because many other sellers are offering milk that is essentially identical. Because each seller can sell all he wants at the going price, he has little reason to charge less, and if he charges more, buyers will go elsewhere. Buyers and sellers in competitive markets must accept the price the market determines and, therefore, are said to be *price takers*.

In addition to the foregoing two conditions for competition, there is a third condition sometimes thought to characterize perfectly competitive markets:

- Firms can freely enter or exit the market.

If, for instance, anyone can decide to start a dairy farm, and if any existing dairy farmer can decide to leave the dairy business, then the dairy industry would satisfy this condition. It should be noted that much of the analysis of competitive firms does not rely on the assumption of free entry and exit because this condition is not necessary for firms to be price takers. But as we will see later in this chapter, entry and exit are often powerful forces shaping the long-run outcome in competitive markets.

The Revenue of a Competitive Firm

A firm in a competitive market, like most other firms in the economy, tries to maximize profit, which equals total revenue minus total cost. To see how it does this, we first consider the revenue of a competitive firm. To keep matters concrete, let's consider a specific firm: the Smith Family Dairy Farm.

The Smith Farm produces a quantity of milk Q and sells each unit at the market price P. The farm's total revenue is $P \times Q$. For example, if a gallon of milk sells for $6 and the farm sells 1,000 gallons, its total revenue is $6,000.

Because the Smith Farm is small compared to the world market for milk, it takes the price as given by market conditions. This means, in particular, that the price of milk does not depend on the quantity of output that the Smith Farm produces and sells. If the Smiths double the amount of milk they produce, the price of milk remains the same, and their total revenue doubles. As a result, total revenue is proportional to the amount of output.

Table 1 shows the revenue for the Smith Family Dairy Farm. The first two columns show the amount of output the farm produces and the price at which it sells its output. The third column is the farm's total revenue. The table assumes that the price of milk is $6 a gallon, so total revenue is simply $6 times the number of gallons.

Just as the concepts of average and marginal were useful in the preceding chapter when analyzing costs, they are also useful when analyzing revenue. To see what these concepts tell us, consider these two questions:

TABLE 1

Total, Average, and Marginal Revenue for a Competitive Firm

Quantity	Price	Total Revenue	Average Revenue	Marginal Revenue
(Q)	(P)	(TR = P × Q)	(AR = TR/Q)	(MR = ΔTR/ΔQ)
1 gallon	$6	$ 6	$6	
				$6
2	6	12	6	
				6
3	6	18	6	
				6
4	6	24	6	
				6
5	6	30	6	
				6
6	6	36	6	
				6
7	6	42	6	
				6
8	6	48	6	

- How much revenue does the farm receive for the typical gallon of milk?
- How much additional revenue does the farm receive if it increases production of milk by 1 gallon?

The last two columns in Table 1 answer these questions.

average revenue
total revenue divided by the quantity sold

The fourth column in the table shows **average revenue,** which is total revenue (from the third column) divided by the amount of output (from the first column). Average revenue tells us how much revenue a firm receives for the typical unit sold. In Table 1, you can see that average revenue equals $6, the price of a gallon of milk. This illustrates a general lesson that applies not only to competitive firms but to other firms as well. Total revenue is the price times the quantity ($P \times Q$), and average revenue is total revenue ($P \times Q$) divided by the quantity (Q). Therefore, *for all firms, average revenue equals the price of the good.*

marginal revenue
the change in total revenue from an additional unit sold

The fifth column shows **marginal revenue,** which is the change in total revenue from the sale of each additional unit of output. In Table 1, marginal revenue equals $6, the price of a gallon of milk. This result illustrates a lesson that applies only to competitive firms. Total revenue is $P \times Q$, and P is fixed for a competitive firm. Therefore, when Q rises by 1 unit, total revenue rises by P dollars. *For competitive firms, marginal revenue equals the price of the good.*

QuickQuiz When a competitive firm doubles the amount it sells, what happens to the price of its output and its total revenue?

PROFIT MAXIMIZATION AND THE COMPETITIVE FIRM'S SUPPLY CURVE

The goal of a competitive firm is to maximize profit, which equals total revenue minus total cost. We have just discussed the firm's revenue, and in the last chapter we discussed the firm's costs. We are now ready to examine how the firm maximizes profit and how that decision leads to its supply curve.

A Simple Example of Profit Maximization

Let's begin our analysis of the firm's supply decision with the example in Table 2. In the first column of the table is the number of gallons of milk the Smith Family Dairy Farm produces. The second column shows the farm's total revenue, which is $6 times the number of gallons. The third column shows the farm's total cost. Total cost includes fixed costs, which are $3 in this example, and variable costs, which depend on the quantity produced.

The fourth column shows the farm's profit, which is computed by subtracting total cost from total revenue. If the farm produces nothing, it has a loss of $3. If it produces 1 gallon, it has a profit of $1. If it produces 2 gallons, it has a profit of $4, and so on. To maximize profit, the Smith Farm chooses the quantity that makes profit as large as possible. In this example, profit is maximized when the farm produces 4 or 5 gallons of milk, when the profit is $7.

TABLE 2

Profit Maximization: A Numerical Example

Quantity	Total Revenue	Total Cost	Profit	Marginal Revenue	Marginal Cost	Change in Profit
(Q)	(TR)	(TC)	(TR – TC)	(MR = $\Delta TR/\Delta Q$)	(MC = $\Delta TC/\Delta Q$)	(MR – MC)
0 gallons	$ 0	$ 3	–$3			
				$6	$2	$4
1	6	5	1			
				6	3	3
2	12	8	4			
				6	4	2
3	18	12	6			
				6	5	1
4	24	17	7			
				6	6	0
5	30	23	7			
				6	7	–1
6	36	30	6			
				6	8	–2
7	42	38	4			
				6	9	–3
8	48	47	1			

There is another way to look at the Smith Farm's decision: The Smiths can find the profit-maximizing quantity by comparing the marginal revenue and marginal cost from each unit produced. The fifth and sixth columns in Table 2 compute marginal revenue and marginal cost from the changes in total revenue and total cost, and the last column shows the change in profit for each additional gallon produced. The first gallon of milk the farm produces has a marginal revenue of $6 and a marginal cost of $2; hence, producing that gallon increases profit by $4 (from –$3 to $1). The second gallon produced has a marginal revenue of $6 and a marginal cost of $3, so that gallon increases profit by $3 (from $1 to $4). As long as marginal revenue exceeds marginal cost, increasing the quantity produced raises profit. Once the Smith Farm has reached 5 gallons of milk, however, the situation is very different. The sixth gallon would have marginal revenue of $6 and marginal cost of $7, so producing it would reduce profit by $1 (from $7 to $6). As a result, the Smiths would not produce beyond 5 gallons.

One of the *Ten Principles of Economics* in Chapter 1 is that rational people think at the margin. We now see how the Smith Family Dairy Farm can apply this principle. If marginal revenue is greater than marginal cost—as it is at 1, 2, or 3 gallons—the Smiths should increase the production of milk. If marginal revenue is less than marginal cost—as it is at 6, 7, or 8 gallons—the Smiths should decrease production. If the Smiths think at the margin and make incremental adjustments to the level of production, they are naturally led to produce the profit-maximizing quantity.

FIGURE 1

Profit Maximization for a Competitive Firm

This figure shows the marginal-cost curve (MC), the average-total-cost curve (ATC), and the average-variable-cost curve (AVC). It also shows the market price (P), which equals marginal revenue (MR) and average revenue (AR). At the quantity Q_1, marginal revenue MR_1 exceeds marginal cost MC_1, so raising production increases profit. At the quantity Q_2, marginal cost MC_2 is above marginal revenue MR_2, so reducing production increases profit. The profit-maximizing quantity Q_{MAX} is found where the horizontal price line intersects the marginal-cost curve.

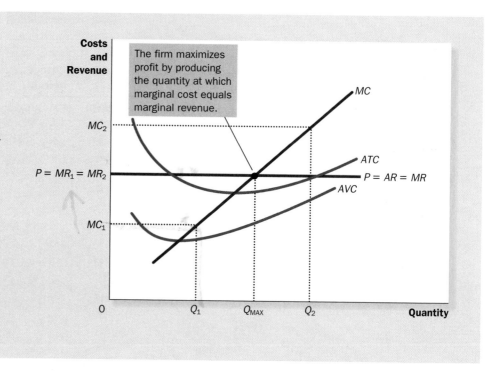

The firm maximizes profit by producing the quantity at which marginal cost equals marginal revenue.

The Marginal-Cost Curve and the Firm's Supply Decision

To extend this analysis of profit maximization, consider the cost curves in Figure 1. These cost curves have the three features that, as we discussed in the previous chapter, are thought to describe most firms: The marginal-cost curve (MC) is upward sloping. The average-total-cost curve (ATC) is U-shaped. And the marginal-cost curve crosses the average-total-cost curve at the minimum of average total cost. The figure also shows a horizontal line at the market price (P). The price line is horizontal because the firm is a price taker: The price of the firm's output is the same regardless of the quantity that the firm decides to produce. Keep in mind that, for a competitive firm, the firm's price equals both its average revenue (AR) and its marginal revenue (MR).

We can use Figure 1 to find the quantity of output that maximizes profit. Imagine that the firm is producing at Q_1. At this level of output, marginal revenue is greater than marginal cost. That is, if the firm raised its level of production and sales by 1 unit, the additional revenue (MR_1) would exceed the additional costs (MC_1). Profit, which equals total revenue minus total cost, would increase. Hence, if marginal revenue is greater than marginal cost, as it is at Q_1, the firm can increase profit by increasing production.

A similar argument applies when output is at Q_2. In this case, marginal cost is greater than marginal revenue. If the firm reduced production by 1 unit, the costs saved (MC_2) would exceed the revenue lost (MR_2). Therefore, if marginal revenue is less than marginal cost, as it is at Q_2, the firm can increase profit by reducing production.

FIGURE 2

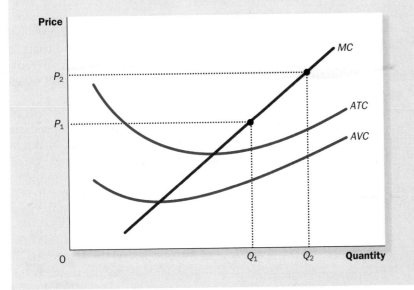

Price

P_2

P_1

MC

ATC

AVC

0   Q_1 Q_2 **Quantity**

Marginal Cost as the Competitive Firm's Supply Curve

An increase in the price from P_1 to P_2 leads to an increase in the firm's profit-maximizing quantity from Q_1 to Q_2. Because the marginal-cost curve shows the quantity supplied by the firm at any given price, it is the firm's supply curve.

Where do these marginal adjustments to level of production end? Regardless of whether the firm begins with production at a low level (such as Q_1) or at a high level (such as Q_2), the firm will eventually adjust production until the quantity produced reaches Q_{MAX}. This analysis shows a general rule for profit maximization: *At the profit-maximizing level of output, marginal revenue and marginal cost are exactly equal.*

We can now see how the competitive firm decides the quantity of its good to supply to the market. Because a competitive firm is a price taker, its marginal revenue equals the market price. For any given price, the competitive firm's profit-maximizing quantity of output is found by looking at the intersection of the price with the marginal-cost curve. In Figure 1, that quantity of output is Q_{MAX}.

Figure 2 shows how a competitive firm responds to an increase in the price. When the price is P_1, the firm produces quantity Q_1, the quantity that equates marginal cost to the price. When the price rises to P_2, the firm finds that marginal revenue is now higher than marginal cost at the previous level of output, so the firm increases production. The new profit-maximizing quantity is Q_2, at which marginal cost equals the new higher price. *In essence, because the firm's marginal-cost curve determines the quantity of the good the firm is willing to supply at any price, it is the competitive firm's supply curve.*

The Firm's Short-Run Decision to Shut Down

So far we have been analyzing the question of how much a competitive firm will produce. In some circumstances, however, the firm will decide to shut down and not produce anything at all.

Here we should distinguish between a temporary shutdown of a firm and the permanent exit of a firm from the market. A *shutdown* refers to a short-run decision not to produce anything during a specific period of time because of current market conditions. *Exit* refers to a long-run decision to leave the market. The short-run and long-run decisions differ because most firms cannot avoid their fixed costs in the short run but can do so in the long run. That is, a firm that shuts down temporarily still has to pay its fixed costs, whereas a firm that exits the market saves both its fixed and its variable costs.

For example, consider the production decision that a farmer faces. The cost of the land is one of the farmer's fixed costs. If the farmer decides not to produce any crops one season, the land lies fallow, and he cannot recover this cost. When making the short-run decision whether to shut down for a season, the fixed cost of land is said to be a *sunk cost*. By contrast, if the farmer decides to leave farming altogether, he can sell the land. When making the long-run decision whether to exit the market, the cost of land is not sunk. (We return to the issue of sunk costs shortly.)

Now let's consider what determines a firm's shutdown decision. If the firm shuts down, it loses all revenue from the sale of its product. At the same time, it saves the variable costs of making its product (but must still pay the fixed costs). Thus, *the firm shuts down if the revenue that it would get from producing is less than its variable costs of production.*

A small bit of mathematics can make this shutdown criterion more useful. If TR stands for total revenue, and VC stands for variable costs, then the firm's decision can be written as

$$\text{Shut down if } TR < VC.$$

The firm shuts down if total revenue is less than variable cost. By dividing both sides of this inequality by the quantity Q, we can write it as

$$\text{Shut down if } TR/Q < VC/Q.$$

Notice that this can be further simplified. TR/Q is total revenue divided by quantity, which is average revenue. As we discussed previously, average revenue for any firm is simply the good's price P. Similarly, VC/Q is average variable cost AVC. Therefore, the firm's shutdown criterion is

$$\text{Shut down if } P < AVC.$$

That is, a firm chooses to shut down if the price of the good is less than the average variable cost of production. This criterion is intuitive: When choosing to produce, the firm compares the price it receives for the typical unit to the average variable cost that it must incur to produce the typical unit. If the price doesn't cover the average variable cost, the firm is better off stopping production altogether. The firm can reopen in the future if conditions change so that price exceeds average variable cost.

We now have a full description of a competitive firm's profit-maximizing strategy. If the firm produces anything, it produces the quantity at which marginal cost equals the price of the good. Yet if the price is less than average variable cost at that quantity, the firm is better off shutting down and not producing anything. These

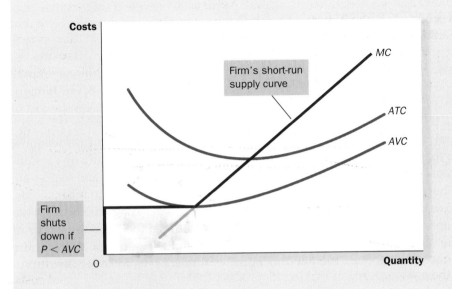

The Competitive Firm's Short-Run Supply Curve

In the short run, the competitive firm's supply curve is its marginal-cost curve (MC) above average variable cost (AVC). If the price falls below average variable cost, the firm is better off shutting down.

results are illustrated in Figure 3. *The competitive firm's short-run supply curve is the portion of its marginal-cost curve that lies above average variable cost.*

Spilt Milk and Other Sunk Costs

Sometime in your life you have probably been told, "Don't cry over spilt milk," or "Let bygones be bygones." These adages hold a deep truth about rational decision-making. Economists say that a cost is a **sunk cost** when it has already been committed and cannot be recovered. In a sense, a sunk cost is the opposite of an opportunity cost: An opportunity cost is what you have to give up if you choose to do one thing instead of another, whereas a sunk cost cannot be avoided, regardless of the choices you make. Because nothing can be done about sunk costs, you can ignore them when making decisions about various aspects of life, including business strategy.

sunk cost
a cost that has already been committed and cannot be recovered

Our analysis of the firm's shutdown decision is one example of the irrelevance of sunk costs. We assume that the firm cannot recover its fixed costs by temporarily stopping production. As a result, the firm's fixed costs are sunk in the short run, and the firm can safely ignore these costs when deciding how much to produce. The firm's short-run supply curve is the part of the marginal-cost curve that lies above average variable cost, and the size of the fixed cost does not matter for this supply decision.

The irrelevance of sunk costs is also important for personal decisions. Imagine, for instance, that you place a $10 value on seeing a newly released movie. You buy a ticket for $7, but before entering the theater, you lose the ticket. Should you buy another ticket? Or should you now go home and refuse to pay a total of $14 to see the movie? The answer is that you should buy another ticket. The benefit of seeing the movie ($10) still exceeds the opportunity cost (the $7 for the second ticket). The $7 you paid for the lost ticket is a sunk cost. As with spilt milk, there is no point in crying about it.

Case Study

NEAR-EMPTY RESTAURANTS AND OFF-SEASON MINIATURE GOLF

Staying open can be profitable, even with many tables empty.

Have you ever walked into a restaurant for lunch and found it almost empty? Why, you might have asked, does the restaurant even bother to stay open? It might seem that the revenue from the few customers could not possibly cover the cost of running the restaurant.

In making the decision whether to open for lunch, a restaurant owner must keep in mind the distinction between fixed and variable costs. Many of a restaurant's costs—the rent, kitchen equipment, tables, plates, silverware, and so on—are fixed. Shutting down during lunch would not reduce these costs. In other words, these costs are sunk in the short run. When the owner is deciding whether to serve lunch, only the variable costs—the price of the additional food and the wages of the extra staff—are relevant. The owner shuts down the restaurant at lunchtime only if the revenue from the few lunchtime customers fails to cover the restaurant's variable costs.

An operator of a miniature-golf course in a summer resort community faces a similar decision. Because revenue varies substantially from season to season, the firm must decide when to open and when to close. Once again, the fixed costs—the costs of buying the land and building the course—are irrelevant. The miniature-golf course should be open for business only during those times of year when its revenue exceeds its variable costs. ●

The Firm's Long-Run Decision to Exit or Enter a Market

The firm's long-run decision to exit the market is similar to its shutdown decision. If the firm exits, it again will lose all revenue from the sale of its product, but now it saves on both fixed and variable costs of production. Thus, *the firm exits the market if the revenue it would get from producing is less than its total costs*.

We can again make this criterion more useful by writing it mathematically. If TR stands for total revenue, and TC stands for total cost, then the firm's criterion can be written as

$$\text{Exit if } TR < TC.$$

The firm exits if total revenue is less than total cost. By dividing both sides of this inequality by quantity Q, we can write it as

$$\text{Exit if } TR/Q < TC/Q.$$

We can simplify this further by noting that TR/Q is average revenue, which equals the price P, and that TC/Q is average total cost ATC. Therefore, the firm's exit criterion is

$$\text{Exit if } P < ATC.$$

FIGURE 4

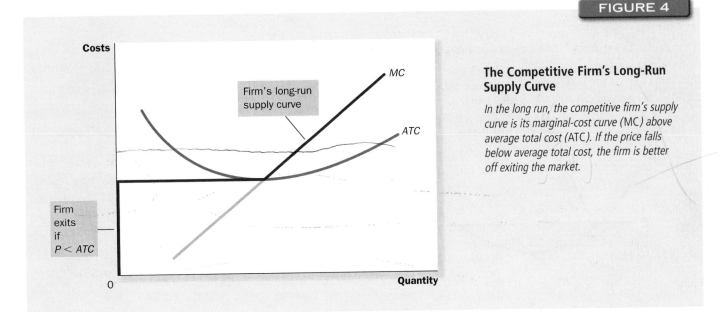

The Competitive Firm's Long-Run Supply Curve

In the long run, the competitive firm's supply curve is its marginal-cost curve (MC) above average total cost (ATC). If the price falls below average total cost, the firm is better off exiting the market.

That is, a firm chooses to exit if the price of the good is less than the average total cost of production.

A parallel analysis applies to an entrepreneur who is considering starting a firm. The firm will enter the market if such an action would be profitable, which occurs if the price of the good exceeds the average total cost of production. The entry criterion is

$$\text{Enter if } P > ATC.$$

The criterion for entry is exactly the opposite of the criterion for exit.

We can now describe a competitive firm's long-run profit-maximizing strategy. If the firm is in the market, it produces the quantity at which marginal cost equals the price of the good. Yet if the price is less than average total cost at that quantity, the firm chooses to exit (or not enter) the market. These results are illustrated in Figure 4. *The competitive firm's long-run supply curve is the portion of its marginal cost curve that lies above average total cost.*

Measuring Profit in Our Graph for the Competitive Firm

As we analyze exit and entry, it is useful to be able to analyze the firm's profit in more detail. Recall that profit equals total revenue (*TR*) minus total cost (*TC*):

$$\text{Profit} = TR - TC.$$

We can rewrite this definition by multiplying and dividing the right-hand side by *Q*:

$$\text{Profit} = (TR/Q - TC/Q) \times Q.$$

FIGURE 5

Profit as the Area between Price and Average Total Cost

The area of the shaded box between price and average total cost represents the firm's profit. The height of this box is price minus average total cost (P − ATC), and the width of the box is the quantity of output (Q). In panel (a), price is above average total cost, so the firm has positive profit. In panel (b), price is less than average total cost, so the firm has losses.

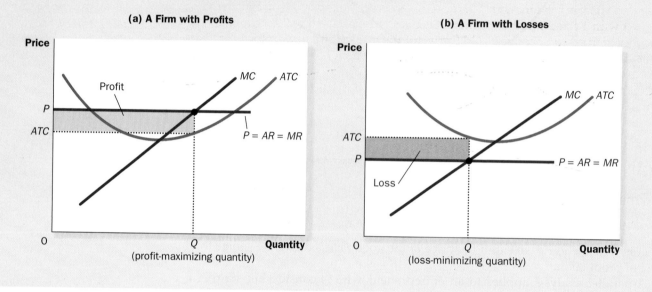

(a) A Firm with Profits

(b) A Firm with Losses

But note that TR/Q is average revenue, which is the price P, and TC/Q is average total cost ATC. Therefore,

$$\text{Profit} = (P - ATC) \times Q.$$

This way of expressing the firm's profit allows us to measure profit in our graphs.

Panel (a) of Figure 5 shows a firm earning positive profit. As we have already discussed, the firm maximizes profit by producing the quantity at which price equals marginal cost. Now look at the shaded rectangle. The height of the rectangle is $P - ATC$, the difference between price and average total cost. The width of the rectangle is Q, the quantity produced. Therefore, the area of the rectangle is $(P - ATC) \times Q$, which is the firm's profit.

Similarly, panel (b) of this figure shows a firm with losses (negative profit). In this case, maximizing profit means minimizing losses, a task accomplished once again by producing the quantity at which price equals marginal cost. Now consider the shaded rectangle. The height of the rectangle is $ATC - P$, and the width is Q. The area is $(ATC - P) \times Q$, which is the firm's loss. Because a firm in this situation is not making enough revenue to cover its average total cost, the firm would choose to exit the market.

QuickQuiz How does the price faced by a profit-maximizing competitive firm compare to its marginal cost? Explain. • When does a profit-maximizing competitive firm decide to shut down? When does a profit-maximizing competitive firm decide to exit a market?

THE SUPPLY CURVE IN A COMPETITIVE MARKET

Now that we have examined the supply decision of a single firm, we can discuss the supply curve for a market. There are two cases to consider. First, we examine a market with a fixed number of firms. Second, we examine a market in which the number of firms can change as old firms exit the market and new firms enter. Both cases are important, for each applies over a specific time horizon. Over short periods of time, it is often difficult for firms to enter and exit, so the assumption of a fixed number of firms is appropriate. But over long periods of time, the number of firms can adjust to changing market conditions.

The Short Run: Market Supply with a Fixed Number of Firms

Consider first a market with 1,000 identical firms. For any given price, each firm supplies a quantity of output so that its marginal cost equals the price, as shown in panel (a) of Figure 6. That is, as long as price is above average variable cost, each firm's marginal-cost curve is its supply curve. The quantity of output supplied to

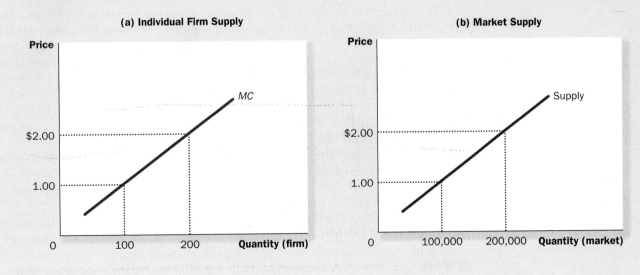

FIGURE 6

Market Supply with a Fixed Number of Firms

When the number of firms in the market is fixed, the market supply curve, shown in panel (b), reflects the individual firms' marginal-cost curves, shown in panel (a). Here, in a market of 1,000 firms, the quantity of output supplied to the market is 1,000 times the quantity supplied by each firm.

the market equals the sum of the quantities supplied by each of the 1,000 individual firms. Thus, to derive the market supply curve, we add the quantity supplied by each firm in the market. As panel (b) of Figure 6 shows, because the firms are identical, the quantity supplied to the market is 1,000 times the quantity supplied by each firm.

The Long Run: Market Supply with Entry and Exit

Now consider what happens if firms are able to enter or exit the market. Let's suppose that everyone has access to the same technology for producing the good and access to the same markets to buy the inputs into production. Therefore, all firms and all potential firms have the same cost curves.

Decisions about entry and exit in a market of this type depend on the incentives facing the owners of existing firms and the entrepreneurs who could start new firms. If firms already in the market are profitable, then new firms will have an incentive to enter the market. This entry will expand the number of firms, increase the quantity of the good supplied, and drive down prices and profits. Conversely, if firms in the market are making losses, then some existing firms will exit the market. Their exit will reduce the number of firms, decrease the quantity of the good supplied, and drive up prices and profits. *At the end of this process of entry and exit, firms that remain in the market must be making zero economic profit.* Recall that we can write a firm's profits as

$$\text{Profit} = (P - ATC) \times Q.$$

This equation shows that an operating firm has zero profit if and only if the price of the good equals the average total cost of producing that good. If price is above average total cost, profit is positive, which encourages new firms to enter. If price is less than average total cost, profit is negative, which encourages some firms to exit. *The process of entry and exit ends only when price and average total cost are driven to equality.*

This analysis has a surprising implication. We noted earlier in the chapter that competitive firms produce so that price equals marginal cost. We just noted that free entry and exit forces price to equal average total cost. But if price is to equal both marginal cost and average total cost, these two measures of cost must equal each other. Marginal cost and average total cost are equal, however, only when the firm is operating at the minimum of average total cost. Recall from the preceding chapter that the level of production with lowest average total cost is called the firm's *efficient scale.* Therefore, *the long-run equilibrium of a competitive market with free entry and exit must have firms operating at their efficient scale.*

Panel (a) of Figure 7 shows a firm in such a long-run equilibrium. In this figure, price *P* equals marginal cost *MC,* so the firm is profit-maximizing. Price also equals average total cost *ATC,* so profits are zero. New firms have no incentive to enter the market, and existing firms have no incentive to leave the market.

From this analysis of firm behavior, we can determine the long-run supply curve for the market. In a market with free entry and exit, there is only one price consistent with zero profit—the minimum of average total cost. As a result, the long-run market supply curve must be horizontal at this price, as in panel (b) of

FIGURE 7

Market Supply with Entry and Exit

Firms will enter or exit the market until profit is driven to zero. Thus, in the long run, price equals the minimum of average total cost, as shown in panel (a). The number of firms adjusts to ensure that all demand is satisfied at this price. The long-run market supply curve is horizontal at this price, as shown in panel (b).

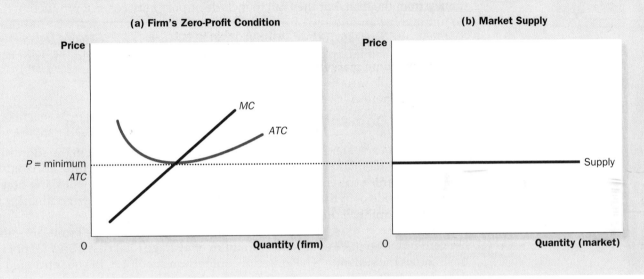

Figure 7. Any price above this level would generate profit, leading to entry and an increase in the total quantity supplied. Any price below this level would generate losses, leading to exit and a decrease in the total quantity supplied. Eventually, the number of firms in the market adjusts so that price equals the minimum of average total cost, and there are enough firms to satisfy all the demand at this price.

Why Do Competitive Firms Stay in Business If They Make Zero Profit?

At first, it might seem odd that competitive firms earn zero profit in the long run. After all, people start businesses to make a profit. If entry eventually drives profit to zero, there might seem to be little reason to stay in business.

To understand the zero-profit condition more fully, recall that profit equals total revenue minus total cost, and that total cost includes all the opportunity costs of the firm. In particular, total cost includes the opportunity cost of the time and money that the firm owners devote to the business. In the zero-profit equilibrium, the firm's revenue must compensate the owners for the time and money that they expend to keep their business going.

Consider an example. Suppose that a farmer had to invest $1 million to open his farm, which otherwise he could have deposited in a bank to earn $50,000 a year in interest. In addition, he had to give up another job that would have paid him

"We're a nonprofit organization—we don't intend to be, but we are!"

$30,000 a year. Then the farmer's opportunity cost of farming includes both the interest he could have earned and the forgone wages—a total of $80,000. Even if his profit is driven to zero, his revenue from farming compensates him for these opportunity costs.

Keep in mind that accountants and economists measure costs differently. As we discussed in the previous chapter, accountants keep track of explicit costs but usually miss implicit costs. That is, they measure costs that require an outflow of money from the firm, but they fail to include opportunity costs of production that do not involve an outflow of money. As a result, in the zero-profit equilibrium, economic profit is zero, but accounting profit is positive. Our farmer's accountant, for instance, would conclude that the farmer earned an accounting profit of $80,000, which is enough to keep the farmer in business.

A Shift in Demand in the Short Run and Long Run

Because firms can enter and exit a market in the long run but not in the short run, the response of a market to a change in demand depends on the time horizon. To see this, let's trace the effects of a shift in demand. This analysis will show how a market responds over time, and it will show how entry and exit drive a market to its long-run equilibrium.

Suppose the market for milk begins in long-run equilibrium. Firms are earning zero profit, so price equals the minimum of average total cost. Panel (a) of Figure 8 shows the situation. The long-run equilibrium is point A, the quantity sold in the market is Q_1, and the price is P_1.

Now suppose scientists discover that milk has miraculous health benefits. As a result, the demand curve for milk shifts outward from D_1 to D_2, as in panel (b). The short-run equilibrium moves from point A to point B; as a result, the quantity rises from Q_1 to Q_2, and the price rises from P_1 to P_2. All of the existing firms respond to the higher price by raising the amount produced. Because each firm's supply curve reflects its marginal-cost curve, how much they each increase production is determined by the marginal-cost curve. In the new short-run equilibrium, the price of milk exceeds average total cost, so the firms are making positive profit.

Over time, the profit in this market encourages new firms to enter. Some farmers may switch to milk from other farm products, for example. As the number of firms grows, the short-run supply curve shifts to the right from S_1 to S_2, as in panel (c), and this shift causes the price of milk to fall. Eventually, the price is driven back down to the minimum of average total cost, profits are zero, and firms stop entering. Thus, the market reaches a new long-run equilibrium, point C. The price of milk has returned to P_1, but the quantity produced has risen to Q_3. Each firm is again producing at its efficient scale, but because more firms are in the dairy business, the quantity of milk produced and sold is higher.

Why the Long-Run Supply Curve Might Slope Upward

So far we have seen that entry and exit can cause the long-run market supply curve to be horizontal. The essence of our analysis is that there are a large number of potential entrants, each of which faces the same costs. As a result, the long-run

FIGURE 8

An Increase in Demand in the Short Run and Long Run

The market starts in a long-run equilibrium, shown as point A in panel (a). In this equilibrium, each firm makes zero profit, and the price equals the minimum average total cost. Panel (b) shows what happens in the short run when demand rises from D₁ to D₂. The equilibrium goes from point A to point B, price rises from P₁ to P₂, and the quantity sold in the market rises from Q₁ to Q₂. Because price now exceeds average total cost, firms make profits, which over time encourage new firms to enter the market. This entry shifts the short-run supply curve to the right from S₁ to S₂, as shown in panel (c). In the new long-run equilibrium, point C, price has returned to P₁ but the quantity sold has increased to Q₃. Profits are again zero, price is back to the minimum of average total cost, but the market has more firms to satisfy the greater demand.

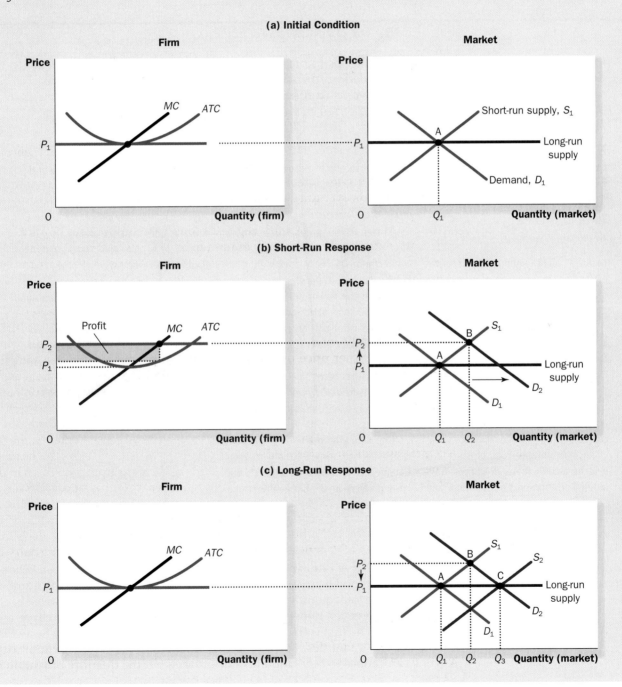

IN THE NEWS

ENTRY OR OVERINVESTMENT?

In competitive markets, strong demand leads to high prices and high profits, which then lead to increased entry, falling prices, and falling profits. To economists, these market forces are one reflection of the invisible hand at work. To the business managers, however, new entry and falling profits can seem like a "problem of overinvestment." Here's an example from a few years ago.

In Some Industries, Executives Foresee Tough Times Ahead; A Key Culprit: High Profits

By Bernard Wysocki, Jr.

MONTEREY, CALIF.—About 20 executives are huddled in a conference room with a team of management consultants, and the mood is surprisingly somber.

It's a fine summer day, the stock market is booming, the U.S. economy is in great shape, and some of the companies represented here are posting stronger-than-expected profits. Best of all, perhaps, these lucky executives are just a chip shot away from the famed Pebble Beach golf course. They ought to be euphoric.

Instead, an undertone of concern is evident among these executives from Mobil Corp., Union Carbide Corp. and other capital-intensive companies. In between golf, fine meals and cigars, they hear a sobering message from their hosts.

"I feel like the prophet of doom" is the welcoming line of R. Duane Dickson, a director of Mercer Management Consulting and host of the meeting. "It's our belief that the downturn has started. I can't tell you how far it's going to go. But it could be a very ugly one."

For two days, the executives and their advisers discuss what they expect in their industries between now and 2000: growing overcapacity, world-wide product gluts, price wars, shakeouts, and consolidations. . . .

One man who attended the Pebble Beach meeting, Joseph Soviero, a Union Carbide vice president, cites an odd but basic problem in chemicals: the strong profits of the past few years. "The profitability that the industry sees during the good times has always led to overinvesting, and it has this time," Mr. Soviero says. He adds that the chemicals business cycle is alive and has peaked. At Union Carbide, he says, "we always talk about the cycle" and try to manage it.

So far, demand isn't a big problem. In many industries, it is still growing steadily, though slowly. What is developing is too much supply, stemming from the recurring problem of overinvestment. . . . The next few years will bring fierce competition and falling prices.

market supply curve is horizontal at the minimum of average total cost. When the demand for the good increases, the long-run result is an increase in the number of firms and in the total quantity supplied, without any change in the price.

There are, however, two reasons that the long-run market supply curve might slope upward. The first is that some resource used in production may be available only in limited quantities. For example, consider the market for farm products. Anyone can choose to buy land and start a farm, but the quantity of land is limited. As more people become farmers, the price of farmland is bid up, which raises the costs of all farmers in the market. Thus, an increase in demand for farm products cannot induce an increase in quantity supplied without also inducing a rise in farmers' costs, which in turn means a rise in price. The result is a long-run market supply curve that is upward sloping, even with free entry into farming.

A second reason for an upward-sloping supply curve is that firms may have different costs. For example, consider the market for painters. Anyone can enter the market for painting services, but not everyone has the same costs. Costs vary in part because some people work faster than others and in part because some people have better alternative uses of their time than others. For any given price, those with lower costs are more likely to enter than those with higher costs. To increase the quantity of painting services supplied, additional entrants must be encouraged to enter the market. Because these new entrants have higher costs, the price must rise to make entry profitable for them. Thus, the market supply curve for painting services slopes upward even with free entry into the market.

Notice that if firms have different costs, some firms earn profit even in the long run. In this case, the price in the market reflects the average total cost of the *marginal firm*—the firm that would exit the market if the price were any lower. This firm earns zero profit, but firms with lower costs earn positive profit. Entry does not eliminate this profit because would-be entrants have higher costs than firms already in the market. Higher-cost firms will enter only if the price rises, making the market profitable for them.

Thus, for these two reasons, the long-run supply curve in a market may be upward sloping rather than horizontal, indicating that a higher price is necessary to induce a larger quantity supplied. Nonetheless, the basic lesson about entry and exit remains true. *Because firms can enter and exit more easily in the long run than in the short run, the long-run supply curve is typically more elastic than the short-run supply curve.*

QuickQuiz In the long run with free entry and exit, is the price in a market equal to marginal cost, average total cost, both, or neither? Explain with a diagram.

CONCLUSION: BEHIND THE SUPPLY CURVE

We have been discussing the behavior of competitive profit-maximizing firms. You may recall from Chapter 1 that one of the *Ten Principles of Economics* is that rational people think at the margin. This chapter has applied this idea to the competitive firm. Marginal analysis has given us a theory of the supply curve in a competitive market and, as a result, a deeper understanding of market outcomes.

We have learned that when you buy a good from a firm in a competitive market, you can be assured that the price you pay is close to the cost of producing that good. In particular, if firms are competitive and profit-maximizing, the price of a good equals the marginal cost of making that good. In addition, if firms can freely enter and exit the market, the price also equals the lowest possible average total cost of production.

Although we have assumed throughout this chapter that firms are price takers, many of the tools developed here are also useful for studying firms in less competitive markets. In the next chapter we will examine the behavior of firms with market power. Marginal analysis will again be useful in analyzing these firms, but it will have quite different implications.

SUMMARY

- Because a competitive firm is a price taker, its revenue is proportional to the amount of output it produces. The price of the good equals both the firm's average revenue and its marginal revenue.

- To maximize profit, a firm chooses a quantity of output such that marginal revenue equals marginal cost. Because marginal revenue for a competitive firm equals the market price, the firm chooses quantity so that price equals marginal cost. Thus, the firm's marginal cost curve is its supply curve.

- In the short run when a firm cannot recover its fixed costs, the firm will choose to shut down temporarily if the price of the good is less than average variable cost. In the long run when the firm can recover both fixed and variable costs, it

will choose to exit if the price is less than average total cost.

- In a market with free entry and exit, profits are driven to zero in the long run. In this long-run equilibrium, all firms produce at the efficient scale, price equals the minimum of average total cost, and the number of firms adjusts to satisfy the quantity demanded at this price.

- Changes in demand have different effects over different time horizons. In the short run, an increase in demand raises prices and leads to profits, and a decrease in demand lowers prices and leads to losses. But if firms can freely enter and exit the market, then in the long run the number of firms adjusts to drive the market back to the zero-profit equilibrium.

KEY CONCEPTS

competitive market, p. 290
average revenue, p. 292

marginal revenue, p. 292

sunk cost, p. 297

QUESTIONS FOR REVIEW

1. What is meant by a competitive firm?

2. Draw the cost curves for a typical firm. For a given price, explain how the firm chooses the level of output that maximizes profit.

3. Under what conditions will a firm shut down temporarily? Explain.

4. Under what conditions will a firm exit a market? Explain.

5. Does a firm's price equal marginal cost in the short run, in the long run, or both? Explain.

6. Does a firm's price equal the minimum of average total cost in the short run, in the long run, or both? Explain.

7. Are market supply curves typically more elastic in the short run or in the long run? Explain.

PROBLEMS AND APPLICATIONS

1. What are the characteristics of a competitive market? Which of the following drinks do you think is best described by these characteristics? Why aren't the others?
   a. tap water
   b. bottled water
   c. cola
   d. beer

2. Your roommate's long hours in Chem lab finally paid off—she discovered a secret formula that lets people do an hour's worth of studying in 5 minutes. So far, she's sold 200 doses, and faces the following average-total-cost schedule:

Q	Average Total Cost
199	$199
200	200
201	201

   If a new customer offers to pay your roommate $300 for one dose, should she make one more? Explain.

3. The licorice industry is competitive. Each firm produces 2 million strings of licorice per year. The strings have an average total cost of $0.20 each, and they sell for $0.30.
   a. What is the marginal cost of a string?
   b. Is this industry in long-run equilibrium? Why or why not?

4. You go out to the best restaurant in town and order a lobster dinner for $40. After eating half of the lobster, you realize that you are quite full. Your date wants you to finish your dinner, because you can't take it home and because "you've already paid for it." What should you do? Relate your answer to the material in this chapter.

5. Bob's lawn-mowing service is a profit-maximizing, competitive firm. Bob mows lawns for $27 each. His total cost each day is $280, of which $30 is a fixed cost. He mows 10 lawns a day. What can you say about Bob's short-run decision regarding shut down and his long-run decision regarding exit?

6. Consider total cost and total revenue given in the table below:

Quantity	0	1	2	3	4	5	6	7
Total Cost	$8	$9	$10	$11	$13	$19	$27	$37
Total Revenue	0	8	16	24	32	40	48	56

   a. Calculate profit for each quantity. How much should the firm produce to maximize profit?
   b. Calculate marginal revenue and marginal cost for each quantity. Graph them. (Hint: Put the points between whole numbers. For example, the marginal cost between 2 and 3 should be graphed at 2 1/2.) At what quantity do these curves cross? How does this relate to your answer to part (a)?
   c. Can you tell whether this firm is in a competitive industry? If so, can you tell whether the industry is in a long-run equilibrium?

7. From *The Wall Street Journal* (July 23, 1991): "Since peaking in 1976, per capita beef consumption in the United States has fallen by 28.6 percent . . . [and] the size of the U.S. cattle herd has shrunk to a 30-year low."
   a. Using firm and industry diagrams, show the short-run effect of declining demand for beef. Label the diagram carefully and write out in words all of the changes you can identify.
   b. On a new diagram, show the long-run effect of declining demand for beef. Explain in words.

8. "High prices traditionally cause expansion in an industry, eventually bringing an end to high

prices and manufacturers' prosperity." Explain, using appropriate diagrams.

9. Suppose the book-printing industry is competitive and begins in a long-run equilibrium.
   a. Draw a diagram describing the typical firm in the industry.
   b. Hi-Tech Printing Company invents a new process that sharply reduces the cost of printing books. What happens to Hi-Tech's profits and the price of books in the short run when Hi-Tech's patent prevents other firms from using the new technology?
   c. What happens in the long run when the patent expires and other firms are free to use the technology?

10. Many small boats are made of fiberglass, which is derived from crude oil. Suppose that the price of oil rises.
   a. Using diagrams, show what happens to the cost curves of an individual boat-making firm and to the market supply curve.
   b. What happens to the profits of boat makers in the short run? What happens to the number of boat makers in the long run?

11. Suppose that the U.S. textile industry is competitive, and there is no international trade in textiles. In long-run equilibrium, the price per unit of cloth is $30.
   a. Describe the equilibrium using graphs for the entire market and for an individual producer.

Now suppose that textile producers in other countries are willing to sell large quantities of cloth in the United States for only $25 per unit.
   b. Assuming that U.S. textile producers have large fixed costs, what is the short-run effect of these imports on the quantity produced by an individual producer? What is the short-run effect on profits? Illustrate your answer with a graph.
   c. What is the long-run effect on the number of U.S. firms in the industry?

12. Suppose there are 1,000 hot-pretzel stands operating in New York City. Each stand has the usual U-shaped average-total-cost curve. The market demand curve for pretzels slopes downward, and the market for pretzels is in long-run competitive equilibrium.
   a. Draw the current equilibrium, using graphs for the entire market and for an individual pretzel stand.
   b. Now the city decides to restrict the number of pretzel-stand licenses, reducing the number of stands to only 800. What effect will this action have on the market and on an individual stand that is still operating? Use graphs to illustrate your answer.
   c. Suppose that the city decides to charge a license fee for the 800 licenses. How will this affect the number of pretzels sold by an individual stand, and the stand's profit? The city wants to raise as much revenue as possible and also wants to ensure that 800

pretzel stands remain in the city. By how much should the city increase the license fee? Show the answer on your graph.

13. Assume that the gold-mining industry is competitive.

   a. Illustrate a long-run equilibrium using diagrams for the gold market and for a representative gold mine.

   b. Suppose that an increase in jewelry demand induces a surge in the demand for gold. Using your diagrams from part (a), show what happens in the short run to the gold market and to each existing gold mine.

   c. If the demand for gold remains high, what would happen to the price over time? Specifically, would the new long-run equilibrium price be above, below, or equal to the short-run equilibrium price in part (b)? Is it possible for the new long-run equilibrium price to be above the original long-run equilibrium price? Explain.

14. (This problem is challenging.) *The New York Times* (July 1, 1994) reported on a Clinton administration proposal to lift the ban on exporting oil from the North Slope of Alaska.

According to the article, the administration said that "the chief effect of the ban has been to provide California refiners with crude oil cheaper than oil on the world market. . . . The ban created a subsidy for California refiners that had not been passed on to consumers." Let's use our analysis of firm behavior to analyze these claims.

   a. Draw the cost curves for a California refiner and for a refiner in another part of the world. Assume that the California refiners have access to inexpensive Alaskan crude oil and that other refiners must buy more expensive crude oil from the Middle East.

   b. All of the refiners produce gasoline for the world gasoline market, which has a single price. In the long-run equilibrium, will this price depend on the costs faced by California producers or the costs faced by other producers? Explain. (Hint: California cannot itself supply the entire world market.) Draw new graphs that illustrate the profits earned by a California refiner and another refiner.

   c. In this model, is there a subsidy to California refiners? Is it passed on to consumers?

http://

For more study tools, please visit http://mankiwXtra.swlearning.com.

MONOPOLY

If you own a personal computer, it probably uses some version of Windows, the operating system sold by the Microsoft Corporation. When Microsoft first designed Windows many years ago, it applied for and received a copyright from the government. The copyright gives Microsoft the exclusive right to make and sell copies of the Windows operating system. So if a person wants to buy a copy of Windows, he or she has little choice but to give Microsoft the approximately $50 that the firm has decided to charge for its product. Microsoft is said to have a *monopoly* in the market for Windows.

Microsoft's business decisions are not well described by the model of firm behavior we developed in the previous chapter. In that chapter we analyzed competitive markets, in which there are many firms offering essentially identical products, so each firm has little influence over the price it receives. By contrast, a monopoly such as Microsoft has no close competitors and, therefore, can influence the market price of its product. While a competitive firm is a *price taker*, a monopoly firm is a *price maker*.

In this chapter we examine the implications of this market power. We will see that market power alters the relationship between a firm's costs and the price at which it sells its product to the market. A competitive firm takes the price of its output as given by the market and then chooses the quantity it will supply so that price equals marginal cost. By contrast, the price charged by a monopoly exceeds marginal cost. This result is clearly true in the case of Microsoft's Windows. The marginal cost of Windows—the extra cost that Microsoft would incur by printing one more copy of the program onto a CD—is only a few dollars. The market price of Windows is many times marginal cost.

It is perhaps not surprising that monopolies charge high prices for their products. Customers of monopolies might seem to have little choice but to pay whatever the monopoly charges. But, if so, why does a copy of Windows not cost $500? Or $5,000? The reason, of course, is that if Microsoft set the price that high, fewer people would buy the product. People would buy fewer computers, switch to other operating systems, or make illegal copies. Monopolies cannot achieve any level of profit they want because high prices reduce the amount that their customers buy. Although monopolies can control the prices of their goods, their profits are not unlimited.

As we examine the production and pricing decisions of monopolies, we also consider the implications of monopoly for society as a whole. Monopoly firms, like competitive firms, aim to maximize profit. But this goal has very different ramifications for competitive and monopoly firms. As we first saw in Chapter 7, self-interested buyers and sellers in competitive markets are unwittingly led by an invisible hand to promote general economic well-being. By contrast, because monopoly firms are unchecked by competition, the outcome in a market with a monopoly is often not in the best interest of society.

One of the *Ten Principles of Economics* in Chapter 1 is that governments can sometimes improve market outcomes. The analysis in this chapter will shed more light on this principle. As we examine the problems that monopolies raise for society, we will also discuss the various ways in which government policymakers might respond to these problems. The U.S. government, for example, keeps a close eye on Microsoft's business decisions. In 1994, it prevented Microsoft from buying Intuit, a software firm that sells the leading program for personal finance, on the grounds that the combination of Microsoft and Intuit would concentrate too much market power in one firm. Similarly, in 1998 the U.S. Justice Department objected when Microsoft started integrating its Internet browser into its Windows operating system, claiming that this would impede competition from other companies, such as Netscape. This concern led the Justice Department to file suit against Microsoft. When the suit was finally settled in 2002, Microsoft agreed to some restrictions on its business practices, but it was allowed to keep the browser as part of Windows.

WHY MONOPOLIES ARISE

monopoly
a firm that is the sole seller of a product without close substitutes

A firm is a **monopoly** if it is the sole seller of its product and if its product does not have close substitutes. The fundamental cause of monopoly is *barriers to entry*: A monopoly remains the only seller in its market because other firms cannot enter the market and compete with it. Barriers to entry, in turn, have three main sources:

- A key resource is owned by a single firm.
- The government gives a single firm the exclusive right to produce some good or service.

- The costs of production make a single producer more efficient than a large number of producers.

Let's briefly discuss each of these.

Monopoly Resources

The simplest way for a monopoly to arise is for a single firm to own a key resource. For example, consider the market for water in a small town in the Old West. If dozens of town residents have working wells, the competitive model discussed in the preceding chapter describes the behavior of sellers. As a result, the price of a gallon of water is driven to equal the marginal cost of pumping an extra gallon. But if there is only one well in town and it is impossible to get water from anywhere else, then the owner of the well has a monopoly on water. Not surprisingly, the monopolist has much greater market power than any single firm in a competitive market. In the case of a necessity like water, the monopolist could command quite a high price, even if the marginal cost is low.

Although exclusive ownership of a key resource is a potential cause of monopoly, in practice monopolies rarely arise for this reason. Actual economies are large, and resources are owned by many people. Indeed, because many goods are traded internationally, the natural scope of their markets is often worldwide. There are, therefore, few examples of firms that own a resource for which there are no close substitutes.

"Rather than a monopoly, we like to consider ourselves 'the only game in town.'"

Case Study
THE DeBEERS DIAMOND MONOPOLY

A classic example of a monopoly that arises from the ownership of a key resource is DeBeers, the South African diamond company. DeBeers controls about 80 percent of the world's production of diamonds. Although the firm's share of the market is not 100 percent, it is large enough to exert substantial influence over the market price of diamonds.

How much market power does DeBeers have? The answer depends in part on whether there are close substitutes for its product. If people view emeralds, rubies, and sapphires as good substitutes for diamonds, then DeBeers has relatively little market power. In this case, any attempt by DeBeers to raise the price of diamonds would cause people to switch to other gemstones. But if people view these other stones as very different from diamonds, then DeBeers can exert substantial influence over the price of its product.

DeBeers pays for large amounts of advertising. At first, this decision might seem surprising. If a monopoly is the sole seller of its product, why does it need to advertise? One goal of the DeBeers ads is to differentiate diamonds from other gems in the minds of consumers. When their slogan tells you that "a diamond is forever," you are meant to think that the same is not true of emeralds, rubies, and sapphires. (And notice that the slogan is applied to all diamonds, not just DeBeers diamonds—a sign of DeBeers's monopoly position.) If the ads are successful, consumers will view diamonds as unique, rather than as one among many gemstones, and this perception will give DeBeers greater market power. ●

Government-Created Monopolies

In many cases, monopolies arise because the government has given one person or firm the exclusive right to sell some good or service. Sometimes the monopoly arises from the sheer political clout of the would-be monopolist. Kings, for example, once granted exclusive business licenses to their friends and allies. At other times, the government grants a monopoly because doing so is viewed to be in the public interest. For instance, the U.S. government has given a monopoly to a company called Network Solutions, Inc., which maintains the database of all .com, .net, and .org Internet addresses, on the grounds that such data need to be centralized and comprehensive.

The patent and copyright laws are two important examples of how the government creates a monopoly to serve the public interest. When a pharmaceutical company discovers a new drug, it can apply to the government for a patent. If the government deems the drug to be truly original, it approves the patent, which gives the company the exclusive right to manufacture and sell the drug for 20 years. Similarly, when a novelist finishes a book, she can copyright it. The copyright is a government guarantee that no one can print and sell the work without the author's permission. The copyright makes the novelist a monopolist in the sale of her novel.

The effects of patent and copyright laws are easy to see. Because these laws give one producer a monopoly, they lead to higher prices than would occur under competition. But by allowing these monopoly producers to charge higher prices and earn higher profits, the laws also encourage some desirable behavior. Drug companies are allowed to be monopolists in the drugs they discover in order to encourage research. Authors are allowed to be monopolists in the sale of their books to encourage them to write more and better books.

Thus, the laws governing patents and copyrights have benefits and costs. The benefits of the patent and copyright laws are the increased incentive for creative activity. These benefits are offset, to some extent, by the costs of monopoly pricing, which we examine fully later in this chapter.

Natural Monopolies

natural monopoly
a monopoly that arises because a single firm can supply a good or service to an entire market at a smaller cost than could two or more firms

An industry is a **natural monopoly** when a single firm can supply a good or service to an entire market at a lower cost than could two or more firms. A natural monopoly arises when there are economies of scale over the relevant range of output. Figure 1 shows the average total costs of a firm with economies of scale. In this case, a single firm can produce any amount of output at least cost. That is, for any given amount of output, a larger number of firms leads to less output per firm and higher average total cost.

An example of a natural monopoly is the distribution of water. To provide water to residents of a town, a firm must build a network of pipes throughout the

FIGURE 1

Economies of Scale as a Cause of Monopoly

When a firm's average-total-cost curve continually declines, the firm has what is called a natural monopoly. In this case, when production is divided among more firms, each firm produces less, and average total cost rises. As a result, a single firm can produce any given amount at the smallest cost.

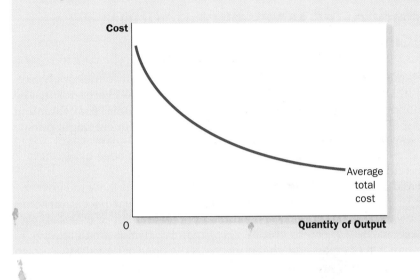

town. If two or more firms were to compete in the provision of this service, each firm would have to pay the fixed cost of building a network. Thus, the average total cost of water is lowest if a single firm serves the entire market.

We saw other examples of natural monopolies when we discussed public goods and common resources in Chapter 11. We noted in passing that some goods in the economy are excludable but not rival. An example is a bridge used so infrequently that it is never congested. The bridge is excludable because a toll collector can prevent someone from using it. The bridge is not rival because use of the bridge by one person does not diminish the ability of others to use it. Because there is a fixed cost of building the bridge and a negligible marginal cost of additional users, the average total cost of a trip across the bridge (the total cost divided by the number of trips) falls as the number of trips rises. Hence, the bridge is a natural monopoly.

When a firm is a natural monopoly, it is less concerned about new entrants eroding its monopoly power. Normally, a firm has trouble maintaining a monopoly position without ownership of a key resource or protection from the government. The monopolist's profit attracts entrants into the market, and these entrants make the market more competitive. By contrast, entering a market in which another firm has a natural monopoly is unattractive. Would-be entrants know that they cannot achieve the same low costs that the monopolist enjoys because, after entry, each firm would have a smaller piece of the market.

In some cases, the size of the market is one determinant of whether an industry is a natural monopoly. Again, consider a bridge across a river. When the population is small, the bridge may be a natural monopoly. A single bridge can satisfy the entire demand for trips across the river at lowest cost. Yet as the population grows and the bridge becomes congested, satisfying the entire demand may require two or more bridges across the same river. Thus, as a market expands, a natural monopoly can evolve into a competitive market.

QuickQuiz What are the three reasons that a market might have a monopoly? • Give two examples of monopolies, and explain the reason for each.

HOW MONOPOLIES MAKE PRODUCTION AND PRICING DECISIONS

Now that we know how monopolies arise, we can consider how a monopoly firm decides how much of its product to make and what price to charge for it. The analysis of monopoly behavior in this section is the starting point for evaluating whether monopolies are desirable and what policies the government might pursue in monopoly markets.

Monopoly versus Competition

The key difference between a competitive firm and a monopoly is the monopoly's ability to influence the price of its output. A competitive firm is small relative to the market in which it operates and, therefore, takes the price of its output as given by market conditions. By contrast, because a monopoly is the sole producer in its market, it can alter the price of its good by adjusting the quantity it supplies to the market.

One way to view this difference between a competitive firm and a monopoly is to consider the demand curve that each firm faces. When we analyzed profit maximization by competitive firms in the preceding chapter, we drew the market price as a horizontal line. Because a competitive firm can sell as much or as little as it wants at this price, the competitive firm faces a horizontal demand curve, as in panel (a) of Figure 2. In effect, because the competitive firm sells a product with many perfect substitutes (the products of all the other firms in its market), the demand curve that any one firm faces is perfectly elastic.

By contrast, because a monopoly is the sole producer in its market, its demand curve is the market demand curve. Thus, the monopolist's demand curve slopes downward for all the usual reasons, as in panel (b) of Figure 2. If the monopolist raises the price of its good, consumers buy less of it. Looked at another way, if the monopolist reduces the quantity of output it sells, the price of its output increases.

The market demand curve provides a constraint on a monopoly's ability to profit from its market power. A monopolist would prefer, if it were possible, to charge a high price and sell a large quantity at that high price. The market demand curve makes that outcome impossible. In particular, the market demand curve describes the combinations of price and quantity that are available to a monopoly firm. By adjusting the quantity produced (or, equivalently, the price charged), the monopolist can choose any point on the demand curve, but it cannot choose a point off the demand curve.

What point on the demand curve will the monopolist choose? As with competitive firms, we assume that the monopolist's goal is to maximize profit. Because the firm's profit is total revenue minus total costs, our next task in explaining monopoly behavior is to examine a monopolist's revenue.

FIGURE 2

Demand Curves for Competitive and Monopoly Firms

Because competitive firms are price takers, they in effect face horizontal demand curves, as in panel (a). Because a monopoly firm is the sole producer in its market, it faces the downward-sloping market demand curve, as in panel (b). As a result, the monopoly has to accept a lower price if it wants to sell more output.

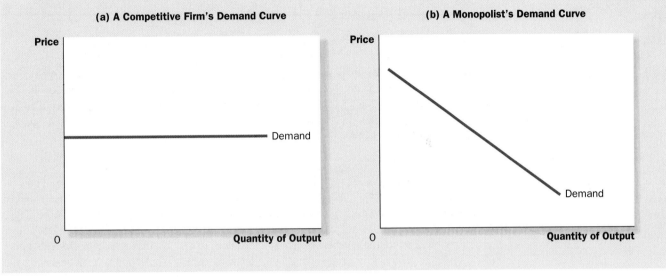

(a) A Competitive Firm's Demand Curve

Price

Demand

0   Quantity of Output

(b) A Monopolist's Demand Curve

Price

Demand

0   Quantity of Output

A Monopoly's Revenue

Consider a town with a single producer of water. Table 1 (p. 320) shows how the monopoly's revenue might depend on the amount of water produced.

The first two columns show the monopolist's demand schedule. If the monopolist produces 1 gallon of water, it can sell that gallon for $10. If it produces 2 gallons, it must lower the price to $9 in order to sell both gallons. And if it produces 3 gallons, it must lower the price to $8. And so on. If you graphed these two columns of numbers, you would get a typical downward-sloping demand curve.

The third column of the table presents the monopolist's *total revenue*. It equals the quantity sold (from the first column) times the price (from the second column). The fourth column computes the firm's *average revenue*, the amount of revenue the firm receives per unit sold. We compute average revenue by taking the number for total revenue in the third column and dividing it by the quantity of output in the first column. As we discussed in the previous chapter, average revenue always equals the price of the good. This is true for monopolists as well as for competitive firms.

The last column of Table 1 computes the firm's *marginal revenue*, the amount of revenue that the firm receives for each additional unit of output. We compute marginal revenue by taking the change in total revenue when output increases by 1 unit. For example, when the firm is producing 3 gallons of water, it receives total revenue of $24. Raising production to 4 gallons increases total revenue to $28. Thus, marginal revenue is $28 minus $24, or $4.

TABLE 1

A Monopoly's Total, Average, and Marginal Revenue

Quantity of Water (Q)	Price (P)	Total Revenue (TR = P × Q)	Average Revenue (AR = TR/Q)	Marginal Revenue (MR = ΔTR/ΔQ)
0 gallons	$11	$ 0	—	
				$10
1	10	10	$10	
				8
2	9	18	9	
				6
3	8	24	8	
				4
4	7	28	7	
				2
5	6	30	6	
				0
6	5	30	5	
				−2
7	4	28	4	
				−4
8	3	24	3	

Table 1 shows a result that is important for understanding monopoly behavior: *A monopolist's marginal revenue is always less than the price of its good.* For example, if the firm raises production of water from 3 to 4 gallons, it will increase total revenue by only $4, even though it will be able to sell each gallon for $7. For a monopoly, marginal revenue is lower than price because a monopoly faces a downward-sloping demand curve. To increase the amount sold, a monopoly firm must lower the price of its good. Hence, to sell the fourth gallon of water, the monopolist must get less revenue for each of the first three gallons.

Marginal revenue for monopolies is very different from marginal revenue for competitive firms. When a monopoly increases the amount it sells, it has two effects on total revenue ($P \times Q$):

- *The output effect:* More output is sold, so Q is higher.
- *The price effect:* The price falls, so P is lower.

Because a competitive firm can sell all it wants at the market price, there is no price effect. When it increases production by 1 unit, it receives the market price for that unit, and it does not receive any less for the units it was already selling. That is, because the competitive firm is a price taker, its marginal revenue equals the price of its good. By contrast, when a monopoly increases production by 1 unit, it must reduce the price it charges for every unit it sells, and this cut in price reduces revenue on the units it was already selling. As a result, a monopoly's marginal revenue is less than its price.

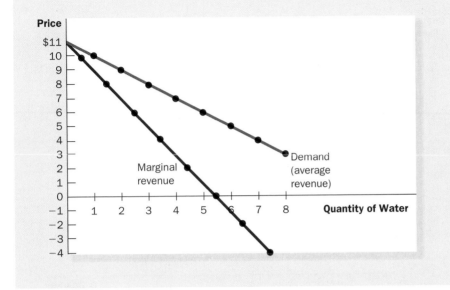

FIGURE 3

Demand and Marginal-Revenue Curves for a Monopoly

The demand curve shows how the quantity affects the price of the good. The marginal-revenue curve shows how the firm's revenue changes when the quantity increases by 1 unit. Because the price on all units sold must fall if the monopoly increases production, marginal revenue is always less than the price.

Figure 3 graphs the demand curve and the marginal-revenue curve for a monopoly firm. (Because the firm's price equals its average revenue, the demand curve is also the average-revenue curve.) These two curves always start at the same point on the vertical axis because the marginal revenue of the first unit sold equals the price of the good. But thereafter, for the reason we just discussed, the monopolist's marginal revenue is less than the price of the good. Thus, a monopoly's marginal-revenue curve lies below its demand curve.

You can see in the figure (as well as in Table 1) that marginal revenue can even become negative. Marginal revenue is negative when the price effect on revenue is greater than the output effect. In this case, when the firm produces an extra unit of output, the price falls by enough to cause the firm's total revenue to decline, even though the firm is selling more units.

Profit Maximization

Now that we have considered the revenue of a monopoly firm, we are ready to examine how such a firm maximizes profit. Recall from Chapter 1 that one of the *Ten Principles of Economics* is that rational people think at the margin. This lesson is as true for monopolists as it is for competitive firms. Here we apply the logic of marginal analysis to the monopolist's decision about how much to produce.

Figure 4 (p. 322) graphs the demand curve, the marginal-revenue curve, and the cost curves for a monopoly firm. All these curves should seem familiar: The demand and marginal-revenue curves are like those in Figure 3, and the cost curves are like those we encountered in the last two chapters. These curves contain all the information we need to determine the level of output that a profit-maximizing monopolist will choose.

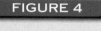

FIGURE 4

Profit Maximization for a Monopoly

A monopoly maximizes profit by choosing the quantity at which marginal revenue equals marginal cost (point A). It then uses the demand curve to find the price that will induce consumers to buy that quantity (point B).

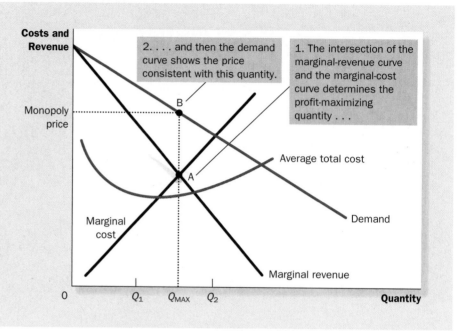

Suppose, first, that the firm is producing at a low level of output, such as Q_1. In this case, marginal cost is less than marginal revenue. If the firm increased production by 1 unit, the additional revenue would exceed the additional costs, and profit would rise. Thus, when marginal cost is less than marginal revenue, the firm can increase profit by producing more units.

A similar argument applies at high levels of output, such as Q_2. In this case, marginal cost is greater than marginal revenue. If the firm reduced production by 1 unit, the costs saved would exceed the revenue lost. Thus, if marginal cost is greater than marginal revenue, the firm can raise profit by reducing production.

In the end, the firm adjusts its level of production until the quantity reaches Q_{MAX}, at which marginal revenue equals marginal cost. *Thus, the monopolist's profit-maximizing quantity of output is determined by the intersection of the marginal-revenue curve and the marginal-cost curve.* In Figure 4, this intersection occurs at point A.

You might recall from the last chapter that competitive firms also choose the quantity of output at which marginal revenue equals marginal cost. In following this rule for profit maximization, competitive firms and monopolies are alike. But there is also an important difference between these types of firm: The marginal revenue of a competitive firm equals its price, whereas the marginal revenue of a monopoly is less than its price. That is,

For a competitive firm: $P = MR = MC$.
For a monopoly firm: $P > MR = MC$.

The equality of marginal revenue and marginal cost at the profit-maximizing quantity is the same for both types of firm. What differs is the relationship of the price to marginal revenue and marginal cost.

WHY A MONOPOLY DOES NOT HAVE A SUPPLY CURVE

You may have noticed that we have analyzed the price in a monopoly market using the market demand curve and the firm's cost curves. We have not made any mention of the market supply curve. By contrast, when we analyzed prices in competitive markets beginning in Chapter 4, the two most important words were always *supply* and *demand*.

What happened to the supply curve? Although monopoly firms make decisions about what quantity to supply (in the way described in this chapter), a monopoly does not have a supply curve. A supply curve tells us the quantity that firms choose to supply at any given price. This concept makes sense when we are analyzing competitive firms, which are price takers. But a monopoly firm is a price maker, not a price taker. It is not meaningful to ask what such a firm would produce at any price because the firm sets the price at the same time it chooses the quantity to supply.

Indeed, the monopolist's decision about how much to supply is impossible to separate from the demand curve it faces. The shape of the demand curve determines the shape of the marginal-revenue curve, which in turn determines the monopolist's profit-maximizing quantity. In a competitive market, supply decisions can be analyzed without knowing the demand curve, but that is not true in a monopoly market. Therefore, we never talk about a monopoly's supply curve.

How does the monopoly find the profit-maximizing price for its product? The demand curve answers this question because the demand curve relates the amount that customers are willing to pay to the quantity sold. Thus, after the monopoly firm chooses the quantity of output that equates marginal revenue and marginal cost, it uses the demand curve to find the price consistent with that quantity. In Figure 4, the profit-maximizing price is found at point B.

We can now see a key difference between markets with competitive firms and markets with a monopoly firm: *In competitive markets, price equals marginal cost. In monopolized markets, price exceeds marginal cost.* As we will see in a moment, this finding is crucial to understanding the social cost of monopoly.

A Monopoly's Profit

How much profit does the monopoly make? To see the monopoly's profit, recall that profit equals total revenue (*TR*) minus total costs (*TC*):

$$\text{Profit} = TR - TC.$$

We can rewrite this as

$$\text{Profit} = (TR/Q - TC/Q) \times Q.$$

TR/Q is average revenue, which equals the price P, and TC/Q is average total cost ATC. Therefore,

$$\text{Profit} = (P - ATC) \times Q.$$

FIGURE 5

The Monopolist's Profit

The area of the box BCDE equals the profit of the monopoly firm. The height of the box (BC) is price minus average total cost, which equals profit per unit sold. The width of the box (DC) is the number of units sold.

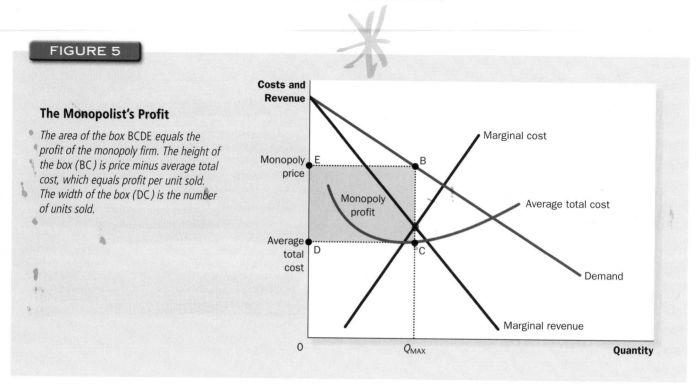

This equation for profit (which is the same as the profit equation for competitive firms) allows us to measure the monopolist's profit in our graph.

Consider the shaded box in Figure 5. The height of the box (the segment BC) is price minus average total cost, $P - ATC$, which is the profit on the typical unit sold. The width of the box (the segment DC) is the quantity sold Q_{MAX}. Therefore, the area of this box is the monopoly firm's total profit.

Case Study

MONOPOLY DRUGS VERSUS GENERIC DRUGS

According to our analysis, prices are determined quite differently in monopolized markets from the way they are in competitive markets. A natural place to test this theory is the market for pharmaceutical drugs because this market takes on both market structures. When a firm discovers a new drug, patent laws give the firm a monopoly on the sale of that drug. But eventually the firm's patent runs out, and any company can make and sell the drug. At that time, the market switches from being monopolistic to being competitive.

What should happen to the price of a drug when the patent runs out? Figure 6 shows the market for a typical drug. In this figure, the marginal cost of producing the drug is constant. (This is approximately true for many drugs.) During the life of the patent, the monopoly firm maximizes profit by producing the quantity at which marginal revenue equals marginal cost and charging a price well above

FIGURE 6

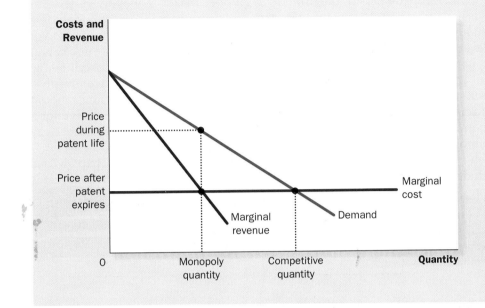

The Market for Drugs

When a patent gives a firm a monopoly over the sale of a drug, the firm charges the monopoly price, which is well above the marginal cost of making the drug. When the patent on a drug runs out, new firms enter the market, making it more competitive. As a result, the price falls from the monopoly price to marginal cost.

marginal cost. But when the patent runs out, the profit from making the drug should encourage new firms to enter the market. As the market becomes more competitive, the price should fall to equal marginal cost.

Experience is, in fact, consistent with our theory. When the patent on a drug expires, other companies quickly enter and begin selling so-called generic products that are chemically identical to the former monopolist's brand-name product. And just as our analysis predicts, the price of the competitively produced generic drug is well below the price that the monopolist was charging.

The expiration of a patent, however, does not cause the monopolist to lose all its market power. Some consumers remain loyal to the brand-name drug, perhaps out of fear that the new generic drugs are not actually the same as the drug they have been using for years. As a result, the former monopolist can continue to charge a price at least somewhat above the price charged by its new competitors. ●

QuickQuiz Explain how a monopolist chooses the quantity of output to produce and the price to charge.

THE WELFARE COST OF MONOPOLY

Is monopoly a good way to organize a market? We have seen that a monopoly, in contrast to a competitive firm, charges a price above marginal cost. From the standpoint of consumers, this high price makes monopoly undesirable. At the same time, however, the monopoly is earning profit from charging this high price. From the standpoint of the owners of the firm, the high price makes monopoly very desirable. Is it possible that the benefits to the firm's owners exceed the costs imposed on consumers, making monopoly desirable from the standpoint of society as a whole?

We can answer this question using the type of analysis we first saw in Chapter 7. As in that chapter, we use total surplus as our measure of economic well-being. Recall that total surplus is the sum of consumer surplus and producer surplus. Consumer surplus is consumers' willingness to pay for a good minus the amount they actually pay for it. Producer surplus is the amount producers receive for a good minus their costs of producing it. In this case, there is a single producer—the monopolist.

You might already be able to guess the result of this analysis. In Chapter 7 we concluded that the equilibrium of supply and demand in a competitive market is not only a natural outcome but a desirable one. In particular, the invisible hand of the market leads to an allocation of resources that makes total surplus as large as it can be. Because a monopoly leads to an allocation of resources different from that in a competitive market, the outcome must, in some way, fail to maximize total economic well-being.

The Deadweight Loss

We begin by considering what the monopoly firm would do if it were run by a benevolent social planner. The social planner cares not only about the profit earned by the firm's owners but also about the benefits received by the firm's consumers. The planner tries to maximize total surplus, which equals producer surplus (profit) plus consumer surplus. Keep in mind that total surplus equals the value of the good to consumers minus the costs of making the good incurred by the monopoly producer.

Figure 7 analyzes what level of output a benevolent social planner would choose. The demand curve reflects the value of the good to consumers, as measured by their willingness to pay for it. The marginal-cost curve reflects the costs of the monopolist. *Thus, the socially efficient quantity is found where the demand curve and the marginal-cost curve intersect.* Below this quantity, the value to consumers exceeds the marginal cost of providing the good, so increasing output would raise total surplus. Above this quantity, the marginal cost exceeds the value to consumers, so decreasing output would raise total surplus.

If the social planner were running the monopoly, the firm could achieve this efficient outcome by charging the price found at the intersection of the demand and marginal-cost curves. Thus, like a competitive firm and unlike a profit-maximizing monopoly, a social planner would charge a price equal to marginal cost. Because this price would give consumers an accurate signal about the cost of producing the good, consumers would buy the efficient quantity.

We can evaluate the welfare effects of monopoly by comparing the level of output that the monopolist chooses to the level of output that a social planner would choose. As we have seen, the monopolist chooses to produce and sell the quantity of output at which the marginal-revenue and marginal-cost curves intersect; the social planner would choose the quantity at which the demand and marginal-cost curves intersect. Figure 8 shows the comparison. *The monopolist produces less than the socially efficient quantity of output.*

FIGURE 7

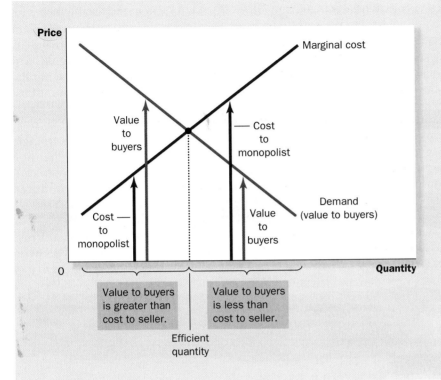

The Efficient Level of Output

A benevolent social planner who wanted to maximize total surplus in the market would choose the level of output where the demand curve and marginal-cost curve intersect. Below this level, the value of the good to the marginal buyer (as reflected in the demand curve) exceeds the marginal cost of making the good. Above this level, the value to the marginal buyer is less than marginal cost.

FIGURE 8

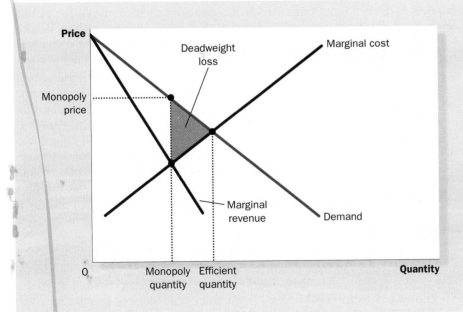

The Inefficiency of Monopoly

Because a monopoly charges a price above marginal cost, not all consumers who value the good at more than its cost buy it. Thus, the quantity produced and sold by a monopoly is below the socially efficient level. The deadweight loss is represented by the area of the triangle between the demand curve (which reflects the value of the good to consumers) and the marginal-cost curve (which reflects the costs of the monopoly producer).

We can also view the inefficiency of monopoly in terms of the monopolist's price. Because the market demand curve describes a negative relationship between the price and quantity of the good, a quantity that is inefficiently low is equivalent to a price that is inefficiently high. When a monopolist charges a price above marginal cost, some potential consumers value the good at more than its marginal cost but less than the monopolist's price. These consumers do not end up buying the good. Because the value these consumers place on the good is greater than the cost of providing it to them, this result is inefficient. Thus, monopoly pricing prevents some mutually beneficial trades from taking place.

Just as we measured the inefficiency of taxes with the deadweight loss triangle in Chapter 8, we can similarly measure the inefficiency of monopoly. Figure 8 shows the deadweight loss. Recall that the demand curve reflects the value to consumers and the marginal-cost curve reflects the costs to the monopoly producer. Thus, the area of the deadweight loss triangle between the demand curve and the marginal-cost curve equals the total surplus lost because of monopoly pricing.

The deadweight loss caused by monopoly is similar to the deadweight loss caused by a tax. Indeed, a monopolist is like a private tax collector. As we saw in Chapter 8, a tax on a good places a wedge between consumers' willingness to pay (as reflected in the demand curve) and producers' costs (as reflected in the supply curve). Because a monopoly exerts its market power by charging a price above marginal cost, it places a similar wedge. In both cases, the wedge causes the quantity sold to fall short of the social optimum. The difference between the two cases is that the government gets the revenue from a tax, whereas a private firm gets the monopoly profit.

The Monopoly's Profit: A Social Cost?

It is tempting to decry monopolies for "profiteering" at the expense of the public. And, indeed, a monopoly firm does earn a higher profit by virtue of its market power. According to the economic analysis of monopoly, however, the firm's profit is not in itself necessarily a problem for society.

Welfare in a monopolized market, like all markets, includes the welfare of both consumers and producers. Whenever a consumer pays an extra dollar to a producer because of a monopoly price, the consumer is worse off by a dollar, and the producer is better off by the same amount. This transfer from the consumers of the good to the owners of the monopoly does not affect the market's total surplus—the sum of consumer and producer surplus. In other words, the monopoly profit itself does not represent a shrinkage in the size of the economic pie; it merely represents a bigger slice for producers and a smaller slice for consumers. Unless consumers are for some reason more deserving than producers—a judgment that goes beyond the realm of economic efficiency—the monopoly profit is not a social problem.

The problem in a monopolized market arises because the firm produces and sells a quantity of output below the level that maximizes total surplus. The deadweight loss measures how much the economic pie shrinks as a result. This inefficiency is connected to the monopoly's high price: Consumers buy fewer units when the firm raises its price above marginal cost. But keep in mind that the profit earned on the units that continue to be sold is not the problem. The problem stems from the inefficiently low quantity of output. Put differently, if the high monopoly price did not discourage some consumers from buying the good, it would raise producer surplus by exactly the amount it reduced consumer surplus, leaving total surplus the same as could be achieved by a benevolent social planner.

There is, however, a possible exception to this conclusion. Suppose that a monopoly firm has to incur additional costs to maintain its monopoly position. For example, a firm with a government-created monopoly might need to hire lobbyists to convince lawmakers to continue its monopoly. In this case, the monopoly may use up some of its monopoly profits paying for these additional costs. If so, the social loss from monopoly includes both these costs and the deadweight loss resulting from a price above marginal cost.

QuickQuiz   How does a monopolist's quantity of output compare to the quantity of output that maximizes total surplus?

PUBLIC POLICY TOWARD MONOPOLIES

We have seen that monopolies, in contrast to competitive markets, fail to allocate resources efficiently. Monopolies produce less than the socially desirable quantity of output and, as a result, charge prices above marginal cost. Policymakers in the government can respond to the problem of monopoly in one of four ways:

- By trying to make monopolized industries more competitive
- By regulating the behavior of the monopolies
- By turning some private monopolies into public enterprises
- By doing nothing at all

Increasing Competition with Antitrust Laws

If Coca-Cola and PepsiCo wanted to merge, the deal would be closely examined by the federal government before it went into effect. The lawyers and economists in the Department of Justice might well decide that a merger between these two large soft drink companies would make the U.S. soft drink market substantially less competitive and, as a result, would reduce the economic well-being of the country as a whole. If so, the Justice Department would challenge the merger in court, and if the judge agreed, the two companies would not be allowed to merge. It is precisely this kind of challenge that prevented software giant Microsoft from buying Intuit in 1994.

The government derives this power over private industry from the antitrust laws, a collection of statutes aimed at curbing monopoly power. The first and most important of these laws was the Sherman Antitrust Act, which Congress passed in 1890 to reduce the market power of the large and powerful "trusts" that were viewed as dominating the economy at the time. The Clayton Act, passed in 1914, strengthened the government's powers and authorized private lawsuits. As the U.S. Supreme Court once put it, the antitrust laws are "a comprehensive charter of economic liberty aimed at preserving free and unfettered competition as the rule of trade."

The antitrust laws give the government various ways to promote competition. They allow the government to prevent mergers, such as our hypothetical merger between Coca-Cola and PepsiCo. They also allow the government to break up

© 2003 BY SIDNEY HARRIS

"But if we do merge with Amalgamated, we'll have enough resources to fight the anti-trust violation caused by the merger."

companies. For example, in 1984 the government split up AT&T, the large telecommunications company, into eight smaller companies. Finally, the antitrust laws prevent companies from coordinating their activities in ways that make markets less competitive; we will discuss some of these uses of the antitrust laws in Chapter 16.

Antitrust laws have costs as well as benefits. Sometimes companies merge not to reduce competition but to lower costs through more efficient joint production. These benefits from mergers are sometimes called *synergies*. For example, many U.S. banks have merged in recent years and, by combining operations, have been able to reduce administrative staff. If antitrust laws are to raise social welfare, the government must be able to determine which mergers are desirable and which are not. That is, it must be able to measure and compare the social benefit from synergies to the social costs of reduced competition. Critics of the antitrust laws are skeptical that the government can perform the necessary cost-benefit analysis with sufficient accuracy.

Regulation

Another way in which the government deals with the problem of monopoly is by regulating the behavior of monopolists. This solution is common in the case of natural monopolies, such as water and electric companies. These companies are not allowed to charge any price they want. Instead, government agencies regulate their prices.

What price should the government set for a natural monopoly? This question is not as easy as it might at first appear. One might conclude that the price should equal the monopolist's marginal cost. If price equals marginal cost, customers will buy the quantity of the monopolist's output that maximizes total surplus, and the allocation of resources will be efficient.

There are, however, two practical problems with marginal-cost pricing as a regulatory system. The first is illustrated in Figure 9. Natural monopolies, by definition, have declining average total cost. As we discussed in Chapter 13, when average total cost is declining, marginal cost is less than average total cost. If regulators are to set price equal to marginal cost, that price will be less than the firm's average total cost, and the firm will lose money. Instead of charging such a low price, the monopoly firm would just exit the industry.

Regulators can respond to this problem in various ways, none of which is perfect. One way is to subsidize the monopolist. In essence, the government picks up the losses inherent in marginal-cost pricing. Yet to pay for the subsidy, the government needs to raise money through taxation, which involves its own deadweight losses. Alternatively, the regulators can allow the monopolist to charge a price higher than marginal cost. If the regulated price equals average total cost, the monopolist earns exactly zero economic profit. Yet average-cost pricing leads to deadweight losses, because the monopolist's price no longer reflects the marginal cost of producing the good. In essence, average-cost pricing is like a tax on the good the monopolist is selling.

The second problem with marginal-cost pricing as a regulatory system (and with average-cost pricing as well) is that it gives the monopolist no incentive to reduce costs. Each firm in a competitive market tries to reduce its costs because lower costs mean higher profits. But if a regulated monopolist knows that regulators will reduce prices whenever costs fall, the monopolist will not benefit from lower costs. In practice, regulators deal with this problem by allowing monopolists

FIGURE 9

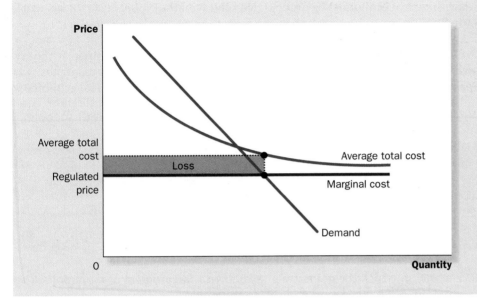

**Marginal-Cost Pricing
for a Natural Monopoly**

*Because a natural monopoly has
declining average total cost, marginal
cost is less than average total cost.
Therefore, if regulators require a natural
monopoly to charge a price equal to
marginal cost, price will be below
average total cost, and the monopoly
will lose money.*

to keep some of the benefits from lower costs in the form of higher profit, a practice that requires some departure from marginal-cost pricing.

Public Ownership

The third policy used by the government to deal with monopoly is public ownership. That is, rather than regulating a natural monopoly that is run by a private
firm, the government can run the monopoly itself. This solution is common in
many European countries, where the government owns and operates utilities such
as the telephone, water, and electric companies. In the United States, the government runs the Postal Service. The delivery of ordinary First Class mail is often
thought to be a natural monopoly.

Economists usually prefer private to public ownership of natural monopolies.
The key issue is how the ownership of the firm affects the costs of production. Private owners have an incentive to minimize costs as long as they reap part of the
benefit in the form of higher profit. If the firm's managers are doing a bad job of
keeping costs down, the firm's owners will fire them. By contrast, if the government bureaucrats who run a monopoly do a bad job, the losers are the customers
and taxpayers, whose only recourse is the political system. The bureaucrats may
become a special-interest group and attempt to block cost-reducing reforms. Put
simply, as a way of ensuring that firms are well run, the voting booth is less reliable than the profit motive.

Doing Nothing

Each of the foregoing policies aimed at reducing the problem of monopoly
has drawbacks. As a result, some economists argue that it is often best for the

government not to try to remedy the inefficiencies of monopoly pricing. Here is the assessment of economist George Stigler, who won the Nobel Prize for his work in industrial organization, writing in the *Fortune Encyclopedia of Economics*:

> A famous theorem in economics states that a competitive enterprise economy will produce the largest possible income from a given stock of resources. No real economy meets the exact conditions of the theorem, and all real economies

IN THE NEWS

PUBLIC TRANSPORT AND PRIVATE ENTERPRISE

In many cities, the mass transit system of buses and subways is a monopoly run by the local government. But is this the best system?

Man with a Van

By John Tierney

Vincent Cummins looks out from his van with the wary eyes of a hardened criminal. It is quiet this evening in downtown Brooklyn . . . too quiet. "Watch my back for me!" he barks into the microphone of his C.B. radio, addressing a fellow outlaw in a van who just drove by him on Livingston Street. He looks left and right. No police cars in sight. None of the usual unmarked cars, either. Cummins pauses for a second—he has heard on the C.B. that cops have just busted two other drivers—but he can't stop himself. "Watch my back!" he repeats into the radio as he ruthlessly pulls over to the curb.

Five seconds later, evil triumphs. *A middle-aged woman with a shopping bag climbs into the van . . . and Cummins drives off with impunity!* His new victim and the other passengers laugh when asked why they're riding this ille-

gal jitney. What fool would pay $1.50 to stand on the bus or subway when you're guaranteed a seat here for $1? Unlike bus drivers, the van drivers make change and accept bills, and the vans run more frequently at every hour of the day. "It takes me an hour to get home if I use the bus," explains Cynthia Peters, a nurse born in Trinidad. "When I'm working late, it's very scary waiting in the dark for the bus and then walking the three blocks home. With Vincent's van, I get home in less than half an hour. He takes me right to the door and waits until I get inside."

Cummins would prefer not to be an outlaw. A native of Barbados, he has been driving his van full time ever since an injury forced him to give up his job as a machinist. "I could be collecting disability," he says, "but it's better to work." He met Federal requirements to run an interstate van service, then spent years trying to get approval to operate in the city. His application, which included more than

900 supporting statements from riders, business groups, and church leaders, was approved by the City Taxi and Limousine Commission as well as by the Department of Transportation. Mayor Giuliani supported him. But this summer the City Council rejected his application for a license, as it has rejected most applications over the past four years, which is why thousands of illegal drivers in Brooklyn and Queens are dodging the police.

Council members claim they're trying to prevent vans from causing accidents and traffic problems, although no one who rides the vans takes these protestations seriously. Vans with accredited and insured drivers like Cummins are no more dangerous or disruptive than taxis. The only danger they pose is to the public transit monopoly, whose union leaders have successfully led the campaign against them.

The van drivers have refuted two modern urban myths: that mass transit

will fall short of the ideal economy—a difference called "market failure." In my view, however, the degree of "market failure" for the American economy is much smaller than the "political failure" arising from the imperfections of economic policies found in real political systems.

As this quotation makes clear, determining the proper role of the government in the economy requires judgments about politics as well as economics.

must lose money and that it must be a public enterprise. Entrepreneurs like Cummins are thriving today in other cities—Seoul and Buenos Aires rely entirely on private, profitable bus companies—and they once made New York the world leader in mass transit. The first horsecars and elevated trains were developed here by private companies. The first subway was partly financed with a loan from the city, but it was otherwise a private operation, built and run quite profitably with the fare set at a nickel—the equivalent of less than a dollar today.

Eventually though, New York's politicians drove most private transit companies out of business by refusing to adjust the fare for inflation. When the enterprises lost money in the 1920's, Mayor John Hylan offered to teach them efficient management. If the city ran the subway, he promised, it would make money while preserving the nickel fare and freeing New Yorkers from "serfdom" and "dictatorship" of the "grasping transportation monopolies." But expenses soared as soon as government merged the private systems into a true monopoly. The fare, which remained a nickel through seven decades of private transit, has risen 2,900 percent under public management—and today the Metropolitan Transportation Authority still manages to lose about $2 per ride. Meanwhile, a jitney driver can provide better

service at lower prices and still make a profit.

"Transit could be profitable again if entrepreneurs are given a chance," says Daniel B. Klein, an economist at Santa Clara University in California and the co-author of *Curb Rights*, a new book from the Brookings Institution on mass transit. "Government has demonstrated that it has no more business producing transit than producing cornflakes. It should concentrate instead on establishing new rules to foster competition." To encourage private operators to make a long-term investment in regular service along a route, the Brookings researchers recommend selling them exclusive "curb rights" to pick up passengers waiting at certain stops along the route. That way part-time opportunists couldn't swoop in to steal regular customers from a long-term operator. But to encourage competition, at other corners along the route there should also be common stops where passengers could be picked up by any licensed jitney or bus.

Elements of this system already exist where jitneys have informally established their own stops separate from the regular buses, but the City Council is trying to eliminate these competitors. Besides denying licenses to new drivers like Cummins, the Council has forbidden veteran drivers with licenses to operate on bus routes. Unless these restrictions are overturned in court—a suit on the

EVAN KAFKA

Vincent Cummins: Outlaw Entrepreneur

drivers' behalf has been filed by the Institute for Justice, a public-interest law firm in Washington—the vans can compete only by breaking the law. At this very moment, despite the best efforts of the police and the Transport Workers Union, somewhere in New York a serial predator like Cummins is luring another unsuspecting victim. He may even be making change for a $5 bill.

Source: *The New York Times Magazine,* August 10, 1997, p. 22. Copyright © 1997 by The New York Times Co. Reprinted by permission.

QuickQuiz Describe the ways policymakers can respond to the inefficiencies caused by monopolies. List a potential problem with each of these policy responses.

PRICE DISCRIMINATION

So far we have been assuming that the monopoly firm charges the same price to all customers. Yet in many cases firms try to sell the same good to different customers for different prices, even though the costs of producing for the two customers are the same. This practice is called **price discrimination.**

price discrimination
the business practice of selling the same good at different prices to different customers

Before discussing the behavior of a price-discriminating monopolist, we should note that price discrimination is not possible when a good is sold in a competitive market. In a competitive market, there are many firms selling the same good at the market price. No firm is willing to charge a lower price to any customer because the firm can sell all it wants at the market price. And if any firm tried to charge a higher price to a customer, that customer would buy from another firm. For a firm to price discriminate, it must have some market power.

A Parable about Pricing

To understand why a monopolist would want to price discriminate, let's consider a simple example. Imagine that you are the president of Readalot Publishing Company. Readalot's best-selling author has just written her latest novel. To keep things simple, let's imagine that you pay the author a flat $2 million for the exclusive rights to publish the book. Let's also assume that the cost of printing the book is zero. Readalot's profit, therefore, is the revenue it gets from selling the book minus the $2 million it has paid to the author. Given these assumptions, how would you, as Readalot's president, decide what price to charge for the book?

Your first step in setting the price is to estimate what the demand for the book is likely to be. Readalot's marketing department tells you that the book will attract two types of readers. The book will appeal to the author's 100,000 die-hard fans. These fans will be willing to pay as much as $30 for the book. In addition, the book will appeal to about 400,000 less enthusiastic readers who will be willing to pay up to $5 for the book.

What price maximizes Readalot's profit? There are two natural prices to consider: $30 is the highest price Readalot can charge and still get the 100,000 die-hard fans, and $5 is the highest price it can charge and still get the entire market of 500,000 potential readers. It is a matter of simple arithmetic to solve Readalot's problem. At a price of $30, Readalot sells 100,000 copies, has revenue of $3 million, and makes profit of $1 million. At a price of $5, it sells 500,000 copies, has revenue of $2.5 million, and makes profit of $500,000. Thus, Readalot maximizes profit by charging $30 and forgoing the opportunity to sell to the 400,000 less enthusiastic readers.

Notice that Readalot's decision causes a deadweight loss. There are 400,000 readers willing to pay $5 for the book, and the marginal cost of providing it to them is zero. Thus, $2 million of total surplus is lost when Readalot charges the higher price. This deadweight loss is the usual inefficiency that arises whenever a monopolist charges a price above marginal cost.

Now suppose that Readalot's marketing department makes an important discovery: These two groups of readers are in separate markets. All the die-hard fans live in Australia, and all the other readers live in the United States. Moreover, it is difficult for readers in one country to buy books in the other. How does this discovery affect Readalot's marketing strategy?

In this case, the company can make even more profit. To the 100,000 Australian readers, it can charge $30 for the book. To the 400,000 American readers, it can charge $5 for the book. In this case, revenue is $3 million in Australia and $2 million in the United States, for a total of $5 million. Profit is then $3 million, which is substantially greater than the $1 million the company could earn charging the same $30 price to all customers. Not surprisingly, Readalot chooses to follow this strategy of price discrimination.

Although the story of Readalot Publishing is hypothetical, it describes accurately the business practice of many publishing companies. Textbooks, for example, are often sold at a lower price in Europe than in the United States. Even more important is the price differential between hardcover books and paperbacks. When a publisher has a new novel, it initially releases an expensive hardcover edition and later releases a cheaper paperback edition. The difference in price between these two editions far exceeds the difference in printing costs. The publisher's goal is just as in our example. By selling the hardcover to die-hard fans and the paperback to less enthusiastic readers, the publisher price discriminates and raises its profit.

The Moral of the Story

Like any parable, the story of Readalot Publishing is stylized. Yet, also like any parable, it teaches some important and general lessons. In this case, there are three lessons to be learned about price discrimination.

The first and most obvious lesson is that price discrimination is a rational strategy for a profit-maximizing monopolist. In other words, by charging different prices to different customers, a monopolist can increase its profit. In essence, a price-discriminating monopolist charges each customer a price closer to his or her willingness to pay than is possible with a single price.

The second lesson is that price discrimination requires the ability to separate customers according to their willingness to pay. In our example, customers were separated geographically. But sometimes monopolists choose other differences, such as age or income, to distinguish among customers.

A corollary to this second lesson is that certain market forces can prevent firms from price discriminating. In particular, one such force is *arbitrage*, the process of buying a good in one market at a low price and selling it in another market at a higher price in order to profit from the price difference. In our example, suppose that Australian bookstores could buy the book in the United States and resell it to Australian readers. This arbitrage would prevent Readalot from price discriminating because no Australian would buy the book at the higher price.

The third lesson from our parable is perhaps the most surprising: Price discrimination can raise economic welfare. Recall that a deadweight loss arises when Readalot charges a single $30 price, because the 400,000 less enthusiastic readers do not end up with the book, even though they value it at more than its marginal cost of production. By contrast, when Readalot price discriminates, all readers end

up with the book, and the outcome is efficient. Thus, price discrimination can eliminate the inefficiency inherent in monopoly pricing.

Note that the increase in welfare from price discrimination shows up as higher
producer surplus rather than higher consumer surplus. In our example, consumers are no better off for having bought the book: The price they pay exactly
equals the value they place on the book, so they receive no consumer surplus. The
entire increase in total surplus from price discrimination accrues to Readalot Publishing in the form of higher profit.

The Analytics of Price Discrimination

Let's consider a bit more formally how price discrimination affects economic welfare. We begin by assuming that the monopolist can price discriminate perfectly.
Perfect price discrimination describes a situation in which the monopolist knows exactly the willingness to pay of each customer and can charge each customer a different price. In this case, the monopolist charges each customer exactly his
willingness to pay, and the monopolist gets the entire surplus in every transaction.

Figure 10 shows producer and consumer surplus with and without price discrimination. Without price discrimination, the firm charges a single price above
marginal cost, as shown in panel (a). Because some potential customers who value
the good at more than marginal cost do not buy it at this high price, the monopoly

---

FIGURE 10

Welfare with and without Price Discrimination

Panel (a) shows a monopolist that charges the same price to all customers. Total surplus in this market equals the sum of profit (producer surplus) and consumer surplus. Panel (b) shows a monopolist that can perfectly price discriminate. Because consumer surplus equals zero, total surplus now equals the firm's profit. Comparing these two panels, you can see that perfect price discrimination raises profit, raises total surplus, and lowers consumer surplus.

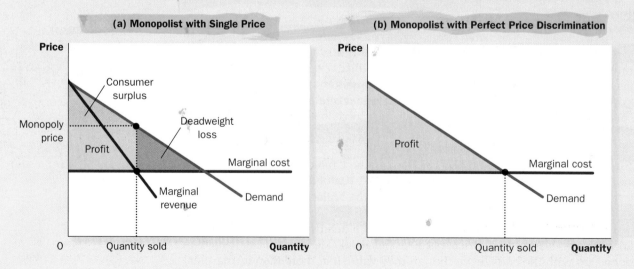

causes a deadweight loss. Yet when a firm can perfectly price discriminate, as shown in panel (b), each customer who values the good at more than marginal cost buys the good and is charged his willingness to pay. All mutually beneficial trades take place, there is no deadweight loss, and the entire surplus derived from the market goes to the monopoly producer in the form of profit.

In reality, of course, price discrimination is not perfect. Customers do not walk into stores with signs displaying their willingness to pay. Instead, firms price discriminate by dividing customers into groups: young versus old, weekday versus weekend shoppers, Americans versus Australians, and so on. Unlike those in our parable of Readalot Publishing, customers within each group differ in their willingness to pay for the product, making perfect price discrimination impossible.

How does this imperfect price discrimination affect welfare? The analysis of these pricing schemes is quite complicated, and it turns out that there is no general answer to this question. Compared to the monopoly outcome with a single price, imperfect price discrimination can raise, lower, or leave unchanged total surplus in a market. The only certain conclusion is that price discrimination raises the monopoly's profit—otherwise the firm would choose to charge all customers the same price.

Examples of Price Discrimination

Firms in our economy use various business strategies aimed at charging different prices to different customers. Now that we understand the economics of price discrimination, let's consider some examples.

Movie Tickets   Many movie theaters charge a lower price for children and senior citizens than for other patrons. This fact is hard to explain in a competitive market. In a competitive market, price equals marginal cost, and the marginal cost of providing a seat for a child or senior citizen is the same as the marginal cost of providing a seat for anyone else. Yet this fact is easily explained if movie theaters have some local monopoly power and if children and senior citizens have a lower willingness to pay for a ticket. In this case, movie theaters raise their profit by price discriminating.

Airline Prices   Seats on airplanes are sold at many different prices. Most airlines charge a lower price for a round-trip ticket between two cities if the traveler stays over a Saturday night. At first this seems odd. Why should it matter to the airline whether a passenger stays over a Saturday night? The reason is that this rule provides a way to separate business travelers and personal travelers. A passenger on a business trip has a high willingness to pay and, most likely, does not want to stay over a Saturday night. By contrast, a passenger traveling for personal reasons has a lower willingness to pay and is more likely to be willing to stay over a Saturday night. Thus, the airlines can successfully price discriminate by charging a lower price for passengers who stay over a Saturday night.

Discount Coupons   Many companies offer discount coupons to the public in newspapers and magazines. A buyer simply has to clip out the coupon in order to get $0.50 off his next purchase. Why do companies offer these coupons? Why don't they just cut the price of the product by $0.50?

"Would it bother you to hear how little I paid for this flight?"

The answer is that coupons allow companies to price discriminate. Companies know that not all customers are willing to spend the time to clip out coupons. Moreover, the willingness to clip coupons is related to the customer's willingness to pay for the good. A rich and busy executive is unlikely to spend her time clipping discount coupons out of the newspaper, and she is probably willing to pay a higher price for many goods. A person who is unemployed is more likely to clip coupons and has a lower willingness to pay. Thus, by charging a lower price only to those customers who clip coupons, firms can successfully price discriminate.

Financial Aid Many colleges and universities give financial aid to needy students. One can view this policy as a type of price discrimination. Wealthy students have greater financial resources and, therefore, a higher willingness to pay than needy students. By charging high tuition and selectively offering financial aid, schools charge prices to customers based on the value they place on going to that school. This behavior is like that of any price-discriminating monopolist.

IN THE NEWS

WHY PEOPLE PAY MORE THAN DOGS

Economist Hal Varian discusses a classic example of price discrimination.

A Big Factor in Prescription Drug Pricing: Location, Location, Location

By Hal R. Varian

Prescription drugs have become politicized. Al Gore recently criticized the manufacturer of the arthritis drug Lodine for selling it for $108 a month when prescribed for humans and $38 when prescribed for dogs. It's not just the doggy divide that has politicians upset; international price differences for drugs are another flash point. The House and Senate recently approved a measure allowing pharmacists to import prescription drugs

from countries where they sell for substantially less than in the United States.

Charging different prices for humans and animals, or different prices to consumers in different countries, is what economists call "third-degree price discrimination." It is a common practice for pharmaceutical companies. A month's supply of the antidepressant Zoloft sells for $29.74 in Austria, $32.91 in Luxembourg, $40.97 in Mexico and $64.67 in the United States.

This kind of differential pricing is motivated in part by drug companies' cost structure and in part by differences in bargaining power. It can cost millions of

dollars to research, develop, test, and market a new drug. Once these fixed costs are incurred, however, actually producing the drug may cost very little. Since the market price is often far greater than the marginal cost of production, there is always a temptation to cut prices to generate incremental sales and profit. The problem is that cutting prices across the board tends to reduce revenue.

The natural strategy is to *selectively* cut prices and set different prices for different markets. Drugs sold for humans generally sell for more than drugs sold for animals. Drugs in rich countries tend to cost more than drugs in poor

Quantity Discounts So far in our examples of price discrimination, the monopolist charges different prices to different customers. Sometimes, however, monopolists price discriminate by charging different prices to the same customer for different units that the customer buys. For example, many firms offer lower prices to customers who buy large quantities. A bakery might charge $0.50 for each donut, but $5 for a dozen. This is a form of price discrimination because the customer pays a higher price for the first unit bought than for the twelfth. Quantity discounts are often a successful way of price discriminating because a customer's willingness to pay for an additional unit declines as the customer buys more units.

QuickQuiz Give two examples of price discrimination. • How does perfect price discrimination affect consumer surplus, producer surplus, and total surplus?

countries. A daily dose of the AIDS drug PLC sells for $18 in the United States and $9 in Uganda, while a generic equivalent sells for $1.50 a day in Brazil. Even at $9 a dose, the drug company makes a profit on incremental sales. But if the drug were sold at $9 to everyone, profits would be substantially lower than they would be under differential pricing.

The United States ends up paying more for drugs since it is much richer than the rest of the world and tends to spend a large fraction of that wealth on health care. Furthermore, in most countries, a single governmental health care provider bargains over drug prices. America's health care system is much more fragmented, which tends to reduce the bargaining power of health care providers in negotiating drug prices.

Price discrimination is not popular with consumers, especially those paying the higher price. What does economics say about whether this kind of differential pricing is good or bad? To answer this question, we have to ask what price would prevail if only one price could be charged.

Imagine that there are only two countries involved, the United States and Uganda, and PLC sells for $18 here and $9 in Uganda. If the drug company had to charge the same price in each country, what would it be? In this case, it is likely that the price would be closer to $18 than to $9. True, sales would drop significantly in Uganda, but that loss in revenue would be very small compared with the revenue loss in the United States from setting a price close to $9 because it is a significantly larger market. In this case, mandating a fixed price makes the Ugandans a lot worse off and does little for American consumers.

But it could work out differently. Imagine an antimalarial drug that lots of people in Uganda might buy at $2 a dose and few people in America might buy at $10 a dose. If the Ugandan market is more than five times the American market, the drug company, if it could set only one price, would make more revenue by setting that price at $2. If the manufactur-

ing cost of the drug is small enough, this would also be the more profitable price.

The critical question, from the viewpoint of economics, is whether differential pricing or a flat price leads to more people getting the drug. In the case of the AIDS drug, differential pricing leads to more total consumption; in the case of the antimalarial drug, it is the other way around. . . .

There is no easy answer as to whether price discrimination, in general, is a good thing or a bad thing. It tends to raise additional revenue that can be plowed back into research and development, which creates better incentives to invest in drug development. When it allows markets to be served that would otherwise be ignored, price discrimination will tend to be socially useful. But if differential pricing is just an excuse to raise prices that would otherwise be low, it doesn't have much to recommend it.

Source: *The New York Times*, September 21, 2000, p. C2. Copyright © 2000 by The New York Times Co. Reprinted by permission.

CONCLUSION: THE PREVALENCE OF MONOPOLY

This chapter has discussed the behavior of firms that have control over the prices they charge. We have seen that these firms behave very differently from the competitive firms studied in the previous chapter. Table 2 summarizes some of the key similarities and differences between competitive and monopoly markets.

From the standpoint of public policy, a crucial result is that monopolists produce less than the socially efficient quantity and charge prices above marginal cost. As a result, they cause deadweight losses. In some cases, these inefficiencies can be mitigated through price discrimination by the monopolist, but other times they call for policymakers to take an active role.

How prevalent are the problems of monopoly? There are two answers to this question.

In one sense, monopolies are common. Most firms have some control over the prices they charge. They are not forced to charge the market price for their goods, because their goods are not exactly the same as those offered by other firms. A Ford Taurus is not the same as a Toyota Camry. Ben and Jerry's ice cream is not the same as Breyer's. Each of these goods has a downward-sloping demand curve, which gives each producer some degree of monopoly power.

Yet firms with substantial monopoly power are quite rare. Few goods are truly unique. Most have substitutes that, even if not exactly the same, are very similar. Ben and Jerry can raise the price of their ice cream a little without losing all their sales; but if they raise it very much, sales will fall substantially.

In the end, monopoly power is a matter of degree. It is true that many firms have some monopoly power. It is also true that their monopoly power is usually limited. In these cases, we will not go far wrong assuming that firms operate in competitive markets, even if that is not precisely the case.

TABLE 2

Competition versus Monopoly: A Summary Comparison

	Competition	Monopoly
Similarities		
Goal of firms	Maximize profits	Maximize profits
Rule for maximizing	$MR = MC$	$MR = MC$
Can earn economic profits in the short run?	Yes	Yes
Differences		
Number of firms	Many	One
Marginal revenue	$MR = P$	$MR < P$
Price	$P = MC$	$P > MC$
Produces welfare-maximizing level of output?	Yes	No
Entry in long run?	Yes	No
Can earn economic profits in long run?	No	Yes
Price discrimination possible?	No	Yes

SUMMARY

- A monopoly is a firm that is the sole seller in its market. A monopoly arises when a single firm owns a key resource, when the government gives a firm the exclusive right to produce a good, or when a single firm can supply the entire market at a smaller cost than many firms could.

- Because a monopoly is the sole producer in its market, it faces a downward-sloping demand curve for its product. When a monopoly increases production by 1 unit, it causes the price of its good to fall, which reduces the amount of revenue earned on all units produced. As a result, a monopoly's marginal revenue is always below the price of its good.

- Like a competitive firm, a monopoly firm maximizes profit by producing the quantity at which marginal revenue equals marginal cost. The monopoly then chooses the price at which that quantity is demanded. Unlike a competitive firm, a monopoly firm's price exceeds its marginal revenue, so its price exceeds marginal cost.

- A monopolist's profit-maximizing level of output is below the level that maximizes the sum of consumer and producer surplus. That is, when the monopoly charges a price above marginal cost, some consumers who value the good more than its cost of production do not buy it. As a result, monopoly causes deadweight losses similar to the deadweight losses caused by taxes.

- Policymakers can respond to the inefficiency of monopoly behavior in four ways. They can use the antitrust laws to try to make the industry more competitive. They can regulate the prices that the monopoly charges. They can turn the monopolist into a government-run enterprise. Or, if the market failure is deemed small compared to the inevitable imperfections of policies, they can do nothing at all.

- Monopolists often can raise their profits by charging different prices for the same good based on a buyer's willingness to pay. This practice of price discrimination can raise economic welfare by getting the good to some consumers who otherwise would not buy it. In the extreme case of perfect price discrimination, the deadweight losses of monopoly are completely eliminated. More generally, when price discrimination is imperfect, it can either raise or lower welfare compared to the outcome with a single monopoly price.

KEY CONCEPTS

monopoly, p. 314   natural monopoly, p. 316   price discrimination, p. 334

QUESTIONS FOR REVIEW

1. Give an example of a government-created monopoly. Is creating this monopoly necessarily bad public policy? Explain.

2. Define natural monopoly. What does the size of a market have to do with whether an industry is a natural monopoly?

3. Why is a monopolist's marginal revenue less than the price of its good? Can marginal revenue ever be negative? Explain.

4. Draw the demand, marginal-revenue, and marginal-cost curves for a monopolist. Show the profit-maximizing level of output. Show the profit-maximizing price.

5. In your diagram from the previous question, show the level of output that maximizes total surplus. Show the deadweight loss from the monopoly. Explain your answer.

6. What gives the government the power to regulate mergers between firms? From the standpoint of the welfare of society, give a good reason and a bad reason that two firms might want to merge.

7. Describe the two problems that arise when regulators tell a natural monopoly

that it must set a price equal to marginal cost.

8. Give two examples of price discrimination. In each case, explain why the monopolist chooses to follow this business strategy.

PROBLEMS AND APPLICATIONS

1. A publisher faces the following demand schedule for the next novel of one of its popular authors:

Price	Quantity Demanded
$100	0
90	100,000
80	200,000
70	300,000
60	400,000
50	500,000
40	600,000
30	700,000
20	800,000
10	900,000
0	1,000,000

The author is paid $2 million to write the book, and the marginal cost of publishing the book is a constant $10 per book.

a. Compute total revenue, total cost, and profit at each quantity. What quantity would a profit-maximizing publisher choose? What price would it charge?

b. Compute marginal revenue. (Recall that MR = ΔTR/ΔQ.) How does marginal revenue compare to the price? Explain.

c. Graph the marginal-revenue, marginal-cost, and demand curves. At what quantity do the marginal-revenue and marginal-cost curves cross? What does this signify?

d. In your graph, shade in the deadweight loss. Explain in words what this means.

e. If the author were paid $3 million instead of $2 million to write the book, how would this affect the publisher's decision regarding the price to charge? Explain.

f. Suppose the publisher was not profit-maximizing but was concerned with

maximizing economic efficiency. What price would it charge for the book? How much profit would it make at this price?

2. Suppose that a natural monopolist was required by law to charge average total cost. On a diagram, label the price charged and the deadweight loss to society relative to marginal-cost pricing.

3. Consider the delivery of mail. In general, what is the shape of the average-total-cost curve? How might the shape differ between isolated rural areas and densely populated urban areas? How might the shape have changed over time? Explain.

4. Suppose the Clean Springs Water Company has a monopoly on bottled water sales in California. If the price of tap water increases, what is the change in Clean Springs' profit-maximizing levels of output, price, and profit? Explain in words and with a graph.

5. A small town is served by many competing supermarkets, which have constant marginal cost.

a. Using a diagram of the market for groceries, show the consumer surplus, producer surplus, and total surplus.

b. Now suppose that the independent supermarkets combine into one chain. Using a new diagram, show the new consumer surplus, producer surplus, and total surplus. Relative to the competitive market, what is the transfer from consumers to producers? What is the deadweight loss?

6. Johnny Rockabilly has just finished recording his latest CD. His record company's marketing department determines that the demand for the CD is as follows:

Price	Number of CDs
$24	10,000
22	20,000
20	30,000
18	40,000
16	50,000
14	60,000

The company can produce the CD with no fixed cost and a variable cost of $5 per CD.

a. Find total revenue for quantity equal to 10,000, 20,000, and so on. What is the marginal revenue for each 10,000 increase in the quantity sold?

b. What quantity of CDs would maximize profit? What would the price be? What would the profit be?

c. If you were Johnny's agent, what recording fee would you advise Johnny to demand from the record company? Why?

7. In 1969 the government charged IBM with monopolizing the computer market. The government argued (correctly) that a large share of all mainframe computers sold in the United States were produced by IBM. IBM argued (correctly) that a much smaller share of the market for *all* types of computers consisted of IBM products. Based on these facts, do you think that the government should have brought suit against IBM for violating the antitrust laws? Explain.

8. A company is considering building a bridge across a river. The bridge would cost $2 million to build and nothing to maintain. The following table shows the company's anticipated demand over the lifetime of the bridge:

Price per Crossing	Number of Crossings (in thousands)
$8	0
7	100
6	200
5	300
4	400
3	500
2	600
1	700
0	800

a. If the company were to build the bridge, what would be its profit-maximizing price?

Would that be the efficient level of output? Why or why not?

b. If the company is interested in maximizing profit, should it build the bridge? What would be its profit or loss?

c. If the government were to build the bridge, what price should it charge?

d. Should the government build the bridge? Explain.

9. The Placebo Drug Company holds a patent on one of its discoveries.

a. Assuming that the production of the drug involves rising marginal cost, draw a diagram to illustrate Placebo's profit-maximizing price and quantity. Also show Placebo's profits.

b. Now suppose that the government imposes a tax on each bottle of the drug produced. On a new diagram, illustrate Placebo's new price and quantity. How does each compare to your answer in part (a)?

c. Although it is not easy to see in your diagrams, the tax reduces Placebo's profit. Explain why this must be true.

d. Instead of the tax per bottle, suppose that the government imposes a tax on Placebo of $10,000 regardless of how many bottles are produced. How does this tax affect Placebo's price, quantity, and profits? Explain.

10. Larry, Curly, and Moe run the only saloon in town. Larry wants to sell as many drinks as possible without losing money. Curly wants the saloon to bring in as much revenue as possible. Moe wants to make the largest possible profits. Using a single diagram of the saloon's demand curve and its cost curves, show the price and quantity combinations favored by each of the three partners. Explain.

11. For many years AT&T was a regulated monopoly, providing both local and long-distance telephone service.

a. Explain why long-distance phone service was originally a natural monopoly.

b. Over the past two decades, many companies have launched communication satellites, each of which can transmit a limited number of calls. How did the growing role of satellites change the cost structure of long-distance phone service?

After a lengthy legal battle with the government, AT&T agreed to compete with other companies in the long-distance market. It also agreed to spin off its local phone service into the "Baby Bells," which remain highly regulated.

   c. Why might it be efficient to have competition in long-distance phone service and regulated monopolies in local phone service?

12. The Best Computer Company just developed a new computer chip, on which it immediately acquires a patent.

   a. Draw a diagram that shows the consumer surplus, producer surplus, and total surplus in the market for this new chip.

   b. What happens to these three measures of surplus if the firm can perfectly price discriminate? What is the change in deadweight loss? What transfers occur?

13. Explain why a monopolist will always produce a quantity at which the demand curve is elastic. (Hint: If demand is inelastic and the firm raises its price, what happens to total revenue and total costs?)

14. Singer Britney Spears has a monopoly over a scarce resource: herself. She is the only person who can produce a Britney Spears concert. Does this fact imply that the government should regulate the prices of her concerts? Why or why not?

15. Napster, the on-line file-swapping service, allowed people to use the Internet to download copies of their favorite songs from other people's computers without cost. In what sense did Napster enhance economic efficiency in the short run? In what sense might Napster have reduced economic efficiency in the long run? Why do you think the courts eventually shut Napster down? Do you think this was the right policy?

16. Many schemes for price discriminating involve some cost. For example, discount coupons take up time and resources from both the buyer and the seller. This question considers the implications of costly price discrimination. To keep things simple, let's assume that our monopolist's production costs are simply proportional to output, so that average total cost and marginal cost are constant and equal to each other.

   a. Draw the cost, demand, and marginal-revenue curves for the monopolist. Show the price the monopolist would charge without price discrimination.

   b. In your diagram, mark the area equal to the monopolist's profit and call it X. Mark the area equal to consumer surplus and call it Y. Mark the area equal to the deadweight loss and call it Z.

   c. Now suppose that the monopolist can perfectly price discriminate. What is the monopolist's profit? (Give your answer in terms of X, Y, and Z.)

   d. What is the change in the monopolist's profit from price discrimination? What is the change in total surplus from price discrimination? Which change is larger? Explain. (Give your answer in terms of X, Y, and Z.)

   e. Now suppose that there is some cost of price discrimination. To model this cost, let's assume that the monopolist has to pay a fixed cost C in order to price discriminate. How would a monopolist make the decision whether to pay this fixed cost? (Give your answer in terms of X, Y, Z, and C.)

   f. How would a benevolent social planner, who cares about total surplus, decide whether the monopolist should price discriminate? (Give your answer in terms of X, Y, Z, and C.)

   g. Compare your answers to parts (e) and (f). How does the monopolist's incentive to price discriminate differ from the social planner's? Is it possible that the monopolist will price discriminate even though it is not socially desirable?

16

OLIGOPOLY

If you go to a store to buy tennis balls, it is likely that you will come home with one of four brands: Wilson, Penn, Dunlop, or Spalding. These four companies make almost all of the tennis balls sold in the United States. Together these firms determine the quantity of tennis balls produced and, given the market demand curve, the price at which tennis balls are sold.

How can we describe the market for tennis balls? The previous two chapters discussed two types of market structure. In a competitive market, each firm is so small compared to the market that it cannot influence the price of its product and, therefore, takes the price as given by market conditions. In a monopolized market, a single firm supplies the entire market for a good, and that firm can choose any price and quantity on the market demand curve.

The market for tennis balls fits neither the competitive nor the monopoly model. Competition and monopoly are extreme forms of market structure. Competition occurs when there are many firms in a market offering essentially identical products; monopoly occurs when there is only one firm in a market. It is natural to start the study of industrial organization with these polar cases, for they are the easiest cases to understand. Yet many industries, including the tennis ball industry, fall somewhere between these two extremes. Firms in these industries have competitors but, at the same time, do not face so much competition that they are price takers. Economists call this situation *imperfect competition*.

In this chapter we discuss the types of imperfect competition and examine a particular type called *oligopoly*. The essence of an oligopolistic market is that there are only a few sellers. As a result, the actions of any one seller in the market can have a large impact on the profits of all the other sellers. That is, oligopolistic firms are interdependent in a way that competitive firms are not. Our goal in this chapter is to see how this interdependence shapes the firms' behavior and what problems it raises for public policy.

BETWEEN MONOPOLY AND PERFECT COMPETITION

The previous two chapters analyzed markets with many competitive firms and markets with a single monopoly firm. In Chapter 14, we saw that the price in a perfectly competitive market always equals the marginal cost of production. We also saw that, in the long run, entry and exit drive economic profit to zero, so the price also equals average total cost. In Chapter 15, we saw how firms with market power can use that power to keep prices above marginal cost, leading to a positive economic profit for the firm and a deadweight loss for society.

The cases of perfect competition and monopoly illustrate some important ideas about how markets work. Most markets in the economy, however, include elements of both these cases and, therefore, are not completely described by either of them. The typical firm in the economy faces competition, but the competition is not so rigorous as to make the firm exactly described by the price-taking firm analyzed in Chapter 14. The typical firm also has some degree of market power, but its market power is not so great that the firm can be exactly described by the monopoly firm analyzed in Chapter 15. In other words, the typical firm in our economy is imperfectly competitive.

oligopoly
a market structure in which only a few sellers offer similar or identical products

monopolistic competition
a market structure in which many firms sell products that are similar but not identical

There are two types of imperfectly competitive markets. An **oligopoly** is a market with only a few sellers, each offering a product similar or identical to the others. One example is the market for tennis balls. Another is the world market for crude oil: A few countries in the Middle East control much of the world's oil reserves. **Monopolistic competition** describes a market structure in which there are many firms selling products that are similar but not identical. Examples include the markets for novels, movies, CDs, and computer games. In a monopolistically competitive market, each firm has a monopoly over the product it makes, but many other firms make similar products that compete for the same customers.

Figure 1 summarizes the four types of market structure. The first question to ask about any market is how many firms there are. If there is only one firm, the market is a monopoly. If there are only a few firms, the market is an oligopoly. If there are many firms, we need to ask another question: Do the firms sell identical or differentiated products? If the many firms sell differentiated products, the market is monopolistically competitive. If the many firms sell identical products, the market is perfectly competitive.

Reality, of course, is never as clear-cut as theory. In some cases, you may find it hard to decide what structure best describes a market. There is, for instance,

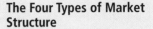

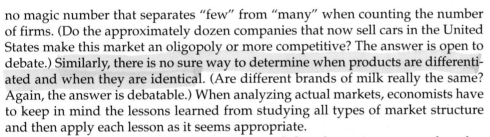

The Four Types of Market Structure

Economists who study industrial organization divide markets into four types—monopoly, oligopoly, monopolistic competition, and perfect competition.

no magic number that separates "few" from "many" when counting the number of firms. (Do the approximately dozen companies that now sell cars in the United States make this market an oligopoly or more competitive? The answer is open to debate.) Similarly, there is no sure way to determine when products are differentiated and when they are identical. (Are different brands of milk really the same? Again, the answer is debatable.) When analyzing actual markets, economists have to keep in mind the lessons learned from studying all types of market structure and then apply each lesson as it seems appropriate.

Now that we understand how economists define the various types of market structure, we can continue our analysis of them. In the next chapter we analyze monopolistic competition. In this chapter we examine oligopoly.

QuickQuiz Define *oligopoly* and *monopolistic competition* and give an example of each.

MARKETS WITH ONLY A FEW SELLERS

Because an oligopolistic market has only a small group of sellers, a key feature of oligopoly is the tension between cooperation and self-interest. The group of oligopolists is best off cooperating and acting like a monopolist—producing a small quantity of output and charging a price above marginal cost. Yet because each oligopolist cares about only its own profit, there are powerful incentives at work that hinder a group of firms from maintaining the monopoly outcome.

A Duopoly Example

To understand the behavior of oligopolies, let's consider an oligopoly with only two members, called a *duopoly*. Duopoly is the simplest type of oligopoly. Oligopolies with three or more members face the same problems as oligopolies with only two members, so we do not lose much by starting with the case of duopoly.

Imagine a town in which only two residents—Jack and Jill—own wells that produce water safe for drinking. Each Saturday, Jack and Jill decide how many gallons of water to pump, bring the water to town, and sell it for whatever price the market will bear. To keep things simple, suppose that Jack and Jill can pump as much water as they want without cost. That is, the marginal cost of water equals zero.

Table 1 shows the town's demand schedule for water. The first column shows the total quantity demanded, and the second column shows the price. If the two well owners sell a total of 10 gallons of water, water goes for $110 a gallon. If they sell a total of 20 gallons, the price falls to $100 a gallon. And so on. If you graphed these two columns of numbers, you would get a standard downward-sloping demand curve.

The last column in Table 1 shows the total revenue from the sale of water. It equals the quantity sold times the price. Because there is no cost to pumping water, the total revenue of the two producers equals their total profit.

Let's now consider how the organization of the town's water industry affects the price of water and the quantity of water sold.

Competition, Monopolies, and Cartels

Before considering the price and quantity of water that would result from the duopoly of Jack and Jill, let's discuss briefly the two market structures we already understand: competition and monopoly.

Consider first what would happen if the market for water were perfectly competitive. In a competitive market, the production decisions of each firm drive price equal to marginal cost. In the market for water, marginal cost is zero. Thus, under competition, the equilibrium price of water would be zero, and the equilibrium quantity would be 120 gallons. The price of water would reflect the cost of producing it, and the efficient quantity of water would be produced and consumed.

Now consider how a monopoly would behave. Table 1 shows that total profit is maximized at a quantity of 60 gallons and a price of $60 a gallon. A profit-maximizing monopolist, therefore, would produce this quantity and charge this price. As is standard for monopolies, price would exceed marginal cost. The result would be inefficient, for the quantity of water produced and consumed would fall short of the socially efficient level of 120 gallons.

What outcome should we expect from our duopolists? One possibility is that Jack and Jill get together and agree on the quantity of water to produce and the price to charge for it. Such an agreement among firms over production and price is called **collusion**, and the group of firms acting in unison is called a **cartel**. Once a cartel is formed, the market is in effect served by a monopoly, and we can apply our analysis from Chapter 15. That is, if Jack and Jill were to collude, they would agree on the monopoly outcome because that outcome maximizes the total profit that the producers can get from the market. Our two producers would produce a total of 60 gallons, which would be sold at a price of $60 a gallon. Once again, price exceeds marginal cost, and the outcome is socially inefficient.

collusion
an agreement among firms in a market about quantities to produce or prices to charge

cartel
a group of firms acting in unison

TABLE 1

The Demand Schedule for Water

Quantity (in gallons)	Price	Total Revenue (and total profit)
0	$120	$ 0
10	110	1,100
20	100	2,000
30	90	2,700
40	80	3,200
50	70	3,500
60	60	3,600
70	50	3,500
80	40	3,200
90	30	2,700
100	20	2,000
110	10	1,100
120	0	0

(handwritten annotations: "← where monopilist would produce.", "P > MC", "← Perfectlly competitive", "Socially effcient →", "P = MC = AR", "P = MR = AR = MC")

A cartel must agree not only on the total level of production but also on the amount produced by each member. In our case, Jack and Jill must agree how to split between themselves the monopoly production of 60 gallons. Each member of the cartel will want a larger share of the market because a larger market share means larger profit. If Jack and Jill agreed to split the market equally, each would produce 30 gallons, the price would be $60 a gallon, and each would get a profit of $1,800.

The Equilibrium for an Oligopoly

Although oligopolists would like to form cartels and earn monopoly profits, often that is not possible. As we discuss later in this chapter, antitrust laws prohibit explicit agreements among oligopolists as a matter of public policy. In addition, squabbling among cartel members over how to divide the profit in the market sometimes makes agreement among them impossible. Let's therefore consider what happens if Jack and Jill decide separately how much water to produce.

At first, one might expect Jack and Jill to reach the monopoly outcome on their own, for this outcome maximizes their joint profit. In the absence of a binding agreement, however, the monopoly outcome is unlikely. To see why, imagine that Jack expects Jill to produce only 30 gallons (half of the monopoly quantity). Jack would reason as follows:

"I could produce 30 gallons as well. In this case, a total of 60 gallons of water would be sold at a price of $60 a gallon. My profit would be $1,800 (30 gallons × $60 a gallon). Alternatively, I could produce 40 gallons. In this case, a total of 70 gallons of water would be sold at a price of $50 a gallon. My profit would be $2,000 (40 gallons × $50 a gallon). Even though total profit in the market would fall, my profit would be higher, because I would have a larger share of the market."

IN THE NEWS

MODERN PIRATES

Cartels are rare, in part because the antitrust laws make them illegal. As the following article describes, however, ocean shipping firms enjoy an unusual exemption from these laws and, as a result, charge higher prices than they otherwise would.

As U.S. Trade Grows, Shipping Cartels Get a Bit More Scrutiny

By Anna Wilde Matthews

RUTHERFORD, N.J.—Every two weeks, in an unobtrusive office building here, about 20 shipping-line managers gather for their usual meeting. They sit around a long conference table, exchange small talk over bagels and coffee and then begin discussing what they will charge to move cargo across the Atlantic Ocean.

All very routine, except for one detail: They don't work for the same company. Each represents a different shipping line, supposedly competing for business. Under U.S. antitrust law, most people doing this would end up in court.

But shipping isn't like other businesses. Many of the world's big shipping lines, from Sea-Land Service Inc. of the U.S. to A.P. Moller/Maersk Line of Denmark, are members of a little-noticed cartel that for many decades has set rates on tens of billions of dollars of cargo.

Most U.S. consumer goods exported or imported by sea are affected to some degree. The cartel—really a series of cartels, one for each major shipping route—can tell importers and exporters when shipping contracts start and when they end. They can favor one port over another, enough to swing badly needed trade away from an entire city. And because the shipping industry has an antitrust exemption from Congress, all of this is legal.

"This is one of the last legalized price-setting arrangements in existence," says Robert Litan, a former Justice De-

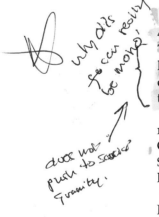

Of course, Jill might reason the same way. If so, Jack and Jill would each bring 40 gallons to town. Total sales would be 80 gallons, and the price would fall to $40. Thus, if the duopolists individually pursue their own self-interest when deciding how much to produce, they produce a total quantity greater than the monopoly quantity, charge a price lower than the monopoly price, and earn total profit less than the monopoly profit.

Although the logic of self-interest increases the duopoly's output above the monopoly level, it does not push the duopolists to reach the competitive allocation. Consider what happens when each duopolist is producing 40 gallons. The price is $40, and each duopolist makes a profit of $1,600. In this case, Jack's self-interested logic leads to a different conclusion:

"Right now, my profit is $1,600. Suppose I increase my production to 50 gallons. In this case, a total of 90 gallons of water would be sold, and the price would be $30 a gallon. Then my profit would be only $1,500. Rather than increasing production and driving down the price, I am better off keeping my production at 40 gallons."

The outcome in which Jack and Jill each produce 40 gallons looks like some sort of equilibrium. In fact, this outcome is called a *Nash equilibrium*. (It is named after

partment antitrust official. Airlines and banks couldn't do this, he says, "but if you're an ocean shipping line, there's nothing to stop you from price fixing."

You could call them the OPEC of shipping, though not quite as powerful because they can't keep members from building too many ships. To get more business, some of the shipping cartels' own members undercut cartel rates or make special deals with big customers. They also face the emergence of new competitors, which are keeping rates down in some markets.

Nonetheless, the industry is playing a bigger role now in the U.S. economy as American companies plunge more deeply into world trade. Exports over the seas have jumped 26% in the past two years and 50% since the start of the decade.

For consumers, the impact is hard to measure. Transportation costs make up 5% to 10% of the price of most goods, and increases in shipping rates are usually passed on to consumers. A limited 1993 survey by the Agriculture Department, examining $5 billion of U.S. farm exports,

concluded that the cartels were raising ocean shipping rates as much as 18%. A different report, by the Federal Trade Commission in 1995, found that when shipping lines broke free of cartel rates, contract prices were about 19% lower.

"The cartels' whole makeup is anti-consumer," says John Taylor, a transportation professor at Wayne State University in Detroit. "They're designed to keep prices up."

Some moves are afoot to change all this. The U.S. Senate is considering a bill that, for the first time in a decade, would weaken the cartels, by reducing their power to police their members. The bill, sponsored by Sen. Kay Bailey Hutchison of Texas, has the support of some other high-ranking Republicans, including Majority Leader Trent Lott. . . .

For eight decades, shipping cartels have been protected by Congress under the Shipping Act of 1916, passed at the behest of American shipping customers, who thought cartels would guarantee reliable service. The law was revised significantly only twice, in 1961 and 1984, but

both times the industry's antitrust immunity was left intact.

The most recent major review was done in 1991 by a congressional commission. It heard more than 100 witnesses, produced a 250-page report—and offered no conclusions or recommendations. . . .

The real reasons for years of inaction in Congress may be apathy and the lobbying by various groups. Dockside labor, for example, fears that secret contracts would enable ship lines to divert cargo to nonunion workers without the union knowing it. David Butz, a University of Michigan economist who has studied shipping, thinks voters aren't likely to weigh in; the cartels aren't a hot topic. "It's below the radar screen," he says. "Consumers don't realize the impact they have."

Source: *The Wall Street Journal*, October 7, 1997, p. A1. © 1997 Dow Jones & Co. Inc. Reproduced with permission of DOW JONES & CO INC in the format Textbook via Copyright Clearance Center.

economic theorist John Nash, whose life was portrayed in the book and movie *A Beautiful Mind*). A **Nash equilibrium** is a situation in which economic actors interacting with one another each choose their best strategy given the strategies the others have chosen. In this case, given that Jill is producing 40 gallons, the best strategy for Jack is to produce 40 gallons. Similarly, given that Jack is producing 40 gallons, the best strategy for Jill is to produce 40 gallons. Once they reach this Nash equilibrium, neither Jack nor Jill has an incentive to make a different decision.

This example illustrates the tension between cooperation and self-interest. Oligopolists would be better off cooperating and reaching the monopoly outcome. Yet because they pursue their own self-interest, they do not end up reaching the monopoly outcome and maximizing their joint profit. Each oligopolist is tempted to raise production and capture a larger share of the market. As each of them tries to do this, total production rises, and the price falls.

At the same time, self-interest does not drive the market all the way to the competitive outcome. Like monopolists, oligopolists are aware that increases in the amount they produce reduce the price of their product. Therefore, they stop short of following the competitive firm's rule of producing up to the point where price equals marginal cost.

Nash equilibrium
a situation in which economic actors interacting with one another each choose their best strategy given the strategies that all the other actors have chosen

In summary, *when firms in an oligopoly individually choose production to maximize profit, they produce a quantity of output greater than the level produced by monopoly and less than the level produced by competition. The oligopoly price is less than the monopoly price but greater than the competitive price (which equals marginal cost).*

How the Size of an Oligopoly Affects the Market Outcome

We can use the insights from this analysis of duopoly to discuss how the size of an oligopoly is likely to affect the outcome in a market. Suppose, for instance, that John and Joan suddenly discover water sources on their property and join Jack and Jill in the water oligopoly. The demand schedule in Table 1 remains the same, but now more producers are available to satisfy this demand. How would an increase in the number of sellers from two to four affect the price and quantity of water in the town?

If the sellers of water could form a cartel, they would once again try to maximize total profit by producing the monopoly quantity and charging the monopoly price. Just as when there were only two sellers, the members of the cartel would need to agree on production levels for each member and find some way to enforce the agreement. As the cartel grows larger, however, this outcome is less likely. Reaching and enforcing an agreement becomes more difficult as the size of the group increases.

If the oligopolists do not form a cartel—perhaps because the antitrust laws prohibit it—they must each decide on their own how much water to produce. To see how the increase in the number of sellers affects the outcome, consider the decision facing each seller. At any time, each well owner has the option to raise production by 1 gallon. In making this decision, the well owner weighs two effects:

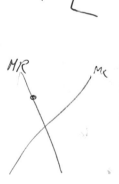

- *The output effect:* Because price is above marginal cost, selling 1 more gallon of water at the going price will raise profit.
- *The price effect:* Raising production will increase the total amount sold, which will lower the price of water and lower the profit on all the other gallons sold.

If the output effect is larger than the price effect, the well owner will increase production. If the price effect is larger than the output effect, the owner will not raise production. (In fact, in this case, it is profitable to reduce production.) Each oligopolist continues to increase production until these two marginal effects exactly balance, taking the other firms' production as given.

Now consider how the number of firms in the industry affects the marginal analysis of each oligopolist. The larger the number of sellers, the less concerned each seller is about its own impact on the market price. That is, as the oligopoly grows in size, the magnitude of the price effect falls. When the oligopoly grows very large, the price effect disappears altogether, leaving only the output effect. In this extreme case, each firm in the oligopoly increases production as long as price is above marginal cost.

We can now see that a large oligopoly is essentially a group of competitive firms. A competitive firm considers only the output effect when deciding how much to produce: Because a competitive firm is a price taker, the price effect is absent. Thus, *as the number of sellers in an oligopoly grows larger, an oligopolistic market looks more and more like a competitive market. The price approaches marginal cost, and the quantity produced approaches the socially efficient level.*

This analysis of oligopoly offers a new perspective on the effects of international trade. Imagine that Toyota and Honda are the only automakers in Japan, Volkswagen and BMW are the only automakers in Germany, and Ford and General Motors are the only automakers in the United States. If these nations prohibited international trade in autos, each would have an auto oligopoly with only two members, and the market outcome would likely depart substantially from the competitive ideal. With international trade, however, the car market is a world market, and the oligopoly in this example has six members. Allowing free trade increases the number of producers from which each consumer can choose, and this increased competition keeps prices closer to marginal cost. Thus, the theory of oligopoly provides another reason, in addition to the theory of comparative advantage discussed in Chapter 3, why all countries can benefit from free trade.

Case Study
OPEC AND THE WORLD OIL MARKET

Our story about the town's market for water is fictional, but if we change water to crude oil, and Jack and Jill to Iran and Iraq, the story is quite close to being true. Much of the world's oil is produced by a few countries, mostly in the Middle East. These countries together make up an oligopoly. Their decisions about how much oil to pump are much the same as Jack and Jill's decisions about how much water to pump.

The countries that produce most of the world's oil have formed a cartel, called the Organization of Petroleum Exporting Countries (OPEC). As originally formed in 1960, OPEC included Iran, Iraq, Kuwait, Saudi Arabia, and Venezuela. By 1973, eight other nations had joined: Qatar, Indonesia, Libya, the United Arab Emirates, Algeria, Nigeria, Ecuador, and Gabon. These countries control about three-fourths of the world's oil reserves. Like any cartel, OPEC tries to raise the price of its product through a coordinated reduction in quantity produced. OPEC tries to set production levels for each of the member countries.

The problem that OPEC faces is much the same as the problem that Jack and Jill face in our story. The OPEC countries would like to maintain a high price of oil. But each member of the cartel is tempted to increase its production in order to get a larger share of the total profit. OPEC members frequently agree to reduce production but then cheat on their agreements.

OPEC was most successful at maintaining cooperation and high prices in the period from 1973 to 1985. The price of crude oil rose from $2.64 a barrel in 1972 to $11.17 in 1974 and then to $35.10 in 1981. But in the early 1980s member countries began arguing about production levels, and OPEC became ineffective at maintaining cooperation. By 1986 the price of crude oil had fallen back to $12.52 a barrel.

In recent years, the members of OPEC have continued to meet regularly, but the cartel has been far less successful at reaching and enforcing agreements. The price of crude oil, adjusted for overall inflation, has remained far below the level OPEC achieved in 1981. While this lack of cooperation has hurt the profits of the oil-producing nations, it has benefited consumers around the world. ●

IN THE NEWS

THE GROWTH OF OLIGOPOLY

This article suggests that oligopolies are becoming a more important part of the economy.

Big Business: Why the Sudden Rise in the Urge to Merge and Form Oligopolies?

Everywhere you look, powerful forces are driving American industries to consolidate into oligopolies—and the obstacles are getting less formidable.

The rewards for getting bigger are growing, particularly in the world of technology, media, and telecommunications, where fixed costs are especially large and the cost of serving each additional customer is small. Some snapshots:

- Twenty years ago, cable television was dominated by a patchwork of thousands of tiny, family-operated companies. Today, a pending deal would leave three companies in control of nearly two-thirds of the market.

- In 1990, three big publishers of college textbooks accounted for 35 percent of the industry. Today, they have 62 percent. . . .
- In 1999, more than 10 significant firms offered help-wanted Web sites. Today, three firms dominate.

Even as economic forces push these industries toward oligopoly, some of the forces that checked this trend in the 1990s are weakening. U.S. antitrust cops, regulators, and judges seem less antagonistic toward bigness. Just last week, a federal appeals court opened the door to another round of media mergers by striking down rules that in effect barred cable companies from buying broadcast networks. . . .

An oligopoly, a market in which a few sellers offer similar products, isn't always avoidable or undesirable. It can produce efficiencies that allow firms to offer consumers better products at lower prices and lead to industry-wide standards that make life smooth for consumers.

But an oligopoly can allow big business to make big profits at the expense of consumers and economic progress. It can destroy competition that is vital to preventing firms from pushing prices well above costs and to forcing companies to change or die. Rates for cable television, for instance, have soared 36 percent, almost triple the rate of overall inflation, since the industry was deregulated in 1996 and then consolidated in a few big firms.

Source: *The Wall Street Journal,* February 25, 2002, p. A1. © 2002 Dow Jones & Co. Inc. Reproduced with permission of DOW JONES & CO INC in the format Textbook via Copyright Clearance Center.

QuickQuiz If the members of an oligopoly could agree on a total quantity to produce, what quantity would they choose? • If the oligopolists do not act together but instead make production decisions individually, do they produce a total quantity more or less than in your answer to the previous question? Why?

GAME THEORY AND THE ECONOMICS OF COOPERATION

As we have seen, oligopolies would like to reach the monopoly outcome, but doing so requires cooperation, which at times is difficult to maintain. In this section we look more closely at the problems people face when cooperation is desirable but difficult. To analyze the economics of cooperation, we need to learn a little about game theory.

Game theory is the study of how people behave in strategic situations. By "strategic" we mean a situation in which each person, when deciding what actions to take, must consider how others might respond to that action. Because the number of firms in an oligopolistic market is small, each firm must act strategically. Each firm knows that its profit depends not only on how much it produces but also on how much the other firms produce. In making its production decision, each firm in an oligopoly should consider how its decision might affect the production decisions of all the other firms.

Game theory is not necessary for understanding competitive or monopoly markets. In a competitive market, each firm is so small compared to the market that strategic interactions with other firms are not important. In a monopolized market, strategic interactions are absent because the market has only one firm. But, as we will see, game theory is quite useful for understanding the behavior of oligopolies.

A particularly important "game" is called the **prisoners' dilemma.** This game provides insight into the difficulty of maintaining cooperation. Many times in life, people fail to cooperate with one another even when cooperation would make them all better off. An oligopoly is just one example. The story of the prisoners' dilemma contains a general lesson that applies to any group trying to maintain cooperation among its members.

game theory
the study of how people behave in strategic situations

prisoners' dilemma
a particular "game" between two captured prisoners that illustrates why cooperation is difficult to maintain even when it is mutually beneficial

The Prisoners' Dilemma

The prisoners' dilemma is a story about two criminals who have been captured by the police. Let's call them Bonnie and Clyde. The police have enough evidence to convict Bonnie and Clyde of the minor crime of carrying an unregistered gun, so that each would spend a year in jail. The police also suspect that the two criminals have committed a bank robbery together, but they lack hard evidence to convict them of this major crime. The police question Bonnie and Clyde in separate rooms, and they offer each of them the following deal:

"Right now, we can lock you up for 1 year. If you confess to the bank robbery and implicate your partner, however, we'll give you immunity and you can go free. Your partner will get 20 years in jail. But if you both confess to the crime, we won't need your testimony and we can avoid the cost of a trial, so you will each get an intermediate sentence of 8 years."

If Bonnie and Clyde, heartless bank robbers that they are, care only about their own sentences, what would you expect them to do? Would they confess or remain silent? Figure 2 (p. 356) shows their choices. Each prisoner has two strategies: confess or remain silent. The sentence each prisoner gets depends on the strategy he or she chooses and the strategy chosen by his or her partner in crime.

Consider first Bonnie's decision. She reasons as follows: "I don't know what Clyde is going to do. If he remains silent, my best strategy is to confess, since then I'll go free rather than spending a year in jail. If he confesses, my best strategy is still to confess, since then I'll spend 8 years in jail rather than 20. So, regardless of what Clyde does, I am better off confessing."

In the language of game theory, a strategy is called a **dominant strategy** if it is the best strategy for a player to follow regardless of the strategies pursued by other

dominant strategy
a strategy that is best for a player in a game regardless of the strategies chosen by the other players

FIGURE 2

The Prisoners' Dilemma

In this game between two criminals suspected of committing a crime, the sentence that each receives depends both on his or her decision whether to confess or remain silent and on the decision made by the other.

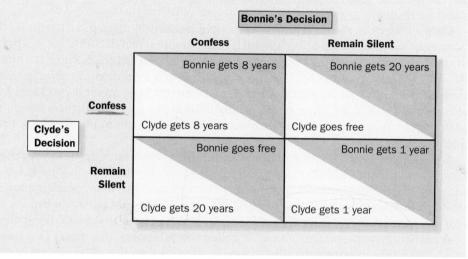

players. In this case, confessing is a dominant strategy for Bonnie. She spends less time in jail if she confesses, regardless of whether Clyde confesses or remains silent.

Now consider Clyde's decision. He faces exactly the same choices as Bonnie, and he reasons in much the same way. Regardless of what Bonnie does, Clyde can reduce his time in jail by confessing. In other words, confessing is also a dominant strategy for Clyde.

In the end, both Bonnie and Clyde confess, and both spend 8 years in jail. Yet, from their standpoint, this is a terrible outcome. If they had *both* remained silent, both of them would have been better off, spending only 1 year in jail on the gun charge. By each pursuing his or her own interests, the two prisoners together reach an outcome that is worse for each of them.

To see how difficult it is to maintain cooperation, imagine that, before the police captured Bonnie and Clyde, the two criminals had made a pact not to confess. Clearly, this agreement would make them both better off *if* they both live up to it, because they would each spend only 1 year in jail. But would the two criminals in fact remain silent, simply because they had agreed to? Once they are being questioned separately, the logic of self-interest takes over and leads them to confess. Cooperation between the two prisoners is difficult to maintain, because cooperation is individually irrational.

Oligopolies as a Prisoners' Dilemma

What does the prisoners' dilemma have to do with markets and imperfect competition? It turns out that the game oligopolists play in trying to reach the monopoly outcome is similar to the game that the two prisoners play in the prisoners' dilemma.

Consider an oligopoly with two members, called Iran and Iraq. Both countries sell crude oil. After prolonged negotiation, the countries agree to keep oil production low in order to keep the world price of oil high. After they agree on production levels, each country must decide whether to cooperate and live up to this

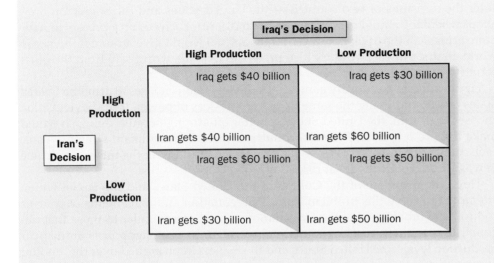

FIGURE 3

An Oligopoly Game

In this game between members of an oligopoly, the profit that each earns depends on both its production decision and the production decision of the other oligopolist.

agreement or to ignore it and produce at a higher level. Figure 3 shows how the profits of the two countries depend on the strategies they choose.

Suppose you are the president of Iraq. You might reason as follows: "I could keep production low as we agreed, or I could raise my production and sell more oil on world markets. If Iran lives up to the agreement and keeps its production low, then my country earns profit of $60 billion with high production and $50 billion with low production. In this case, Iraq is better off with high production. If Iran fails to live up to the agreement and produces at a high level, then my country earns $40 billion with high production and $30 billion with low production. Once again, Iraq is better off with high production. So, regardless of what Iran chooses to do, my country is better off reneging on our agreement and producing at a high level."

Producing at a high level is a dominant strategy for Iraq. Of course, Iran reasons in exactly the same way, and so both countries produce at a high level. The result is the inferior outcome (from Iran and Iraq's standpoint) with low profits for each country.

This example illustrates why oligopolies have trouble maintaining monopoly profits. The monopoly outcome is jointly rational for the oligopoly, but each oligopolist has an incentive to cheat. Just as self-interest drives the prisoners in the prisoners' dilemma to confess, self-interest makes it difficult for the oligopoly to maintain the cooperative outcome with low production, high prices, and monopoly profits.

Other Examples of the Prisoners' Dilemma

We have seen how the prisoners' dilemma can be used to understand the problem facing oligopolies. The same logic applies to many other situations as well. Here we consider three examples in which self-interest prevents cooperation and leads to an inferior outcome for the parties involved.

Arms Races   An arms race is much like the prisoners' dilemma. To see this, consider the decisions of two countries—the United States and the Soviet Union—about whether to build new weapons or to disarm. Each country prefers to have more arms than the other because a larger arsenal would give it more influence in world affairs. But each country also prefers to live in a world safe from the other country's weapons.

Figure 4 shows the deadly game. If the Soviet Union chooses to arm, the United States is better off doing the same to prevent the loss of power. If the Soviet Union chooses to disarm, the United States is better off arming because doing so would make it more powerful. For each country, arming is a dominant strategy. Thus, each country chooses to continue the arms race, resulting in the inferior outcome in which both countries are at risk.

Throughout the era of the Cold War, the United States and the Soviet Union attempted to solve this problem through negotiation and agreements over arms control. The problems that the two countries faced were similar to those that oligopolists encounter in trying to maintain a cartel. Just as oligopolists argue over production levels, the United States and the Soviet Union argued over the amount of arms that each country would be allowed. And just as cartels have trouble enforcing production levels, the United States and the Soviet Union each feared that the other country would cheat on any agreement. In both arms races and oligopolies, the relentless logic of self-interest drives the participants toward a noncooperative outcome that is worse for each party.

Advertising   When two firms advertise to attract the same customers, they face a problem similar to the prisoners' dilemma. For example, consider the decisions facing two cigarette companies, Marlboro and Camel. If neither company advertises, the two companies split the market. If both advertise, they again split the market, but profits are lower, since each company must bear the cost of advertis-

---

FIGURE 4

An Arms-Race Game

In this game between two countries, the safety and power of each country depends on both its decision whether to arm and the decision made by the other country.

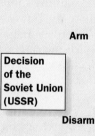

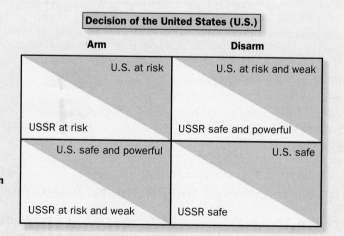

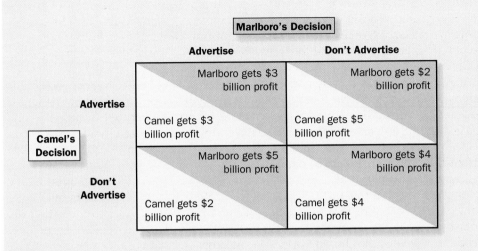

FIGURE 5

An Advertising Game

In this game between firms selling similar products, the profit that each earns depends on both its own advertising decision and the advertising decision of the other firm.

ing. Yet if one company advertises while the other does not, the one that advertises attracts customers from the other.

Figure 5 shows how the profits of the two companies depend on their actions. You can see that advertising is a dominant strategy for each firm. Thus, both firms choose to advertise, even though both firms would be better off if neither firm advertised.

A test of this theory of advertising occurred in 1971, when Congress passed a law banning cigarette advertisements on television. To the surprise of many observers, cigarette companies did not use their considerable political clout to oppose the law. When the law went into effect, cigarette advertising fell, and the profits of cigarette companies rose. The law did for the cigarette companies what they could not do on their own: It solved the prisoners' dilemma by enforcing the cooperative outcome with low advertising and high profit.

Common Resources   In Chapter 11 we saw that people tend to overuse common resources. One can view this problem as an example of the prisoners' dilemma.

Imagine that two oil companies—Exxon and Texaco—own adjacent oil fields. Under the fields is a common pool of oil worth $12 million. Drilling a well to recover the oil costs $1 million. If each company drills one well, each will get half of the oil and earn a $5 million profit ($6 million in revenue minus $1 million in costs).

Because the pool of oil is a common resource, the companies will not use it efficiently. Suppose that either company could drill a second well. If one company has two of the three wells, that company gets two-thirds of the oil, which yields a profit of $6 million. The other company gets one-third of the oil, for a profit of $3 million. Yet if each company drills a second well, the two companies again split the oil. In this case, each bears the cost of a second well, so profit is only $4 million for each company.

FIGURE 6

A Common-Resources Game

In this game between firms pumping oil from a common pool, the profit that each earns depends on both the number of wells it drills and the number of wells drilled by the other firm.

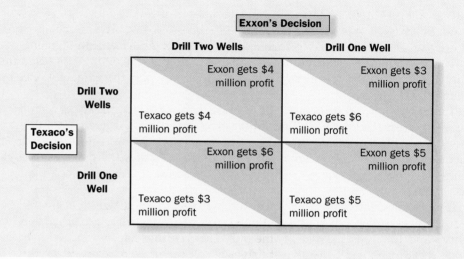

Exxon's Decision

	Drill Two Wells	Drill One Well
Drill Two Wells	Exxon gets $4 million profit / Texaco gets $4 million profit	Exxon gets $3 million profit / Texaco gets $6 million profit
Drill One Well	Exxon gets $6 million profit / Texaco gets $3 million profit	Exxon gets $5 million profit / Texaco gets $5 million profit

Texaco's Decision

Figure 6 shows the game. Drilling two wells is a dominant strategy for each company. Once again, the self-interest of the two players leads them to an inferior outcome.

The Prisoners' Dilemma and the Welfare of Society

The prisoners' dilemma describes many of life's situations, and it shows that co-operation can be difficult to maintain, even when cooperation would make both players in the game better off. Clearly, this lack of cooperation is a problem for those involved in these situations. But is lack of cooperation a problem from the standpoint of society as a whole? The answer depends on the circumstances.

In some cases, the noncooperative equilibrium is bad for society as well as the players. In the arms-race game in Figure 4, both the United States and the Soviet Union end up at risk. In the common-resources game in Figure 6, the extra wells dug by Texaco and Exxon are pure waste. In both cases, society would be better off if the two players could reach the cooperative outcome.

By contrast, in the case of oligopolists trying to maintain monopoly profits, lack of cooperation is desirable from the standpoint of society as a whole. The monopoly outcome is good for the oligopolists, but it is bad for the consumers of the product. As we first saw in Chapter 7, the competitive outcome is best for society because it maximizes total surplus. When oligopolists fail to cooperate, the quantity they produce is closer to this optimal level. Put differently, the invisible hand guides markets to allocate resources efficiently only when markets are competitive, and markets are competitive only when firms in the market fail to cooperate with one another.

Similarly, consider the case of the police questioning two suspects. Lack of co-operation between the suspects is desirable, for it allows the police to convict more criminals. The prisoners' dilemma is a dilemma for the prisoners, but it can be a boon to everyone else.

Why People Sometimes Cooperate

The prisoners' dilemma shows that cooperation is difficult. But is it impossible? Not all prisoners, when questioned by the police, decide to turn in their partners in crime. Cartels sometimes do manage to maintain collusive arrangements, despite the incentive for individual members to defect. Very often, the reason that players can solve the prisoners' dilemma is that they play the game not once but many times.

To see why cooperation is easier to enforce in repeated games, let's return to our duopolists, Jack and Jill. Recall that Jack and Jill would like to maintain the monopoly outcome in which each produces 30 gallons, but self-interest drives them to an equilibrium in which each produces 40 gallons. Figure 7 shows the game they play. Producing 40 gallons is a dominant strategy for each player in this game.

Imagine that Jack and Jill try to form a cartel. To maximize total profit, they would agree to the cooperative outcome in which each produces 30 gallons. Yet, if Jack and Jill are to play this game only once, neither has any incentive to live up to this agreement. Self-interest drives each of them to renege and produce 40 gallons.

Now suppose that Jack and Jill know that they will play the same game every week. When they make their initial agreement to keep production low, they can also specify what happens if one party reneges. They might agree, for instance, that once one of them reneges and produces 40 gallons, both of them will produce 40 gallons forever after. This penalty is easy to enforce, for if one party is producing at a high level, the other has every reason to do the same.

The threat of this penalty may be all that is needed to maintain cooperation. Each person knows that defecting would raise his or her profit from $1,800 to $2,000. But this benefit would last for only one week. Thereafter, profit would fall to $1,600 and stay there. As long as the players care enough about future profits, they will choose to forgo the one-time gain from defection. Thus, in a game of

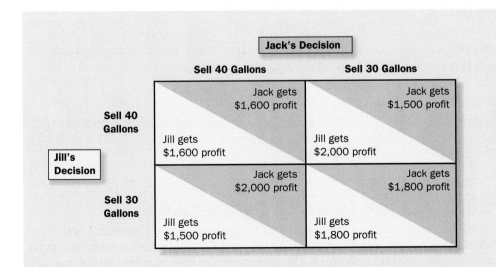

FIGURE 7

Jack and Jill's Oligopoly Game

In this game between Jack and Jill, the profit that each earns from selling water depends on both the quantity he or she chooses to sell and the quantity the other chooses to sell.

Jack's Decision

Jill's Decision	Sell 40 Gallons	Sell 30 Gallons
Sell 40 Gallons	Jack gets $1,600 profit / Jill gets $1,600 profit	Jack gets $1,500 profit / Jill gets $2,000 profit
Sell 30 Gallons	Jack gets $2,000 profit / Jill gets $1,500 profit	Jack gets $1,800 profit / Jill gets $1,800 profit

repeated prisoners' dilemma, the two players may well be able to reach the cooperative outcome.

Case Study
THE PRISONERS' DILEMMA TOURNAMENT

Imagine that you are playing a game of prisoners' dilemma with a person being "questioned" in a separate room. Moreover, imagine that you are going to play not once but many times. Your score at the end of the game is the total number of years in jail. You would like to make this score as small as possible. What strategy would you play? Would you begin by confessing or remaining silent? How would the other player's actions affect your subsequent decisions about confessing?

Repeated prisoners' dilemma is quite a complicated game. To encourage cooperation, players must penalize each other for not cooperating. Yet the strategy described earlier for Jack and Jill's water cartel—defect forever as soon as the other player defects—is not very forgiving. In a game repeated many times, a strategy that allows players to return to the cooperative outcome after a period of noncooperation may be preferable.

To see what strategies work best, political scientist Robert Axelrod held a tournament. People entered by sending computer programs designed to play repeated prisoners' dilemma. Each program then played the game against all the other programs. The "winner" was the program that received the fewest total years in jail.

The winner turned out to be a simple strategy called *tit-for-tat*. According to tit-for-tat, a player should start by cooperating and then do whatever the other player did last time. Thus, a tit-for-tat player cooperates until the other player defects; he then defects until the other player cooperates again. In other words, this strategy starts out friendly, penalizes unfriendly players, and forgives them if warranted. To Axelrod's surprise, this simple strategy did better than all the more complicated strategies that people had sent in.

The tit-for-tat strategy has a long history. It is essentially the biblical strategy of "an eye for an eye, a tooth for a tooth." The prisoners' dilemma tournament suggests that this may be a good rule of thumb for playing some of the games of life. ●

QuickQuiz Tell the story of the prisoners' dilemma. Write down a table showing the prisoners' choices and explain what outcome is likely. • What does the prisoners' dilemma teach us about oligopolies?

PUBLIC POLICY TOWARD OLIGOPOLIES

One of the *Ten Principles of Economics* in Chapter 1 is that governments can sometimes improve market outcomes. The application of this principle to oligopolistic markets is, as a general matter, straightforward. As we have seen, cooperation among oligopolists is undesirable from the standpoint of society as a whole, because it leads to production that is too low and prices that are too high. To move the allocation of resources closer to the social optimum, policymakers should try to induce firms in an oligopoly to compete rather than cooperate. Let's consider how policymakers do this and then examine the controversies that arise in this area of public policy.

Restraint of Trade and the Antitrust Laws

One way that policy discourages cooperation is through the common law. Normally, freedom of contract is an essential part of a market economy. Businesses and households use contracts to arrange mutually advantageous trades. In doing this, they rely on the court system to enforce contracts. Yet, for many centuries, judges in England and the United States have deemed agreements among competitors to reduce quantities and raise prices to be contrary to the public good. They have therefore refused to enforce such agreements.

The Sherman Antitrust Act of 1890 codified and reinforced this policy:

> Every contract, combination in the form of trust or otherwise, or conspiracy, in restraint of trade or commerce among the several States, or with foreign nations, is declared to be illegal. . . . Every person who shall monopolize, or attempt to monopolize, or combine or conspire with any person or persons to monopolize any part of the trade or commerce among the several States, or with foreign nations, shall be deemed guilty of a misdemeanor, and on conviction therefor, shall be punished by fine not exceeding fifty thousand dollars, or by imprisonment not exceeding one year, or by both said punishments, in the discretion of the court.

The Sherman Act elevated agreements among oligopolists from an unenforceable contract to a criminal conspiracy.

The Clayton Act of 1914 further strengthened the antitrust laws. According to this law, if a person could prove that he was damaged by an illegal arrangement to restrain trade, that person could sue and recover three times the damages he sustained. The purpose of this unusual rule of triple damages is to encourage private lawsuits against conspiring oligopolists.

Today, both the U.S. Justice Department and private parties have the authority to bring legal suits to enforce the antitrust laws. As we discussed in Chapter 15, these laws are used to prevent mergers that would lead to excessive market power in any single firm. In addition, these laws are used to prevent oligopolists from acting together in ways that would make their markets less competitive.

Case Study

AN ILLEGAL PHONE CALL

Firms in oligopolies have a strong incentive to collude in order to reduce production, raise price, and increase profit. The great eighteenth-century economist Adam

Smith was well aware of this potential market failure. In *The Wealth of Nations* he wrote, "People of the same trade seldom meet together, but the conversation ends in a conspiracy against the public, or in some diversion to raise prices."

To see a modern example of Smith's observation, consider the following excerpt of a phone conversation between two airline executives in the early 1980s. The call was reported in *The New York Times* on February 24, 1983. Robert Crandall was president of American Airlines, and Howard Putnam was president of Braniff Airways.

CRANDALL: I think it's dumb as hell . . . to sit here and pound the @#$% out of each other and neither one of us making a #$%& dime.

PUTNAM: Do you have a suggestion for me?

CRANDALL: Yes, I have a suggestion for you. Raise your $%*& fares 20 percent. I'll raise mine the next morning.

PUTNAM: Robert, we . . .

CRANDALL: You'll make more money, and I will, too.

PUTNAM: We can't talk about pricing!

CRANDALL: Oh @#$%, Howard. We can talk about any &*#@ thing we want to talk about.

Putnam was right: The Sherman Antitrust Act prohibits competing executives from even talking about fixing prices. When Putnam gave a tape of this conversation to the Justice Department, the Justice Department filed suit against Crandall.

Two years later, Crandall and the Justice Department reached a settlement in which Crandall agreed to various restrictions on his business activities, including his contacts with officials at other airlines. The Justice Department said that the terms of settlement would "protect competition in the airline industry, by preventing American and Crandall from any further attempts to monopolize passenger airline service on any route through discussions with competitors about the prices of airline services." ●

Controversies over Antitrust Policy

Over time, much controversy has centered on the question of what kinds of behavior the antitrust laws should prohibit. Most commentators agree that price-fixing agreements among competing firms should be illegal. Yet the antitrust laws have been used to condemn some business practices whose effects are not obvious. Here we consider three examples.

Resale Price Maintenance   One example of a controversial business practice is *resale price maintenance,* also called *fair trade.* Imagine that Superduper Electronics sells DVD players to retail stores for $300. If Superduper requires the retailers to charge customers $350, it is said to engage in resale price maintenance. Any retailer that charged less than $350 would have violated its contract with Superduper.

At first, resale price maintenance might seem anticompetitive and, therefore, detrimental to society. Like an agreement among members of a cartel, it prevents the retailers from competing on price. For this reason, the courts have often viewed resale price maintenance as a violation of the antitrust laws.

Yet some economists defend resale price maintenance on two grounds. First, they deny that it is aimed at reducing competition. To the extent that Superduper Electronics has any market power, it can exert that power through the wholesale price, rather than through resale price maintenance. Moreover, Superduper has no incentive to discourage competition among its retailers. Indeed, because a cartel of retailers sells less than a group of competitive retailers, Superduper would be worse off if its retailers were a cartel.

Second, economists believe that resale price maintenance has a legitimate goal. Superduper may want its retailers to provide customers with a pleasant showroom and a knowledgeable sales force. Yet, without resale price maintenance, some customers would take advantage of one store's service to learn about the DVD player's special features and then buy the item at a discount retailer that does not provide this service. To some extent, good service is a public good among the retailers that sell Superduper products. As we discussed in Chapter 11, when one person provides a public good, others are able to enjoy it without paying for it. In this case, discount retailers would free ride on the service provided by other retailers, leading to less service than is desirable. Resale price maintenance is one way for Superduper to solve this free-rider problem.

The example of resale price maintenance illustrates an important principle: *Business practices that appear to reduce competition may in fact have legitimate purposes.* This principle makes the application of the antitrust laws all the more difficult. The economists, lawyers, and judges in charge of enforcing these laws must determine what kinds of behavior public policy should prohibit as impeding competition and reducing economic well-being. Often that job is not easy.

Predatory Pricing   Firms with market power normally use that power to raise prices above the competitive level. But should policymakers ever be concerned that firms with market power might charge prices that are too low? This question is at the heart of a second debate over antitrust policy.

Imagine that a large airline, call it Coyote Air, has a monopoly on some route. Then Roadrunner Express enters and takes 20 percent of the market, leaving Coyote with 80 percent. In response to this competition, Coyote starts slashing its fares. Some antitrust analysts argue that Coyote's move could be anticompetitive: The price cuts may be intended to drive Roadrunner out of the market so Coyote can recapture its monopoly and raise prices again. Such behavior is called *predatory pricing.*

Although predatory pricing is a common claim in antitrust suits, some economists are skeptical of this argument and believe that predatory pricing is rarely, and perhaps never, a profitable business strategy. Why? For a price war to drive out a rival, prices have to be driven below cost. Yet if Coyote starts selling cheap tickets at a loss, it had better be ready to fly more planes, because low fares will attract more customers. Roadrunner, meanwhile, can respond to Coyote's predatory move by cutting back on flights. As a result, Coyote ends up bearing more than 80 percent of the losses, putting Roadrunner in a good position to survive the price war. As in the old Roadrunner–Coyote cartoons, the predator suffers more than the prey.

Economists continue to debate whether predatory pricing should be a concern for antitrust policymakers. Various questions remain unresolved. Is predatory pricing ever a profitable business strategy? If so, when? Are the courts capable of telling which price cuts are competitive and thus good for consumers and which are predatory? There are no simple answers.

Tying   A third example of a controversial business practice is *tying*. Suppose that Makemoney Movies produces two new films—*Spiderman* and *Hamlet*. If Makemoney offers theaters the two films together at a single price, rather than separately, the studio is said to be tying its two products.

When the practice of tying movies was challenged in the courts, the Supreme Court banned it. The Court reasoned as follows: Imagine that *Spiderman* is a blockbuster, whereas *Hamlet* is an unprofitable art film. Then the studio could use the high demand for *Spiderman* to force theaters to buy *Hamlet*. It seemed that the studio could use tying as a mechanism for expanding its market power.

Many economists are skeptical of this argument. Imagine that theaters are willing to pay $20,000 for *Spiderman* and nothing for *Hamlet*. Then the most that a theater would pay for the two movies together is $20,000—the same as it would pay for *Spiderman* by itself. Forcing the theater to accept a worthless movie as part of the deal does not increase the theater's willingness to pay. Makemoney cannot increase its market power simply by bundling the two movies together.

Why, then, does tying exist? One possibility is that it is a form of price discrimination. Suppose there are two theaters. City Theater is willing to pay $15,000 for *Spiderman* and $5,000 for *Hamlet*. Country Theater is just the opposite: It is willing to pay $5,000 for *Spiderman* and $15,000 for *Hamlet*. If Makemoney charges separate prices for the two films, its best strategy is to charge $15,000 for each film, and each theater chooses to show only one film. Yet if Makemoney offers the two movies as a bundle, it can charge each theater $20,000 for the movies. Thus, if different theaters value the films differently, tying may allow the studio to increase profit by charging a combined price closer to the buyers' total willingness to pay.

Tying remains a controversial business practice. The Supreme Court's argument that tying allows a firm to extend its market power to other goods is not well founded, at least in its simplest form. Yet economists have proposed more elaborate theories for how tying can impede competition. Given our current economic knowledge, it is unclear whether tying has adverse effects for society as a whole.

Case Study
THE MICROSOFT CASE

The most important and controversial antitrust case in recent years has been the U.S. government's suit against the Microsoft Corporation, filed in 1998. Certainly, the case did not lack drama. It pitted one of the world's richest men (Bill Gates) against one of the world's most powerful regulatory agencies (the U.S. Justice Department). Testifying for the government was a prominent economist (MIT professor Franklin

Fisher). Testifying for Microsoft was an equally prominent economist (MIT professor Richard Schmalensee). At stake was the future of one of the world's most valuable companies (Microsoft) in one of the economy's fastest growing industries (computer software).

A central issue in the Microsoft case involved tying—in particular, whether Microsoft should be allowed to integrate its Internet browser into its Windows operating system. The government claimed that Microsoft was bundling these two products together to expand the market power it had in the market for computer operating systems into an unrelated market (for Internet browsers). Allowing Microsoft to incorporate such products into its operating system, the government argued, would deter other software companies such as Netscape from entering the market and offering new products.

Microsoft responded by pointing out that putting new features into old products is a natural part of technological progress. Cars today include stereos and air conditioners, which were once sold separately, and cameras come with built-in flashes. The same is true with operating systems. Over time, Microsoft has added many features to Windows that were previously stand-alone products. This has made computers more reliable and easier to use because consumers can be confident that the pieces work together. The integration of Internet technology, Microsoft argued, was the natural next step.

One point of disagreement concerned the extent of Microsoft's market power. Noting that more than 80 percent of new personal computers use a Microsoft operating system, the government argued that the company had substantial monopoly power, which it was trying to expand. Microsoft replied that the software market is always changing and that Microsoft's Windows was constantly being challenged by competitors, such as the Apple Mac and Linux operating systems. It also argued that the low price it charged for Windows—about $50, or only 3 percent of the price of a typical computer—was evidence that its market power was severely limited.

Like many large antitrust suits, the Microsoft case became a legal morass. In November 1999, after a long trial, Judge Penfield Jackson ruled that Microsoft had great monopoly power and that it had illegally abused that power. In June 2000, after hearings about possible remedies, he ordered that Microsoft be broken up into two companies—one that sold the operating system and one that sold applications software. A year later, an appeals court overturned Jackson's breakup order and handed the case to a new judge. In September 2001, the Justice Department announced that it no longer sought a breakup of the company and wanted to settle the case quickly.

A settlement was finally reached in November 2002. Microsoft accepted some restrictions on its business practices. The government accepted that a browser would remain part of the Windows operating system. ●

"Me? A monopolist? Now just wait a minute . . ."

QuickQuiz What kind of agreement is illegal for businesses to make? • Why are the antitrust laws controversial?

IN THE NEWS

ANTITRUST IN THE NEW ECONOMY

Many modern technologies, such as software, have the characteristics of natural monopoly. What does this mean for antitrust enforcement?

For Policymakers, Microsoft Suggests Need to Recast Models

By Alan Murray

The Microsoft case is just the beginning.

As government policymakers grapple with a rapidly changing American marketplace, they are increasingly struck by this fact: In the New Economy, monopoly is becoming the rule, not the exception.

Whether today's hot companies deal in Web services, business-to-business exchanges, or MP3 songs, many have the look of what economics textbooks used to call "natural monopolies." The products and services often involve a relatively big upfront investment. But they cost little or nothing to manufacture and distribute, thanks in part to the ease of spreading digital information over the Internet.

In such a business, it's inexpensive to expand rapidly into a dominant position, and dangerous not to. Competition of the traditional variety, with multiple firms offering nearly identical products and services, can quickly push prices to zero.

But how, if at all, should the government respond to these new monopolylike businesses? . . . Does this mean the government's antitrust forces will have to get more active, doing to other companies what they have done to Microsoft?

The Clinton administration's top economist, Treasury Secretary Lawrence Summers, steadfastly refuses to comment on the Microsoft case, as do other administration officials. But he gave an intriguing speech in San Francisco last month, titled "The New Wealth of Nations," that suggested the proliferation of natural monopolies is more good than bad.

In an information-based economy, he said, "the only incentive to produce anything is the possession of temporary monopoly power—because without that power the price will be bid down to the marginal cost and the high fixed costs cannot be recouped. . . . So the constant pursuit of that monopoly power becomes the central driving thrust of the New Economy. And the creative destruction that results from all that striving becomes the essential spur of economic growth."

Source: *The Wall Street Journal*, June 9, 2000, pp. A1, A8. © 2000 by Dow Jones & Co. Inc. Reproduced with permission of DOW JONES & CO INC in the format Textbook via Copyright Clearance Center.

CONCLUSION

Oligopolies would like to act like monopolies, but self-interest drives them closer to competition. Thus, oligopolies can end up looking either more like monopolies or more like competitive markets, depending on the number of firms in the oligopoly and how cooperative the firms are. The story of the prisoners' dilemma shows why oligopolies can fail to maintain cooperation, even when cooperation is in their best interest.

Policymakers regulate the behavior of oligopolists through the antitrust laws. The proper scope of these laws is the subject of ongoing controversy. Although price fixing among competing firms clearly reduces economic welfare and should be illegal, some business practices that appear to reduce competition may have legitimate if subtle purposes. As a result, policymakers need to be careful when they use the substantial powers of the antitrust laws to place limits on firm behavior.

SUMMARY

- Oligopolists maximize their total profits by forming a cartel and acting like a monopolist. Yet, if oligopolists make decisions about production levels individually, the result is a greater quantity and a lower price than under the monopoly outcome. The larger the number of firms in the oligopoly, the closer the quantity and price will be to the levels that would prevail under competition.

- The prisoners' dilemma shows that self-interest can prevent people from maintaining cooperation, even when cooperation is in their mutual interest. The logic of the prisoners' dilemma applies in many situations, including arms races, advertising, common-resource problems, and oligopolies.

- Policymakers use the antitrust laws to prevent oligopolies from engaging in behavior that reduces competition. The application of these laws can be controversial, because some behavior that may seem to reduce competition may in fact have legitimate business purposes.

KEY CONCEPTS

oligopoly, p. 346
monopolistic competition, p. 346
collusion, p. 348

cartel, p. 348
Nash equilibrium, p. 351
game theory, p. 355

prisoners' dilemma, p. 355
dominant strategy, p. 355

QUESTIONS FOR REVIEW

1. If a group of sellers could form a cartel, what quantity and price would they try to set?

2. Compare the quantity and price of an oligopoly to those of a monopoly.

3. Compare the quantity and price of an oligopoly to those of a competitive market.

4. How does the number of firms in an oligopoly affect the outcome in its market?

5. What is the prisoners' dilemma, and what does it have to do with oligopoly?

6. Give two examples other than oligopoly to show how the prisoners' dilemma helps to explain behavior.

7. What kinds of behavior do the antitrust laws prohibit?

8. What is resale price maintenance, and why is it controversial?

PROBLEMS AND APPLICATIONS

1. *The New York Times* (Nov. 30, 1993) reported that "the inability of OPEC to agree last week to cut production has sent the oil market into turmoil . . . [leading to] the lowest price for domestic crude oil since June 1990."
   a. Why were the members of OPEC trying to agree to cut production?

   b. Why do you suppose OPEC was unable to agree on cutting production? Why did the oil market go into "turmoil" as a result?

   c. The newspaper also noted OPEC's view "that producing nations outside the organization, like Norway and Britain, should do their share and cut production."

What does the phrase "do their share" suggest about OPEC's desired relationship with Norway and Britain?

2. A large share of the world supply of diamonds comes from Russia and South Africa. Suppose that the marginal cost of mining diamonds is constant at $1,000 per diamond, and the demand for diamonds is described by the following schedule:

Price	Quantity
$8,000	5,000
7,000	6,000
6,000	7,000
5,000	8,000
4,000	9,000
3,000	10,000
2,000	11,000
1,000	12,000

a. If there were many suppliers of diamonds, what would be the price and quantity?

b. If there were only one supplier of diamonds, what would be the price and quantity?

c. If Russia and South Africa formed a cartel, what would be the price and quantity? If the countries split the market evenly, what would be South Africa's production and profit? What would happen to South Africa's profit if it increased its production by 1,000 while Russia stuck to the cartel agreement?

d. Use your answer to part (c) to explain why cartel agreements are often not successful.

3. This chapter discusses companies that are oligopolists in the market for the goods they sell. Many of the same ideas apply to companies that are oligopolists in the market for the inputs they buy.

a. If sellers who are oligopolists try to increase the price of goods they sell, what is the goal of buyers who are oligopolists?

b. Major League Baseball team owners have an oligopoly in the market for baseball players. What is the owners' goal regarding players' salaries? Why is this goal difficult to achieve?

c. Baseball players went on strike in 1994 because they would not accept the salary cap that the owners wanted to impose. If the owners were already colluding over salaries, why did the owners feel the need for a salary cap?

4. Describe several activities in your life in which game theory could be useful. What is the common link among these activities?

5. Consider trade relations between the United States and Mexico. Assume that the leaders of the two countries believe the payoffs to alternative trade policies are as follows:

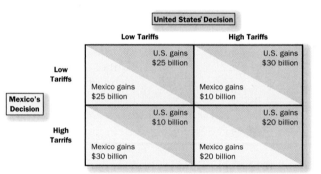

a. What is the dominant strategy for the United States? For Mexico? Explain.

b. Define *Nash equilibrium*. What is the Nash equilibrium for trade policy?

c. In 1993 the U.S. Congress ratified the North American Free Trade Agreement (NAFTA), in which the United States and Mexico agreed to reduce trade barriers simultaneously. Do the perceived payoffs shown here justify this approach to trade policy?

d. Based on your understanding of the gains from trade (discussed in Chapters 3 and 9), do you think that these payoffs actually reflect a nation's welfare under the four possible outcomes?

6. Suppose that you and a classmate are assigned a project on which you will receive one combined grade. You each want to receive a good grade, but you also want to do as little work as possible. The decision box and payoffs are as follows:

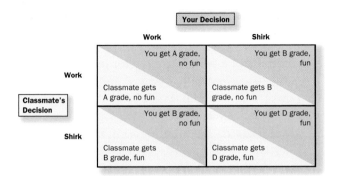

Assume that having fun is your normal state, but having no fun is as unpleasant as receiving a grade that is two letters lower.

a. Write out the decision box that combines the letter grade and the amount of fun you have into a single payoff for each outcome.

b. If neither you nor your classmate knows how much work the other person is doing, what is the likely outcome? Does it matter whether you are likely to work with this person again? Explain your answer.

7. The chapter states that the ban on cigarette advertising on television in 1971 increased the profits of cigarette companies. Could the ban still be good public policy? Explain your answer.

8. A case study in the chapter describes a phone conversation between the presidents of American Airlines and Braniff Airways. Let's analyze the game between the two companies. Suppose that each company can charge either a high price for tickets or a low price. If one company charges $100, it earns low profits if the other company charges $100 also, and high profits if the other company charges $200. On the other hand, if the company charges $200, it earns very low profits if the other company charges $100, and medium profits if the other company charges $200 also.

a. Draw the decision box for this game.

b. What is the Nash equilibrium in this game? Explain.

c. Is there an outcome that would be better than the Nash equilibrium for both airlines?

How could it be achieved? Who would lose if it were achieved?

9. Farmer Jones and Farmer Smith graze their cattle on the same field. If there are 20 cows grazing in the field, each cow produces $4,000 of milk over its lifetime. If there are more cows in the field, then each cow can eat less grass, and its milk production falls. With 30 cows on the field, each produces $3,000 of milk; with 40 cows, each produces $2,000 of milk. Cows cost $1,000 apiece.

a. Assume that Farmer Jones and Farmer Smith can each purchase either 10 or 20 cows, but that neither knows how many the other is buying when she makes her purchase. Calculate the payoffs of each outcome.

b. What is the likely outcome of this game? What would be the best outcome? Explain.

c. There used to be more common fields than there are today. Why? (For more discussion of this topic, reread Chapter 11.)

10. Little Kona is a small coffee company that is considering entering a market dominated by Big Brew. Each company's profit depends on whether Little Kona enters and whether Big Brew sets a high price or a low price:

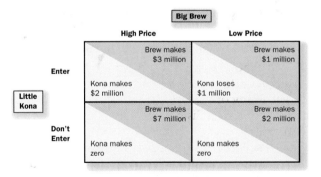

Big Brew threatens Little Kona by saying, "If you enter, we're going to set a low price, so you had better stay out." Do you think Little Kona should believe the threat? Why or why not? What do you think Little Kona should do?

11. Jeff and Steve are playing tennis. Every point comes down to whether Steve guesses correctly whether Jeff will hit the ball to Steve's left or right. The outcomes are:

Does either player have a dominant strategy? If Jeff chooses a particular strategy (Left or Right) and sticks with it, what will Steve do? So, can you think of a better strategy for Jeff to follow?

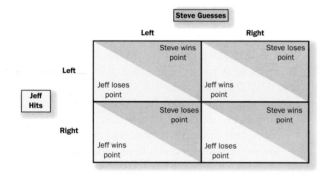

http://   For more study tools, please visit http://mankiwXtra.swlearning.com.

17

MONOPOLISTIC COMPETITION

You walk into a bookstore to buy a book to read during your next vacation. On the store's shelves you find a John Grisham mystery, a Stephen King thriller, a Danielle Steel romance, a Frank McCourt memoir, and many other choices. When you pick out a book and buy it, what kind of market are you participating in?

On the one hand, the market for books seems competitive. As you look over the shelves at your bookstore, you find many authors and many publishers vying for your attention. A buyer in this market has thousands of competing products from which to choose. And because anyone can enter the industry by writing and publishing a book, the book business is not very profitable. For every highly paid novelist, there are hundreds of struggling ones.

On the other hand, the market for books seems monopolistic. Because each book is unique, publishers have some latitude in choosing what price to charge. The sellers in this market are price makers rather than price takers. And, indeed, the price of books greatly exceeds marginal cost. The price of a typical hardcover novel, for instance, is about $25, whereas the cost of printing one additional copy of the novel is less than $5.

monopolistic competition
a market structure in which many firms sell products that are similar but not identical

In this chapter we examine markets that have some features of competition and some features of monopoly. This market structure is called **monopolistic competition.** Monopolistic competition describes a market with the following attributes:

- *Many sellers:* There are many firms competing for the same group of customers.
- *Product differentiation:* Each firm produces a product that is at least slightly different from those of other firms. Thus, rather than being a price taker, each firm faces a downward-sloping demand curve.
- *Free entry:* Firms can enter (or exit) the market without restriction. Thus, the number of firms in the market adjusts until economic profits are driven to zero.

A moment's thought reveals a long list of markets with these attributes: books, CDs, movies, computer games, restaurants, piano lessons, cookies, furniture, and so on.

Monopolistic competition, like oligopoly, is a market structure that lies between the extreme cases of competition and monopoly. But oligopoly and monopolistic competition are quite different. Oligopoly departs from the perfectly competitive ideal of Chapter 14 because there are only a few sellers in the market. The small number of sellers makes rigorous competition less likely, and it makes strategic interactions among them vitally important. By contrast, under monopolistic competition, there are many sellers, each of which is small compared to the market. A monopolistically competitive market departs from the perfectly competitive ideal because each of the sellers offers a somewhat different product.

COMPETITION WITH DIFFERENTIATED PRODUCTS

To understand monopolistically competitive markets, we first consider the decisions facing an individual firm. We then examine what happens in the long run as firms enter and exit the industry. Next, we compare the equilibrium under monopolistic competition to the equilibrium under perfect competition that we examined in Chapter 14. Finally, we consider whether the outcome in a monopolistically competitive market is desirable from the standpoint of society as a whole.

The Monopolistically Competitive Firm in the Short Run

Each firm in a monopolistically competitive market is, in many ways, like a monopoly. Because its product is different from those offered by other firms, it faces a downward-sloping demand curve. (By contrast, a perfectly competitive firm faces a horizontal demand curve at the market price.) Thus, the monopolistically competitive firm follows a monopolist's rule for profit maximization: It chooses the quantity at which marginal revenue equals marginal cost and then uses its demand curve to find the price consistent with that quantity.

Figure 1 shows the cost, demand, and marginal-revenue curves for two typical firms, each in a different monopolistically competitive industry. In both panels of this figure, the profit-maximizing quantity is found at the intersection of the marginal-revenue and marginal-cost curves. The two panels in this figure show different outcomes for the firm's profit. In panel (a), price exceeds average total cost, so the firm makes a profit. In panel (b), price is below average total cost. In this case, the firm is unable to make a positive profit, so the best the firm can do is to minimize its losses.

FIGURE 1

Monopolistic Competitors in the Short Run

Monopolistic competitors, like monopolists, maximize profit by producing the quantity at which marginal revenue equals marginal cost. The firm in panel (a) makes a profit because, at this quantity, price is above average total cost. The firm in panel (b) makes losses because, at this quantity, price is less than average total cost.

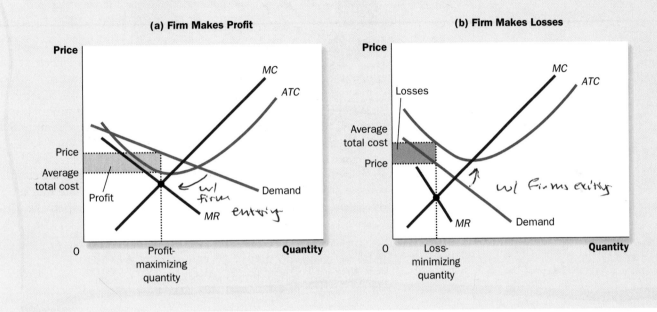

All this should seem familiar. A monopolistically competitive firm chooses its quantity and price just as a monopoly does. In the short run, these two types of market structure are similar.

The Long-Run Equilibrium

The situations depicted in Figure 1 do not last long. When firms are making profits, as in panel (a), new firms have an incentive to enter the market. This entry increases the number of products from which customers can choose and, therefore, reduces the demand faced by each firm already in the market. In other words, profit encourages entry, and entry shifts the demand curves faced by the incumbent firms to the left. As the demand for incumbent firms' products fall, these firms experience declining profit.

Conversely, when firms are making losses, as in panel (b), firms in the market have an incentive to exit. As firms exit, customers have fewer products from which to choose. This decrease in the number of firms expands the demand faced by those firms that stay in the market. In other words, losses encourage exit, and exit shifts the demand curves of the remaining firms to the right. As the demand for the remaining firms' products rises, these firms experience rising profit (that is, declining losses).

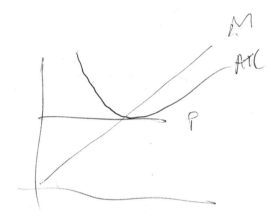

"GIVEN THE DOWNWARD SLOPE OF OUR DEMAND CURVE, AND THE EASE WITH WHICH OTHER FIRMS CAN ENTER THE INDUSTRY WE CAN STRENGTHEN OUR PROFIT POSITION ONLY BY EQUATING MARGINAL COST AND MARGINAL REVENUE. ORDER MORE JELLY BEANS."

This process of entry and exit continues until the firms in the market are making exactly zero economic profit. Figure 2 depicts the long-run equilibrium. Once the market reaches this equilibrium, new firms have no incentive to enter, and existing firms have no incentive to exit.

Notice that the demand curve in this figure just barely touches the average-total-cost curve. Mathematically, we say the two curves are *tangent* to each other. These two curves must be tangent once entry and exit have driven profit to zero. Because profit per unit sold is the difference between price (found on the demand curve) and average total cost, the maximum profit is zero only if these two curves touch each other without crossing.

To sum up, two characteristics describe the long-run equilibrium in a monopolistically competitive market:

- As in a monopoly market, price exceeds marginal cost. This conclusion arises because profit maximization requires marginal revenue to equal marginal cost and because the downward-sloping demand curve makes marginal revenue less than the price.
- As in a competitive market, price equals average total cost. This conclusion arises because free entry and exit drive economic profit to zero.

The second characteristic shows how monopolistic competition differs from monopoly. Because a monopoly is the sole seller of a product without close substi-

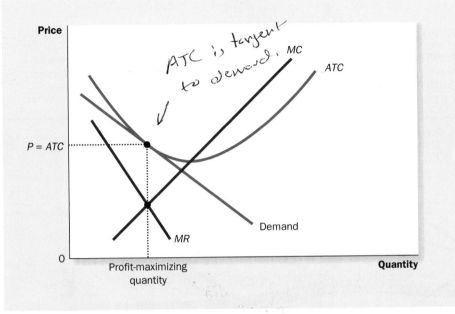

ATC is tangent
to demand.

**A Monopolistic Competitor
in the Long Run**

*In a monopolistically competitive market,
if firms are making profit, new firms
enter, and the demand curves for the
incumbent firms shift to the left. Similarly,
if firms are making losses, old firms exit,
and the demand curves of the remaining
firms shift to the right. Because of these
shifts in demand, a monopolistically
competitive firm eventually finds itself
in the long-run equilibrium shown
here. In this long-run equilibrium, price
equals average total cost, and the firm
earns zero profit.*

tutes, it can earn positive economic profit, even in the long run. By contrast, because there is free entry into a monopolistically competitive market, the economic
profit of a firm in this type of market is driven to zero.

Monopolistic versus Perfect Competition

Figure 3 (p. 378) compares the long-run equilibrium under monopolistic competition to the long-run equilibrium under perfect competition. (Chapter 14 discussed
the equilibrium with perfect competition.) There are two noteworthy differences
between monopolistic and perfect competition—excess capacity and the markup.

Excess Capacity   As we have just seen, entry and exit drive each firm in a monopolistically competitive market to a point of tangency between its demand and
average-total-cost curves. Panel (a) of Figure 3 shows that the quantity of output
at this point is smaller than the quantity that minimizes average total cost. Thus,
under monopolistic competition, firms produce on the downward-sloping portion of their average-total-cost curves. In this way, monopolistic competition
contrasts starkly with perfect competition. As panel (b) of Figure 3 shows, free entry in competitive markets drives firms to produce at the minimum of average total cost.

The quantity that minimizes average total cost is called the *efficient scale* of the
firm. In the long run, perfectly competitive firms produce at the efficient scale,
whereas monopolistically competitive firms produce below this level. Firms are
said to have *excess capacity* under monopolistic competition. In other words, a
monopolistically competitive firm, unlike a perfectly competitive firm, could increase the quantity it produces and lower the average total cost of production.

FIGURE 3

Monopolistic versus Perfect Competition

Panel (a) shows the long-run equilibrium in a monopolistically competitive market, and panel (b) shows the long-run equilibrium in a perfectly competitive market. Two differences are notable. (1) The perfectly competitive firm produces at the efficient scale, where average total cost is minimized. By contrast, the monopolistically competitive firm produces at less than the efficient scale. (2) Price equals marginal cost under perfect competition, but price is above marginal cost under monopolistic competition.

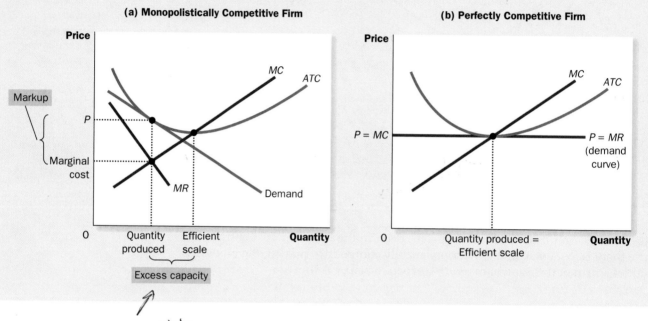

[handwritten] economists cannot decide if this is bad.

[handwritten] Huge

Markup over Marginal Cost A second difference between perfect competition and monopolistic competition is the relationship between price and marginal cost. For a competitive firm, such as that shown in panel (b) of Figure 3, price equals marginal cost. For a monopolistically competitive firm, such as that shown in panel (a), price exceeds marginal cost, because the firm always has some market power.

How is this markup over marginal cost consistent with free entry and zero profit? The zero-profit condition ensures only that price equals average total cost. It does *not* ensure that price equals marginal cost. Indeed, in the long-run equilibrium, monopolistically competitive firms operate on the declining portion of their average-total-cost curves, so marginal cost is below average total cost. Thus, for price to equal average total cost, price must be above marginal cost.

In this relationship between price and marginal cost, we see a key behavioral difference between perfect competitors and monopolistic competitors. Imagine that you were to ask a firm the following question: "Would you like to see another customer come through your door ready to buy from you at your current price?" A perfectly competitive firm would answer that it didn't care. Because price exactly equals marginal cost, the profit from an extra unit sold is zero. By contrast, a monopolistically competitive firm is always eager to get another customer. Because its price exceeds marginal cost, an extra unit sold at the posted price means more profit. According to an old quip, monopolistically competitive markets are those in which sellers send Christmas cards to the buyers.

Monopolistic Competition and the Welfare of Society

Is the outcome in a monopolistically competitive market desirable from the standpoint of society as a whole? Can policymakers improve on the market outcome? There are no simple answers to these questions.

One source of inefficiency is the markup of price over marginal cost. Because of the markup, some consumers who value the good at more than the marginal cost of production (but less than the price) will be deterred from buying it. Thus, a monopolistically competitive market has the normal deadweight loss of monopoly pricing. We first saw this type of inefficiency when we discussed monopoly in Chapter 15.

Although this outcome is clearly undesirable compared to the first-best outcome of price equal to marginal cost, there is no easy way for policymakers to fix the problem. To enforce marginal-cost pricing, policymakers would need to regulate all firms that produce differentiated products. Because such products are so common in the economy, the administrative burden of such regulation would be overwhelming.

Moreover, regulating monopolistic competitors would entail all the problems of regulating natural monopolies. In particular, because monopolistic competitors are making zero profits already, requiring them to lower their prices to equal marginal cost would cause them to make losses. To keep these firms in business, the government would need to help them cover these losses. Rather than raising taxes to pay for these subsidies, policymakers may decide it is better to live with the inefficiency of monopolistic pricing.

Another way in which monopolistic competition may be socially inefficient is that the number of firms in the market may not be the "ideal" one. That is, there may be too much or too little entry. One way to think about this problem is in terms of the externalities associated with entry. Whenever a new firm considers entering the market with a new product, it considers only the profit it would make. Yet its entry would also have two external effects:

- *The product-variety externality:* Because consumers get some consumer surplus from the introduction of a new product, entry of a new firm conveys a positive externality on consumers.
- *The business-stealing externality:* Because other firms lose customers and profits from the entry of a new competitor, entry of a new firm imposes a negative externality on existing firms.

Thus, in a monopolistically competitive market, there are both positive and negative externalities associated with the entry of new firms. Depending on which externality is larger, a monopolistically competitive market could have either too few or too many products.

Both of these externalities are closely related to the conditions for monopolistic competition. The product-variety externality arises because a new firm would offer a product different from those of the existing firms. The business-stealing externality arises because firms post a price above marginal cost and, therefore, are always eager to sell additional units. Conversely, because perfectly competitive firms produce identical goods and charge a price equal to marginal cost, neither of these externalities exists under perfect competition.

In the end, we can conclude only that monopolistically competitive markets do not have all the desirable welfare properties of perfectly competitive markets.

IS EXCESS CAPACITY A SOCIAL PROBLEM?

As we have seen, monopolistically competitive firms produce a quantity of output below the level that minimizes average total cost. By contrast, firms in perfectly competitive markets are driven to produce at the quantity that minimizes average total cost. This comparison between perfect and monopolistic competition led some

economists in the past to argue that the excess capacity of monopolistic competitors was a source of inefficiency.

Today economists understand that the excess capacity of monopolistic competitors is not directly relevant for evaluating economic welfare. There is no reason that society should want all firms to produce at the minimum of average total cost. For example, consider a publishing firm. Producing a novel might take a fixed cost of $50,000 (the author's time) and variable costs of $5 per book (the cost of printing). In this case, the average total cost of a book declines as the number of books increases because the fixed cost gets spread over more and more units. The average total cost is minimized by printing an infinite number of books. But in no sense is infinity the right number of books for society to produce.

In short, monopolistic competitors do have excess capacity, but this fact tells us little about the desirability of the market outcome.

That is, the invisible hand does not ensure that total surplus is maximized under monopolistic competition. Yet because the inefficiencies are subtle, hard to measure, and hard to fix, there is no easy way for public policy to improve the market outcome.

QuickQuiz List the three key attributes of monopolistic competition. • Draw and explain a diagram to show the long-run equilibrium in a monopolistically competitive market. How does this equilibrium differ from that in a perfectly competitive market?

ADVERTISING

It is nearly impossible to go through a typical day in a modern economy without being bombarded with advertising. Whether you are reading a newspaper, watching television, or driving down the highway, some firm will try to convince you to buy its product. Such behavior is a natural feature of monopolistic competition. When firms sell differentiated products and charge prices above marginal cost, each firm has an incentive to advertise in order to attract more buyers to its particular product.

The amount of advertising varies substantially across products. Firms that sell highly differentiated consumer goods, such as over-the-counter drugs, perfumes, soft drinks, razor blades, breakfast cereals, and dog food, typically spend between 10 and 20 percent of revenue for advertising. Firms that sell industrial products, such as drill presses and communications satellites, typically spend very little on advertising. And firms that sell homogeneous products, such as wheat, peanuts, or crude oil, spend nothing at all. For the economy as a whole, spending on advertising comprises about 2 percent of total firm revenue, or about $200 billion per year.

Advertising takes many forms. Most advertising spending is for commercials on television and radio (31 percent of total spending in 2001), space in newspapers and magazines (24 percent), direct mail (19 percent), the yellow pages (6 percent), and the Internet (3 percent). The remainder (17 percent) is for miscellaneous other ways of reaching customers, such as billboards and the Goodyear blimp.

The Debate over Advertising

← May/May not be wasteful.

Is society wasting the resources it devotes to advertising? Or does advertising serve a valuable purpose? Assessing the social value of advertising is difficult and often generates heated argument among economists. Let's consider both sides of the debate.

The Critique of Advertising Critics of advertising argue that firms advertise in order to manipulate people's tastes. Much advertising is psychological rather than informational. Consider, for example, the typical television commercial for some brand of soft drink. The commercial most likely does not tell the viewer about the product's price or quality. Instead, it might show a group of happy people at a party on a beach on a beautiful sunny day. In their hands are cans of the soft drink. The goal of the commercial is to convey a subconscious (if not subtle) message: "You too can have many friends and be happy, if only you drink our product." Critics of advertising argue that such a commercial creates a desire that otherwise might not exist.

Critics also argue that advertising impedes competition. Advertising often tries to convince consumers that products are more different than they truly are. By increasing the perception of product differentiation and fostering brand loyalty, advertising makes buyers less concerned with price differences among similar goods. With a less elastic demand curve, each firm charges a larger markup over marginal cost.

try to make product more differentiated than it actually is.

The Defense of Advertising Defenders of advertising argue that firms use advertising to provide information to customers. Advertising conveys the prices of the goods being offered for sale, the existence of new products, and the locations of retail outlets. This information allows customers to make better choices about what to buy and, thus, enhances the ability of markets to allocate resources efficiently.

Defenders also argue that advertising fosters competition. Because advertising allows customers to be more fully informed about all the firms in the market, customers can more easily take advantage of price differences. Thus, each firm has less market power. In addition, advertising allows new firms to enter more easily, because it gives entrants a means to attract customers from existing firms.

argue makes market more efficient and competitive

Over time, policymakers have come to accept the view that advertising can make markets more competitive. One important example is the regulation of advertising for certain professions, such as lawyers, doctors, and pharmacists. In the past, these groups succeeded in getting state governments to prohibit advertising in their fields on the grounds that advertising was "unprofessional." In recent years, however, the courts have concluded that the primary effect of these restrictions on advertising was to curtail competition. They have, therefore, overturned many of the laws that prohibit advertising by members of these professions.

low makes ad free.

Case Study

ADVERTISING AND THE PRICE OF EYEGLASSES

differenciate or more competitive?

What effect does advertising have on the price of a good? On the one hand, advertising might make consumers view products as being more different than they otherwise would. If so, it would make markets less competitive and firms' demand curves less elastic, and this would lead firms to charge higher prices. On the other hand, advertising might make it easier for consumers to find the firms offering the best prices. In this case, it would make markets more competitive and firms' demand curves more elastic, and this would lead to lower prices.

In an article published in the *Journal of Law and Economics* in 1972, economist Lee Benham tested these two views of advertising. In the United States during the 1960s, the various state governments had vastly different rules about advertising by optometrists. Some states allowed advertising for eyeglasses and eye examinations. Many states, however, prohibited it. For example, the Florida law read as follows:

> It is unlawful for any person, firm, or corporation to . . . advertise either directly or indirectly by any means whatsoever any definite or indefinite price or credit terms on prescriptive or corrective lens, frames, complete prescriptive or corrective glasses, or any optometric service. . . . This section is passed in the interest of public health, safety, and welfare, and its provisions shall be liberally construed to carry out its objects and purposes.

Professional optometrists enthusiastically endorsed these restrictions on advertising.

Benham used the differences in state law as a natural experiment to test the two views of advertising. The results were striking. In those states that prohibited advertising, the average price paid for a pair of eyeglasses was $33. (This number is not as low as it seems, for this price is from 1963, when all prices were much lower than they are today. To convert 1963 prices into today's dollars, you can multiply them by 5.) In those states that did not restrict advertising, the average price was $26. Thus, advertising reduced average prices by more than 20 percent. In the market for eyeglasses, and probably in many other markets as well, advertising fosters competition and leads to lower prices for consumers. ●

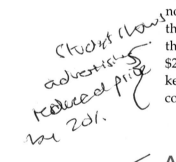

(two) laws advertising reduced price by 20%.

Advertising as a Signal of Quality

Expensive ad's mean good product?

Many types of advertising contain little apparent information about the product being advertised. Consider a firm introducing a new breakfast cereal. A typical advertisement might have some highly paid actor eating the cereal and exclaiming how wonderful it tastes. How much information does the advertisement really provide?

The answer is: more than you might think. Defenders of advertising argue that even advertising that appears to contain little hard information may in fact tell consumers something about product quality. The willingness of the firm to spend a large amount of money on advertising can itself be a *signal* to consumers about the quality of the product being offered.

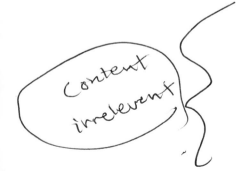

Content irrelevant

Consider the problem facing two firms—Post and Kellogg. Each company has just come up with a recipe for a new cereal, which it would sell for $3 a box. To keep things simple, let's assume that the marginal cost of making cereal is zero, so the $3 is all profit. Each company knows that if it spends $10 million on advertising, it will get 1 million consumers to try its new cereal. And each company knows that if consumers like the cereal, they will buy it not once but many times.

First consider Post's decision. Based on market research, Post knows that its cereal is only mediocre. Although advertising would sell one box to each of 1 million consumers, the consumers would quickly learn that the cereal is not very good and stop buying it. Post decides it is not worth paying $10 million in advertising to get only $3 million in sales. So it does not bother to advertise. It sends its cooks back to the drawing board to find another recipe.

Kellogg, on the other hand, knows that its cereal is great. Each person who tries it will buy a box a month for the next year. Thus, the $10 million in advertising will bring in $36 million in sales. Advertising is profitable here because Kellogg has a good product that consumers will buy repeatedly. Thus, Kellogg chooses to advertise.

Now that we have considered the behavior of the two firms, let's consider the behavior of consumers. We began by asserting that consumers are inclined to try a new cereal that they see advertised. But is this behavior rational? Should a consumer try a new cereal just because the seller has chosen to advertise it?

In fact, it may be completely rational for consumers to try new products that they see advertised. In our story, consumers decide to try Kellogg's new cereal because Kellogg advertises. Kellogg chooses to advertise because it knows that its cereal is quite good, while Post chooses not to advertise because it knows that its cereal is only mediocre. By its willingness to spend money on advertising, Kellogg signals to consumers the quality of its cereal. Each consumer thinks, quite sensibly, "Boy, if the Kellogg Company is willing to spend so much money advertising this new cereal, it must be really good."

What is most surprising about this theory of advertising is that the content of the advertisement is irrelevant. Kellogg signals the quality of its product by its willingness to spend money on advertising. What the advertisements say is not as important as the fact that consumers know ads are expensive. By contrast, cheap advertising cannot be effective at signaling quality to consumers. In our example, if an advertising campaign cost less than $3 million, both Post and Kellogg would use it to market their new cereals. Because both good and mediocre cereals would be advertised, consumers could not infer the quality of a new cereal from the fact that it is advertised. Over time, consumers would learn to ignore such cheap advertising.

This theory can explain why firms pay famous actors large amounts of money to make advertisements that, on the surface, appear to convey no information at all. The information is not in the advertisement's content, but simply in its existence and expense.

Brand Names

Advertising is closely related to the existence of brand names. In many markets, there are two types of firms. Some firms sell products with widely recognized brand names, while other firms sell generic substitutes. For example, in a typical drugstore, you can find Bayer aspirin on the shelf next to a generic aspirin. In a typical grocery store, you can find Pepsi next to less familiar colas. Most often, the firm with the brand name spends more on advertising and charges a higher price for its product.

Just as there is disagreement about the economics of advertising, there is disagreement about the economics of brand names. Let's consider both sides of the debate.

Critics of brand names argue that brand names cause consumers to perceive differences that do not really exist. In many cases, the generic good is almost indistinguishable from the brand-name good. Consumers' willingness to pay more for the brand-name good, these critics assert, is a form of irrationality fostered by advertising. Economist Edward Chamberlin, one of the early developers of the theory of monopolistic competition, concluded from this argument that brand names were bad for the economy. He proposed that the government discourage their use by refusing to enforce the exclusive trademarks that companies use to identify their products.

More recently, economists have defended brand names as a useful way for consumers to ensure that the goods they buy are of high quality. There are two related arguments. First, brand names provide consumers with *information* about quality when quality cannot be easily judged in advance of purchase. Second, brand names give firms an *incentive* to maintain high quality, because firms have a financial stake in maintaining the reputation of their brand names.

To see how these arguments work in practice, consider a famous brand name: McDonald's hamburgers. Imagine that you are driving through an unfamiliar town and want to stop for lunch. You see a McDonald's and a local restaurant next to it. Which do you choose? The local restaurant may in fact offer better food at lower prices, but you have no way of knowing that. By contrast, McDonald's offers a consistent product across many cities. Its brand name is useful to you as a way of judging the quality of what you are about to buy.

The McDonald's brand name also ensures that the company has an incentive to maintain quality. For example, if some customers were to become ill from bad food sold at a McDonald's, the news would be disastrous for the company. McDonald's would lose much of the valuable reputation that it has built up with years of expensive advertising. As a result, it would lose sales and profit not just in the outlet that sold the bad food but in its many outlets throughout the country. By contrast, if some customers were to become ill from bad food at a local restaurant, that restaurant might have to close down, but the lost profits would be much smaller. Hence, McDonald's has a greater incentive to ensure that its food is safe.

The debate over brand names thus centers on the question of whether consumers are rational in preferring brand names over generic substitutes. Critics of brand names argue that brand names are the result of an irrational consumer response to advertising. Defenders of brand names argue that consumers have good reason to pay more for brand-name products because they can be more confident in the quality of these products.

QuickQuiz How might advertising make markets less competitive? How might it make markets more competitive? • Give the arguments for and against brand names.

CONCLUSION

Monopolistic competition is true to its name: It is a hybrid of monopoly and competition. Like a monopoly, each monopolistic competitor faces a downward-sloping demand curve and, as a result, charges a price above marginal cost. As in a perfectly competitive market, there are many firms, and entry and exit drive the profit of each monopolistic competitor toward zero. Table 1 summarizes these lessons.

TABLE 1

Monopolistic Competition: Between Perfect Competition and Monopoly

	Market Structure		
	Perfect Competition	Monopolistic Competition	Monopoly
Features that all three market structures share			
Goal of firms	Maximize profits	Maximize profits	Maximize profits
Rule for maximizing	$MR = MC$	$MR = MC$	$MR = MC$
Can earn economic profits in the short run?	Yes	Yes	Yes
Features that monopoly and monopolistic competition share			
Price taker?	Yes	No	No
Price	$P = MC$	$P > MC$	$P > MC$
Produces welfare-maximizing level of output?	Yes	No	No
Features that perfect competition and monopolistic competition share			
Number of firms	Many	Many	One
Entry in long run?	Yes	Yes	No
Can earn economic profits in long run?	No	No	Yes

Because monopolistically competitive firms produce differentiated products, each firm advertises in order to attract customers to its own brand. To some extent, advertising manipulates consumers' tastes, promotes irrational brand loyalty, and impedes competition. To a larger extent, advertising provides information, establishes brand names of reliable quality, and fosters competition.

The theory of monopolistic competition seems to describe many markets in the economy. It is somewhat disappointing, therefore, that the theory does not yield simple and compelling advice for public policy. From the standpoint of the economic theorist, the allocation of resources in monopolistically competitive markets is not perfect. Yet, from the standpoint of a practical policymaker, there may be little that can be done to improve it.

SUMMARY

- A monopolistically competitive market is characterized by three attributes: many firms, differentiated products, and free entry.

- The equilibrium in a monopolistically competitive market differs from that in a perfectly competitive market in two related ways. First, each firm in a monopolistically competitive market has excess capacity. That is, it operates on the downward-sloping portion of the average-total-cost curve. Second, each firm charges a price above marginal cost.

- Monopolistic competition does not have all the desirable properties of perfect competition. There is the standard deadweight loss of monopoly caused by the markup of price over marginal cost. In addition, the number of firms (and thus the variety of products) can be too large or too small. In practice, the ability of policymakers to correct these inefficiencies is limited.

- The product differentiation inherent in monopolistic competition leads to the use of advertising and brand names. Critics of advertising and brand names argue that firms use them to take advantage of consumer irrationality and to reduce competition. Defenders of advertising and brand names argue that firms use them to inform consumers and to compete more vigorously on price and product quality.

KEY CONCEPTS

monopolistic competition, p. 374

QUESTIONS FOR REVIEW

1. Describe the three attributes of monopolistic competition. How is monopolistic competition like monopoly? How is it like perfect competition?

2. Draw a diagram depicting a firm in a monopolistically competitive market that is making profits. Now show what happens to this firm as new firms enter the industry.

3. Draw a diagram of the long-run equilibrium in a monopolistically competitive market. How is price related to average total cost? How is price related to marginal cost?

4. Does a monopolistic competitor produce too much or too little output compared to the most efficient level? What practical considerations make it difficult for policymakers to solve this problem?

5. How might advertising reduce economic well-being? How might advertising increase economic well-being?

6. How might advertising with no apparent informational content in fact convey information to consumers?

7. Explain two benefits that might arise from the existence of brand names.

PROBLEMS AND APPLICATIONS

1. Classify the following markets as perfectly competitive, monopolistic, or monopolistically competitive, and explain your answers.
   a. wooden #2 pencils
   b. bottled water
   c. copper
   d. local telephone service
   e. peanut butter
   f. lipstick

2. What feature of the product being sold distinguishes a monopolistically competitive firm from a monopolistic firm?

3. The chapter states that monopolistically competitive firms could increase the quantity they produce and lower the average total cost of production. Why don't they do so?

4. Sparkle is one firm of many in the market for toothpaste, which is in long-run equilibrium.
   a. Draw a diagram showing Sparkle's demand curve, marginal-revenue curve, average-total-cost curve, and marginal-cost curve. Label Sparkle's profit-maximizing output and price.
   b. What is Sparkle's profit? Explain.
   c. On your diagram, show the consumer surplus derived from the purchase of Sparkle toothpaste. Also show the deadweight loss relative to the efficient level of output.
   d. If the government forced Sparkle to produce the efficient level of output, what would happen to the firm? What would happen to Sparkle's customers?

5. Do monopolistically competitive markets typically have the optimal number of products? Explain.

6. The chapter says that monopolistically competitive firms may send Christmas cards to their customers. What do they accomplish by this? Explain in words and with a diagram.

7. If you were thinking of entering the ice-cream business, would you try to make ice cream that is just like one of the existing brands? Explain your decision using the ideas of this chapter.

8. Describe three commercials that you have seen on TV. In what ways, if any, were each of these commercials socially useful? In what ways were they socially wasteful? Did the commercials affect the likelihood of your buying the product? Why or why not?

9. For each of the following pairs of firms, explain which firm would be more likely to engage in advertising:
   a. a family-owned farm or a family-owned restaurant
   b. a manufacturer of forklifts or a manufacturer of cars
   c. a company that invented a very reliable watch or a company that invented a less reliable watch that costs the same amount to make

10. Twenty years ago the market for chicken was perfectly competitive. Then Frank Perdue began marketing chicken under his name.
    a. How do you suppose Perdue created a brand name for chicken? What did he gain from doing so?
    b. What did society gain from having brand-name chicken? What did society lose?

11. The makers of Tylenol pain reliever do a lot of advertising and have very loyal customers. In contrast, the makers of generic acetaminophen do no advertising, and their customers shop only for the lowest price. Assume that the marginal costs of Tylenol and generic acetaminophen are the same and constant.
    a. Draw a diagram showing Tylenol's demand, marginal-revenue, and marginal-cost curves. Label Tylenol's price and markup over marginal cost.
    b. Repeat part (a) for a producer of generic acetaminophen. How do the diagrams differ? Which company has the bigger markup? Explain.
    c. Which company has the bigger incentive for careful quality control? Why?

6

THE ECONOMICS OF LABOR MARKETS

THE MARKETS FOR
THE FACTORS OF PRODUCTION

When you finish school, your income will be determined largely by what kind of job you take. If you become a computer programmer, you will earn more than if you become a gas station attendant. This fact is not surprising, but it is not obvious why it is true. No law requires that computer programmers be paid more than gas station attendants. No ethical principle says that programmers are more deserving. What then determines which job will pay you the higher wage?

Your income, of course, is a small piece of a larger economic picture. In 2002 the total income of all U.S. residents was about $10 trillion. People earned this income in various ways. Workers earned about three-fourths of it in the form of wages and fringe benefits. The rest went to landowners and to the owners of *capital*—the economy's stock of equipment and structures—in the form of rent, profit, and interest. What determines how much goes to workers? To landowners? To the owners of capital? Why do some workers earn higher wages than others, some landowners higher rental income than others, and some capital owners greater profit than others? Why, in particular, do computer programmers earn more than gas station attendants?

factors of production
the inputs used to produce goods
and services

The answers to these questions, like most in economics, hinge on supply and demand. The supply and demand for labor, land, and capital determine the prices paid to workers, landowners, and capital owners. To understand why some people have higher incomes than others, therefore, we need to look more deeply at the markets for the services they provide. That is our job in this and the next two chapters.

This chapter provides the basic theory for the analysis of factor markets. As you may recall from Chapter 2, the **factors of production** are the inputs used to produce goods and services. Labor, land, and capital are the three most important factors of production. When a computer firm produces a new software program, it uses programmers' time (labor), the physical space on which its offices sit (land), and an office building and computer equipment (capital). Similarly, when a gas station sells gas, it uses attendants' time (labor), the physical space (land), and the gas tanks and pumps (capital).

Although in many ways factor markets resemble the goods markets we have analyzed in previous chapters, they are different in one important way: The demand for a factor of production is a *derived demand*. That is, a firm's demand for a factor of production is derived from its decision to supply a good in another market. The demand for computer programmers is inextricably tied to the supply of computer software, and the demand for gas station attendants is inextricably tied to the supply of gasoline.

In this chapter we analyze factor demand by considering how a competitive, profit-maximizing firm decides how much of any factor to buy. We begin our analysis by examining the demand for labor. Labor is the most important factor of production, for workers receive most of the total income earned in the U.S. economy. Later in the chapter, we see that the lessons we learn about the labor market apply directly to the markets for the other factors of production.

The basic theory of factor markets developed in this chapter takes a large step toward explaining how the income of the U.S. economy is distributed among workers, landowners, and owners of capital. Chapter 19 will build on this analysis to examine in more detail why some workers earn more than others. Chapter 20 will examine how much inequality results from this process and then consider what role the government should and does play in altering the distribution of income.

THE DEMAND FOR LABOR

Labor markets, like other markets in the economy, are governed by the forces of supply and demand. This is illustrated in Figure 1. In panel (a) the supply and demand for apples determine the price of apples. In panel (b) the supply and demand for apple pickers determine the price, or wage, of apple pickers.

As we have already noted, labor markets are different from most other markets because labor demand is a derived demand. Most labor services, rather than being final goods ready to be enjoyed by consumers, are inputs into the production of other goods. To understand labor demand, we need to focus on the firms that hire the labor and use it to produce goods for sale. By examining the link between the production of goods and the demand for labor, we gain insight into the determination of equilibrium wages.

FIGURE 1

The Versatility of Supply and Demand

The basic tools of supply and demand apply to goods and to labor services. Panel (a) shows how the supply and demand for apples determine the price of apples. Panel (b) shows how the supply and demand for apple pickers determine the wage of apple pickers.

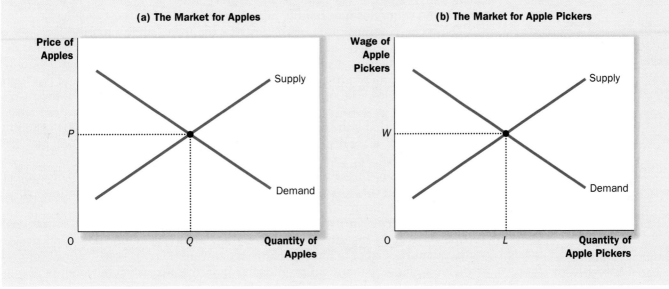

The Competitive Profit-Maximizing Firm

Let's look at how a typical firm, such as an apple producer, decides the quantity of labor to demand. The firm owns an apple orchard and each week must decide how many apple pickers to hire to harvest its crop. After the firm makes its hiring decision, the workers pick as many apples as they can. The firm then sells the apples, pays the workers, and keeps what is left as profit.

We make two assumptions about our firm. First, we assume that our firm is *competitive* both in the market for apples (where the firm is a seller) and in the market for apple pickers (where the firm is a buyer). Recall from Chapter 14 that a competitive firm is a price taker. Because there are many other firms selling apples and hiring apple pickers, a single firm has little influence over the price it gets for apples or the wage it pays apple pickers. The firm takes the price and the wage as given by market conditions. It only has to decide how many workers to hire and how many apples to sell.

Second, we assume that the firm is *profit-maximizing*. Thus, the firm does not directly care about the number of workers it has or the number of apples it produces. It cares only about profit, which equals the total revenue from the sale of apples minus the total cost of producing them. The firm's supply of apples and its demand for workers are derived from its primary goal of maximizing profit.

The Production Function and the Marginal Product of Labor

To make its hiring decision, the firm must consider how the size of its workforce affects the amount of output produced. In other words, it must consider how the number of apple pickers affects the quantity of apples it can harvest and sell. Table 1 gives a numerical example. In the first column is the number of workers. In the second column is the quantity of apples the workers harvest each week.

production function
the relationship between the quantity of inputs used to make a good and the quantity of output of that good

These two columns of numbers describe the firm's ability to produce. As we noted in Chapter 13, economists use the term **production function** to describe the relationship between the quantity of the inputs used in production and the quantity of output from production. Here the "input" is the apple pickers and the "output" is the apples. The other inputs—the trees themselves, the land, the firm's trucks and tractors, and so on—are held fixed for now. This firm's production function shows that if the firm hires 1 worker, that worker will pick 100 bushels of apples per week. If the firm hires 2 workers, the two workers together will pick 180 bushels per week, and so on.

Figure 2 graphs the data on labor and output presented in Table 1. The number of workers is on the horizontal axis, and the amount of output is on the vertical axis. This figure illustrates the production function.

One of the *Ten Principles of Economics* introduced in Chapter 1 is that rational people think at the margin. This idea is the key to understanding how firms decide what quantity of labor to hire. To take a step toward this decision, the third column in Table 1 gives the **marginal product of labor**, the increase in the amount of output from an additional unit of labor. When the firm increases the number of work-

marginal product of labor
the increase in the amount of output from an additional unit of labor

---

TABLE 1

How the Competitive Firm Decides How Much Labor to Hire

Labor	Output	Marginal Product of Labor	Value of the Marginal Product of Labor	Wage	Marginal Profit
L (number of workers)	Q (bushels per week)	$MPL = \Delta Q / \Delta L$ (bushels per week)	$VMPL = P \times MPL$	W	$\Delta Profit = VMPL - W$
0	0				
		100	$1,000	$500	$500
1	100				
		80	800	500	300
2	180				
		60	600	500	100
3	240				
		40	400	500	−100
4	280				
		20	200	500	−300
5	300				

FIGURE 2

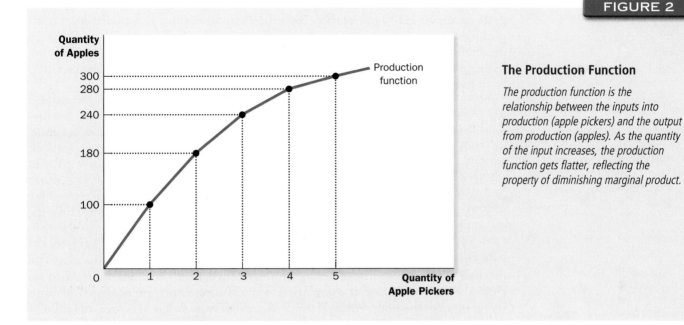

The Production Function

The production function is the relationship between the inputs into production (apple pickers) and the output from production (apples). As the quantity of the input increases, the production function gets flatter, reflecting the property of diminishing marginal product.

ers from 1 to 2, for example, the amount of apples produced rises from 100 to 180 bushels. Therefore, the marginal product of the second worker is 80 bushels.

Notice that as the number of workers increases, the marginal product of labor declines. As you may recall from Chapter 13, this property is called **diminishing marginal product.** At first, when only a few workers are hired, they pick apples from the best trees in the orchard. As the number of workers increases, additional workers have to pick from the trees with fewer apples. Hence, as more and more workers are hired, each additional worker contributes less to the production of apples. For this reason, the production function in Figure 2 becomes flatter as the number of workers rises.

diminishing marginal product the property whereby the marginal product of an input declines as the quantity of the input increases

The Value of the Marginal Product and the Demand for Labor

Our profit-maximizing firm is concerned more with money than with apples. As a result, when deciding how many workers to hire, the firm considers how much profit each worker would bring in. Because profit is total revenue minus total cost, the profit from an additional worker is the worker's contribution to revenue minus the worker's wage.

To find the worker's contribution to revenue, we must convert the marginal product of labor (which is measured in bushels of apples) into the *value* of the marginal product (which is measured in dollars). We do this using the price of apples. To continue our example, if a bushel of apples sells for $10 and if an additional worker produces 80 bushels of apples, then the worker produces $800 of revenue.

The **value of the marginal product** of any input is the marginal product of that input multiplied by the market price of the output. The fourth column in Table 1

value of the marginal product the marginal product of an input times the price of the output

shows the value of the marginal product of labor in our example, assuming the price of apples is $10 per bushel. Because the market price is constant for a competitive firm, the value of the marginal product (like the marginal product itself) diminishes as the number of workers rises. Economists sometimes call this column of numbers the firm's *marginal revenue product:* It is the extra revenue the firm gets from hiring an additional unit of a factor of production.

Now consider how many workers the firm will hire. Suppose that the market wage for apple pickers is $500 per week. In this case, as you see in Table 1, the first worker that the firm hires is profitable: The first worker yields $1,000 in revenue, or $500 in profit. Similarly, the second worker yields $800 in additional revenue, or $300 in profit. The third worker produces $600 in additional revenue, or $100 in profit. After the third worker, however, hiring workers is unprofitable. The fourth worker would yield only $400 of additional revenue. Because the worker's wage is $500, hiring the fourth worker would mean a $100 reduction in profit. Thus, the firm hires only three workers.

It is instructive to consider the firm's decision graphically. Figure 3 graphs the value of the marginal product. This curve slopes downward because the marginal product of labor diminishes as the number of workers rises. The figure also includes a horizontal line at the market wage. To maximize profit, the firm hires workers up to the point where these two curves cross. Below this level of employment, the value of the marginal product exceeds the wage, so hiring another worker would increase profit. Above this level of employment, the value of the marginal product is less than the wage, so the marginal worker is unprofitable. Thus, *a competitive, profit-maximizing firm hires workers up to the point where the value of the marginal product of labor equals the wage.*

Having explained the profit-maximizing hiring strategy for a competitive firm, we can now offer a theory of labor demand. Recall that a firm's labor demand

---

FIGURE 3

The Value of the Marginal Product of Labor

This figure shows how the value of the marginal product (the marginal product times the price of the output) depends on the number of workers. The curve slopes downward because of diminishing marginal product. For a competitive, profit-maximizing firm, this value-of-marginal-product curve is also the firm's labor demand curve.

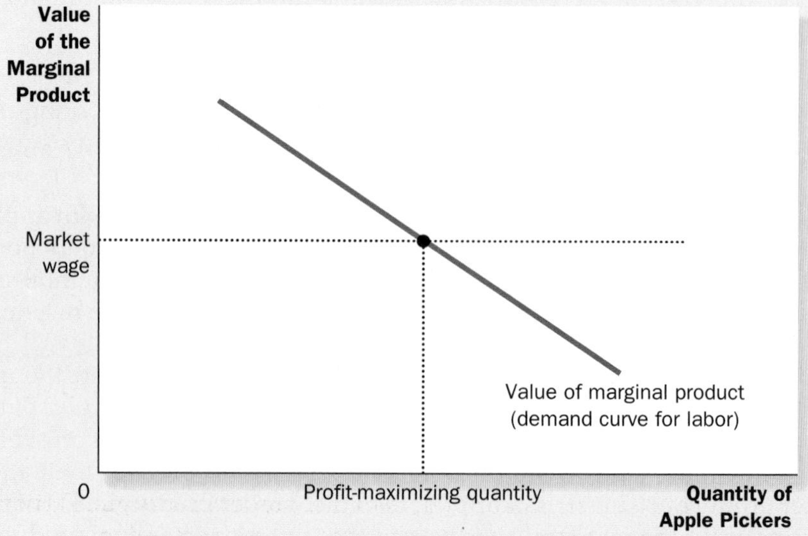

FYI

INPUT DEMAND AND OUTPUT SUPPLY: TWO SIDES OF THE SAME COIN

In Chapter 14 we saw how a competitive, profit-maximizing firm decides how much of its output to sell: It chooses the quantity of output at which the price of the good equals the marginal cost of production. We have just seen how such a firm decides how much labor to hire: It chooses the quantity of labor at which the wage equals the value of the marginal product. Because the production function links the quantity of inputs to the quantity of output, you should not be surprised to learn that the firm's decision about input demand is closely linked to its decision about output supply. In fact, these two decisions are two sides of the same coin.

To see this relationship more fully, let's consider how the marginal product of labor (*MPL*) and marginal cost (*MC*) are related. Suppose an additional worker costs $500 and has a marginal product of 50 bushels of apples. In this case, producing 50 more bushels costs $500; the marginal cost of a bushel is $500/50, or $10. More generally, if *W* is the wage, and an extra unit of labor produces *MPL* units of output, then the marginal cost of a unit of output is $MC = W/MPL$.

This analysis shows that diminishing marginal product is closely related to increasing marginal cost. When our apple orchard grows crowded with workers, each additional worker adds less to the production of apples (*MPL* falls). Similarly, when the apple firm is producing a large quantity of apples, the orchard is already crowded with workers, so it is more costly to produce an additional bushel of apples (*MC* rises).

Now consider our criterion for profit maximization. We determined earlier that a profit-maximizing firm chooses the quantity of labor so that the value of the marginal product ($P \times MPL$) equals the wage (*W*). We can write this mathematically as

$$P \times MPL = W.$$

If we divide both sides of this equation by *MPL*, we obtain

$$P = W/MPL.$$

We just noted that W/MPL equals marginal cost *MC*. Therefore, we can substitute to obtain

$$P = MC.$$

This equation states that the price of the firm's output is equal to the marginal cost of producing a unit of output. *Thus, when a competitive firm hires labor up to the point at which the value of the marginal product equals the wage, it also produces up to the point at which the price equals marginal cost.* Our analysis of labor demand in this chapter is just another way of looking at the production decision we first saw in Chapter 14.

---

curve tells us the quantity of labor that a firm demands at any given wage. We have just seen in Figure 3 that the firm makes that decision by choosing the quantity of labor at which the value of the marginal product equals the wage. As a result, *the value-of-marginal-product curve is the labor demand curve for a competitive, profit-maximizing firm.*

What Causes the Labor Demand Curve to Shift?

We now understand the labor demand curve: It reflects the value of the marginal product of labor. With this insight in mind, let's consider a few of the things that might cause the labor demand curve to shift.

The Output Price   The value of the marginal product is marginal product times the price of the firm's output. Thus, when the output price changes, the value of the marginal product changes, and the labor demand curve shifts. An increase in the price of apples, for instance, raises the value of the marginal product of each worker who picks apples and, therefore, increases labor demand from the firms that supply apples. Conversely, a decrease in the price of apples reduces the value of the marginal product and decreases labor demand.

Technological Change   Between 1960 and 2000, the amount of output a typical U.S. worker produced in an hour rose by 140 percent. Why? The most important reason is technological progress: Scientists and engineers are constantly figuring out new and better ways of doing things. This has profound implications for the labor market. Technological advance raises the marginal product of labor, which in turn increases the demand for labor. Such technological advance explains persistently rising employment in the face of rising wages: Even though wages (adjusted for inflation) increased by 131 percent over these four decades, firms nonetheless increased by 80 percent the amount of labor they employed.

The Supply of Other Factors   The quantity available of one factor of production can affect the marginal product of other factors. A fall in the supply of ladders, for instance, will reduce the marginal product of apple pickers and thus the demand for apple pickers. We consider this linkage among the factors of production more fully later in the chapter.

QuickQuiz Define *marginal product of labor* and *value of the marginal product of labor.* • Describe how a competitive, profit-maximizing firm decides how many workers to hire.

THE SUPPLY OF LABOR

Having analyzed labor demand in detail, let's turn to the other side of the market and consider labor supply. A formal model of labor supply is included in Chapter 21, where we develop the theory of household decisionmaking. Here we discuss briefly and informally the decisions that lie behind the labor supply curve.

The Tradeoff between Work and Leisure

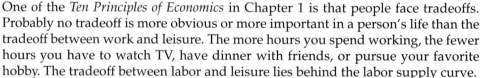

One of the *Ten Principles of Economics* in Chapter 1 is that people face tradeoffs. Probably no tradeoff is more obvious or more important in a person's life than the tradeoff between work and leisure. The more hours you spend working, the fewer hours you have to watch TV, have dinner with friends, or pursue your favorite hobby. The tradeoff between labor and leisure lies behind the labor supply curve.

Another of the *Ten Principles of Economics* is that the cost of something is what you give up to get it. What do you give up to get an hour of leisure? You give up an hour of work, which in turn means an hour of wages. Thus, if your wage is $15 per hour, the opportunity cost of an hour of leisure is $15. And when you get a raise to $20 per hour, the opportunity cost of enjoying leisure goes up.

The labor supply curve reflects how workers' decisions about the labor–leisure tradeoff respond to a change in that opportunity cost. An upward-sloping labor supply curve means that an increase in the wage induces workers to increase the quantity of labor they supply. Because time is limited, more hours of work means that workers are enjoying less leisure. That is, workers respond to the increase in the opportunity cost of leisure by taking less of it.

It is worth noting that the labor supply curve need not be upward sloping. Imagine you got that raise from $15 to $20 per hour. The opportunity cost of leisure is now greater, but you are also richer than you were before. You might decide that with your extra wealth you can now afford to enjoy more leisure. That is, at the higher wage, you might choose to work fewer hours. If so, your labor supply curve would slope backwards. In Chapter 21, we discuss this possibility in terms of conflicting effects on your labor-supply decision (called the income and substitution effects). For now, we ignore the possibility of backward-sloping labor supply and assume that the labor supply curve is upward sloping.

What Causes the Labor Supply Curve to Shift?

The labor supply curve shifts whenever people change the amount they want to work at a given wage. Let's now consider some of the events that might cause such a shift.

Changes in Tastes In 1950, 34 percent of women were employed at paid jobs or looking for work. In 2000, the number had risen to 60 percent. There are, of course, many explanations for this development, but one of them is changing tastes, or attitudes toward work. A generation or two ago, it was the norm for women to stay at home while raising children. Today, family sizes are smaller, and more mothers choose to work. The result is an increase in the supply of labor.

Changes in Alternative Opportunities The supply of labor in any one labor market depends on the opportunities available in other labor markets. If the wage earned by pear pickers suddenly rises, some apple pickers may choose to switch occupations. The supply of labor in the market for apple pickers falls.

Immigration Movement of workers from region to region, or country to country, is an obvious and often important source of shifts in labor supply. When immigrants come to the United States, for instance, the supply of labor in the United States increases and the supply of labor in the immigrants' home countries contracts. In fact, much of the policy debate about immigration centers on its effect on labor supply and, thereby, equilibrium in the labor market.

QuickQuiz Who has a greater opportunity cost of enjoying leisure—a janitor or a brain surgeon? Explain. Can this help explain why doctors work such long hours?

EQUILIBRIUM IN THE LABOR MARKET

So far we have established two facts about how wages are determined in competitive labor markets:

FIGURE 4

Equilibrium in a Labor Market

Like all prices, the price of labor (the wage) depends on supply and demand. Because the demand curve reflects the value of the marginal product of labor, in equilibrium workers receive the value of their marginal contribution to the production of goods and services.

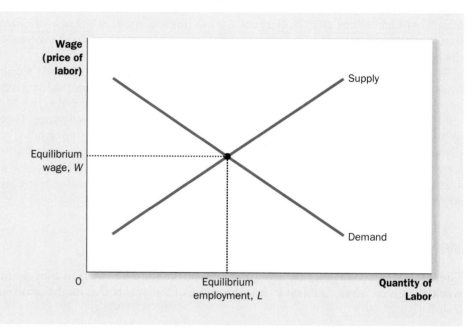

- The wage adjusts to balance the supply and demand for labor.
- The wage equals the value of the marginal product of labor.

At first, it might seem surprising that the wage can do both these things at once. In fact, there is no real puzzle here, but understanding why there is no puzzle is an important step to understanding wage determination.

Figure 4 shows the labor market in equilibrium. The wage and the quantity of labor have adjusted to balance supply and demand. When the market is in this equilibrium, each firm has bought as much labor as it finds profitable at the equilibrium wage. That is, each firm has followed the rule for profit maximization: It has hired workers until the value of the marginal product equals the wage. Hence, the wage must equal the value of the marginal product of labor once it has brought supply and demand into equilibrium.

This brings us to an important lesson: *Any event that changes the supply or demand for labor must change the equilibrium wage and the value of the marginal product by the same amount, because these must always be equal.* To see how this works, let's consider some events that shift these curves.

Shifts in Labor Supply

Suppose that immigration increases the number of workers willing to pick apples. As Figure 5 shows, the supply of labor shifts to the right from S_1 to S_2. At the initial wage W_1, the quantity of labor supplied now exceeds the quantity demanded. This surplus of labor puts downward pressure on the wage of apple pickers, and the fall in the wage from W_1 to W_2 in turn makes it profitable for firms to hire more workers. As the number of workers employed in each apple orchard rises, the

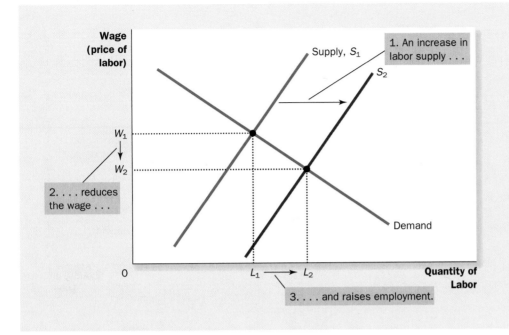

FIGURE 5

A Shift in Labor Supply

When labor supply increases from S₁ to S₂, perhaps because of an immigration of new workers, the equilibrium wage falls from W₁ to W₂. At this lower wage, firms hire more labor, so employment rises from L₁ to L₂. The change in the wage reflects a change in the value of the marginal product of labor: With more workers, the added output from an extra worker is smaller.

marginal product of a worker falls, and so does the value of the marginal product. In the new equilibrium, both the wage and the value of the marginal product of labor are lower than they were before the influx of new workers.

An episode from Israel illustrates how a shift in labor supply can alter the equilibrium in a labor market. During most of the 1980s, many thousands of Palestinians regularly commuted from their homes in the Israeli-occupied West Bank and Gaza Strip to jobs in Israel, primarily in the construction and agriculture industries. In 1988, however, political unrest in these occupied areas induced the Israeli government to take steps that, as a by-product, reduced this supply of workers. Curfews were imposed, work permits were checked more thoroughly, and a ban on overnight stays of Palestinians in Israel was enforced more rigorously. The economic impact of these steps was exactly as theory predicts: The number of Palestinians with jobs in Israel fell by half, while those who continued to work in Israel enjoyed wage increases of about 50 percent. With a reduced number of Palestinian workers in Israel, the value of the marginal product of the remaining workers was much higher.

Shifts in Labor Demand

Now suppose that an increase in the popularity of apples causes their price to rise. This price increase does not change the marginal product of labor for any given number of workers, but it does raise the *value* of the marginal product. With a higher price of apples, hiring more apple pickers is now profitable. As Figure 6 (p. 402) shows, when the demand for labor shifts to the right from D_1 to D_2, the equilibrium wage rises from W_1 to W_2, and equilibrium employment rises from L_1

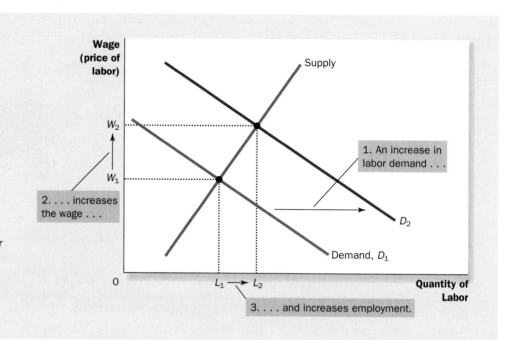

FIGURE 6

A Shift in Labor Demand

When labor demand increases from D_1 to D_2, perhaps because of an increase in the price of the firms' output, the equilibrium wage rises from W_1 to W_2, and employment rises from L_1 to L_2. Again, the change in the wage reflects a change in the value of the marginal product of labor: With a higher output price, the added output from an extra worker is more valuable.

to L_2. Once again, the wage and the value of the marginal product of labor move together.

This analysis shows that prosperity for firms in an industry is often linked to prosperity for workers in that industry. When the price of apples rises, apple producers make greater profit, and apple pickers earn higher wages. When the price of apples falls, apple producers earn smaller profit, and apple pickers earn lower wages. This lesson is well known to workers in industries with highly volatile prices. Workers in oil fields, for instance, know from experience that their earnings are closely linked to the world price of crude oil.

From these examples, you should now have a good understanding of how wages are set in competitive labor markets. Labor supply and labor demand together determine the equilibrium wage, and shifts in the supply or demand curve for labor cause the equilibrium wage to change. At the same time, profit maximization by the firms that demand labor ensures that the equilibrium wage always equals the value of the marginal product of labor.

Case Study

PRODUCTIVITY AND WAGES

One of the *Ten Principles of Economics* in Chapter 1 is that our standard of living depends on our ability to produce goods and services. We can now see how this principle works in the market for labor. In particular, our analysis of labor demand

TABLE 2

Productivity and Wage Growth in the United States.

Time Period	Growth Rate of Productivity	Growth Rate of Real Wages
1959–2000	2.0	2.0
1959–1973	2.9	3.0
1973–1995	1.3	1.1
1995–2000	2.6	2.9

Source: *Economic Report of the President 2002,* table B-49, p. 378. Growth in productivity is measured here as the annualized rate of change in output per hour in the nonfarm business sector. Growth in real wages is measured as the annualized change in compensation per hour in the nonfarm business sector divided by the implicit price deflator for that sector. These productivity data measure average productivity—the quantity of output divided by the quantity of labor—rather than marginal productivity, but average and marginal productivity are thought to move closely together.

shows that wages equal productivity as measured by the value of the marginal product of labor. Put simply, highly productive workers are highly paid, and less productive workers are less highly paid.

This lesson is key to understanding why workers today are better off than workers in previous generations. Table 2 presents some data on growth in productivity and growth in real wages (that is, wages adjusted for inflation). From 1959 to 2000, productivity as measured by output per hour of work grew about 2.0 percent per year. Real wages grew at the same rate. With a growth rate of 2.0 percent per year, productivity and real wages double about every 35 years.

Table 2 also shows the rates of growth for three shorter periods of time. Notice that from 1973 to 1995 growth in productivity was slow compared to either the period before 1973 or the period since 1995. The cause of the productivity slowdown in 1973 is not well understood, but the link between productivity and real wages that we find in the data is exactly as standard theory predicts. The slowdown in productivity growth from 2.9 to 1.3 percent per year coincided with a slowdown in real wage growth from 3.0 to 1.1 percent per year.

Productivity growth picked up again in 1995. Many observers attribute this phenomenon to the spread of computers and information technology. As theory predicts, growth in real wages picked up as well. From 1995 to 2000, productivity grew by 2.6 percent per year, while real wages grew by 2.9 percent per year. Both theory and history confirm the close connection between productivity and real wages. ●

QuickQuiz How does an immigration of workers affect labor supply, labor demand, the marginal product of labor, and the equilibrium wage?

MONOPSONY

On the preceding pages, we built our analysis of the labor market with the tools of supply and demand. In doing so, we assumed that the labor market was competitive. That is, we assumed that there were many buyers of labor and many sellers of labor, so each buyer or seller had a negligible effect on the wage.

Yet imagine the labor market in a small town dominated by a single large employer. That employer can exert a large influence on the going wage, and it may well use that market power to alter the outcome. Such a market in which there is a single buyer is called a *monopsony.*

A monopsony (a market with one buyer) is in many ways similar to a monopoly (a market with one seller). Recall from Chapter 15 that a monopoly firm produces less of the good than would a competitive firm; by reducing the quantity offered for sale, the monopoly firm moves along the product's demand curve, raising the price and also its profits. Similarly, a monopsony firm in a labor market hires fewer workers than would a competitive firm; by reducing the number of jobs available, the monopsony firm moves along the labor supply curve, reducing the wage it pays and raising its profits. Thus, both monopolists and monopsonists reduce economic activity in a market below the socially optimal level. In both cases, the existence of market power distorts the outcome and causes deadweight losses.

This book does not present the formal model of monopsony because, in the world, monopsonies are rare. In most labor markets, workers have many possible employers, and firms compete with one another to attract workers. In this case, the model of supply and demand is the best one to use.

THE OTHER FACTORS OF PRODUCTION: LAND AND CAPITAL

We have seen how firms decide how much labor to hire and how these decisions determine workers' wages. At the same time that firms are hiring workers, they are also deciding about other inputs to production. For example, our apple-producing firm might have to choose the size of its apple orchard and the number of ladders to make available to its apple pickers. We can think of the firm's factors of production as falling into three categories: labor, land, and capital.

capital
the equipment and structures used to produce goods and services

The meaning of the terms *labor* and *land* is clear, but the definition of *capital* is somewhat tricky. Economists use the term **capital** to refer to the stock of equipment and structures used for production. That is, the economy's capital represents the accumulation of goods produced in the past that are being used in the present to produce new goods and services. For our apple firm, the capital stock includes the ladders used to climb the trees, the trucks used to transport the apples, the buildings used to store the apples, and even the trees themselves.

Equilibrium in the Markets for Land and Capital

What determines how much the owners of land and capital earn for their contribution to the production process? Before answering this question, we need to distinguish between two prices: the purchase price and the rental price. The *purchase price* of land or capital is the price a person pays to own that factor of production indefinitely. The *rental price* is the price a person pays to use that factor for a limited period of time. It is important to keep this distinction in mind because, as we will see, these prices are determined by somewhat different economic forces.

Having defined these terms, we can now apply the theory of factor demand that we developed for the labor market to the markets for land and capital. The wage is, after all, simply the rental price of labor. Therefore, much of what we have learned about wage determination applies also to the rental prices of land and capital. As Figure 7 illustrates, the rental price of land, shown in panel (a), and the rental price of capital, shown in panel (b), are determined by supply and demand. Moreover, the demand for land and capital is determined just like the demand for labor. That is, when our apple-producing firm is deciding how much land and how many ladders to rent, it follows the same logic as when deciding how many workers to hire. For both land and capital, the firm increases the quantity hired until the value of the factor's marginal product equals the factor's price. Thus, the demand curve for each factor reflects the marginal productivity of that factor.

We can now explain how much income goes to labor, how much goes to landowners, and how much goes to the owners of capital. As long as the firms using the factors of production are competitive and profit-maximizing, each factor's rental price must equal the value of the marginal product for that factor. *Labor, land, and capital each earn the value of their marginal contribution to the production process.*

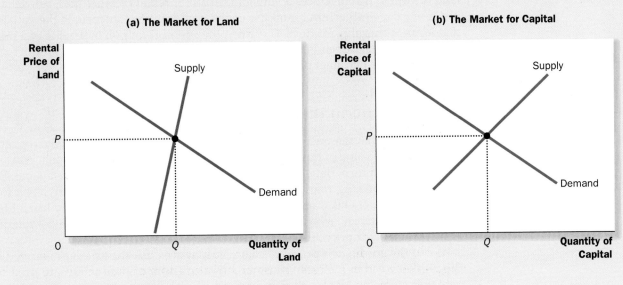

FIGURE 7

The Markets for Land and Capital

Supply and demand determine the compensation paid to the owners of land, as shown in panel (a), and the compensation paid to the owners of capital, as shown in panel (b). The demand for each factor, in turn, depends on the value of the marginal product of that factor.

(a) The Market for Land

Rental Price of Land

Supply

P

Demand

0   Q   Quantity of Land

(b) The Market for Capital

Rental Price of Capital

Supply

P

Demand

0   Q   Quantity of Capital

WHAT IS CAPITAL INCOME?

Labor income is an easy concept to understand: It is the paycheck that workers get from their employers. The income earned by capital, however, is less obvious.

In our analysis, we have been implicitly assuming that households own the economy's stock of capital—ladders, drill presses, warehouses, and so forth—and rent it to the firms that use it. Capital income, in this case, is the rent that households receive for the use of their capital. This assumption simplified our analysis of how capital owners are compensated, but it is not entirely realistic. In fact, firms usually own the capital they use and, therefore, they receive the earnings from this capital.

These earnings from capital, however, eventually get paid to households. Some of the earnings are paid in the form of interest to those households who have lent money to firms. Bondholders and bank depositors are two examples of recipients of interest. Thus, when you receive interest on your bank account, that income is part of the economy's capital income.

In addition, some of the earnings from capital are paid to households in the form of dividends. Dividends are payments by a firm to the firm's stockholders. A stockholder is a person who has bought a share in the ownership of the firm and, therefore, is entitled to share in the firm's profits.

A firm does not have to pay out all of its earnings to households in the form of interest and dividends. Instead, it can retain some earnings within the firm and use these earnings to buy additional capital. Although these retained earnings do not get paid to the firm's stockholders, the stockholders benefit from them nonetheless. Because retained earnings increase the amount of capital the firm owns, they tend to increase future earnings and, thereby, the value of the firm's stock.

These institutional details are interesting and important, but they do not alter our conclusion about the income earned by the owners of capital. Capital is paid according to the value of its marginal product, regardless of whether this income gets transmitted to households in the form of interest or dividends or whether it is kept within firms as retained earnings.

Now consider the purchase price of land and capital. The rental price and the purchase price are obviously related: Buyers are willing to pay more for a piece of land or capital if it produces a valuable stream of rental income. And, as we have just seen, the equilibrium rental income at any point in time equals the value of that factor's marginal product. Therefore, the equilibrium purchase price of a piece of land or capital depends on both the current value of the marginal product and the value of the marginal product expected to prevail in the future.

Linkages among the Factors of Production

We have seen that the price paid to any factor of production—labor, land, or capital—equals the value of the marginal product of that factor. The marginal product of any factor, in turn, depends on the quantity of that factor that is available. Because of diminishing marginal product, a factor in abundant supply has a low marginal product and thus a low price, and a factor in scarce supply has a high marginal product and a high price. As a result, when the supply of a factor falls, its equilibrium factor price rises.

When the supply of any factor changes, however, the effects are not limited to the market for that factor. In most situations, factors of production are used together in a way that makes the productivity of each factor dependent on the quantities of the other factors available to be used in the production process. As a result, a change in the supply of any one factor alters the earnings of all the factors.

For example, suppose a hurricane destroys many of the ladders that workers use to pick apples from the orchards. What happens to the earnings of the various factors of production? Most obviously, the supply of ladders falls and, therefore, the equilibrium rental price of ladders rises. Those owners who were lucky enough to avoid damage to their ladders now earn a higher return when they rent out their ladders to the firms that produce apples.

Yet the effects of this event do not stop at the ladder market. Because there are fewer ladders with which to work, the workers who pick apples have a smaller marginal product. Thus, the reduction in the supply of ladders reduces the demand for the labor of apple pickers, and this causes the equilibrium wage to fall.

This story shows a general lesson: An event that changes the supply of any factor of production can alter the earnings of all the factors. The change in earnings of any factor can be found by analyzing the impact of the event on the value of the marginal product of that factor.

Case Study

THE ECONOMICS OF THE BLACK DEATH

In fourteenth-century Europe, the bubonic plague wiped out about one-third of the population within a few years. This event, called the *Black Death*, provides a grisly natural experiment to test the theory of factor markets that we have just developed. Consider the effects of the Black Death on those who were lucky enough to survive. What do you think happened to the wages earned by workers and the rents earned by landowners?

To answer this question, let's examine the effects of a reduced population on the marginal product of labor and the marginal product of land. With a smaller supply of workers, the marginal product of labor rises. (This is simply diminishing marginal product working in reverse.) Thus, we would expect the Black Death to raise wages.

Because land and labor are used together in production, a smaller supply of workers also affects the market for land, the other major factor of production in medieval Europe. With fewer workers available to farm the land, an additional unit of land produced less additional output. In other words, the marginal product of land fell. Thus, we would expect the Black Death to lower rents.

In fact, both predictions are consistent with the historical evidence. Wages approximately doubled during this period, and rents declined 50 percent or more. The Black Death led to economic prosperity for the peasant classes and reduced incomes for the landed classes. ●

Workers who survived the plague were lucky in more ways than one.

QuickQuiz What determines the income of the owners of land and capital? ● How would an increase in the quantity of capital affect the incomes of those who already own capital? How would it affect the incomes of workers?

CONCLUSION

This chapter explained how labor, land, and capital are compensated for the roles they play in the production process. The theory developed here is called the *neoclassical theory of distribution*. According to the neoclassical theory, the amount paid to each factor of production depends on the supply and demand for that factor. The demand, in turn, depends on that particular factor's marginal productivity. In equilibrium, each factor of production earns the value of its marginal contribution to the production of goods and services.

The neoclassical theory of distribution is widely accepted. Most economists begin with the neoclassical theory when trying to explain how the U.S. economy's $10 trillion of income is distributed among the economy's various members. In the following two chapters, we consider the distribution of income in more detail. As you will see, the neoclassical theory provides the framework for this discussion.

Even at this point you can use the theory to answer the question that began this chapter: Why are computer programmers paid more than gas station attendants? It is because programmers can produce a good of greater market value than can a gas station attendant. People are willing to pay dearly for a good computer game, but they are willing to pay little to have their gas pumped and their windshield washed. The wages of these workers reflect the market prices of the goods they produce. If people suddenly got tired of using computers and decided to spend more time driving, the prices of these goods would change, and so would the equilibrium wages of these two groups of workers.

SUMMARY

- The economy's income is distributed in the markets for the factors of production. The three most important factors of production are labor, land, and capital.

- The demand for factors, such as labor, is a derived demand that comes from firms that use the factors to produce goods and services. Competitive, profit-maximizing firms hire each factor up to the point at which the value of the marginal product of the factor equals its price.

- The supply of labor arises from individuals' tradeoff between work and leisure. An upward-sloping labor supply curve means that people respond to an increase in the wage by enjoying less leisure and working more hours.

- The price paid to each factor adjusts to balance the supply and demand for that factor. Because factor demand reflects the value of the marginal product of that factor, in equilibrium each factor is compensated according to its marginal contribution to the production of goods and services.

- Because factors of production are used together, the marginal product of any one factor depends on the quantities of all factors that are available. As a result, a change in the supply of one factor alters the equilibrium earnings of all the factors.

KEY CONCEPTS

factors of production, p. 392
production function, p. 394
marginal product of
    labor, p. 394

diminishing marginal
    product, p. 395
value of the marginal
    product, p. 395

capital, p. 404

QUESTIONS FOR REVIEW

1. Explain how a firm's production function is related to its marginal product of labor, how a firm's marginal product of labor is related to the value of its marginal product, and how a firm's value of marginal product is related to its demand for labor.

2. Give two examples of events that could shift the demand for labor.

3. Give two examples of events that could shift the supply of labor.

4. Explain how the wage can adjust to balance the supply and demand for labor while simultaneously equaling the value of the marginal product of labor.

5. If the population of the United States suddenly grew because of a large immigration, what would happen to wages? What would happen to the rents earned by the owners of land and capital?

PROBLEMS AND APPLICATIONS

1. Suppose that the president proposes a new law aimed at reducing heath care costs: All Americans are to be required to eat one apple daily.
   a. How would this apple-a-day law affect the demand and equilibrium price of apples?
   b. How would the law affect the marginal product and the value of the marginal product of apple pickers?
   c. How would the law affect the demand and equilibrium wage for apple pickers?

2. Henry Ford once said: "It is not the employer who pays wages—he only handles the money. It is the product that pays wages." Explain.

3. Show the effect of each of the following events on the market for labor in the computer manufacturing industry.
   a. Congress buys personal computers for all U.S. college students.
   b. More college students major in engineering and computer science.
   c. Computer firms build new manufacturing plants.

4. Your enterprising uncle opens a sandwich shop that employs 7 people. The employees are paid $6 per hour, and a sandwich sells for $3. If your uncle is maximizing his profit, what is the value of the marginal product of the last worker he hired? What is that worker's marginal product?

5. Imagine a firm that hires two types of workers—some with computer skills and some

without. If technology advances so that computers become more useful to the firm, what happens to the marginal product of the two types? What happens to equilibrium wages? Explain, using appropriate diagrams.

6. Suppose a freeze in Florida destroys part of the Florida orange crop.
   a. Explain what happens to the price of oranges and the marginal product of orange pickers as a result of the freeze. Can you say what happens to the demand for orange pickers? Why or why not?
   b. Suppose the price of oranges doubles and the marginal product falls by 30 percent. What happens to the equilibrium wage of orange pickers?
   c. Suppose the price of oranges rises by 30 percent and the marginal product falls by 50 percent. What happens to the equilibrium wage of orange pickers?

7. During the 1980s and 1990s the United States experienced a significant inflow of capital from other countries. For example, Toyota, BMW, and other foreign car companies built auto plants in the United States.
   a. Using a diagram of the U.S. capital market, show the effect of this inflow on the rental price of capital in the United States and on the quantity of capital in use.
   b. Using a diagram of the U.S. labor market, show the effect of the capital inflow on the average wage paid to U.S. workers.

8. Suppose that labor is the only input used by a perfectly competitive firm that can hire workers for $50 per day. The firm's production function is as follows:

Days of Labor	Units of Output
0	0
1	7
2	13
3	19
4	25
5	28
6	29

Each unit of output sells for $10. Plot the firm's demand for labor. How many days of labor should the firm hire? Show this point on your graph.

9. (This question is challenging.) In recent years some policymakers have proposed requiring firms to give workers certain fringe benefits. For example, in 1993 President Clinton proposed requiring firms to provide health insurance to their workers. Let's consider the effects of such a policy on the labor market.
   a. Suppose that a law required firms to give each worker $3 of fringe benefits for every hour that the worker is employed by the firm. How does this law affect the marginal profit that a firm earns from each worker? How does the law affect the demand curve for labor? Draw your answer on a graph with the cash wage on the vertical axis.

b. If there is no change in labor supply, how would this law affect employment and wages?
   c. Why might the labor supply curve shift in response to this law? Would this shift in labor supply raise or lower the impact of the law on wages and employment?
   d. As Chapter 6 discussed, the wages of some workers, particularly the unskilled and inexperienced, are kept above the equilibrium level by minimum-wage laws. What effect would a fringe-benefit mandate have for these workers?

10. (This question is challenging.) This chapter has assumed that labor is supplied by individual workers acting competitively. In some markets, however, the supply of labor is determined by a union of workers.
   a. Explain why the situation faced by a labor union may resemble the situation faced by a monopoly firm.
   b. The goal of a monopoly firm is to maximize profits. Is there an analogous goal for labor unions?
   c. Now extend the analogy between monopoly firms and unions. How do you suppose that the wage set by a union compares to the wage in a competitive market? How do you suppose employment differs in the two cases?
   d. What other goals might unions have that make unions different from monopoly firms?

http:// For more study tools, please visit http://mankiwXtra.swlearning.com.

19

EARNINGS AND DISCRIMINATION

In the United States today, the typical physician earns about $200,000 a year, the typical police officer about $50,000, and the typical farmworker about $20,000. These examples illustrate the large differences in earnings that are so common in our economy. These differences explain why some people live in mansions, ride in limousines, and vacation on the French Riviera, while other people live in small apartments, ride the bus, and vacation in their own backyards.

Why do earnings vary so much from person to person? Chapter 18, which developed the basic neoclassical theory of the labor market, offers an answer to this question. There we saw that wages are governed by labor supply and labor demand. Labor demand, in turn, reflects the marginal productivity of labor. In equilibrium, each worker is paid the value of his or her marginal contribution to the economy's production of goods and services.

This theory of the labor market, though widely accepted by economists, is only the beginning of the story. To understand the wide variation in earnings that we observe, we must go beyond this general framework and examine more precisely what determines the supply and demand for different types of labor. That is our goal in this chapter.

SOME DETERMINANTS OF EQUILIBRIUM WAGES

Workers differ from one another in many ways. Jobs also have differing characteristics—both in terms of the wage they pay and in terms of their nonmonetary attributes. In this section we consider how the characteristics of workers and jobs affect labor supply, labor demand, and equilibrium wages.

Compensating Differentials

When a worker is deciding whether to take a job, the wage is only one of many job attributes that the worker takes into account. Some jobs are easy, fun, and safe; others are hard, dull, and dangerous. The better the job as gauged by these nonmonetary characteristics, the more people there are who are willing to do the job at any given wage. In other words, the supply of labor for easy, fun, and safe jobs is greater than the supply of labor for hard, dull, and dangerous jobs. As a result, "good" jobs will tend to have lower equilibrium wages than "bad" jobs.

For example, imagine you are looking for a summer job in a local beach community. Two kinds of jobs are available. You can take a job as a beach-badge checker, or you can take a job as a garbage collector. The beach-badge checkers take leisurely strolls along the beach during the day and check to make sure the tourists have bought the required beach permits. The garbage collectors wake up before dawn to drive dirty, noisy trucks around town to pick up garbage. Which job would you want? Most people would prefer the beach job if the wages were the same. To induce people to become garbage collectors, the town has to offer higher wages to garbage collectors than to beach-badge checkers.

Economists use the term **compensating differential** to refer to a difference in wages that arises from nonmonetary characteristics of different jobs. Compensating differentials are prevalent in the economy. Here are some examples:

- Coal miners are paid more than other workers with similar levels of education. Their higher wage compensates them for the dirty and dangerous nature of coal mining, as well as the long-term health problems that coal miners experience.
- Workers who work the night shift at factories are paid more than similar workers who work the day shift. The higher wage compensates them for having to work at night and sleep during the day, a lifestyle that most people find undesirable.
- Professors are paid less than lawyers and doctors, who have similar amounts of education. Professors' lower wages compensate them for the great intellectual and personal satisfaction that their jobs offer. (Indeed, teaching economics is so much fun that it is surprising that economics professors get paid anything at all!)

Human Capital

As we discussed in the previous chapter, the word *capital* usually refers to the economy's stock of equipment and structures. The capital stock includes the farmer's tractor, the manufacturer's factory, and the teacher's blackboard. The essence of capital is that it is a factor of production that itself has been produced.

There is another type of capital that, while less tangible than physical capital, is just as important to the economy's production. **Human capital** is the accumulation

"On the one hand, I know I could make more money if I left public service for the private sector, but, on the other hand, I couldn't chop off heads."

compensating differential
a difference in wages that arises to offset the nonmonetary characteristics of different jobs

human capital
the accumulation of investments in people, such as education and on-the-job training

of investments in people. The most important type of human capital is education. Like all forms of capital, education represents an expenditure of resources at one point in time to raise productivity in the future. But, unlike an investment in other forms of capital, an investment in education is tied to a specific person, and this linkage is what makes it human capital.

Not surprisingly, workers with more human capital on average earn more than those with less human capital. College graduates in the United States, for example, earn almost twice as much as those workers who end their education with a high school diploma. This large difference has been documented in many countries around the world. It tends to be even larger in less developed countries, where educated workers are in scarce supply.

It is easy to see why education raises wages from the perspective of supply and demand. Firms—the demanders of labor—are willing to pay more for the highly educated because highly educated workers have higher marginal products. Workers—the suppliers of labor—are willing to pay the cost of becoming educated only if there is a reward for doing so. In essence, the difference in wages between highly educated workers and less educated workers may be considered a compensating differential for the cost of becoming educated.

Case Study
THE INCREASING VALUE OF SKILLS

"The rich get richer, and the poor get poorer." Like many adages, this one is not always true, but recently it has been. Many studies have documented that the earnings gap between workers with high skills and workers with low skills has increased over the past two decades.

Table 1 (p. 414) presents data on the average earnings of college graduates and of high school graduates without any additional education. These data show the increase in the financial reward from education. In 1980, a man on average earned 44 percent more with a college degree than without one; by 2000, this figure had risen to 89 percent. For a woman, the reward for attending college rose from a 35 percent increase in earnings to a 70 percent increase. The incentive to stay in school is as great today as it has ever been.

Why has the gap in earnings between skilled and unskilled workers widened in recent years? No one knows for sure, but economists have proposed two hypotheses to explain this trend. Both hypotheses suggest that the demand for skilled labor has risen over time relative to the demand for unskilled labor. The shift in demand has led to a corresponding change in wages, which in turn has led to greater inequality.

The first hypothesis is that international trade has altered the relative demand for skilled and unskilled labor. In recent years, the amount of trade with other countries has increased substantially. As a percentage of total U.S. production, imports have risen from 5 percent in 1970 to 15 percent in 2000, and exports have risen from 5 percent in 1970 to 11 percent in 2000. Because unskilled labor is plentiful and cheap in many foreign countries, the United States tends to import goods produced with unskilled labor and export goods produced with skilled labor.

TABLE 1

Average Annual Earnings by Educational Attainment

College graduates have always earned more than workers without the benefit of college, but the salary gap grew even larger during the 1980s and 1990s.

	1980	2000
Men		
High school, no college	$36,430	$36,770
College graduates	$52,492	$69,421
Percent extra for college grads	+44%	+89%
Women		
High school, no college	$21,969	$24,970
College graduates	$29,663	$42,575
Percent extra for college grads	+35%	+70%

Note: Earnings data are adjusted for inflation and are expressed in 2000 dollars. Data apply to full-time, year-round workers age 18 and over. Data for college graduates exclude workers with additional schooling beyond college.

Source: U.S. Bureau of the Census and author's calculations.

Thus, when international trade expands, the domestic demand for skilled labor rises, and the domestic demand for unskilled labor falls.

The second hypothesis is that changes in technology have altered the relative demand for skilled and unskilled labor. Consider, for instance, the introduction of computers. Computers raise the demand for skilled workers who can use the new machines and reduce the demand for the unskilled workers whose jobs are replaced by the computers. For example, many companies now rely more on computer databases, and less on filing cabinets, to keep business records. This change raises the demand for computer programmers and reduces the demand for filing clerks. Thus, as more firms use computers, the demand for skilled labor rises, and the demand for unskilled labor falls.

Economists have found it difficult to gauge the validity of these two hypotheses. It is possible, of course, that both are true: Increasing international trade and technological change may share responsibility for the increasing inequality we have observed in recent decades. ●

Ability, Effort, and Chance

Why do baseball players in the major leagues get paid more than those in the minor leagues? Certainly, the higher wage is not a compensating differential. Playing in the major leagues is not a less pleasant task than playing in the minor leagues; in fact, the opposite is true. The major leagues do not require more years of schooling or more experience. To a large extent, players in the major leagues earn more just because they have greater natural ability.

LOOKING FOR TRUE LOVE? GO TO SCHOOL

Economists spend much time studying how education affects a person's income. But schooling has benefits beyond those measured in dollars and cents. Some of these nonmonetary benefits showed up in a poll of the American public conducted by *The New York Times Magazine* (reported in the May 7, 2000, issue).

In one question, people were asked, "Do you agree or disagree with the following statement: It bothers me sometimes that my life did not turn out as I expected." Among those who ended their education with a high school diploma, 38 percent agreed with this statement. Among those with a college degree, only 28 percent agreed. And the percentage fell to 23 percent for those with some education beyond college. Schooling is clearly related to overall satisfaction with life.

Part of this higher satisfaction reflects the higher income that schooling yields. As the nineteenth-century writer Jane Austen put it, "A large income is the best recipe for happiness I ever heard of." But education produces satisfaction in other ways as well.

The *Times* poll asked, "Do you agree or disagree with the following statement: It has become more difficult to find true love in society." Among high school graduates, 67 percent agreed with the statement. Among college graduates, 53 percent agreed. And among those with some graduate education, only 39 percent agreed. Apparently, education improves not only financial security but also a person's love life.

Perhaps this result is not surprising. As any reader of Jane Austen's novels is well aware, success with money and success with love often go hand in hand.

Natural ability is important for workers in all occupations. Because of heredity and upbringing, people differ in their physical and mental attributes. Some people are strong, others weak. Some people are smart, others less so. Some people are outgoing, others awkward in social situations. These and many other personal characteristics determine how productive workers are and, therefore, play a role in determining the wages they earn.

Closely related to ability is effort. Some people work hard, others are lazy. We should not be surprised to find that those who work hard are more productive and earn higher wages. To some extent, firms reward workers directly by paying people on the basis of what they produce. Salespeople, for instance, are often paid as a percentage of the sales they make. At other times, hard work is rewarded less directly in the form of a higher annual salary or a bonus.

Chance also plays a role in determining wages. If a person attended a trade school to learn how to repair televisions with vacuum tubes and then found this skill made obsolete by the invention of solid-state electronics, he or she would end up earning a low wage compared to others with similar years of training. The low wage of this worker is due to chance—a phenomenon that economists recognize but do not shed much light on.

How important are ability, effort, and chance in determining wages? It is hard to say, because ability, effort, and chance are hard to measure. But indirect evidence suggests that they are very important. When labor economists study wages, they relate a worker's wage to those variables that can be measured—years of schooling, years of experience, age, and job characteristics. Although all of these measured variables affect a worker's wage as theory predicts, they account for less than half of the variation in wages in our economy. Because so much of the variation in wages is left unexplained, omitted variables, including ability, effort, and chance, must play an important role.

Case Study

THE BENEFITS OF BEAUTY

Good looks pay.

People differ in many ways. One difference is in how attractive they are. The actor Brad Pitt, for instance, is a handsome man. In part for this reason, his movies attract large audiences. Not surprisingly, the large audiences mean a large income for Mr. Pitt.

How prevalent are the economic benefits of beauty? Labor economists Daniel Hamermesh and Jeff Biddle tried to answer this question in a study published in the December 1994 issue of the *American Economic Review*. Hamermesh and Biddle examined data from surveys of individuals in the United States and Canada. The interviewers who conducted the survey were asked to rate each respondent's physical appearance. Hamermesh and Biddle then examined how much the wages of the respondents depended on the standard determinants—education, experience, and so on—and how much they depended on physical appearance.

Hamermesh and Biddle found that beauty pays. People who are deemed to be more attractive than average earn 5 percent more than people of average looks. People of average looks earn 5 to 10 percent more than people considered less attractive than average. Similar results were found for men and women.

What explains these differences in wages? There are several ways to interpret the "beauty premium."

One interpretation is that good looks are themselves a type of innate ability determining productivity and wages. Some people are born with the attributes of a movie star; other people are not. Good looks are useful in any job in which workers present themselves to the public—such as acting, sales, and waiting on tables. In this case, an attractive worker is more valuable to the firm than an unattractive worker. The firm's willingness to pay more to attractive workers reflects its customers' preferences.

A second interpretation is that reported beauty is an indirect measure of other types of ability. How attractive a person appears depends on more than just heredity. It also depends on dress, hairstyle, personal demeanor, and other attributes that a person can control. Perhaps a person who successfully projects an attractive image in a survey interview is more likely to be an intelligent person who succeeds at other tasks as well.

A third interpretation is that the beauty premium is a type of discrimination, a topic to which we return later. ●

An Alternative View of Education: Signaling

Earlier we discussed the human-capital view of education, according to which schooling raises workers' wages because it makes them more productive. Although this view is widely accepted, some economists have proposed an alternative theory, which emphasizes that firms use educational attainment as a way of sorting between high-ability and low-ability workers. According to this alternative view, when people earn a college degree, for instance, they do not become more productive, but they do *signal* their high ability to prospective employers. Because it is easier for high-ability people to earn a college degree than it is for low-ability people, more high-ability people get college degrees. As a result, it is rational for firms to interpret a college degree as a signal of ability.

The signaling theory of education is similar to the signaling theory of advertising discussed in Chapter 17. In the signaling theory of advertising, the advertisement itself contains no real information, but the firm signals the quality of its product to consumers by its willingness to spend money on advertising. In the signaling theory of education, schooling has no real productivity benefit, but the worker signals his innate productivity to employers by his willingness to spend years at school. In both cases, an action is being taken not for its intrinsic benefit but because the willingness to take that action conveys private information to someone observing it.

Thus, we now have two views of education: the human-capital theory and the signaling theory. Both views can explain why more educated workers tend to earn more than less educated workers. According to the human-capital view, education makes workers more productive; according to the signaling view, education is correlated with natural ability. But the two views have radically different predictions for the effects of policies that aim to increase educational attainment. According to the human-capital view, increasing educational levels for all workers would raise all workers' productivity and thereby their wages. According to the signaling view, education does not enhance productivity, so raising all workers' educational levels would not affect wages.

Most likely, truth lies somewhere between these two extremes. The benefits to education are probably a combination of the productivity-enhancing effects of human capital and the productivity-revealing effects of signaling. The open question is the relative size of these two effects.

The Superstar Phenomenon

Although most actors earn little and often take jobs as waiters to support themselves, Robin Williams earns millions of dollars for each film he makes. Similarly, while most people who play tennis do it for free as a hobby, Venus Williams earns millions on the pro tour. Robin Williams and Venus Williams are superstars in their fields, and their great public appeal is reflected in astronomical incomes.

Why do Robin Williams and Venus Williams earn so much? It is not surprising that there are differences in incomes within occupations. Good carpenters earn more than mediocre carpenters, and good plumbers earn more than mediocre plumbers. People vary in ability and effort, and these differences lead to differences in income. Yet the best carpenters and plumbers do not earn the many millions that are common among the best actors and athletes. What explains the difference?

To understand the tremendous incomes of Robin Williams and Venus Williams, we must examine the special features of the markets in which they sell their services. Superstars arise in markets that have two characteristics:

- Every customer in the market wants to enjoy the good supplied by the best producer.
- The good is produced with a technology that makes it possible for the best producer to supply every customer at low cost.

If Robin Williams is the funniest actor around, then everyone will want to see his next movie; seeing twice as many movies by an actor half as funny is not a good

ARE ELITE COLLEGES WORTH THE COST?

Economist Alan Krueger teaches at Princeton University, one of the most expensive colleges in the country. According to his research, however, his students would do just as well attending a less expensive school.

Children Smart Enough to Get into Elite Schools May Not Need to Bother

By Alan B. Krueger

Your son or daughter has just been accepted to both the University of Pennsylvania and to Penn State. The deadline for decision is May 1. Where should he or she go?

Many factors should be considered, of course, but lots of parents and stu-

dents are particularly interested in the potential economic payoff from higher education. Until recently, there was a consensus among economists that students who attend more selective colleges—ones with tougher admissions standards—land better paying jobs as a result. Having smart, motivated classmates and a prestigious degree were thought to enhance learning and give students access to job networks.

But is it true?

A study that I conducted with Stacy Dale of the Andrew W. Mellon Foundation, "Estimating the Payoff to Attending a More Selective College" (available online at http://papers.nber.org/), has unintentionally undermined this consensus.

It is easy to see how one could think that elite colleges enhance their graduates' earnings. According to the College and Beyond Survey, data collected by the Mellon Foundation, the average student who entered a highly selective college

substitute. Moreover, it is *possible* for everyone to enjoy the comedy of Robin Williams. Because it is easy to make multiple copies of a film, Robin Williams can provide his service to millions of people simultaneously. Similarly, because tennis games are broadcast on television, millions of fans can enjoy the extraordinary athletic skills of Venus Williams.

We can now see why there are no superstar carpenters and plumbers. Other things equal, everyone prefers to employ the best carpenter, but a carpenter, unlike a movie actor, can provide his services to only a limited number of customers. Although the best carpenter will be able to command a somewhat higher wage than the average carpenter, the average carpenter will still be able to earn a good living.

Above-Equilibrium Wages: Minimum-Wage Laws, Unions, and Efficiency Wages

Most analyses of wage differences among workers are based on the equilibrium model of the labor market—that is, wages are assumed to adjust to balance labor supply and labor demand. But this assumption does not always apply. For some

like Yale, Swarthmore or the University of Pennsylvania in 1976, earned $92,000 in 1995. The average student from a moderately selective college, like Penn State, Denison or Tulane, earned $22,000 less.

The problem with this comparison is that students who attend more selective colleges are likely to have higher earnings regardless of where they attend college for the very reasons that they were admitted to the more selective colleges in the first place.

Trying to address the problem, earlier studies compared students with similar standardized test scores and grade point averages who attended more and less selective schools. But this approach takes account of much less information than admissions committees see. There is no guarantee that all the relevant differences among students have been held constant.

This problem is known as selection bias. More selective schools accept students with greater earnings potential, and students with greater earnings po-

tential are more likely to apply to more selective schools.

To overcome the problem, Ms. Dale and I restricted the comparison to students who applied to and were accepted by comparable colleges. Some students chose more selective schools; some less selective ones. . . .

Our research found that earnings were unrelated to the selectivity of the college that students had attended among those who had comparable options. For example, the average earnings for the 519 students who were accepted by both moderately selective (average College Board scores of 1,000 to 1,099) and highly selective schools (average scores greater than 1,275) varied little, no matter which type of college they attended.

One group of students, however, clearly benefited from attending a highly selective college: those from lower-income families—defined approximately as the bottom quarter of families who

send children to college. For them, attending a more selective school increased earnings significantly. . . .

My advice to students: Don't believe that the only school worth attending is one that would not admit you. That you go to college is more important than *where* you go. Find a school whose academic strengths match your interests and which devotes resources to instruction in those fields. Recognize that your own motivation, ambition, and talents will determine your success more than the college name on your diploma.

My advice to elite colleges: Recognize that the most disadvantaged students benefit most from your instruction. Set financial aid and admission policies accordingly.

Source: *The New York Times*, April 27, 2000, p. C2. Copyright © 2000 by The New York Times Co. Reprinted by permission.

workers, wages are set above the level that brings supply and demand into equilibrium. Let's consider three reasons why this might be so.

One reason for above-equilibrium wages is minimum-wage laws, as we first saw in Chapter 6. Most workers in the economy are not affected by these laws because their equilibrium wages are well above the legal minimum. But for some workers, especially the least skilled and experienced, minimum-wage laws raise wages above the level they would earn in an unregulated labor market.

A second reason that wages might rise above their equilibrium level is the market power of labor unions. A **union** is a worker association that bargains with employers over wages and working conditions. Unions often raise wages above the level that would prevail without a union, perhaps because they can threaten to withhold labor from the firm by calling a **strike**. Studies suggest that union workers earn about 10 to 20 percent more than similar nonunion workers.

A third reason for above-equilibrium wages is suggested by the theory of **efficiency wages.** This theory holds that a firm can find it profitable to pay high wages because doing so increases the productivity of its workers. In particular, high wages may reduce worker turnover, increase worker effort, and raise the quality of workers who apply for jobs at the firm. If this theory is correct, then some firms may choose to pay their workers more than they would normally earn.

union
a worker association that bargains with employers over wages and working conditions

strike
the organized withdrawal of labor from a firm by a union

efficiency wages
above-equilibrium wages paid by firms in order to increase worker productivity

Above-equilibrium wages, whether caused by minimum-wage laws, unions, or efficiency wages, have similar effects on the labor market. In particular, pushing a wage above the equilibrium level raises the quantity of labor supplied and reduces the quantity of labor demanded. The result is a surplus of labor, or unemployment. The study of unemployment and the public policies aimed to deal with it is usually considered a topic within macroeconomics, so it goes beyond the scope of this chapter. But it would be a mistake to ignore these issues completely when analyzing earnings. Although most wage differences can be understood while maintaining the assumption of equilibrium in the labor market, above-equilibrium wages play a role in some cases.

QuickQuiz Define *compensating differential* and give an example. • Give two reasons why more educated workers earn more than less educated workers.

THE ECONOMICS OF DISCRIMINATION

discrimination
the offering of different opportunities to similar individuals who differ only by race, ethnic group, sex, age, or other personal characteristics

Another source of differences in wages is discrimination. **Discrimination** occurs when the marketplace offers different opportunities to similar individuals who differ only by race, ethnic group, sex, age, or other personal characteristics. Discrimination reflects some people's prejudice against certain groups in society. Although discrimination is an emotionally charged topic that often generates heated debate, economists try to study the topic objectively in order to separate myth from reality.

Measuring Labor-Market Discrimination

How much does discrimination in labor markets affect the earnings of different groups of workers? This question is important, but answering it is not easy.

There is no doubt that different groups of workers earn substantially different wages, as Table 2 demonstrates. The median black man in the United States is paid 22 percent less than the median white man, and the median black woman is paid 11 percent less than the median white woman. The differences by sex show even larger differences. The median white woman is paid 28 percent less than the median white man, and the median black woman is paid 17 percent less than the median black man. Taken at face value, these differentials look like evidence that employers discriminate against blacks and women.

Yet there is a potential problem with this inference. Even in a labor market free of discrimination, different people have different wages. People differ in the amount of human capital they have and in the kinds of work they are able and willing to do. The wage differences we observe in the economy are, to some extent, attributable to the determinants of equilibrium wages we discussed in the preceding section. Simply observing differences in wages among broad groups—whites and blacks, men and women—does not prove that employers discriminate.

Consider, for example, the role of human capital. Among male workers, whites are about 75 percent more likely to have a college degree than blacks. Thus, at least some of the difference between the wages of whites and the wages of blacks can be traced to differences in educational attainment. Among white workers, men and

TABLE 2

	White	Black	Percent Earnings Are Lower for Black Workers
Men	$38,870	$30,403	22%
Women	28,080	25,107	11%
Percent Earnings Are Lower for Women Workers	28%	17%	

Median Annual Earnings by Race and Sex

Note: Earnings data are for the year 2000 and apply to full-time, year-round workers aged 14 and over.
Source: U.S. Bureau of the Census.

women are now about equally likely to have a college degree, but men are about 11 percent more likely to earn a graduate or professional degree after college, indicating that some of the wage differential between men and women is attributable to educational attainment.

Moreover, human capital may be more important in explaining wage differentials than measures of years of schooling suggest. Historically, public schools in predominantly black areas have been of lower quality—as measured by expenditure, class size, and so on—than public schools in predominantly white areas. Similarly, for many years, schools directed girls away from science and math courses, even though these subjects may have had greater value in the marketplace than some of the alternatives. If we could measure the quality as well as the quantity of education, the differences in human capital among these groups would seem even larger.

Human capital acquired in the form of job experience can also help explain wage differences. In particular, women tend to have less job experience on average than men. One reason is that female labor-force participation has increased over the past several decades. Because of this historic change, the average female worker today is younger than the average male worker. In addition, women are more likely to interrupt their careers to raise children. For both reasons, the experience of the average female worker is less than the experience of the average male worker.

Yet another source of wage differences is compensating differentials. Men and women do not always choose the same type of work, and this fact may help explain some of the earnings differential between men and women. For example, women are more likely to be secretaries, and men are more likely to be truck drivers. The relative wages of secretaries and truck drivers depend in part on the working conditions of each job. Because these nonmonetary aspects are hard to measure, it is difficult to gauge the practical importance of compensating differentials in explaining the wage differences that we observe.

In the end, the study of wage differences among groups does not establish any clear conclusion about the prevalence of discrimination in U.S. labor markets. Most economists believe that some of the observed wage differentials are attributable to discrimination, but there is no consensus about how much. The only conclusion about which economists are in consensus is a negative one: Because the differences in average wages among groups in part reflect differences in human capital and job characteristics, they do not by themselves say anything about how much discrimination there is in the labor market.

Of course, differences in human capital among groups of workers may themselves reflect discrimination. The less rigorous curriculums historically offered to female students, for instance, can be considered a discriminatory practice. Similarly, the inferior schools historically available to black students may be traced to prejudice on the part of city councils and school boards. But this kind of discrimination occurs long before the worker enters the labor market. In this case, the disease is political, even if the symptom is economic.

Discrimination by Employers

Let's now turn from measurement to the economic forces that lie behind discrimination in labor markets. If one group in society receives a lower wage than another group, even after controlling for human capital and job characteristics, who is to blame for this differential?

The answer is not obvious. It might seem natural to blame employers for discriminatory wage differences. After all, employers make the hiring decisions that determine labor demand and wages. If some groups of workers earn lower wages than they should, then it seems that employers are responsible. Yet many economists are skeptical of this easy answer. They believe that competitive, market economies provide a natural antidote to employer discrimination. That antidote is called the profit motive.

Imagine an economy in which workers are differentiated by their hair color. Blondes and brunettes have the same skills, experience, and work ethic. Yet, because of discrimination, employers prefer not to hire workers with blonde hair. Thus, the demand for blondes is lower than it otherwise would be. As a result, blondes earn a lower wage than brunettes.

How long can this wage differential persist? In this economy, there is an easy way for a firm to beat out its competitors: It can hire blonde workers. By hiring blondes, a firm pays lower wages and thus has lower costs than firms that hire brunettes. Over time, more and more "blonde" firms enter the market to take advantage of this cost advantage. The existing "brunette" firms have higher costs and, therefore, begin to lose money when faced with the new competitors. These losses induce the brunette firms to go out of business. Eventually, the entry of blonde firms and the exit of brunette firms cause the demand for blonde workers to rise and the demand for brunette workers to fall. This process continues until the wage differential disappears.

Put simply, business owners who care only about making money are at an advantage when competing against those who also care about discriminating. As a result, firms that do not discriminate tend to replace those that do. In this way, competitive markets have a natural remedy for employer discrimination.

Case Study

SEGREGATED STREETCARS AND THE PROFIT MOTIVE

In the early twentieth century, streetcars in many southern cities were segregated by race. White passengers sat in the front of the streetcars, and black passengers sat in the back. What do you suppose caused and maintained this discriminatory practice? And how was this practice viewed by the firms that ran the streetcars?

In a 1986 article in the *Journal of Economic History,* economic historian Jennifer Roback looked at these questions. Roback found that the segregation of races on streetcars was the result of laws that required such segregation. Before these laws were passed, racial discrimination in seating was rare. It was far more common to segregate smokers and nonsmokers.

Moreover, the firms that ran the streetcars often opposed the laws requiring racial segregation. Providing separate seating for different races raised the firms' costs and reduced their profit. One railroad company manager complained to the city council that, under the segregation laws, "the company has to haul around a good deal of empty space."

Here is how Roback describes the situation in one southern city:

> The railroad company did not initiate the segregation policy and was not at all eager to abide by it. State legislation, public agitation, and a threat to arrest the president of the railroad were all required to induce them to separate the races on their cars. . . . There is no indication that the management was motivated by belief in civil rights or racial equality. The evidence indicates their primary motives were economic; separation was costly. . . . Officials of the company may or may not have disliked blacks, but they were not willing to forgo the profits necessary to indulge such prejudice.

The story of southern streetcars illustrates a general lesson: Business owners are usually more interested in making profit than in discriminating against a particular group. When firms engage in discriminatory practices, the ultimate source of the discrimination often lies not with the firms themselves but elsewhere. In this particular case, the streetcar companies segregated whites and blacks because discriminatory laws, which the companies opposed, required them to do so. ●

Discrimination by Customers and Governments

Although the profit motive is a strong force acting to eliminate discriminatory wage differentials, there are limits to its corrective abilities. Here we consider two of the most important limits: *customer preferences* and *government policies.*

To see how customer preferences for discrimination can affect wages, consider again our imaginary economy with blondes and brunettes. Suppose that restaurant owners discriminate against blondes when hiring waiters. As a result, blonde waiters earn lower wages than brunette waiters. In this case, a restaurant could open up with blonde waiters and charge lower prices. If customers only cared about the quality and price of their meals, the discriminatory firms would be driven out of business, and the wage differential would disappear.

On the other hand, it is possible that customers prefer being served by brunette waiters. If this preference for discrimination is strong, the entry of blonde restaurants need not succeed in eliminating the wage differential between brunettes and blondes. That is, if customers have discriminatory preferences, a competitive market is consistent with a discriminatory wage differential. An economy with such discrimination would contain two types of restaurants. Blonde restaurants hire blondes, have lower costs, and charge lower prices. Brunette restaurants hire brunettes, have higher costs, and charge higher prices. Customers who did not care about the hair color of their waiters would be attracted to the lower prices at the blonde restaurants. Bigoted customers would go to the brunette restaurants. They would pay for their discriminatory preference in the form of higher prices.

Another way for discrimination to persist in competitive markets is for the government to mandate discriminatory practices. If, for instance, the government passed a law stating that blondes could wash dishes in restaurants but could not work as waiters, then a wage differential could persist in a competitive market. The example of segregated streetcars in the foregoing case study is one example of government-mandated discrimination. More recently, before South Africa abandoned its system of apartheid, blacks were prohibited from working in some jobs. Discriminatory governments pass such laws to suppress the normal equalizing force of free and competitive markets.

To sum up: *Competitive markets contain a natural remedy for employer discrimination. The entry into the market of firms that care only about profit tends to eliminate discriminatory wage differentials. These wage differentials persist in competitive markets only when customers are willing to pay to maintain the discriminatory practice or when the government mandates it.*

Case Study
DISCRIMINATION IN SPORTS

As we have seen, measuring discrimination is often difficult. To determine whether one group of workers is discriminated against, a researcher must correct for differences in the productivity between that group and other workers in the economy. Yet, in most firms, it is difficult to measure a particular worker's contribution to the production of goods and services.

One type of firm in which such corrections are easier is the sports team. Professional teams have many objective measures of productivity. In baseball, for instance, we can measure a player's batting average, the frequency of home runs, the number of stolen bases, and so on.

Studies of sports teams suggest that racial discrimination is, in fact, common and that much of the blame lies with customers. One study, published in the *Journal of Labor Economics* in 1988, examined the salaries of basketball players. It found that black players earned 20 percent less than white players of comparable ability. The study also found that attendance at basketball games was larger for teams with a greater proportion of white players. One interpretation of these facts is that, at least at the time of the study, customer discrimination made black players less profitable than white players for team owners. In the presence of such customer discrimination, a discriminatory wage gap can persist, even if team owners care only about profit.

A similar situation once existed for baseball players. A study using data from the late 1960s showed that black players earned less than comparable white players. Moreover, fewer fans attended games pitched by blacks than games pitched by whites, even though black pitchers had better records than white pitchers. Studies of more recent salaries in baseball, however, have found no evidence of discriminatory wage differentials.

Another study, published in the *Quarterly Journal of Economics* in 1990, examined the market prices of old baseball cards. This study found similar evidence of discrimination. The cards of black hitters sold for 10 percent less than the cards of comparable white hitters. The cards of black pitchers sold for 13 percent less than the cards of comparable white pitchers. These results suggest customer discrimination among baseball fans. ●

QuickQuiz Why is it hard to establish whether a group of workers is being discriminated against? ● Explain how profit-maximizing firms tend to eliminate discriminatory wage differentials. ● How might a discriminatory wage differential persist?

CONCLUSION

In competitive markets, workers earn a wage equal to the value of their marginal contribution to the production of goods and services. There are, however, many things that affect the value of the marginal product. Firms pay more for workers who are more talented, more diligent, more experienced, and more educated because these workers are more productive. Firms pay less to those workers against whom customers discriminate because these workers contribute less to revenue.

The theory of the labor market we have developed in the last two chapters explains why some workers earn higher wages than other workers. The theory does not say that the resulting distribution of income is equal, fair, or desirable in any way. That is the topic we take up in Chapter 20.

SUMMARY

- Workers earn different wages for many reasons. To some extent, wage differentials compensate workers for job attributes. Other things equal, workers in hard, unpleasant jobs get paid more than workers in easy, pleasant jobs.

- Workers with more human capital get paid more than workers with less human capital. The return to accumulating human capital is high and has increased over the past two decades.

- Although years of education, experience, and job characteristics affect earnings as theory predicts, there is much variation in earnings that cannot be explained by things that economists can

measure. The unexplained variation in earnings is largely attributable to natural ability, effort, and chance.

- Some economists have suggested that more educated workers earn higher wages not because education raises productivity but because workers with high natural ability use education as a way to signal their high ability to employers. If this signaling theory is correct, then increasing the educational attainment of all workers would not raise the overall level of wages.

- Wages are sometimes pushed above the level that brings supply and demand into balance. Three reasons for above-equilibrium wages are minimum-wage laws, unions, and efficiency wages.

- Some differences in earnings are attributable to discrimination on the basis of race, sex, or other factors. Measuring the amount of discrimination is difficult, however, because one must correct for differences in human capital and job characteristics.

- Competitive markets tend to limit the impact of discrimination on wages. If the wages of a group of workers are lower than those of another group for reasons not related to marginal productivity, then nondiscriminatory firms will be more profitable than discriminatory firms. Profit-maximizing behavior, therefore, can reduce discriminatory wage differentials. Discrimination persists in competitive markets, however, if customers are willing to pay more to discriminatory firms or if the government passes laws requiring firms to discriminate.

KEY CONCEPTS

compensating differential, p. 412
human capital, p. 412

union, p. 419
strike, p. 419

efficiency wages, p. 419
discrimination, p. 420

QUESTIONS FOR REVIEW

1. Why do coal miners get paid more than other workers with similar amounts of education?

2. In what sense is education a type of capital?

3. How might education raise a worker's wage without raising the worker's productivity?

4. What conditions lead to economic superstars? Would you expect to see superstars in dentistry? In music? Explain.

5. Give three reasons why a worker's wage might be above the level that balances supply and demand.

6. What difficulties arise in deciding whether a group of workers has a lower wage because of discrimination?

7. Do the forces of economic competition tend to exacerbate or ameliorate discrimination on the basis of race?

8. Give an example of how discrimination might persist in a competitive market.

PROBLEMS AND APPLICATIONS

1. College students sometimes work as summer interns for private firms or the government. Many of these positions pay little or nothing.
   a. What is the opportunity cost of taking such a job?
   b. Explain why students are willing to take these jobs.
   c. If you were to compare the earnings later in life of workers who had worked as interns and those who had taken summer jobs that paid more, what would you expect to find?

2. As explained in Chapter 6, a minimum-wage law distorts the market for low-wage labor. To reduce this distortion, some economists advocate a two-tiered minimum-wage system, with a regular minimum wage for adult workers and a lower, "sub-minimum" wage for teenage workers. Give two reasons why a single minimum wage might distort the labor market for teenage workers more than it would the market for adult workers.

3. A basic finding of labor economics is that workers who have more experience in the

labor force are paid more than workers who have less experience (holding constant the amount of formal education). Why might this be so? Some studies have also found that experience at the same job (called "job tenure") has an extra positive influence on wages. Explain.

4. At some colleges and universities, economics professors receive higher salaries than professors in some other fields.
   a. Why might this be true?
   b. Some other colleges and universities have a policy of paying equal salaries to professors in all fields. At some of these schools, economics professors have lighter teaching loads than professors in some other fields. What role do the differences in teaching loads play?

5. Sara works for Steve, whom she hates because of his snobbish attitude. Yet when she looks for other jobs, the best she can do is find a job paying $10,000 less than her current salary. Should she take the job? Analyze Sara's situation from an economic point of view.

6. Imagine that someone were to offer you a choice: You could spend four years studying at the world's best university, but you would have to keep your attendance there a secret. Or you could be awarded an official degree from the world's best university, but you couldn't actually attend. Which choice do you think would enhance your future earnings more? What does your answer say about the debate over signaling versus human capital in the role of education?

7. When recording devices were first invented almost 100 years ago, musicians could suddenly supply their music to large audiences at low cost. How do you suppose this development affected the income of the best musicians? How do you suppose it affected the income of average musicians?

8. When Alan Greenspan (future chairman of the Federal Reserve) ran an economic consulting firm in the 1960s, he hired primarily female economists. He once told *The New York Times*, "I always valued men and women equally, and I found that because others did not, good

women economists were cheaper than men." Is Greenspan's behavior profit-maximizing? Is it admirable or despicable? If more employers were like Greenspan, what would happen to the wage differential between men and women? Why might other economic consulting firms at the time not have followed Greenspan's business strategy?

9. A case study in this chapter described how customer discrimination in sports seems to have an important effect on players' earnings. Note that this is possible because sports fans know the players' characteristics, including their race. Why is this knowledge important for the existence of discrimination? Give some specific examples of industries where customer discrimination is and is not likely to influence wages.

10. Suppose that all young women were channeled into careers as secretaries, nurses, and teachers; at the same time, young men were encouraged to consider these three careers and many others as well.
   a. Draw a diagram showing the combined labor market for secretaries, nurses, and teachers. Draw a diagram showing the combined labor market for all other fields. In which market is the wage higher? Do men or women receive higher wages on average?
   b. Now suppose that society changed and encouraged both young women and young men to consider a wide range of careers. Over time, what effect would this change have on the wages in the two markets you illustrated in part (a)? What effect would the change have on the average wages of men and women?

11. Economist June O'Neill argues that "until family roles are more equal, women are not likely to have the same pattern of market work and earnings as men." What does she mean by the "pattern" of market work? How do these characteristics of jobs and careers affect earnings?

12. This chapter considers the economics of discrimination by employers, customers, and governments. Now consider discrimination by workers. Suppose that some brunette workers

did not like working with blonde workers. Do you think this worker discrimination could explain lower wages for blonde workers? If such a wage differential existed, what would a profit-maximizing entrepreneur do? If there were many such entrepreneurs, what would happen over time?

http://

For more study tools, please visit http://mankiwXtra.swlearning.com.

INCOME INEQUALITY AND POVERTY

"The only difference between the rich and other people," Mary Colum once said to Ernest Hemingway, "is that the rich have more money." Maybe so. But this claim leaves many questions unanswered. The gap between rich and poor is a fascinating and important topic of study—for the comfortable rich, for the struggling poor, and for the aspiring and worried middle class.

From the previous two chapters you should have some understanding about why different people have different incomes. A person's earnings depend on the supply and demand for that person's labor, which in turn depend on natural ability, human capital, compensating differentials, discrimination, and so on. Because labor earnings make up about three-fourths of the total income in the U.S. economy, the factors that determine wages are also largely responsible for determining how the economy's total income is distributed among the various members of society. In other words, they determine who is rich and who is poor.

In this chapter we discuss the distribution of income—a topic that raises some fundamental questions about the role of economic policy. One of the *Ten Principles of Economics* in Chapter 1 is that governments can sometimes improve market outcomes. This possibility is particularly important when considering the distribution of income. The invisible hand of the marketplace acts to allocate resources efficiently, but it does not necessarily ensure that resources are allocated fairly. As a result, many economists—though not all—believe that the government should redistribute income to achieve greater equality. In doing so, however, the government runs into another of the *Ten Principles of Economics:* People face tradeoffs. When the government enacts policies to make the distribution of income more equitable, it distorts incentives, alters behavior, and makes the allocation of resources less efficient.

Our discussion of the distribution of income proceeds in three steps. First, we assess how much inequality there is in our society. Second, we consider some different views about what role the government should play in altering the distribution of income. Third, we discuss various public policies aimed at helping society's poorest members.

THE MEASUREMENT OF INEQUALITY

We begin our study of the distribution of income by addressing four questions of measurement:

- How much inequality is there in our society?
- How many people live in poverty?
- What problems arise in measuring the amount of inequality?
- How often do people move among income classes?

These measurement questions are the natural starting point from which to discuss public policies aimed at changing the distribution of income.

U.S. Income Inequality

Imagine that you lined up all the families in the economy according to their annual income. Then you divided the families into five equal groups: the bottom fifth, the second fifth, the middle fifth, the fourth fifth, and the top fifth. Table 1 shows the income ranges for each of these groups. It also shows the cutoff for the top 5 percent. You can use this table to find where your family lies in the income distribution.

TABLE 1

The Distribution of Income in the United States: 2000

Source: U.S. Bureau of the Census.

Group	Annual Family Income
Bottom fifth	Under $24,000
Second fifth	$24,001–$41,000
Middle fifth	$41,001–$61,378
Fourth fifth	$61,379–$91,700
Top fifth	$91,701 and over
Top 5%	$160,250 and over

TABLE 2

Year	Bottom Fifth	Second Fifth	Middle Fifth	Fourth Fifth	Top Fifth	Top 5%
2000	4.3%	9.8%	15.5%	22.8%	47.4%	20.8%
1990	4.6	10.8	16.6	23.8	44.3	17.4
1980	5.2	11.5	17.5	24.3	41.5	15.3
1970	5.5	12.2	17.6	23.8	40.9	15.6
1960	4.8	12.2	17.8	24.0	41.3	15.9
1950	4.5	12.0	17.4	23.4	42.7	17.3
1935	4.1	9.2	14.1	20.9	51.7	26.5

Income Inequality in the United States

This table shows the percent of total before-tax income received by families in each fifth of the income distribution and by those families in the top 5 percent.

Source: U.S. Bureau of the Census.

For examining differences in the income distribution over time, economists find it useful to present the income data as in Table 2. This table shows the share of total income that each group of families received. In 2000 the bottom fifth of all families received 4.3 percent of all income, and the top fifth of all families received 47.4 percent of all income. In other words, even though the top and bottom fifths include the same number of families, the top fifth has about ten times as much income as the bottom fifth.

The last column in the table shows the share of total income received by the very richest families. In 2000, the top 5 percent of families received 20.8 percent of total income. The total income of the richest 5 percent of families was greater than the total income of the poorest 40 percent.

Table 2 also shows the distribution of income in various years beginning in 1935. At first glance, the distribution of income appears to have been remarkably stable over time. Throughout the past several decades, the bottom fifth of families has received about 4 to 5 percent of income, while the top fifth has received about 40 to 50 percent of income. Closer inspection of the table reveals some trends in the degree of inequality. From 1935 to 1970, the distribution gradually became more equal. The share of the bottom fifth rose from 4.1 to 5.5 percent, and the share of the top fifth fell from 51.7 percent to 40.9 percent. In more recent years, this trend has reversed itself. From 1970 to 2000, the share of the bottom fifth fell from 5.5 percent to 4.3 percent, and the share of the top fifth rose from 40.9 to 47.4 percent.

In Chapter 19 we discussed some explanations for this recent rise in inequality. Increases in international trade with low-wage countries and changes in technology have tended to reduce the demand for unskilled labor and raise the demand for skilled labor. As a result, the wages of unskilled workers have fallen relative to the wages of skilled workers, and this change in relative wages has increased inequality in family incomes.

Case Study

THE WOMEN'S MOVEMENT AND THE INCOME DISTRIBUTION

Over the past several decades, there has been a dramatic change in women's role in the economy. The percentage of women who hold jobs has risen from about

32 percent in the 1950s to about 54 percent in the 1990s. As full-time homemakers have become less common, a woman's earnings have become a more important determinant of the total income of a typical family.

While the women's movement has led to more equality between men and women in access to education and jobs, it has also led to less equality in family incomes. The reason is that the rise in women's labor-force participation has not been the same across all income groups. In particular, the women's movement has had its greatest impact on women from high-income households. Women from low-income households have long had high rates of participation in the labor force, even in the 1950s, and their behavior has changed much less.

In essence, the women's movement has changed the behavior of the wives of high-income men. In the 1950s, a male executive or physician was likely to marry a woman who would stay at home and raise their children. Today, the wife of a male executive or physician is more likely to be an executive or physician herself. The result is that rich households have become even richer, a pattern that increases the inequality in family incomes.

As this example shows, there are social as well as economic determinants of the distribution of income. Moreover, the simplistic view that "income inequality is bad" can be misleading. Increasing the opportunities available to women was surely a good change for society, even if one effect was greater inequality in family incomes. When evaluating any change in the distribution of income, policymakers must look at the reasons for that change before deciding whether it presents a problem for society. ●

Equality for women has meant less equality for family incomes.

Case Study
INEQUALITY AROUND THE WORLD

How does the amount of inequality in the United States compare to that in other countries? This question is interesting, but answering it is problematic. For some countries, data are not available. Even when they are, not every country collects data in the same way; for example, some countries collect data on individual incomes, whereas other countries collect data on family incomes, and still others collect data on expenditure rather than income. As a result, whenever we find a difference between two countries, we can never be sure whether it reflects a true difference in the economies or merely a difference in the way data are collected.

With this warning in mind, consider Table 3, which compares inequality in 12 countries. The countries are ranked from the most equal to the most unequal. On the top of the list is Japan, where the richest tenth of the population has income only 4.5 times that of the poorest tenth. On the bottom of the list is Brazil, where the richest tenth has income of 46.7 times that of the poorest tenth. Although all countries have substantial inequality, the degree of inequality varies substantially around the world.

Country	Lowest 10%	Highest 10%	Ratio
Japan	4.8%	21.7%	4.5
Germany	3.3	23.7	7.2
Canada	2.8	23.8	8.5
India	3.5	33.5	9.6
United Kingdom	2.6	27.3	10.5
China	2.4	30.4	12.7
United States	1.8	30.5	16.9
Russia	1.7	38.7	22.8
Nigeria	1.6	40.8	25.5
Mexico	1.6	41.1	25.7
South Africa	1.1	45.9	41.7
Brazil	1.0	46.7	46.7

Inequality around the World

This table shows the percent of income or expenditure of the lowest and highest 10 percent of the population. The ratio of these two numbers measures the gap between rich and poor.

Source: *World Development Report: 2002*, pp. 234–235. Copyright © 2002 World Bank. Reproduced with permission of World Bank in the format Textbook via Copyright Clearance Center.

When countries are ranked by inequality, the United States ends up around the middle of the pack. Compared to other economically advanced countries, such as Japan, Germany, and Canada, the United States has substantial inequality. But the United States has a more equal income distribution than many developing countries, such as Mexico, South Africa, and Brazil. ●

The Poverty Rate

A commonly used gauge of the distribution of income is the poverty rate. The **poverty rate** is the percentage of the population whose family income falls below an absolute level called the **poverty line.** The poverty line is set by the federal government at roughly three times the cost of providing an adequate diet. This line is adjusted every year to account for changes in the level of prices, and it depends on family size.

To get some idea about what the poverty rate tells us, consider the data for 2000. In that year, the median family had an income of $50,890, and the poverty line for a family of four was $17,603. The poverty rate was 11.3 percent. In other words, 11.3 percent of the population were members of families with incomes below the poverty line for their family size.

Figure 1 (p. 434) shows the poverty rate since 1959, when the official data begin. You can see that the poverty rate fell from 22.4 percent in 1959 to a low of 11.1 percent in 1973. This decline is not surprising, for average income in the economy (adjusted for inflation) rose more than 50 percent during this period. Because the poverty line is an absolute rather than a relative standard, more families are pushed above the poverty line as economic growth pushes the entire income distribution upward. As John F. Kennedy once put it, a rising tide lifts all boats.

Since the early 1970s, however, the economy's rising tide has left some boats behind. Despite continued growth in average income, the poverty rate has not declined below the level reached in 1973. This lack of progress in reducing poverty in recent decades is closely related to the increasing inequality we saw in Table 2.

poverty rate
the percentage of the population whose family income falls below an absolute level called the poverty line

poverty line
an absolute level of income set by the federal government for each family size below which a family is deemed to be in poverty

FIGURE 1

The Poverty Rate

The poverty rate shows the percentage of the population with incomes below an absolute level called the poverty line.

Source: U.S. Bureau of the Census.

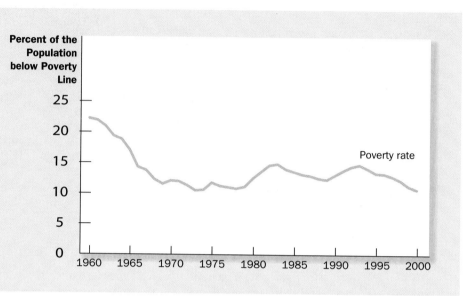

Although economic growth has raised the income of the typical family, the increase in inequality has prevented the poorest families from sharing in this greater economic prosperity.

Poverty is an economic malady that affects all groups within the population, but it does not affect all groups with equal frequency. Table 4 shows the poverty rates for several groups, and it reveals three striking facts:

- Poverty is correlated with race. Blacks and Hispanics are about three times more likely to live in poverty than are whites.
- Poverty is correlated with age. Children are more likely than average to be members of poor families, and the elderly are less likely than average to be poor.
- Poverty is correlated with family composition. Families headed by a female adult and without a spouse present are about five times as likely to live in poverty as a family headed by a married couple.

These three facts have described U.S. society for many years, and they show which people are most likely to be poor. These effects also work together: Among black and Hispanic children in female-headed households, about half live in poverty.

Problems in Measuring Inequality

Although data on the income distribution and the poverty rate help to give us some idea about the degree of inequality in our society, interpreting these data is not as straightforward as it might first appear. The data are based on households' annual incomes. What people care about, however, is not their incomes but their ability to maintain a good standard of living. For various reasons, data on the income distribution and the poverty rate give an incomplete picture of inequality in living standards. We examine these reasons below.

TABLE 4

Group	Poverty Rate
All persons	11.3%
White, not Hispanic	7.5
Black	22.0
Hispanic	21.2
Asian, Pacific Islander	10.7
Children (under age 18)	16.1
Elderly (over age 64)	10.2
Married-couple families	5.6
Female household, no spouse present	27.9

Who Is Poor?

This table shows that the poverty rate varies greatly among different groups within the population.

Source: U.S. Bureau of the Census. Data are for 2000.

In-Kind Transfers   Measurements of the distribution of income and the poverty rate are based on families' *money* income. Through various government programs, however, the poor receive many nonmonetary items, including food stamps, housing vouchers, and medical services. Transfers to the poor given in the form of goods and services rather than cash are called **in-kind transfers.** Standard measurements of the degree of inequality do not take account of these in-kind transfers.

Because in-kind transfers are received mostly by the poorest members of society, the failure to include in-kind transfers as part of income greatly affects the measured poverty rate. According to a study by the Census Bureau, if in-kind transfers were included in income at their market value, the number of families in poverty would be about 10 percent lower than the standard data indicate.

The important role of in-kind transfers makes evaluating changes in poverty more difficult. Over time, as public policies to help the poor evolve, the composition of assistance between cash and in-kind transfers changes. Some of the fluctuations in the measured poverty rate, therefore, reflect the form of government assistance rather than the true extent of economic deprivation.

in-kind transfers
transfers to the poor given in the form of goods and services rather than cash

The Economic Life Cycle   Incomes vary predictably over people's lives. A young worker, especially one in school, has a low income. Income rises as the worker gains maturity and experience, peaks at around age 50, and then falls sharply when the worker retires at around age 65. This regular pattern of income variation is called the **life cycle.**

Because people can borrow and save to smooth out life cycle changes in income, their standard of living in any year depends more on lifetime income than on that year's income. The young often borrow, perhaps to go to school or to buy a house, and then repay these loans later when their incomes rise. People have their highest saving rates when they are middle-aged. Because people can save in anticipation of retirement, the large declines in incomes at retirement need not lead to similar declines in the standard of living.

This normal life cycle pattern causes inequality in the distribution of annual income, but it does not represent true inequality in living standards. To gauge the inequality of living standards in our society, the distribution of lifetime incomes is more relevant than the distribution of annual incomes. Unfortunately, data on

life cycle
the regular pattern of income variation over a person's life

lifetime incomes are not readily available. When looking at any data on inequality, however, it is important to keep the life cycle in mind. Because a person's lifetime income smooths out the highs and lows of the life cycle, lifetime incomes are surely more equally distributed across the population than are annual incomes.

Transitory versus Permanent Income   Incomes vary over people's lives not only because of predictable life cycle variation but also because of random and transitory forces. One year a frost kills off the Florida orange crop, and Florida orange growers see their incomes fall temporarily. At the same time, the Florida frost drives up the price of oranges, and California orange growers see their incomes temporarily rise. The next year the reverse might happen.

Just as people can borrow and lend to smooth out life cycle variation in income, they can also borrow and lend to smooth out transitory variation in income. When California orange growers experience a good year, as in our example above, they would be foolish to spend all of their additional income. Instead, they save some of it, knowing that their good fortune is unlikely to persist. Similarly, the Florida orange growers respond to their temporarily low incomes by drawing down their savings or by borrowing. To the extent that a family saves and borrows to buffer itself from transitory changes in income, these changes do not affect its standard of living. A family's ability to buy goods and services depends largely on its **permanent income,** which is its normal, or average, income.

To gauge inequality of living standards, the distribution of permanent income is more relevant than the distribution of annual income. Although permanent income is hard to measure, it is an important concept. Because permanent income excludes transitory changes in income, permanent income is more equally distributed than is current income.

permanent income
a person's normal income

Economic Mobility

People sometimes speak of "the rich" and "the poor" as if these groups consisted of the same families year after year. In fact, this is not at all the case. Economic mobility, the movement of people among income classes, is substantial in the U.S. economy. Movements up the income ladder can be due to good luck or hard work, and movements down the ladder can be due to bad luck or laziness. Some of this mobility reflects transitory variation in income, while some reflects more persistent changes in income.

Because economic mobility is so great, many of those below the poverty line are there only temporarily. Poverty is a long-term problem for relatively few families. In a typical ten-year period, about one in four families falls below the poverty line in at least one year. Yet fewer than 3 percent of families are poor for eight or more years. Because it is likely that the temporarily poor and the persistently poor face different problems, policies that aim to combat poverty need to distinguish between these groups.

Another way to gauge economic mobility is the persistence of economic success from generation to generation. Economists who have studied this topic find substantial mobility. If a father earns 20 percent above his generation's average income, his son will most likely earn 8 percent above his generation's average income. There is almost no correlation between the income of a grandfather and the income of a grandson. There is much truth to the old saying, "From shirtsleeves to shirtsleeves in three generations."

One result of this great economic mobility is that the U.S. economy is filled with self-made millionaires (as well as with heirs who squandered the fortunes they inherited). According to estimates for 1996, about 2.7 million households in the United States had net worth (assets minus debts) that exceeded $1 million. These households represented the richest 2.8 percent of the population. About four out of five of these millionaires made their money on their own, such as by starting and building a business or by climbing the corporate ladder. Only one in five millionaires inherited their fortunes.

QuickQuiz What does the poverty rate measure? • Describe three potential problems in interpreting the measured poverty rate.

THE POLITICAL PHILOSOPHY OF REDISTRIBUTING INCOME

We have just seen how the economy's income is distributed and have considered some of the problems in interpreting measured inequality. This discussion was *positive* in the sense that it merely described the world as it is. We now turn to the *normative* question facing policymakers: What should the government do about economic inequality?

This question is not just about economics. Economic analysis alone cannot tell us whether policymakers should try to make our society more egalitarian. Our views on this question are, to a large extent, a matter of political philosophy. Yet because the government's role in redistributing income is central to so many debates over economic policy, here we digress from economic science to consider a bit of political philosophy.

Utilitarianism

A prominent school of thought in political philosophy is **utilitarianism.** The founders of utilitarianism are the English philosophers Jeremy Bentham (1748–1832) and John Stuart Mill (1806–1873). To a large extent, the goal of utilitarians is to apply the logic of individual decisionmaking to questions concerning morality and public policy.

The starting point of utilitarianism is the notion of **utility**—the level of happiness or satisfaction that a person receives from his or her circumstances. Utility is a measure of well-being and, according to utilitarians, is the ultimate objective of all public and private actions. The proper goal of the government, they claim, is to maximize the sum of utility of everyone in society.

The utilitarian case for redistributing income is based on the assumption of *diminishing marginal utility.* It seems reasonable that an extra dollar of income to a poor person provides that person with more additional utility than does an extra dollar to a rich person. In other words, as a person's income rises, the extra well-being derived from an additional dollar of income falls. This plausible assumption, together with the utilitarian goal of maximizing total utility, implies that the government should try to achieve a more equal distribution of income.

The argument is simple. Imagine that Peter and Paul are the same, except that Peter earns $80,000 and Paul earns $20,000. In this case, taking a dollar from Peter

utilitarianism
the political philosophy according to which the government should choose policies to maximize the total utility of everyone in society

utility
a measure of happiness or satisfaction

to pay Paul will reduce Peter's utility and raise Paul's utility. But, because of diminishing marginal utility, Peter's utility falls by less than Paul's utility rises. Thus, this redistribution of income raises total utility, which is the utilitarian's objective.

At first, this utilitarian argument might seem to imply that the government should continue to redistribute income until everyone in society has exactly the same income. Indeed, that would be the case if the total amount of income—$100,000 in our example—were fixed. But, in fact, it is not. Utilitarians reject complete equalization of incomes because they accept one of the *Ten Principles of Economics* presented in Chapter 1: People respond to incentives.

To take from Peter to pay Paul, the government must pursue policies that redistribute income, such as the U.S. federal income tax and welfare system. Under these policies, people with high incomes pay high taxes, and people with low incomes receive income transfers. Yet, as we have seen in Chapters 8 and 12, taxes distort incentives and cause deadweight losses. If the government takes away additional income a person might earn through higher income taxes or reduced transfers, both Peter and Paul have less incentive to work hard. As they work less, society's income falls, and so does total utility. The utilitarian government has to balance the gains from greater equality against the losses from distorted incentives. To maximize total utility, therefore, the government stops short of making society fully egalitarian.

A famous parable sheds light on the utilitarian's logic. Imagine that Peter and Paul are thirsty travelers trapped at different places in the desert. Peter's oasis has much water; Paul's has little. If the government could transfer water from one oasis to the other without cost, it would maximize total utility from water by equalizing the amount in the two places. But suppose that the government has only a leaky bucket. As it tries to move water from one place to the other, some of the water is lost in transit. In this case, a utilitarian government might still try to move some water from Peter to Paul, depending on how thirsty Paul is and how leaky the bucket is. But, with only a leaky bucket at its disposal, a utilitarian government will not try to reach complete equality.

Liberalism

liberalism
the political philosophy according to which the government should choose policies deemed to be just, as evaluated by an impartial observer behind a "veil of ignorance"

A second way of thinking about inequality might be called **liberalism**. Philosopher John Rawls develops this view in his book *A Theory of Justice*. This book was first published in 1971, and it quickly became a classic in political philosophy.

Rawls begins with the premise that a society's institutions, laws, and policies should be just. He then takes up the natural question: How can we, the members of society, ever agree on what justice means? It might seem that every person's point of view is inevitably based on his or her particular circumstances—whether he or she is talented or less talented, diligent or lazy, educated or less educated, born to a wealthy family or a poor one. Could we ever *objectively* determine what a just society would be?

To answer this question, Rawls proposes the following thought experiment. Imagine that before any of us is born, we all get together for a meeting to design the rules that govern society. At this point, we are all ignorant about the station in life each of us will end up filling. In Rawls's words, we are sitting in an "original position" behind a "veil of ignorance." In this original position, Rawls argues, we can choose a just set of rules for society because we must consider how those rules will affect every person. As Rawls puts it, "Since all are similarly situated and no one is able to design principles to favor his particular conditions, the principles of justice are the result of fair agreement or bargain." Designing public policies and institutions in this way allows us to be objective about what policies are just.

Rawls then considers what public policy designed behind this veil of ignorance would try to achieve. In particular, he considers what income distribution a person would consider fair if that person did not know whether he or she would end up at the top, bottom, or middle of the distribution. Rawls argues that a person in the original position would be especially concerned about the possibility of being at the *bottom* of the income distribution. In designing public policies, therefore, we should aim to raise the welfare of the worst-off person in society. That is, rather than maximizing the sum of everyone's utility, as a utilitarian would do, Rawls would maximize the minimum utility. Rawls's rule is called the **maximin criterion.**

Because the maximin criterion emphasizes the least fortunate person in society, it justifies public policies aimed at equalizing the distribution of income. By transferring income from the rich to the poor, society raises the well-being of the least fortunate. The maximin criterion would not, however, lead to a completely egalitarian society. If the government promised to equalize incomes completely, people would have no incentive to work hard, society's total income would fall substantially, and the least fortunate person would be worse off. Thus, the maximin criterion still allows disparities in income, because such disparities can improve incentives and thereby raise society's ability to help the poor. Nonetheless, because Rawls's philosophy puts weight on only the least fortunate members of society, it calls for more income redistribution than does utilitarianism.

Rawls's views are controversial, but the thought experiment he proposes has much appeal. In particular, this thought experiment allows us to consider the redistribution of income as a form of *social insurance.* That is, from the perspective of the original position behind the veil of ignorance, income redistribution is like an insurance policy. Homeowners buy fire insurance to protect themselves from the risk of their housing burning down. Similarly, when we as a society choose policies that tax the rich to supplement the incomes of the poor, we are all insuring ourselves against the possibility that we might have been a member of a poor family. Because people dislike risk, we should be happy to have been born into a society that provides us this insurance.

It is not at all clear, however, that rational people behind the veil of ignorance would truly be so averse to risk as to follow the maximin criterion. Indeed, because a person in the original position might end up anywhere in the distribution of outcomes, he or she might treat all possible outcomes equally when designing public policies. In this case, the best policy behind the veil of ignorance would be to maximize the average utility of members of society, and the resulting notion of justice would be more utilitarian than Rawlsian.

maximin criterion
the claim that the government should aim to maximize the well-being of the worst-off person in society

Libertarianism

A third view of inequality is called **libertarianism.** The two views we have considered so far—utilitarianism and liberalism—both view the total income of society as a shared resource that a social planner can freely redistribute to achieve

libertarianism
the political philosophy according to which the government should punish crimes and enforce voluntary agreements but not redistribute income

some social goal. By contrast, libertarians argue that society itself earns no income—only individual members of society earn income. According to libertarians, the government should not take from some individuals and give to others in order to achieve any particular distribution of income.

For instance, philosopher Robert Nozick writes the following in his famous 1974 book *Anarchy, State, and Utopia*:

> We are not in the position of children who have been given portions of pie by someone who now makes last minute adjustments to rectify careless cutting. There is no *central* distribution, no person or group entitled to control all the resources, jointly deciding how they are to be doled out. What each person gets, he gets from others who give to him in exchange for something, or as a gift. In a free society, diverse persons control different resources, and new holdings arise out of the voluntary exchanges and actions of persons.

Whereas utilitarians and liberals try to judge what amount of inequality is desirable in a society, Nozick denies the validity of this very question.

The libertarian alternative to evaluating economic *outcomes* is to evaluate the *process* by which these outcomes arise. When the distribution of income is achieved unfairly—for instance, when one person steals from another—the government has the right and duty to remedy the problem. But, as long as the process determining the distribution of income is just, the resulting distribution is fair, no matter how unequal.

Nozick criticizes Rawls's liberalism by drawing an analogy between the distribution of income in society and the distribution of grades in a course. Suppose you were asked to judge the fairness of the grades in the economics course you are now taking. Would you imagine yourself behind a veil of ignorance and choose a grade distribution without knowing the talents and efforts of each student? Or would you ensure that the process of assigning grades to students is fair without regard for whether the resulting distribution is equal or unequal? For the case of grades at least, the libertarian emphasis on process over outcomes is compelling.

Libertarians conclude that equality of opportunities is more important than equality of incomes. They believe that the government should enforce individual rights to ensure that everyone has the same opportunity to use his or her talents and achieve success. Once these rules of the game are established, the government has no reason to alter the resulting distribution of income.

QuickQuiz Pam earns more than Pauline. Someone proposes taxing Pam in order to supplement Pauline's income. How would a utilitarian, a liberal, and a libertarian evaluate this proposal?

POLICIES TO REDUCE POVERTY

As we have just seen, political philosophers hold various views about what role the government should take in altering the distribution of income. Political debate among the larger population of voters reflects a similar disagreement. Despite these continuing debates, however, most people believe that, at the very least, the government should try to help those most in need. According to a popular metaphor, the government should provide a "safety net" to prevent any citizen from falling too far.

Poverty is one of the most difficult problems that policymakers face. Poor families are more likely than the overall population to experience homelessness, drug dependency, domestic violence, health problems, teenage pregnancy, illiteracy, unemployment, and low educational attainment. Members of poor families are both more likely to commit crimes and more likely to be victims of crimes. Although it is hard to separate the causes of poverty from the effects, there is no doubt that poverty is associated with various economic and social ills.

Suppose that you were a policymaker in the government, and your goal was to reduce the number of people living in poverty. How would you achieve this goal? Here we consider some of the policy options that you might consider. Although each of these options does help some people escape poverty, none of them is perfect, and deciding which is best is not easy.

Minimum-Wage Laws

Laws setting a minimum wage that employers can pay workers are a perennial source of debate. Advocates view the minimum wage as a way of helping the working poor without any cost to the government. Critics view it as hurting those it is intended to help.

The minimum wage is easily understood using the tools of supply and demand, as we first saw in Chapter 6. For workers with low levels of skill and experience, a high minimum wage forces the wage above the level that balances supply and demand. It therefore raises the cost of labor to firms and reduces the quantity of labor that those firms demand. The result is higher unemployment among those groups of workers affected by the minimum wage. Although those workers who remain employed benefit from a higher wage, those who might have been employed at a lower wage are worse off.

The magnitude of these effects depends crucially on the elasticity of demand. Advocates of a high minimum wage argue that the demand for unskilled labor is relatively inelastic, so that a high minimum wage depresses employment only slightly. Critics of the minimum wage argue that labor demand is more elastic, especially in the long run when firms can adjust employment and production more fully. They also note that many minimum-wage workers are teenagers from middle-class families, so that a high minimum wage is imperfectly targeted as a policy for helping the poor.

Welfare

One way to raise the living standards of the poor is for the government to supplement their incomes. The primary way in which the government does this is through the welfare system. **Welfare** is a broad term that encompasses various government programs. Temporary Assistance for Needy Families (TANF) is a program that assists families where there are children but no adult able to support the family. In a typical family receiving such assistance, the father is absent, and the mother is at home raising small children. Another welfare program is Supplemental

welfare
government programs that supplement the incomes of the needy

IN THE NEWS

SHOULD THE GOVERNMENT TRY TO HELP POOR REGIONS?

Many antipoverty programs are targeted at poor areas of the country. Economist Edward Glaeser presents the case against this geographic approach.

Help Poor People, Not Poor Places

By Edward L. Glaeser

President Clinton's six-city "New Markets" tour earlier this summer signaled a renewed focus on the problems of the poor. But while the president's concern is appreciated by all of us who care about the islands of poverty in America's sea of affluence, his proposals are fundamentally flawed. They may still help some of the poor, but also risk repeating some of the worst mistakes of the Johnson era.

The trouble with the president's recommendations is that they violate the first economic rule of urban poverty policy: Programs should be person-based, not place-based.

Economists have long argued that place-based programs are a mistake. They strongly prefer person-based policies that create transfers, entitlements, or relief from regulation on the basis of personal characteristics. Examples of person-based policies include the Earned Income Tax Credit and the GI Bill.

Place-based policies, on the other hand, give transfers or other government

Security Income (SSI), which provides assistance to the poor who are sick or disabled. Note that for both of these welfare programs, a poor person cannot qualify for assistance simply by having a low income. He or she must also establish some additional "need," such as small children or a disability.

A common criticism of welfare programs is that they create incentives for people to become "needy." For example, these programs may encourage families to break up, for many families qualify for financial assistance only if the father is absent. The programs may also encourage illegitimate births, for many poor, single women qualify for assistance only if they have children. Because poor, single mothers are such an important part of the poverty problem and because welfare programs seem to raise the number of poor, single mothers, critics of the welfare system assert that these policies exacerbate the very problems they are supposed to cure. As a result of these arguments, the welfare system was revised in a 1996 law that limited the amount of time recipients could stay on welfare.

How severe are these potential problems with the welfare system? No one knows for sure. Proponents of the welfare system point out that being a poor, single mother on welfare is a difficult existence at best, and they are skeptical that many people would be encouraged to pursue such a life if it were not thrust upon them. Moreover, trends over time do not support the view that the decline of the two-parent family is largely a symptom of the welfare system, as the system's critics sometimes claim. Since the early 1970s, welfare benefits (adjusted for inflation) have declined, yet the percentage of children living with only one parent has risen.

support on the basis of location. Examples of such policies are housing projects and enterprise zones. President Clinton's recent Rural Housing and Economic Development Assistance for Kentucky or the new Empowerment Zone Grant for East St. Louis, Ill., are quintessential place-based policies.

The problem with place-based programs is that they create incentives to keep the poor in the ghetto. By subsidizing the place, not the person living there, these policies make it more attractive for the poor to stay in high-poverty areas. Indeed, current research shows that supposedly benevolent pro-poor housing and transfer policies play a major role in herding the poor into inner cities.

It's hard to see the logic in artificially limiting migration and concentrating the poor in areas with low productivity. Movement out of low-productivity, high-unemployment areas is one reason that unemployment rates in the U.S. stay low. Moreover, flight from the ghettos has enabled many African-Americans to avoid the social costs of the inner city, and black-white segregation in the U.S. has declined substantially because of it.

Place-based programs also suffer from the fact that their benefits go disproportionately to property owners in the targeting areas—and not to the intended beneficiaries. If the government offers tax credits to firms that invest in a poor region, for instance, then firms will locate there, pushing up property values and rents. But the benefits of increased economic activity will evaporate as higher housing costs eat away the planned benefits to the needy. . . .

If place-based policies are so bad, why are they so popular? A cynic might say that the residents of wealthy suburbs prefer that the poor remain in ghettos. A more practical explanation is that we have place-based politicians who lobby for place-based policies. . . .

A wise alternative to such faulty place-based poverty assistance would be a program that offers tax credits to companies that employ the disadvantaged. This would be a less distortionary means of assisting the poor.

Source: *The Wall Street Journal,* August 12, 1999, p. A22. Copyright © 1999 by Dow Jones & Co. Inc. Reproduced with permission of DOW JONES & CO INC in the format Textbook via Copyright Clearance Center.

Negative Income Tax

Whenever the government chooses a system to collect taxes, it affects the distribution of income. This is clearly true in the case of a progressive income tax, whereby high-income families pay a larger percentage of their income in taxes than do low-income families. As we discussed in Chapter 12, equity across income groups is an important criterion in the design of a tax system.

Many economists have advocated supplementing the income of the poor using a **negative income tax.** According to this policy, every family would report its income to the government. High-income families would pay a tax based on their incomes. Low-income families would receive a subsidy. In other words, they would "pay" a "negative tax."

For example, suppose the government used the following formula to compute a family's tax liability:

$$\text{Taxes owed} = (1/3 \text{ of income}) - \$10,000.$$

In this case, a family that earned $60,000 would pay $10,000 in taxes, and a family that earned $90,000 would pay $20,000 in taxes. A family that earned $30,000 would owe nothing. And a family that earned $15,000 would "owe" −$5,000. In other words, the government would send this family a check for $5,000.

Under a negative income tax, poor families would receive financial assistance without having to demonstrate need. The only qualification required to receive

negative income tax
a tax system that collects revenue from high-income households and gives transfers to low-income households

assistance would be a low income. Depending on one's point of view, this feature can be either an advantage or a disadvantage. On the one hand, a negative income tax does not encourage illegitimate births and the breakup of families, as critics of the welfare system believe current policy does. On the other hand, a negative income tax would subsidize those who are simply lazy and, in some people's eyes, undeserving of government support.

One actual tax provision that works much like a negative income tax is the Earned Income Tax Credit (EITC). This credit allows poor working families to receive income tax refunds greater than the taxes they paid during the year. Because the Earned Income Tax Credit applies only to the working poor, it does not discourage recipients from working, as other antipoverty programs are claimed to do. For the same reason, however, it also does not help alleviate poverty due to unemployment, sickness, or other inability to work.

In-Kind Transfers

Another way to help the poor is to provide them directly with some of the goods and services they need to raise their living standards. For example, charities provide the needy with food, shelter, and toys at Christmas. The government gives poor families *food stamps*, which are government vouchers that can be used to buy food at stores; the stores then redeem the vouchers for money. The government also gives many poor people health care through a program called *Medicaid*.

Is it better to help the poor with these in-kind transfers or with direct cash payments? There is no clear answer.

Advocates of in-kind transfers argue that such transfers ensure that the poor get what they need most. Among the poorest members of society, alcohol and drug addiction is more common than it is in society as a whole. By providing the poor with food and shelter, society can be more confident that it is not helping to support such addictions. This is one reason why in-kind transfers are more politically popular than cash payments to the poor.

Advocates of cash payments, on the other hand, argue that in-kind transfers are inefficient and disrespectful. The government does not know what goods and services the poor need most. Many of the poor are ordinary people down on their luck. Despite their misfortune, they are in the best position to decide how to raise their own living standards. Rather than giving the poor in-kind transfers of goods and services that they may not want, it may be better to give them cash and allow them to buy what they think they need most.

Antipoverty Programs and Work Incentives

Many policies aimed at helping the poor can have the unintended effect of discouraging the poor from escaping poverty on their own. To see why, consider the following example. Suppose that a family needs an income of $15,000 to maintain a reasonable standard of living. And suppose that, out of concern for the poor, the government promises to guarantee every family that income. Whatever a family earns, the government makes up the difference between that income and $15,000. What effect would you expect this policy to have?

The incentive effects of this policy are obvious: Any person who would make under $15,000 by working has no incentive to find and keep a job. For every dollar that the person would earn, the government would reduce the income supplement by a dollar. In effect, the government taxes 100 percent of additional earnings. An effective marginal tax rate of 100 percent is surely a policy with a large deadweight loss.

The adverse effects of this high effective tax rate can persist over time. A person discouraged from working loses the on-the-job training that a job might offer. In addition, his or her children miss the lessons learned by observing a parent with a full-time job, and this may adversely affect their own ability to find and hold a job.

Although the antipoverty program we have been discussing is hypothetical, it is not as unrealistic as it might first appear. Welfare, Medicaid, food stamps, and the Earned Income Tax Credit are all programs aimed at helping the poor, and they are all tied to family income. As a family's income rises, the family becomes ineligible for these programs. When all these programs are taken together, it is common for families to face effective marginal tax rates that are very high. Sometimes the effective marginal tax rates even exceed 100 percent, so that poor families are worse off when they earn more. By trying to help the poor, the government discourages those families from working. According to critics of antipoverty programs, these programs alter work attitudes and create a "culture of poverty."

It might seem that there is an easy solution to this problem: Reduce benefits to poor families more gradually as their incomes rise. For example, if a poor family loses 30 cents of benefits for every dollar it earns, then it faces an effective marginal tax rate of 30 percent. Although this effective tax reduces work effort to some extent, it does not eliminate the incentive to work completely.

The problem with this solution is that it greatly increases the cost of programs to combat poverty. If benefits are phased out gradually as a poor family's income rises, then families just above the poverty level will also be eligible for substantial benefits. The more gradual the phase-out, the more families are eligible—and the more the program costs. Thus, policymakers face a tradeoff between burdening the poor with high effective marginal tax rates and burdening taxpayers with costly programs to reduce poverty.

There are various other ways to try to reduce the work disincentive of antipoverty programs. One is to require any person collecting benefits to accept a government-provided job—a system sometimes called *workfare*. Another possibility is to provide benefits for only a limited period of time. This route was taken in the 1996 welfare reform bill. Advocates of time limits point to the falling poverty rate in the late 1990s as evidence supporting this approach. Critics argue that time limits are cruel to the least fortunate members of society and that the falling poverty rate in the late 1990s was due more to a strong economy than to welfare reform.

QuickQuiz List three policies aimed at helping the poor, and discuss the pros and cons of each.

CONCLUSION

People have long reflected on the distribution of income in society. Plato, the ancient Greek philosopher, concluded that in an ideal society the income of the

IN THE NEWS

SCHOOL VOUCHERS

One aim of universal education is to shrink the gap between rich and poor. But government-financed education does not require government-run schools.

The Market Can Transform Our Schools

By Milton Friedman

The Supreme Court's voucher decision clears the way for a major expansion of parental school choice. Opponents of choice can no longer use the First Amendment's religious Establishment Clause to attack voucher programs, now that the Supreme Court has declared the Cleveland program constitutionally acceptable even though most voucher recipients went to parochial schools.

The state of Ohio provided vouchers worth up to $2,250 to low-income parents in Cleveland who chose to send their children to private schools that charge them tuition of no more than $2,500 per child. The voucher was offered as an alternative to government schooling costing nearly three times as much per student. Yet some 4,000 low-income parents still found the private alternative preferable—enough so to pay 10 percent of private school tuition out of their own pockets. What an indictment of government schools.

Most schools that accept vouchers are religious for a simple reason, and one that is easily corrected. That reason is the low value of the voucher. It is not easy, perhaps not possible, to provide a satisfactory education for $2,500 per student. Most private schools spend more than that. But parochial schools are able to accept that low voucher amount because they are subsidized by their churches.

Raise the voucher amount to $7,000—the sum that Ohio state and local governments now spend per child in government schools—and make it

richest person would be no more than four times the income of the poorest person. Although the measurement of inequality is difficult, it is clear that our society has much more inequality than Plato recommended.

One of the *Ten Principles of Economics* discussed in Chapter 1 is that governments can sometimes improve market outcomes. There is little consensus, however, about how this principle should be applied to the distribution of income. Philosophers and policymakers today do not agree on how much income inequality is desirable, or even whether public policy should aim to alter the distribution of income. Much of public debate reflects this disagreement. Whenever taxes are raised, for instance, lawmakers argue over how much of the tax hike should fall on the rich, the middle class, and the poor.

Another of the *Ten Principles of Economics* is that people face tradeoffs. This principle is important to keep in mind when thinking about economic inequality. Policies that penalize the successful and reward the unsuccessful reduce the incentive to succeed. Thus, policymakers face a tradeoff between equality and efficiency. The more equally the pie is divided, the smaller the pie becomes. This is the one lesson concerning the distribution of income about which almost everyone agrees.

available to all students, not simply to students from low-income families, and most private schools accepting vouchers would no longer be religious. A host of new nonprofit and for-profit schools would emerge. Voucher-bearing students would then be less dependent on low-tuition parochial schools.

Parents would then truly have a choice, and the quality of schooling—in both public and private schools—would soar as competition worked its magic. This has happened in Milwaukee, where the voucher program has evolved over the past 10 years. Since that program's creation, 37 new schools have opened, nearly two-thirds of them nonreligious.

Assumption of responsibility by government for educating all children does not require that schooling be delivered in government-run institutions—just as government food stamps need not be spent in government grocery stores.

Besides, an emphasis on school choice is not new, even in public programs. The G.I. Bill enacted at the end of World War II

demonstrates how well choice can work. That program provided vouchers for higher education—for use in religious and nonreligious institutions—to millions of veterans; it transformed higher education and provided the educational leadership that has played a major role in political and economic change in the postwar period.

When the G.I. Bill was enacted, doubts were expressed that the colleges could expand rapidly enough to handle the flood of new students. Yet the number of students enrolled in colleges nearly doubled in the two years after the end of the war. The supply expanded to meet the surge in demand.

The market will respond as fully and rapidly to the increased demand for private schools generated by the expansion of vouchers for elementary and secondary education. Private voucher programs, financed by foundations and individuals, plus the limited government programs so far enacted have already brought forth a market response.

School vouchers can push elementary and secondary education out of the 19th century and into the 21st by introducing market competition on a broad scale, just as competition has made progress possible in every other area of economic and civic life.

The biggest winner from such an educational revolution would be American society as a whole. A better schooled work force promises higher productivity and more rapid economic growth. Even more important, improved education could help narrow the income gap between the less skilled and more skilled workers and would fend off the prospect of a society divided between the haves and have-nots, of a society in which an educated elite provides for a permanent class of unemployables.

Source: *The New York Times,* July 2, 2002, p. A21. Copyright © 2002 by The New York Times Co. Reprinted by permission.

SUMMARY

- Data on the distribution of income show wide disparity in our society. The richest fifth of families earns about ten times as much income as the poorest fifth.

- Because in-kind transfers, the economic life cycle, transitory income, and economic mobility are so important for understanding variation in income, it is difficult to gauge the degree of inequality in our society using data on the distribution of income in a single year. When these other factors are taken into account, they tend to suggest that economic well-being is more equally distributed than is annual income.

- Political philosophers differ in their views about the role of government in altering the

distribution of income. Utilitarians (such as John Stuart Mill) would choose the distribution of income to maximize the sum of utility of everyone in society. Liberals (such as John Rawls) would determine the distribution of income as if we were behind a "veil of ignorance" that prevented us from knowing our own stations in life. Libertarians (such as Robert Nozick) would have the government enforce individual rights to ensure a fair process but then not be concerned about inequality in the resulting distribution of income.

- Various policies aim to help the poor—minimum-wage laws, welfare, negative income taxes, and in-kind transfers. Although each of these policies helps some families escape poverty, they also have unintended side effects. Because financial assistance declines as income rises, the poor often face effective marginal tax rates that are very high. Such high effective tax rates discourage poor families from escaping poverty on their own.

KEY CONCEPTS

poverty rate, p. 433
poverty line, p. 433
in-kind transfers, p. 435
life cycle, p. 435

permanent income, p. 436
utilitarianism, p. 437
utility, p. 437
liberalism, p. 438

maximin criterion, p. 439
libertarianism, p. 439
welfare, p. 441
negative income tax, p. 443

QUESTIONS FOR REVIEW

1. Does the richest fifth of the U.S. population earn two, four, or ten times the income of the poorest fifth?

2. How does the extent of income inequality in the United States compare to that of other nations around the world?

3. What groups in the population are most likely to live in poverty?

4. When gauging the amount of inequality, why do transitory and life cycle variations in income cause difficulties?

5. How would a utilitarian, a liberal, and a libertarian determine how much income inequality is permissible?

6. What are the pros and cons of in-kind (rather than cash) transfers to the poor?

7. Describe how antipoverty programs can discourage the poor from working. How might you reduce this disincentive? What are the disadvantages with your proposed policy?

PROBLEMS AND APPLICATIONS

1. Table 2 shows that income inequality in the United States has increased during the past 20 years. Some factors contributing to this increase were discussed in Chapter 19. What are they?

2. Table 4 shows that the percentage of children in families with income below the poverty line far exceeds the percentage of the elderly in such families. How might the allocation of government money across different social programs have contributed to this phenomenon? (Hint: See Chapter 12.)

3. Economists often view life cycle variation in income as one form of transitory variation in income around people's lifetime, or permanent, income. In this sense, how does your current income compare to your permanent income? Do you think your current income accurately reflects your standard of living?

4. The chapter discusses the importance of economic mobility.
   a. What policies might the government pursue to increase economic mobility *within* a generation?
   b. What policies might the government pursue to increase economic mobility *across* generations?
   c. Do you think we should reduce spending on current welfare programs in order to increase spending on programs that enhance economic mobility? What are some of the advantages and disadvantages of doing so?

5. Consider two communities. In one community, ten families have incomes of $100 each and ten families have incomes of $20 each. In the other community, ten families have incomes of $200 each and ten families have incomes of $22 each.

a. In which community is the distribution of income more unequal? In which community is the problem of poverty likely to be worse?

b. Which distribution of income would Rawls prefer? Explain.

c. Which distribution of income do you prefer? Explain.

6. The chapter uses the analogy of a "leaky bucket" to explain one constraint on the redistribution of income.

a. What elements of the U.S. system for redistributing income create the leaks in the bucket? Be specific.

b. Do you think that Republicans or Democrats generally believe that the bucket used for redistributing income is more leaky? How does that belief affect their views about the amount of income redistribution that the government should undertake?

7. Suppose there are two possible income distributions in a society of ten people. In the first distribution, nine people would have incomes of $30,000 and one person would have an income of $10,000. In the second distribution, all ten people would have incomes of $25,000.

a. If the society had the first income distribution, what would be the utilitarian argument for redistributing income?

b. Which income distribution would Rawls consider more equitable? Explain.

c. Which income distribution would Nozick consider more equitable? Explain.

8. The poverty rate would be substantially lower if the market value of in-kind transfers were added to family income. The government spends more money on Medicaid than on any other in-kind transfer, with expenditures per recipient family amounting to roughly $5,000 annually.

a. If the government gave each recipient family a check for this amount instead of enrolling them in the Medicaid program, do you think that most of these families would spend that much to purchase health insurance? (Recall that the poverty line is below $15,000 for a family of four.) Why?

b. How does your answer to part (a) affect your view about whether we should determine

the poverty rate by valuing in-kind transfers at the price the government pays for them? Explain.

c. How does your answer to part (a) affect your view about whether we should provide assistance to the poor in the form of cash transfers or in-kind transfers? Explain.

9. Suppose that a family's tax liability equaled its income multiplied by one-half, minus $10,000. Under this system, some families would pay taxes to the government, and some families would receive money from the government through a "negative income tax."

a. Consider families with pre-tax incomes of $0, $10,000, $20,000, $30,000, and $40,000. Make a table showing pre-tax income, taxes paid to the government or money received from the government, and after-tax income for each family.

b. What is the marginal tax rate in this system? (See Chapter 12 if you need to review the definition of marginal tax rate.) What is the maximum amount of income at which a family *receives* money from the government?

c. Now suppose that the tax schedule is changed, so that a family's tax liability equals its income multiplied by one-quarter, minus $10,000. What is the marginal tax rate in this new system? What is the maximum amount of income at which a family receives money from the government?

d. What is the main advantage of each of the tax schedules discussed here?

10. John and Jeremy are utilitarians. John believes that labor supply is highly elastic, whereas Jeremy believes that labor supply is quite inelastic. How do you suppose their views about income redistribution differ?

11. Do you agree or disagree with each of the following statements? What do your views imply for public policies, such as taxes on inheritance?

a. "Every parent has the right to work hard and save in order to give his or her children a better life."

b. "No child should be disadvantaged by the sloth or bad luck of his or her parents."

7

TOPICS FOR FURTHER STUDY

THE THEORY OF CONSUMER CHOICE

When you walk into a store, you are confronted with thousands of goods that you might buy. Of course, because your financial resources are limited, you cannot buy everything that you want. You therefore consider the prices of the various goods being offered for sale and buy a bundle of goods that, given your resources, best suits your needs and desires.

In this chapter we develop the theory that describes how consumers make decisions about what to buy. So far throughout this book, we have summarized consumers' decisions with the demand curve. As we discussed in Chapters 4 through 7, the demand curve for a good reflects consumers' willingness to pay for it. When the price of a good rises, consumers are willing to pay for fewer units, so the quantity demanded falls. We now look more deeply at the decisions that lie behind the demand curve. The theory of consumer choice presented in this chapter provides a more complete understanding of demand, just as the theory of the competitive firm in Chapter 14 provides a more complete understanding of supply.

One of the *Ten Principles of Economics* discussed in Chapter 1 is that people face tradeoffs. The theory of consumer choice examines the tradeoffs that people face in their role as consumers. When a consumer buys more of one good, he can afford less of other goods. When he spends more time enjoying leisure and less time working, he has lower income and can afford less consumption. When he spends more of his income in the present and saves less of it, he must accept a lower level of consumption in the future. The theory of consumer choice examines how consumers facing these tradeoffs make decisions and how they respond to changes in their environment.

After developing the basic theory of consumer choice, we apply it to three questions about household decisions. In particular, we ask:

- Do all demand curves slope downward?
- How do wages affect labor supply?
- How do interest rates affect household saving?

At first, these questions might seem unrelated. But, as we will see, we can use the theory of consumer choice to address each of them.

THE BUDGET CONSTRAINT: WHAT THE CONSUMER CAN AFFORD

Most people would like to increase the quantity or quality of the goods they consume—to take longer vacations, drive fancier cars, or eat at better restaurants. People consume less than they desire because their spending is *constrained,* or limited, by their income. We begin our study of consumer choice by examining this link between income and spending.

To keep things simple, we examine the decision facing a consumer who buys only two goods: Pepsi and pizza. Of course, real people buy thousands of different kinds of goods. Yet assuming there are only two goods greatly simplifies the problem without altering the basic insights about consumer choice.

We first consider how the consumer's income constrains the amount he spends on Pepsi and pizza. Suppose that the consumer has an income of $1,000 per month and that he spends his entire income each month on Pepsi and pizza. The price of a pint of Pepsi is $2, and the price of a pizza is $10.

The table in Figure 1 shows some of the many combinations of Pepsi and pizza that the consumer can buy. The first line in the table shows that if the consumer spends all his income on pizza, he can eat 100 pizzas during the month, but he would not be able to buy any Pepsi at all. The second line shows another possible consumption bundle: 90 pizzas and 50 pints of Pepsi. And so on. Each consumption bundle in the table costs exactly $1,000.

The graph in Figure 1 illustrates the consumption bundles that the consumer can choose. The vertical axis measures the number of pints of Pepsi, and the horizontal axis measures the number of pizzas. Three points are marked on this figure. At point A, the consumer buys no Pepsi and consumes 100 pizzas. At point B, the consumer buys no pizza and consumes 500 pints of Pepsi. At point C, the consumer buys 50 pizzas and 250 pints of Pepsi. Point C, which is exactly at the middle of the line from A to B, is the point at which the consumer spends an equal amount ($500) on Pepsi and pizza. Of course, these are only three of the many combinations of Pepsi and pizza that the consumer can choose. All the points on

FIGURE 1

The Consumer's Budget Constraint

The budget constraint shows the various bundles of goods that the consumer can afford for a given income. Here the consumer buys bundles of Pepsi and pizza. The table and graph show what the consumer can afford if his income is $1,000, the price of Pepsi is $2, and the price of pizza is $10.

Pints of Pepsi	Number of Pizzas	Spending on Pepsi	Spending on Pizza	Total Spending
0	100	$ 0	$1,000	$1,000
50	90	100	900	1,000
100	80	200	800	1,000
150	70	300	700	1,000
200	60	400	600	1,000
250	50	500	500	1,000
300	40	600	400	1,000
350	30	700	300	1,000
400	20	800	200	1,000
450	10	900	100	1,000
500	0	1,000	0	1,000

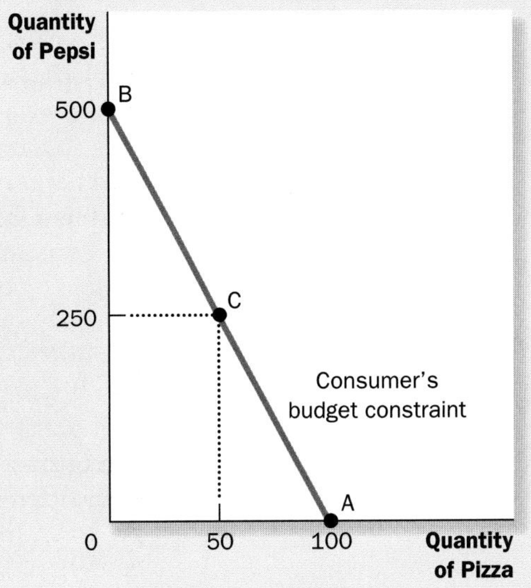

the line from A to B are possible. This line, called the **budget constraint,** shows the consumption bundles that the consumer can afford. In this case, it shows the trade-off between Pepsi and pizza that the consumer faces.

The slope of the budget constraint measures the rate at which the consumer can trade one good for the other. Recall from the appendix to Chapter 2 that the slope between two points is calculated as the change in the vertical distance divided by the change in the horizontal distance ("rise over run"). From point A to point B, the vertical distance is 500 pints, and the horizontal distance is 100 pizzas. Thus, the slope is 5 pints per pizza. (Actually, because the budget constraint slopes downward, the slope is a negative number. But for our purposes we can ignore the minus sign.)

Notice that the slope of the budget constraint equals the *relative price* of the two goods—the price of one good compared to the price of the other. A pizza costs 5 times as much as a pint of Pepsi, so the opportunity cost of a pizza is 5 pints of Pepsi. The budget constraint's slope of 5 reflects the tradeoff the market is offering the consumer: 1 pizza for 5 pints of Pepsi.

budget constraint
the limit on the consumption bundles that a consumer can afford

QuickQuiz Draw the budget constraint for a person with income of $1,000 if the price of Pepsi is $5 and the price of pizza is $10. What is the slope of this budget constraint?

PREFERENCES: WHAT THE CONSUMER WANTS

Our goal in this chapter is to see how consumers make choices. The budget constraint is one piece of the analysis: It shows what combination of goods the consumer can afford given his income and the prices of the goods. The consumer's choices, however, depend not only on his budget constraint but also on his preferences regarding the two goods. Therefore, the consumer's preferences are the next piece of our analysis.

Representing Preferences with Indifference Curves

indifference curve
a curve that shows consumption bundles that give the consumer the same level of satisfaction

The consumer's preferences allow him to choose among different bundles of Pepsi and pizza. If you offer the consumer two different bundles, he chooses the bundle that best suits his tastes. If the two bundles suit his tastes equally well, we say that the consumer is *indifferent* between the two bundles.

Just as we have represented the consumer's budget constraint graphically, we can also represent his preferences graphically. We do this with indifference curves. An **indifference curve** shows the bundles of consumption that make the consumer equally happy. In this case, the indifference curves show the combinations of Pepsi and pizza with which the consumer is equally satisfied.

Figure 2 shows two of the consumer's many indifference curves. The consumer is indifferent among combinations A, B, and C, because they are all on the same

---

FIGURE 2

The Consumer's Preferences

The consumer's preferences are represented with indifference curves, which show the combinations of Pepsi and pizza that make the consumer equally satisfied. Because the consumer prefers more of a good, points on a higher indifference curve (I_2 here) are preferred to points on a lower indifference curve (I_1). The marginal rate of substitution (MRS) shows the rate at which the consumer is willing to trade Pepsi for pizza.

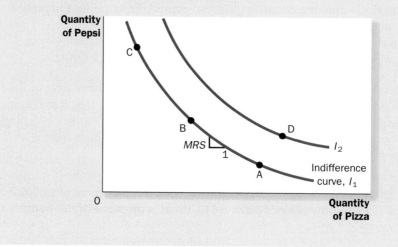

curve. Not surprisingly, if the consumer's consumption of pizza is reduced, say from point A to point B, consumption of Pepsi must increase to keep him equally happy. If consumption of pizza is reduced again, from point B to point C, the amount of Pepsi consumed must increase yet again.

The slope at any point on an indifference curve equals the rate at which the consumer is willing to substitute one good for the other. This rate is called the **marginal rate of substitution** (*MRS*). In this case, the marginal rate of substitution measures how much Pepsi the consumer requires in order to be compensated for a one-unit reduction in pizza consumption. Notice that because the indifference curves are not straight lines, the marginal rate of substitution is not the same at all points on a given indifference curve. The rate at which a consumer is willing to trade one good for the other depends on the amounts of the goods he is already consuming. That is, the rate at which a consumer is willing to trade pizza for Pepsi depends on whether he is more hungry or more thirsty, which in turn depends on how much pizza and Pepsi he has.

The consumer is equally happy at all points on any given indifference curve, but he prefers some indifference curves to others. Because he prefers more consumption to less, higher indifference curves are preferred to lower ones. In Figure 2, any point on curve I_2 is preferred to any point on curve I_1.

A consumer's set of indifference curves gives a complete ranking of the consumer's preferences. That is, we can use the indifference curves to rank any two bundles of goods. For example, the indifference curves tell us that point D is preferred to point A because point D is on a higher indifference curve than point A. (That conclusion may be obvious, however, because point D offers the consumer both more pizza and more Pepsi.) The indifference curves also tell us that point D is preferred to point C because point D is on a higher indifference curve. Even though point D has less Pepsi than point C, it has more than enough extra pizza to make the consumer prefer it. By seeing which point is on the higher indifference curve, we can use the set of indifference curves to rank any combinations of Pepsi and pizza.

> **marginal rate of substitution**
> the rate at which a consumer is willing to trade one good for another

Four Properties of Indifference Curves

Because indifference curves represent a consumer's preferences, they have certain properties that reflect those preferences. Here we consider four properties that describe most indifference curves:

- *Property 1: Higher indifference curves are preferred to lower ones.* Consumers usually prefer more of something to less of it. This preference for greater quantities is reflected in the indifference curves. As Figure 2 shows, higher indifference curves represent larger quantities of goods than lower indifference curves. Thus, the consumer prefers being on higher indifference curves.
- *Property 2: Indifference curves are downward sloping.* The slope of an indifference curve reflects the rate at which the consumer is willing to substitute one good for the other. In most cases, the consumer likes both goods. Therefore, if the quantity of one good is reduced, the quantity of the other good must increase in order for the consumer to be equally happy. For this reason, most indifference curves slope downward.
- *Property 3: Indifference curves do not cross.* To see why this is true, suppose that two indifference curves did cross, as in Figure 3 (p. 458). Then, because point A is on the same indifference curve as point B, the two points would make the

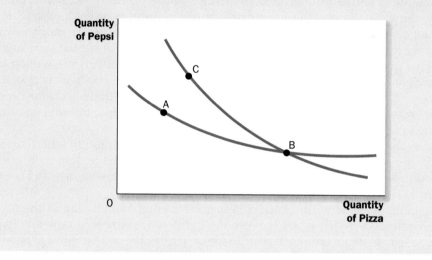

FIGURE 3

The Impossibility of Intersecting Indifference Curves

A situation like this can never happen. According to these indifference curves, the consumer would be equally satisfied at points A, B, and C, even though point C has more of both goods than point A.

consumer equally happy. In addition, because point B is on the same indifference curve as point C, these two points would make the consumer equally happy. But these conclusions imply that points A and C would also make the consumer equally happy, even though point C has more of both goods. This contradicts our assumption that the consumer always prefers more of both goods to less. Thus, indifference curves cannot cross.

- *Property 4: Indifference curves are bowed inward.* The slope of an indifference curve is the marginal rate of substitution—the rate at which the consumer is willing to trade off one good for the other. The marginal rate of substitution (*MRS*) usually depends on the amount of each good the consumer is currently consuming. In particular, because people are more willing to trade away goods that they have in abundance and less willing to trade away goods of which they have little, the indifference curves are bowed inward. As an example, consider Figure 4. At point A, because the consumer has a lot of Pepsi and only a little pizza, he is very hungry but not very thirsty. To induce the consumer to give up 1 pizza, the consumer has to be given 6 pints of Pepsi: The marginal rate of substitution is 6 pints per pizza. By contrast, at point B, the consumer has little Pepsi and a lot of pizza, so he is very thirsty but not very hungry. At this point, he would be willing to give up 1 pizza to get 1 pint of Pepsi: The marginal rate of substitution is 1 pint per pizza. Thus, the bowed shape of the indifference curve reflects the consumer's greater willingness to give up a good that he already has in large quantity.

Two Extreme Examples of Indifference Curves

The shape of an indifference curve tells us about the consumer's willingness to trade one good for the other. When the goods are easy to substitute for each other,

FIGURE 4

Bowed Indifference Curves

Indifference curves are usually bowed inward. This shape implies that the marginal rate of substitution (MRS) depends on the quantity of the two goods the consumer is consuming. At point A, the consumer has little pizza and much Pepsi, so he requires a lot of extra Pepsi to induce him to give up one of the pizzas: The marginal rate of substitution is 6 pints of Pepsi per pizza. At point B, the consumer has much pizza and little Pepsi, so he requires only a little extra Pepsi to induce him to give up one of the pizzas: The marginal rate of substitution is 1 pint of Pepsi per pizza.

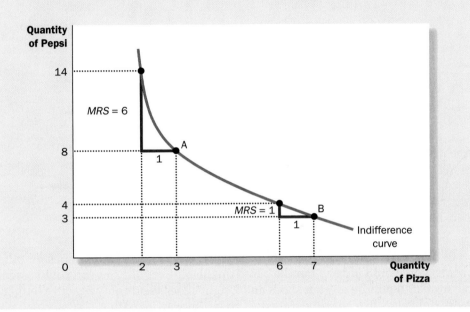

the indifference curves are less bowed; when the goods are hard to substitute, the indifference curves are very bowed. To see why this is true, let's consider the extreme cases.

Perfect Substitutes   Suppose that someone offered you bundles of nickels and dimes. How would you rank the different bundles?

Most likely, you would care only about the total monetary value of each bundle. If so, you would judge a bundle based on the number of nickels plus twice the number of dimes. In other words, you would always be willing to trade 1 dime for 2 nickels, regardless of the number of nickels and dimes in the bundle. Your marginal rate of substitution between nickels and dimes would be a fixed number: 2.

We can represent your preferences over nickels and dimes with the indifference curves in panel (a) of Figure 5 (p. 460). Because the marginal rate of substitution is constant, the indifference curves are straight lines. In this extreme case of straight indifference curves, we say that the two goods are **perfect substitutes.**

perfect substitutes
two goods with straight-line indifference curves

Perfect Complements   Suppose now that someone offered you bundles of shoes. Some of the shoes fit your left foot, others your right foot. How would you rank these different bundles?

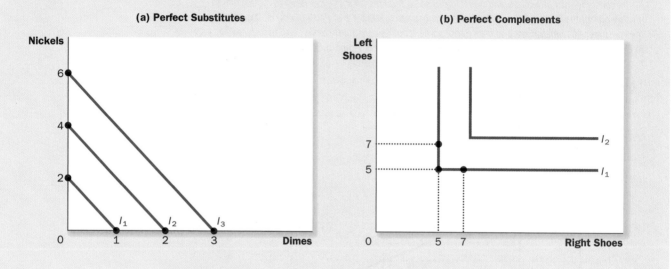

FIGURE 5

Perfect Substitutes and Perfect Complements

When two goods are easily substitutable, such as nickels and dimes, the indifference curves are straight lines, as shown in panel (a). When two goods are strongly complementary, such as left shoes and right shoes, the indifference curves are right angles, as shown in panel (b).

perfect complements
two goods with right-angle indifference curves

In this case, you might care only about the number of pairs of shoes. In other words, you would judge a bundle based on the number of pairs you could assemble from it. A bundle of 5 left shoes and 7 right shoes yields only 5 pairs. Getting 1 more right shoe has no value if there is no left shoe to go with it.

We can represent your preferences for right and left shoes with the indifference curves in panel (b) of Figure 5. In this case, a bundle with 5 left shoes and 5 right shoes is just as good as a bundle with 5 left shoes and 7 right shoes. It is also just as good as a bundle with 7 left shoes and 5 right shoes. The indifference curves, therefore, are right angles. In this extreme case of right-angle indifference curves, we say that the two goods are **perfect complements.**

In the real world, of course, most goods are neither perfect substitutes (like nickels and dimes) nor perfect complements (like right shoes and left shoes). More typically, the indifference curves are bowed inward, but not so bowed as to become right angles.

QuickQuiz Draw some indifference curves for Pepsi and pizza. Explain the four properties of these indifference curves.

OPTIMIZATION: WHAT THE CONSUMER CHOOSES

The goal of this chapter is to understand how a consumer makes choices. We have the two pieces necessary for this analysis: the consumer's budget constraint and the consumer's preferences. Now we put these two pieces together and consider the consumer's decision about what to buy.

The Consumer's Optimal Choices

Consider once again our Pepsi and pizza example. The consumer would like to end up with the best possible combination of Pepsi and pizza—that is, the combination on the highest possible indifference curve. But the consumer must also end up on or below his budget constraint, which measures the total resources available to him.

Figure 6 shows the consumer's budget constraint and three of his many indifference curves. The highest indifference curve that the consumer can reach (I_2 in the figure) is the one that just barely touches the budget constraint. The point at which this indifference curve and the budget constraint touch is called the *optimum*. The consumer would prefer point A, but he cannot afford that point because it lies above his budget constraint. The consumer can afford point B, but that point is on a lower indifference curve and, therefore, provides the consumer less satisfaction. The optimum represents the best combination of consumption of Pepsi and pizza available to the consumer.

Notice that, at the optimum, the slope of the indifference curve equals the slope of the budget constraint. We say that the indifference curve is *tangent* to the budget constraint. The slope of the indifference curve is the marginal rate of substitution between Pepsi and pizza, and the slope of the budget constraint is the relative price of Pepsi and pizza. Thus, *the consumer chooses consumption of the two goods so that the marginal rate of substitution equals the relative price.*

In Chapter 7 we saw how market prices reflect the marginal value that consumers place on goods. This analysis of consumer choice shows the same result in another way. In making his consumption choices, the consumer takes as given the relative price of the two goods and then chooses an optimum at which his marginal rate of substitution equals this relative price. The relative price is the rate at which the *market* is willing to trade one good for the other, whereas the marginal rate of substitution is the rate at which the *consumer* is willing to trade one good for the other. At the consumer's optimum, the consumer's valuation of the two goods (as measured by the marginal rate of substitution) equals the market's valuation

FIGURE 6

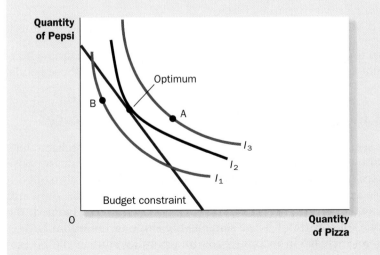

The Consumer's Optimum

The consumer chooses the point on his budget constraint that lies on the highest indifference curve. At this point, called the optimum, the marginal rate of substitution equals the relative price of the two goods. Here the highest indifference curve the consumer can reach is I_2. The consumer prefers point A, which lies on indifference curve I_3, but the consumer cannot afford this bundle of Pepsi and pizza. By contrast, point B is affordable, but because it lies on a lower indifference curve, the consumer does not prefer it.

UTILITY: AN ALTERNATIVE WAY TO DESCRIBE PREFERENCES AND OPTIMIZATION

We have used indifference curves to represent the consumer's preferences. Another common way to represent preferences is with the concept of *utility.* Utility is an abstract measure of the satisfaction or happiness that a consumer receives from a bundle of goods. Economists say that a consumer prefers one bundle of goods to another if the first provides more utility than the second.

Indifference curves and utility are closely related. Because the consumer prefers points on higher indifference curves, bundles of goods on higher indifference curves provide higher utility. Because the consumer is equally happy with all points on the same indifference curve, all these bundles provide the same utility. You can think of an indifference curve as an "equal-utility" curve.

The *marginal utility* of any good is the increase in utility that the consumer gets from an additional unit of that good. Most goods are assumed to exhibit *diminishing marginal utility:* The more of the good the consumer already has, the lower the marginal utility provided by an extra unit of that good.

The marginal rate of substitution between two goods depends on their marginal utilities. For example, if the marginal utility of good X is twice the marginal utility of good Y, then a person would need 2 units of good Y to compensate for losing one unit of good X, and the

marginal rate of substitution equals 2. More generally, the marginal rate of substitution (and thus the slope of the indifference curve) equals the marginal utility of one good divided by the marginal utility of the other good.

Utility analysis provides another way to describe consumer optimization. Recall that at the consumer's optimum, the marginal rate of substitution equals the ratio of prices. That is,

$$MRS = P_X/P_Y.$$

Because the marginal rate of substitution equals the ratio of marginal utilities, we can write this condition for optimization as

$$MU_X/MU_Y = P_X/P_Y.$$

Now rearrange this expression to become

$$MU_X/P_X = MU_Y/P_Y.$$

This equation has a simple interpretation: At the optimum, the marginal utility per dollar spent on good X equals the marginal utility per dollar spent on good Y. (Why? If this equality did not hold, the consumer could increase utility by spending less on the good that provided lower marginal utility per dollar and more on the good that provided higher marginal utility per dollar.)

When economists discuss the theory of consumer choice, they might express the theory using different words. One economist might say that the goal of the consumer is to maximize utility. Another economist might say that the goal of the consumer is to end up on the highest possible indifference curve. The first economist would conclude that at the consumer's optimum, the marginal utility per dollar is the same for all goods, whereas the second would conclude that the indifference curve is tangent to the budget constraint. In essence, these are two ways of saying the same thing.

(as measured by the relative price). As a result of this consumer optimization, market prices of different goods reflect the value that consumers place on those goods.

How Changes in Income Affect the Consumer's Choices

Now that we have seen how the consumer makes the consumption decision, let's examine how consumption responds to changes in income. To be specific, suppose that income increases. With higher income, the consumer can afford more of both goods. The increase in income, therefore, shifts the budget constraint outward, as in Figure 7. Because the relative price of the two goods has not changed, the slope of the new budget constraint is the same as the slope of the initial budget constraint. That is, an increase in income leads to a parallel shift in the budget constraint.

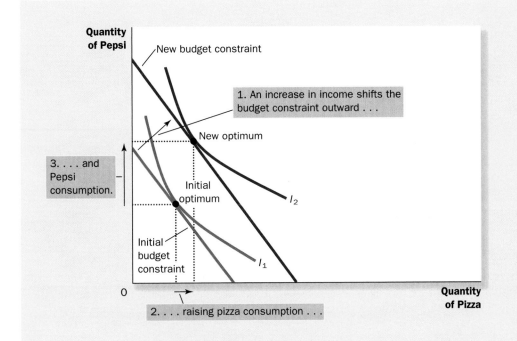

FIGURE 7

An Increase in Income

When the consumer's income rises, the budget constraint shifts out. If both goods are normal goods, the consumer responds to the increase in income by buying more of both of them. Here the consumer buys more pizza and more Pepsi.

The expanded budget constraint allows the consumer to choose a better combination of Pepsi and pizza. In other words, the consumer can now reach a higher indifference curve. Given the shift in the budget constraint and the consumer's preferences as represented by his indifference curves, the consumer's optimum moves from the point labeled "initial optimum" to the point labeled "new optimum."

Notice that, in Figure 7, the consumer chooses to consume more Pepsi and more pizza. Although the logic of the model does not require increased consumption of both goods in response to increased income, this situation is the most common one. As you may recall from Chapter 4, if a consumer wants more of a good when his income rises, economists call it a **normal good.** The indifference curves in Figure 7 are drawn under the assumption that both Pepsi and pizza are normal goods.

Figure 8 (p. 464) shows an example in which an increase in income induces the consumer to buy more pizza but less Pepsi. If a consumer buys less of a good when his income rises, economists call it an **inferior good.** Figure 8 is drawn under the assumption that pizza is a normal good and Pepsi is an inferior good.

Although most goods are normal goods, there are some inferior goods in the world. One example is bus rides. High-income consumers are more likely to own cars and less likely to ride the bus than low-income consumers. Bus rides, therefore, are an inferior good.

normal good
a good for which an increase in income raises the quantity demanded

inferior good
a good for which an increase in income reduces the quantity demanded

How Changes in Prices Affect the Consumer's Choices

Let's now use this model of consumer choice to consider how a change in the price of one of the goods alters the consumer's choices. Suppose, in particular, that the

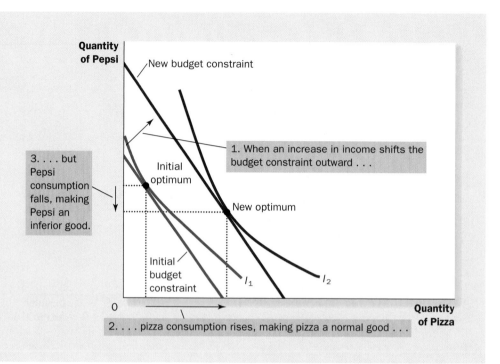

FIGURE 8

An Inferior Good

A good is an inferior good if the consumer buys less of it when his income rises. Here Pepsi is an inferior good: When the consumer's income increases and the budget constraint shifts outward, the consumer buys more pizza but less Pepsi.

price of Pepsi falls from $2 to $1 a pint. It is no surprise that the lower price expands the consumer's set of buying opportunities. In other words, a fall in the price of any good shifts the budget constraint outward.

Figure 9 considers more specifically how the fall in price affects the budget constraint. If the consumer spends his entire $1,000 income on pizza, then the price of Pepsi is irrelevant. Thus, point A in the figure stays the same. Yet if the consumer spends his entire income of $1,000 on Pepsi, he can now buy 1,000 rather than only 500 pints. Thus, the end point of the budget constraint moves from point B to point D.

Notice that in this case the outward shift in the budget constraint changes its slope. (This differs from what happened previously when prices stayed the same but the consumer's income changed.) As we have discussed, the slope of the budget constraint reflects the relative price of Pepsi and pizza. Because the price of Pepsi has fallen to $1 from $2, while the price of pizza has remained $10, the consumer can now trade a pizza for 10 rather than 5 pints of Pepsi. As a result, the new budget constraint is more steeply sloped.

How such a change in the budget constraint alters the consumption of both goods depends on the consumer's preferences. For the indifference curves drawn in this figure, the consumer buys more Pepsi and less pizza.

income effect
the change in consumption that results when a price change moves the consumer to a higher or lower indifference curve

substitution effect
the change in consumption that results when a price change moves the consumer along a given indifference curve to a point with a new marginal rate of substitution

Income and Substitution Effects

The impact of a change in the price of a good on consumption can be decomposed into two effects: an **income effect** and a **substitution effect.** To see what these two

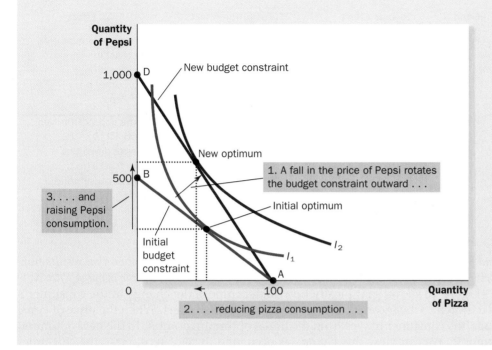

FIGURE 9

Quantity
of Pepsi

1,000 • D   New budget constraint

New optimum

500 • B

1. A fall in the price of Pepsi rotates
the budget constraint outward . . .

3. . . . and
raising Pepsi
consumption.

Initial optimum

Initial
budget
constraint

I_2

I_1

A

0   100

2. . . . reducing pizza consumption . . .

Quantity
of Pizza

A Change in Price

*When the price of Pepsi falls, the
consumer's budget constraint
shifts outward and changes
slope. The consumer moves from
the initial optimum to the new
optimum, which changes his
purchases of both Pepsi and
pizza. In this case, the quantity
of Pepsi consumed rises, and the
quantity of pizza consumed falls.*

effects are, consider how our consumer might respond when he learns that the price of Pepsi has fallen. He might reason in the following ways:

- "Great news! Now that Pepsi is cheaper, my income has greater purchasing power. I am, in effect, richer than I was. Because I am richer, I can buy both more Pepsi and more pizza." (This is the income effect.)
- "Now that the price of Pepsi has fallen, I get more pints of Pepsi for every pizza that I give up. Because pizza is now relatively more expensive, I should buy less pizza and more Pepsi." (This is the substitution effect.)

Which statement do you find more compelling?

In fact, both of these statements make sense. The decrease in the price of Pepsi makes the consumer better off. If Pepsi and pizza are both normal goods, the consumer will want to spread this improvement in his purchasing power over both goods. This income effect tends to make the consumer buy more pizza and more Pepsi. Yet, at the same time, consumption of Pepsi has become less expensive relative to consumption of pizza. This substitution effect tends to make the consumer choose more Pepsi and less pizza.

Now consider the end result of these two effects. The consumer certainly buys more Pepsi, because the income and substitution effects both act to raise purchases of Pepsi. But it is ambiguous whether the consumer buys more pizza, because the income and substitution effects work in opposite directions. This conclusion is summarized in Table 1 (p. 466).

We can interpret the income and substitution effects using indifference curves. *The income effect is the change in consumption that results from the movement to a higher*

	Good	Income Effect	Substitution Effect	Total Effect
TABLE 1 Income and Substitution Effects When the Price of Pepsi Falls	Pepsi	Consumer is richer, so he buys more Pepsi.	Pepsi is relatively cheaper, so consumer buys more Pepsi.	Income and substitution effects act in same direction, so consumer buys more Pepsi.
	Pizza	Consumer is richer, so he buys more pizza.	Pizza is relatively more expensive, so consumer buys less pizza.	Income and substitution effects act in opposite directions, so the total effect on pizza consumption is ambiguous.

indifference curve. The substitution effect is the change in consumption that results from being at a point on an indifference curve with a different marginal rate of substitution.

Figure 10 shows graphically how to decompose the change in the consumer's decision into the income effect and the substitution effect. When the price of Pepsi falls, the consumer moves from the initial optimum, point A, to the new optimum, point C. We can view this change as occurring in two steps. First, the consumer moves *along* the initial indifference curve I_1 from point A to point B. The consumer is equally happy at these two points, but at point B, the marginal rate of substitution reflects the new relative price. (The dashed line through point B reflects the new relative price by being parallel to the new budget constraint.) Next, the consumer *shifts* to the higher indifference curve I_2 by moving from point B to point C. Even though point B and point C are on different indifference curves, they have the same marginal rate of substitution. That is, the slope of the indifference curve I_1 at point B equals the slope of the indifference curve I_2 at point C.

Although the consumer never actually chooses point B, this hypothetical point is useful to clarify the two effects that determine the consumer's decision. Notice that the change from point A to point B represents a pure change in the marginal rate of substitution without any change in the consumer's welfare. Similarly, the change from point B to point C represents a pure change in welfare without any change in the marginal rate of substitution. Thus, the movement from A to B shows the substitution effect, and the movement from B to C shows the income effect.

Deriving the Demand Curve

We have just seen how changes in the price of a good alter the consumer's budget constraint and, therefore, the quantities of the two goods that he chooses to buy. The demand curve for any good reflects these consumption decisions. Recall that a demand curve shows the quantity demanded of a good for any given price. We can view a consumer's demand curve as a summary of the optimal decisions that arise from his budget constraint and indifference curves.

For example, Figure 11 considers the demand for Pepsi. Panel (a) shows that when the price of a pint falls from $2 to $1, the consumer's budget constraint shifts outward. Because of both income and substitution effects, the consumer increases his purchases of Pepsi from 250 to 750 pints. Panel (b) shows the demand curve

FIGURE 10

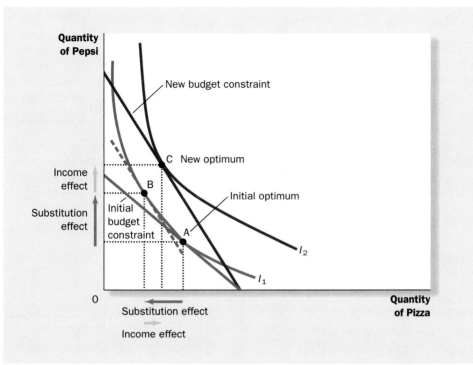

Income and Substitution Effects

The effect of a change in price can be broken down into an income effect and a substitution effect. The substitution effect—the movement along an indifference curve to a point with a different marginal rate of substitution—is shown here as the change from point A to point B along indifference curve I₁. The income effect—the shift to a higher indifference curve—is shown here as the change from point B on indifference curve I₁ to point C on indifference curve I₂.

FIGURE 11

Deriving the Demand Curve

Panel (a) shows that when the price of Pepsi falls from $2 to $1, the consumer's optimum moves from point A to point B, and the quantity of Pepsi consumed rises from 250 to 750 pints. The demand curve in panel (b) reflects this relationship between the price and the quantity demanded.

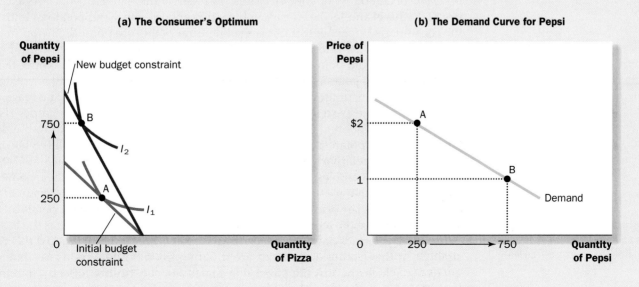

that results from this consumer's decisions. In this way, the theory of consumer choice provides the theoretical foundation for the consumer's demand curve, which we first introduced in Chapter 4.

Although it is comforting to know that the demand curve arises naturally from the theory of consumer choice, this exercise by itself does not justify developing the theory. There is no need for a rigorous, analytic framework just to establish that people respond to changes in prices. The theory of consumer choice is, however, very useful. As we see in the next section, we can use the theory to delve more deeply into the determinants of household behavior.

QuickQuiz   Draw a budget constraint and indifference curves for Pepsi and pizza. Show what happens to the budget constraint and the consumer's optimum when the price of pizza rises. In your diagram, decompose the change into an income effect and a substitution effect.

THREE APPLICATIONS

Now that we have developed the basic theory of consumer choice, let's use it to shed light on three questions about how the economy works. These three questions might at first seem unrelated. But because each question involves household decisionmaking, we can address it with the model of consumer behavior we have just developed.

Do All Demand Curves Slope Downward?

Normally, when the price of a good rises, people buy less of it. Chapter 4 called this usual behavior the *law of demand.* This law is reflected in the downward slope of the demand curve.

As a matter of economic theory, however, demand curves can sometimes slope upward. In other words, consumers can sometimes violate the law of demand and buy *more* of a good when the price rises. To see how this can happen, consider Figure 12. In this example, the consumer buys two goods—meat and potatoes. Initially, the consumer's budget constraint is the line from point A to point B. The optimum is point C. When the price of potatoes rises, the budget constraint shifts inward and is now the line from point A to point D. The optimum is now point E. Notice that a rise in the price of potatoes has led the consumer to buy a larger quantity of potatoes.

Why is the consumer responding in a seemingly perverse way? The reason is that potatoes here are a strongly inferior good. When the price of potatoes rises, the consumer is poorer. The income effect makes the consumer want to buy less meat and more potatoes. At the same time, because the potatoes have become more expensive relative to meat, the substitution effect makes the consumer want to buy more meat and less potatoes. In this particular case, however, the income effect is so strong that it exceeds the substitution effect. In the end, the consumer responds to the higher price of potatoes by buying less meat and more potatoes.

Economists use the term **Giffen good** to describe a good that violates the law of demand. (The term is named for economist Robert Giffen, who first noted this possibility.) In this example, potatoes are a Giffen good. Giffen goods are inferior goods for which the income effect dominates the substitution effect. Therefore, they have demand curves that slope upward.

Giffen good
a good for which an increase in the price raises the quantity demanded

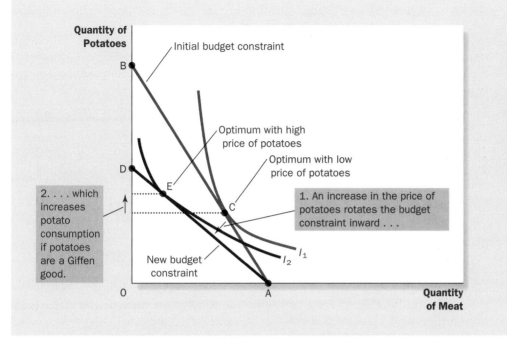

FIGURE 12

A Giffen Good

In this example, when the price of potatoes rises, the consumer's optimum shifts from point C to point E. In this case, the consumer responds to a higher price of potatoes by buying less meat and more potatoes.

Economists disagree about whether any Giffen good has ever been discovered. Some historians suggest that potatoes were in fact a Giffen good during the Irish potato famine of the nineteenth century. Potatoes were such a large part of people's diet that when the price of potatoes rose, it had a large income effect. People responded to their reduced living standard by cutting back on the luxury of meat and buying more of the staple food of potatoes. Thus, it is argued that a higher price of potatoes actually raised the quantity of potatoes demanded.

Whether or not this historical account is true, it is safe to say that Giffen goods are very rare. The theory of consumer choice does allow demand curves to slope upward. Yet such occurrences are so unusual that the law of demand is as reliable a law as any in economics.

How Do Wages Affect Labor Supply?

So far we have used the theory of consumer choice to analyze how a person decides how to allocate his income between two goods. We can use the same theory to analyze how a person decides to allocate his time between work and leisure.

Consider the decision facing Sally, a freelance software designer. Sally is awake for 100 hours per week. She spends some of this time enjoying leisure—riding her bike, watching television, studying economics, and so on. She spends the rest of this time developing software at her computer. For every hour she spends developing software, she earns $50, which she spends on consumption goods. Thus, her wage ($50) reflects the tradeoff Sally faces between leisure and consumption. For every hour of leisure she gives up, she works one more hour and gets $50 of consumption.

Figure 13 (p. 470) shows Sally's budget constraint. If she spends all 100 hours enjoying leisure, she has no consumption. If she spends all 100 hours working, she

FIGURE 13

The Work–Leisure Decision

This figure shows Sally's budget constraint for deciding how much to work, her indifference curves for consumption and leisure, and her optimum.

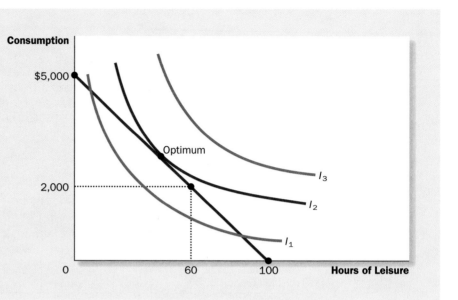

earns a weekly consumption of $5,000 but has no time for leisure. If she works a normal 40-hour week, she enjoys 60 hours of leisure and has weekly consumption of $2,000.

Figure 13 uses indifference curves to represent Sally's preferences for consumption and leisure. Here consumption and leisure are the two "goods" between which Sally is choosing. Because Sally always prefers more leisure and more consumption, she prefers points on higher indifference curves to points on lower ones. At a wage of $50 per hour, Sally chooses a combination of consumption and leisure represented by the point labeled "optimum." This is the point on the budget constraint that is on the highest possible indifference curve, which is curve I_2.

Now consider what happens when Sally's wage increases from $50 to $60 per hour. Figure 14 shows two possible outcomes. In each case, the budget constraint, shown in the left-hand graph, shifts outward from BC_1 to BC_2. In the process, the budget constraint becomes steeper, reflecting the change in relative price: At the higher wage, Sally gets more consumption for every hour of leisure that she gives up.

Sally's preferences, as represented by her indifference curves, determine the resulting responses of consumption and leisure to the higher wage. In both panels, consumption rises. Yet the response of leisure to the change in the wage is different in the two cases. In panel (a), Sally responds to the higher wage by enjoying less leisure. In panel (b), Sally responds by enjoying more leisure.

Sally's decision between leisure and consumption determines her supply of labor because the more leisure she enjoys, the less time she has left to work. In each panel, the right-hand graph in Figure 14 shows the labor supply curve implied by Sally's decision. In panel (a), a higher wage induces Sally to enjoy less leisure and work more, so the labor supply curve slopes upward. In panel (b), a higher wage induces Sally to enjoy more leisure and work less, so the labor supply curve slopes "backward."

At first, the backward-sloping labor supply curve is puzzling. Why would a person respond to a higher wage by working less? The answer comes from considering the income and substitution effects of a higher wage.

FIGURE 14

An Increase in the Wage

The two panels of this figure show how a person might respond to an increase in the wage. The graphs on the left show the consumer's initial budget constraint BC_1 and new budget constraint BC_2, as well as the consumer's optimal choices over consumption and leisure. The graphs on the right show the resulting labor supply curve. Because hours worked equal total hours available minus hours of leisure, any change in leisure implies an opposite change in the quantity of labor supplied. In panel (a), when the wage rises, consumption rises and leisure falls, resulting in a labor supply curve that slopes upward. In panel (b), when the wage rises, both consumption and leisure rise, resulting in a labor supply curve that slopes backward.

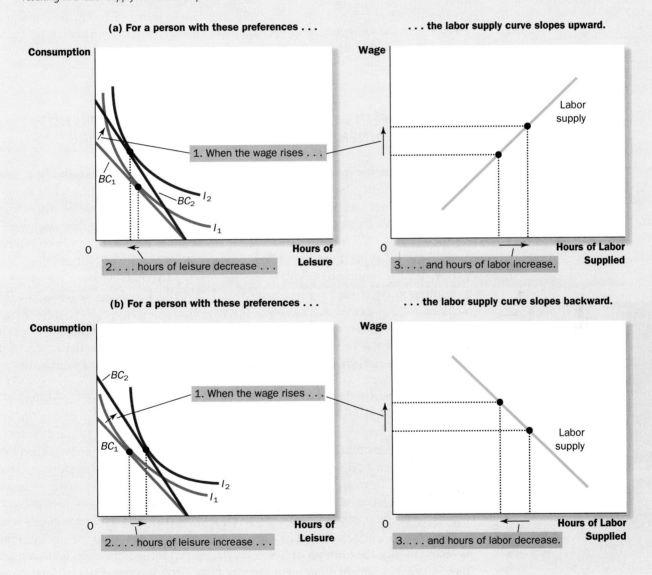

Consider first the substitution effect. When Sally's wage rises, leisure becomes more costly relative to consumption, and this encourages Sally to substitute consumption for leisure. In other words, the substitution effect induces Sally to work harder in response to higher wages, which tends to make the labor supply curve slope upward.

Now consider the income effect. When Sally's wage rises, she moves to a higher indifference curve. She is now better off than she was. As long as consumption and leisure are both normal goods, she tends to want to use this increase in well-being to enjoy both higher consumption and greater leisure. In other words, the income effect induces her to work less, which tends to make the labor supply curve slope backward.

In the end, economic theory does not give a clear prediction about whether an increase in the wage induces Sally to work more or less. If the substitution effect is greater than the income effect for Sally, she works more. If the income effect is greater than the substitution effect, she works less. The labor supply curve, therefore, could be either upward or backward sloping.

Case Study

INCOME EFFECTS ON LABOR SUPPLY: HISTORICAL TRENDS, LOTTERY WINNERS, AND THE CARNEGIE CONJECTURE

The idea of a backward-sloping labor supply curve might at first seem like a mere theoretical curiosity, but in fact it is not. Evidence indicates that the labor supply curve, considered over long periods of time, does in fact slope backward. A hundred years ago many people worked six days a week. Today five-day workweeks are the norm. At the same time that the length of the workweek has been falling, the wage of the typical worker (adjusted for inflation) has been rising.

Here is how economists explain this historical pattern: Over time, advances in technology raise workers' productivity and, thereby, the demand for labor. The increase in labor demand raises equilibrium wages. As wages rise, so does the reward for working. Yet rather than responding to this increased incentive by working more, most workers choose to take part of their greater prosperity in the form of more leisure. In other words, the income effect of higher wages dominates the substitution effect.

Further evidence that the income effect on labor supply is strong comes from a very different kind of data: winners of lotteries. Winners of large prizes in the lottery see large increases in their incomes and, as a result, large outward shifts in their budget constraints. Because the winners' wages have not changed, however, the *slopes* of their budget constraints remain the same. There is, therefore, no substitution effect. By examining the behavior of lottery winners, we can isolate the income effect on labor supply.

The results from studies of lottery winners are striking. Of those winners who win more than $50,000, almost 25 percent quit working within a year, and another 9 percent reduce the number of hours they work. Of those winners who win more than $1 million, almost 40 percent stop working. The income effect on labor supply of winning such a large prize is substantial.

Similar results were found in a study, published in the May 1993 issue of the *Quarterly Journal of Economics,* of how receiving a bequest affects a person's labor supply. The study found that a single person who inherits more than $150,000 is

"No more 9-to-5 for us."

four times as likely to stop working as a single person who inherits less than $25,000. This finding would not have surprised the nineteenth-century industrialist Andrew Carnegie. Carnegie warned that "the parent who leaves his son enormous wealth generally deadens the talents and energies of the son, and tempts him to lead a less useful and less worthy life than he otherwise would." That is, Carnegie viewed the income effect on labor supply to be substantial and, from his paternalistic perspective, regrettable. During his life and at his death, Carnegie gave much of his vast fortune to charity. ●

How Do Interest Rates Affect Household Saving?

An important decision that every person faces is how much income to consume today and how much to save for the future. We can use the theory of consumer choice to analyze how people make this decision and how the amount they save depends on the interest rate their savings will earn.

Consider the decision facing Sam, a worker planning ahead for retirement. To keep things simple, let's divide Sam's life into two periods. In the first period, Sam is young and working. In the second period, he is old and retired. When young, Sam earns $100,000. He divides this income between current consumption and saving. When he is old, Sam will consume what he has saved, including the interest that his savings have earned.

Suppose that the interest rate is 10 percent. Then for every dollar that Sam saves when young, he can consume $1.10 when old. We can view "consumption when young" and "consumption when old" as the two goods that Sam must choose between. The interest rate determines the relative price of these two goods.

Figure 15 shows Sam's budget constraint. If he saves nothing, he consumes $100,000 when young and nothing when old. If he saves everything, he consumes

FIGURE 15

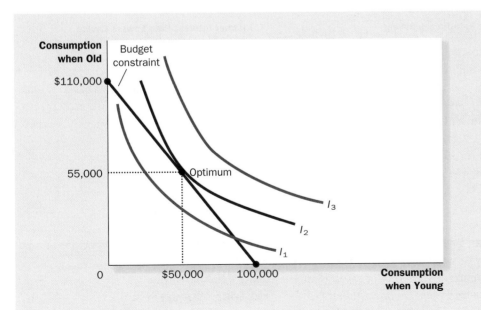

The Consumption–Saving Decision

This figure shows the budget constraint for a person deciding how much to consume in the two periods of his life, the indifference curves representing his preferences, and the optimum.

nothing when young and $110,000 when old. The budget constraint shows these and all the intermediate possibilities.

Figure 15 uses indifference curves to represent Sam's preferences for consumption in the two periods. Because Sam prefers more consumption in both periods, he prefers points on higher indifference curves to points on lower ones. Given his preferences, Sam chooses the optimal combination of consumption in both periods of life, which is the point on the budget constraint that is on the highest possible indifference curve. At this optimum, Sam consumes $50,000 when young and $55,000 when old.

Now consider what happens when the interest rate increases from 10 percent to 20 percent. Figure 16 shows two possible outcomes. In both cases, the budget constraint shifts outward and becomes steeper. At the new higher interest rate, Sam gets more consumption when old for every dollar of consumption that he gives up when young.

The two panels show different preferences for Sam and the resulting response to the higher interest rate. In both cases, consumption when old rises. Yet the response of consumption when young to the change in the interest rate is different in the two cases. In panel (a), Sam responds to the higher interest rate by consuming less when young. In panel (b), Sam responds by consuming more when young.

Sam's saving, of course, is his income when young minus the amount he consumes when young. In panel (a), consumption when young falls when the interest

FIGURE 16

An Increase in the Interest Rate

In both panels, an increase in the interest rate shifts the budget constraint outward. In panel (a), consumption when young falls, and consumption when old rises. The result is an increase in saving when young. In panel (b), consumption in both periods rises. The result is a decrease in saving when young.

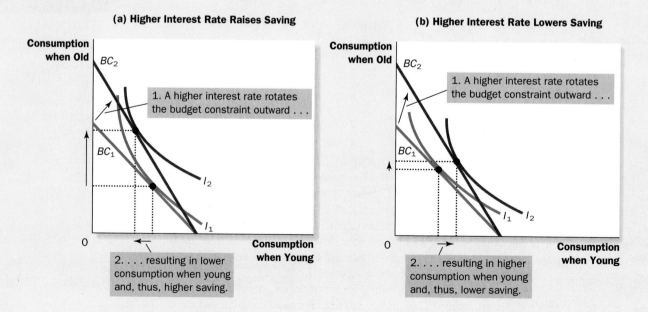

rate rises, so saving must rise. In panel (b), Sam consumes more when young, so saving must fall.

The case shown in panel (b) might at first seem odd: Sam responds to an increase in the return to saving by saving less. Yet this behavior is not as peculiar as it might seem. We can understand it by considering the income and substitution effects of a higher interest rate.

Consider first the substitution effect. When the interest rate rises, consumption when old becomes less costly relative to consumption when young. Therefore, the substitution effect induces Sam to consume more when old and less when young. In other words, the substitution effect induces Sam to save more.

Now consider the income effect. When the interest rate rises, Sam moves to a higher indifference curve. He is now better off than he was. As long as consumption in both periods consists of normal goods, he tends to want to use this increase in well-being to enjoy higher consumption in both periods. In other words, the income effect induces him to save less.

The end result, of course, depends on both the income and substitution effects. If the substitution effect of a higher interest rate is greater than the income effect, Sam saves more. If the income effect is greater than the substitution effect, Sam saves less. Thus, the theory of consumer choice says that an increase in the interest rate could either encourage or discourage saving.

Although this ambiguous result is interesting from the standpoint of economic theory, it is disappointing from the standpoint of economic policy. It turns out that an important issue in tax policy hinges in part on how saving responds to interest rates. Some economists have advocated reducing the taxation of interest and other capital income, arguing that such a policy change would raise the after-tax interest rate that savers can earn and would thereby encourage people to save more. Other economists have argued that because of offsetting income and substitution effects, such a tax change might not increase saving and could even reduce it. Unfortunately, research has not led to a consensus about how interest rates affect saving. As a result, there remains disagreement among economists about whether changes in tax policy aimed to encourage saving would, in fact, have the intended effect.

QuickQuiz   Explain how an increase in the wage can potentially decrease the amount that a person wants to work.

CONCLUSION: DO PEOPLE REALLY THINK THIS WAY?

The theory of consumer choice describes how people make decisions. As we have seen, it has broad applicability. It can explain how a person chooses between Pepsi and pizza, work and leisure, consumption and saving, and on and on.

At this point, however, you might be tempted to treat the theory of consumer choice with some skepticism. After all, you are a consumer. You decide what to buy every time you walk into a store. And you know that you do not decide by writing down budget constraints and indifference curves. Doesn't this knowledge about your own decisionmaking provide evidence against the theory?

The answer is no. The theory of consumer choice does not try to present a literal account of how people make decisions. It is a model. And, as we first discussed in Chapter 2, models are not intended to be completely realistic.

The best way to view the theory of consumer choice is as a metaphor for how consumers make decisions. No consumer (except an occasional economist) goes through the explicit optimization envisioned in the theory. Yet consumers are aware that their choices are constrained by their financial resources. And, given those constraints, they do the best they can to achieve the highest level of satisfaction. The theory of consumer choice tries to describe this implicit, psychological process in a way that permits explicit, economic analysis.

The proof of the pudding is in the eating. And the test of a theory is in its applications. In the last section of this chapter we applied the theory of consumer choice to three practical issues about the economy. If you take more advanced courses in economics, you will see that this theory provides the framework for much additional analysis.

SUMMARY

- A consumer's budget constraint shows the possible combinations of different goods he can buy given his income and the prices of the goods. The slope of the budget constraint equals the relative price of the goods.

- The consumer's indifference curves represent his preferences. An indifference curve shows the various bundles of goods that make the consumer equally happy. Points on higher indifference curves are preferred to points on lower indifference curves. The slope of an indifference curve at any point is the consumer's marginal rate of substitution—the rate at which the consumer is willing to trade one good for the other.

- The consumer optimizes by choosing the point on his budget constraint that lies on the highest indifference curve. At this point, the slope of the indifference curve (the marginal rate of substitution between the goods) equals the slope of the budget constraint (the relative price of the goods).

- When the price of a good falls, the impact on the consumer's choices can be broken down into an income effect and a substitution effect. The income effect is the change in consumption that arises because a lower price makes the consumer better off. The substitution effect is the change in consumption that arises because a price change encourages greater consumption of the good that has become relatively cheaper. The income effect is reflected in the movement from a lower to a higher indifference curve, whereas the substitution effect is reflected by a movement along an indifference curve to a point with a different slope.

- The theory of consumer choice can be applied in many situations. It can explain why demand curves can potentially slope upward, why higher wages could either increase or decrease the quantity of labor supplied, and why higher interest rates could either increase or decrease saving.

KEY CONCEPTS

budget constraint, p. 455
indifference curve, p. 456
marginal rate of
   substitution, p. 457

perfect substitutes, p. 459
perfect complements, p. 460
normal good, p. 463
inferior good, p. 463

income effect, p. 464
substitution effect, p. 464
Giffen good, p. 468

QUESTIONS FOR REVIEW

1. A consumer has income of $3,000. Wine costs $3 a glass, and cheese costs $6 a pound. Draw the consumer's budget constraint. What is the slope of this budget constraint?

2. Draw a consumer's indifference curves for wine and cheese. Describe and explain four properties of these indifference curves.

3. Pick a point on an indifference curve for wine and cheese and show the marginal rate of substitution. What does the marginal rate of substitution tell us?

4. Show a consumer's budget constraint and indifference curves for wine and cheese. Show the optimal consumption choice. If the price of wine is $3 a glass and the price of cheese is $6 a pound, what is the marginal rate of substitution at this optimum?

5. A person who consumes wine and cheese gets a raise, so his income increases from $3,000 to $4,000. Show what happens if both wine and cheese are normal goods. Now show what happens if cheese is an inferior good.

6. The price of cheese rises from $6 to $10 a pound, while the price of wine remains $3 a glass. For a consumer with a constant income of $3,000, show what happens to consumption of wine and cheese. Decompose the change into income and substitution effects.

7. Can an increase in the price of cheese possibly induce a consumer to buy more cheese? Explain.

PROBLEMS AND APPLICATIONS

1. Jennifer divides her income between coffee and croissants (both of which are normal goods). An early frost in Brazil causes a large increase in the price of coffee in the United States.
   a. Show the effect of the frost on Jennifer's budget constraint.
   b. Show the effect of the frost on Jennifer's optimal consumption bundle assuming that the substitution effect outweighs the income effect for croissants.
   c. Show the effect of the frost on Jennifer's optimal consumption bundle assuming that the income effect outweighs the substitution effect for croissants.

2. Compare the following two pairs of goods:

   • Coke and Pepsi
   • Skis and ski bindings

   In which case do you expect the indifference curves to be fairly straight, and in which case do you expect the indifference curves to be very bowed? In which case will the consumer respond more to a change in the relative price of the two goods?

3. Mario consumes only cheese and crackers.
   a. Could cheese and crackers both be inferior goods for Mario? Explain.
   b. Suppose that cheese is a normal good for Mario while crackers are an inferior good. If the price of cheese falls, what happens to Mario's consumption of crackers? What happens to his consumption of cheese? Explain.

4. Jim buys only milk and cookies.
   a. In 2003, Jim earns $100, milk costs $2 per quart, and cookies cost $4 per dozen. Draw Jim's budget constraint.
   b. Now suppose that all prices increase by 10 percent in 2004 and that Jim's salary increases by 10 percent as well. Draw Jim's new budget constraint. How would Jim's optimal combination of milk and cookies in 2004 compare to his optimal combination in 2003?

5. Consider your decision about how many hours to work.
   a. Draw your budget constraint assuming that you pay no taxes on your income. On the same diagram, draw another budget constraint assuming that you pay a 15 percent tax.
   b. Show how the tax might lead to more hours of work, fewer hours, or the same number of hours. Explain.

6. Sarah is awake for 100 hours per week. Using one diagram, show Sarah's budget constraints if she earns $6 per hour, $8 per hour, and $10 per hour. Now draw indifference curves such that Sarah's labor supply curve is upward sloping when the wage is between $6 and $8 per hour, and backward sloping when the wage is between $8 and $10 per hour.

7. Draw the indifference curve for someone deciding how much to work. Suppose the wage increases. Is it possible that the person's consumption would fall? Is this plausible?

Discuss. (Hint: Think about income and substitution effects.)

8. Suppose you take a job that pays $30,000 and set some of this income aside in a savings account that pays an annual interest rate of 5 percent. Use a diagram with a budget constraint and indifference curves to show how your consumption changes in each of the following situations. To keep things simple, assume that you pay no taxes on your income.
   a. Your salary increases to $40,000.
   b. The interest rate on your bank account rises to 8 percent.

9. As discussed in the text, we can divide an individual's life into two hypothetical periods: "young" and "old." Suppose that the individual earns income only when young and saves some of that income to consume when old. If the interest rate on savings falls, can you tell what happens to consumption when young? Can you tell what happens to consumption when old? Explain.

10. (This problem is challenging.) The welfare system provides income to some needy families. Typically, the maximum payment goes to families that earn no income; then, as families begin to earn income, the welfare payment declines gradually and eventually disappears. Let's consider the possible effects of this program on a family's labor supply.
   a. Draw a budget constraint for a family assuming that the welfare system did not exist. On the same diagram, draw a budget constraint that reflects the existence of the welfare system.
   b. Adding indifference curves to your diagram, show how the welfare system could reduce the number of hours worked by the family. Explain, with reference to both the income and substitution effects.
   c. Using your diagram from part (b), show the effect of the welfare system on the well-being of the family.

11. (This problem is challenging.) Suppose that an individual owed no taxes on the first $10,000 she earned and 15 percent of any income she earned over $10,000. (This is a simplified version of the actual U.S. income tax.) Now suppose that Congress is considering two ways to reduce the tax burden: a reduction in the tax rate and an increase in the amount on which no tax is owed.
   a. What effect would a reduction in the tax rate have on the individual's labor supply if she earned $30,000 to start? Explain in words using the income and substitution effects. You do not need to use a diagram.
   b. What effect would an increase in the amount on which no tax is owed have on the individual's labor supply? Again, explain in words using the income and substitution effects.

12. (This problem is challenging.) Consider a person deciding how much to consume and how much to save for retirement. This person has particular preferences: Her lifetime utility depends on the lowest level of consumption during the two periods of her life. That is,

   Utility = Minimum {consumption when young, consumption when old}.

   a. Draw this person's indifference curves. (Hint: Recall that indifference curves show the combinations of consumption in the two periods that yield the same level of utility.)
   b. Draw the budget constraint and the optimum.
   c. When the interest rate increases, does this person save more or less? Explain your answer using income and substitution effects.

13. Economist George Stigler once wrote that, according to consumer theory, "if consumers do not buy less of a commodity when their incomes rise, they will surely buy less when the price of the commodity rises." Explain this statement.

http://

For more study tools, please visit http://mankiwXtra.swlearning.com.

FRONTIERS OF MICROECONOMICS

Economics is a study of the choices that people make and the resulting interactions they have with one another. This study has many facets, as we have seen in the preceding chapters. Yet it would be a mistake to think that all the facets we have seen make up a finished jewel, perfect and unchanging. Like all scientists, economists are always on the lookout for new areas to study and new phenomena to explain. This final chapter on microeconomics offers an assortment of three topics at the discipline's frontier to see how economists are trying to expand their understanding of human behavior and society.

The first topic is the economics of *asymmetric information*. Many times in life, some people are better informed than others, and this difference in information can affect the choices they make and how they deal with one another. Thinking about this asymmetry can shed light on many aspects of the world, from the market for used cars to the custom of gift giving.

The second topic we examine in this chapter is *political economy*. Throughout this book we have seen many examples where markets fail and government policy can potentially improve matters. But "potentially" is a needed qualifier: Whether this potential is realized depends on how well our political institutions work. The field of political economy applies the tools of economics to understand the functioning of government.

The third topic in this chapter is *behavioral economics*. This field brings some of the insights from psychology into the study of economic issues. It offers a view of human behavior that is more subtle and complex than that found in conventional economic theory, but this view may also be more realistic.

This chapter covers a lot of ground. To do so, it offers not a full helping of these three topics but, instead, a taste of each. One goal is to show a few of the directions economists are heading in their effort to expand knowledge of how the economy works. Another goal is to whet your appetite for more courses in economics.

ASYMMETRIC INFORMATION

"I know something you don't know." This statement is a common taunt among children, but it also conveys a deep truth about how people sometimes interact with one another. Many times in life, one person knows more about what is going on than another. A difference in access to relevant knowledge is called an *information asymmetry*.

Examples abound. A worker knows more than his employer about how much effort he puts into his job. A seller of a used car knows more than the buyer about the car's condition. The first is an example of a *hidden action*, whereas the second is an example of a *hidden characteristic*. In each case, the party in the dark (the employer, the car buyer) would like to know the relevant information, but the informed party (the worker, the car seller) may have an incentive to conceal it.

Because asymmetric information is so prevalent, economists have devoted much effort in recent decades to studying its effects. And, indeed, the 2001 Nobel Prize in economics was awarded to three economists (George Akerlof, Michael Spence, and Joseph Stiglitz) for their pioneering work on this topic. Let's discuss some of the insights that this study has revealed.

Hidden Actions: Principals, Agents, and Moral Hazard

moral hazard
the tendency of a person who is imperfectly monitored to engage in dishonest or otherwise undesirable behavior

agent
a person who is performing an act for another person, called the principal

principal
a person for whom another person, called the agent, is performing some act

Moral hazard is a problem that arises when one person, called the **agent,** is performing some task on behalf of another person, called the **principal.** If the principal cannot perfectly monitor the agent's behavior, the agent tends to undertake less effort than the principal considers desirable. The phrase *moral hazard* refers to the risk, or "hazard," of inappropriate or otherwise "immoral" behavior by the agent. In such a situation, the principal tries various ways to encourage the agent to act more responsibly.

The employment relationship is the classic example. The employer is the principal, and the worker is the agent. The moral-hazard problem is the temptation of imperfectly monitored workers to shirk their responsibilities. Employers can respond to this problem in various ways:

- *Better monitoring.* Parents hiring nannies have been known to plant hidden video cameras in their homes to record the nanny's behavior when the parents are away. The aim is to catch irresponsible behavior.
- *High wages.* According to *efficiency-wage theories* (discussed in Chapter 19), some employers may choose to pay their workers a wage above the level that equilibrates supply and demand in the labor market. A worker who earns an above-

equilibrium wage is less likely to shirk, because if he is caught and fired, he might not be able to find another high-paying job.

- *Delayed payment.* Firms can delay part of a worker's compensation, so if the worker is caught shirking and is fired, he suffers a larger penalty. One example of delayed compensation is the year-end bonus. Similarly, a firm may choose to pay its workers more later in their lives. Thus, the wage increases that workers get as they age may reflect not just the benefits of experience but also a response to moral hazard.

These various mechanisms to reduce the problem of moral hazard need not be used alone. Employers can use a combination of them.

Beyond the workplace, there are many other examples of moral hazard. A homeowner with fire insurance will likely buy too few fire extinguishers because the homeowner bears the cost of the extinguisher while the insurance company receives much of the benefit. A family may live near a river with a high risk of flooding because the family enjoys the scenic views, while the government bears the cost of disaster relief after a flood. Many regulations are aimed at addressing the problem: An insurance company may require homeowners to buy extinguishers, and the government may prohibit building homes on land with high risk of flooding. But the insurance company does not have perfect information about how cautious homeowners are, and the government does not have perfect information about the risk that families undertake when choosing where to live. As a result, the problem of moral hazard persists.

Hidden Characteristics: Adverse Selection and the Lemons Problem

Adverse selection is a problem that arises in markets where the seller knows more about the attributes of the good being sold than the buyer does. As a result, the buyer runs the risk of being sold a good of low quality. That is, the "selection" of goods being sold may be "adverse" from the standpoint of the uninformed buyer.

adverse selection
the tendency for the mix of unobserved attributes to become undesirable from the standpoint of an uninformed party

The classic example of adverse selection is the market for used cars. Sellers of used cars know their vehicles' defects while buyers often do not. Because owners of the worst cars are more likely to sell them than are the owners of the best cars, buyers are apprehensive about getting a "lemon." As a result, many people avoid buying vehicles in the used car market. This lemons problem can explain why a used car only a few weeks old sells for thousands of dollars less than a new car of the same type. A buyer of the used car might surmise that the seller is getting rid of the car quickly because the seller knows something about it that the buyer does not.

A second example of adverse selection occurs in the labor market. According to another efficiency-wage theory, workers vary in their abilities, and they may know their own abilities better than do the firms that hire them. When a firm cuts the wage it pays, the more talented workers are more likely to quit, knowing they are better able to find other employment. Conversely, a firm may choose to pay an above-equilibrium wage to attract a better mix of workers.

A third example of adverse selection occurs in markets for insurance. For example, buyers of health insurance know more about their own health problems than do insurance companies. Because people with greater hidden health problems are more likely to buy health insurance than are other people, the price of health insurance reflects the costs of a sicker-than-average person. As a result, people in average health may be discouraged from buying health insurance by the high price.

When markets suffer from adverse selection, the invisible hand does not necessarily work its magic. In the used car market, owners of good cars may choose to keep them rather than sell them at the low price that skeptical buyers are willing to pay. In the labor market, wages may be stuck above the level that balances supply and demand, resulting in unemployment. In insurance markets, buyers with low risk may choose to remain uninsured, because the policies they are offered fail to reflect their true characteristics. Advocates of government-provided health insurance sometimes point to the problem of adverse selection as one reason not to trust the private market to provide the right amount of health insurance on its own.

Signaling to Convey Private Information

Although asymmetric information is sometimes a motivation for public policy, it also motivates some individual behavior that otherwise might be hard to explain. Markets respond to problems of asymmetric information in many ways. One of them is **signaling,** which refers to actions taken by an informed party for the sole purpose of credibly revealing his private information.

signaling
an action taken by an informed party to reveal private information to an uninformed party

We have seen examples of signaling in previous chapters. As we saw in Chapter 17, firms may spend money on advertising to signal to potential customers that they have high-quality products. As we saw in Chapter 20, students may earn college and postgraduate degrees to signal to potential employers that they are high-ability individuals. Recall that the signaling theory of education contrasts with the human-capital theory, which asserts that education increases a person's productivity, rather than merely conveying information about innate talent. These two examples of signaling (advertising, education) may seem very different, but below the surface they are much the same: In both cases, the informed party (the firm, the student) is using the signal to convince the uninformed party (the customer, the employer) that the informed party is offering something of high quality.

What does it take for an action to be an effective signal? Obviously, it must be costly. If a signal were free, everyone would use it, and it would convey no information. For the same reason, there is another requirement: The signal must be less costly, or more beneficial, to the person with the higher-quality product. Otherwise, everyone would have the same incentive to use the signal, and the signal would reveal nothing.

Consider again our two examples. In the advertising case, a firm with a good product reaps a larger benefit from advertising because customers who try the product once are more likely to become repeat customers. Thus, it is rational for the firm with the good product to pay for the cost of the signal (advertising), and it is rational for the customer to use the signal as a piece of information about the product's quality. In the education case, a talented person can get through school more easily than a less talented one. Thus, it is rational for the talented person to pay for the cost of the signal (education), and it is rational for the employer to use the signal as a piece of information about the person's talent.

The world is replete with instances of signaling. Magazine ads sometimes include the phrase "as seen on TV." Why does a firm selling a product in a magazine choose to stress this fact? One possibility is that the firm is trying to convey its willingness to pay for an expensive signal (a spot on television) in the hope that you will infer that its product is of high quality. For the same reason, graduates of elite schools are always sure to put that fact on their résumés.

Case Study
GIFTS AS SIGNALS

A man is debating what to give his girlfriend for her birthday. "I know," he says to himself, "I'll give her cash. After all, I don't know her tastes as well as she does, and with cash, she can buy anything she wants." But when he hands her the money, she is offended. Convinced he doesn't really love her, she breaks off the relationship.

What's the economics behind this story?

In some ways, gift giving is a strange custom. As the man in our story suggests, people typically know their own preferences better than others do, so we might expect everyone to prefer cash to in-kind transfers. If your employer substituted merchandise for your paycheck, you would likely object to the means of payment. But your reaction is very different when someone who (you hope) loves you does the same thing.

One interpretation of gift giving is that it reflects asymmetric information and signaling. The man in our story has private information that the girlfriend would like to know: Does he really love her? Choosing a good gift for her is a signal of his love. Certainly, picking out a gift has the right characteristics to be a signal. It is costly (it takes time), and its cost depends on the private information (how much he loves her). If he really loves her, choosing a good gift is easy because he is thinking about her all the time. If he doesn't love her, finding the right gift is more difficult. Thus, giving a gift that suits the girlfriend is one way for him to convey the private information of his love for her. Giving cash shows that he isn't even bothering to try.

The signaling theory of gift giving is consistent with another observation: People care most about the custom when the strength of affection is most in question. Thus, giving cash to a girlfriend or boyfriend is usually a bad move. But when college students receive a check from their parents, they are less often offended. The parents' love is less likely to be in doubt, so the recipient probably won't interpret the cash gift as a signal of lack of affection. ●

"Now we'll see how much he loves me."

Screening to Induce Information Revelation

When an informed party takes actions to reveal his private information, the phenomenon is called signaling. When an uninformed party takes actions to induce the informed party to reveal private information, the phenomenon is called **screening.**

Some screening is common sense. A person buying a used car may ask that it be checked by an auto mechanic before the sale. A seller who refuses this request reveals his private information that the car is a lemon. The buyer may decide to offer a lower price or to look for another car.

Other examples of screening are more subtle. For example, consider a firm that sells car insurance. The firm would like to charge a low premium to safe drivers and a high premium to risky drivers. But how can it tell them apart? Drivers know whether they are safe or risky, but the risky ones won't admit to it. A driver's history is one piece of information (which insurance companies in fact use), but

screening
an action taken by an uninformed party to induce an informed party to reveal information

because of the intrinsic randomness of car accidents, history is an imperfect indicator of future risks.

The insurance company might be able to sort out the two kinds of drivers by offering different insurance policies that would induce them to separate themselves. One policy would have a high premium and cover the full cost of any accidents that occur. Another policy would have low premiums but would have, say, a $1,000 deductible. (That is, the driver would be responsible for the first $1,000 of damage, and the insurance company would cover the remaining risk.) Notice that the deductible is more of a burden for risky drivers because they are more likely to have an accident. Thus, with a large enough deductible, the low-premium policy with a deductible would attract the safe drivers, while the high-premium policy without a deductible would attract the risky drivers. Faced with these two policies, the two kinds of drivers would reveal their private information by choosing different insurance policies.

Asymmetric Information and Public Policy

We have examined two kinds of asymmetric information—moral hazard and adverse selection. And we have seen how individuals may respond to the problem with signaling or screening. Now let's consider what the study of asymmetric information suggests about the proper scope of public policy.

The tension between market success and market failure is central in microeconomics. We learned in Chapter 7 that the equilibrium of supply and demand is efficient in the sense that it maximizes the total surplus that society can obtain in a market. Adam Smith's invisible hand seemed to reign supreme. This conclusion was then tempered with the study of externalities (Chapter 10), public goods (Chapter 11), imperfect competition (Chapters 15 through 17), and poverty (Chapter 20). These examples of market failure showed that government can sometimes improve market outcomes.

The study of asymmetric information gives us new reason to be wary of markets. When some people know more than others, the market may fail to put resources to their best use. People with high-quality used cars may have trouble selling them because buyers will be afraid of getting a lemon. People with few health problems may have trouble getting low-cost health insurance because insurance companies lump them together with those who have significant (but hidden) health problems.

Although asymmetric information may call for government action in some cases, three facts complicate the issue. First, as we have seen, the private market can sometimes deal with information asymmetries on its own using a combination of signaling and screening. Second, the government rarely has more information than the private parties. Even if the market's allocation of resources is not first-best, it may be second-best. That is, when there are information asymmetries, policymakers may find it hard to improve upon the market's admittedly imperfect outcome. Third, the government is itself an imperfect institution—a topic we take up in the next section.

QuickQuiz A person who buys a life insurance policy pays a certain amount per year and receives for his family a much larger payment in the event of his death. Would you expect buyers of life insurance to have higher or lower death rates than the average person? How might this be an example of moral hazard? Of adverse selection? How might a life insurance company deal with these problems?

POLITICAL ECONOMY

As we have seen, markets left on their own do not always reach a desirable allocation of resources. When we judge the market's outcome to be either inefficient or inequitable, there may be a role for the government to step in and improve the situation. Yet before we embrace an activist government, we need to consider one more fact: The government is also an imperfect institution. The field of *political economy* (sometimes called the field of *public choice*) applies the methods of economics to study how government works.

The Condorcet Voting Paradox

Most advanced societies rely on democratic principles to set government policy. When a city is deciding between two locations to build a new park, for example, we have a simple way to choose: The majority gets its way. Yet, for most policy issues, the number of possible outcomes far exceeds two. A new park, for instance, could be placed in many possible locations. In this case, as the eighteenth-century French political theorist Marquis de Condorcet famously noted, democracy might run into some problems trying to choose one of the outcomes.

For example, suppose there are three possible outcomes, labeled A, B, and C, and there are three voter types with the preferences shown in Table 1. The mayor of our town wants to aggregate these individual preferences into preferences for society as a whole. How should he do it?

At first, he might try some pairwise votes. If he asks voters to choose first between B and C, voter types 1 and 2 will vote for B, giving B the majority. If he then asks voters to choose between A and B, voter types 1 and 3 will vote for A, giving A the majority. Observing that A beats B, and B beats C, the mayor might conclude that A is the voters' clear choice.

But wait: Suppose the mayor then asks voters to choose between A and C. In this case, voter types 2 and 3 vote for C, giving C the majority. That is, under pairwise majority voting, A beats B, B beats C, and C beats A. Normally, we expect preferences to exhibit a property called *transitivity:* If A is preferred to B, and B is preferred to C, then we would expect A to be preferred to C. The **Condorcet paradox** is that democratic outcomes do not always obey this property. Pairwise voting might

Condorcet paradox
the failure of majority rule to produce transitive preferences for society

TABLE 1

The Condorcet Paradox

If voters have these preferences over outcomes A, B, and C, then in pairwise majority voting, A beats B, B beats C, and C beats A.

	Voter Type		
	Type 1	**Type 2**	**Type 3**
Percent of electorate	35	45	20
First choice	A	B	C
Second choice	B	C	A
Third choice	C	A	B

produce transitive preferences for a society, depending on the pattern of individual preferences, but as our example in the table shows, it cannot be counted on to do so.

One implication of the Condorcet paradox is that the order on which things are voted can affect the result. If the mayor suggests choosing first between A and B and then comparing the winner to C, the town ends up choosing C. But if the voters choose first between B and C and then compare the winner to A, the town ends up with A. And if the voters choose first between A and C and then compare the winner to B, the town ends up with B.

There are two lessons to be learned from the Condorcet paradox. The narrow lesson is that when there are more than two options, setting the agenda (that is, deciding the order in which items are voted) can have a powerful impact on the outcome of a democratic election. The broad lesson is that majority voting by itself does not tell us what outcome a society really wants.

Arrow's Impossibility Theorem

Since political theorists first noticed Condorcet's paradox, they have spent much energy studying voting systems and proposing new ones. For example, as an alternative to pairwise majority voting, the mayor of our town could ask each voter to rank the possible outcomes. For each voter, we could give 1 point for last place, 2 points for second to last, 3 points for third to last, and so on. The outcome that receives the most total points wins. With the preferences in Table 1, outcome B is the winner. (You can do the arithmetic yourself.) This voting method is called a *Borda count*, for the eighteenth-century French mathematician and political scientist who devised it. It is often used in polls that rank sports teams.

Is there a perfect voting system? Economist Kenneth Arrow took up this question in his 1951 book *Social Choice and Individual Values*. Arrow started by defining what a perfect voting system would be. He assumes that individuals in society have preferences over the various possible outcomes: A, B, C, and so on. He then assumes that society wants a voting scheme to choose among these outcomes that satisfies several properties:

- *Unanimity:* If everyone prefers A to B, then A should beat B.
- *Transitivity:* If A beats B, and B beats C, then A should beat C.
- *Independence of irrelevant alternatives:* The ranking between any two outcomes A and B should not depend on whether some third outcome C is also available.
- *No dictators:* There is no person that always gets his way, regardless of everyone else's preferences.

These all seem like desirable properties for a voting system to have. Yet Arrow proved, mathematically and incontrovertibly, that *no voting system can satisfy all of these properties.* This amazing result is called **Arrow's impossibility theorem.**

The mathematics needed to prove Arrow's theorem is beyond the scope of this book, but we can get some sense of why the theorem is true from a couple of examples. We have already seen the problem with the method of majority rule. The Condorcet paradox shows that majority rule fails to produce a ranking among the outcomes that always satisfies transitivity.

As another example, the Borda count fails to satisfy the independence of irrelevant alternatives. Recall that, using the preferences in Table 1, outcome B wins with a Borda count. But suppose that suddenly C disappears as an alternative. If the Borda count method is applied only to outcomes A and B, then A wins. (Once again,

Arrow's impossibility theorem
a mathematical result showing that, under certain assumed conditions, there is no scheme for aggregating individual preferences into a valid set of social preferences

you can do the arithmetic on your own.) Thus, eliminating alternative C changes the ranking between A and B. The reason for this change is that the result of the Borda count depends on the number of points that A and B receive, and the number of points depends on whether the irrelevant alternative, C, is also available.

Arrow's impossibility theorem is a deep and disturbing result. It doesn't say that we should abandon democracy as a form of government. But it does say that, no matter what voting scheme society adopts for aggregating the preferences of its members, in some way it will be flawed as a mechanism for social choice.

The Median Voter Is King

Despite Arrow's theorem, voting is how most societies choose their leaders and public policies, often by majority rule. The next step in studying government is to examine how governments run by majority rule work. That is, in a democratic society, who determines what policy is chosen? In some cases, the theory of democratic government yields a surprisingly simple answer.

Let's consider an example. Imagine that society is deciding on how much money to spend on some public good, such as the army or the national parks. Each voter has his own most preferred budget, and he always prefers outcomes closer to his most preferred value to outcomes further away. Thus, we can line up voters from those who prefer the smallest budget to those who prefer the largest. Figure 1 is an example. Here there are 100 voters, and the budget size varies from zero to $20 billion. Given these preferences, what outcome would you expect democracy to produce?

According to a famous result called the **median voter theorem,** majority rule will produce the outcome most preferred by the median voter. The *median voter* is the voter exactly in the middle of the distribution. In this example, if you take the line of voters ordered by their preferred budgets and count 50 voters from either end of the line, you will find that the median voter wants a budget of $10 billion. By contrast, the average preferred outcome (calculated by adding the preferred

median voter theorem
a mathematical result showing that if voters are choosing a point along a line and each voter wants the point closest to his most preferred point, then majority rule will pick the most preferred point of the median voter

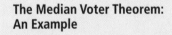
FIGURE 1

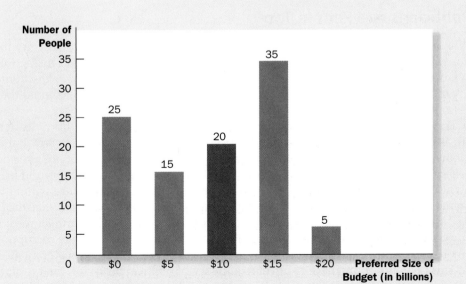

The Median Voter Theorem: An Example

This bar chart shows how 100 voters' most preferred budget is distributed over five options, ranging from zero to $20 billion. If society makes its choice by majority rule, the median voter (who here prefers $10 billion) determines the outcome.

outcomes and dividing by the number of voters) is $9 billion, and the modal outcome (the one preferred by the greatest number of voters) is $15 billion.

The median voter rules the day because his preferred outcome beats any other proposal in a two-way race. In our example, more than half the voters want $10 billion or more, and more than half want $10 billion or less. If someone proposes, say, $8 billion instead of $10 billion, everyone who prefers $10 billion or more will vote with the median voter. Similarly, if someone proposes $12 billion instead of $10 billion, everyone who wants $10 billion or less will vote with the median voter. In either case, the median voter has more than half the voters on his side.

What about the Condorcet voting paradox? It turns out that when the voters are picking a point along a line and each voter aims for his own most preferred point, the Condorcet paradox cannot arise. The median voter's most preferred outcome beats all comers.

One implication of the median voter theorem is that if two political parties are each trying to maximize their chance of election, they will both move their positions toward the median voter. Suppose, for example, that the Democratic party advocates a budget of $15 billion, while the Republican party advocates a budget of $10 billion. The Democratic position is more popular in the sense that $15 billion has more proponents than any other single choice. Nonetheless, the Republicans get more than 50 percent of the vote: They will attract the 20 voters who want $10 billion, the 15 voters who want $5 billion, and the 25 voters who want zero. If the Democrats want to win, they will move their platform toward the median voter. Thus, this theory can explain why the parties in a two-party system are similar to each other: They are both moving toward the median voter.

Another implication of the median voter theorem is that minority views are not given much weight. Imagine that 40 percent of the population want a lot of money spent on the national parks, and 60 percent want nothing spent. In this case, the median voter's preference is zero, regardless of the intensity of the minority's view. Such is the logic of democracy. Rather than reaching a compromise that takes into account everyone's preferences, majority rule looks only to the person in the exact middle of the distribution.

Politicians Are People Too

When economists study consumer behavior, they assume that consumers buy the bundle of goods and services that gives them the greatest level of satisfaction. When economists study firm behavior, they assume that firms produce the quantity of goods and services that yields the greatest level of profits. What should they assume when they study people involved in the practice of politics?

Politicians also have objectives. It would be nice to assume that political leaders are always looking out for the well-being of society as a whole, that they are aiming for an optimal combination of efficiency and equity. Nice, perhaps, but not realistic. Self-interest is as powerful a motive for political actors as it is for consumers and firm owners. Some politicians are motivated by desire for reelection and are willing to sacrifice the national interest when doing so solidifies their base of voters. (See the *In the News* box on pages 490–491.) Other politicians are motivated by simple greed. If you have any doubt, you should look at the world's poor nations, where corruption among government officials is a common impediment to economic development.

This book is not the place to develop a theory of political behavior. That topic is best left to the political scientists. But when thinking about economic policy, remember that this policy is made not by a benevolent king, but by real people with their own all-too-human desires. Sometimes they are motivated to further the national interest, but sometimes they are motivated by their own political and financial ambitions. We shouldn't be surprised when economic policy fails to resemble the ideals derived in economics textbooks.

QuickQuiz A public school district is voting on the school budget and the resulting student–teacher ratio. A poll finds that 35 percent of the voters want a ratio of 9:1, 25 percent want a ratio of 10:1, and 40 percent want a ratio of 12:1. What outcome would you expect the district to end up with?

BEHAVIORAL ECONOMICS

Economics is a study of human behavior, but it is not the only field that can make that claim. The social science of psychology also sheds light on the choices that people make in their lives. The fields of economics and psychology usually proceed independently, in part because they address a different range of questions. But recently a field called *behavioral economics* has emerged in which economists are making use of basic psychological insights. Let's consider some of these insights here.

People Aren't Always Rational

Economic theory is populated by a particular species of organism, sometimes called *homo economicus*. Members of this species are always rational. As firm managers, they maximize profits. As consumers, they maximize utility (or, equivalently, pick the point on the highest indifference curve). Given the constraints they face, they rationally weigh all the costs and benefits and always choose the best possible course of action.

Real people, however, are *homo sapiens*. Although in many ways they resemble the rational, calculating people assumed in economic theory, they are far more complex. They can be forgetful, impulsive, confused, emotional, and shortsighted. These imperfections of human reasoning are the bread-and-butter of psychologists, but until recently, economists have neglected them.

Herbert Simon, one of the first social scientists to work at the boundary of economics and psychology, suggested that humans should be viewed not as rational maximizers but as *satisficers*. Rather than always choosing the best course of action, they make decisions that are merely good enough. Similarly, other economists have suggested that humans are only "near rational" or that they exhibit "bounded rationality."

Studies of human decisionmaking have tried to detect systematic mistakes that people make. Here are a few of the findings:

• *People are overconfident.* Imagine that you were asked some numerical questions, such as the number of African countries in the United Nations, the height of the tallest mountain in North America, and so on. Instead of being asked for a single estimate, however, you were asked to give a 90 percent confidence interval—a range such that you were 90 percent confident the true number falls within it. When psychologists run experiments like this, they find that most people give ranges that are too small: The true number falls within their intervals far less than 90 percent of the time. That is, most people are too sure of their own abilities.

IN THE NEWS

FARM POLICY AND POLITICS

Humorist Dave Barry takes aim at the Farm Security Act, which the U.S. Congress passed and President Bush signed in 2002.

Farmer on the Dole

By Dave Barry

If you're like most American taxpayers, you often wake up in the middle of the night in a cold sweat and ask yourself: "Am I doing enough to support mohair producers?"

I am pleased to report that you are, thanks to bold action taken recently by the United States Congress (motto: "Hey, it's not OUR money!"). I am referring to the 2002 Farm Security Act, which recently emerged from the legislative process very much the way a steaming wad of processed vegetation emerges from the digestive tract of a cow.

The purpose of the Farm Security Act is to provide farmers with "price stability." What do we mean by "price stability"? We mean: your money. You have already been very generous about this: Last year alone, you gave more than $20 billion worth of price stability to farmers. Since 1996, you've given more than a million dollars apiece to more than 1,000 lucky recipients, many of which are actually big agribusinesses. Some of the "farmers" you've sent your money to are billionaires, such as Ted Turner and Charles Schwab, as well as major corporations, such as Chevron, DuPont and John Hancock Mutual Life Insurance.

But that is NOTHING compared with how generous you're about to get, taxpayers! Thanks to the Farm Security Act, over the next 10 years, you'll be providing farmers with 70 percent MORE stability, for a total of $180 billion. At this rate, in a few years farmers will be so stable that they'll have to huddle in their root cellars for fear of being struck by bales of taxpayer-supplied cash raining down on the Heartland states from Air Force bombers.

- *People give too much weight to a small number of vivid observations.* Imagine that you are thinking about buying a car of brand X. To learn about its reliability, you read *Consumer Reports*, which has surveyed 1,000 owners of car X. Then you run into a friend who owns car X, and she tells you that her car is a lemon. How do you treat your friend's observation? If you think rationally, you will realize that she has only increased your sample size from 1,000 to 1,001, which does not provide much new information. But because your friend's story is so vivid, you may be tempted to give it more weight in your decisionmaking than you should.
- *People are reluctant to change their minds.* People tend to interpret evidence to confirm beliefs they already hold. In one study, subjects were asked to read and evaluate a research report on whether capital punishment deters crime. After reading the report, those who initially favored the death penalty said they were more sure in their view, and those who initially opposed the death penalty also said they were more sure in their view. The two groups interpreted the same evidence in exactly opposite ways.

Think about decisions you have made in your own life. Do you exhibit some of these traits?

Perhaps you are asking yourself: "Wait a minute! Isn't this kind of like, I don't know . . . *welfare*?"

No, it is not. Welfare is when the government gives money to people who produce nothing. Whereas the farm-money recipients produce something that is critical to our nation: votes. Powerful congresspersons from both parties, as well as President Bush, believe that if they dump enough of your money on farm states, the farm states will re-elect them, thus enabling them to continue the vital work of dumping your money on the farm states. So as we see, it's not welfare at all! It's bribery.

But let us not forget the element of National Security. This is where your mohair comes in. As you know, "mohair" is the hair of any animal whose name begins with "mo," such as moose, mouse, mongoose or moray eel.

No, wait, sorry. "Mohair" is actually wool made from the hair of a goat. During WWII, mohair was used to make military uniforms, so it was considered to be a strategic material, and Congress decided that you, the taxpayer, should pay people to produce it. But of course today mohair has no vital military purpose, and so . . . you are STILL paying people to produce it! And thanks to the Farm Security Act, you will continue to pay millions and millions of dollars, every year, to mohair producers!

As I say, this is for National Security. If terrorists, God forbid, ever manage to construct a giant time machine and transport the United States back to 1941, and we have to fight World War II again, WE WILL BE READY.

You will also be thrilled, as a taxpayer, to learn that the Farm Security Act provides new subsidies for producers of lentils and chickpeas. And not a moment too soon. This nation has become far too dependent on imported lentils and chickpeas. Try to picture the horror of living in a world in which foreigners, in foreign countries, suddenly cut off our lentil and chickpea supply. Imagine how you would feel if you had to look your small child in the eye and say, "I'm sorry, little Billy or Suzy as the case may be, but there will be no lentils or chickpeas tonight, and all because we taxpayers were too short-sighted to fork over millions of dollars in support for domestic lentil and chickpea producers, who thus were forced to compete in the market like everybody else, and . . . HEY, COME BACK HERE!"

Yes, that would be a horrible world, all right. And that is why I totally support the Farm Security Act. I hope you agree with me, though I realize that some of you may not; in fact, some of you may be so angry about this column that you've decided to never read anything by me again.

Well, guess what: I don't care! Thanks to the Humor Security Act recently passed by Congress, I'll be getting huge sums of money from the federal government to continue grinding out these columns, year after year, even if nobody wants to read them!

No, that would be stupid.

A hotly debated issue is whether deviations from rationality are important for understanding economic phenomena. An intriguing example arises in the study of 401(k) plans, the tax-advantaged retirement savings accounts that some firms offer their workers. In some firms, workers can choose to participate in the plan by filling out a simple form. In other firms, workers are automatically enrolled and can opt out of the plan by filling out a simple form. It turns out many more workers participate in the second case than in the first. If workers were perfectly rational maximizers, they would choose the optimal amount of retirement saving, regardless of the default offered by their employer. In fact, workers' behavior appears to exhibit substantial inertia. Understanding their behavior seems easier once we abandon the model of rational man.

Why, you might ask, is economics built on the rationality assumption when psychology and common sense cast doubt on it? One answer is that the assumption, even if not exactly true, is still a good approximation. For example, when we studied the differences between competitive and monopoly firms, the assumption that firms rationally maximize profit yielded many important and valid insights. Recall from Chapter 2 that economic models are not meant to replicate reality but are supposed to show the essence of the problem at hand as an aid to understanding.

Another reason that economists so often assume rationality may be that economists are themselves not rational maximizers. Like most people, they are overconfident, and they are reluctant to change their minds. Their choice among alternative theories of human behavior may exhibit excessive inertia. Moreover, economists may be content with a theory that is not perfect but is good enough. The model of rational man may be the theory of choice for a satisficing social scientist.

People Care About Fairness

Another insight about human behavior is best illustrated with an experiment called the *ultimatum game.* The game works like this: Two volunteers (who are otherwise strangers to each other) are told that they are going to play a game and could win a total of $100. Before they play, they learn the rules. The game begins with a coin flip, which is used to assign the volunteers to the roles of player A and player B. Player A's job is to propose a division of the $100 prize between himself and the other player. After player A makes his proposal, player B decides whether to accept or reject it. If he accepts it, both players are paid according to the proposal. If player B rejects the proposal, both players walk away with nothing. In either case, the game then ends.

Before proceeding, stop and think about what you would do in this situation. If you were player A, what division of the $100 would you propose? If you were player B, what proposals would you accept?

Conventional economic theory assumes in this situation that people are rational wealth-maximizers. This assumption leads to a simple prediction: Player A should propose that he gets $99 and player B gets $1, and player B should accept the proposal. After all, once the proposal is made, player B is better off accepting it as long as he gets something out of it. Moreover, because player A knows that accepting the proposal is in player's B interest, player A has no reason to offer him more than $1. In the language of game theory (discussed in Chapter 16), the 99–1 split is the Nash equilibrium.

Yet when experimental economists ask real people to play the ultimatum game, the results are very different from this prediction. People in the role of player B usually reject proposals that give them only $1 or a similarly small amount. Knowing this, people in the role of player A usually propose giving player B much more than $1. Some people will offer a 50–50 split, but it is more common for player A to propose giving player B an amount such as $30 or $40, keeping the larger share for himself. In this case, player B usually accepts the proposal.

What's going on here? The natural interpretation is that people are driven in part by some innate sense of fairness. A 99–1 split seems so wildly unfair to many people that they reject it, even to their own detriment. By contrast, a 70–30 split is still unfair, but it is not so unfair that it induces people to abandon their normal self-interest.

Throughout our study of household and firm behavior, the innate sense of fairness has not played any role. But the results of the ultimatum game suggest that perhaps it should. For example, in Chapters 18 and 19 we discussed how wages were determined by labor supply and labor demand. Some economists have suggested that the perceived fairness of what a firm pays its workers should also enter the picture. Thus, when a firm has an especially profitable year, workers (like player B) may expect to be paid a fair share of the prize, even if the standard equilibrium does not dictate it. The firm (like player A) might well decide to give workers more than the equilibrium wage for fear that the workers might otherwise try to punish the firm with reduced effort, strikes, or even vandalism.

People Are Inconsistent over Time

Imagine some dreary task, such as doing your laundry, shoveling snow off your driveway, or filling out your income tax forms. Now consider the following questions:

1. Would you prefer (A) to spend 50 minutes doing the task immediately or (B) to spend 60 minutes doing the task tomorrow?
2. Would you prefer (A) to spend 50 minutes doing the task in 90 days or (B) to spend 60 minutes doing the task in 91 days?

When asked questions like these, many people choose B to question 1 and A to question 2. When looking ahead to the future (as in question 2), they minimize the amount of time spent on the dreary task. But faced with the prospect of doing the task immediately (as in question 1), they choose to put it off.

In some ways, this behavior is not surprising: Everyone procrastinates from time to time. But from the standpoint of the theory of rational man, it is puzzling. Suppose that, in response to question 2, a person chooses to spend 50 minutes in 90 days. Then, when the 90th day arrives, we allow him to change his mind. In effect, he then faces question 1, so he opts for doing the task the next day. But why should the mere passage of time affect the choices he makes?

Many times in life, people make plans for themselves, but then they fail to follow through. A smoker promises himself that he will quit, but within a few hours of smoking his last cigarette, he craves another and breaks his promise. A person trying to lose weight promises that he will stop eating dessert, but when the waiter brings the dessert cart, the promise is forgotten. In both cases, the desire for instant gratification induces the decisionmaker to abandon his own past plans.

Some economists believe that the consumption–saving decision is an important instance where people exhibit this inconsistency over time. For many people, spending provides a type of instant gratification. Saving, like passing up the cigarette or the dessert, requires a sacrifice in the present for a reward in the distant future. And just as many smokers wish they could quit and many overweight individuals wish they ate less, many consumers wish they saved more. According to one survey, 76 percent of Americans said they were not saving enough for retirement.

An implication of this inconsistency over time is that people should try to find ways to commit their future selves to following through on their plans. A smoker trying to quit may throw away his cigarettes, and a person on a diet may put a lock on the refrigerator. What can a person who saves too little do? He should find some way to lock up his money before he spends it. Some retirement accounts, such as 401(k) plans, do exactly that. A worker can agree to have some money taken out of his paycheck before he ever sees it. The money is deposited in an account that can be used before retirement only with a penalty. Perhaps that is one reason why these retirement accounts are so popular: They protect people from their own desires for instant gratification.

QuickQuiz Describe at least three ways in which human decisionmaking differs from that of the rational individual of conventional economic theory.

CONCLUSION

This chapter has examined the frontier of microeconomics. You may have noticed that we have sketched out ideas rather than fully developing them. This is no accident. One reason is that you might study these topics in more detail in advanced courses. Another reason is that these topics remain active areas of research and, therefore, are still being fleshed out.

To see how these topics fit into the broader picture, recall the *Ten Principles of Economics* from Chapter 1. One principle states that markets are usually a good way to organize economic activity. Another principle states that governments can sometimes improve market outcomes. As you study economics, you can more fully appreciate the truth of these principles as well as the caveats that go with them. The study of asymmetric information should make you more wary of market outcomes. The study of political economy should make you more wary of government solutions. And the study of behavioral economics should make you wary of any institution that relies on human decisionmaking—including both the market and the government.

If there is a unifying theme to these topics, it is that life is messy. Information is imperfect, government is imperfect, and people are imperfect. Of course, you knew this long before you started studying economics, but economists need to understand these imperfections as precisely as they can if they are to explain, and perhaps even improve, the world around them.

SUMMARY

- In many economic transactions, information is asymmetric. When there are hidden actions, principals may be concerned that agents suffer from the problem of moral hazard. When there are hidden characteristics, buyers may be concerned about the problem of adverse selection among the sellers. Private markets sometimes deal with asymmetric information with signaling and screening.

- Although government policy can sometimes improve market outcomes, governments are themselves imperfect institutions. The Condorcet paradox shows that majority rule fails to produce transitive preferences for society, and Arrow's impossibility theorem shows that no voting

scheme will be perfect. In many situations, democratic institutions will produce the outcome desired by the median voter, regardless of the preferences of the rest of the electorate. Moreover, the individuals who set government policy may be motivated by self-interest rather than the national interest.

- The study of psychology and economics reveals that human decisionmaking is more complex than is assumed in conventional economic theory. People are not always rational, they care about the fairness of economic outcomes (even to their own detriment), and they can be inconsistent over time.

KEY CONCEPTS

moral hazard, p. 480
agent, p. 480
principal, p. 480
adverse selection, p. 481

signaling, p. 482
screening, p. 483
Condorcet paradox, p. 485

Arrow's impossibility
    theorem, p. 486
median voter theorem, p. 487

QUESTIONS FOR REVIEW

1. What is moral hazard? List three things an employer might do to reduce the severity of this problem.

2. What is adverse selection? Give an example of a market in which adverse selection might be a problem.

3. Define *signaling* and *screening*, and give an example of each.

4. What unusual property of voting did Condorcet notice?

5. Explain why majority rule respects the preferences of the median voter rather than the average voter.

6. Describe the ultimatum game. What outcome from this game would conventional economic theory predict? Do experiments confirm this prediction? Explain.

PROBLEMS AND APPLICATIONS

1. Each of the following situations involves moral hazard. In each case, identify the principal and the agent, and explain why there is asymmetric information. How does the action described reduce the problem of moral hazard?
   a. Landlords require tenants to pay security deposits.
   b. Firms compensate top executives with options to buy company stock at a given price in the future.
   c. Car insurance companies offer discounts to customers who install antitheft devices in their cars.

2. Suppose that the Live-Long-and-Prosper Health Insurance Company charges $5,000 annually for a family insurance policy. The company's president suggests that the company raise the annual price to $6,000 in order to increase its profits. If the firm followed this suggestion, what economic problem might arise? Would the firm's pool of customers tend to become more or less healthy on average? Would the company's profits necessarily increase?

3. The case study in this chapter describes how a boyfriend can signal to a girlfriend that he loves her by giving an appropriate gift. Do you think saying "I love you" can also serve as a signal? Why or why not?

4. Some AIDS activists believe that health insurance companies should not be allowed to ask applicants if they are infected with the HIV virus that causes AIDS. Would this rule help or hurt those who are HIV-positive? Would it help or hurt those who are not HIV-positive? Would it exacerbate or mitigate the problem of adverse selection in the market for health insurance? Do you think it would increase or decrease the number of people without health insurance? In your opinion, would this be a good policy?

5. The government is considering two ways to help the needy: giving them cash, or giving them free meals at soup kitchens. Give an argument for giving cash. Give an argument, based on asymmetric information, for why the soup kitchen may be better than the cash handout.

6. Ken walks into an ice-cream parlor.

   WAITER: We have vanilla and chocolate today.
   KEN: I'll take vanilla.
   WAITER: I almost forgot. We also have strawberry.
   KEN: In that case, I'll take chocolate.

   What standard property of decisionmaking is Ken violating? (Hint: Reread the section on Arrow's impossibility theorem.)

7. Why might a political party in a two-party system choose not to move toward the median voter? (Hint: Think about abstentions from voting and political contributions.)

8. Two ice-cream stands are deciding where to locate along a one-mile beach. Each person sitting on the beach buys exactly one ice-cream cone per day from the stand nearest to him. Each ice-cream seller wants the maximum number of customers. Where along the beach will the two stands locate?

9. After a widely reported earthquake in California, many people call their insurance company to apply for earthquake insurance. Might this reaction reflect some deviation from rationality? Discuss.

ability-to-pay principle   the idea that taxes should be levied on a person according to how well that person can shoulder the burden

absolute advantage   the comparison among producers of a good according to their productivity

accounting profit   total revenue minus total explicit cost

adverse selection   the tendency for the mix of unobserved attributes to become undesirable from the standpoint of an uninformed party

agent   a person who is performing an act for another person, called the principal

Arrow's impossibility theorem   a mathematical result showing that, under certain assumed conditions, there is no scheme for aggregating individual preferences into a valid set of social preferences

average fixed cost   fixed costs divided by the quantity of output

average revenue   total revenue divided by the quantity sold

average tax rate   total taxes paid divided by total income

average total cost   total cost divided by the quantity of output

average variable cost   variable costs divided by the quantity of output

benefits principle   the idea that people should pay taxes based on the benefits they receive from government services

budget constraint   the limit on the consumption bundles that a consumer can afford

budget deficit   an excess of government spending over government receipts

budget surplus   an excess of government receipts over government spending

business cycle   fluctuations in economic activity, such as employment and production

capital   the equipment and structures used to produce goods and services

cartel   a group of firms acting in unison

circular-flow diagram   a visual model of the economy that shows how dollars flow through markets among households and firms

Coase theorem   the proposition that if private parties can bargain without cost over the allocation of resources, they can solve the problem of externalities on their own

collusion   an agreement among firms in a market about quantities to produce or prices to charge

common resources   goods that are rival but not excludable

comparative advantage   the comparison among producers of a good according to their opportunity cost

compensating differential   a difference in wages that arises to offset the nonmonetary characteristics of different jobs

competitive market   a market with many buyers and sellers trading identical products so that each buyer and seller is a price taker

complements   two goods for which an increase in the price of one leads to a decrease in the demand for the other

Condorcet paradox   the failure of majority rule to produce transitive preferences for society

constant returns to scale   the property whereby long-run average total cost stays the same as the quantity of output changes

consumer surplus   a buyer's willingness to pay minus the amount the buyer actually pays

cost   the value of everything a seller must give up to produce a good

cost-benefit analysis   a study that compares the costs and benefits to society of providing a public good

cross-price elasticity of demand   a measure of how much the quantity demanded of one good responds to a change in the price of another good, computed as the percentage change in quantity demanded of the first good divided by the percentage change in the price of the second good

deadweight loss   the fall in total surplus that results from a market distortion, such as a tax

demand curve   a graph of the relationship between the price of a good and the quantity demanded

demand schedule   a table that shows the relationship between the price of a good and the quantity demanded

diminishing marginal product   the property whereby the marginal product of an input declines as the quantity of the input increases

discrimination   the offering of different opportunities to similar individuals who differ only by race, ethnic group, sex, age, or other personal characteristics

diseconomies of scale   the property whereby long-run average total cost rises as the quantity of output increases

dominant strategy   a strategy that is best for a player in a game regardless of the strategies chosen by the other players

economic profit   total revenue minus total cost, including both explicit and implicit costs

economics   the study of how society manages its scarce resources

economies of scale   the property whereby long-run average total cost falls as the quantity of output increases

efficiency   the property of society getting the most it can from its scarce resources

efficiency wages   above-equilibrium wages paid by firms in order to increase worker productivity

efficient scale   the quantity of output that minimizes average total cost

elasticity a measure of the responsiveness of quantity demanded or quantity supplied to one of its determinants

equilibrium a situation in which the price has reached the level where quantity supplied equals quantity demanded

equilibrium price the price that balances quantity supplied and quantity demanded

equilibrium quantity the quantity supplied and the quantity demanded at the equilibrium price

equity the property of distributing economic prosperity fairly among the members of society

excludability the property of a good whereby a person can be prevented from using it

explicit costs input costs that require an outlay of money by the firm

exports goods produced domestically and sold abroad

externality the uncompensated impact of one person's actions on the well-being of a bystander

factors of production the inputs used to produce goods and services

fixed costs costs that do not vary with the quantity of output produced

free rider a person who receives the benefit of a good but avoids paying for it

game theory the study of how people behave in strategic situations

Giffen good a good for which an increase in the price raises the quantity demanded

horizontal equity the idea that taxpayers with similar abilities to pay taxes should pay the same amount

human capital the accumulation of investments in people, such as education and on-the-job training

implicit costs input costs that do not require an outlay of money by the firm

import quota a limit on the quantity of a good that can be produced abroad and sold domestically

imports goods produced abroad and sold domestically

income effect the change in consumption that results when a price change moves the consumer to a higher or lower indifference curve

income elasticity of demand a measure of how much the quantity demanded of a good responds to a change in consumers' income, computed as the percentage change in quantity demanded divided by the percentage change in income

indifference curve a curve that shows consumption bundles that give the consumer the same level of satisfaction

inferior good a good for which, other things equal, an increase in income leads to a decrease in demand

inflation an increase in the overall level of prices in the economy

in-kind transfers transfers to the poor given in the form of goods and services rather than cash

internalizing an externality altering incentives so that people take account of the external effects of their actions

law of demand the claim that, other things equal, the quantity demanded of a good falls when the price of the good rises

law of supply the claim that, other things equal, the quantity supplied of a good rises when the price of the good rises

law of supply and demand the claim that the price of any good adjusts to bring the quantity supplied and the quantity demanded for that good into balance

liberalism the political philosophy according to which the government should choose policies deemed to be just, as evaluated by an impartial observer behind a "veil of ignorance"

libertarianism the political philosophy according to which the government should punish crimes and enforce voluntary agreements but not redistribute income

life cycle the regular pattern of income variation over a person's life

lump-sum tax a tax that is the same amount for every person

macroeconomics the study of economy-wide phenomena, including inflation, unemployment, and economic growth

marginal changes small incremental adjustments to a plan of action

marginal cost the increase in total cost that arises from an extra unit of production

marginal product the increase in output that arises from an additional unit of input

marginal product of labor the increase in the amount of output from an additional unit of labor

marginal rate of substitution the rate at which a consumer is willing to trade one good for another

marginal revenue the change in total revenue from an additional unit sold

marginal tax rate the extra taxes paid on an additional dollar of income

market a group of buyers and sellers of a particular good or service

market economy an economy that allocates resources through the decentralized decisions of many firms and households as they interact in markets for goods and services

market failure a situation in which a market left on its own fails to allocate resources efficiently

market power the ability of a single economic actor (or small group of actors) to have a substantial influence on market prices

maximin criterion   the claim that the government should aim to maximize the well-being of the worst-off person in society

median voter theorem   a mathematical result showing that if voters are choosing a point along a line and each voter wants the point closest to his most preferred point, then majority rule will pick the most preferred point of the median voter

microeconomics   the study of how households and firms make decisions and how they interact in markets

monopolistic competition   a market structure in which many firms sell products that are similar but not identical

monopoly   a firm that is the sole seller of a product without close substitutes

moral hazard   the tendency of a person who is imperfectly monitored to engage in dishonest or otherwise undesirable behavior

Nash equilibrium   a situation in which economic actors interacting with one another each choose their best strategy given the strategies that all the other actors have chosen

natural monopoly   a monopoly that arises because a single firm can supply a good or service to an entire market at a smaller cost than could two or more firms

negative income tax   a tax system that collects revenue from high-income households and gives transfers to low-income households

normal good   a good for which, other things equal, an increase in income leads to an increase in demand

normative statements   claims that attempt to prescribe how the world should be

oligopoly   a market structure in which only a few sellers offer similar or identical products

opportunity cost   whatever must be given up to obtain some item

perfect complements   two goods with right-angle indifference curves

perfect substitutes   two goods with straight-line indifference curves

permanent income   a person's normal income

Phillips curve   a curve that shows the short-run tradeoff between inflation and unemployment

Pigovian tax   a tax enacted to correct the effects of a negative externality

positive statements   claims that attempt to describe the world as it is

poverty line   an absolute level of income set by the federal government for each family size below which a family is deemed to be in poverty

poverty rate   the percentage of the population whose family income falls below an absolute level called the poverty line

price ceiling   a legal maximum on the price at which a good can be sold

price discrimination   the business practice of selling the same good at different prices to different customers

price elasticity of demand   a measure of how much the quantity demanded of a good responds to a change in the price of that good, computed as the percentage change in quantity demanded divided by the percentage change in price

price elasticity of supply   a measure of how much the quantity supplied of a good responds to a change in the price of that good, computed as the percentage change in quantity supplied divided by the percentage change in price

price floor   a legal minimum on the price at which a good can be sold

principal   a person for whom another person, called the agent, is performing some act

prisoners' dilemma   a particular "game" between two captured prisoners that illustrates why cooperation is difficult to maintain even when it is mutually beneficial

private goods   goods that are both excludable and rival

producer surplus   the amount a seller is paid for a good minus the seller's cost

production function   the relationship between quantity of inputs used to make a good and the quantity of output of that good

production possibilities frontier   a graph that shows the combinations of output that the economy can possibly produce given the available factors of production and the available production technology

productivity   the quantity of goods and services produced from each hour of a worker's time

profit   total revenue minus total cost

progressive tax   a tax for which high-income taxpayers pay a larger fraction of their income than do low-income taxpayers

proportional tax   a tax for which high-income and low-income taxpayers pay the same fraction of income

public goods   goods that are neither excludable nor rival

quantity demanded   the amount of a good that buyers are willing and able to purchase

quantity supplied   the amount of a good that sellers are willing and able to sell

regressive tax   a tax for which high-income taxpayers pay a smaller fraction of their income than do low-income taxpayers

rivalry   the property of a good whereby one person's use diminishes other people's use

scarcity   the limited nature of society's resources

screening   an action taken by an uninformed party to induce an informed party to reveal information

shortage   a situation in which quantity demanded is greater than quantity supplied

signaling   an action taken by an informed party to reveal private information to an uninformed party

strike   the organized withdrawal of labor from a firm by a union

substitutes   two goods for which an increase in the price of one leads to an increase in the demand for the other

substitution effect   the change in consumption that results when a price change moves the consumer along a given indifference curve to a point with a new marginal rate of substitution

sunk cost   a cost that has already been committed and cannot be recovered

supply curve   a graph of the relationship between the price of a good and the quantity supplied

supply schedule   a table that shows the relationship between the price of a good and the quantity supplied

surplus   a situation in which quantity supplied is greater than quantity demanded

tariff   a tax on goods produced abroad and sold domestically

tax incidence   the manner in which the burden of a tax is shared among participants in a market

total cost   the market value of the inputs a firm uses in production

total revenue (for a firm)   the amount a firm receives for the sale of its output

total revenue (in a market)   the amount paid by buyers and received by sellers of a good, computed as the price of the good times the quantity sold

Tragedy of the Commons   a parable that illustrates why common resources get used more than is desirable from the standpoint of society as a whole

transaction costs   the costs that parties incur in the process of agreeing and following through on a bargain

union   a worker association that bargains with employers over wages and working conditions

utilitarianism   the political philosophy according to which the government should choose policies to maximize the total utility of everyone in society

utility   a measure of happiness or satisfaction

value of the marginal product   the marginal product of an input times the price of the output

variable costs   costs that vary with the quantity of output produced

vertical equity   the idea that taxpayers with a greater ability to pay taxes should pay larger amounts

welfare   government programs that supplement the incomes of the needy

welfare economics   the study of how the allocation of resources affects economic well-being

willingness to pay   the maximum amount that a buyer will pay for a good

world price   the price of a good that prevails in the world market for that good

INDEX

Note: Page numbers in **boldface** refer to pages where key terms are defined.

A

Ability, wages and, 414–416
Ability-to-pay principle, **254**, 254–258
Absolute advantage, **51**
Absolute value, 92
Accidents, associated with driving, 214
Accounting profit, **270**
Adverse selection, **481**, 481–482
Advertising, 380–385
  brand names and, 383–385
  critique of, 381
  defense of, 381
  prices and, 382
  as prisoners' dilemma, 358–359
  as signal of quality, 382–383
AFC (average fixed cost) curve, 278, 280, 281
Africa. *See also specific countries*
Agents, **480**
Agriculture, wheat market and, 104–106
Air, clean, as common resource, 233
Airline industry, price discrimination in, 337
Akerlof, George, 480
Alston, Richard M., 32
Alternative opportunities, labor supply curve and, 399
Aluminum market, externalities and, 205–207
American Airlines, 364
American Sheep Industry Association, 54, 55
Anarchy, State, and Utopia (Nozick), 440
Anderson, Terry L., 119
Antipoverty programs, 441–445
  place-based, 442–443
  taxes to provide, 254
Antitrust laws, 329–330
  controversies over, 364–367
  restraint of trade and, 363–364
A.P. Moller/Maersk Line, 350
Apartheid, 424
Appearance, wages and, 416
Apple Mac operating system, 367
Arms races, as prisoners' dilemmas, 358
Arrow, Kenneth, 486
Arrow's impossibility theorem, **486**, 486–487
Asia Pacific Economic Cooperation, 55
Assumptions, 21–22
Asymmetric information, 479, 480–484
  adverse selection and, 481–482
  moral hazard and, 480–481
  public policy and, 484
  screening to induce information revelation and, 483–484
  signaling to convey information and, 482–483
ATC (average total cost) curve, 278, 279, 280, 281
AT&T, 330
Austen, Jane, 415
Australia, lamb imports from, 54–55
Austria, drug prices in, 338
Automobile industry
  costs in, 280, 282
  trade restriction and, 190

B

AVC (average variable cost) curve, 278, 280, 281
Average fixed cost, 275, **277**, 284
Average fixed cost *(AFC)* curve, 278, 280, 281
Average revenue, 291, **292**
  of monopolies, 319
Average tax rates, **250**
  marginal tax rates versus, 250–251
Average total cost, 275, **277**, 284
  marginal cost related to, 279
  short-and long-run, relationship between, 280, 282
Average total cost *(ATC)* curve, 278, 279, 280, 281
Average variable cost, 275, **277**, 284
Average variable cost *(AVC)* curve, 278, 280, 281

Bangladesh, child labor in, 192–193
Banks
  central, 29
  mergers of, 330
Bar graphs, 36, 37
Barriers to entry, monopoly and, 314–315
Barry, Dave, 490–491
Basic research, as public good, 227–228
Basketball players, salaries of, 424
Baucus, Max, 55
Baum, Caroline, 153
Baumol, William J., 151
Bayer aspirin, 383
Beauty, wages and, 416
Beef, demand for, 234–236
Behavioral economics, 480, 489–493
  deviations from rationality and, 489–492
  fairness and, 492
  inconsistency over time and, 493
Benefits
  cost-benefit analysis and, **229**
  marginal, 6–7
Benefits principle, **254**
Benham, Lee, 382
Bentham, Jeremy, 437
Biddle, Jeff, 416
Black Plague, 407
Book market, 373
Borda counts, 486–487
Botswana, elephants in, 236
Bradford, William, 153
Brand names, 383–385
Braniff Airlines, 364
Brazil
  drug prices in, 339
  income inequality in, 432, 433
  tax burden in, 243
Bryant, Kobe, 7
Bubonic plague, 407
Budget constraint, 454–455, **455**
Budget deficits, **246**
Budget surpluses, **246**
Bush, George H. W., 159
Bush, George W., 159, 166
  tariffs under, 31, 184
  tax cut under, 261

Business cycle, **14**
Butz, David, 351
Buyers. *See also* Consumer *entries*
  marginal, 139
  number of, shifts in demand curve and, 69
  taxes on, effect on market outcomes, 124–126

C

Cable television market, 354
Calfee, John, 99
California
  citrus crop in, 81
  water shortage in, 119
Camel, 358–359
Canada
  income inequality in, 433
  international trade of, 193
  tax burden in, 243
Capital, **404**
  human, **412**, 412–414
Capital income, 406
  taxation of, 259
Capital market, equilibrium in, 404–406
Capone, Al "Scarface," 241
Carnegie, Andrew, 473
Cartels, **348**, 348–349, 350–351, 352. *See also* Organization of Petroleum Exporting Countries (OPEC)
Cattle, demand for beef and, 234–236
Cause and effect, 42–44
Centrally planned economies. *See also specific countries*
  collapse of, 9
Chamberlin, Edward, 384
Chance, wages and, 415–416
Chevron, 490
Chicken market, in India, 191
Child labor, globalization and, 192–193
Children, as externalities, 218–219
Chile, international trade of, 192
China
  income inequality in, 433
  "Permanent Normal Trade Relations" status for, 194
Choice. *See* Consumer choice; Optimization
Cigarettes
  advertising of, 358–359
  prices of, quantity of smoking and, 70–71
Circular-flow diagram, **23**, 23–24
Citrus crop, 81
Clayton Act of 1914, 329, 363
Clean Air Act, 119
Clean air and water, as common resource, 233
Clinton, Bill, 55, 159, 171
  antipoverty programs under, 442, 443
  tax increase under, 261
Coase, Ronald, 210
Coase theorem, **210**, 210–211, 217
Coca-Cola Company, 329
Cold War, 358
Collusion, **348**
Colum, Mary, 429
Command-and-control policies, 212

Common resources, **225**, 231–236
 clean air and water as, 233
 congested roads as, 233–234
 as prisoners' dilemmas, 359–360
 Tragedy of the Commons and, **231**, 231–232
 wildlife as, 234
Communism, collapse in Soviet Union and Eastern Europe, 9
Compaq, 8
Comparative advantage, 50–56, **52**
 absolute advantage and, 51
 applications of, 54–56
 opportunity cost and, 51–52
 trade and, 52–53
 world price and, 177
Comparative statics, 78
Compensating differentials, **412**, 421
Competition, 64–65
 imperfect, 346. *See also* Monopolistic competition; Oligopoly
 monopoly versus, 318, 319
 oligopoly and, 348–349
 perfect, 64
 unfair-competition argument for trade restriction and, 190
Competitive firms, 314
 graphical measurement of profit of, 299–300
 labor demand of, 393
 long-fun decision to exit or enter markets, 298–299
 profit maximization by, 292–293
 revenue of, 291–292
 short-run decision to shut down, 295–297
 sunk costs and, 297
 supply decision of, 294–295
Competitive markets, **64**, 64–65, 289–308, **290**. *See also* Price takers
 demand shifts in short and long fun, 304, 305
 firms in. *See* Competitive firms
 market supply with entry and exit in, 302–303
 market supply with fixed number of firms in, 301–302
 upward sloping long-run supply curve in, 304, 306–307
 zero profit and, 303–304
Complements, **69**
 perfect, 459–460, **460**
Condorcet, Marquis de (Marie-Jean Caritat), 485
Condorcet paradox, **485**, 485–486, 488
Congressional Budget Office, 29
Constant returns to scale, **283**
Consumer choice, 453–476
 budget constraint and, 454–455
 demand curves and, 468–469
 interest rates and saving and, 473–475
 optimization and. *See* Optimization
 preferences and, 456–460
 tastes and, 69, 399
 wages and labor supply and, 469–473
Consumer surplus, 138–143, **139**
 efficiency and, 147–148
 at equilibrium, 148–149

as measure of economic well-being, 141–142
 measuring with demand curve, 139–140, 141
 raising of, by lower prices, 140–141, 142
 willingness to pay and, 138–139
Consumption taxes, 249–250
Cooperation
 prisoners' dilemma and, 355–360, 362
 reasons for, 361–362
Coordinate system, 36
Coordination problems, diseconomies of scale and, 283
Corporate income tax, 244–245, 247
 burden of, 260
Correlation, positive and negative, 37
Cost(s), **143**, 268–285
 average, 277
 of capital, 269–270
 economies of scale and. *See* Diseconomies of scale; Economies of scale
 explicit, **269**, 284
 fixed, 275, **276**, 277, 284, 298
 implicit, **269**, 284
 marginal. *See* Marginal cost
 opportunity. *See* Opportunity cost
 producer surplus and, 143–144
 production and, 271–275
 in short and long run, 180, 282–284
 social. *See* Social costs
 sunk, 296, **297**
 total, **268**, 275, 277, 279, 280, 282, 284
 transaction, **211**
 true versus fictitious measurement of, 271
 variable, 275, **276**, 276–277, 277, 284, 298
Cost-benefit analysis, **229**
Cost curves, 278–280, 281
 firm's supply decision and, 294–295
 shapes of, 278–279
 total-cost, production function and, 273–275
 typical, 279–280
Council of Economic Advisers, 29
Coupons, discount, 337–338
Crandall, Robert, 364
Crime, drug-related, drug interdiction and, 108–109
Cross-price elasticity of demand, **100**
Cummins, Vincent, 332, 333
Curb Rights (Klein), 333
Curves, 37–41. *See also specific curves*
 movement along, 40, 79–80
 shifts of, 40–41, 79–80
 slope of, 41–42
Customers, labor-market discrimination by, 423–424

D

Dale, Stacy, 418–419
Deadweight losses, 160–171, **163**, 242, 248–250
 determinants of, 164–167
 gains from trade and, 163–164
 of monopoly, 326–328
 tax effects on market participants and, 161–163
 tax revenue and, 167–171

DeBeers, 315–316
Decisions, 3–8
 incentives and, 7–8
 marginal changes and, 6–7
 mistakes in making, 489–490
 opportunity cost and, 5–6
 tradeoffs and, 4–5
Deficits, budget. *See* Budget deficits
Delta (Δ), 42, 277
Delta Air Lines, 268
Demand, 65–71. *See also* Equilibrium
 applications of, 104–109
 change in, 81–82
 decreases in, 68
 derived, 392
 elastic, 90, 93
 elasticity of. *See* Demand elasticity
 excess, 76–77
 increases in, 68
 individual, 67
 inelastic, 90, 93
 for labor. *See* Labor demand
 law of, 66
 market, 66–67
 perfectly elastic, 93
 perfectly inelastic, 93
 shifts in short and long run, in competitive markets, 304, 305
Demand curve, 38–41, 65–66, **66**
 derivation of, 466–468
 for labor, shifts in, 397–398
 measuring consumer surplus using, 139–140, 141
 price elasticity of demand and, 93, 94
 shifts in, 67–71, 304, 305, 397–398
 slope of, 468–469
Demand elasticity, 90–100
 cross-price, **100**
 deadweight losses and, 166
 income, **99**, 99–100
 price, **90**, 90–99
Demand schedule, **66**
Denison, 419
Derived demand, 392
Dickson, R. Duane, 306
Diminishing marginal product, **273**, **395**
Diminishing marginal utility, 437, 462
Discount(s), quantity, 339
Discount coupons, 337–338
Discrimination, **420**
 in labor market. *See* Labor-market discrimination
 price. *See* Price discrimination
 racial, in South Africa, 424
Diseconomies of scale, **283**
Distribution, neoclassical theory of, 408
Dividends, 406
Dole, Bob, 171
Dominant strategy, **355**, 355–356
Drug interdiction, drug-related crime and, 108–109
Dugger, Celia W., 191
Dunlop, 345
Duopoly, 348
DuPont, 490
Dynegy, 271

E

Earned Income Tax Credit (EITC), 123, 442, 444, 445
East Asia. *See specific countries*
Eastern Europe, collapse of communism in, 9
Economic interdependence, 45–57. *See also* International trade; Trade
Economic life cycle, 435–436
Economic mobility, 436–437
Economic models, 22–26. *See also specific models*
Economic policy, economists as policy advisers and, 28–30
Economic profit, **270**
Economic Report of the President, 29
Economics, **4**
Economic welfare
    consumer surplus as measure of, 141–142
    externalities and, 205–209
    monopoly and, 325–329
    tax effects on, 161–163
Economies
    centrally planned, 9
    market, **9**
    underground, 167
Economies of scale, **283**
    monopoly and, 316, 317
Economists
    disagreement among, 30–32
    as policy advisers, 28–30
    as scientists, 20–28
Education. *See also* Human capital
    at elite colleges, 418–419
    human capital view of, 412–414
    school vouchers and, 446–447
    signaling and, 416–417
    state and local spending for, 247
    value of, 415
Efficiency, **5**, 147–154, **148**
    market equilibrium and, 148–150
    market failure and, 154
    production-possibility frontier and, 25
    taxes and, 248–253
    total surplus and, 147–148
    tradeoff with equity, 260–261
Efficiency wages, **419**
Efficiency-wage theories, moral-hazard problem and, 480–481
Efficient scale, **279**, 377
Effort, wages and, 415–416
Einstein, Albert, 20, 21
Eissa, Nada, 252, 253
EITC (Earned Income Tax Credit), 123, 442, 444, 445
Elastic demand, 90, 93
Elasticity, 89–110, **90**
    applications of, 104–109
    of demand. *See* Demand elasticity
    of supply, 100–104, 165–166
    tax incidence and, 128–130
Elastic supply, 100
Elephants, as common resource, 234, 236
Employment, jobs argument for trade restriction and, 188–189

Empowerment Zone Grant, 443
England. *See* United Kingdom
Enron, 271
Entry into industry
    barriers to, monopoly and, 314–315
    externalities associated with, in monopolistic competition, 379
    market supply and, 302–303
    profits and, 306
Environmental Protection Agency (EPA), 212–213, 215–216
Equilibrium, **75**, 75–83
    changes in, analyzing, 77–82
    efficiency and, 148–150
    in labor market, 399–404
    Nash, 350–351, **351**, 492
    for oligopoly, 349–352
    without international trade, 176–177
Equilibrium price, **75**, 76–77
Equilibrium quantity, **75**, 76
Equity, **5, 148**
    horizontal, **254**, 256–258
    tradeoff with efficiency, 260–261
    vertical, **254**, 255–256
Europe. *See also specific countries*
    bubonic plague in, 407
Excess capacity, of monopolistically competitive firms, 377, 380
Excise taxes, 245
Excludability, of goods, **224**
Exit from industry, market supply and, 302–303
Expectations
    causality and, 44
    shifts in demand curve and, 69
    shifts in supply curve and, 74–75
Explicit costs, **269**, 284
Exports, **56**. *See also* International trade
    gains and losses of exporting countries and, 178–180
Externalities, **11**, 154, 203–219, **204**
    associated with driving, 214
    associated with market entry, in monopolistic competition, 379
    children as, 218–219
    internalizing, **207**
    market inefficiency and, 204–209
    negative, 204, 206–207. *See also* Pollution
    positive, 204, 207
    private solutions to, 209–212
    public policies toward, 212–217
Eyeglass advertising, 382

F

Factor markets, 24, 391–408
    equilibrium in, 399–406
    for labor. *See* Labor *entries*
    linkages among factors of production and, 406–407
Factors of production, 23, **392**. *See also* Capital; Labor
    linkages among, 406–407
    markets for. *See* Factor markets; Labor *entries*
    prices of, shift in supply curve related to, 74

Fairness, 492
Fair trade, 364–365
Farming, wheat market and, 104–106
Farm Security Act of 2002, 490–491
Federal government, 244–246
    budget of. *See* Budget *entries*
    economists in, 29–30
    receipts of, 244–245
    size of, taxes and, 166–167
    spending by, 245–246
    Web sites for agencies of, 29
Federal Insurance Contribution Act (FICA) taxes, 127
Federal Reserve System (Fed), 29
FICA (Federal Insurance Contribution Act) taxes, 127
Financial aid, 338
Firms
    in circular-flow diagram, 23–24
    competitive. *See* Competitive firms
    labor demand of. *See* Labor demand
    monopolistically competitive. *See* Monopolistic competition
    monopoly. *See* Monopoly
Fish, as common resource, 234
Fisher, Franklin, 366–367
Fixed costs, 275, **276**, 284
    average, 275, **277**, 284
    variable costs versus, 298
Flows, international. *See* Exports; Import(s); International trade
Flypaper theory of tax incidence, 258
Food Stamp program, 246, 444, 445
Ford, Gerald, 12
Ford Motor Company, 8, 280, 282
401(k) plans, 250
France, tax burden in, 243
Franklin, Ben, 241
Free riders, **226**
Free trade, 192–194
Friedman, Milton, 168, 446–447

G

Gains from trade
    deadweight losses and, 163–164
    of exporting countries, 178–180
    of importing countries, 180–182
Game theory, 354–362, **355**
    dominant strategy and, 355–356
    prisoners' dilemma and, 355–360, 362
    reasons for cooperation and, 361–362
Gasoline
    price ceiling in market for, 116–117
    taxation of, 214, 254
Gates, Bill, 366, 367
GATT (General Agreement on Tariffs and Trade), 193
Gender. *See also* Women
    labor-market discrimination based on, 420–421
General Agreement on Tariffs and Trade (GATT), 193
General Electric, 267
General Mills, 267
General Motors, 267
George, Henry, 168

Germany
  income inequality in, 433
  inflation in, 12, 13
  tax burden in, 243
GI Bill, 442, 447
Giffen, Robert, 468
Giffen goods, **468**, 468–469
Gifts, as signals, 483
Giuliani, Rudolph, 332
Glaeser, Edward L., 442–443
Globalization, of world trade, 192–193
Goods
  complements, **69**, 459–460, **460**
  excludability of, **224**
  Giffen, **468**, 468–469
  inferior, **68**, 100, **463**
  markets for, 24
  normal, **68**, 99–100, **463**
  private, **224**, 224–225
  public, **225**, 225–230
  related, prices of, demand and, 68–69
  rivalry of, **224**
  substitutes, **69**, 90, **459**, 460
Gore, Al, 338
Government
  benefits of, 10–11
  labor-market discrimination by, 424
  ownership of monopolies by, 331
  of United States. *See* Federal government;
    Local government; State government
Government spending
  by federal government, 245–246
  by state and local government, 247–248
Grand Canyon National Park, 235
Graphs, 36–44
  cause and effect and, 42–44
  curves and, 37–41
  profit measurement using, 299–300
  of single variable, 36, 37
  slope and, 41–42
  of two variables, 36–37, 38
Great Britain, international trade of, 192
Grisham, John, 373
"Guns and butter" tradeoff, 5

H

Hamermesh, Daniel, 416
Harkin, Tom, 192
Hemingway, Ernest, 429
Holmes, Oliver Wendell, 171
Horizontal equity, **254**, 256–258
Households
  in circular-flow diagram, 23–24
  decisions faced by, 3
  saving by, interest rates and, 473–475
Hubbard, Glenn, 184
Human capital, **412**, 412–414
Human life, value of, 229–230
Hutchison, Kay Bailey, 351
Hylan, John, 333
Hyperinflation, in Germany, 12, 13

I

Iceland, tax system of, 251
Immigration, labor supply curve and, 399
Imperfect competition, 346. *See also*
    Monopolistic competition; Oligopoly

Implicit costs, **269**, 284
Import(s), **56**. *See also* International trade
  gains and losses of importing countries
    and, 180–182
  restrictions on. *See* Trade restriction
Import quotas, **185**, 185–187
Incentives, 7–8
  antipoverty programs and, 444–445
Income
  capital, 406
  consumer choice and, 363, 462–463
  permanent, **436**
  shifts in demand curve and, 68
Income distribution. *See* Income inequality;
    Income redistribution; Poverty
Income effect, **464**
  consumer choice and, 464–466
Income elasticity of demand, **99**
Income inequality, 430–437. *See also* Poverty
  economic mobility and, 436–437
  measurement problems with, 434–436
  poverty rate and, 433–434, 435
  in United States, 430–433
  women's movement and, 431–432
  world, 432–433
Income redistribution, 437–440
  liberalism and, 438–439
  libertarianism and, 439–440
  utilitarianism and, 437–438
Income security, federal spending for, 246
Income taxes. *See* Tax *entries*
India
  income inequality in, 433
  tax burden in, 242, 243
  trade policy in, 191
Indifference curves, **456**, 456–460
  extreme examples of, 458–460
  properties of, 457–458, 459
Individual demand, 67
  market demand versus, 66–67
Individual income taxes, 247. *See also* Tax
    entries
  on capital income, 259
  labor supply of married women and,
    252–253
  marriage, 257–258
Individual Retirement Accounts
    (IRAs), 250
Individual supply, 72–73
Indonesia, tax burden in, 243
Industrial organization, 267–268
Industrial policy, 208–209
Industries. *See also specific industries*
  entry into. *See* Entry into industry
  exit from, market supply and, 302–303
Inefficiency, externalities and, 204–209
Inelastic demand, 90, 93
Inelastic supply, 100
Infant-industry argument for trade
    restriction, 190
Inferior goods, **68**, 100, **463**
Inflation, **12**, 12–13. *See also* Hyperinflation
  tradeoff with unemployment. *See* Phillips
    curve
Information, asymmetric. *See* Asymmetric
    information
In-kind transfers, **435**, 444

Inputs. *See* Factors of production; *specific
    factors of production*
*An Inquiry into the Nature and Causes of the
    Wealth of Nations* (Smith), 9, 10, 53, 283,
    364
Insurance, social. *See* Social insurance;
    Welfare programs
Insurance, social, tax for, 166
Interest, 406
Interest rate(s), saving and, 473–475
Internalizing the externality, **207**
International trade, 175–195
  benefits of, 189
  comparative advantage and. *See*
    Comparative advantage
  determinants of, 176–177
  equilibrium without, 176–177
  free, 192–194
  gains and losses of exporting countries
    and, 178–180
  gains and losses of importing countries
    and, 180–182
  gains from. *See* Gains from trade
  globalization and, 192–193
  restriction of. *See* Trade restriction
  trade policy and, 187–188
  of United States, 56
  world price and, 177
Intuit, 329
Invisible hand, 9–11, 150, 153
IRAs (Individual Retirement Accounts), 250
Irwin, Douglas A., 54
Israel, shift in labor supply in, 401

J

Jackson, Penfield, 367
Japan, income inequality in, 432, 433
Jitneys, 332–333
Jobs argument for trade restriction, 188–189
John Hancock Mutual Life Insurance, 490

K

Kearl, J. B., 32
Kennedy, John F., 433
Kenya, elephants in, 236
Keogh plans, 250
Keynes, John Maynard, 29–30, 32–33
Kidneys (human), market for, 152
King, Stephen, 373
Klein, Daniel B., 333
Krueger, Alan B., 418–419
Krugman, Paul, 192–193, 271

L

Labor
  child, 192–193
  marginal product of. *See* Marginal product
    of labor
  taxes on, 166–167
Labor demand, 392–398
  of competitive profit-maximizing firms,
    393
  marginal product of labor and, 394–397
  shifts in, 397–398, 401–403
Labor-market discrimination, 420–425
  by customers, 423–424
  by employers, 422–423

measurement of, 420–422
    racial, 422–423, 424–425
Labor-market equilibrium, 399–404
Labor supply, 398–399
    shifts in, 399, 400–401
    tradeoff between work and leisure and, 398–399
    wages and, 469–473
Labor unions. *See* Union(s)
Laffer, Arthur, 169–171
Laffer curve, 169–171
Laissez-faire policy, 150
Lamb imports, 54–55
Land market, equilibrium in, 404–406
Landry, Clay J., 119
Landsburg, Steven E., 259
Land tax, 168
Latin America. *See specific countries*
Law of demand, **66**
Law of supply, **71**
Law of supply and demand, **77**
Legislation
    antitrust. *See* Antitrust laws
    Clean Air Act, 119
    Farm Security Act of 2002, 490–491
    minimum-wage laws, 419, 441
    Shipping Act of 1916, 351
    Temporary Assistance for Needy Families Act, 441
Leisure, tradeoff between work and, 398–399
Liberalism, **438,** 438–439
Libertarianism, **439,** 439–440
Life cycle, **435,** 435–436
Lighthouses, as public goods, 228–229
Lindsey, Lawrence, 184
Linux operating system, 367
Litan, Robert, 350–351
Living standards, determinants of, 11–12
Local government, 246–248
    receipts of, 246–247
    spending by, 247–248
Long, Russell, 253
Long run
    costs in, 280, 282–283
    demand shifts in, 304, 305
    market supply with entry and exit in, 302–303
Long-run equilibrium, in monopolistic competition, 375–377
Long-run supply curve, upward-sloping, 303, 306–307
Losses
    deadweight. *See* Deadweight losses
    of exporting countries, 178–180
    of importing countries, 180–182
Lott, Trent, 351
Lump-sum taxes, **251,** 251–252
Luxembourg, drug prices in, 338
Luxuries, price elasticity of demand and, 90–91
Luxury tax, 130

M

McCourt, Frank, 373
McDonald's, 384
Mac operating system, 367
Macroeconomics, **27**

Malawi, elephants in, 236
Marginal buyers, 139
Marginal changes, **6,** 6–7
Marginal cost, 6–7, 275, **277,** 284
    average total cost related to, 279
    marginal product of labor related to, 397
    markup over, of monopolistically competitive firms, 378
    rising, 278–279
Marginal cost *(MC)* curve, 278, 279, 280, 281
    firm's supply decision and, 294–295
Marginal product, **272,** 272–273
    diminishing, **273,** 395
    value of, **395,** 395–397
Marginal product of labor, **394,** 394–397
    diminishing, 395
    marginal cost related to, 397
    production function and, 394–395
    value of, demand for labor and, 395–397
Marginal rate of substitution *(MRS)*, **457**
Marginal revenue, 291, **292**
    of monopolies, 319
Marginal-revenue curve, for monopoly firms, 321
Marginal revenue product, 396
Marginal tax rates, 166, 244, **250**
    average tax rates versus, 250–251
Marginal utility, 462
    diminishing, 437, 462
Market(s), **64,** 64–65. *See also specific markets*
    competitive. *See* Competitive markets
    definition of, price elasticity of demand and, 91
    for factors of production, 24
    for goods and services, 24
    organization of economic activity by, 9–10
Market-based policies, 212
Market-clearing price, 75, 76–77
Market demand, 66–67
    individual demand versus, 66–67
Market economy, **9**
Market efficiency. *See* Efficiency
Market failures, **11,** 154, 364
Market power, **11,** 154, 313–314
    of labor unions, 419
Market supply, 72–73
    in competitive markets. *See* Competitive markets
Markup, over marginal cost, of monopolistically competitive firms, 378
Marlboro, 358–359
Marriage tax, 257–258
Marx, Karl, 259
Mass transit systems, public versus private, 332–333
Matthews, Anna Wilde, 350–351
Maximum criterion, **439**
MC (marginal cost) curve, 278, 279, 280, 281
    firm's supply decision and, 294–295
Median voter theorem, **487,** 487–488
Medicaid program, 444, 445
Medicare spending, 246
Medicare tax, 166
Mercer Management Consulting, 306
Mergers, antitrust laws and, 329–330
Metropolitan Transportation Authority, 333
Mexico

drug prices in, 338
    income inequality in, 433
    international trade of, 193
    living standard in, 11
    tax burden in, 243
Microeconomics, **27**
Microsoft Corporation, 313, 329, 366–367, 368
Middle East. *See* Organization of Petroleum Exporting Countries (OPEC); *specific countries*
Midpoint method, for calculating price elasticity of demand, 92, 94
Mill, John Stuart, 437
Minimum wage, 121–123
Minimum-wage laws, 419, 441
Mobil Corp., 306
Money supply, inflation and, 12–13
Monopolistic competition, 65, **346,** 373–380, **374,** 385
    excess capacity of, 377, 380
    long-run equilibrium and, 375–377
    perfect competition versus, 377–378
    in short run, 374–375
    welfare of society and, 379–380
Monopoly, 65, 313–341, **316,** 385
    antitrust laws and, 329–330
    competition versus, 318, 319
    deadweight loss and, 326–328
    economies of scale and, 316, 317
    government-created, 316
    lack of interference with, 331–333
    lack of supply curve for, 323
    natural, **316,** 316–318
    prevalence of, 340
    price discrimination and. *See* Price discrimination
    prices charged by, 314
    profit maximization by, 321–323
    profits of, 323–325, 328–329
    proliferation of, 368
    public ownership of, 331
    reasons for, 314–318
    regulation of, 330–331
    revenue of, 319–321
Monopsony, 404
Moral hazard, **480,** 480–481
Movements along curves, 40
Movie industry, price discrimination in, 337
MRS (marginal rate of substitution), **457**
Murray, Alan, 368
Museum admission prices, 98–99
Muskie, Edmund, 216

N

Nader, Ralph, 7
NAFTA (North American Free Trade Agreement), 193
Namibia, elephants in, 236
Nash, John, 351
Nash equilibrium, 350–351, **351,** 492
National defense
    federal spending for, 246
    as public good, 226–227
National Institutes of Health, 227
National park admission fees, 235
National Park Service, 235
National saving, **59**

National Science Foundation, 227
National-security argument for trade restriction, 189–190
Natural monopoly, **316,** 316–318
Necessities, price elasticity of demand and, 90–91
Negative correlation, 37
Negative externalities, 204, 206–207
Negative income tax, **443,** 443–444
Negative relationships, 39
Neoclassical theory of distribution, 408
Netscape, 314, 367
Newton, Isaac, 21
"The New Wealth of Nations" (Summers), 368
New Zealand, lamb imports from, 54–55
Nigeria
  income inequality in, 433
  living standard in, 11
Normal goods, **68,** 99–100, **463**
Normative statements, **28,** 28–29
North American Free Trade Agreement (NAFTA), 193
Nozick, Robert, 440

O

Observation, 21
Ocean shipping firms, 350–351
Oil prices
  OPEC increases in, 116–117
  OPEC's failure to keep high, 106–107
  OPEC's means of controlling, 353
Oligopoly, 65, 345–369, **346**
  competition and monopoly and, 348–349
  duopoly example of, 348
  equilibrium for, 349–352
  game theory and. See Game theory; Prisoners' dilemma
  OPEC and. See Organization of Petroleum Exporting Countries (OPEC)
  public policy toward. See Antitrust laws
  size of, market outcome and, 352–353
Omitted variables, causality and, 43
OPEC. See Organization of Petroleum Exporting Countries (OPEC)
Opportunity cost, 5–6, **6, 51,** 268–269
  comparative advantage and, 51–52
  of leisure, 398–399
  production-possibility frontier and, 26
Optimization, 460–468
  consumer's optimal choices and, 461–462
  demand curve derivation and, 466–468
  income changes and, 462–463, 464
  income effect and, 464–466
  price changes and, 463–464, 465
  substitution effect and, 464–466
  utility and, 462
Ordered pairs, 36–37
Organization of Petroleum Exporting Countries (OPEC)
  failure to keep oil prices high, 106–107
  oil price increases of, 116–117
  world oil market and, 353
Organs (human), market for, 152
Origin, of graph, 37
Output effect
  on oligopoly, 352

on total revenue of monopoly, 320
Output price, demand curve for labor and, 397–398
Overconfidence, in decisionmaking, 489

P

Pakistan, tax burden in, 242, 243
Palestinian workers, shift in labor supply and, 401
Payroll taxes, 244, 245
  burden of, 127–128
Pearlstein, Steven, 98–99
Peltzman, Sam, 7–8
Penn, 345
Penn State, 419
PepsiCo, 329, 383
Perception, reality versus, 31–32
Perdue, 191
Perfect competition, 64, 385
  monopolistic competition versus, 377–378
Perfect complements, **460**
  indifference curves and, 459–460
Perfectly competitive markets. See Competitive markets
Perfectly elastic demand, 93
Perfectly elastic supply, 103
Perfectly inelastic demand, 93
Perfectly inelastic supply, 103
Perfect price discrimination, 336
Perfect substitutes, **459**
  indifference curves and, 459, 460
Permanent income, **436**
Peters, Cynthia, 332
Petroleum market. See Gasoline; Oil prices
Pharmaceutical industry
  monopoly versus generic drugs in, 324–325
  price discrimination in, 338–339
Phillips curve, **13,** 13–14
Physical appearance, wages and, 416
Pie charts, 36, 37
Pigou, Arthur, 213
Pigovian taxes, **213,** 213–214, 215–216
Pilgrims, 153
Pitt, Brad, 416
Plato, 445–446
Plymouth Bay Colony, 153
Political behavior, 488–489
Political economy, 479–480, 485–489
  Arrow's impossibility theorem and, 486–487
  Condorcet voting paradox and, 485–486
  median voter theorem and, 487–488
  political behavior and, 488–489
Pollution. See also Externalities
  associated with driving, 214
  economic analysis of, objections to, 216–217
Pollution permits, tradable, 215–216
Positive correlation, 37
Positive externalities, 204, 207
Positive relationships, 39
Positive statements, **28,** 28–29
Postrel, Virginia, 252–253
Poverty, 440–445
  in-kind transfers and, 444
  minimum-wage laws and, 441
  negative income tax and, 443–444

welfare and, 441–442
work incentives and, 444–445
Poverty line, **433**
Poverty rate, **433,** 433–434, 435
Predatory pricing, 365–366
Preferences, 456–460. See also Tastes
Price(s)
  advertising and, 382
  charged by monopoly, 314
  consumer choice and, 463–464, 465
  equilibrium (market-clearing), **75,** 76–77
  higher, raising of producer surplus by, 146–147
  of inputs, shift in supply curve related to, 74
  lower, raising of consumer surplus by, 140–141, 142
  of output, demand curve for labor and, 397–398
  purchase, for land or capital, 404–405
  quantity demanded related to, 65–66
  quantity supplied related to, 71–72
  of related goods, shifts in demand curve and, 68–69
  rental, for land or capital, 404–405
  resource allocation by, 83–84
  world, **177**
Price ceilings, **114,** 114–119
  binding, 114–115
  evaluation of, 123
  not binding, 114
  rent control as, 117–118
Price discrimination, **334,** 334–339
  analytics of, 336–337
  examples of, 337–339
  perfect, 336
Price effect
  on oligopoly, 352
  on total revenue of monopoly, 320
Price elasticity of demand, **90,** 90–99
  computing, 91, 92–94
  demand curve and, 93, 94
  determinants of, 90–91
  total revenue and, 94–98
Price elasticity of supply, **100,** 100–104
  computing, 101
  determinants of, 100–101
  supply curves and, 101–103
Price fixing, 364
Price floors, **114,** 120–123
  evaluation of, 123
Price makers. See Monopoly
Price takers, 290. See also Competitive markets
Pricing
  monopoly decisions regarding, 318–325
  predatory, 365–366
Principals, **480**
Principles of Political Economy and Taxation (Ricardo), 53
Prisoners' dilemma, **355,** 355–360, 362
  examples of, 357–360
  oligopolies as, 356–357
  welfare of society and, 360
Private goods, **224,** 224–225
Private saving, **59**
Producer surplus, 143–147, **144**

cost and willingness to sell and, 143–144
efficiency and, 147–148
at equilibrium, 148–149
measuring with supply curve, 144–146
raising of, by higher prices, 146–147
Product differentiation, on monopolistic
competition. *See* Monopolistic
competition
Production
costs and, 271–275
factors of. *See* Capital; Factors of
production; Labor *entries*
monopoly decisions regarding, 318–325
Production function, **272,** 272–273, **394,** 395
total-cost curve and, 273–275
Production-possibility frontier, 24–26, **25,** 27,
36–38
Productivity, **12**
living standard and, 12
wages and, 402–403
Profit(s), **268**
accounting, **270**
economic, **270**
graphical measurement of, 299–300
market entry and, 306
of monopoly, 323–325, 328–237
true versus fictitious measurement of, 271
zero, competitive firms with, 303–304
Profit maximization
by competitive firm, 292–293
labor demand of competitive firms
and, 393
by monopoly firms, 321–323
Progress and Poverty (George), 168
Progressive taxes, **255**
Property rights, 236–237
over technology, 209
Property taxes, 246, 247
Proportional taxes, **255**
Protection-as-bargaining-chip argument for
trade restriction, 191–194
Public choice. *See* Political economy
Public goods, **225,** 225–230
antipoverty programs as, 228
basic research as, 227–228
cost-benefit analysis and, 229–230
free-rider problem and, 226
lighthouses as, 228–229
national defense as, 226–227
value of human life and, 229–230
Public ownership, of monopolies, 331
Public policy. *See also* Antitrust laws;
Legislation; Regulation
asymmetric information and, 484
command-and-control, 212
toward externalities, 212–217
market-based, 212
Public saving, **59**
Public transportation, 332–333
Purdum, Todd S., 81
Putnam, Howard, 364

Q

Quality, advertising as signal of, 382–383
Quantity, equilibrium, **75,** 76
Quantity demanded, **65**
price related to, 65–66

Quantity discounts, 339
Quantity supplied, **71**
price related to, 71–72
Quintiles, 255
Quotas, import, **185,** 185–187

R

Racial discrimination, 422–423
in labor market, 420–421, 423–424
in South Africa, 424
in sports, 424–425
Rationing, price ceilings for, 114–118
Rawls, John, 438–439
Reagan, Ronald, 30, 159, 170–171
tax cut under, 261
Reality, perception versus, 31–32
Regressive taxes, **255**
Regulation
of externalities, 212–213
of monopolies, 330–331
Relative prices, budget constraint and, 455
Rent control, 123
in short and long run, 117–118
Rents, Black Plague and, 407
Resale price maintenance, 364–365
Research, basic, as public good, 227–228
Resource(s)
common, **225,** 231–236, 359–360
scarcity of, 4
Resource allocation, by prices, 83–84
Retained earnings, 406
Retirement plans
401(k) plans as, 250
IRAs as, 250
Keogh plans as, 250
Return(s), to scale, constant, **283**
Revenue
average, 291, **292,** 319
of competitive firms, 291–292
of federal government, 244–245
marginal, 291, **292,** 319
of monopolies, 319–321
of state and local government, 246–247
tax, deadweight loss and, 167–171
total. *See* Total revenue
true versus fictitious measurement of, 271
Reverse causality, 42–44
Ricardo, David, 53
Rivalry, of goods, **224**
Road congestion
associated with driving, 214
as common resource, 233–234
tolls as solution to, 232–233
Roback, Jennifer, 423
Robots, 208
Roosevelt, Theodore, 168
Rural Housing and Economic Development
Assistance, 443
Russia. *See also* Soviet Union
income inequality in, 433
tax burden in, 243

S

Salaries, of professional athletes, 424
Sales taxes, 246–247
Sanderson, Allen R., 235
Sanger, David E., 184

Satisficers, 489
Saving, **59**
interest rates and, 473–475
national, **59**
private, **59**
public, **59**
for retirement. *See* Retirement plans
Scale
constant returns to, **283**
diseconomies of, **283**
economies of, **283,** 316, 317
efficient, **279,** 377
Scarcity, **4**
Scatterplots, 37
Schmalensee, Richard, 367
School vouchers, 446–447
Schwab, Charles, 490
Scientific judgments, differences among
economists in, 30–31
Scientific method, 20, 21
Screening, **483**
to induce information revelation, 483–484
Sea-Land Service Inc., 350
Selection bias, 419
Sellers
number of, shift in supply curve related
to, 75
taxes on, effect on market outcomes,
126–128
Services, markets for, 24
Shaw, George Bernard, 30
Sherman Antitrust Act of 1890, 329, 363, 364
Shifts of curves, 40
Shipping Act of 1916, 351
Shortages, **76,** 76–77
of water, 119
Short run
costs in, 280, 282–283
demand shifts in, 304, 305
firm's decision to shut down and, 295–297
market supply with fixed number of firms
in, 301–302
monopolistically competitive firms in,
374–375
Shutdown, firm's short-run decision to shut
down and, 295–297
Sierra Club, 209
Signaling, **482**
to convey private information, 482–483
education and, 416–417
Simon, Herbert, 489
Singapore, toll roads in, 232–233
Skills, value of, 413–414
Slope, of curves, 41–42
Smith, Adam, 9, 10, 53, 283, 363–364
Smith, Roger, 190
Smoking, reducing, 70–71
Social Choice and Individual Values (Arrow),
486
Social costs
of externalities, 206
monopoly profit as, 328–329
Social insurance, 439. *See also* Welfare
programs
Medicaid, 444, 445
Medicare, 166, 246
taxes for, 166, 244

Social Security, taxation for, 166
Society
  decisions faced by, 3
  monopolistic competition and, 379–380
  prisoners' dilemma and, 360
South Africa
  apartheid in, 424
  income inequality in, 433
South Korea, international trade of, 192
Soviero, Joseph, 306
Soviet Union. *See also* Russia
  Cold War and, 358
  collapse of, 9
Spalding, 345
Specialization, 48–50
  economies of scale and, 283
Spence, Michael, 480
Sports
  racial discrimination in, 424–425
  salaries of professional athletes and, 424
SSI (Supplemental Security Income), 441–442
Standard of living, determinants of, 11–12
State government, 246–248
  receipts of, 246–247
  spending by, 247–248
Steele, Danielle, 373
Steel market, international trade in, 176
Stephens, Susan, 152
Stigler, George, 332–333
Stiglitz, Joseph, 480
Stockman, David, 170
Strikes, **419**
Study suggestions, 14
Substitutes, **69**
  perfect, **459,** 460
  price elasticity of demand and, 90
Substitution, marginal rate of, **457**
Substitution effect, **464**
  consumer choice and, 464–466
Summers, Lawrence H., 368
Sunk costs, 296, **297**
Supplemental Security Income (SSI), 441–442
Supply, 71–75. *See also* Equilibrium
  applications of, 104–109
  change in, 81–82
  decrease in, 74
  elastic, 100
  elasticity of, 100–104, 165–166
  excess, 76
  increase in, 74
  individual, 73
  inelastic, 100
  of labor, 398–399
  law of, **71**
  marginal-cost curve and firm's supply
    decision and, 294–295
  market, 72–73. *See also* Competitive
    markets
  of money, inflation and, 12–13
  of other factors, demand curve for labor
    and, 398
  perfectly elastic, 103
  perfectly inelastic, 103
Supply and demand, law of, **77**
Supply curve, 71–72, **72**
  in competitive markets. *See* Competitive
    markets

  for labor, shifts in, 399
  lack of, for monopoly firms, 323
  long-run, upward-sloping, 303, 306–307
  measuring producer surplus using,
    144–146
  price elasticity of supply and, 101–103
  shifts in, 73–75
Supply elasticity, 100–104
  deadweight losses and, 165–166
Supply schedule, **72**
Supply-side economics, 169–171
Surpluses, **76**
  budget, **246**
  consumer. *See* Consumer surplus
  producer. *See* Producer surplus
  total, efficiency and, 147–148
Swarthmore, 419
Synergies, 330

T

TANF (Temporary Assistance for Needy
  Families), 228, 246, 441
Tanzania, elephants in, 236
Tariffs, **182,** 182–185
  of G. W. Bush administration, 31, 184
  on lamb imports, 54–55
Tastes. *See also* Preferences
  labor supply curve and, 399
  shifts in demand curve and, 69
Tax(es), 124–131, 159–172, 241
  administrative burden of, 250
  burden of. *See* Tax burden
  on buyers, effect on market outcomes,
    124–126
  consumption, 249–250
  corporate income taxes, 244–245, 247
  cuts under G. W. Bush, 261
  cuts under Reagan, 261
  deadweight losses and. *See* Deadweight
    losses
  efficiency and, 248–253
  equity and, 253–260
  excise, 245
  on gasoline, 214, 254
  incidence of, 124, 128–130
  increase under Clinton, 261
  individual income taxes, 244, 247
  on labor, 166–167
  on land, 168
  loopholes and, 250
  lump-sum, **251,** 251–252
  luxury, 130
  negative income tax and, **443**
  payroll, 127–128, 244, 245
  Pigovian, **213,** 213–214, 215–216
  progressive, **255**
  property, 246, 247
  proportional, **255**
  regressive, **255**
  revenue from, deadweight loss and,
    167–171
  sales, 246–247
  on sellers, effect on market outcomes,
    126–128
  social insurance, 166, 244, 245
Tax burden
  ability-to-pay principle of, 254–258

  benefits principle of, 254
  distribution of, 255–256
  international comparison of, 242, 243
Tax equity, tax incidence and, 258, 260
Tax incidence, **124**
  elasticity and, 128–130
  tax equity and, 258, 260
Tax liability, 244
Tax rates
  average, **250,** 250–251
  marginal, 166, 244, **250,** 250–251
Taylor, John, 351
Technology
  change in, demand curve for labor and,
    398
  shift in supply curve related to, 74
Technology spillovers, 208–209
Temporary Assistance for Needy Families
  (TANF), 228, 246, 441
Tennis ball market, 345–346
Thanksgiving, 153
Theory, 21
Thomas, Kevin, 151
Thurow, Lester C., 232–233
Ticket scalping, 151
Tierney, John, 151, 332–333
Time horizon. *See also* Long run; Long-run
  entries; Short run; Short-run *entries*
  price elasticity of demand and, 91
Time inconsistency, of people, 493
Time-series graphs, 36, 37
Toll roads, 98–99, 232–233
Toshiba, 8
Total cost, **268,** 275, 284
  average, 275, **277,** 279, 280, 282, 284
Total-cost curve, production function and,
  273–275
Total revenue, **94, 268,** 291
  along linear demand curve, 96–97
  of monopolies, 319
  price elasticity of demand and, 94–97
Total surplus, efficiency and, 147–148
Toyota, 8
Tradable pollution permits, 215–216
Trade
  benefits of, 8–9
  comparative advantage and. *See*
    Comparative advantage
  gains from. *See* Gains from trade
  international. *See* International trade; Trade
    restriction
  production possibilities and, 46–48
  specialization and, 48–50
Trade Act of 1974, 54
Tradeoffs, 4–5
  between equity and efficiency, 260–261
  between inflation and unemployment. *See*
    Phillips curve
  policy decisions and, 29
  production-possibility frontier and, 26, 48
  between unemployment and inflation. *See*
    Phillips curve
  between work and leisure, 398–399
Trade policy, 187–188
  in India, 191
Trade restriction
  infant-industry argument for, 190

jobs argument for, 188–189
national-security argument for, 189–190
protection-as-bargaining-chip argument
  for, 191–194
quotas, 185–187
tariffs, 31, 54–55, 182–185
unfair-competition argument for, 190
Tragedy of the Commons, **231,** 231–232
Transaction costs, **211**
Transfer payments, 245–246
Transitivity, 485–486
Transport Workers Union, 333
Truman, Harry, 29, 55
Tulane, 419
Turner, Ted, 490
Tying, 366

U

Uganda
  drug prices in, 339
  elephants in, 236
Underground economy, 167
Unemployment, tradeoff with inflation,
  13–14
Unfair-competition argument for trade
  restriction, 190
Union(s), **419**
Union Carbide Corp., 306
United Kingdom
  income inequality in, 433
  tax burden in, 243
United States
  Cold War and, 358
  drug prices in, 338–339
  income inequality in, 430–433, 433
  international trade of, 56, 193
  living standard in, 11
  tax burden in, 242, 243, 255–256
U.S. government, 242–248
  federal, 29, 242, 244–246
  receipts of, 244–245, 246–247
  spending by, 245–246, 247–248
  state and local, 246–248
U.S. International Trade Commission, 55
U.S. Justice Department, 29, 329, 363, 364, 366
  case against Microsoft and, 314

U.S. Labor Department, 29
U.S. Postal Service, 331
U.S. Treasury Department, 29
University of Pennsylvania, 419
Unsafe at Any Speed (Nader), 7
Utilitarianism, **437,** 437–438
Utility, 462
  marginal, 462

V

Value
  absolute, 92
  of human life, 229–230
  of marginal product, **395,** 395–397
  of skills, 413–414
Values, differences among economists in, 31
Variable(s), omitted, causality and, 43
Variable costs, 275, **276,** 276–277, 284
  average, **277,** 284
  fixed costs versus, 298
Varian, Hal R., 338–339
Vaughn, Michael B., 32
Vertical equity, **254,** 255–256

W

Wages
  ability, effort, and chance and, 414–416
  above-equilibrium, 418–420
  Black Plague and, 407
  compensating differentials and, 412
  discrimination and. *See* Labor-market
    discrimination
  efficiency, **419**
  equilibrium, determinants of, 412–420
  human capital and, 412–414
  labor supply and, 469–473
  minimum, 121–123, 419, 441
  productivity and, 402–403
  signaling and, 416–417
  subsidization of, 123
  superstar phenomenon and, 417–418
Wal-Mart, 192
Water
  clean, as common resource, 233
  shortages of, 119
Welfare, economic. *See* Economic welfare

Welfare economics, **138**
Welfare programs, 246, **441,** 441–442, 445
  federal spending for, 246
  Food Stamp program, 246, 444, 445
  as public good, 228
  state and local spending for, 247
  TANF, 228, 246, 441
West Germany. *See* Germany
Whales, as common resource, 234
Wheat market, 104–106
Wildlife, as common resource, 234
Williams, Robin, 417–418
Williams, Venus, 417, 418
Willingness to pay, **138,** 138–139
Willingness to sell, producer surplus and,
  143–144
Wilson, 345
Windows operating system, 313, 314, 366–367
Winston, Clifford, 99
Women. *See also* Gender
  married, income taxes and, 252
Women's movement, income distribution
  and, 431–432
Woods, Tiger, 54–56
Work, tradeoff between leisure and, 398–399
Workfare, 445
Work incentives, antipoverty programs and,
  444–445
WorldCom, 271
World price, **177**
World trade. *See* International trade; Trade
  restriction
World Trade Organization (WTO), 55, 193
Wysocki, Bernard, Jr., 306

X

x-coordinate, 37

Y

Yale, 419
y-coordinate, 37
Yellowstone National Park, 235

Z

Zimbabwe, elephants in, 236
Zoellick, Robert B., 184

SUGGESTIONS FOR SUMMER READING

IF YOU ENJOYED THE ECONOMICS COURSE THAT YOU HAVE JUST FINISHED, YOU MIGHT LIKE READING MORE ABOUT ECONOMIC ISSUES IN THE FOLLOWING BOOKS.

ROBERT J. BARRO

Nothing Is Sacred:
Economic Ideas for the New Millennium
Cambridge, Mass.: MIT Press, 2002

In this collection of essays, economist Robert Barro offers his views about economists, the economy, and the proper scope of public policy.

ALAN S. BLINDER AND JANET L. YELLEN

The Fabulous Decade:
Macroeconomic Lessons from the 1990s
Twentieth Century Fund, 2001

Two economic advisers to President Bill Clinton look back at a prosperous decade for the U.S. economy.

TODD G. BUCHHOLZ

New Ideas from Dead Economists
New York: Penguin Books, 1989

This amusing book provides an overview of the history of economic thought.

COUNCIL OF ECONOMIC ADVISERS

Economic Report of the President
U.S. Government Printing Office, released every year

The annual report of the CEA surveys the state of economy and presents the case for the president's economic program.

AVINASH DIXIT AND BARRY NALEBUFF

Thinking Strategically: A Competitive Edge in Business, Politics, and Everyday Life
New York: Norton, 1991

This introduction to game theory discusses how all people – from corporate executives to criminals under arrest – should and do make strategic decisions.

WILLIAM EASTERLY

The Elusive Quest for Growth: Economists' Adventures and Misadventures in the Tropics
Cambridge, Mass.: MIT Press, 2001

A World Bank economist examines the many attempts to help the world's poorest nations and why they have so often failed.